Conflict in Afghanistan

Roots of Modern Conflict

Conflict in Afghanistan
Ludwig W. Adamec and Frank A. Clements

Conflict in the Former Yugoslavia
John B. Allcock, Marko Milivojevic, and John J. Horton, editors

Conflict in Korea
James E. Hoares and Susan Pares

Conflict in Northern Ireland
Sydney Elliott and W. D. Flackes

Conflict in Afghanistan

A Historical Encyclopedia

Ludwig W. Adamec and
Frank A. Clements

A B C ⬥ C L I O

Santa Barbara, California   Denver, Colorado   Oxford, England

Library of Congress Cataloging-in-Publication Data
Adamec, Ludwig W.
Clements, Frank, 1942–
    Conflict in Afghanistan : a historical encyclopedia / Ludwig W. Adamec and Frank A. Clements.
        p.   cm. — (Roots of modern conflict)
    Includes bibliographical references and index.
    ISBN 1-85109-402-4 (hardcover : alk. paper)
    1. Afghanistan—History—Encyclopedias.   I. Title.   II. Series.
DS351.C54   2003
958.1'003—dc22

2003021334

07   06   05   04   03   10 9 8 7 6 5 4 3 2 1

This book is also available on the World Wide Web as an e-book. Visit http://www.abc-clio.com for details.

ABC-CLIO, Inc.
130 Cremona Drive, P.O. Box 1911
Santa Barbara, California 93116–1911

This book is printed on acid-free paper.

Manufactured in the United States of America

Contents

Conflict in Afghanistan
A Historical Encyclopedia

About This Encyclopedia

This encyclopedia offers the reader a guide to the conflict in contemporary Afghanistan by providing a series of entries covering key figures, events, and organizations relevant to the subject. However, to understand the current situation, it is essential to have a grasp of the history of the country. An appropriate starting point is the creation of the modern state of Afghanistan in 1747 and the rule of Ahmad Shah Durrani.

The reader will note that some entries for individuals do not have dates of birth or, where relevant, dates of death. In many instances, records simply do not exist, and Afghans often do not know their dates of birth. In other cases, people have disappeared from Afghanistan leaving no information as to whether they are dead or alive.

Names are also confusing because there are so many variants, and I have endeavored to standardize the names in this volume based on what seems to be the accepted Western versions and spellings. Afghans also tend to use only their given names, which can lead to confusion for outsiders; for example, the Afghan foreign minister, Dr. Abdullah Abdullah, is known only as Abdullah. In other cases, the given name is attached to an honorific title, such as Isma'il Khan, Governor of Herat. This, too, can be confusing, and again, I have adopted the most frequently used version of a name and, where necessary, indicated a common variant.

The introduction to the volume presents a brief history of Afghanistan in an attempt to lay out the foundations that underpin the current conflict. However, as of August 2003, the situation in Afghanistan is extremely volatile, and the reader can do no better than consult the various Web sites listed in the bibliography to obtain details of the evolving history of the conflict.

Acknowledgments

I wish to record my thanks to Professor Shaista Wahab of the University of Nebraska, Omaha, for her assistance and kindness during my visit to the Afghan Research Center, funded by a grant from my college. As always, I owe a great deal to my wife for her continuing patience and forbearance with my pastimes.

Introduction

Afghanistan came to the fore on the international scene in recent decades with the Soviet intervention in 1979, the guerrilla war waged against the Soviets and the Communist regime in Kabul, the civil war after the collapse of the Marxist government, and the rise of the Taliban with its fundamentalist regime, its human rights abuses, and its harboring of Osama bin Laden and al-Qaeda terrorists. However, the country was really thrust into the limelight with the launching of Operation Enduring Freedom in October 2001 by an alliance of Coalition forces—mainly composed of U.S. and British troops but with special forces from other participating countries—and Afghan anti-Taliban forces; their objectives were to overthrow the Taliban regime, capture Osama bin Laden, and destroy al-Qaeda in the aftermath of the terrorist attacks on the United States on 11 September 2001. An understanding of contemporary events in Afghanistan requires a grasp of the country's geopolitical situation, its ethnic composition, and the impact that these two factors have had on its history.

Geopolitics of Afghanistan

The political significance of Afghanistan began to attract the attention of the Western world when the Soviet Union intervened in support of the Marxist government in Kabul in December 1979. However, Afghanistan's strategic position had been recognized for centuries, for the country was part of the Silk Road and, in the nineteenth century, a key player in the "Great Game" played between the two colonial powers of Great Britain and Russia. Events in the twentieth century can be seen as a legacy of the politics of the Great Game.

British concerns over the possibility of a Russian invasion of British India prompted interest in Afghanistan and eventually led to three Anglo-Afghan wars. After Afghanistan acquired responsibility for its own foreign policy in 1919, the country used its geopolitical situation and the concept of neutrality to preserve its independence and to extract

whatever benefits it could from its more powerful neighbors, and this continued until the Saur Revolt of April 1978, which brought the Communists to power. The geopolitics of Afghanistan are critical to an understanding of Afghan history; they are also critical in terms of the diversity of the population, achieved through trade and migration. The present-day ethnic composition is a vital factor in the politics of Afghanistan and its current instability.

However, the country now known as Afghanistan has a long and rich history due, in large part, to the fact that it lies at the crossroads of many cultures and of Asian migration routes. As a result, the country has a rich heritage of archaeological remains, art, and architecture, much of which has been damaged or destroyed over twenty-three years of war in recent times. Although the country did not emerge in its present form until the reign of Ahmad Shah Durrani in 1747, it was soon to become significant in European history as part of the Great Game played out by Britain and Russia. In this game, Britain sought two things: to prevent an increase of Russian influence in Central Asia and to safeguard British interests in India by using Afghanistan as a buffer zone. Britain's experiences fighting in Afghanistan during the nineteenth and early twentieth centuries should have served as valuable lessons for other invaders, such as the Soviets in 1979.

Ethnic Composition

Population statistics for Afghanistan have always been difficult to determine, and the statistics-gathering arm of the administration has never been a strong feature of the government. Thus, population figures and ethnic breakdowns are always suspect, with figures sometimes manipulated to improve international funding on a per capita basis. However, there is little doubt that the Pashtuns are the largest of the ethnic groups, forming about 40 percent of the population, followed by the Tajiks, who make up about 20 percent. The other main groups—the Hazaras, the Uzbeks, and the Aimaq— are roughly equal, with each composing about 9 percent of the population. The balance of the population is made up of a number of ethnic minorities, including Turkomans, Kazakhs, Qizilbash, Wakhis, Nuristanis, Baluchis, and Kyrgyz together with extremely small numbers of Hindus, Sikhs, and Jews.

The urban areas of Afghanistan have generally had mixed populations, whereas villages have usually been single ethnic communities; Afghan ethnic groups tend to be identified by location, but, apart from the Hazaras of the Hazarajat and the Wakhis of the Wakhan Corridor, they are not designated as such by name. Although the Kabul government has attempted to engineer ethnic integration over the years by, for example, transplanting Pashtuns into the north of the country, such attempts have failed. After all internal conflicts, the north of Afghanistan has always gone back to single ethnic community patterns, especially in the rural areas. Kabul is the most ethnically mixed city due to its position as the seat of government, but other cities, such as Herat and Mazar-i Sharif, reflect the dominant ethnic characteristics of the region in which they are located.

In the main, the distribution of the various ethnic groups in Afghanistan resulted from the international borders drawn in the nineteenth century by the British and Russian Empires, which often split up tribal communities. For instance, the Durand Agreement of 1893 split the Pashtun community between Afghanistan and the northwest area of British India (now Pakistan). Afghanistan's geographic position straddling the migration routes of Iranian tribes and Indo-Aryan, Turkic, and Arab groups has also left a presence of small ethnic groups protected in isolated villages in the numerous mountain valleys and hillsides. Such migrations have gone on for thousands of years and have continued until recent times, with influxes of people fleeing the Bolshevik Revolution, Stalinist Russia, and the arrival of Marxism in China.

Trade can account for some diversity, with small trading communities of Hindus and Sikhs and a declining Jewish presence in Kabul and Mazar-i Sharif. Afghanistan has also become a refuge for persecuted groups. For other ethnic groups, such as the Nuristanis and the Wakhis, geographic isolation has meant that they have retained their languages and cultures. However, the diversity of the communities in Afghanistan and the geographic impediments to integration have all contributed to the fragmentation and disunity of the country.

Originally, the term *Afghan* referred to the dominant Pashtun majority (though the word's origins are unclear), and it was not until the Pashtuns carved out a home for themselves in Central Asia during the eighteenth century that the name *Afghanistan* became used to describe the territory controlled by the Pashtuns. This meant that other ethnic groups living in this area also became known to outsiders as Afghans. As a result of Kabul extending control throughout the area to the north and west of Kabul, present-day Afghanistan was created as a multiethnic country, though it took nearly a century before Kabul obtained even nominal allegiance to its rule. As the country continued to develop, some integration gradually took place, largely as a result of the public education system, conscription into the armed forces, development of the media, and public sector employment. However, these developments were shallow and soon disappeared in the face of internal conflict, with the civil war from 1992 to 1996 exposing acute rifts between the various ethnic groups.

The Pashtuns, as the largest ethnic group, have been dominant in ruling the country, particularly from 1747 with the reign of Ahmad Shah Durrani, regarded as the father of modern Afghanistan. They speak Pashtu and have dominated the political scene since that time (except for a small break under the Tajik ruler Habibullah Kalakani in 1929) until the arrival of the Marxist government in 1978. Even in the post-Soviet and mujahideen periods, the Pashtuns retained their dominance through the Taliban regime, as the movement had emerged from the Pashtun tribes of southern and eastern Afghanistan. In the north, the other ethnic groups, such as the Dari-speaking Tajiks, the Uzbeks, and the Hazaras, have only barely or begrudgingly accepted control from a central administration in Kabul, dominated by the Pashtuns, and this link has been exposed throughout Afghanistan's history with various internal conflicts, uprisings, and interethnic clashes. In addition, there is the religious divide between the Shi'a Hazara population and the predominantly Sunni population of the rest of Afghanistan.

The historical, linguistic, and cultural differences between the various ethnic groups in Afghanistan have also led to an unstable political situation, with the civil war, following the downfall of the Najibullah government in 1992, having thrust these differences to the fore. After four years of internal conflict and shifting alliances, the divisions were so deep that Afghan society had disintegrated in a series of regions dominated by majority ethnic groups backed by well-armed militias; further, evidence shows ethnic cleansing was used to settle old scores or in revenge for perceived atrocities or other human rights abuses. The Taliban reinforced these divisions between the Pashtuns and the other ethnic groups that opposed their regime and their concept of an Afghan society based on the strict application of Shari'a law; they were also responsible for atrocities and egregious human rights abuses, particularly against the Shi'a Hazaras and women. These divisions and rivalries have contributed to the instability of post-Taliban Afghanistan, and an awareness of these issues is critical to an understanding of Afghan history and the problems now faced by the Transitional Government of President Hamid Karzai. Ideally, these pressing concerns should be resolved before the elections scheduled for June 2004.

Early History

Evidence exists of early Stone Age settlement in Afghanistan, with plant remains in the foothills of the Hindu Kush suggesting that this was one of the earliest places in which plants and animals were domesticated. Between 300 B.C. and 2000 B.C., urban centers grew up in the area. Mundigak, sited near present-day Kandahar, was an economic center for raising wheat, barley, sheep, and goats, and it possibly served as a regional capital for the Indus Valley civilization. In about 600 B.C., Zoroaster introduced the new Zoroastrian religion into Bactria (now Balkh Province), and he died there in 522 B.C. Between 522 B.C. and 486 B.C., the Persians occupied the bulk of modern Afghanistan under Darius the Great, but their rule was beset by constant tribal revolts in the present-day Kandahar and Quetta areas.

After conquering Persia, Alexander the Great invaded Afghanistan between 329–326 B.C., but again, the tribes were never really subdued, and there were constant uprisings against the Greek rulers. In the end, the Greeks only really controlled northern Afghanistan from the present-day Balkh. This era was followed by a period of changing influences, with Seleucid, Roman, Arab, and Chinese influences in the area until the invasion of the Huns in A.D. 400, which resulted in the destruction of Buddhist culture and a country left in ruins. In A.D. 550, the Persians again ruled over a rebellious people who were constantly in revolt against the occupiers.

From the Arrival of Islam to Ahmad Shah Durrani (652–1747)

The Arabs in A.D. 652 introduced Islam into the region, but it was not until A.D. 962 that the first Islamic era was established, with the Ghaznaid dynasty that ruled until 1140. The dynasty was of Turkic origin and was founded by Nasir al-Daulav Sebuktegin, who ruled from 977 to 997; Ghazni was its administrative capital. The empire of the Ghazni extended from the Tigris to the Ganges Rivers and from the Indian Ocean to the Amu Daria River. The city of Ghazni became extremely rich and also was a center of culture, though it started to decline in influence after the death of Mahmud Ghazi. In 1221, the forces of Genghis Khan sacked the city, and it became part of the Ilkhanid Empire, but with the destruction of its irrigation systems, the fertile soil of the region was turned into permanent desert. The period following the first Mogul invasion was marked by recurrent invasions of Turkic Central Asians into the region, with Afghanistan still retaining its strategic significance. However, Afghan resistance continued to manifest itself throughout the fourteenth and fifteenth centuries, albeit with limited success.

In the early sixteenth century, the Afghans again revolted against the Mogul government. They were led by an intellectual named Bayazid Roshan, who was killed in 1579 in a battle against the Moguls, though the struggles continued. It was not until the following century that further national uprisings continued, with a 1613 campaign led by Khushhal Khan Khattack. The region was also subjected to occupation by the Safavid regime from Persia, which ruled in Kandahar from 1622 until a revolt led by Mir Wais Khan, a Ghilzai Pashtun, in 1708; this revolt succeeded in ending Persian domination in the region and led to an Afghan invasion of Persia in 1722, wherein the Safavids were soundly defeated at the Battle of Gulnabad. At the same time, the Durrani tribes rose up in revolt against the Persians and succeeded in wresting from them control over Herat.

Afghan control of Persia was short-lived. In 1725, the occupation began to weaken, with Nadir Shah, ruler of Persia, retaking southeast Persia and occupying southwest Afghanistan in 1726. In 1738, Nadir Shah retook Kandahar, and Persian rule was again established over most of Afghanistan, though it could never be regarded as secure. In 1747, Nadir Shah was assassinated, and the Afghans again rose up in revolt under the leadership of Ahmad Shah Abdali (Durrani), taking control of Kandahar and beginning a campaign to gain control over the territory that is now Afghanistan.

From the Emergence of Modern Afghanistan to the Great Game

After taking Kandahar from the Persians, Ahmad Shah Durrani consolidated his position in the region before beginning a campaign to extend his control. In the period from 1747 until his death in 1773, be captured further territory, defeated the Moguls in the area to the west of the Indus, and ejected the Persians from Herat. At the time of his death, he controlled an empire that ran from Central Asia to Delhi and from Kashmir to the Arabian Sea, creating the greatest Muslim empire in the eighteenth century. Timur Shah, who ruled from 1773 to 1793, replaced Durrani, but his rule was not secure; further, because of tribal opposition, he moved his capital from Kandahar to Kabul in an attempt to weaken the power of the Durrani chiefs. He was regarded as a humane ruler who was more of a scholar than a soldier, and he never realized his ambition of creating a truly centralized state.

In 1793, Timur Shah died, and his five sons, who had been made governors of Afghan provinces, began an internecine struggle for power. He was succeeded by Shah Zaman in 1793, but Zaman's rule was constantly threatened by internal unrest. He was an authoritarian, harsh ruler who was eventually overthrown in 1801, while on a visit to the Punjab. He was replaced by Shah Mahmud, whose reign only lasted until 1803, when Shah Shuja took the reins of power. Shah Shuja's rule lasted until 1809 and was marked by an unsuccessful Persian attack on Herat and further internal strife, resulting in the

return of Shah Mahmud, who continued to rule until 1818; the period brought further struggles against the Persians and continued internal strife. From 1818 to 1826, anarchy and civil war prevailed, with the sons of Timur Shah struggling for control of the throne, and during this period, the Afghans finally lost control of Sind Province.

From the Great Game to the Independent Monarchy (1826–1919)

This period of Afghanistan's history was marked by the increasing interest of Britain in the internal affairs of the country, largely because of the Great Game being played out in the region with Russia. Afghanistan was seen by Britain as a crucial buffer state, given the increasing power and widening interests of the Russian Empire in the region; British policy was determined by the desire to protect the security of its Indian Empire against the Russians, who were deemed to be the greatest threat to British interests in the region.

In 1826, Amir Dost Muhammad Khan, known as "the Great Amir," took the throne and ruled initially until 1838, when he was ousted by Britain. His rule over the whole of Afghanistan was established in 1834 when he defeated Shah Shuja at Kandahar; this was followed in 1837 by the defeat of the Sikhs at Jamrud, in which the great Sikh military leader Hari Singh was killed. However, Dost Muhammad failed to capitalize on this victory, and a bid to take Peshawar was unsuccessful largely because of disunity among the Afghan forces.

Dost Muhammad soon found himself at odds with the British India government when he was suspected of having opened negotiations with Russia, a view reinforced by the arrival in Kabul of a Russian emissary, Capt. Ivan Vitkevich, who had come to establish commercial relations with Afghanistan. At the same time, Alexander Burnes, a British East India Company representative, was also in Kabul, and he advised Dost Muhammad to abandon any hopes of getting Peshawar back from the Sikhs and to make peace instead. This led Dost Muhammad to open negotiations with Captain Vitkevich over assistance for Afghanistan, but the Russian government repudiated these moves. At the same time, the British in India were negotiating with the deposed Shah Shuja and Ranjit Shah, ruler of the Sikh nation, and they concluded the Simla Manifesto of 1838, which recognized the independence of the Sikhs from Afghanistan and was to become effective once Shah Shuja had regained the Afghan throne.

In effect, the manifesto was a declaration of war against Dost Muhammad, and Afghanistan was invaded by Britain in July 1839; Kabul was taken on 23 July. On 2 November, Dost Muhammad surrendered to the British and was exiled to India, and Shah Shuja was restored to the throne, a position he held with British support until 1842. The British occupation of Afghanistan was never secure, and the army found its lines of communication being disrupted and garrisons in outlying settlements being ousted by Afghan tribesmen. The position of the army in Kabul became critical, and army leaders were forced to negotiate conditions for a withdrawal. The withdrawal became a death march, with the troops being massacred while trying to cross back into India; only one survived.

In April 1842, Shah Shuja was assassinated, and Dost Muhammad was restored to the throne one year later and ruled until 1863. In 1855, Afghanistan finally concluded a peace treaty with the Indian government, but in 1859, the British India government took Baluchistan, making Afghanistan a totally landlocked country. After the death of Dost Muhammad, his son Shir Ali assumed the throne and ruled until 1866. But in 1865, Bukhara, Tashkent, and Samarkand were taken by the Russians, and his reign was characterized by constant power struggles with his brothers, who held positions as provincial governors. In 1866, Muhammed Afzal occupied Kabul and proclaimed himself amir, but he died in October 1867 and was replaced by Muhammad Azam, who ruled until 1868, when he was forced to flee to Persia. Thereafter, Shir Ali regained the throne, ruling until 1879.

In 1869, Shir Ali traveled to India to try to obtain support against Russian aggression and to secure recognition for his son as his successor. However, the viceroy would not accede to his requests and only provided a few pieces of artillery and some funds. As a direct result of this rejection, Shir Ali listened to approaches from the Russian government, who sent General Stolietoff to Kabul on 22 July 1878 to negotiate an agreement, following up on the Russian agreement with Afghanistan over fixed boundaries in 1873 and with a promise to respect the country's territorial integrity. These moves

alarmed the British, who tried to send an emissary to Kabul. That emissary was refused entry to Afghanistan, leading to an ultimatum from the India government, followed by the invasion by a British army.

Shir Ali had left Kabul for northern Afghanistan, leaving his son Yaqub in charge, and he was advised by the Russians to make peace with the British. The Afghans again put up strong resistance to the British, but Yaqub Khan was forced to agree to the Treaty of Gandomak in 1879, which resulted in Afghanistan giving up a number of frontier districts, including those controlling the Khyber Pass, and these became permanently lost to Afghanistan. In the same year, Shir Ali died of natural causes in Mazar-i Sharif. The lost districts were to prove troublesome in the twentieth century when Pakistan was created in 1947 and the Pashtun frontier districts became part of the new state. In 1880, the Afghans inflicted a major defeat on the British at the Battle of Maiwand, near Kandahar, but a force under Sir Frederick Roberts in turn inflicted a heavy defeat on the Afghans and retrieved the situation. However, the British recognized the futility of trying to impose direct rule in Afghanistan, determining instead to install a government stable enough to combat Russian aggression without posing a threat to British India.

The British invited Abdur Rahman, who was a nephew of the deceased Shir Ali and had been living in exile in Tashkent, to become the ruler of Afghanistan, and he was made amir in 1880, ruling until 1901. At the accession of Abdur Rahman, the British withdrew from Afghanistan but still retained the right to control the country's foreign relations. The borders of Afghanistan were fixed, and Abdur Rahman was forced to accept the territorial losses inflicted by the Treaty of Gandomak. In 1881, he took possession of Kandahar and Herat and became the undisputed ruler of Afghanistan. However, in 1895, Russian forces seized the oasis at Panjdeh, north of the River Amu Daria, and the Afghans failed in attempts to retake it, though they secured a Russian agreement to respect Afghanistan's territorial integrity thereafter. Border problems continued, however, with the 1893 Durand Agreement with Britain, which fixed the borders with British India but split the tribal areas of Afghanistan. The amir always maintained that he signed the agreement under duress, and the outcome was to continue to affect relations with British India and, after 1947, with the new state of Pakistan.

Abdur Rahman died in 1901, he was succeeded by his son Habibullah, who began attempts to modernize the kingdom. One of the most crucial decisions taken was to introduce modern education for civilians and military personnel and to use foreign teachers. The institutions created by Habibullah were to form the foundations for the elite governmental and military bureaucracy. The political system was also liberalized, which encouraged some Afghan exiles to return home and, in turn, accelerate the reform process. Other infrastructure projects were undertaken in the health sector and communications, and trade with Central Asia and India was encouraged. It was also during Habibullah's reign that modern journalism came to Afghanistan, with the founding of a number of newspapers almost totally the work of Mahmud Tarzi, a returned exile; his papers advocated further developments in education and political liberalization.

Habibullah maintained a policy of neutrality during World War I and resisted pressure from both the Ottoman and German governments to enter the war by supporting anti-British activity in India. However, the ruler's modernizing policies led to the growth of an opposition movement, and plots against the amir were discovered, leading to a number of arrests and executions. The neutrality policy during World War I (which in reality was somewhat biased toward the British) caused opposing factions to draw together, and there was also a great deal of popular resentment at the Allies' treatment of the Muslim Ottoman Empire at the end of the war. Opposition to the amir was drawn from the traditional and conservative sectors of the elite and the general population and from the modernists led by the amir's son Amanullah and influenced by the newspapers of Tarzi, who wanted more modernization and a nationalist agenda.

The reign of Habibullah had established the Afghan monarchy as a modernizing force in Afghanistan, but it became critical to ensure a balance between the modernizers and the traditional, conservative elements that formed the bulk of Afghan society. The threat of foreign intervention had not disappeared, and the formation of the Soviet Empire meant that Afghanistan again became a buffer state between Russia and Britain.

The Independent Monarchy (1919–1973)

Throughout this period, Afghanistan operated as a constitutional monarchy, and the role of the legislative branch of government was largely restricted to the endorsement of programs presented by the king or his immediate officials. Also during this period, Afghanistan became able to determine its own, independent foreign policy.

King Amanullah succeeded his father in 1919, having defeated his uncle Nasrullah, who had attempted to seize the throne. One of his first acts was to proclaim a jihad against the British in May 1919, leading to the third and final Anglo-Afghan war. However, the war was only of short duration, fought largely in the border regions and concluded with Afghanistan having secured complete independence but, in turn, having to forfeit all British subsidies and guarantees of protection against foreign aggression. Amanullah also harbored pan-Islamic aspirations and attempted to aid the besieged amir of Bukhara, who was engaged in a struggle against the Red Army and local Bolshevik sympathizers. However, when the Bolsheviks established control in Central Asia, Amanullah withdrew his support, though he did give refuge to the deposed amir of Bukhara and harbor to Ibrahim Beg, who had been a leading commander of the Basmachi in the insurgency against the Red Army. Afghanistan also became a safe haven for thousands of Central Asians fleeing from Bolshevik rule. In the 1921 treaty concluded with the Soviet Union, Amanullah tried to secure the independence of Bukhara and Khiva and the return of Panjdeh (seized by the Russians in 1885) but to no avail.

The domestic policies of Amanullah were largely concerned with an overhaul of the state to make it conform to the king's concept of a modern nation. One aspect of the reform program was the drawing up of the 1923 Constitution, which established the basis for the formal structure of government, set the role of the constitutional monarch, and attempted to regulate relations between the state and Islam. Amanullah also established schools using English, French, and German as the main languages of education, and he ended Afghanistan's international isolation by establishing diplomatic relations in Europe and Asia. On the social scene, Amanullah encourage government employees to wear Western dress and allowed women to go without veils. However, the reform program angered the conservative elements of society, particularly the *ulama* (Islamic scholars and clerics).

Opposition manifested itself through a rebellion at Khost in eastern Afghanistan in 1924, which was only put down with great difficulty after the army received support from tribes traditionally opposed to the rebels. In 1927 and 1928, Amanullah went on a tour of European and Middle Eastern capitals, returning with a determination to advance the modernization program. However, he had succeeded in alienating the most powerful forces in the country, including the military, the religious leaders, and the Pashtun tribes, and in 1928, the Shinwari Pashtun tribe rebelled in the area to the east of Jalalabad. At the same time, Khost rebels, led by a Tajik named Habibullah Kalakani, attacked and laid siege to Kabul. Amanullah abdicated in favor of his brother Inaytullah, who soon abdicated as well, and Amanullah and his immediate family fled to India in May 1929.

The Afghan throne then passed to Habibullah Kalakani, the son of a water carrier; this was the only occasion on which the monarchy was assumed by a non-Pashtun. Habibullah had only a tenuous hold on the country outside of Kabul, and his aspirations to be accepted as monarch were hampered by his common background and the fact that he was a Tajik, though his Khoistani supporters regarded him as a hero. He only ruled for nine months, but the period of his reign saw confirmation of the severity of ethnic divisions in Afghanistan and revealed the difficulty of changing the attitudes of an isolated people.

Habibullah's main policies were directed at reversing the reforms of Amanullah, particularly in the areas of marriage customs, the status of women, and education. Severe veiling for women was introduced, and cultural institutions such as museums and libraries were sacked. Government workers associated with the former king were subjected to beatings, imprisonment, and exile, with students from the new schools also coming under suspicion. Other reforms on the abolition of conscription and the lowering of taxes were reversed, and the schools and courts were returned to the control of the clergy. Meanwhile, the economy of the country became unstable, the Pashtun tribes became disaffected with Habibullah's rule, and the Soviets and British feared an unstable Afghanistan. All these factors helped to bring an end to Habibullah's rule.

Nadir Shah, a Muhammadzai Durrani, returned from exile in India in 1929 with tribal support from Waziristan and British acquiesence, to defeat Habibullah. He took Kabul on 13 October 1929. He was proclaimed king two days later, and Habibullah, who had been taken prisoner, was hanged together with a number of his followers. Nadir Shah continued to reverse the modernization process and courted favor with the religious extremists. However, he did put in train a restructuring program that included provision of schooling and the founding of a faculty of medicine in Kabul in 1932. One year earlier, he had promulgated a new constitution that provided for a parliament, a national council, a senate, and an advisory council.

During his reign, Nadir Shah also had to deal with attempts to restore Amanullah to the throne. Part of his strategy for defeating the opposition was to set ethnic groups against each other, particularly the Tajiks and Pashtuns, resulting in the destruction of the Shamali area north of Kabul. Many Afghans regarded his rule as oppressive, and he was assassinated by a Hazara, the adopted son of an Amanullah supporter named Ghulam Nabi who had been executed for treason in 1932.

Nadir Shah was succeeded by his nineteen-year-old son, Zahir, who was to rule until 1973, though in the early years the country was effectively run by two of his uncles and then a cousin holding the post of prime minister. Until 1946, Muhammad Hashim was prime minister, minister of war, and commander-in-chief; he was replaced by Shah Mahmud Ghazi, who was prime minister until 1953. Ghazi, in turn, was replaced by the king's cousin and brother-in-law Muhammad Daud, who held the position of prime minister until 1963, when he was forced to resign by the king.

During the early period of Zahir's rule, a proliferation of newspapers and journals began to encourage debate on the problems of modernization, the relationship of Islam with society and the individual, and the relationship between Islam and modernization. At the same time, the French were excavating archaeological remains and revealing the glory of Afghanistan's past, which encouraged secular thinkers to see in the past an opportunity to restore Afghan glory, with a diminished role for religion. However, these discussions and thoughts were restricted to the elite and did not permeate through to the general population until much later in the reign.

The Afghan economy also developed, with the introduction of banking institutions, the growth of the trade in agricultural exports, and transit trade through Soviet Central Asia, which increased as relations with the Soviet Union improved. Afghanistan also benefited from remaining neutral during World War II, and it became a refuge for many citizens from Central Europe who provided important but inexpensive technical assistance for development. During the premiership of Shah Mahmud Ghazi, the political agenda was dominated by political relaxation and the expansion of international ties, especially with the United States. The government also wanted to improve irrigation and agriculture and to find a third-party state to avoid it again becoming a buffer between Russia and the Indian subcontinent.

Political reform was also instituted in 1949, and reformists made up one-third of the new assembly; in addition, laws were passed to establish a free press, and new newspapers sprang up overnight. The free press called for an elected constitutional assembly, an end to corruption, improved living conditions, and an end to import-export monopolies established by local capitalists under government sponsorship. A student union was formed at Kabul University, and students began to protest the abuses of the royal family and the misuse of Islam to sustain injustice. However, in 1951, the government became alarmed at such developments, and it closed down the student union; in the following year, there were a number of enforced press closures.

In 1953, the king's cousin and brother-in-law, Muhammad Daud, became prime minister, and he shared the aspirations of the reformists, feeling that the government was too conservative, the religious establishment too reactionary, and the newly emergent capitalists too powerful. Daud was determined to pursue a reformist program by harnessing the skills of the intellectuals to run the government and to build up a strong military to ensure regime stability; he sought support for the latter among the Pashtun tribes by reviving aspirations with regard to the question of Pashtunistan. Daud's preferred choice of supplier was the United States, but Washington refused to supply military material, and he was forced to turn to the Soviet Union for supplies and technical assistance. Cold War relationships meant that the West ignored Afghanistan, but it was courted by the Soviets, and Daud became reliant on the Soviet government for all types of military assistance.

In the social arena, Daud also introduced reforms aimed at enhancing educational opportunities, and he made the wearing of the veil and the *chadari* optional. One outcome of these reforms was that women enrolled at Kabul University, and others began to enter the workforce and the government, but the reforms had little impact outside of Kabul. At the same time, a major road construction program, partially financed by the United States, linked the main cities of Afghanistan and provided ties into Pakistan. However, the Pashtunistan problem, which involved Afghanistan's efforts to secure the return of the Pashtuns in Pakistan to Afghan control or at least attain independence or autonomy for the region, bedeviled relations with Pakistan, and 1961 saw the two countries on the brink of war. The tense relations with Pakistan and the autocratic nature of Daud's premiership led the ruling elite and the king to believe that Daud was becoming a liability. This, coupled with his opposition to the 1963 constitution proposed by King Zahir (which, among other things, banned close members of the royal family from high office), caused the ruler to demand Daud's resignation. In 1963, Daud departed the scene, and the Loya Jirga adopted the constitution in 1964.

The last decade of Zahir's rule was marked by some political instability, for the new constitution encouraged feverish political activity with heavily contested elections, the rise of multiple political parties, and a free press. However, the king did not seize the reins of power in order to shape the direction of the new government, and his rule was characterized by indecision and procrastination. During this period, the Afghan Communist party, known as the People's Democratic Party of Afghanistan (PDPA), was secretly formed in 1965, with Babrak Karmal as one of its leaders. In September 1965, the first elections under the new constitution were held, and Babrak Karmal was elected to parliament, and in the 1969 elections, both Karmal and Hafizullah Amin, another secret Communist, were elected to parliament.

From the Republic to the Saur Revolt of April 1978
In July 1973, King Zahir was on vacation in Europe, and on 17 July, with the backing of one wing of the

Communist party, Muhammad Daud seized power, abolished the monarchy, and declared himself president of the Republic of Afghanistan. Unbeknownst to Daud, sleepers had been placed within the Afghan bureaucracy and the military following the founding of the PDPA in 1965. After the coup, they suddenly emerged in positions of authority within the ministries, much to the surprise of their former superiors; one sleeper actually became the official interpreter to President Daud. The inherent inefficiency of the Afghan bureaucracy meant that many of these sleepers went undetected until the Marxist coup of 1978.

However, Daud was keen to divorce himself from his backers in the PDPA, and by 1975, he had eased most members of the Parchami wing out of office and had began the process of rapprochement with Pakistan. In the same year, he undertook visits to Saudi Arabia and Iran and secured much-needed financial support for his reformist program. He also began to restore friendly relations with Pakistan by resolving a dispute over Baluchistan and promising to settle the issue of Pashtunistan. In a visit to Lahore in 1976, Daud was warned by Pakistan's Inter-Service Intelligence (ISI) unit about meetings between members of the PDPA, Soviet officials, and supposedly loyal Daud supporters.

In 1977, Daud announced a new constitution, which called for deep and fundamental socioeconomic reform and an end to the exploitation of ordinary Afghan citizens. The constitutional program also promised land reform, the nationalization of key industries, and the regulation of business to eliminate exploitation. In addition, the constitution declared that power was to be exercised by the people, the majority of whom were deemed farmers, workers, the enlightened, and youth, with the new legislature having to draw 50 percent of its membership from among farmers and workers. The armed forces were given a political role through the High Council of the Armed Forces, and only one party was allowed to operate. This was the National Revolutionary Party founded by Daud in 1975, and it excluded his PDPA collaborators in the coup. However, its Central Committee, formed in 1977, was appointed by Daud and was criticized for being full of his cronies or corrupt officials. The party was supposed to be a short-term expedient until the people achieved political maturity, but it had the power to nominate all candidates for the forthcoming elections. The constitution also confirmed the rights for women already introduced by Daud.

In April 1977, Daud visited Moscow for high-level negotiations, but these talks became acrimonious due to Soviet objections to Afghanistan's use of foreign experts from other countries, a situation that Daud refused to change. However, while he was in Moscow, the two wings of the PDPA—the Khalq and the Parchami—were holding reunification talks, and their differences were resolved in July 1977, with Nur Muhammad Taraki becoming party secretary, Babrak Karmal secretary of the Central Committee, and both factions being equally represented on the committee.

Although President Daud had repeatedly made it clear that he wished to maintain good relations with the Soviet Union, he also wanted Afghanistan to remain a nonaligned state. By this stage, the Soviet Union was unwilling to risk losing its considerable investment in Afghanistan—and its sleepers in the bureaucracy and the military—to be replaced by oil-rich Arab states. It therefore instructed the PDPA to plan a coup to oust the Daud regime, and Hafizullah Amin, from the Khalq faction, was assigned to garner support from among the military, though the Parchami faction was to be secretly operating through Mir Akbar Khaibar. Neither faction was aware of those within the military who were already under the control of the Soviet State Security Committee (KGB) and the Chief Intelligence Directorate (GRU). Leaders of the PDPA considered that they had been betrayed by Daud because of his refusal to share power and because he had abandoned the Pashtuns in Pakistan in return for Iranian and Saudi gold. However, he was still feared by the PDPA leadership, and his execution was to become a deliberate part of the coup being planned.

From the Saur Revolt to Soviet Intervention (April 1978–December 1979)

The Saur Revolt of 27 April 1978 brought with it a Marxist government and total dependence on the Soviet Union. The coup was led by the PDPA and members of the party within the military, together with hitherto unidentified Soviet sleepers, who secured military and key public facilities. The royal palace was also stormed, and despite a spirited defense by Daud's guards, the president and his family were killed. Such was the degree of infiltration within the government and the military that the coup was a complete success and was met by only minimal opposition.

However, the new Marxist regime was full of inexperienced administrators who thought that they were the leaders of a social and political revolution, aided by the military. The Central Committee of the PDPA also operated under the illusion that it controlled the relationship with the Soviet Union and that the Soviets would allow the committee to freely reconstruct Afghan society. In fact, the Soviets cared nothing for the transformation of Afghan society but sought only control over Afghanistan as a secure base for further possible incursion in the Middle East and South Asia. They saw this as their reward for decades of patience and considerable financial investment.

The new regime was also incapable of understanding the need for a balance in foreign and domestic policies and the importance of pursuing gradual change, so they operated under the illusion that everything was possible. As a result, they attempted to bring about change by issuing orders from the center and following a policy of ruthless brutality to eliminate actual or perceived opposition, which succeeded in driving away potential allies from within the ranks of the modernists and the traditionalists. The Marxist regime also failed to expand its base among the urban intellectuals or to overcome the many years of suspicion with which Afghans regarded their Soviet neighbors. Failure was also to be the result of trying to create a national, democratic revolution in a country that had yet to become a nation and the inability to fully realize the conservative nature of the traditional Afghan rural communities.

After the coup, Nur Muhammad Taraki became president and prime minister, with Babrak Karmal as deputy prime minister and Abdul Qadir, a Pashtun air force officer, as minister of defense. The Foreign Ministry was given to Hafizullah Amin, who also became second deputy prime minister, meaning that the Khalq faction controlled the critical ministry in terms of relations with the Soviet Union. Soviet advisers and political officers also heavily staffed the military and the government. In Afghanistan, the Pashtuns have always dominated the political scene, but the Soviet political officers directed their initial programs toward northern Afghanistan and the non-Pashtun minorities. The policy was to

appeal to the minorities on the basis of cultural and linguistic equality and, in the process, act against the domination of the Pashtuns, particularly in the north. The advisers were Dari-, Uzbek-, or Turkoman-speakers, and they stressed the links between these communities and those of the Central Asian republics of the Soviet Union.

The Khalq faction dominated the regime in Kabul, with all pronouncements coming from Taraki or his close aide Hafizullah Amin. In the media, a cult of personality was developing, with Taraki being called "the Great Leader" of the revolution, and the Parchamis, led by Babrak Karmal, were ousted from the government; many were sent into exile through diplomatic postings abroad. It was not long before they were accused of plotting a coup, and Parchami ambassadors were recalled but wisely remained overseas, with many of them seeking the protection of the Soviet Union. Those left within Afghanistan were arrested, removed from government and party positions, and charged with treason.

At no time did the Soviets attempt to interfere, probably in the belief that the strong Khalqis in the military were best suited to Soviet control over Afghanistan rather than the Parchamis who tended to be urban elites, though they were not totally abandoned by the Soviet Union. In 1979, political instability increased, with mass arrests and killings and factional unrest within the military. A major mutiny took place in Herat in March 1979 when the Seventeenth Division massacred their Soviet advisers and their families. In addition, the land distribution program reforms introduced by the regime were a complete socioeconomic disaster, bringing chaos and hardship to all levels of society. The party continued to suffer from internal divisions, and in September 1979, the clash between Taraki and Amin came to a head. Amin came out on top, having removed Taraki from office and arranged for him to be suffocated in prison.

At the same time, opposition to the Marxist regime had begun to develop, starting in June 1979 and becoming active mainly in the rural areas. The situation within Afghanistan had dramatically changed as the Soviets' supposedly compliant regional ally was descending into chaos. The authority of the PDPA was being challenged in the provinces by a resistance that was based on national, social, ethnic, and religious grounds and was developing with covert assistance from Pakistan.

The army was beginning to experience desertions in large numbers; conscripts were refusing to report for service; and military units fought among themselves, mutinied, or deserted wholesale to the opposition.

Amin was convinced that the Soviets would support him because he controlled the military, which was vital for securing the nation against the mujahideen guerrillas. As a result, he raised no objections when the Soviets increased the numbers of advisers within the military, even down to the company level, and he also allowed Soviet combat units into the country in order to relieve Afghan units from the defense of Kabul and to move on the offensive within the provinces. However, Soviet Special Forces moved on the presidential palace on 27 December 1979 and executed Amin while he was trying to negotiate protection against what he thought was a Parchami coup.

The Period of the Soviet Intervention (1979–1989)

The Soviets replaced Amin with Babrak Karmal, leader of the Parchami faction of the PDPA, but the situation within Afghanistan continued to deteriorate. The regime had effectively lost control of the countryside, which meant that it had lost 85 percent of the population. This situation led the Soviets to consider whether they should intervene to preserve the Marxist regime in Kabul from a humiliating defeat—a defeat that would also damage the credibility of the Soviet Union, particularly as Afghanistan was on its borders. Equally, defeat for the Afghan army would also reflect badly on the Soviets, for the troops had been advised, trained, and equipped by the Soviet Union. Afghanistan's position as a buffer state was once again to be thrust to the fore of international politics. However, the Soviets decided that military intervention was an acceptable option, particularly because they believed that the United States was preoccupied elsewhere, with its attention in the region being centered on Iran and Pakistan.

The Soviet army crossed the border on 24 December 1979 when, it was correctly assumed, Western embassies and governments would be on vacation, thus ensuring that any response would be delayed. The Soviets also counted on international opposition being short-lived and felt that the world would soon accept the situation in Afghanistan as a fait accompli. The initial aspects of the operation were a complete success, and Moscow expected resistance to cease at that point. But, as with previous invaders, the Soviets had miscalculated and had ignored the traditional Afghan values that had manifested themselves throughout recent history. They were soon to be faced by an enemy that had values, a love of freedom—even from central control emanating from Kabul—and, of course, an immutable faith in Islam.

It would have been reasonable to assume that the Soviet military would prevail. The Soviets, after all, had an extensive knowledge of Afghanistan, having constructed many of the country's airfields, part of the highway network, and the Salang Tunnel, and they also had superior technology. The Soviet objective was to stabilize the situation in Afghanistan and to hold key objectives, including the urban areas, leaving Afghan forces to deal with the mujahideen in the countryside. The Soviet forces intended to have only minor contact with the local population, to provide air support and logistics to the Afghan military, and to keep their own casualties to a minimum. It was intended that the Soviet forces should strengthen the resistance of the Afghan military so that the mujahideen could be quickly defeated and a Soviet withdrawal effected.

However, an occupation designed to last for a few months was to endure for ten years. With just cause, it has been described as the Soviet Union's Vietnam. In the end, the Soviets lost about 40,000 troops killed in action, but a large number were murdered, some committed suicide, many became drug addicts, and many others succumbed to disease due to their poor support services and inadequate food and equipment. The Soviets came prepared to fight a conventional European war with a battle plan designed to destroy their ill-equipped opposition or to so terrify them that they would flee across the borders into Iran or Pakistan. However, the Soviet military had miscalculated and had underestimated the capacity of the mujahideen, who were from a traditional warrior society. They proved to be resourceful and implacable enemies who utilized their topographical knowledge and became adept at withdrawing in the face of Soviet attacks and then returning to strike when their opponents were unprepared or when units had become exposed or isolated. The mujahideen also had the advantage of the support of the local population, who opposed and obstructed the Soviets and government forces at every turn; even women became involved in the resistance.

The Afghan government legitimized the Soviet presence, but it soon grew beyond the original Limited Contingency Force; its strength eventually varied from 90,000 to 104,000, with troops operating on a rotational basis. They were also backed by other troops and air support operating from bases in the Central Asian republics of the Soviet Union. Even with this commitment, the Soviet and Afghan forces could only provide a measure of control over the main centers of population and the main communication routes, with the countryside belonging to the mujahideen. The Soviets were extremely slow to change tactics, and the mujahideen refused to fight a conventional war; rather, they pursued guerrilla tactics and struck at roads and pipelines in order to disrupt Soviet supply lines.

The mujahideen saw themselves as fighters in a jihad directed against an infidel government backed by the Communist regime in Moscow. However, it must be realized that the mujahideen were never a unified force and represented the factional interests of Afghan society, which hardened the acute differences that already existed in the country. The mujahideen were split between Sunni Muslim and Shi'a Muslim groups, Islamic radicals, and moderates: the only unifying factor was their opposition to the government of Babrak Karmal and the Soviet presence. The guerrillas also operated with their own external backers, which was to cause problems at a later date; the northern Afghan groups drew support from their ethnic counterparts in Central Asia, the Shi'a groups were backed by Iran, and the Islamic radicals were supported by Saudi Arabia, with Pakistan eventually becoming a conduit for Western aid.

The mujahideen mainly operated from bases outside Afghanistan, with the largest number of groups in Peshawar, Pakistan. However, the group led by the Tajik leader Ahmad Shah Masood operated out of the Panjshir Valley in northern Afghanistan, which was never taken by the government forces despite several determined assaults. The Shi'a groups operated largely out of western Afghanistan and had support from the Iranian government. The vast number of groups were Sunni Muslims, and the leaders operated out of Peshawar in a somewhat tenuous alliance of seven groups that received support initially from the Pakistan government and

then, as the war progressed, from the United States through covert aid provided by the Central Intelligence Agency and distributed by Pakistan's Inter-Services Intelligence unit.

The mujahideen movement was always in a state of flux, with shifting alliances and power bases whose allegiances reflected regional, tribal, and ethnic origins; all of this would return to haunt Afghanistan in the post-Communist era. It was not long before Western aid began to reach the mujahideen in an overt manner as the struggle became embroiled in Cold War politics. Afghanistan once again became a buffer state and a pawn in the twentieth-century version of the Great Game. The mujahideen forces in Afghanistan were also becoming stronger and better equipped, being able to counter Soviet airpower and helicopter gunships by the use of Stinger missiles supplied by the United States. They benefited, as well, from equipment captured from the Soviets or brought over by Afghan military deserters. By the middle of the 1980s, it was becoming evident to the Soviets that they were engaged in a war that they could not win and that it was necessary to secure a political solution in Afghanistan to enable their troops to be withdrawn.

All of this was having a devastating effect on the Afghans themselves, resulting in millions of refugees fleeing the conflict and creating major humanitarian problems for Pakistan and Iran. At one stage, it was estimated that there were some 5 million Afghan refugees, most of whom were in refugee camps in Pakistan and totally reliant on UN agencies or nongovernmental organizations (NGOs) for their survival. In Iran, because of other international problems, the bulk of the burden was borne by the Iranian government on its own at a time of economic hardship with Iran. Inside Afghanistan, there was also the problem of displaced populations moving from areas of conflict or because of the scorched-earth policies being adopted by Afghan forces and their Soviet allies in areas considered to be hostile.

At the same time, the ruling PDPA was in a state of disarray, and the internal divisions within the party were continuing to cause problems. The Soviets attempted to force unity by bringing Khalq personnel into the Parchami-led government, and they also brought back Dr. Muhammad Najibullah from Moscow in 1980 to head the state security service,

KHAD; at that time, he was loyal to Karmal, having once been his bodyguard. However, the war between the two factions continued. Assassinations were commonplace, and the feuds were solely concerned with the acquistion of power. The strength of the party was only growing in the urban areas, where it was safe to be a declared party member because of security, though most of the new members were opportunists taking advantage of the favorable treatment accorded to party members. Karmal made several attempts to bring about party unity, but all of them foundered, so that by 1985, he was becoming an embarrassment to the Soviets and their changing policy.

In the Soviet Union, Mikhail Gorbachev had come to power, and his policy of glasnost, or openness, meant that the costs of the Afghan war were no longer secret, in terms of either financial losses or casualties, though accurate casualty figures were never released and the drug problem was never acknowledged. UN-sponsored negotiations were also going in Geneva, having started in 1982, between Afghanistan and Pakistan, with the Soviet Union and the United States in attendance. Gorbachev felt that agreement was not going to be reached with Karmal in power because his known allegiance to the Soviet Union meant that he would not be acceptable to any national reconciliation process designed to appeal to the ordinary Afghan's desire for peace. In 1985, Karmal was replace by Najibullah, but PDPA disunity did not disappear and was to come to a head in 1990 with an attempted coup by the minister of defense, Gen. Shanawaz Tanai, who led the Khalq faction.

In 1987, Najibullah tried to negotiate a cease-fire, but the mujahideen refused to deal with him, as he was considered a puppet of the Soviet Union. Meanwhile, the mujahideen were having even more success, and the Soviets were in danger of experiencing an ignominious defeat. In 1988, the Geneva Accords were signed, and the Soviet government agreed to withdraw from Afghanistan within nine months. For his part, Najibullah tried to move his government away from its Marxist roots by introducing Islamic-friendly policies but to no avail. The last Soviet troops departed from Afghanistan on 15 February 1989, leaving the Najibullah government to its own devices. The Soviets left a great deal of military equipment behind for the Afghan military, and although

many observers expected the Najibullah regime to collapse within weeks, it continued to survive.

From the Fall of Najibullah to the Arrival of the Taliban (1989–1994)

Najibullah's government continued to survive after the Soviet withdrawal largely by holding on to a reduced territory, concentrating on the urban areas and on keeping open the main communication routes. This was only possible with continuing Soviet aid, Soviet air force missions, and some Soviet troops in civilian clothing operating SCUD missile batteries. In addition, support from the United States and Pakistan to the mujahideen had been reduced, as the prime objective of securing a Soviet withdrawal had been achieved. The mujahideen had not been able to defeat the Marxist government militarily, which was illustrated by the attack on Jalalabad in March 1989 when a garrison of some 4,500 troops successfully repulsed a mujahideen force of some 10,000 men. The mujahideen siege of Kabul was also not proving to bring about the gains that they had hoped for, mainly due to the lack of cohesion between the various groups and poor battle discipline.

During the period after the Soviet withdrawal, Najibullah attempted to pursue a policy of reconciliation, and he tried to draw mujahideen military leaders into the Afghan armed forces, provided they observed a cease-fire. Najibullah was also prepared to allow them to consolidate control over their own localities and to support them against any fundamentalist incursions, but the mujahideen were reluctant to cooperate. Meanwhile, the United States had begun to restore supplies to the mujahideen, and these groups mounted attacks against the urban areas held by government forces. But disunity between the groups had increased, and they again failed in an attempt to take Jalalabad.

However, the Soviet Union was beginning to loosen its grip on Eastern Europe, and the Cold War was coming to an end. By 1990, support for the mujahideen was reducing, and the U.S. administration also began to form the opinion that the mujahideen were unlikely to overthrow the Najibullah regime. At the same time, the Soviet support was also being reduced, and the Afghan military forces were beginning to run out of fuel and money. In addition, commodity prices were spiraling out of control. The collapse of the Kabul regime was an internal collapse due to the differences within the government as to the best way forward. By 1992, Najibullah had abandoned all plans to form a coalition government, and he tried to obtain support for a transfer of power to all parties involved in the struggle.

The factions loyal to Babrak Karmal wanted to form a coalition with the mujahideen, but this plan excluded the Islamic Party of Gulbuddin Hekmatyar. Najibullah had also fallen out with Gen. Abdul Rashid Dostum, but he failed to remove him from the scene; consequently, the northern militia loyal to Dostum switched allegiances and joined the Northern Alliance forces led by Masood. On 14 April 1992, Najibullah was forced to resign, and the Kabul government came under the control of Babrak Karmal. Agreement was reached with some elements of the mujahideen over the formation of a coalition government. The coalition consisted of supporters of Karmal, the Islamist Movement of Rabbani backed by Masood, the Uzbeks under Dostum, and the Isma'ili faction of Nadari.

The coalition envisaged control of the cities and the major communication routes by the Afghan army and all political parties fused into the civil administration. Hekmatyar, who saw no need for a compromise with the Communists, rejected this move, and he also rejected a move by Najibullah to form a link between the Islamic Party and the PDPA (now renamed Watan, or Homeland Party). Instead, Hekmatyar ordered his forces to move on Kabul and to take control of the cities from the Communists. The whole situation came to a head on 15 April 1992 when a mujahideen group, formerly allied to the government, seized the Kabul airport and prevented Najibullah from leaving Afghanistan. On 25 April, the forces of Masood entered Kabul and reached agreement on a coalition government that excluded Gulbuddin Hekmatyar, leading to a period of intense and bloody conflict. Najibullah was forced to seek refuge in the UN compound in Kabul.

The mujahideen government suffered from two significant weaknesses: their agreement for power sharing in Kabul was basically flawed and their Islamic unity was shaken by the ethnic rivalries and desire for power. The planned rotating two-month leadership, leading to ineffectiveness within the government, demonstrated the mistrust that existed between the mujahideen leaders. This also led to

each group consolidating its position in Kabul and its environs, with the massing of fighters and weapons to protect these interests. The first president of the coalition government was Sabghatullah Mujaddidi, who served his two-month period and was replaced by Burhannudin Rabbani in June. But Rabbani deviated from the agreement by having his period of office extended after packing a meeting with his supporters.

The mujahideen coalition as a legitimate government was totally eroded by its disunity and by its multiple ethnicity, which undermined the Islamic fervor that had been its strength in the war against the Soviets and had accorded the movement respectability in the eyes of the Afghan people. The struggle for power in Kabul, however, was to bring Pashtun chauvinism and minority ethnic irredentism to the fore, and these divisive factors were to dominate internal relations in Afghanistan from 1992 onward. Rabbani's struggle to retain the presidency led to fears by other groups that this was an attempt by the Tajiks to seize power, leading to the Pashtuns opposing Rabbani. The opposition was expressed through the mobilizing of other ethnic groups against Rabbani and his military commander Masood in a series of shifting alliances; it is clear that these ethnic rivalries also extended to the Hazaras and Uzbeks as major forces, as well as the less critical Nuristanis and Isma'ilis.

The net result of these ethnic and factional rivalries was a civil war largely fought out in Kabul and its immediate environs. In the process, significant parts of the city were reduced to rubble, and another wave of refugees fled to the eastern provinces and Pakistan. Tales of murder, mutilation, abduction, and rape marked the conflict, with all groups being equally guilty. In essence, the civil war was not just a breakdown in law and order but a complete disintegration of Afghan society, and the interethnic atrocities traumatized the civilian population. Pakistan attempted to mediate between the combatants in March 1993 and succeeded in securing an agreement whereby Rabbani was to continue as president for a further eighteen months and Gulbuddin Hekmatyar was to be prime minister; Dostum was totally excluded at Hekmatyar's insistence because of his prior support for the Communists. This situation led to Dostum withdrawing his forces and returning to the north and his power base in Mazar-i Sharif.

Afghanistan was again a divided nation. Dostum controlled six of the northern provinces, from the Central Asian republics to the outskirts of Kabul. In Kabul, the alliance between Rabbani and Hekmatyar was beginning to unravel, and in October 1993, fighting broke out between the two groups. In January 1994, Dostum abandoned his policy of neutrality and launched attacks on Rabbani's forces in Kabul, having been joined by his erstwhile enemy Hekmatyar. In June 1994, Rabbani refused to step down as president and the civil war intensified, with all efforts to bring about peace by the United Nations and other countries in the region doomed to failure. It appeared that Russia and the U.S. administration were content to see the internecine rivalry continue, as they feared that a stable Islamic Afghanistan would damage their interests in the region and could also provide assistance to Islamic militant forces in areas such as Tajikistan.

Afghanistan was in a state of total anarchy, with a complete breakdown of law and order, no semblance of government, and a population suffering from the effects of military action and starvation; many were kept alive only through the intervention of the United Nations and NGOs. Apart from the area under the control of General Dostum, the rest of Afghanistan, outside of Kabul, had been carved up among a number of mujahideen commanders who had set themselves up as regional warlords. The local populations had no security from murder, looting, rape, and extortion. Even the aid agencies found it difficult to operate, and there were instances of offices being ransacked, vehicles commandeered at gunpoint, and staff members intimidated.

From the Rise of the Taliban to Operation Enduring Freedom (1994–2001)

In the midst of the anarchy and chaos, the Taliban movement emerged in 1994 in Kandahar Province, formed by a number of Pashtun mullahs who were veterans of the war against the Soviets and wished to see an end to the civil war. A few mujahideen leaders who had become disillusioned with the anarchy that had followed their victory joined the mullahs. The movement began to center on a former mujahideen commander, Mullah Muhammad Omar, from the village of Singesar in Kandahar Province. Commanders from other Pashtun parties,

Khalqi PDPA members, and students from the Afghan *madrasas* (religious schools) soon swelled the group.

The movement became known as the Taliban, standing for students, as the bulk of the membership came from the students of the religious schools, primarily in Afghanistan and then from the North-West Frontier Province of Pakistan; it also recruited from the young in the refugee camps. The Taliban's objectives were the restoration of peace, the disarming of civilians, and the full application of Shari'a law. Mullah Omar soon began to restore law and order in the areas under his control, and he was then approached by truckers from Pakistan trying to secure safe passage through areas dominated by warlords who demanded tolls from the truckers. Taliban successes in this respect resulted in their receiving support from Pakistan because of that country's concern about the trade routes to the Central Asian republics.

The Taliban armed themselves by seizing a munitions depot near Spin Boldak and the border with Pakistan and then began a move on Kandahar. The city was taken after the local commander, loyal to Rabbani, ordered his troops not to resist; this allowed the Taliban to acquire heavy weapons, tanks, and aircraft. The ranks of the Taliban were then greatly increased by volunteer fighters from Pakistan, who crossed the border with the knowledge of the Pakistani authorities. Toward the end of 1994, the Taliban spread north and east to the suburbs of Kabul and west toward Herat, with strong financial backing from Pakistani merchants who had markets in Central Asia.

The Taliban program was based on a promise to end the fighting and to restore law and order under the Shari'a, and this meant that in areas taken by the group, bad local commanders were removed whereas commanders who had followed Islamic values were confirmed in their posts. The Taliban began to make inroads in the country. Ghazni fell at the end of January 1994, followed by Maidanshahr in Wardak Province, and then Hekmatyar's headquarters at Charasyab, south of Kabul, were taken. The defeat of Hekmatyar was a significant development for the forces of Rabbani, as the Taliban then attempted to adopt a neutral position in Kabul by separating the opposing forces. But in March 1994, Masood took advantage of the situation to drive the Taliban and Wahdat forces from Kabul. The Taliban had also tried to take Herat but were driven back by the forces of Isma'il Khan, which had air support provided by Masood.

In 1995, the Kabul government attempted to regain international recognition, for the city was no longer under attack and the international airport was reopened. However, in September 1996, the Taliban again attacked Herat, and this time it was taken, with Isma'il Khan being forced to seek refuge in Iran. This left the Taliban free to concentrate on Kabul, which fell to their forces on 27 September, following on from a number of successes elsewhere in eastern and southern Afghanistan. However, Masood had already withdrawn his forces in good order and retired to his stronghold in the Panjshir Valley in northern Afghanistan. It was evident that the presence of Masood in the Panjshir region and Dostum in Mazar-i Sharif could not be tolerated by the Taliban: they represented a threat to their aim of ending the power of the regional warlords, former Communists, and former mujahideen leaders in order to form a unified country under an Islamic government.

By the spring of 1997, the Taliban controlled about 90 percent of the country, with the anti-Taliban forces of Masood holding only an area in the Panjshir Valley and an enclave in the eastern mountains. However, the military campaigns of the Taliban had been marked by abuses of human rights, particularly in relation to women, and ethnic cleansing, especially during the retaking of Mazar-i Sharif. Both sides have been equally guilty of atrocities, with incidents of massacres, mutilations, prisoners being suffocated in containers, and other abuses being recorded by the United Nations, NGOs, and the U.S.-based Human Rights Watch. This form of human rights violations only served to heighten the ethnic rivalry between the Pashtun-dominated Taliban and Afghanistan's other ethnic minorities. In the case of the Hazarajat region, the conflict was also one of religion, for the Taliban regarded the Hazaras as inferior beings because they belonged to the Shi'a sect of Islam. The whole character of the Taliban military campaign and the reactions of the resistance were to provide a legacy of mistrust and a desire for revenge in some areas in the post-Taliban period.

The ranks of the Taliban had been strengthened by foreign fighters, largely coming from the Arab states, Chechnya, and Pakistan, many of who were also part of al-Qaeda. In 1996, Osama bin Laden had returned to Afghanistan following his expulsion from the Sudan. He had already been accused of complicity in a number of terrorist incidents, including the attempted bombing of the World Trade Center and attacks on the U.S. embassies in Kenya and Tanzania. It is ironic to note that bin Laden had been a mujahideen leader during the jihad against the Soviets and had been the recipient of U.S. aid, in large part because of his military capabilities in the field. However, in 1996, he was organizing training camps for terrorists in eastern Afghanistan and attracting recruits from within the Islamic world to his al-Qaeda organization.

The presence of bin Laden and al-Qaeda again thrust Afghanistan to the forefront of international politics. Pressure mounted for the Taliban regime to extradite bin Laden to face charges in relation to a variety of terrorist acts, but Mullah Omar, who insisted that bin Laden was a guest of Afghanistan, refused to respond to these demands. The UN Security Council imposed limited sanctions on Afghanistan, but bin Laden was still given shelter, though the Taliban insisted that his activities had been curbed and that he was under house arrest. The Security Council was not satisfied with this response, and further sanctions were imposed, but their impact was limited because they did not cover the land routes from Pakistan.

Meanwhile, there was considerable international condemnation of the human rights record of the Taliban regime. All representations were rejected by the regime, for the Taliban maintained that they were acting in accordance with Shari'a law and that it was no concern of the outside world. International adverse reaction to the regime was further fueled by the decision taken in March 2001 to destroy all statues and monuments relating to Afghanistan's pre-Islamic heritage, including the world-famous statues of the Buddha in Bamian Province. Despite pleas from countries around the world, including Islamic states, as well as international organizations such as UNESCO and museums that were prepared to house the relics, the process of destruction continued unabated. It has been argued that some of the actions of the Taliban and their refusal to respond to the international community can be attributed to their total naïveté with regard to foreign affairs and diplomacy.

All of this was to pale into insignificance, however, with the 11 September 2001 terrorist attacks in the United States on the World Trade Center and the Pentagon, resulting in just under 4,000 deaths of civilians from several countries. The U.S. and UK governments named the al-Qaeda organization as responsible for these atrocities, with Osama bin Laden as the instigator and financier of the operation. This contention seemed to be reinforced by a video released by bin Laden and broadcast by the Arab satellite television station al-Jazeera, operating out of Qatar, in which he welcomed the attacks on the United States. Further investigations revealed that al-Qaeda members had been warned to return to Afghanistan before 11 September, as a momentous event was to take place on that day. The whole world was shaken and moved by this tragedy and the bloodshed and carnage, and the UN Security Council again demanded that Osama bin Laden be handed over to face justice—a demand that was again rejected by the Taliban.

In Afghanistan, the charismatic leader of the Northern Alliance, Ahmad Shah Masood, had been assassinated by Arabs posing as reporters and thought to be from al-Qaeda. These events had an immediate impact with respect to the countries that had recognized the Taliban regime: Saudi Arabia, the United Arab Emirates, and, most significantly, Pakistan withdrew their recognition. The U.S. administration had already determined to bring the perpetrators of these atrocities to account, and it declared a "War on Terror," with the immediate objectives being the overthrow of the Taliban regime, the capture of Osama bin Laden, and the destruction of al-Qaeda. The Pakistan government of President Pervez Musharraf immediately declared its support for the concept, as did the Central Asian republics that were fearful of Islamic fundamentalists causing unrest in their countries. Even the regime in Iran was opposed to the Taliban because of their treatment of the Shi'a minorities in the Hazarajat and the death of Iranian diplomats during the Taliban campaign in western Afghanistan.

The campaign against the Taliban and al-Qaeda began on 7 October 2001 with an air assault designed to destroy Taliban installations and infrastructure and attacks on al-Qaeda training camps. Further objectives were to pave the way for ground attacks by conventional forces and to aid anti-Taliban Afghan forces. Intelligence for the air campaign was provided by U.S. and UK Special Forces who were already in Afghanistan, working with Northern Alliance troops or operating independently in Taliban-held territory. The air attacks provided the impetus for Northern Alliance forces to move against the Taliban, with the tactic then changing to provide support for anti-Taliban forces by attacking Taliban frontline positions. This change in emphasis took place toward the end of October 2001, though the Northern Alliance was frustrated by the delay and by the fact that the air attacks were not as sustained and comprehensive as they would have wished.

The Coalition land campaign was initially launched by special forces, primarily from the United States and the United Kingdom but with contributions from Australia, France, Germany, and New Zealand. The operations were conducted with anti-Taliban forces providing advice and intelligence or guiding U.S. Cruise missile attacks, while others worked behind enemy lines mounting covert operations against enemy installations. One such attack was carried out by U.S. Army Rangers and Delta Force commandos on the compound of Mullah Omar at Kandahar. Small groups were also operating in eastern Afghanistan, trying to destabilize the Taliban or working with CIA and ISI operatives attempting to bribe local warlords to turn against the regime.

The Coalition strategy to overthrow the Taliban was based on supporting the Northern Alliance as it attacked from the north while special forces kept up the pressure in southern Afghanistan. It was clear that the Northern Alliance was the only military alliance on the ground; despite the efforts of Afghans (such as Abdul Haq, who was later executed by the Taliban, and Hamid Karzai), there was no real Pashtun resistance in southern Afghanistan, and any resistance that occurred was uncoordinated and minimal. However, the Northern Alliance was seen as problematic, for it was distrusted by the Pashtuns because it was composed of ethnic-minority Tajiks and Uzbeks. This mistrust was understandable, as it was based on the bitter experience of four years of mujahideen rule in Kabul between 1992 and 1996. The bulk of the ground fighting against the Taliban and al-Qaeda was carried out by Northern Alliance forces. Coalition ground troops, apart from the special forces, only became involved in November 2001, primarily to hunt down the retreating Taliban and al-Qaeda fighters. Anti-Taliban forces took the main Taliban stronghold of Kandahar on 6 December 2001 after Taliban and al-Qaeda fighters had fled the city for the mountains.

The Post-Taliban Period (December 2001–2003)

At a conference held in Bonn, Germany, under the auspices of the United Nations, agreement was reached between anti-Taliban groups on the formation of an interim government for Afghanistan. This accord was announced on 5 December 2001, with Hamid Karzai having been elected as president of the interim cabinet. This cabinet was scheduled to last for six months, to be replaced by an interim government approved by a *loya jirga* (grand council), with a life of eighteen months. Thereafter, Afghanistan was to have a democratically elected government, with balloting to take place in 2004. To help the new government maintain order, the UN Security Council authorized the formation of the International Security Assistance Force (ISAF), with a mandate to police Kabul and its immediate environs. The force was multinational and initially headed by the United Kingdom, which had provided the bulk of the forces; Turkey and other countries would then take turns as head of the ISAF, on a rotating basis.

Although the main thrust of UN involvement was the installation of the new administration, Coalition forces were still pursuing the remaining Taliban and al-Qaeda fighters, of whom there were a few thousand. As a consequence, major operations were mounted in December 2001 against opposition forces in the Tora Bora hills area, some 30 miles south of Kandahar. However, despite air attacks on the complex of caves and assaults by Coalition forces, it is estimated that some 2,000 fighters fled the area, with the majority crossing into the tribal borderlands of Pakistan. It has been accepted that Osama bin Laden was part of this exodus. Further operations were mounted throughout 2002 against Taliban and al-Qaeda refugees in Operations Anaconda, Snipe, Mountain Lion, and Ptarmigan, and although successes were achieved, a number of the enemy were still active in southern Afghanistan. The geography of the area is such that fighters are able to cross and recross the border with Pakistan by using mountain tracks that are not charted on any maps. They find a welcome haven among the Pashtuns in the North-West Frontier Province of Pakistan, which is only loosely under the control of Islamabad.

In June 2002, a loya jirga was held by President Karzai to form the Transitional Government, as provided for by the Bonn Agreement. The reelection of Karzai as president was the first decision of the council, but this outcome was aided by the fact that the former king wished to take no active role in Afghan politics and the former president, Burhanuddin Rabbani, had withdrawn. The compilation of the government proposed by Karzai for approval by the council was a compromise, for he tried to represent all of the various factional and ethnic interests in the country. An indication of the weakness of Karzai's position was seen in the hasty appointment of General Dostum as a deputy defense minister after he had been omitted from the Interim Government and had therefore refused to recognize the Bonn Agreement. Both administrations also had significant Northern Alliance representation as a result of the military campaigns, but this caused a great deal of suspicion and mistrust within the Pashtun majority.

Coalition operations continued in 2003, with actions being mounted in Paktia and Helmand Provinces to counter raids by Taliban and al-Qaeda fighters. Some successes were achieved, the most striking being the capture of Khalid Sheikh Mohammad—the number three man in the al-Qaeda hierarchy—on 1 March 2003 in Rawalpindi, Pakistan, as a result of a combined operation between CIA operatives and Pakistan security forces. However, activity still continues in southern and eastern Afghanistan with sporadic raids on Coalition forces and bases, and there is some evidence that al-Qaeda training camps have been reestablished in eastern Afghanistan and the tribal borderlands of Pakistan. Operations are taking place in geographically difficult areas against small groups of guerrilla fighters and close to a border that is difficult to police and impossible to seal. Also, in some areas of Afghanistan, there is still some sympathy for the Taliban, and the North-West Frontier Province of Pakistan also houses a largely sympathetic population.

The situation in Afghanistan is still unstable. President Karzai's authority does not run much beyond Kabul under the protection of the ISAF, though this has not prevented attempts on his life. As a result, the regional warlords in the provinces have filled the security vacuum, and their militias are again rising. The anarchy prevailing in some provinces, especially in southern and northern Afghanistan, partially explains the continuing sympathy for the Taliban, who are remembered for bringing law and order to the areas under their control. Unrest has been prevalent with the fighting between rival factions in the eastern and northern provinces, and the situation has not been helped by the failure of the international community to expand the operations of the ISAF (despite many pleas by President Karzai) and the slow progress being made in the creation of a national Afghan army and police force.

In parallel with the security issue is the major task of reconstruction faced by Afghanistan and the international community. The country has been ravaged by twenty-three years of war and several years of drought. An environmental impact assessment undertaken by the UN Environmental Program has painted a bleak picture of deforestation, water shortages, infrastructure breakdown, and environmental pollution in urban and rural areas alike. In addition, there are the ravages of war, with enormous destruction in Kabul and other cities, together with severe damage to roads, power supplies, and telecommunications. The scale of the problem is enormous, promised aid has been slow to arrive, and it is clear that if Operation Enduring Freedom is to have been a success, the international community must demonstrate a long-term commitment to Afghanistan.

Afghanistan is also faced with the problem of assimilating returning refugees and trying to resettle the thousands of internally displaced persons. At least 600,000 refugees still remain in Pakistan as of March 2003, but it is expected that many of those will begin to make their way back to Afghanistan as the mountain roads clear of winter snows. A meaningful reconstruction program is an essential prerequisite for restoring stability in Afghanistan and to enable it to stand on its own. Although $4.5 billion was pledged over a period of five years by the international community at the Tokyo Conference in January 2002, as well as $1.24 billion at the Oslo Conference of 18 December 2002, assistance has been slow in arriving, with President Karzai stating that more aid is needed.

However, some positive measures are being put in place. Six Afghan agencies, working with the UN Mine Action Program, have been allocated $7.5 million to clear mines along the sides of the road from Kabul to Kandahar. The Kabul-Kandahar-Herat road has been under reconstruction since November 2002 with aid from Japan, Saudi Arabia, and the United States, and the mine-clearing program is scheduled for completion by the end of 2003. Some of the funding is also to be used to clear land mines from construction sites earmarked for building schools and bridges. Under another project from the U.S. Agency for International Development, worth $60 million, 1,200 primary schools across the country are to be repaired or built, and 10 million textbooks will be printed in Dari and Pashto. The issue of reconstruction has remained at the forefront of the agenda, with a meeting held at Brussels on 17 March 2003 to discuss the deficit being faced in the ordinary budget of the Afghan government and in the budget needed for reconstruction. At this meeting, Canada pledged C$250 million over two years specifically for the development program.

Progress in the areas of security, dealing with the regional warlords, and reconstruction must be significant if the credibility of the Karzai government is to be established. This is also seen as critical to the success of the democratic elections, which are scheduled for 2004 under the terms of the Bonn Agreement. Until the start of planning for the elections, political parties are not recognized in Afghanistan, and a program of registration is planned to take place before the elections. However, this did not stop several small political groups and former mujahideen leaders from coming together to launch the National Democratic Front on 12 March 2003. The coalition consists of fifteen political parties and thirty other groups, including labor unions, and it claims a membership of 40,000 and growing. Coalition members believe that Western-style democracy is the best way to counter the power of the militias, ethnic divisions, and Islamic fundamentalism.

A spokesman for the coalition stated that the main objective was to curb extremist ideas and to pursue Western concepts such as human rights, freedom for women, social justice, and democracy. He also warned against the power of the Tajiks in the Kabul government who were pursuing a fundamentalist agenda and stressed that armed factions, doubling as political parties, must be disarmed before they could enter the democratic process. The new coalition is still small, but it does show some political development in Afghanistan. Meanwhile, the situation in the country is fluid, and the nation will again descend into anarchy unless the international community maintains its interest and support, possibly for decades to come. Political stability is critical to the country's economic development, but with its oil and gas and its geographically strategic position, Afghanistan could face a brighter future at the crossroads of many of the world's economic and political powers.

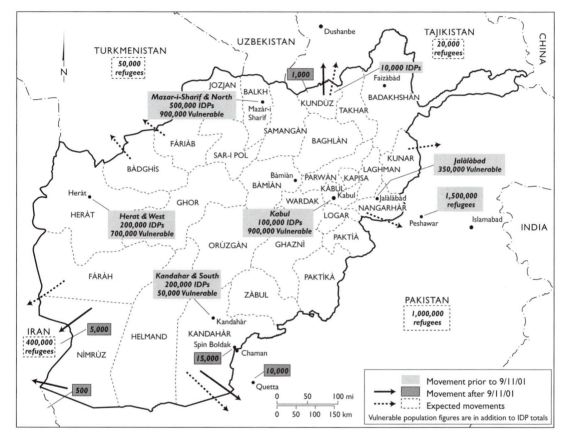

Map 1 Afghanistan Humanitarian Situation, September 25, 2001. (Courtesy Government of the UK, Department for International Development)

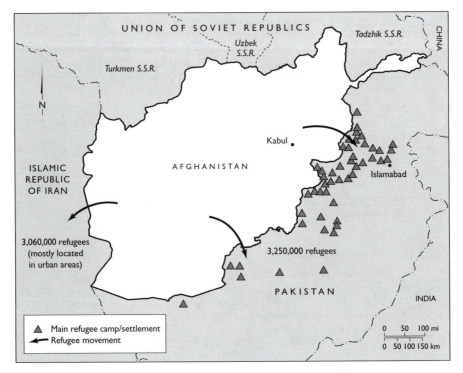

Map 2   Main Afghan Refugee Flows, 1979–1990 (Courtesy UN Refugee Agency/Europa Technologies Ltd.)

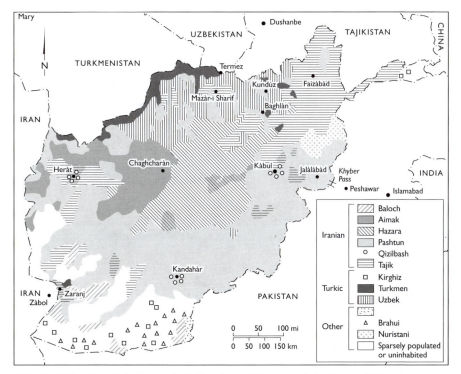

Map 3   Ethnolinguistic Groups in Afghanistan. (Courtesy of the General Libraries, University of Texas at Austin)

Map 4   Political map of Afghanistan. (Courtesy of the General Libraries, University of Texas at Austin)

Map 5   Pakistan/Afghan border. (Courtesy of the General Libraries, University of Texas at Austin)

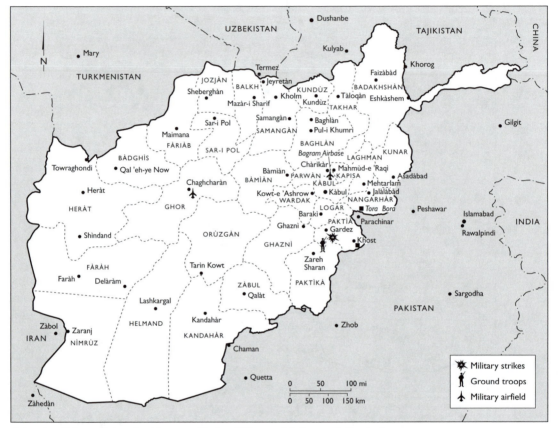

Map 6   Cities and Attacks. (Courtesy National Geographic Image Collection)

ABDULLAH ABDULLAH (1958–)

Abdullah Abdullah is the foreign minister in President Hamid Karzai's Transitional Government and emerged as one of the main spokesmen of the Northern Alliance following the assassination of Ahmad Shah Masood, the military leader of the alliance. He has become a pivotal figure in many of the diplomatic talks and negotiations on Afghanistan's future, both within the country and overseas, meeting in Iran with UK foreign secretary Jack Straw and in Uzbekistan with U.S. envoy James Dobbins.

Abdullah is a qualified doctor who speaks several languages, is fluent in English and French, and is typically dressed in Western-style suits. He received his M.D. degree in ophthalmology at Kabul University's Department of Medicine in 1983, and from 1985 to 1986, he worked in the Ophthalmology Hospital for Afghan Refugees in Peshawar, Pakistan. In 1986, he became special adviser and personal assistant to Masood, a position he held until 1992, when the mujahideen coalition seized power in Kabul. In 1993, he was appointed director-general in the Ministry of Defense in Burhanuddin Rabbani's government in Kabul, a position he held until 1996 when Kabul fell to the Taliban and the Northern Alliance forces withdrew to northern Afghanistan. He continued as Masood's personal assistant and accompanied him on a visit to Europe in 2001 to appeal for international support in the struggle against the Taliban.

It is clear that Abdullah represents a brand-new type of Afghan politician, and he has recruited to his ministry articulate, educated Afghans from around the world, all of whom have much-needed expertise and skills gained outside Afghanistan. However, most of them are ethnic Tajiks, with their family origins in the Panjshir region of northwest Afghanistan. Some observers believe this could present problems in the future from the Pashtun majority in southern and eastern Afghanistan and from supporters of the former king Zahir Shah,

A

though the exiled monarch has continued to maintain that he has no political aspirations. It is recognized by the United Nations and foreign diplomats that Abdullah has done an excellent job since his appointment following the December 2001 Bonn Conference and the June 2002 Loya Jirga (Great Council), but ethnic divisions within Afghanistan still make these loyalties as important as competence in terms of political legitimacy. In Abdullah's favor is the fact that, with no funds and many internal difficulties, Afghanistan has retained the support of the United States without alienating Iran or letting tensions on the borders of Afghanistan get out of control.

As foreign minister, Abdullah has tried to project calm and confidence despite the ongoing tumult within the country and has insisted, for example, that there is unity within the Karzai administration on the question of stabilization. He has continually stressed that the maintenance of peace and the rebuilding of the country are paramount goals, with the government having been given a historic opportunity that cannot be wasted. In this respect, Abdullah has the advantage of having a Pashtun father and a Tajik mother and is thus able to bridge the ethnic divide, which will be important in the reconstruction process and bringing an end to ethnic cleansing.

In terms of foreign relations, the major problem faced by the Interim and Transitional Governments has been the need to mend fences with Afghanistan's neighbors after decades of war. Many Afghans, for example, have a deep distrust of Pakistan because of its support of the Taliban and the presence of thousands of Islamic militants from Pakistan fighting in Afghanistan with the Taliban or al-Qaeda. Underlying all of

Foreign Minister of Afghanistan Abdullah Abdullah (Patrick Robert/Corbis)

this current distrust is the vexed Pashtunistan issue in the North-West Frontier Province of Afghanistan, with many Afghans still believing that the Pashtuns in this region should return to Afghan control or at least that the area should become an independent or autonomous region. Abdullah has been keen to forge a new relationship with Pakistan in order to deal with the threat posed by Taliban and al-Qaeda elements sheltering in Pakistan's tribal borderlands. Relations with Iran are also seen as important because of the Shi'a population in the areas bordering Iran, and although the anti-Taliban support from Iran had been welcomed, there is some concern that anti-Kabul elements are being armed by Iran, such as the forces of Isma'il Khan in Herat.

In terms of internal security, Abdullah has been keen to see an increased role for the International Security Assistance Forces (ISAF) in order to give Afghanistan time to organize a national police force and form a national army. He has also been concerned about ensuring that the aid pledges from foreign governments are met so that reconstruction work can begin, particularly on roads, to get the economy moving and enable the government to realize its objectives. He has been conscious of the need for the government to fulfill its promises and to deal with the returning refugees and the internal displaced population, many of whom have migrated to Kabul. Abdullah has also expressed confidence in the peace process despite the attempt on President Karzai's life on 5 September 2002, which he has described as a desperate attempt to destabilize the government. It is clear that the problem of the warlords in the provinces is crucial, hence the pressure from Karzai and Abdullah to expand the role of the ISAF.

Abdullah was instrumental in securing a nonaggression agreement on 22 December 2002 with five of Afghanistan's neighbors—China, Iran, Pakistan, Tajikistan, and Uzbekistan—at a conference in Kabul that was also attended by representatives from India, Saudi Arabia, Turkey, the European Union, and the United Nations. The Kabul Declaration, as the agreement is titled, was designed to emphasize amicable relations, to foster respect for territorial integrity, and to discourage actions intended to threaten peace and stability in the region. Despite this agreement, however, concerns are still being voiced by the United States over Iran's continued support for Gulbuddin Hekmatyar, an avowed opponent of President Karzai and the U.S. presence in Afghanistan, and by elements in the Karzai administration who are worried about continuing support for the Taliban by the Inter-Services Intelligence unit of Pakistan.

Nonetheless, it is evident that Abdullah has faith in this declaration as a foundation for building a stable relationship within the region, and he has shown himself to be a committed supporter of President Karzai and the policies of the Transitional Government.

References

Rubin, Barnett R. 2002. *The Fragmentation of Afghanistan: State Formation and Collapse in the International System.* 2nd ed. New Haven, CT: Yale University Press.

ABDUR RAHIM, NAIB SULAR (1896?–1941?)

Naib Sular Abdur Rahim was a Tajik from Kohdaman and was born in Kohistan. At age sixteen, he went into service at the court of Amir Habibullah, and he served in Kabul for a period of five years. Between 1903 and 1913, he was the supervisor of bridge construction in the eastern provinces before being promoted to the rank of major and posted to the Cavalry Division based in Herat Province. In 1921, he was promoted to brigadier, recalled to Kabul in 1927, and then transferred to the Cavalry Division at Mazar-i Sharif.

In 1927, he returned to Kabul and joined Bacha-i-Saqqau in his second attempt to seize Kabul. January 1928 saw Abdur Rahim sent to Mazar-i Sharif to organize a revolt; he deposed the governor and then left for Maimana and Herat where, on 4 May 1929, he defeated the Herati forces under Gen. Muhammad Ghaus. As a result, he was appointed civil and military governor of Herat, and Muhammad Nadir Shah reconfirmed him in the post in October 1929.

After the military successes of Nadir Shah's commander, Shah Mahmud, in the spring of 1931, he decided to accept the rule of Nadir Shah, and in September 1932, he was confirmed as governor of Herat and the adjoining areas. In June 1934, he was appointed minister of public works, and in September, he became head of the Persian-Afghan Boundary Commission, returning to resume his post in the ministry in 1936. Two years later, he became deputy prime minister, a post he held until 1940.

References
Ikbal, Ali Shah. 1939. *Modern Afghanistan.* London: S. Low, Marstons.

ADMINISTRATIVE DIVISIONS

Kabul has been the capital and center of Afghanistan since the reign of Timur Shah, who ruled from 1773 to 1793, with the provinces—including Badakhshan, Herat, Kandahar, Qataghan, and Turkstan—being largely autonomous under the rule of various princes. Not until the reign of Abdur Rahman from 1880 to 1901 were various provinces incorporated into Afghanistan and brought under the control of Kabul. The country was divided into five major and four minor provinces during the reign of Nadir Shah from 1929 to 1933.

The present structure of Afghanistan was largely settled by the 1964 Constitution, when the country was divided into twenty-six provinces graded according to their importance, with the most important being controlled by a governor (*wali*), who may also have controlled an adjacent minor province. The governor is responsible to the Ministry of the Interior in Kabul, but representatives of various departments in the provinces also report directly to Kabul.

The administrative structure of the provinces is quite complex, as they are further divided into sub-provinces, districts, and subdistricts. Each district has an administrator, who may also be responsible for adjacent subdistricts and who reports directly to the provincial governor. Administrators of subdistricts reside in a major village and are responsible to the district administrator, working with village headmen in the rural areas (who are also linked to the district administrator). In major centers of population, such as Mazar-i Sharif, they are divided into wards, with each ward official being responsible to the city administrator. In the 1970s, 27 provinces were divided into 6 subprovinces, 175 districts, and 11 subdistricts, but changes were often made by the central government in response to a particular political need or objective.

The provinces and administrative centers are as follows:

Province	Administrative Center
Badakhshan	Faizabad
Badghis	Qala-i-Nau

Amir Abdur Rahman, whose isolationist policies rebuilt Afghanistan after the Second Anglo-Afghan War (Illustrated London News Group)

Baghlan	Baghlan
Balkh	Mazar-i Sharif
Bamian	Bamian
Farah	Farah
Fariab	Maimana
Ghazni	Ghazni
Ghor	Chaghahaman
Helmand	Lashkargah
Herat	Herat
Jozjan	Sheberghan
Kabul	Kabul
Kandahar	Kandahar
Kapisa	Mahmud Raqi
Kunduz	Kunduz
Laghman	Mehtarlam
Logar	Pul-i-Alam
Nangarhar (including Kunar)	Jalalabad
Nimruz	Zaranj
Oruzgan	Trinkot
Paktia (including Paktika)	Gardez
Parwan	Charikar
Samangan	Ajbak
Takhar	Taloqan
Wardak	Kotu-i-Ashro
Zabul	Qalat

References

Adamec, Ludwig W. 1972–1985. *Historical and Political Gazetteer of Afghanistan.* 6 vols. Graz, Austria: Akademische Druck-uVerlagsansalt.

AFGHAN ARABS

A large number of Afghan Arabs live in different parts of Afghan Turkestan, and they are mainly nomadic or seminomadic. Estimates are impossible to obtain, but several thousand families reside in the valleys and graze their animals on the slopes of the mountains in the summer. They tend to be well off, owning large flocks of sheep and herds of cattle. Most speak Persian, and they live in yurts, or conical tents of Turkoman origin. At one time, they were much more widely dispersed, but they retreated from areas such as Maimana in the face of occupation by the Turkomans. However, they are to be found in the Sar-i-Pul, a large hill district in Afghan Turkestan.

A small colony of Arabs live in the Jalalabad district, their ancestors having arrived with Timur Shah in the eighteenth century. They speak Persian and have retained some of their nomadic instincts and are primarily engaged in agricultural and pastoral pursuits. The colony has also migrated over the centuries to Pagham and Basud, near Kabul.

References

Bellew, H. D. 1880. *The Races of Afghanistan: Being a Brief Account of the Principal Nations Inhabiting That Country.* London: Thacker.

AFGHAN ARMY

A new national army for Afghanistan has been in training since April 2002 with U.S., British, and French expertise, but by the end of 2002, only 1,700 men, arrayed in five battalions, had completed the course. This situation does not bode well for President Hamid Karzai and his goal of having in place a force of 70,000 by 2009, loyal to the central government in Kabul. Further, there is the danger of a security vacuum, with the International Security Assistance Force (ISAF) restricted to Kabul. Recruitment to the new force has been hampered by the reluctance of regional warlords to send good recruits to join the army for fear of weakening their own power base. Dropout and desertion rates have also been high, largely due to the low rates of pay—$30 a month during training and $50 a month after graduation (raised to $70 a month in January 2003).

Historically, Afghanistan's army evolved from traditional beginnings, but it was not until the reigns of Amir Dost Muhammad and Shir Ali Khan in the early nineteenth century that a process of modernization began. However, the army lacked the modern weaponry of the neighboring states and did not have a modern officer corps, for officers were appointed on the basis of loyalty rather than ability. Western technology and ideas only came to Afghanistan through means of prisoners of war or foreign mercenaries. Army troops were paid partially in cash and partially in kind and almost always in arrears, and recruitment was often accomplished through the seizure of able-bodied men, regardless of age. A militia of riflemen and tribal irregular forces enhanced the regular army. The modernization process was continued by Amir Shir Ali, who obtained a number of artillery pieces and some 5,000 Snider rifles in 1875, but civil war put an end to any other advancement. Amir Abdur Rahman was responsible for reequipping the regular army and expanding the production of weaponry in Afghanistan.

Kabul parade, on 23 January 2002, of a unit of Afghanistan's new multiethnic National Army (© Reuters NewMedia Inc./CORBIS)

It was not until the beginning of the twentieth century (in 1904) that Amir Habibullah founded the Royal Military College, with the aim of creating a modern officer corps. The recruits were mostly the sons of Durrani chiefs, and the college was headed by a Turkish officer, Mahmud Sami, marking the beginning of Turkish influence in the Afghan army; this trend continued after World War I during the reign of King Amanullah, though advisers from Germany and other countries were also used. Amanullah's army comprised an infantry of 38,000 men, a cavalry force of 8,000, and some 4,000 artillerymen, with mainly German field pieces.

Nadir Shah, on coming to power in 1930, reconstituted the army; established military schools for the artillery, cavalry, and infantry; increased pay for the armed forces; and improved accommodations and clothing. By 1936, the army, some 60,000 strong, utilized German, Italian, and Turkish officers and played a significant role in internal security. The troops were now regularly paid and housed in better accommodations, but this army was still inferior to the British India army in terms of equipment and levels of training. King Zahir continued the modernization process, for he realized that to ensure domestic stability and defend against external aggression, he needed a strong, modern force. The minister of war and commander-in-chief of the army, Shah Mahmud, embarked on a major program of reorganization and reequipping the troops. New officer training schools were established at Maimana and Mazar-i Sharif, and those in Kabul and Herat were expanded, with officers being sent abroad for additional training. Major weapons purchases were also made from Britain, Czechoslovakia, Germany, and Italy, together with the acquisition of tanks and aircraft to create the first mechanized forces. As a result of a voluntary enlistment process combined with compulsory service, the force had risen to 80,000 by 1936 and was consuming about half of the revenues of the government.

At the end of World War II, the force stood at 90,000 men, but by then its equipment was largely obsolete. Shah Mahmud, now prime minister, reduced the size of the army by half in order to focus on internal security and increased the size of the central police force. The Afghan government repeatedly tried to buy weapons from the United States, but these efforts were rebuffed, and in 1955, Prime Minister Muhammad Daud turned to the Soviet

Union for assistance. In July 1956, the Soviet Union granted a loan of $32.4 million, which was used to modernize the army, but this arrangement resulted in Afghanistan becoming dependent on Soviet supplies and expertise, with nearly 4,000 Afghan personnel going to the USSR for training.

At the time of the Saur Revolt of April 1978, which brought the Communists to power, the Afghan army comprised infantry divisions, mechanized forces, paratroops, commandos, and artillery brigades and was actively involved in the coup against President Muhammad Daud. The armed forces had a sizable tank force and an air force of some 170 fighter planes and 60 helicopters. In 1979, following the Soviet intervention in Afghanistan, the army became embroiled in the war against the mujahideen guerrilla forces, largely under Soviet direction. As part of the planning, the Afghan army was used in the field against guerrilla forces, with the Soviets concentrating on providing security for the urban areas and airpower for campaigns against the mujahideen. However, during the ten-year Soviet presence, from 1979 to 1989, large numbers of the Afghan troops deserted to join the mujahideen.

After the fall of Muhammad Najibullah's government in 1992, the Afghan army disintegrated, with troops breaking up to support various mujahideen groups depending on their ethnic or political allegiances. The period from the mujahideen government of 1992 to the fall of the Taliban in 2001 was marked by factional fighting, and no formal armed forces structure remained.

It is deemed crucial to the survival of Afghanistan as an integrated state for a new national army to be formed in order to support a central government and to break the hold of the various regional warlords, each with his own armed forces. At present, however, the signs are not promising, and the new national army is still a distant dream that may take many years to come to fruition.

Many of the rival warlords made promises of integrating their forces within a new Afghan army once the Interim Government was established, but to date, none has made any attempt to disarm or to transfer troops to government control. Also, the Taliban and al-Qaeda are not a spent force, as they still enjoy a measure of popular support in southern Afghanistan and the tribal borderlands in Pakistan. Moreover, the force now being trained is not linked to a command structure that reflects Afghanistan's ethnic diversity, no plans exist to integrate or demobilize the forces of the regional warlords, and opposition is not being decisively handled. One possible concept would be to use the new force for operations designed to encourage public support and engender cohesion and experience among the troops, with involvement in weapons disposal, mine clearing, and disaster relief operations. Another possible solution might be the creation of a small professional army that is answerable to the central government and a national guard, drawn from the tribal and warlord militias, that is answerable to the provincial governments.

The Defense Ministry decided, in February 2003, to redress the ethnic imbalance by replacing fifteen Tajik generals with officers from the Pashtun, Uzbek, and Hazara ethnic groups. The post of a fourth deputy defense minister has also been created and given to Gen. Zarak Zadran, a Pashtun. Further, the generals in charge of the artillery, special forces, education, logistics, and military investigations were all replaced. The ousted generals have been given jobs elsewhere in the ministry, with the changes being designed to create a sound and healthy administration that would earn the trust of all the people of Afghanistan.

Support has also been forthcoming from the Pakistan army, which, on 16 February 2003, turned over to the Afghan army 500 submachine guns, 180 82-mm mortars, rocket-propelled grenades, and 50,000 rounds of ammunition. The Pakistan army has also offered to train Afghan personnel at bases in Pakistan, but no start date for this program has been determined.

References

Manuel, Anja, and P. W. Singer. 2002. "A New Model Afghan Army." *Foreign Affairs* 81, no. 4: 44–89.

AFGHAN-GERMAN RELATIONS

Relations between Afghanistan and Germany date from August 1915, when members of the Hentig-Niedermayer Expedition first established contact with the rulers of Afghanistan. The country's lack of contact with other Europeans resulted from its self-imposed isolation and the refusal of the British India government to allow entry into Afghanistan, except for its own nationals. Some German and Austrian prisoners of war had reached Kabul, having escaped from Russia, and were interned by the authorities but contributed their skills to various public work projects.

However, the Hentig-Niedermayer Expedition, which also had Indian and Turkish representation, was the first official contact. Its mission was to establish relations with Afghanistan and persuade Amir Habibullah to attack India as part of Sultan Abdul Hamid's holy war. Although the amir wished to secure Afghanistan's independence from British control, he did not want to enter into a conflict that did not offer guaranteed success, and he agreed with Britain to remain neutral in return for a subsidy and recognition of Afghanistan's independence. Despite this agreement, however, the British were forced to maintain troops on the northwest frontier—forces that could have been released for the European theater of war.

One way in which Germany helped Afghanistan was by concluding the Treaty of Brest-Litovsk with Russia, signed on 3 March 1918. This agreement ended Russia's participation in World War I and also recognized the independence of Afghanistan. During the reign of King Amanullah (1919–1929), Afghanistan's independence was secured as a result of the Third Anglo-Afghan War of 1919, and the king sought to open up diplomatic relations with the major powers of the world. In 1923, the German minister plenipotentiary, Fritz Grobba, was sent to Kabul, and it was clear that Afghanistan and Germany had mutual interests, as the king desperately needed expertise to develop his modernization projects but found that, for a number of reasons, other powers were not able or willing to participate. Also, Germany had been an ally of the Ottomans and the caliphate during World War I, which led to a sympathetic relationship between the two states. Beyond that, Germany offered to provide industrial hardware and skilled engineers and technicians at highly competitive rates.

Commercial relations developed through a consortium of German companies, which formed the Deutsch-Afghanische Companie and established an office in Kabul. In 1923, King Amanullah founded a German-language high school, together with French- and English-language schools, and German influence grew in Afghanistan to the extent that, by 1926, the German colony was the largest after the Russian community; it soon became the largest foreign group in the country.

In October 1936, Germany and Afghanistan entered into a "confidential protocol" under which Germany provided DM 15 million of war matériel on credit, to be repaid in part with products from Afghanistan. Germany became an important player in the economy of Afghanistan and was regarded as politically significant in the country's attempt to balance the influences of Britain and Russia. In 1937, the German airline, Lufthansa, established a regular service between Berlin and Kabul, with a view to extending the service into China, and in the summer of 1939, a German delegation arrived in Kabul with the objective of expanding trade.

However, events in Europe—particularly the German annexation of Austria in March 1938 and Czechoslovakia in the following year, as well as a nonaggression pact signed with the Soviet Union in August 1939—were omens of war, and the Kabul government decided it did not want closer ties with the Nazi regime in Berlin. At the declaration of war, Zahir Shah immediately proclaimed Afghanistan's neutrality; the amir was determined to keep his country out of the conflict. Germany, conscious of Afghanistan's strategic location, considered supporting a pro-Amanullah coup to establish a sympathetic government in Kabul. German officials and Afghan supporters of the former king were sent to Moscow to test Russian reaction to the idea, but they received a noncommittal response and the project was shelved.

Following the German invasion of the Soviet Union in June 1941, Russia and Britain were allied again and adopted a common stance with regard to the situation in Afghanistan. In separate moves, the two governments demanded the evacuation of all Axis nationals in October 1941, a move that Afghanistan resented as an infringement of its sovereignty but still complied with, and all Axis nationals left for India under the promise of free passage to a neutral country. Although Axis diplomats were allowed to remain, their attempts to foment a rising against Britain among the Pashtun tribes on the Indian side of the border were unsuccessful. Despite sympathy for the Germans because of their traditional enmity with Britain, armed cooperation with Germany was never a realistic proposition for Kabul.

After Germany was defeated in World War II, the revival of the economy in West Germany caused German expertise to be in demand again in Kabul, and although they were unable to immediately supply industrial products, German nationals became a major factor in Afghan development projects. One of the first of these was a dam and hydroelectric power station at Sarobi. This project was followed by the building of the Kabul University campus by German contractors using financial aid from the United States, and German teachers were employed in the Faculties of Economics and Science. German aid grew to such an extent that by the 1970s, Germany ranked third after the Soviet Union and the United States in terms of assistance provided to Kabul. The German-language school became a model institution, the German Development Service brought volunteers with needed skills to Afghanistan, and the Goethe Institute was opened in Kabul to promote the German language and culture. Additionally, West German universities offered Afghans opportunities to further their studies in Germany. The East German regime was not recognized by Afghanistan, but it appeared on the scene with offers of aid, and its nationals gradually replaced those of West Germany after the Soviet occupation of Afghanistan began in 1979, though West German influence was not totally ousted. German nationals have enjoyed a good reputation in Kabul, and it is likely that they will play a significant part in the post-Taliban reconstruction program.

See also Hentig-Niedermayer Expedition
References
Adamec, Ludwig W. 1979. *Afghanistan's Foreign Affairs to the Mid-twentieth Century: Relations with the USSR, Germany and Britain.* Tucson: University of Arizona Press.

AFGHAN-IRANIAN RELATIONS

Relations between Afghanistan and Iran have been strained in recent years, primarily due to the war against the Soviet intervention (during which Iran supported the Shi'a mujahideen groups), the burden of Afghan refugees in Iran, and the Taliban's treatment of the Shi'a minority Afghan population. The Iranian regime has also been gravely concerned about the drug traffic coming from Afghanistan and has adopted harsh measures to stem the trade. Since October 2001, relations have also been strained because of Iranian suspicion about the large number of U.S. military personnel in Afghanistan, and President Hamid Karzai has had the difficult task of trying to repair fences with Iran without alienating U.S. support for his Transitional Government.

Iranian involvement in the affairs of Afghanistan goes back to the sixteenth century, when Afghanistan had no separate identity and was shared between the Iranians (then Persians) and the Mogul Empire of India. Not until 1722 was Iranian rule overthrown, with the occupation of Isfahan, in Iran, by Mir Mahmud (a leader of the Afghan northern tribes), though the period of independence was short-lived because Iran again took control of the country in 1736. However, in 1747, the Iranian ruler Nadir Shah was assassinated, the Afghans rose again, and Afghanistan was established with the retaking of Kandahar by forces under Ahmad Shah Durrani, followed by the expulsion of the Iranians from Herat. Iran continued to interfere in the affairs of Afghanistan and made several inroads, particularly against Herat in 1805, 1816, 1833, 1837, and for six months between 1856 and 1857.

In 1921, a treaty of friendship was signed with Iran, followed on 27 November 1927 by a treaty of neutrality and nonaggression. However, the border between the two states remained in contention, and in 1935, Turkey led arbitration to settle the border issue. Problems between the two countries came to the fore again in September 1947, when Iran claimed that Afghanistan's diversion of the Helmand River had caused crop failures in the Iranian province of Sistan. Relations improved in 1956 when an air service was established between Kabul and Tehran, and this was followed on 3 December 1960 with a joint agreement on trade and transit; on 20 April 1962, a new five-year agreement was concluded.

On 18 September 1961, Iran offered to mediate in a dispute between Afghanistan and Pakistan, and between 27 and 31 July 1962, representatives from Afghanistan and Pakistan met in Tehran to try to resolve the dispute over Pashtunistan. (Pashtunistan was an area that had been part of Afghanistan; many Afghans wanted the area to be returned or, alternatively, to be given independence or autonomy.) On 12 March 1973, agreement was finally reached between Afghanistan and Iran to settle the dispute over the Helmand River, but this issue continued to be a matter of contention, and it was not until 24 July 1975 that the two countries agreed to jointly develop the Helmand River region.

The seeds of historical animosity are also to be found in Islam—with Iran being a Shi'a state whereas Afghanistan is primarily Sunni—and the

Tehran government has always been concerned about the treatment of the Shi'a minority in Afghanistan, particularly by the Taliban. However, it is also apparent that Shi'as in Afghanistan have only been lukewarm in their support for Iran and have tended to resent Iranian interference in their affairs. The Taliban were militantly anti-Shi'a, and relations with Iran were almost pushed to the breaking point when the Taliban closed the Iranian embassy in Kabul in 1997 and then especially after the Iranian consulate in Mazar-i Sharif was attacked in August 1998 and eight staff members and an Iranian journalist were killed. At the same time, some seventy Iranian citizens, half of them truck drivers, were also seized, though they were gradually released between September and November 1998. Iran reacted to this atrocity by mustering 70,000 troops along the border and carrying out military exercises. These moves were significant in that they provided a breathing space for beleaguered Northern Alliance forces, for the Taliban was forced to deploy 5,000 troops to the area to counter a possible Iranian attack.

The Iranian government has always supported the various Shi'a mujahideen groups in Afghanistan, which had begun operations against the occupying Soviet forces in 1979. But they were small, independent, geographically based groups, and on 5 March 1985, Iran announced a merger between four of the mujahideen groups. Such unity did not last, however, and fighting broke out between the groups after the fall of Muhammad Najibullah's government in Afghanistan in 1992, forcing Iran to broker a cease-fire between the groups on 25 September 1993. This situation was also a trigger for Iran to begin to provide the regime of Burhanuddin Rabbani and Abdul Rashid Dostum with substantial military aid. Iran continued to aid the Northern Alliance, particularly the forces of Dostum and Ahmad Shad Masood, but it also rearmed Isma'il Khan, the former governor of Herat, who had taken refuge in Iran and returned to Afghanistan in 1996 to bolster opposition to the Taliban. By 1998, it was thought that Iran was providing more arms, fuel, and other materials to the Northern Alliance than was Russia. Planeloads of arms were flown in to equip the Shi'a Hazaras, and Iranian truck drivers provided a regular flow of materials. It was also thought that Iranian personnel were working with the Taliban's opposition and that Iran was providing covert training assistance from a base in Mashad,

Iran. In addition, it was providing technical assistance—for example, helping in the construction of a new bridge over the Amu Daria River, near the headquarters of Masood.

In November 1999, a slight thaw in relations between Iran and the Taliban regime occurred when Iran reopened a border post near Herat to allow trade between the two countries; it had been closed in August 1988 after the Mazar-i Sharif incident. Iran joined with Pakistan in December 1999 to try to find ways of encouraging Afghans to set up a broad-based government but to no avail. In January 2000, an Iranian delegation held trade talks with the Taliban and continued efforts, with Pakistan, to restrain the Taliban, mainly because Iran held the chair of the Organization of the Islamic Conference. However, relations were still not good; in March 2000, Isma'il Khan escaped from the Kandahar prison and again sought refuge in Iran and was rearmed by Iran on his return to Afghanistan in May 2001. Following the collapse of the Taliban, Isma'il Khan again became governor of Herat, and Iran continues to support him militarily and by the construction of a road from Herat to the Iranian border.

Tehran has been gravely concerned about the flow of narcotics across the border from Afghanistan and has estimated the trade at about 3,000 tons annually, with the drugs destined for Iranian and European markets. It is thought that Iran has, despite its draconian laws, about 1.2 million addicts, which greatly alarms the Iranian regime. Attempts to combat the drug trade are costing Iran about $800 million a year, and a number of security personnel have been killed by drug smugglers, who are well armed and well organized.

The war against drugs has been escalating, with confrontations taking place in the border regions. On 27 March 1999, a number of drug traffickers were killed by Iranian police in eastern Iran, and on 12 July 1999, the border was sealed in an endeavor to halt the trade. That these moves were unsuccessful is illustrated by the fact that eleven Afghan drug smugglers were shot near the town of Tabat-e-Heydarieh on 14 September 2000, which was followed by the death of a further thirteen smugglers in the border region on 7 November 2000. This situation led the Iranian authorities to declare a shoot-on-sight policy with regard to drug smugglers, but the trade still continues because the rewards are high.

On 17 May 2000, the Iranian parliament voted to seal the 625-mile border with Afghanistan and to fund the construction of electronically equipped walls and fences.

A further irritant in relations between Iran and Afghanistan is the presence of a large number of Afghan refugees in Iran, probably numbering some 1.4 million at the beginning of 2003. These refugees receive minimal outside assistance, and their presence has caused problems because Iran is suffering from a deteriorating economy and high unemployment itself; thus, tensions build between refugees and locals. Iran began a repatriation program in 1995 and on 12 March announced plans to repatriate 500,000 refugees. As part of the program and to achieve the target, the Iranian government withdrew temporary living permits, refused to renew work permits, and cut off all welfare facilities.

These steps were followed on 22 June by the repatriation of a further 400,000 refugees through Herat and then by additional repatriations from Sistan Province in Iran during August. However, on 6 September 1995, repatriations ceased when Iran closed the border after Herat fell to the Taliban. The program was resumed on 13 March 1996, when another 250,000 refugees were returned to northern Afghanistan via Turkmenistan. In September 1996, 250,000 more were repatriated through the same route but this time with the cooperation of the United Nations and the UN High Commission for Refugees (UNHCR).

Iran called a further halt to the program because of the worsening situation in Afghanistan, given the intense Taliban military activity in the northern part of the country, but on 25 February 1999, the program recommended after an agreement with the Taliban and the provision of logistical support by the United Nations. On 31 July 1999, a further 65,000 illegal Afghan refugees were expelled by Iran under a UN-devised plan. Since the fall of the Taliban in 2001, additional voluntary and compulsory repatriations have taken place.

In May 2002, it was announced that the Iranian president, Mahmud Khatami, was to visit Afghanistan on 8 and 9 June, prior to the holding of the Loya Jirga (Great Council); he hoped to build on the personal relationship he had established with Afghan president Hamid Karzai during the latter's visit to Tehran in February 2002. Karzai has had to tread a narrow path in order to improve relations with Iran without upsetting the United States, as both nations are critical to Afghanistan's stability. As a result, Kabul has adopted a neutral stance with regard to U.S.-Iranian relations, stressing that it favors an improvement in bilateral relations and would not be influenced by U.S. views on Iran.

Among the main topics discussed during President Khatami's visit was the question of the return of Afghan refugees; Tehran felt the repatriation process was too slow and that there was a danger the refugees were becoming too well integrated into Iranian society and would not wish to return home. This discussion took place against a backdrop of UN concern over Iran's apparent policy of forced repatriations. Security was also another major worry, with Iranian leaders trying to determine how to deal with the movement of Taliban and al-Qaeda fighters on their territory. It is not clear whether the Iranian authorities are trying to arrest the fighters and return them to their home countries or merely turning a blind eye to their presence.

More significant are concerns over Iran's relationship with regional rulers, especially Isma'il Khan in Herat. President Karzai is worried that Iran is preventing his government from consolidating its control in western Afghanistan. However, Tehran feels justified in retaining a measure of control over Herat in case the Afghan Interim Government does not survive, in order to protect its own security. Although Kabul would prefer that Iran stopped supplying arms to Isma'il Khan, the Tehran government believes that it has a special role in supporting the Northern Alliance, which helped topple the Taliban.

The appointment of Hamid Karzai was welcomed by the Iranians. Iran believes the interim body is one that it could tolerate and work with, as it wishes to see a moderate, Islamic government on its eastern border. However, Tehran is also concerned that Afghanistan is still in danger of disintegration, which would force the Karzai government to rely more heavily on U.S. support. To date, Karzai has managed to balance Afghanistan's relations with the two powers.

However, conservative elements in Iran view these developments with concern, as they consider the Karzai administration as pro–United States; indeed, they have accused the Afghan interim administration of being in league with the Central Intelligence Agency (CIA). Yet many Iranians believe that ties between Iran and Afghanistan could lead to economic growth and improved living standards and might serve as a bridge that could eventually bring Iran and the United States together.

See also Civil War; Guardians of the Islamic Revolution; Herat Province; Human Rights Violations; Isma'il Khan; Mazar-i Sharif; Refugee Problem; Shi'a Mujahideen Groups; Victory Organization

References
Ahady, Anwar-ul-Haq. 1998. "Saudi Arabia, Iran and the Conflict in Afghanistan." In *Fundamentalism Reborn? Afghanistan and the Taliban,* edited by William Maley, 117–134. London: Hurst.
Entekhabi-Fard, Camelia. 2002. "Iranian Leader Plans Visit to Afghanistan." http://www.eurasianet.org/departments/insight/articles/eav052402.shtml (cited 25 May 2002).
Goodson, Larry P. 2001. *Afghanistan's Endless War: State Failure, Regional Politics and the Rise of the Taliban.* Seattle: University of Washington Press.
Moaveni, Azedeh. 2002. "In Bush's Shadow." http://www.ahran.org.eg/2002/600/re4.htm (cited 22 August 2002).

AFGHAN NATIONAL LIBERATION FRONT

The Afghan National Liberation Front was founded after the Saur Revolt of 27 April 1978 to promote a united front against the new Communist regime in Kabul. During the revolt, some 12,000 people lost their lives and thousands were persecuted, including religious leaders, soldiers, civil servants, and students of religion; many were tortured and killed. The National Liberation Front calls for:

- Sincere and true application of Islamic principles as the only salvation for the Afghan nation
- Opposition to every element of disunity based on religious denomination, ethnic origin, or regionalism
- A society based on equality, brotherhood, and social justice
- Political power belonging to the people, which is necessary to fight for the rights of the individual—the right to live, the right to be free, the right to equality, and the right to personal property
- Fighting all elements of imperialism, feudalism, and economic slavery, which hinder the establishment of a free, independent, and prosperous Afghanistan

that is developed politically, economically, and socially

Members of the movement also pledge to:

- Support sovereign neutrality, nonalliance, and full recognition of human rights in Afghanistan
- Promote close relations with all friendly nations, especially neighbors
- Advocate noninterference in internal affairs of other countries, which is essential for the maintenance of peace and security in the region

References
Afghan National Liberation Front. N.d. *The Objectives of Afghan National Liberation Front.* Peshawar, Pakistan: Afghan National Liberation Front.

AFGHAN-PAKISTANI RELATIONS

Relations between Afghanistan and Pakistan have been determined by the history of the region since the end of the British Empire in India in 1947, which saw the birth of the state of Pakistan, created from the northwest part of British India. Included in this area was the North-West Frontier Province, which had become part of British India under the Durand Agreement of 1893. This border agreement was subsequently repudiated by Afghanistan, as it claimed that the Pashtuns' area should be part of Afghanistan. The question of Pashtunistan was to bedevil relations between the two states for decades and is still to be completely resolved.

The tone was set on 30 September 1947, when Afghanistan was the only state to vote against Pakistan's membership in the United Nations because of concern about the future of the Pashtuns in the border regions. In the following year, there were major signs of unrest among the Pashtuns in Pakistan, and on 16 June 1948, Pakistan arrested Abdul Ghaffer Khan and other Pashtun dissidents, which motivated Afghanistan to mount a media campaign for an independent Pashtunistan. The unrest between the two states persisted throughout 1949, with Afghanistan continuing to argue against the validity of the Pakistani claim that the tribal territories were an integral part of Pakistan. On 2 April, Afghanistan withdrew its diplomats from Karachi after a Pakistani bombing in Waziristan and followed this action by instituting border restrictions.

Further tension arose when, on 14 June, a Pakistani plane bombed Moghalgai, in Afghanistan. Pakistan attempted to defuse the situation by offering to hold talks on economic issues while still rejecting Afghanistan's claim to the tribal territories. The response by Afghanistan's National Assembly was to repudiate all the treaties with Britain that related to the tribal territories, at a meeting on 26 July 1949.

Relations between the states continued to be difficult, and on 26 May 1950, Pakistan was asked to recall a member of its embassy staff for breaking Afghan laws. It was not until 1953 that talks were held between the two countries to try to improve relations, but no real progress was made because of the Pashtun question. In November 1953, Afghanistan's foreign minister, Muhammad Naim, maintained that the issue of Pashtunistan was not a question of territory but one of allowing the Pashtuns to express their own wishes. Matters remained relatively quiet until 29 March 1955, when Prime Minister Muhammad Daud warned Pakistan not to include the Pashtun areas into West Pakistan, and on the following day, there were demonstrations outside the Pakistan embassy in Kabul and the ambassador's residence in Kandahar. On 1 April, demonstrations took place at the Pakistan consulate at Jalalabad, and the Afghan consulate in Peshawar was attacked.

On 12 April, Pakistan rejected Afghan replies to its protests and evacuated all families of its diplomats and other nationals and closed its consulate in Jalalabad. The situation worsened in May when Pakistan demanded the closure of all Afghan diplomatic facilities within its borders and closed all of its consulates in Afghanistan. On 4 May, Afghanistan mobilized its army but nine days later agreed with Pakistan that Saudi Arabia should arbitrate the dispute; however, Saudi arbitration was rejected by both countries on 28 June 1955. Afghanistan ended its state of emergency on 28 July, and in September, both countries agreed to stop hostile propaganda. Diplomatic relations were restored on 13 September.

Throughout the remainder of the decade, relations remained strained, and there were a variety of diplomatic incidents. Afghanistan's case was weakened by the Southeast Asia Treaty Organization's decision to uphold the Durand Agreement in 1956, though the Soviet Union assured Afghanistan in 1960 of its support in regard to the Pashtun question. The situation became truly critical beginning in May 1961, when Pakistan accused the Afghans of using troops to create unrest across the borders among the Pashtuns, an accusation that was rejected by Kabul. On 6 June, Afghanistan accused Pakistan of bombing Afghan border villages with arms supplied by the United States, and in Pakistan, 1,200 Pashtun leaders were arrested in Peshawar.

At the National Assembly meeting in June 1961, King Zahir stressed Afghan support for the self-determination of Pashtunistan, but on 22 June, Afghan nomads were banned from reentering Afghanistan unless they held valid passports, visas, and health certificates. By August, tensions were high, punctuated by threats and counterthreats, and on 6 September, Afghanistan severed diplomatic links with Pakistan. Six days later, the Islamic Congress of Jerusalem appealed for the resolution of differences between the two Islamic states, with Iran agreeing to act as a mediator, Saudi Arabia looking after Pakistani interests in Afghanistan, and the United Arab Republic looking after Afghani interests in Pakistan. Toward the end of September, Afghanistan refused to allow its transit goods to pass through Pakistan without the opening of consular and trade offices, a move that was rejected by Pakistani president Ayub Khan, who maintained that such offices would be used for subversive activities. It was not until 29 January 1962 that the border was reopened, albeit only for a period of eight weeks to allow U.S. humanitarian aid to reach Afghanistan.

In May 1963, it was announced that Iranian arbitration between Afghanistan and Pakistan had been successful, as was formally declared on 28 May. Diplomatic and commercial relations were soon reestablished, with the first trucks crossing the border on 25 July 1963. The situation had been successfully defused, and in 1965, the two countries signed a new five-year trade and transit agreement. Relations began to deteriorate again in 1975, when, on 28 July, a terrorist group was captured in the Panjshir Valley district of Afghanistan and Pakistan was accused of arming the group. This incident was followed in December by an accusation from Pakistan that Afghanistan was mobilizing troops on the Pakistan border. However, by 1977, relations between the two countries had resumed, and a semblance of accord had been established.

The Soviet invasion of Afghanistan in 1979 had a marked effect on relations with Pakistan. The Islamabad government promoted itself as an ally against the Soviet forces, in the hope that it would become a hub in the Cold War agenda of the West in the region. Pakistan therefore invited the Western powers to use its territory, the capabilities of its Inter-Services Intelligence (ISI) unit, and its infrastructure in order to mount anti-Soviet operations in Afghanistan. This prospect fitted in with Pakistan's strategy of using Afghanistan as a buffer state on its western flank and trying to bring to power in Kabul a government that would also see India as a common enemy. The Islamabad policy was a disposition to use Afghan resistance groups as surrogates for a "creeping invasion" of Afghanistan, but there is some doubt as to whether the Pakistan government fully understood the highly complex political environment in Afghanistan, particularly in the area of intercommunal relations.

However, Pakistan's involvement in the affairs of Afghanistan brought with it numerous problems. The Pakistani economy suffered from huge expenditures on military and intelligence services, and there was large-scale cross-border smuggling, together with the domestic problem of low taxation and poor excise collection rates. In addition, Afghan refugees competed with Pakistani nationals for jobs and business opportunities, causing tensions between the two societies, and there was also an increase in criminal activity. The large number of refugees, which had grown to 2 million by May 1981, and the fact that Pakistan was housing Afghan mujahideen groups led to strained relations with the Communist government in Kabul. The training of mujahideen groups was also reported to have begun in February 1979, using a Pakistani military establishment near Peshawar.

The mujahideen were operating from bases in Pakistan and were supported by the government in Islamabad and the United States, with covert military supplies being channeled through the Central Intelligence Agency (CIA). However, Northern Alliance forces under Ahmad Shah Masood were operating in northern Afghanistan from their base in the Panjshir Valley. Pakistan attempted to control the activities of the various mujahideen groups by stating that it would only recognize six groups to receive support and that refugees would only receive aid if they were allied to one of these six groups.

In 1982, the United Nations sponsored direct talks between Afghanistan and Pakistan at Geneva, with the first meeting taking place from 16 to 25 June. But these talks were inconclusive, and they were carried on, intermittently, until 1988, when agreement was finally reached. Throughout this period, problems still occurred—for example, Pakistan denounced a raid by Afghan troops on a border post and a refugee camp at Khuram that caused six deaths. The ISI also attempted to control military activity in Afghanistan and to steer the political outcome by directing raids, selecting targets, and mainly supporting the Islamic groups, especially that led by Gulbuddin Hekmatyar, as it was felt that these groups best served Pakistan's interests. The policy was guided by a belief that the religion-based groups would remain loyal to Pakistan whereas nationalist groups would assert their independence from Pakistan as soon as it suited their interests.

In 1989, the Soviet Union withdrew its forces from Afghanistan. The Kabul Communist government lasted until 1992, when Muhammad Najibullah resigned in an endeavor to bring the conflict to a close. The replacement government was based on a mujahideen coalition headed by Burhanuddin Rabbani, but civil war soon broke out between the various groups; a series of shifting alliances took place throughout the four-year conflict. This chaos gave rise to the fundamentalist Taliban group, which emerged on the scene in the autumn of 1994, with considerable backing from Pakistan. The Taliban was a network of clerics and students who had either fought against the Soviets or were products of the *madrasas* (religious schools) in Afghanistan and Pakistan.

The leaders of the Taliban, such as Mullah Muhammad Omar, had very close links with the religious schools in Pakistan, especially in the large concentration of schools along the Afghan-Pakistan border. The Taliban rigidly interpreted the Koran and followed the restrictive lifestyle preached in the religious schools. The Taliban saw themselves as the rightful enforcers of God's will and as the undisputed representatives of the Pashtun majority. Pakistan was a loyal supporter of the Taliban's cause, although it had its own agenda in relation to Afghanistan. The Taliban recognized this situation but were prepared to accept it because of their total dependence on Pakistan's support. However, the Northern Alliance, which once regarded Pakistan as a friendly and supportive neighbor, now regarded it as a traitor, with no role to play as a peace broker in Afghanistan.

The problem of Pashtunistan ceased to exist for the Taliban because they did not accept state borders, and members frequently made visits, long and short, to Pakistan to further their objectives; at the same time, some 3,000 to 5,000 Pakistani fundamentalists were operating out of Kabul in support of the Taliban. However, the Taliban refused to accept responsibility for cross-border activity, which spawned an increase in sectarian violence and criminality linked to the Taliban presence in Pakistan. Although the Taliban were able to guarantee safe land routes for Pakistan to ship goods to the Central Asian republics, smuggling also grew at an alarming rate, with cloth, arms and ammunition, vehicles, spare parts, electronics, cigarettes, and drugs regularly moving into Pakistan. In terms of recognition, Pakistan was one of only three states to recognize the Taliban regime as the legitimate government in Afghanistan, the others being Saudi Arabia and the United Arab Emirates. The remainder of the international community continued to recognize the government of President Rabbani. Pakistan also supplied regular troops, ammunition, and equipment to Taliban forces while simultaneously launching a number of halfhearted peace initiatives that yielded no benefits.

Within Pakistan, one effect of this relationship has been the widening impact of militant Islamist groups, such that after the 2002 election, they became a significant partner in the coalition government. Pakistan did adopt the economic sanctions imposed by the United Nations against the Taliban on 15 October 1999 by freezing the group's assets and closing all Afghan banks in Pakistan. However, by the time the action was taken, the Taliban regime had moved the bulk of its assets; since Afghanistan's land routes were not mentioned in the sanctions, trade continued normally.

However, Pakistan paid a price for its support of the Taliban, including the overthrow of a democratic government by the military, the rise of sectarian violence, and accusations by the international community of supporting terrorism emanating from Afghanistan under the auspices of al-Qaeda. Pressure gradually mounted on the Pakistan government to rein in terrorism and the training of terrorists, with that pressure coming from the United States, Russia (because of Taliban support for Chechnya), and China (whose leaders were concerned about the activities of Shi'a militants in

their country). The military government of Gen. Pervez Musharraf began to respond to these pressures and also advised the Taliban that they should cease to provide a safe haven for Osama bin Laden, largely because of the price it was paying in terms of economic and diplomatic isolation. However, the government did nothing to disturb the Taliban and al-Qaeda training camps in Pakistan, particularly in the tribal borderlands of the North-West Frontier Province. It is also evident that Pakistan brought on itself the rise of the fundamentalist groups (or, as it has been called, the Talibanization of Pakistan), with the resultant societal unrest, sectarian violence, and terrorist attacks against foreign interests in Pakistan.

The terrorist attacks on the United States on 11 September 2001 radically changed the situation. Pakistan withdrew recognition of the Taliban regime and agreed to join the United States in its War on Terror. Pakistan attempted to prevent armed conflict by sending a delegation of military personnel and *ulama* (Islamic scholars and clergymen) to Afghanistan on 29 September to try to persuade the Taliban to surrender bin Laden albeit to no avail. This effort was closely followed by the United Arab Emirates and Saudi Arabia withdrawing recognition of the Taliban regime, arguing that, in harboring al-Qaeda and bin Laden, the regime was harming Islam and marring the reputation of Muslims throughout the world. Further moves were taken by General Musharraf with regard to the ISI. The head of the organization, Gen. Mohmand Ahmad, was removed and replaced by the moderate head of military intelligence, Gen. Ehansul Haq, who was charged with purging the ISI of Taliban supporters. As a result, the ISI found itself deprived of its backing from the leaders of the military officers corps, and its economic and political lifelines were severed.

Pakistan also demonstrated its support by allowing the United States to utilize its military bases during Operation Enduring Freedom, and it cooperated with moves to arrest al-Qaeda and Taliban fighters working from bases in Pakistan, though the authority of the Islamabad government does not run deep in the tribal borderlands. The post-Taliban era has presented new challenges for Pakistan because of its own fundamentalist movements. In addition, the Interim Government formed in Kabul in December 2001 and the Transitional Government approved by the Loya Jirga (Great Council) in June

2002 have a significant representation from the Northern Alliance, which is still suspicious of Pakistan's policy relating to Afghanistan. However, meetings have taken place between Karzai and Musharraf, with both leaders expressing their belief that, despite the bitterness of recent events, the two countries shared enough history to overcome these problems.

Afghanistan has expressed its gratitude to Pakistan for taking in millions of refugees from the time of the Soviet invasion and for aid sent after the March 2002 earthquake in Baghlan Province. Pakistan has also expressed its willingness to help Afghanistan rebuild and to assist its neighbor in any way possible. Arrangements have been discussed for the release or transfer of Pakistanis being held prisoner in Afghanistan after fighting with al-Qaeda or the Taliban. And both leaders have stressed the need to deal with terrorist elements within each other's states, though General Musharraf has made it plain that Pakistan, though welcoming intelligence from the Coalition, would deal with issues on its territory through actions taken by its own law enforcement agencies and the armed forces. Pakistan has also made it clear that neither the ISI nor religious extremists in Pakistan would be allowed to thwart the objectives of forging friendly relations between the two states.

Suspicions still remain in Afghanistan because of Pakistan's past support for the Taliban, the presence of Pakistanis fighting against Afghans, and, some argue, the poor treatment of refugees in camps in Pakistan. A feeling exists in many quarters that Pakistan has consistently interfered in the internal affairs of Afghanistan and merely changed policies as a result of U.S. pressure and economic assistance. Despite Pakistan having given Afghanistan $10 million for reconstruction projects in April 2002, many Afghans feel that Pakistan has to prove that it is prepared to enter into a new era of relations between the two states.

See also Civil War; Coalition Air Campaign against the Taliban; Coalition Land Campaign against the Taliban; Durand Agreement; Geneva Accords; Mujahideen; Pashtunistan Dispute; Soviet War in Afghanistan; Taliban

References

Hiro, Dilip. 2002. Rev. ed. *War without End. The Rise of Islamic Terrorism and Global Response.* London: Routledge.

Hussein, Waseem. 1999. *Afghan-Pakistani Relations: The Afghan Perspective.* Bern: Swiss Peace Foundation Institute for Conflict Resolution.

Kartha, Tara. 2000. "Pakistan and the Taliban: Flux in an Old Relationship." http://www.instute-for-afghan-studies.org . . ./2001_kartha_idsa_pakistan_and_the _taliban.ht (cited 12 December 2001).

Krushelnysky, Askold. 2002. " Afghanistan: Musharraf and Karzai Exchange Warm Words and Pledge Cooperation." http://www.rferl.org/nca/features/2002/04/02042094 053.asp (cited 2 April 2002).

Maley, William, ed. 1998. *Fundamentalism Reborn? Afghanistan and the Taliban.* London: Hurst.

Rashid, Ahmed. 2001. *Taliban: The Story of the Afghan Warlords.* Rev. ed. London: Pan Books.

AFGHAN SECURITY SERVICE

The government of Nur Muhammad Taraki (1978–1979) established a security service after the April 1978 Saur Revolt in which the Communists took power in Afghanistan. Known as the Afghan Security Service Department (AGSA), the organization was headed from May 1978 to August 1979 by Asadullah Sarwari. The service was renamed the Workers' Security Institution, or KAM, after the coming to power of Hafizullah Amin in 1979. But almost immediately, the service was purged of Khalq supporters by the Parchami wing of government, and it was renamed the State Information Service, or KHAD. The renamed service was headed by Dr. Muhammad Najibullah until 1986, when he became general secretary of the People's Democratic Party of Afghanistan (PDPA). On becoming president of Afghanistan, Najibullah accorded the security service ministry status, and it was renamed the Ministry of State Security, or WAD, and headed by Ghulam Faruq Yaqubi. The new organization was modeled on the Soviet State Security Committee, or KGB, and was said to have between 15,000 and 30,000 operatives, with the infrastructure thought to have been set up with the assistance of Soviet and East German intelligence personnel. WAD had its own military units and a national guard and was charged with detecting and eradicating all internal domestic opposition, subverting armed resistance, penetrating opposition groups abroad, and providing intelligence for the armed forces. However, Yaqubi did not survive the fall of the Marxist government: he either committed suicide on 16 April 1992 or was assassinated by a Parchami rival. A new security service was established by President Burhanuddin Rabbani and was also known as KHAD.

See also KAM; KHAD; *Khalq; Parcham;* Yaqubi, Gen. Ghulam Faruq

References

Rubin, Barnett R. 2002. *The Fragmentation of Afghanistan.* 2nd ed. New Haven, CT: Yale University Press.

AFGHAN SOCIAL DEMOCRATIC PARTY

The Afghan Social Democratic Party (ASDP) was founded on 8 March 1966 by Ghulam Muhammad Farhad as a protector of the religious values and the national culture and cultural heritage of Afghanistan. The ASDP aims were to:

- Achieve and preserve national independence
- Support democracy and the election of a government representing the wishes of the people
- Abolish social inequality, introduce a system of social justice, and maintain national sovereignty
- Defend national security
- Condemn all forces seeking to exploit religious, linguistic, ethnic, and sectarian differences
- Provide primary education in the native idiom as the right of each ethnic group
- Improve the national economy, exploit natural resources, implement all development plans, fairly distribute national wealth, and kindle Afghan patriotism

The party was also opposed to all forms of colonialism, Zionism, fascism, capitalism, communism, apartheid, and aggression, and it committed itself to the struggle against all types of material, physical, moral, and ideological exploitation.

In terms of foreign policy, the party stood for:

- Free and positive judgment in international affairs through a policy of genuine nonalignment
- Opposition to aggressive powers of both the East and the West
- Support for the UN Charter and the Universal Declaration of Human Rights
- Peaceful coexistence with neighbors

The party considered that the Afghan people had a sacred duty to defend their homeland against imperialist Russia and its puppet regime and that the ASDP had to take responsibility for leading the struggle for national independence. Being opposed to the hegemony of both the East and the West, the mottoes of the party were "God-Soil-Nation" and "Afghanistan for the Afghans." The party considered that it had a responsibility to struggle against the Soviet invasion because of the bloodshed and cruelties that ensued, which posed a threat to world peace and security. The ASDP welcomed all initiatives to stop the killing in Afghanistan and sought the withdrawal of all Soviet troops, promising that friendly relations could be established if aggression ceased and if Afghan independence was recognized by the Soviet Union.

The ASDP was also prepared to cooperate and coordinate activities with all other groups involved in the struggle for national independence, as it recognized that there was a serious need for the unity of political parties and groups fighting against foreign aggression. The party was ready to become involved in independent and joint fronts mounted against the puppet regime and had participated in fighting in various parts of the country.

See also Farhad, Ghulam Muhammad

References

Supreme Council of the Afghan Social Democratic Party. 1988. *Aims and Objectives of the Afghan Social Democratic Party.* Peshawar, Pakistan: Afghan Social Democratic Party.

AFGHAN-SOVIET RELATIONS

Afghan-Soviet relations were, in recent years, marked by the dependence of a Marxist regime in Kabul on the Soviet Union, intervention by the Soviet military in 1979, and a decade of civil war during which Afghan government and Soviet forces were opposed by the various mujahideen groups. The Soviet troops were withdrawn in 1989, having been badly mauled by the mujahideen forces, and Afghanistan was left to its own devices. However, the breakup of the Soviet Union changed the situation, and relations with significant neighbors that are now independent states as well as relations with Russia have improved in recent years.

Afghanistan had always been pivotal to the strategic objectives of the Russian Empire of the czars and then the Soviet Union, mainly because it opened up the route to India. Thus, British policy in the region was aimed at the containment of Russian aspirations, which became part of what was known as the "Great Game." While Britain controlled Afghanistan's external affairs, this containment was possible.

However, the Third Anglo-Afghan War of 1919 secured Afghanistan's independence, and King Amanullah attempted to demonstrate this newfound freedom by establishing diplomatic relations with European powers and the United States. A mission was sent to Tashkent and Moscow, led by Muhammad Ali, and it was well received by the Soviet authorities, as was a letter from King Amanullah to Vladimir Lenin, seeking Soviet assistance in the emancipation of Afghanistan. A Soviet diplomat, Michael K. Bravin, was sent to Kabul to prepare the way for the establishment of diplomatic relations, to be followed by a Soviet delegation charged with negotiating a treaty of friendship. The result was the Afghan-Soviet Treaty of Friendship of 1921, by which the two states recognized their mutual independence and agreed to be bound not to enter into any political or military accord with a third state that might prejudice either of the signatories. The terms of the treaty had serious implications for the content of the Anglo-Afghan Treaty of 1921, under which Britain endeavored to exclude Russia from involvement in Afghanistan.

The Soviet Union allowed the free and untaxed transit of Afghan goods into its territory and recognized the independence of Khiva and Bukhara to meet the wishes of the people. The agreement also made provision for Soviet technical assistance, aid of 1 million rubles, and return of the area of Panjdeh, which had been part of Afghanistan in the nineteenth century before its annexation by Russia. This last was a significant development for King Amanullah, as it allowed Afghanistan to open up a new route for goods bought in Europe and avoided the monopoly on the supply of military equipment exercised by Britain; previously, the goods had to be shipped via India. Evidence for the use of this new route was provided by King Amanullah's successful suppression of the Khost Rebellion in 1924, which saw the deployment of Soviet aircraft and foreign pilots, including some Russians.

Nonetheless, relations were not always cordial, for the freedom of Khiva and Bukhara did not materialize because the population revolted against these moves and opted to join the Soviet Union, thus destroying Amanullah's dream of a Central Asian confederation. The Soviets defended their retention of the possessions of the former Russian Empire by pointing out that they were responding to the wishes of the people, as provided for under the 1921 treaty. A more serious conflict stemmed from the Soviet occupation of Dargad Island on the Amu Daria River in December 1925. The island was considered by Afghanistan to be its territory, and due to a change of river course, the island was now located south of that course. The island had become a haven for refugees from Bolshevik Russia, including Basmachi revolutionaries who used it as a base for incursions into Soviet territory. However, to retain good relations with King Amanullah, the Soviets defused the situation by withdrawing their troops on 28 February 1926, having dealt with the Basmachi bases on the island.

Because of Russia's internal economic problems, the subsidy promised under the 1921 treaty was paid by Moscow on an irregular basis, but this was offset by the expansion of Afghanistan's diplomatic relations, reducing its dependence on the Soviet Union. In 1929, civil war came to Afghanistan, resulting in the overthrow of King Amanullah. The Soviets maintained their embassy in Kabul and immediately recognized the government established under Nadir Shah. The new ruler appointed his half brother, Muhammad Aziz, to be ambassador to Moscow in recognition of the significance of the post, but at the same time, he was opposed to Soviet influence in Afghanistan. Nadir Shah opened up negotiations for a review of the 1921 treaty, and the new Afghan-Soviet treaty signed on 24 June 1931 included a clause specifically calling for the prohibition in both states of activities that might cause either military or political damage. The Soviets were concerned with the threat from the Basmachis, whereas Nadir Shah was concerned about the possible return to power of King Amanullah.

Although a commercial treaty was signed in 1936, Afghanistan failed to renew a Soviet airline concession and dismissed all Soviet pilots and mechanics, turning to Germany for its technological and development requirements. The move caused alarm in Moscow, especially as a special relationship with Germany began to evolve, and in Britain, the change was regarded as the lesser of two evils. After the outbreak of World War II and the short-lived alliance between Germany and the Soviet Union, there were fears in Afghanistan and London that the Soviets might mount a coup in support of King Amanullah. Such a view was reinforced by the fact that the Germans regarded Zahir Shah as pro-British and seriously considered mounting a coup in Afghanistan, to the extent that the Soviet foreign minister was asked if he would allow the transport of German troops into northern Afghanistan. The response from the Soviet Union was noncommittal, and the proposal went no further.

Germany launched an attack on the Soviet Union on 22 June 1941, and Moscow joined the Western alliance, causing considerable concern in Kabul. Afghanistan's foreign policy had always been based on protection of its territorial integrity by fostering the continuing rivalry between its important neighbors and exploiting the "Great Game," but Britain and the Soviet Union were now allies. Afghan fears were soon to be realized, for in October 1941, Britain and Russia presented separate notes to the Kabul government demanding the expulsion of all Axis nationals from the country. The government had no option but to comply, stipulating only that these individuals be given passage to a neutral country; the decision was retrospectively endorsed by a *loya jirga* (great council). In an effort to protect its neutrality, Afghanistan closed its northern border except for diplomatic exchanges, but it also continued to trade with the Soviet Union.

In 1946, good relations were restored with the Soviet Union, with Afghanistan agreeing to accept the middle of the Amu Daria River as its international boundary. This turn of events was followed by the establishment of a telegraph link with Tashkent in 1947. But Afghanistan's strategic insecurity was heightened by the creation of Pakistan in 1947, when India became independent, and then with the impact of the Cold War. In response, it repudiated the treaties that had established the Durand Line as its international boundary, and it issued a demand that the Afghans inhabiting the North-West Frontier Province of Pakistan be given the option of joining Afghanistan or becoming independent. Pakistan rejected these overtures, and Afghanistan was subsequently the only nation to vote against Pakistan's admission to the United Nations; as a consequence, relations between the two states became strained and hostile.

Relations with the United States were not helped by the policy followed by President Dwight Eisenhower's administration of containing Soviet expansionism by forming alliances with key nations and supporting the creation of the Baghdad Pact, which included Pakistan as part of the defensive alliance. Although the pact guaranteed the international borders of its signatories, it ignored irredentist and nationalist aspirations, such as those expressed by people in the North-West Frontier Province of Pakistan.

Therefore, Afghanistan began to direct its attentions again to the Soviet Union, and in 1950, it signed a four-year trade agreement with the Soviets, while maintaining a position of neutrality. In 1955, Nikita Khrushchev and Nikolay Bulganin visited Kabul and praised Afghanistan's policy of positive neutrality, and the two sides renewed the treaty of 1931 for a further ten-year period. As part of the renewed agreement, the Soviet Union agreed to loan Afghanistan $100 million at 2 percent interest, to be used for projects selected by a joint Afghan-Soviet committee. In 1965, Afghanistan started flights to Tashkent, which were subsequently extended to Moscow and then to other European countries.

Relations with the Soviet Union were strengthened further in 1956, when, following a refusal from the United States, Afghanistan turned to the Soviets for the supply of military equipment. This supply was accompanied by thousands of Soviet advisers who arrived to train the Afghan military, and thousands of Afghan technicians and military officers were sent to the Soviet Union for training. Through this arrangement, Muhammad Daud, the Afghan prime minister, had created a growing corps of military officers, technicians, and students with left-wing and, in some cases, pro-Soviet tendencies. Daud used this left-wing group in 1973 when he mounted a coup to depose King Zahir and establish Afghanistan as a republic. The coup had, in effect, laid the groundwork for the Saur Revolt of April 1978, which led to the downfall of Daud, who was murdered, and brought the Communists to power.

The new Afghan government under Nur Mohammad Taraki accepted the Soviet offer to supply advisers in all branches of government and concluded a series of treaties making the Soviets the dominant power in Afghanistan. On 5 December 1978, Taraki concluded a treaty of friendship with the Soviets that provided for military assistance from the Soviet Union and was used as a justification for the intervention that followed in 1979. The Marxist regime in Kabul was beginning to encounter resistance from other elements in Afghanistan, which became known as the mujahideen, and the foremost opponents were among the Hazaras, the Islamists, and the Tajiks in northern Afghanistan, with opposition growing as conflict escalated. Taraki requested military assistance in March 1979, but this was initially refused by the Soviets, who were nervous about the international reaction to such a move and the long-term reaction of the Afghan people.

In September 1979, Taraki was overthrown and executed, with his prime minister, Hafizullah Amin, seizing power. However, by the end of 1979, the situation had deteriorated to such an extent that the Soviets agreed to intervene to prop up the Kabul regime. The move was seen by the Soviet Politburo as a temporary measure to prevent the Marxist regime being defeated by the mujahideen, not as a venture designed ultimately to provide access to the oil fields and warm-water ports of the Persian Gulf. The Kabul government legalized the Soviet occupation by the April 1980 Status of Armed Forces Agreement, which justified the presence of the Limited Contingent of Soviet Forces in Afghanistan (LCSFA) as a response to foreign intervention on behalf of the rebels, and stipulated that Soviet forces would withdraw when foreign intervention ceased.

Soviet troops entered Afghanistan on 27 December 1979 after two airborne assault brigades had secured the Bagram air base, some 40 miles north of Kabul. The Soviet Fortieth Army entered Afghanistan, the Salang Pass and Salang Tunnel were secured by special forces, and two motorized rifle divisions crossed into Afghanistan over the Amu Daria River. The Soviet troops moved quickly to Herat, Shindand, Kabul, and Kandahar, and after about seven days, some 50,000 troops were stationed in Afghanistan, together with 350 tanks and some 450 other armored vehicles. The main objective was to secure the cities and the key lines of communications; about one-third of the forces were stationed in Kabul, and there were large garrisons in Herat, Jalalabad, Kandahar, Kunduz, Mazar-i Sharif, and Shindand, with smaller garrisons in other towns.

The Soviet command intended to have its own troops protect the towns and lines of communication, with the Afghan army being left to handle all counterinsurgency activity. However, it was not long before the Soviet presence reached some 85,000 ground troops, 25,000 support troops, and 10,000 airborne troops, together with a further 30,000 troops and air force pilots who operated from Soviet territory. The Soviets were equipped for conventional warfare, and had, among other units, an SA-4 antiaircraft missile brigade and chemical decontamination teams.

However, the Soviet objective of not becoming involved in counterinsurgency was not to be realized, and as the situation deteriorated, Soviet troops were drawn into actions against mujahideen forces outside the urban areas and suffered heavy casualties. After a ten-year presence in Afghanistan, the Soviets were thoroughly demoralized, as they were enduring heavy casualties, troops had become involved in the drug trade, and it was obvious that the mujahideen, with backing from the United States and Pakistan, were gaining the upper hand. The Soviets were unable to adapt to guerrilla warfare, and the acquisition by the mujahideen of Stinger missiles led to heavy losses of Soviet transport and attack helicopters and armor.

See also Afghan-German Relations; Amanullah, King; Anglo-Afghan Treaty of 1921; Daud, Sardar Muhammad; Saur Revolt; Soviet War in Afghanistan; Taraki, Nur Muhammad; Third Anglo-Afghan War

References

Arnold, Anthony. 1993. *The Fateful Pebble: Afghanistan's Role in the Fall of the Soviet Empire*. Novato, CA: Presidio Press.

Bocharov, G. 1990. *Russian Roulette: Afghanistan through Russian Eyes*. New York: Hamish Hamilton.

Ganjoo, Satish. 1990. *Soviet-Afghan Relations*. Delhi, India: Ahashdeep Publishing.

Hauner, Milan, and Robert Leroy Canfield, eds. 1989. *Afghanistan and the Soviet Union: Collision and Transformation*. Boulder, CO: Westview Press.

AFGHANI, SAYYID JAMALUDDIN (1838–1897)

Sayyid Jamaluddin Afghani is widely regarded as the originator of the pan-Islamic movement and a modernist who advocated the unity of the Islamic world but was prepared to borrow from the West if that would enable Islam to resist Western imperialism. His memory is revered by Afghans, who believe him to be descended from a family of Sayyids from

Asadabad in Kunar Province, whereas Western scholars believe him to be of Iranian origin. Afghani became a political adviser to rulers across the Islamic world and was a political activist in Afghanistan, Egypt, Iran, and the Ottoman Empire. He was often at odds with authority, on the run from arrest, opposed by the *ulama* (Islamic scholars and clergymen), and suspected by the secular authorities. A follower of Afghani assassinated the Persian ruler Nasruddin Shah in 1896, and Sultan Abdul Hamid placed Afghani under house arrest. Afghani died in Istanbul in 1897, but his ideas and his memory are still revered throughout the Islamic world.

References
Keddie, N. R., ed. 1983. *An Islamic Response to Imperialism: Political and Religious Writings of Sayyid Jamal al-Din al-Afghani.* Berkeley: University of California Press.

AFGHANIS

The Afghanis are the radical Islamists, mainly Arab but also from other Muslim countries, who went to Afghanistan to fight in the holy war against the Marxist regime and the Soviet occupation from 1979 to 1989. They fought, for the most part, in the groups led by Gulbuddin Hekmatyar, Maulawi Husain Jamilurrahman, and Abdul Rasul Sayyaf. Accurate figures are difficult to determine, but it is estimated that at the height of the war, there were 5,000 Saudis, 3,000 Yemenis, 2,800 Algerians, 2,000 Tunisians, 370 Iraqis, and 200 Jordanians, as well as citizens from other Muslim countries, fighting in Afghanistan. Between 1987 and 1993, some 3,350 Arab citizens left Pakistan, and many returned to their own countries with the objective of setting up Islamic states by force of arms. As such, they have been a major threat in Algeria, are responsible for terrorist attacks in Egypt, and have been engaged in fighting in regional wars in areas such as Bosnia, Kashmir, and the Philippines.

However, almost 3,000 Afghanis were left in Afghanistan and Pakistan after the fall of the Marxist regime, and many of them joined the Taliban and presented a major threat to the Northern Alliance and their supporters in the war against the Taliban between 1996 and 2001, as they usually fought to the bitter end. A number of these experienced fighters also joined the ranks of al-Qaeda, for that group's leader, Osama bin Laden, had financed various Islamist groups prior to seeking refuge in Afghanistan as a "guest" of the Taliban.

See also Laden, Osama bin; Taliban
References
Cogan, Charles. 1993. *Holy Blood: An Inside View of the Afghan War.* Westport, CT: Praeger.

AFGHANISTAN INTERIM CABINET

An interim cabinet with thirty members was announced in Afghanistan on 27 December 2001, following the talks on the new Interim Government that were held in Bonn. The cabinet was agreed to by four main Afghan factions representing the Northern Alliance, the Rome group that is loyal to the former king, Zahir Shah, and the smaller exile groups based in Cyprus and Peshawar, Pakistan. However, the formation of the cabinet was beset by problems, with some factions refusing to accept the membership composition, and Gen. Abdul Rashid Dostum was given a post to secure his support for the new government.

The cabinet members and their allegiances were as follows:

Chair:
Hamid Karzai (Pashtun)

Vice-chairs:
Women's Affairs: Sima Samar (Rome group, Hazara)
Defense: Mohammad Fahim (Northern Alliance, Tajik)
Deputy Defense: Gen. Abdul Rashid Dostum (Northern Alliance, Uzbek)
Planning: Haji Mohammad Mohaqqaq (Northern Alliance, Hazara)
Water and Electricity: Shaker Kargar (Northern Alliance, Uzbek)
Finance: Hedayat group (Pashtun)

Members:
Foreign Affairs: Dr. Abdullah Abdullah (Northern Alliance, Tajik)
Interior: Younis Qanooni (Northern Alliance, Tajik)
Commerce: Seyyed Mustafa Kazemi (Northern Alliance)
Mines and Industries: Mohammed Alem Razm (Uzbek)
Small Industries: Araf Noorzai (Northern Alliance)

Hamid Karzai (3rd R-front), his cabinet members, and dignitaries stand as the national anthem of Afghanistan is played at the inauguration of the new interim government in Kabul, 22 December 2001. (Reuters NewMedia Inc./CORBIS)

Information and Culture: Rahin Makhdoom (Rome group)

Communication: Abdul Rahim (Northern Alliance)

Labor and Social Affairs: Mir Wais Sadeq (Northern Alliance)

Hajj (Pilgrimage): Maulawi Balkhi

Martyrs and Disabled: Abdullah Wardak (Northern Alliance)

Education: Abdul Salam Azimi (Rome group)

Higher Education: Dr. Sharif Faez (Northern Alliance)

Public Health: Suhaila Seddiqi (Independent)

Public Works: Juma Mohammad Mohammadi (Rome group)

Rural Development: Abdul Malik Anwar (Northern Alliance)

Urban Development: Haji Abdul Qadir (Northern Alliance)

Reconstruction: Sardar Mohammed Roshan (Rome group)

Transport: Ishaq Shahryar (Peshawar group)

Return of Refugees: Enayatullah Nazeri (Northern Alliance)

Agriculture: Seyyed Hussein Anwari (United Front)

Irrigation: Haji Mangal Hussein (Peshawar group, Pashtun)

Justice: Abdul Rahmi Karimi (Northern Alliance)

Air Transport and Tourism: Rahim Wardak (Rome group); Wardak was lynched by a crowd of pilgrims at the Kabul airport on 14 February 2002 and was replaced by Zalmai Rassoul

Department of Border Affairs: Amanullah Dzadran (Rome group)

References
"Interim Government." 2001. http://www.afghanland.com/history/interim.html (cited 12 February 2003).

AFGHANISTAN INTERIM GOVERNMENT

Late in 2001, the United Nations sponsored talks in Bonn with the various groups opposed to the Taliban in order to establish an interim Afghan government for a period of six months, until a permanent administration could be established. The talks were chaired by the UN chief envoy for Afghanistan,

Lackdar Brahimi, and lasted for nine days, with agreement being reached on 5 December 2001. The interim administration was to take power in Kabul on 22 December.

The administration would be headed by Hamid Karzai, a Pashtun leader and relative of the former king (King Zahir), and would consist of a chair, five vice chair, and twenty-three other ministers. The agreement effectively put an end to the administration of the former president, Burhanuddin Rabbani.

It is clear that the winners in this arrangement have been the new generation of Afghan leaders drawn from the Northern Alliance and other anti-Taliban groups, as they occupy the key posts. Women are also represented, with two posts in the interim cabinet. The losers are the old guard: a generational change appears to have taken place. The new administration, with a significant number of exiled Afghans, will face problems in imposing its will on a divided country that has been controlled by warlords for generations. But it has the advantage of international political support and access to external aid for reconstruction and development.

The agreement in Bonn also included a number of other significant recommendations:

- The UN Security Council would be asked to organize a multinational security force for Kabul and the surrounding areas.
- A special commission would be appointed within a month to organize the calling of an emergency *loya jirga* (great council), which would be able to revise the interim cabinet and create a transitional government to last for a period of two years.
- The loya jirga would be required to include representatives of Afghan refugees living in Iran, Pakistan, and elsewhere; members of the Afghan diaspora; and prominent Islamic intellectuals, scholars, and traders. Due attention would be paid to the inclusion of women.
- The former king would open the emergency loya jirga and preside over the first session.

The agreement was endorsed by the UN Security Council at a meeting on 6 December 2001.

See also Karzai, Hamid; Loya Jirga; Rabbani, Burhanuddin

References
United Nations. 2001. *United Nations Security Council Resolution 1383.* New York: United Nations.

AFGHANISTAN PEACE ASSOCIATION (APA)

The Afghanistan Peace Association was established on 11 November 1989 as an independent, non-aligned, but responsible organization that is not seeking political power but continuing to rely on the national powers of Afghanistan. Organizers hoped to make the association a social power in order to play a role in conflict resolution and to try to prevent internal conflicts in the future. The APA is striving to become a protector of the people and of all the social forces in Afghanistan that would, in the political arena, like to legally and legitimately rule the country. Based in the United States, the APA has some 3,000 Afghan members within Afghanistan and around the world.

The APA has articulated the following goals and principles, which were revised on 11 November 1995, the sixth anniversary of the organization:

1. To establish and preserve peace and national unity through negotiations and understanding by banning fighting and disarming the citizenry, political groups, and military, while maintaining basic policing.
2. To preserve the national sovereignty, national integrity, political independence, and indivisibility of Afghanistan.
3. To organize Afghan refugees in order to effectively participate in the restoration and preservation of peace in Afghanistan.
4. To encourage all social and political groups to partake in the formation of a broad national peace coalition.
5. To promote and support the practice of democratic and free electoral system ideals in Afghanistan's political arena on a national as well as an organizational level in accordance with Afghan traditions.
6. To encourage a sense of brotherhood and equality among Afghans in order to uproot all existing prejudices. With this goal as the basis, the APA will strive to create grounds for positive and constructive competition

in all aspects of life for sociopolitical growth and development.

7. To help provide the necessary assistance to the disabled, the maimed, and the refugee Afghans and to encourage them to willfully repatriate when there is peace, safety, and security in Afghanistan.

8. To promote education and awareness and to abolish illiteracy, since it is the enemy of peace and national unity.

9. To succeed against all forms of destructive military and detrimental political interferences by foreign countries in Afghanistan's internal affairs.

10. To establish the legitimate right of Afghanistan as a permanently nonaligned and demilitarized country.

11. To establish and preserve close, effective relations with internal and international peace organizations and to support and abide by the Universal Declaration of Human Rights, the UN Charter, and international norms.

The APA is not seeking political power in Afghanistan as a whole; however, its members have the right to partake in any political candidacy or vote for others as they choose. The APA would also support any legitimate government that would come to power through the people's vote. Having its political independence, the APA, on the basis of nonviolent principles conceived of as the God-given birthrights of individuals, will respect the rights of all Afghan citizens in terms of equal rights for men and women and will always sustain its nonalliance in regard to any individual, organization, political party, ethnicity, tribe, locality, language, and nationality.

The APA was formed to help empower the notions of peace and national duty among the various ethnic groups and to foster the natural course of development in society, which has been destroyed by foreign aggression and internal fratricidal war, pushing Afghanistan toward national disparity and chaos. The movement recognizes that great parts of the country have been destroyed, hundreds of thousands of Afghans killed, millions scattered as refugees, and society rendered so fragile that it could break apart at any moment. The founders of the APA believe that the people of Afghanistan do not deserve all of these misfortunes and that the survival of the country depends on national unity and achieving a permanent peace based on the establishment of the political and social rights of all its citizens, without any discrimination.

The APA has been promoting its objectives by holding conferences such as the Intra-Afghan International Conference in Search of Peace, held in New York in 1996, and it presented a peace plan in 1998 to the Hamburg conference in Germany. It also publishes a monthly newsletter, *Voice of Peace*, and sponsors the now independent, bimonthly *Afghan Communication: Voice of the Young Generation.* In addition, the APA has sponsored a number of cultural and social events and founded regional offices in Europe, Central Asia, and South Asia. It has also fostered links with organizations within Afghanistan and provided advice on structuring these organizations and helping them organize events and activities to meet the needs of people in postconflict Afghanistan.

The APA has also been involved in projects at a practical level in Afghanistan through the following type of activities:

* Raising funds for orphaned children in 1991
* Founding an orphanage in Khost, Paktia Province, in 1997
* Providing medical supplies worth $24,000 for earthquake victims in 1998
* Founding Maihan High School in Peshawar, Pakistan, in 1999 to provide education for 300 refugee children

In addition, the APA has been actively involved in relevant international conferences and has become a member of the Conference of NGOs at the United Nations. On 2 June 2002, it sponsored and organized the Conference of Afghan Organizations of New York in Support of the Emergency Loya Jirga, which was attended by sixteen Afghan organizations. Future plans include more networking within Afghanistan, organizing local meetings in Afghanistan to promote the peace message, investing in the youth of Afghanistan, and utilizing the United Nations and other international organizations to foster peace proposals.

The main goal of the APA is the restoration of peace and national unity, as mentioned, and its members believe it is the only organization that struggles for the people on this basis. The fact that the opinions and views of the Afghan people are respected is seen as distinguishing the APA from other groups and political bodies. According to the organization, only a government that has risen to power through free elections can be considered legitimate. Members of the APA believe that the key to conflict resolution rests with Afghans themselves, that they should not wait for foreigners to bring peace to their country, and that Afghans must not to leave a legacy of war and fratricide for their children.

See also Humanitarian Relief
References
http://www.AfghanistanPeace.com

AFGHANISTAN TRANSITIONAL GOVERNMENT

At the emergency *loya jirga* (great council) held in June 2002, Hamid Karzai was unanimously re-elected as president, following behind-the-scenes negotiations that removed the former king Zahir and former president Burhanuddin Rabbani as possible candidates. After much delay due to the need to achieve a compromise between the various power blocs, President Karzai presented his government for approval on 21 June 2002. The following individuals were appointed to serve until the democratic elections that are to be held in 2004:

President: Hamid Karzai (Pashtun)
Deputy presidents: Mohammad Fahim (Tajik), Karim Khalili (Hazara), Abdul Qadir (Pashtun)
Special adviser on security: Younis Qanooni (Tajik)

Cabinet:
Defense minister   Mohammad Fahim (Tajik)
Foreign minister   Abdullah Abdullah (Tajik)
Finance minister   Ashraf Ghani (Pashtun)
Interior minister   Taj Mohammad Wardak (Pashtun) (The interior minister was replaced on 29 January 2003 by Ali Ahmad Jalali, a former mujahideen leader who had been head of the Pashtu and Persian service for the Voice of America radio station in the United States. Wardak's handling of the student demonstrations at Kabul University on 14 November 2002, when one student was killed and a number were injured, brought about the change.)

Planning minister   Mohammad Mohaqik (Hazara)
Communications minister   Masoom Stanakzai (Pashtun)
Borders minister   Araf Noorzai (Pashtun but from a Tajik-dominated party)
Refugees minister   Enayatullah Nazeri (Tajik)
Mines minister   Juma M. Mahammadi (Pashtun)
Light industries minister   Mohammed Alem Razm (Uzbek)
Public health minister   Dr. Sohaila Siddiqi (Pashtun)
Commerce minister   Seyyed Mustafa Kazemi (Shi'a Muslim)
Agriculture minister   Seyyed Hussein Anwari (United Front)
Justice minister   Abbas Karimi (Uzbek)
Information and culture minister   Saeed Makhdoom Rahim (Tajik)
Reconstruction minister   Mohammad Gahim Farhang (Pashtun)
Hajj and mosques minister   Mohammad Amin Naziryar (Pashtun)
Urban affairs minister   Yusuf Pashtun (Pashtun)
Social affairs minister   Noor Mohammed Karkin (Turkman)
Water and power minister   Ahmed Shakar Karkar (Uzbek)
Irrigation and environment minister   Ahmed Yusuf Nuristani (Pashtun)
Martyrs and disabled minister   Abdullah Wardak (Pashtun)
Higher education minister   Sharif Faez (Tajik)
Civil aviation and tourism minister   Mir Wais Sadeq (Tajik)
Transportation minister   Saeed Mohammad Ali Jawad (Shi'a Muslim)
Education minister   Younis Qanooni (Tajik)
Rural development minister   Hanif Asmar (Pashtun)

Courts:
Supreme Court chief justice   Sheikh Kamal Shinwari

However, many observers felt at the time that the Loya Jirga had provided Karzai with a government composed of religious extremists and warlords who would pose a threat to the creation of a more open and stable society. Some have contended that Karzai is an Afghan loner with devoted Western friends but no personal support base. The Kabul representative of the International Crisis Group maintained that the Loya Jirga had been a missed opportunity to break the power of the Afghan warlords. However, UN officials in Kabul praised the proceeding as a first step on the long road to democracy.

Among possible dangers that have been identified is the appointment of Mohammad Fahim as defense minister and a deputy president, as he has been accused of using his secret intelligence officers to consolidate his power base. In addition to his control of government forces, Fahim also has his own private army of 10,000 well-armed fighters, he leads the Northern Alliance, and he is close to Burhanuddin Rabbani.

Another possible area of future conflict is in the legal arena, for the chief justice, Judge Kamal Shinwari, is a strict Islamist who, in January 2003, called for the full implementation of Shari'a law. This appointment and the influence on the government of Islamists such as Rabbani and Sayyaf are also seen as increasing the devaluation of the role of women in Afghanistan, a sector that Karzai has sought to promote.

The new administration has been faced with a formidable task, and it is evident that there is a need for a strong, viable, and authoritative administration to lead the nation until the democratic elections in 2004. The following are the priorities for the new government:

- Paving the way for a representative parliament
- Beginning the process of writing a new draft constitution, expected to be ready in March 2003 and now out for selective consultation, without the proposals having been published
- Embarking on the creation and training of a new national army and a national police force
- Dealing with the power of the regional warlords
- Developing a viable central authority with equal representation for all provinces and upholding the rule of law
- Reviving the country's dilapidated economic structure
- Aiding the needy and looking after returning refugees
- Fighting hunger and disease
- Upholding human rights without any form of discrimination
- Embarking on conflict resolution
- Providing a secure environment in order for Afghans to peacefully work, live, and prosper

Criticism of the performance of the government is now beginning to be heard, with the administration being accused of not establishing its priorities and with ministries engaging in nonproductive rounds of paperwork. The power of the regional warlords has certainly not been tackled, and although orders were issued for militias to disarm, no time frame was put in place, nor was it made clear how the task was to be carried out and who was responsible for seeing the policy through. Further dissent also emerged from a gathering of Afghan elders held in Peshawar, Pakistan, on 28 January 2003. This meeting concluded that the Karzai government was a failure and called for a broad-based government in Kabul. Those attending the meeting also appealed to the United Nations for more peacekeepers to be sent to Afghanistan to ensure peace and stability and to deal with the banditry that has taken place in the provinces.

On 28 January 2003, the government revealed that participants in the legislature that was soon to be created would not be allowed to represent political parties, as there were no laws to mandate their involvement. Former president Rabbani, leader of the Islamist Movement, immediately challenged this pronouncement on the grounds that party politics were ingrained in Afghan culture and that, because of the past conflicts, all Afghans had the right to give voice to their party. However, the president's spokesman declared that political parties could not be permitted a platform in the legislature until legislation had been passed granting them representation.

Support for Karzai's position came from Sayyed Ahmad Gailani, a moderate mujahideen leader, who took the view that representatives in the legislature were likely to be those elected to the Loya Jirga on a nonparty basis and that they should therefore refrain from pursuing a particular political agenda. He argued that party members had participated in the

Loya Jirga as representatives of the people and that this status should continue until legislation on political parties was passed. The government view is that the legislature should be an unelected body designed to serve the country until fully democratic elections are held in 2004. On 24 February, President Karzai stated that he was still committed to holding national elections as scheduled but that he may not seek reelection himself. He wanted the government to be judged on whether it had delivered security and reconstruction for Afghanistan.

See also Afghan Army; Loya Jirga

References

"Afghan President Karzai Says He May Not Be a Candidate in Elections." 2003. http://www.afgha. com/?af=article&sid=29914 (cited 15 May 2003).
"Afghan Transitional Government." 2002. http://www. afghanland.com/history/transitional.html (cited 11 February 2003).
Roashan, G. Rauf. 2002. "Is the Afghan Government Meeting the Challenge?" http://www.institute-for-afghan-studies.org/Contribution/Commentaries/DRRoshan/7-1 (cited 5 February 2003).
Smucker, Philip. 2002. "New Afghan Leader Faces a Rogues Gallery." http://www.csmonitor.com/2002/0621/p07s02-wosc.htm (cited 21 June 2002).

AFRIDI TRIBE

The Afridis are members of a Pashtun-speaking tribe located in the area of the Khyber Pass on the Pakistan side of the border with Afghanistan. They have always seen themselves as protectors of the gateway to India, and they have usually extracted payment for safe transit through the pass. At times, the Afridis were accepted into the service of Afghan rulers, primarily as bodyguards or militia, but they have also supported Afghan rulers in various military campaigns between Afghanistan and British India. It is thought that the tribe can muster an armed force of 50,000 men, and in the 1980s, the Kabul government attempted to recruit the tribe into a militia to attack the supply lines of the mujahideen. The Afridis accepted payment but did not fulfill their assigned functions, though they exercised their own tolls on supplies passing through their territory.

References

Hammerton, J. A. 1984. *Tribes, Races and Cultures of India and Her Neighbouring Countries: Afghanistan, Bhutan, Burma, Ceylon, Nepal and Tibet.* Delhi, India: Mittal.
Hart, David M. 1985. *Guardians of the Khaibar Pass: The Social Organization and History of the Afridis of Pakistan.* Lahore, Pakistan: Vanguard Books.

AHMAD, ALI (1883–1929)

Ali Ahmad was governor of Kabul during the reign of King Amanullah and was proclaimed king by the tribesmen in Nangarhar Province following the abdication of King Amanullah in 1929. He was born in 1883, the son of Loinab Khushdil Khan, and was educated in India before serving as chamberlain of Amir Habibullah. He was in charge of the Afghan Peace Delegation to the talks at Rawalpindi in 1919, which resulted in the Anglo-Afghan Treaty of 1919. He was a successful commander in King Amanullah's army, which put down the Khost Rebellion in 1924, and he was similarly engaged in the Shinwari Rebellion of 1928. After the abdication of Amanullah, he fought with Habibullah Kalakani but was defeated. He was taken as a prisoner to Kabul and executed in July 1929.

See also Khost Rebellion; Shinwari Tribe

References

Wild, Roland. 1933. *Amanullah: Ex-King of Afghanistan.* London: Hurst and Blackett.

AHMAD, SHAH (1943–)

Shah Ahmad was a member of the Islamic Union for the Liberation of Afghanistan, founded by Abdul Rasul Sayyaf, and in 1998, he was prime minister of the interim cabinet of the Islamic Unity of Mujahideen, which was an umbrella group of seven mujahideen parties recognized by Pakistan. He was born in 1943 in a village near Kabul and educated at Kabul Polytechnic Institute and Kabul University, graduating in 1958 with a degree in engineering and then taking up a post in the Department of Agriculture and Irrigation. In 1972, Ahmad went to the United States and gained an M.A. in engineering at Colorado State University in 1974 before taking up a teaching post at King Faisal University in Saudi Arabia. He went to Peshawar, Pakistan, after the Soviet invasion of Afghanistan, where he joined Sayyaf's mujahideen party, becoming president of the education committee and later of the finance committee. In May 1996, after Gulbuddin Hekmatyar entered the government of Burhanuddin Rabbani, Ahmad became minister of education, but he was forced to flee Afghanistan after the Taliban captured Kabul.

A British India Army Officer signing the register when entering independent Afridis territory (Bettman/Corbis)

See also Islamic Union for the Liberation of Afghanistan
References
Saikal, Amin. 1999. *The Rabbani Government,
    1992–1996.* In *Fundamentalism Reborn? Afghanistan
    and the Taliban,* edited by William Maley, 29–42..
    London: Hurst.

AHMADZAI TRIBE

The Ahmadzai tribe is a section of the Sulaiman Khel division of the Ghazi tribe, largely found in a triangle formed by lines drawn from Kabul to Jalalabad and Gardez. The Ahmadzais are mainly sedentary, though a small number are nomadic, and most are engaged in trade, with many of them having become extremely wealthy. The Ahmadzais have also been represented in positions of importance in various Afghan governments, and they have a history of intermarrying with the powerful Durrani tribe. Such has been the power of the Ahmadzais that Amir Abdur Rahman forcibly settled a number of families in northern Afghanistan in an attempt to weaken their power and to serve as Pashtun colonists in a predominantly Turkic region.

References
Wilber, Donald Newton. 1962. *Afghanistan: Its People,
    Its Society, Its Culture.* New Haven, CT: HRAF Press.

AKBAR, SARDAR MUHAMMAD (1816–1845)

A major figure in the defeat of the British in the First Anglo-Afghan War (1839–1842), Sardar Muhammad Akbar was the son of Amir Dost Muhammad. He was the leader of the Afghan chiefs who negotiated with the British occupation forces over guarantees of safety during the retreat from Kabul to India, but during the negotiations, he lost his temper with the British negotiator, Sir William Macnaghten, and killed him. Yet he saved the lives of British women, children, and some officers he had taken into protective custody during the retreat, which very few survived. Akbar was also keen to regain territory lost in the Punjab, but his father wanted to reach a compromise with the British, and in 1845, Akbar rebelled against his father. However, he died of poisoning before any serious threat could be mounted (his unidentified poisoner was probably a paid assassin). As a result of his part in the First Anglo-Afghan War, Akbar was revered by Afghans and accorded the name Ghazi, meaning "victor against infidels."

See also First Anglo-Afghan War

References
Eyre, Vincent. 1879. *The Kabul Insurrection of 1841–42.*
    London: W. H. Allen.

AMANULLAH, KING (1892–1960)

Amanullah, also called Ghazi, ruled Afghanistan from 1919 to 1929. He was the son of Amir Habibullah and was governor of Kabul when his father was assassinated at Jalalabad in February 1919. Due to his position, he controlled the Afghanistan treasury and the main arsenal of the army, and he lost no time in having himself proclaimed king in Kabul. In doing so, he defied the claim of his uncle, Nasrullah Khan, whom he denounced as an accomplice in the murder of Amir Habibullah and a usurper. Although proclaimed as king in Peshawar, Nasrullah did not have the support of the army, and he was arrested and later assassinated while imprisoned in Kabul.

Amanullah had a modernizing and reformist zeal and greatly admired the policies of Kamal Ataturk in Turkey and Muhammad Reza in Iran. One of his first acts was to challenge British policy in relation to Afghanistan. To that end, he sought to renegotiate the Anglo-Afghan agreements concluded with Amir Abdur Rahman, that left Britain in charge of Afghanistan's foreign relations in return for subsidies, military assistance, and a guarantee of protection against any unprovoked Russian aggression. Britain refused to renegotiate the agreements and thereby provoked Afghani aggression, culminating in the Third Anglo-Afghan War, which broke out on 4 May 1919 and lasted only until June 1919. The war was largely fought in the border regions and Waziristan, and Britain was reluctant to become involved in a protracted campaign due to the war-weariness following World War I. Lengthy negotiations took place between the two sides at Rawalpindi, Mussoorie, and Kabul, and the resultant Anglo-Afghan Treaty of 1919 left Afghanistan free from British control and an independent nation.

Regarded as a national hero thereafter, Amanullah turned his attentions to reforming and modernizing his kingdom. He was instrumental in establishing schools in which English, French, and German were the main languages of instruction, and he promulgated a constitution that guaranteed equal rights and personal freedom for all Afghans. He also ended the international isolation of Afghanistan by establishing diplomatic and commercial relations in European and Asian capitals. Amanullah built a new capital called Darulaman (meaning "Abode of Peace"), which housed a new parliament building, major government offices, and villas for the Afghan elite.

King Amanullah was also active as a social reformer. He encouraged government employees to wear Western dress and introduced a new dress code that allowed women in Kabul to go without veils. However, reforms were expensive and also angered the traditional elements of Afghan society, especially the *ulama* (Islamic scholars and clergymen). Opposition manifested itself through the Khost Rebellion of 1924, which was put down by the king's forces with great difficulty. In December 1927, Amanullah visited Europe, but on his return in 1928, he was faced by yet another rebellion—this time by Shinwari tribesmen. This rebellion led to further attacks from the forces of Habibullah Kalakani (leader of the antireformist action against Amanullah), forcing the king into exile. Amanullah made one unsuccessful attempt to regain his throne but finally fled to India in May 1929. He then lived In Italy and Switzerland until his death on 26 April 1960. He was buried in Jalalabad beside the tomb of Amir Habibullah.

See also Anglo-Afghan Treaty of 1919; Khost Rebellion; Mussoorie Conference; Shinwari Tribe; Third Anglo-Afghan War

References

Gregorian, Vartan. 1969. *The Emergence of Modern Afghanistan: Politics of Reformed Modernization, 1880–1946.* Stanford, CA: Stanford University Press.

Poullada, Leon B. 1973. *Reform and Rebellion in Afghanistan, 1919–1929.* Omaha: University of Nebraska at Omaha.

Wild, Roland. 1933. *Amanullah, Ex-King of Afghanistan.* London: Hurst and Blackett.

AMBALA CONFERENCE (1869)

A meeting was held in March 1969 between Amir Shir Ali and Lord Mayo, the viceroy of India, at which the amir sought to effect an alliance with Britain. The amir had recaptured the Afghan throne and consolidated his position, such that he accepted an invitation to meet the viceroy at Ambala, a town some 200 miles north of Delhi. The amir was afraid of Russian intentions regarding Afghanistan after the Amirate of Bukhara on his northern borders had become a czarist protectorate, and he was looking for British support against Russian incursions. He was also anxious to quell any possible domestic unrest and to obtain British recognition for the legitimacy of his position, as well as recognition of his son Abdullah Jas as his immediate successor. The viceroy assured the amir of the sympathies of the British government but made no specific promises; however, as a sign of friendship, the Indian government gave the amir a gift of 600,000 rupees, 6,500 muskets, and various pieces of artillery.

References

Malleson, George B. 1879. *History of Afghanistan from the Earliest Period to the Outbreak of the War of 1878.* London: W. H. Allen.

AMIN, HAFIZULLAH (1929–1979)

Hafizullah Amin was president of the Democratic Republic of Afghanistan from 16 September 1979 until he was assassinated by Soviet troops on 27 December 1979. He was born in Pagham in Kabul Province in 1929 of the Kharati tribe, which is part of the Ghilzai Pashtuns. He was educated in Afghanistan and the United States, where he earned a reputation as a Pashtun nationalist, and on his return to Afghanistan, he became a teacher and then principal of the Ibn Sina and Teacher Training Schools in Kabul. It is thought that he became a convert to Marxism in 1964, and in 1969, he was elected to parliament as the representative from Pagham. During the period of the Afghan republic, from 1973 to 1978, he was engaged in the successful recruitment of supporters in the army, in competition with the Parchami faction of the People's Democratic Party of Afghanistan (named after its newspaper, *Parcham*). After the Saur Revolt of April 1978, through which the Communists seized power, he became vice-premier and minister of foreign affairs. In April 1979, he was named prime minister, but the Khalq faction split, and he accused Nur Muhammad Taraki of being unfit to lead the country. After a brief struggle, Taraki was ousted and secretly executed, leaving Hafizullah Amin in control; he became president on 16 September 1979.

At the outset, Amin was in conflict with the Soviet ambassador to Kabul, Alexandr Puzamov, and successfully demanded his recall to Moscow. Amin, very much a nationalist, wanted to be independent of outside influences, and he was ruthless with any opposition, being accused of ordering thousands of

President Hafizullah Amin (L) addresses a press conference nine days after taking power. Hafizullah was partly responsible for the outbreak of civil war and was assassinated by Soviet Special Forces on 27 December 1979. (Bettman/Corbis)

assassinations. He was attacked by Soviet Special Forces at Darulaman and assassinated on 27 December 1979, being replaced by Babrak Karmal from the Parchami faction of the People's Democratic Party of Afghanistan (PDPA).

See also Khalq; *Parcham;* People's Democratic Party of
Afghanistan
References
Arnold, Anthony. 1983. *Afghanistan's Two-Party
Communism: Parcham and Khalq.* Stanford, CA:
Hoover Institution Press.

AMIR, MUHAMMAD (?–1936)

Amir Muhammad was also known as the Chacknau Mullah and exercised a great deal of influence among the Mohmand tribes. In 1915, he twice led the Mohmands in actions against British forces at Shabkadar in the eastern provinces on the British India side of the Durand Line. (This line set the boundary between Afghanistan and British India in 1893, resulting in the Pashtun tribes being split between the two countries.) He was ordered arrested

in March 1919 by King Amanullah on the grounds that he supported the cause of Nasrullah Khan, but he escaped from custody. He was again involved in actions against the British at Dakka and remained active among the Mohmands. In 1921, in company with other mullahs, he arrived at Haddra to advise, if required, on negotiations with the British at the Kabul Conference, which eventually led to the Anglo-Afghan Treaty of 1921.

In 1924, he attended the Loya Jirga (Great Council) at Pagham and participated in the debates, and in the following year, he embarked on a propaganda tour from August to September on behalf of King Amanullah. In 1926, he was on pilgrimage to Mecca and was recalled from the hajj to assist in resolving problems among the Mohmands; funds were made available to appease the tribes by improving the infrastructure and public services in the tribal areas. However, in the following year, the king again had to try to curb his influence by forbidding him to maintain an armed retinue as part of his political activities within the Mohmand tribe.

In 1928, during the Shinwari Rebellion, Amir Muhammad successfully kept the Mohmands in check during the conflict. In June 1930, he was summoned to Kabul by Nadir Shah to prevent him from becoming involved in disturbances that were taking place in the northwest frontier regions. He was permitted to return home later that year, and until 1936, he remained the most important mullah among the Mohmand tribes in the eastern provinces.

See also Mohmand Tribe

References

Mark, William Rudolph Henry. 1984. *The Mohmands.* Lahore, Pakistan.: Vanguard Books.

AMU DARIA

The Amu Daria River, known as the Oxus by the Greeks, forms the boundary between Afghanistan and the states of Uzbekistan and Tajikistan for a distance of some 280 miles. The river and its tributaries flow in a northwesterly direction before running into the Aral Sea. Although some 1,500 miles in length, the river is navigable only in parts but was bridged at Hairaton in 1982, providing a link from Mazar-i Sharif to the Uzbek rail terminal Tarmez by way of the Afghan highway. The river is also bridged at Sharkham and at Qala Kutarma in the province of Kunduz, and both of these bridges were vital strategic links for the supply of Afghan and Soviet forces during the war waged against the mujahideen from 1979 to 1989.

References

Field, Neil C. 1954. "The Amu Daria: A Study in Resource Geography." *Geographical Review* 44, no. 2: 528–542.

ANGLO-AFGHAN TREATY OF 1905

Through the Anglo-Afghan Treaty of 1905, the government of India wanted to ensure that Afghanistan would recognize the existing border with India and cease to interfere in the politics of the transborder tribes while also pursuing a more liberal commercial policy. The treaty was, in effect, to be a renewal of an agreement reached in correspondence between Amir Abdul Rahman and Britain's chief political officer in Afghanistan in 1880 but with these additional objectives satisfied. To secure agreement, Britain prohibited the import of arms into Afghanistan and suspended subsidies to it. However, Amir Habibullah, who had ascended the throne in 1901,

was a hard negotiator, and after three months of talks, a treaty was signed on 21 March 1905 without any of the British objectives having been realized. Britain also agreed not to interfere in the internal affairs of Afghanistan, and the subsidy was restored and arrears paid. The treaty was repudiated in 1919 by Amir Amanullah.

References

Adamec, Ludwig W. 1967. *Afghanistan, 1900–1923: A Diplomatic History.* Berkeley: University of California Press.

ANGLO-AFGHAN TREATY OF 1919

The Anglo-Afghan Treaty of 1919 was concluded after the Third Anglo-Afghan War and signed on 8 August 1919. The peace treaty was designed to restore the previous relationship between the two states, but this outcome would be dependent on negotiations commencing six months after the signing ceremony. Until final agreement was reached, subsidies from Britain were suspended, the payment of arrears was canceled, and Afghanistan was not permitted to import arms and munitions through India. On border issues, Afghanistan was required to recognize the Indo-Afghan frontier as defined, and areas of Khalibar, which were undefined, were to be demarcated by a British commission.

Britain had anticipated that Amir Amanullah would enter into an exclusive alliance, but he proceeded to send missions to Russia, Europe, and the United States to assert Afghanistan's right to control its own external affairs. In fact, it took two conferences—at Mussoorie in 1920 and Kabul in 1921—to restore relations between the two states with the concluding of a new treaty.

See also Mussoorie Conference

References

Adamec, Ludwig W. 1967. *Afghanistan, 1900–1923: A Diplomatic History.* Berkeley: University of California Press.

ANGLO-AFGHAN TREATY OF 1921

The Anglo-Afghan Treaty of 1921 was concluded after negotiations that lasted almost a year, with conferences held at Mussoorie and Rawalpindi finally restoring friendly relations after the Third Anglo-Afghan War. The treaty was also known as the Treaty of Kabul and was signed by Henry R. C. Dobbs, the British envoy, and Mahmud Tarzi, representing the Afghan delegation. Negotiations throughout the period were difficult, as Afghanistan was seeking territorial concessions whereas Britain wanted Kabul to revoke diplomatic ties with Russia in return for increased subsidies and arms.

Britain failed in its bid to exclude Russia from Afghanistan, for the Russo-Afghan Treaty of 1921 was ratified. However, the Afghans failed to secure any meaningful territorial concessions. The treaty stated that:

- Both governments would respect each other's rights of internal and external independence
- The boundary west of the Khalibar would be accepted by Afghanistan, following a minor realignment
- Legations were to be opened in London and Kabul and consulates opened in Afghanistan and India
- India would permit its territory to be used for the import of arms and munitions by Afghanistan, and customs duties would not be imposed on goods in transit to Afghanistan
- Each side would notify the other of military operations in the frontier area

It was also agreed that negotiations should be opened on a trade convention, and a document to that end was signed in June 1923.

References
Adamec, Ludwig W. *Afghanistan, 1900–1923: A Diplomatic History.* Berkeley: University of California Press.

ANGLO-RUSSIAN CONVENTION (1907)

The Anglo-Russian Convention was concluded on 31 August 1907, with the objective of ensuring "perfect security on their respective frontiers in Central Asia and to maintain in these regions a solid and lasting peace." The two powers divided Iran into spheres of influence, and Tibet was to be under Chinese sovereignty. However, Britain was free to deal with the Tibetans on commercial matters and the Buddhists in Russia could deal with the Dalai Lama on religious matters. Russia was also permitted to have relations of a nonpolitical nature with Afghan leaders in northern Afghanistan and to have equal access with Britain to commercial opportunities.

Britain did not repudiate its 1905 treaty with Afghanistan to protect it from unprovoked Russian aggression, and the latter declared the country to be outside its sphere of influence. However, Amir Habibullah saw the convention as an attempt by the two powers to resolve the Afghan question without his involvement. The amir was on a state visit to India when the agreement was concluded, but he was not informed of its existence by Britain until 10 September 1907. He felt that he had been betrayed, and when requested to agree to the convention, he deliberated for a year and then refused ratification. As far as Afghanistan was concerned, the convention had no validity, and Russia failed to obtain the promised benefits. The Bolshevik government repudiated the convention in 1918 as a sign of goodwill to its Asian neighbors.

See also Habibullah, Amir

References
Edwardes, Michael. 1975. *Playing the Great Game: A Victorian Cold War.* London: Hamish Hamilton.

ARIAN, ABDUL RASHID (1941–)

Abdul Rashid Arian was a member of the Khalq faction of the People's Democratic Party of Afghanistan (PDPA) from 1964 and a member of the Khalqi Central Committee from 1977. When the Communists took the reins of power after the Saur Revolt of April 1978, he held the post of deputy minister of information from April to October 1978 and became ambassador to Islamabad until 1980. He was then appointed by Babrak Karmal as deputy prime minister and minister of justice, as well as president of the High Judiciary Council and attorney general, holding these posts until 1981. In that year, he lost all of his ministerial posts but was elected vice-president of the Revolutionary Council from 1981 to 1988 and elected to the Senate in 1988.

Arian was born in 1941 in Kandahar of a Pashtun family and worked as a typesetter and journalist. He was expelled from the PDPA for complicity in the attempted coup mounted by the minister of defense, Gen. Shanawaz Tanai, against the government of President Muhammad Najibullah in March 1990.

See also Khalq; People's Democratic Party of Afghanistan

References
Arnold, Anthony. 1983. *Afghanistan's Two-Party Communism: Parcham and Khalq.* Stanford, CA: Hoover Institution Press.

ARSARI TRIBE

The Arsari tribe is one of the most numerous and wealthy of the Turkoman tribes and is concentrated mainly in districts adjacent to the Amu Daria River. The Arsaris occupy the fertile plains of the river, though the northern banks of the Amu Daria are shared with Uzbeks. There is also a small Arsari presence in Balkh Province. The tribespeople have traditionally been devoted to agriculture, primarily raising sheep and cattle, but they also make carpet and felts, and there is some silk production. The carpets they produce are not of the highest quality among Afghan carpets, but their silk—which has been traditionally sent to Bukhara to be woven and is known as *labiabi* (riverbank silk)—is superb. Unlike most of the tribes in Afghanistan, the Arsaris do not have a tradition of raiding or fighting with other tribes, except in self-defense.

References
Clifford, Mary Louise. 1973. *The Land and People of Afghanistan.* Philadelphia: Lippincott.

ASGHAR, MUHAMMAD (1914–)

Muhammad Asghar held several positions in Afghanistan, being president of Kabul University from 1954 to 1960, deputy minister of the interior from 1960 to 1962, and minister of justice from 1967 to 1969. However, in October 1989, he became president of the National Salvation Society, which was made up of officials who were opposed to the bloody conflict in Afghanistan and wanted a political solution to the war. The members of the society had no affiliation to the People's Democratic Party of Afghanistan.

ATA, MUHAMMAD (DATES OF BIRTH AND DEATH UNKNOWN)

Muhammad Ata was the son of the governor of Mazar-i Sharif at the time of Amir Habibullah (1901–1919). He was present in Jalalabad when the amir was assassinated and was implicated in the murder; he was arrested, condemned to death, and then pardoned at the last minute. In the following year, there was an attack on King Amanullah, and Ata was arrested in Pagham on suspicion of complicity but was later released without charge.

In 1920, he was appointed by King Amanullah as diplomatic representative at Bukhara, but this event coincided with a Bolshevik revolt, so he never assumed the post. He returned to Mazar-i Sharif, where he was ordered to render secret assistance to Enver Pasha of Turkey in Central Asia in his struggles against the Bolsheviks in the eastern provinces of the Turkish Empire. In 1928, he was appointed as governor of Balkh Province, and during the civil war (November 1928 to March 1929), he fought against the forces of Habibullah Kalakani but was defeated; he fled across the border into Tashkent. In April 1929, he accompanied Ghulam Nabi Charkhi in an attempt to recapture northern Afghanistan but was again unsuccessful and retired with his supporters across the Soviet border.

He returned to Afghanistan when Nadir Shah came to power, and in March 1930, he was appointed to the Mission of Reconstruction that was sent to Mazar-i Sharif under the control of Muhammad Yaqub. In 1931, he commanded part of the force during operations against Ibrahim Beg, an Uzbek Basmachi. Beg had originally fought against the Bolsheviks, mounting raids from his bases inside Afghanistan. However, under pressure from the Soviets, Nadir Shah prevented him from raiding across the border, and so Beg began to raid within Afghanistan but was defeated by the amir's forces; he retreated across the Soviet border and was caught by Soviet troops and executed in April 1931. In December 1931, as a reward for his actions in Mazar-i Sharif, Ata was appointed a member of the Council of Notables.

See also Amanullah, King; Nadir, Shah Muhammad
References
Gregorian, Vartan. 1969. *The Emergence of Modern Afghanistan: Politics of Reformed Modernization, 1880–1946.* Stanford, CA: Stanford University Press.

AUCKLAND, LORD GEORGE EDEN (1784–1849)

Lord Auckland was the governor-general of India from 1836 to 1842 and was responsible for involving Britain in the First Anglo-Afghan War but at variance with the wishes of the directors of the British East India Company. The objective of the action carried out by Lord Auckland was to replace Amir Dost Muhammad with Shah Shuja; the Simla Manifesto of 1 October 1838, issued by Auckland, was, in effect, a declaration of war. Auckland stressed that the situation in Afghanistan was critical because of Russian and Persian influences on Dost Muhammad and that he was compelled to act without the prior consent of the company's board of directors.

The plan devised by Auckland initially envisaged using the army of Ranjit Singh of the Sikh nation to restore Shah Shuja to the Afghan throne, but Ranjit Singh was reluctant to become involved, so Auckland concluded that he could not be trusted to conclude the venture successfully, even if persuaded to act. It was therefore left to the British India army to wage the war, and early successes led to Auckland being awarded a peerage in 1839. However, the disastrous war led to him being denounced and recalled to London.

See also Burnes, Alexander; First Anglo-Afghan War; Shuja, Shah; Simla Manifesto

References

Heathcote, T. A. 1980. *The Afghan Wars, 1839–1919.* London: Osprey.

AUSTRALIAN SPECIAL FORCES

The Australian government committed a rotating squadron of special forces to Afghanistan in 2002, and they were involved in a number of critical actions, including Operations Mountain Lion and Condor. In company with special forces from other members of the Coalition, their operations were directed to finding concentrations of Taliban and al-Qaeda forces, especially in the mountainous region of Paktia Province, bordering Afghanistan.

Operation Mountain Lion was conducted in the immediate area around the town of Khost, which is only some 20 miles from the Pakistan border, and commenced in April 2002. The Australian Special Air Service (SAS) squadron of 150 men was charged with gathering intelligence to enable the Coalition to counter al-Qaeda fighters who were infiltrating from Pakistan in order to harass Coalition forces and attack the civilian population. The mission was carried out by soldiers operating in small groups of four, five, or six men, working in areas known to be traversed by the enemy. Such actions were dangerous, and on 30 April, a small patrol was discovered by an enemy group; the enemies engaged them, but the patrol withdrew after killing two of the attackers. A rapid-reaction force from the U.S. airborne division launched a follow-up search of the area but without success: the al-Qaeda group had almost certainly crossed back into Pakistan. However, the troops did discover large quantities of mortar rounds, grenades, and ammunition in buildings and caves, together with evidence showing that the enemy had dragged away injured or dead comrades.

A similar incident occurred on the following day, with another patrol coming under heavy fire from rocket-propelled grenades and small arms. The patrol reported killing two of the enemy and was again able to withdraw without casualties. It was evident from this further engagement that al-Qaeda fighters had now dispersed into small units to cause maximum damage but without exposing themselves to the effects of the U.S. air strikes that any large concentration would attract. The Australian SAS continued operations in the area without further incidents, and none of the Coalition forces were successful in locating large groups of enemy troops.

Australian Special Forces were again in combat on 16 May, when two separate patrols were engaged by enemy forces in Paktia Province. A five-man patrol was attacked by an estimated ninety al-Qaeda fighters. A second patrol attempting to join these men also came under attack, and Coalition air strikes had to be called up to enable the patrols to withdraw. It is estimated that the patrols killed three of the enemy and the air strikes a further ten, but a follow-up operation mounted by 1,000 British Royal Marines, known as Operation Condor, failed to locate the enemy force, which had almost certainly melted away across the border.

No further combat took place between June and July, although patrols continued in the area around Kabul and Gardez in Paktia Province, the objective being to deny territory to al-Qaeda and Taliban fighters. At first, the Australians were treated with hostility by the local population, but they worked hard at convincing the locals that their fight was with al-Qaeda and the Taliban, not the Afghan people or Muslims in general. The Australian patrols provided a level of security that enabled UN mine-clearing teams to return, other aid agencies to resume operations, and the government to reopen schools. A third rotation of Australian Special Forces arrived in Afghanistan in August 2002, joining what was now considered to be a counterinsurgency operation, with al-Qaeda and Taliban fighters deemed unlikely to mount any mass attack that would leave them vulnerable to U.S. air power.

Prime Minister Helen Clark finally confirmed a New Zealand SAS presence in Afghanistan, but no details have been released as to its strength, deployment, or actions undertaken.

See also al-Qaeda; UK Special Forces; U.S. Special Forces

References

Beaumont, Peter. 2002. "Special Forces Take Over Hunt for al-Qaeda." *Observer* (London), 4 August.

Berger, Julien, and Richard Norton-Taylor. 2001. "Special Forces in Afghanistan." *Guardian* (London), 29 September.

Evans, Michael. 2001. "SAS Already Gathering Intelligence in Afghanistan." *Times* (London), 21 September.

AWAKENED YOUTH (WISH ZALMAYAN)

Awakened Youth, one of the earliest political parties in Afghanistan, was a liberal organization founded in Kandahar in 1947 by literary figures and Pashtun nationalists. It included such individuals as Shamsuddin Majruh, Mir Ghulam Muhammad Ghobar, and Nur Muhammad Taraki, and its objective was the reform of Afghan society. The aims of the organization were to advance education, eradicate corruption, promote national welfare, and increase understanding and respect among the people. The party eventually split over the issue of Pashtun nationalism, with the nationalists leaving to support the Red Shirt movement of Khan Abdul Ghaffar Khan.

See also Ghobar, Mir Ghulam Muhammad; Red Shirts; Taraki, Nur Muhammad

References

Newell, Richard S. 1972. *The Politics of Afghanistan.* Ithaca, NY: Cornell University Press.

AYUB, KHAN MUHAMMAD (1857–1914)

Muhammad Ayub was the son of Amir Shir Ali and brother of Yaqub Khan. He became governor of Herat at his father's death on 21 February 1879, while his brother was being crowned king at Kabul. On hearing that the British had occupied Kabul, Ayub raised a force to expel them from Afghanistan, and he was proclaimed as amir by the *ulama* (Islamic scholars and clergymen) in Herat. He marched against Kandahar on 27 July 1880, and at the Battle of Maiwand, he virtually destroyed the force of Gen. George Burrows. His troops then besieged Kandahar, but the intervention of another British force, under Gen. Frederick Roberts, compelled Ayub to retreat to Herat, though with his forces largely intact. He moved again on Kandahar in June 1881, but by then, Abdur Rahman had been recognized as amir by Britain, and his forces easily routed Muhammad Ayub at Kandahar in September. At the same time, one of his generals, Abdul Quddus, had been sent to Herat to capture the city, which had been left bereft of forces, and Ayub was forced to flee to Iran with his immediate entourage. After a few years in Iran, he accepted asylum for himself and his followers in India.

See also Maiwand, Battle of; Quddus, Abdul; Shir Ali, Amir; Yaqub Khan, Amir Muhammad

References

Forbes, A. 1982. *The Afghan Wars, 1839–42 and 1878–80.* London: Seeley.

BADAKHSHAN PROVINCE

Badakhshan is a province in northeastern Afghanistan with an area of 15,786 square miles and a population of about 484,000. The province includes the Wakhan Corridor, which is a narrow valley separating Tajikstan from the Indo-Pakistan subcontinent and extending to the border with China. The administrative capital of this largely mountainous province with high valleys and peaks of 16,000 feet is Faizabad. The province is extremely rich in mineral resources, including, silver, copper, lead, and precious stones, particularly lapis lazuli, with Badahkshan being the most important source for this gemstone in Afghanistan. A further economic development in the past was a lucrative tourist industry based on wealthy foreigners hunting ibex and snow leopards, but this was totally disrupted by all of the conflicts in recent years.

The population is largely Tajik, though there are communities of Uzbeks in the west and Wakhis and Qirghiz in the Wakhan Corridor (most of the latter fled after the Soviet invasion, however). Until 1850, autonomous chiefs had ruled the province before being brought under the control of Kabul by Amir Dost Muhammad, and under Amir Abdur Rahman, Badakhshan became an integral part of the kingdom. In 1893, the Durand Agreement demarcated Afghanistan's northern border, allocating the Wakhan Corridor to Afghanistan, but Abdur Rahman was reluctant to accept the territory because it was difficult to defend. However, he ultimately agreed to do so, considering it as a buffer between the British and Russian Empires, after his subsidy from Britain was increased by 650,000 rupees. During the period of the Soviet occupation and the rule of the Taliban (1979–2001), the province was under the control of the Northern Alliance.

See also Durand Agreement; Wakhan District
References
Adamec, Ludwig. 1972–1985. *Historical and Political Gazetteer of Afghanistan.* 6 vols. Graz, Austria: Akademische Druck-u Verlagsansalt.

B

BADAKHSHI, TAHIR (?–1979)

Together with Babrak Karmal and Nur Muhammad Taraki, Tahir Badakhshi was one of the founders of the People's Democratic Party of Afghanistan (PDPA) and a member of the party's Central Committee in 1965. In 1967, he sided with the Parcham faction of the PDPA in a dispute with the Khalq arm of the party but then left the PDPA to form National Oppression (Setam-i-Milli), established in 1968 as a Marxist, anti-Pashtun party. He was born in Faizabad in Badakhshan Province and educated in Kabul at the Habibia School before studying in the Faculty of Economics at Kabul University. In the summer of 1978, he was arrested and imprisoned in the Pul-i Charkhi jail. He was executed on 17 September 1979 during the rule of Hafizullah Amin.

See also People's Democratic Party of Afghanistan
References
Arnold, Anthony. 1983. *Afghanistan's Two-Party Communism: Parcham and Khalq.* Stanford, CA: Hoover Institution Press.

BADGHIS PROVINCE

Badghis is a province of northwestern Afghanistan and was part of Herat Province until 1964. Its area is 8,438 square miles, and it has a population of about 47,000 and borders on Turkmenistan in the north and Herat in the west. The climate is cold in the winter and hot in the summer, and the province has an abundance of good water and grassy hills but is almost totally devoid of bushes and trees. The economy is largely dependent on agriculture, with the main crops being barley, wheat, and pistachio nuts. The population was mainly nomadic in the past because of the fear of Turkoman raids from the north, but it is now largely composed of Pashtuns, Jamshidis, Hazaras, and small communities of other ethnic groups.

References

Adamec, Ludwig. 1972–1985. *Historical and Political Gazetteer of Afghanistan*. 6 vols. Graz, Austria: Akademische Druck-u Verlagsansalt.

BAGHLAN PROVINCE

Baghlan Province in northeastern Afghanistan has an area of 6,627 square miles and a population of some 486,000. Baghlan is also the name of the administrative capital, which has around 39,000 inhabitants. The province includes the northern slopes of the Hindu Kush range crossed by the Robatak, Barabi, Khawak, and Salang Passes, the latter having been a crucial supply route for the Soviets during the occupation of Afghanistan from 1979 to 1989. The north of the province is mainly agricultural, with irrigation provided by the rivers and sugar beets and cotton being the major crops; in addition, grapes, pistachio nuts, and pomegranates are significant export crops. Karakul sheep are also raised in the northern part of the province. An important industry is sugar production, which was started in 1940 with technical assistance from Czech industrialists. Coal is extracted in the Karkar Valley near Pul-i-Khumri, and a silk industry was begun in 1951.

References

Amin, H. 1974. *Agricultural Geography of Afghanistan*. Kabul: Kabul University Press.

Jettmar, Karl. 1974. *Cultures of the Hindukush*. Wiesbaden, Germany: Franz Steiner.

BAGRAM

The town of Bagram is located to the north of Kabul, near the confluence of the Panjshir and Ghorband Rivers, just to the west of Charikar. It lies on the site of an ancient city and has a number of Buddhist, Greco-Roman, and Phoenician artifacts, many of which were destroyed by the Taliban in March 2001. The present town is small and is the center of the district of the same name in Parwan Province, whose significance is now linked to the presence of the air base, built with Soviet assistance in the 1950s. The base was occupied by Soviet paratroops on 7 July 1979 in preparation for the invasion of Afghanistan in December 1979, when the 105th Guard Airborne Division landed there. Bagram be-

came a major strategic base for the Soviet defense of Kabul and the Salang highway. The air base was constantly under attack by the mujahideen, with one attack on 3 June 1985 destroying some 70 Soviet aircraft and killing about 100 Soviet troops. Following the fall of the Marxist regime and the Soviet withdrawal in 1989, the base was much fought over by rival mujahideen groups before becoming a strategic base for the government of Burhanuddin Rabbani until it was captured by the Taliban on 24 September 1996. Following the collapse of the Taliban regime, the Bagram air base was taken over by the Coalition forces in the campaign against the Taliban and al-Qaeda.

See also Civil War; Coalition Land Campaign against the Taliban; Taliban

References

Maley, William. 1999. *Fundamentalism Reborn? Afghanistan and the Taliban*. London: Hurst.

BALKH PROVINCE

Balkh Province in north-central Afghanistan has an area of 4,633 square miles and a population of about 570,000. The administrative capital of the province is Mazar-i Sharif, which, prior to the War on Terror declared by U.S. President George W. Bush in 2001, had a population of about 103,000 inhabitants. It is also the location of a shrine believed to be the burial place of the caliph Ali, who died in A.D. 640. Another town of historical importance is Balkh, which is about 14 miles west of Mazar-i Sharif on the Balkh River. According to local tradition, it was founded by Noah, and Zoroastrian tradition has it as the birthplace of Zoroaster, but it became secondary to Mazar-i Sharif after the discovery of Ali's tomb. The province has been colonized by the Greeks, the Turkomans, and the Kushkans and was ravaged by the invading armies of Genghis Khan. Mazar-i Sharif has been of great strategic significance, was the scene of massacres by the Taliban, and was a major trophy in the advance by the Northern Alliance on Kabul in December 2001.

See also Mazar-i Sharif

References

Adamec, Ludwig. 1972–1985. *Historical and Political Gazetteer of Afghanistan*. 6 vols. Graz, Austria: Akademische Druck-u Verlagsansalt.

Dupree, Nancy Hatch. 1967. *The Road to Balkh*. Kabul: Afghan Tourist Organization.

The fifteenth-century mosque at Mazar-i Sharif in northern Afghanistan. Revered by Afghans because of the belief that the tomb of Ali, fourth caliph of Islam and son-in-law of Muhammad, the founder of Islam, lies within the mosque. (Charles and Josette Lenars/Corbis)

BALUCHS

The Baluchs make up one of Afghanistan's ethnic minorities and are found primarily in Nimruz Province, but there are also small, scattered communities in Badakhshan, Farah, Fariab, Helmand, Herat, Jozjan, and Kunduz Provinces. No accurate figures exist as to their numbers, which are estimated to be between 100,000 and 200,000, and all are Sunni Muslims speaking the Baluchi language, except for the Qatagham Baluchs, who speak Dari. The Baluchs are largely sedentary, and they are no longer organized into specific tribes. The main concentrations of Baluchs are in the Baluchistan provinces of Iran and Pakistan, where they number some 5 million, with small communities existing in provinces of the former Soviet Union. Since the mid-1970s, some 2,500 Baluch guerrillas have been sheltering in southern Afghanistan following struggles for Baluch autonomy in Pakistan.

References
Clifford, Mary Louise. 1973. *The Land and People of Afghanistan*. Philadelphia: Lippincott.
Raverty, H. G. 1976. *Notes on Afghanistan and Baluchistan*. Quetta, Pakistan: Gosha-a-Adeb.

BAMIAN PROVINCE

Bamian Province is located in central Afghanistan, occupies an area of 6,757 square miles, and has a population of about 285,00, with the administrative capital being a town of the same name. Bamian is about 205 miles north of Kabul and is about 8,200 feet above sea level. The province is part of the mountainous Hazarajat region of central Afghanistan and is inhabited primarily by the Hazaras, who were severely persecuted by the Taliban. The province was famous for its two statues of the Buddha, which were 120 and 175 feet high and dated from the third and fifth centuries A.D. The cliffs where they were carved from solid rock were decorated with stucco works and wall paintings, in a mix of Indian, Central Asian, Iranian, and classical European styles. The cliffs were honeycombed with caves serving as living quarters for the Buddhist monks and are still inhabited by Afghanis. Despite an international outcry by governments and organizations, such as the UN Educational, Scientific, and Cultural Organization (UNESCO), the Taliban blew up the statues in March 2001, as they considered them an affront to their Islamic state.

See also Destruction of Pre-Islamic Heritage; Hazaras; Taliban

References
Adamec, Ludwig W. 1972–1985. *Historical and Political Gazetteer of Afghanistan*. 6 vols. Graz, Austria: Akademische Druck-u Verlagsansalt.

BARAKI TRIBE

The Baraki tribe is made up of Tajiks who have mixed with the Ghilzais and who inhabit Logar and parts of Butkhak. They are thought to have arrived in the 11th century with Sultan Mahmud, their origins uncertain, and their lands were extensive. They considered themselves to be descended from Arabs, although others feel that they may be of Kurdish origin. Traditionally, they have provided soldiers for the government forces, and they were part of the force Mahmud Shah took with him on his incursions into India. In return for their military service, the amir granted them land rights. The tribe is divided into two divisions, with those in Logar speaking Persian and the others speaking Baraki.

See also Durrani Tribe; Ghilzai Tribe

References
Bellew, H. D. 1880. *The Races of Afghanistan: Being an Account of the Nations Inhabiting That Country*. London: Thacker.

BARAKZAIS

The Barakzais are a significant section of the Zirah branch of the Durrani tribe, which has been the ruling family in Afghanistan, and in terms of numbers, economic standing, and political influence, they have been the paramount tribe in Afghanistan. The Barakzais are the majority in the area to the south of Kandahar, the valley of the Arghastan River, and along the banks and plains of the Helmand River. The Barakzais had been soldiers in Iran, serving Nadir Shah, the founder of the Afshamid dynasty, and following his successful invasion of Afghanistan and the capture of Herat, they were settled on land taken from the Ghilzais. This situation caused friction and rivalry between the Durranis and the Ghilzais, which has continued to the present day. The link between the Barakzais and the rulers of Afghanistan continued with their service under Ahmad Shah Durrani, and they rose to complete power when their chief Dost Muhammad came to power in 1792. The Barakzais are large landowners

and raise extensive flocks of livestock in the land between Herat and Kandahar.

See also Durrani Tribe; Ghilzai Tribe

References
Wilber, Donald Newton. 1962. *Afghanistan: Its People, Its Society, Its Culture*. New Haven, CT: HRAF Press.

BARECHI TRIBE

The Barechis are Sunni Muslims who inhabit the Sharawak region to the south of Kandahar in Kandahar Province and own most of the cultivable area. They are divided into the Badalzais, Manodozais, Zakozais, and Shiranis, with the first three sections tracing their ancestry back to Barech, the ancestor of all Pashtuns. The Barechis are agriculturalists and irrigate their lands from the River Lora, which flows through the Sharawak Valley; they also breed camels, with the wool being exported to Kandahar. Wheat is the main crop grown in the rich alluvial soil. The Barechis are known as a peaceful tribe but, at the same time, are closely knit and are skilled swordsmen, having provided men for the armies of Ahmad Shah and Shah Shuja. Despite their peaceful nature, there is bitter enmity between the tribe and the Achakzais. A significant amount of intermarriage has taken place with their Brahui neighbors.

See also Brahuis

References
Wilber, Donald Newton. 1962. *Afghanistan: Its people, Its Society, Its Culture*. New Haven, CT: HRAF Press.

BAREQ-SHAFI'I, MUHAMMAD HASAN (1932–)

Muhammad Hasan Bareq-Shafi'i is a noted Afghan poet and writer and was also a high-ranking member of the People's Democratic Party of Afghanistan (PDPA). He had been editor of a number of newspapers and journals, including *Pashtun Voice* (*Pashtun Zhagh*), *Message of the Day* (*Payam-i-Imruz*), *Theatre* (*Nanderi*), and *Life* (*Zhuandin*) and was a member of the Parchami faction of the PDPA from the outset.

Bareq-Shafi'i is a Pashtun who was born in 1932 in Kabul and educated at Ghazi High School and at the Theological College in Kabul. In 1966, he became editor of *Khalq*, which was the party organ of the PDPA. After the Saur Revolt of April 1978, which brought the Communists to power, he became minister of information and culture and, in 1979, minister of transport. During the period of Khalq dominance, Bareq-Shafi'i was forced to denounce Babrak Karmal, and when Karmal rose to power, he was demoted to being only an alternate member of the Central Committee of the PDPA. In 1982, he was appointed vice-president of the Central Council of the National Fatherland Front and governor of Herat Province. Three years later, he was appointed second secretary to the Afghan embassy in Libya, and in May 1987, he took over control of the party paper and was chair of the union of journalists. After the fall of the Marxist government in 1992, he is thought to have fled to Europe.

See also National Fatherland Front; People's Democratic Party of Afghanistan

References
Guistozzi, Antonio. 2000. *War, Politics and Society in Afghanistan, 1978–1992.* Washington, DC: Georgetown University Press.

BARYALAI, MAHMUD (1944–)

Mahmud Baryalai was appointed as first deputy prime minister in May 1990 by Dr. Muhammad Najibullah (president of Afghanistan and leader of the People's Democratic Party of Afghanistan, or PDPA) and was a member of the executive board of the Central Council of the Islamic Unity Party (Hizb-i Wahdat). He was born in Kabul and educated at the Habibia School, at Kabul University, and in the Soviet Union, where he received an M.A. degree in political economics. Baryalai is a half brother of Babrak Karmal (a leading member of the PDPA) and the son-in-law of Anahita Ratebzad (a prominent female member of parliament and the PDPA). He was also a charter member of the PDPA. After the Saur Revolt of April 1978 and the advent of Communist rule in Kabul, he became the Afghan ambassador to Pakistan in July 1978 but was recalled as part of the Khalq purge in October 1978, though he did not return to Kabul. Following the ousting of Hafizullah Amin, he became head of the International Relations Department of the PDPA and editor of the party newspaper in 1980. He was expelled from the party in July 1991 prior to Babrak Karmal's return to Afghanistan. After the fall of the Marxist regime, he moved into the region controlled by Gen. Abdul Rashid Dostum but is thought to have sought asylum abroad thereafter.

See also People's Democratic Party of Afghanistan

References
Arnold, Anthony. 1983. *Afghanistan's Two-Party Communism: Parcham and Khalq.* Stanford, CA: Hoover Institution Press.

BEHESHTI, SAYYID ALI

Sayyid Ali Beheshti was president of the Revolutionary Council of the Islamic Union of Afghanistan, which controlled large parts of the Hazarajat region in central Afghanistan in 1982. He was born in Bamian Province and was educated in Saudi Arabia and Iraq, where he was in close contact with the exiled Ayatollah Khomeini. On his return to Afghanistan, he opened a *madrasa* (religious school) at Waras in Ghor Province in order to spread his revivalist ideas among the Hazara population. He was also a speaker in the parliament at Kabul until the Saur Revolt of April 1978, which brought the communists to power. In September 1979, he was elected president of the Shura (the elected ruling council in the Hazarajat) by a council of elders and set up a traditional Islamic resistance group, led by Sayyid Muhammad Hasan Jagran. The group operated out of Waras and was a major force in the Hazarajat until losing ground to the Islamist forces of Nasr, a group founded by Sheikh Mir Husain Sadeqi. Beheshti had set up an infrastructure in the Hazarajat by disarming the population, appointing mayors and governors of towns, and creating an administration based on traditional lines. However, the Shura was torn by internal factionalism and pressured by radical Islamist movements, and the area controlled by the movement dwindled. Beheshti joined forces with Burhanuddin Rabbani, the political leader of the Northern Alliance, but was driven out of Kabul by the arrival of the Taliban in 1996.

See also Shi'a Mujahideen Groups
References
Olesen, A. 1995. *Islam and Politics in Afghanistan.* London: Curzon Press.

BONN CONFERENCE (2 DECEMBER 2002)

Following the Bonn Conference of December 2001, which was sponsored by the United Nations and helped set up the Afghanistan Interim Government, a second conference was held at Bonn on 2 December 2002. It was attended by representatives from Afghanistan, led by President Hamid Karzai, and thirty-one other nations. The conference was convened to discuss the rebuilding of Afghanistan, to find ways of speeding up the creation of a new national army, and to discuss the security problems in Afghanistan in order to find ways to increase the government's authority outside of Kabul.

At the time of the conference, the security question was brought to the fore by reports of fighting between rival warlords in Paktia Province, leading to appeals from President Karzai for more assistance in respect to security problems. The United States is now training the new Afghan army with French assistance, and Germany is leading efforts to set up a national police force, but progress has been slow due to resistance from Afghan leaders keen to retain their own positions of power. Although President Karzai has called for the role of the International Security Assistance Force (ISAF) to be extended to the rest of the country, such a move has been resisted by contributing nations, mainly from Europe.

The closing statement from the conference also reaffirmed the need for international aid for Afghanistan but stressed that the country had to implement economic reforms, to guarantee human rights for women and ethnic minorities, and to effectively combat the drug trade. The progress of rebuilding, with the opening of schools and the reconstruction of roads, was also recognized, but the conference attendees acknowledged that real progress would depend on an improved security situation. One of the main areas of concern was how to bring the warlords and their militias under the control of the Kabul government. This issue was seen as a major factor in ensuring that the timetable set out at Bonn in December 2001 regarding a new constitution and democratic elections could still be met. The conference also concluded that the fight of the civilized world against international terrorism, irrational fanaticism, and the evils of the drug trade was at stake in Afghanistan.

See also Afghan Army; Disarmament Program; Reconstruction Program
References
Czacka, Tony. 2002. "Afghanistan Conference Sets Track for Army, Election, a Year after Taliban Ousted." http://www.story.news.yahoo.com/news?tmpl=story 2&cid:524=u=/ap/20021202/ap (cited 3 December 2002).
Graham, Stephen. 2003. "Afghan Leader Appeals for More Security." http://www.afghan.com (cited 2 December 2002).

"Summit to Tackle Afghan Woes." 2002. http://www.afgfha.com (cited 2 December 2002).

BRAHUIS

The Brahuis are members of one of Afghanistan's small ethnic communities and speak a Dravidian language; they are found in the southern parts of the provinces of Kandahar and Nimruz. They are of ancient origin and were mentioned by Pliny in his accounts of Bactria. Historically, these people were essentially nomadic. The community numbers somewhat in excess of 20,000 today, and members speak Pashtu and Baluchi and consider themselves akin to the Baluchs. The majority of the Brahuis live in the Pakistan province of Baluchistan, and the community is composed of Sunni Muslims of the Hanifa School. The Brahuis in Pakistan are divided into two main tribes, with members of the Sarawa tribe considering themselves to be of Afghan descent, but the tribal structure is compact and united (though there is intermarriage with their Barechi neighbors).

See also Barechi Tribe
References
Bray, Denys. 1913. *The Life and History of a Brahui.* London: Royal Asiatic Society.
———. 1986. *The Brahui Language, an Old Dravidian Language Spoken in Parts of Baluchistan and Sind.* Delhi, India: Gian Publishing House.
Raverty, H. G. 1976. *Notes on Afghanistan and Baluchistan.* Quetta, Pakistan: Gosho-a-Adeb.

BURNES, ALEXANDER (1805–1841)

Alexander Burnes was a captain in the British Indian army who was sent by the British East India Company in September 1837 to the court of Amir Dost Muhammad in Afghanistan. The objectives of the mission were to conclude an alliance between the amir and Britain and to reach a peace agreement with Ranjit Singh of the Sikh nation, who had captured Kashmir and entered Peshawar. Burnes was well received by the amir, and a settlement looked promising, but Lord Auckland of the East India Company refused to make any commitments other than to recommend that the amir drop his claim to Peshawar and make peace with the Sikhs. Tensions between the British and the amir were heightened by correspondence conducted by the amir with the Russian government, as well as the presence in Kabul of a Russian emissary, Capt. Ivan

Vitkevich, all of which led to the invasion of Afghanistan and the outbreak of the First Anglo-Afghan War in 1839. Burnes had returned to Kabul with the British army to serve as deputy to Sir William Macnaghten, head of the British mission at Kabul. However, there was an uprising in Kabul among the civilian population and members of the army, who sacked the British mission. Burnes was among the staff assassinated on 2 November 1841. The war was a complete disaster for the British army and the British India government.

See also Capitulation, Treaty of; First Anglo-Afghan War;
    Macnaghten, Sir William
References
Norris, James A. 1967. *The First Afghan War, 1838–42.*
    London: Cambridge University Press.

CAPITULATION, TREATY OF (1841)

On 11 December 1841, during the First Anglo-Afghan War, British forces opened negotiations with Afghan chiefs when it was evident that they could not defend themselves against further Afghan attacks. A treaty was signed by Eldred Pottinger, the political agent at Kabul, and Maj. Gen. William Elphinstone, commander of the British forces in Afghanistan, as well as a number of Afghan chiefs, including Muhammad Akbar Khan, son of Amir Dost Muhammad. The treaty demanded that the British withdraw from Afghanistan and never return, that they hand over all weapons as a sign of friendship, and that all the seized property of the amir be returned. Six British officers were to remain behind as a gesture of goodwill, and they were to be released, together with the sick and wounded at Kabul, once the British had crossed the border. The retreating army was to be accompanied to the border to prevent molestation by Afghan tribesmen during the withdrawal. Britain was still to be bound by earlier agreements to offer assistance in the event of a foreign invasion of Afghanistan.

The treaty, however, was never implemented because of mutual distrust between the two parties, and the British representative at Kabul, Sir William Macnaghten, was killed by Sardar Akbar Khan, commander of the Afghan forces, when he discovered that the British had been trying to reach a deal with rival chiefs. The British refused to hand over their weapons and began to evacuate Kabul on 6 January 1842 but were almost totally wiped out on the march to the border. Despite this outcome, British officers and families left behind under the protection of Akbar Khan were returned safely to India.

See also Burnes, Alexander; First Anglo-Afghan War; Pottinger, Maj. Eldred

References

Norris, James A. *The First Anglo-Afghan War, 1838–42.* London: Cambridge University Press.

C

CAVAGNARI, SIR PIERRE LOUIS (1841–1879)

Pierre Louis Cavagnari was of mixed British and French ancestry, was commissioner of Peshawar, and was the British government's signatory for the 1879 Treaty of Gandomak concluded with Yaqub Khan, ruler of Afghanistan from February to October 1879. On 21 September 1878, he had crossed the Afghan border with a small entourage to prepare for the mission of Sir Neville Chamberlain to Kabul. The party was stopped at Ali Masjid by Afghan troops under the command of Gen. Faiz Muhammad, and this action was used by Britain as an excuse to invade Afghanistan on 21 November 1878, thus beginning the Second Anglo-Afghan War. At the end of the war, Cavagnari was appointed as the British envoy to the amir's court at Kabul, where he arrived in July 1879. However, on 3 September 1879, mutinous Afghan soldiers and Kabuli civilians attacked the British mission, and Cavagnari and his staff were killed. The British feared a repeat of the debacle of the First Anglo-Afghan War and withdrew their army, having recognized Abdur Rahman Khan as amir.

See also Gandomak, Treaty of; Second Anglo-Afghan War; Yaqub Khan, Amir Muhammad

References

Cardew, F. G. 1908. *The Second Afghan War, 1878–80.* London: J. Murray.

Dey, Kelly Prosono. 1881. *The Life and Career of Major Sir Louis Cavagnari, C.S.I., K.C.B. British Envoy at Cabul, with a Brief Outline of the Second Anglo-Afghan War.* Calcutta, India: J. N. Ghose.

CENTRAL INTELLIGENCE AGENCY AND ITS SUPPORT FOR THE MUJAHIDEEN

In the ten years following the 1979–1989 Soviet occupation of Afghanistan, the United States provided

Sir Pierre Louis Cavagnari, British envoy to Afghanistan, photographed on his way to Kabul in July 1879. He was killed two months later during an Afghan uprising in Kabul, which led to the Second Anglo-Afghan War. (Hulton-Deutsch Collection/Corbis)

between $2 billion and $3 billion to the coalition of seven mujahideen groups recognized by Pakistan. However, this coalition, known as the Afghan Interim Government, was on the fringes of Afghan politics, as it failed to include representatives of key Afghan constituencies, such as field commanders. It was more representative of Pakistani interests and policies rather than fully meeting Afghan interests, as evidenced by the fact that Gulbuddin Hekmatyar's group received the bulk of U.S. aid because he was favored by Pakistan authorities as the leader they wished to deal with. The group had an inability to attract support inside Afghanistan and was only held together by the jihad against the Marxist government in Kabul, as well as the Soviet occupying forces.

Officials in the Central Intelligence Agency (CIA) thought that the Soviet withdrawal would result in the mujahideen instantly toppling the regime of Muhammad Najibullah and that the conflict would only last a few weeks or at most six months.

However, by 1989, the military campaign had stagnated, for the alliance was unable to command a national consensus to continue the jihad and the attempt to take Jalalabad had foundered badly against government forces. The United States had portrayed the Afghan war as a battle between Najibullah's foreign-backed forces and those of the U.S.-backed patriots. Both were, in fact, mirror images, as neither side in the conflict was indigenous or broad-based and 40 percent of the population were refugees, living either in urban areas or refugee camps.

The whole nature of the mujahideen movement was complex, as it included both Islamic revolutionaries and elite traditionalists, with a working alliance being the price of continued U.S. support. The United States also used Pakistan as a conduit for this support, and President Mohammad Zia al Haq would only recognize seven groups for receiving funds and arms. Power accrued to the Afghan Interim Government because its members were seen as approved middlemen, and the field commanders cooperated with the arrangement, either because of affinities or because it was the only way to obtain sophisticated arms and equipment. Beyond the belief that the Soviets must be expelled from Afghanistan and the Communist government brought down, there was little agreement between any of the groups in Peshawar. The role of the Inter-Services Intelligence (ISI) unit of Pakistan, whose representatives sat in on all meetings, and the financing provided for some groups from Saudi Arabia or Iran caused the Peshawar groups to be regarded as tools of external policies rather than Afghan interests.

See also Inter-Services Intelligence Service
References
Bonosky, Phillip. 1985. *Washington's Secret War against Afghanistan.* New York: International Publishers.
Lohbeck, Kurt. 1993. *Holy War, Unholy Victory: Eyewitness to the CIA's Secret War in Afghanistan.* Washington, DC: Regnery Gateway.

CHAHAR AIMAQS

The Chahar Aimaqs are an ethnic group of some 800,000 Sunni Muslims who are seminomadic and live in the typical Asian yurt, a conical structure made of felt. Their language is Dari but with a mix of some Turki, and the group includes Firuzkuhis, Jamshidis, Taimaris, and the Sunni Hazaras of Qalai-Nau. Due to their seminomadic lifestyle, they were, in the past, largely independent, but they also allied themselves with the ruling Durrani princes of Herat. Amir Abdur Rahman was instrumental in curbing their power, and he placed them under the direct control of the governor of Herat. The economy of the Aimaqs is primarily based on raising sheep and cattle, and they live mainly in the provinces of Badghis, Ghor, and Herat.

See also Jamshidi Tribe; Taimaris
References
Pedersen, G. 1994. *Afghan Nomads in Transition.* London: Thames and Hudson.

CHARKHI, GHULAM NABI (?–1932)

Ghulam was a general under Amir Habibullah who was appointed as ambassador to Moscow from 1922 to 1924 by King Amanullah and then deputy minister of foreign affairs. He was heavily involved in pacification campaigns on behalf of the king and served in the Logar Valley during the Khost Rebellion between 1924 and 1925. He then served for short periods as Afghanistan's ambassador in Paris and

Moscow but returned in 1929 to lead an army, officered by Afghan cadets who had been in Turkey, in an attempt to restore Amanullah to the throne. However, he was unable to defeat the forces of Habibullah Kalakani and was forced to withdraw into the Soviet Union. In 1932, he was pardoned and returned to Afghanistan but was later accused of subversive activities against Nadir Shah and executed.

See also Amanullah, King; Habibullah Kalakani; Khost Rebellion
References
Poullada, Leon B. 1973. *Reform and Rebellion in Afghanistan, 1919–1929.* Ithaca, NY: Cornell University Press.

CIVIL WAR
Soviet Withdrawal from Afghanistan

After ten years of intervention in Afghanistan and an occupation in all but name, the Soviet Union finally withdrew its forces in 1989. The Soviets had arrived in Afghanistan on 25 December 1979, and with the death of Hafizullah Amin at the hands of Soviet Special Forces, Babrak Karmal was installed as the new head of a Parcham-based government. The Soviet actions were justified on the grounds that the USSR was coming to the aid of an endangered, friendly socialist government, but it was also clear that the Soviets had become increasingly alarmed at the unstable and unpredictable nature of the Afghan regime on their southern borders.

The Soviet intervention resulted in large numbers of Afghans becoming refugees in Iran and Afghanistan, a significant internal displacement of the population, international condemnation, and recognition by the United States that Pakistan was now a frontline state in the battle against communism. Among the refugees in Pakistan and Iran, groups began to emerge as a resistance movement whose objective was to oust the Communist-backed government in Kabul. The resultant ten-year war against the Kabul regime of the People's Democratic Party of Afghanistan (PDPA), backed by the Soviet Union, was waged by the mujahideen groups based primarily in Pakistan but also in Iran and by leaders such as Ahmad Shah Masood who had remained in Afghanistan. The guerrilla war was fought with intensity on both sides, without concern for the usual rules of warfare and at enormous cost to both sides, so that by 1985, the Soviet Union was beginning to look for a face-saving exit strategy.

A Soviet tank crosses the Friendship Bridge linking the USSR and Afghanistan over the Amu Daria River. (Reuters NewMedia Inc./CORBIS)

In 1985, Mikhail Gorbachev became the leader of the Soviet Union and began to pursue a policy of opening up the country (perestroika) and seeking accommodation with the West. But the situation in Afghanistan proved to be a stumbling block. The situation had also changed in Afghanistan as Babrak Karmal resigned as secretary-general of the PDPA and was replaced by Muhammad Najibullah, who had been the head of state security, the Khedamat-i Ettela'at-i Daulati (KHAD). Although Karmal continued as president for a few months, power really rested with Najibullah, who tried to reach an accommodation with the mujahideen, partially through a reassertion of Islamic values. However, the mujahideen rejected all moves made by the Najibullah government out of hand and refused to enter into any compromise agreement.

At the same time, proximity talks were being held in Geneva under the sponsorship of the United Nations, and on 14 April 1988, agreement was reached between Afghanistan and Pakistan on the withdrawal of Soviet troops in nine months, the creation of a neutral state in Afghanistan, and the repatriation of Afghan refugees. The terms of the agreement, known as the Geneva Accords, were underwritten by the Soviet Union and the United States, but the mujahideen were still bitterly opposed to the Najibullah government. However, the accords held, and the Soviet Union began to withdraw from Afghanistan, with the last troops leaving Afghan soil on 15 February 1989.

It was anticipated by many observers that the Najibullah government would collapse within weeks of the Soviet withdrawal, but to everyone's surprise, it survived, despite continuing pressure from mujahideen forces that were unable to oust government troops from cities such as Jalalabad. However, the situation soon began to deteriorate because financial and military aid from the Soviet Union had all but ceased, the military was running out of fuel and money, commodity prices had risen beyond the reach of most people, and the mujahideen were besieging Kabul. The government forces had lost all semblance of morale, and even within the government, differences had begun to emerge as to the best way forward. One governmental faction wanted to transfer power to the mujahideen under the Geneva Accords; another faction wanted to form a coalition government with certain elements of the mujahideen.

Following the collapse of the concept of a coalition government, Najibullah declared his support for a transfer of power to all the parties involved in the struggle, and he made his views public on 18 March 1992. However, followers of Babrak Karmal within the government wanted to form a coalition government with elements of the mujahideen, excluding the Islamic Party of Gulbuddin Hekmatyar, and it was this faction that held power within the military and the militias. In April 1992, an attempt was made to assassinate Gen. Abdul Rashid Dostum, but Najibullah's efforts to remove the general from the scene were foiled. On 14 April 1992, Najibullah was forced to relinquish power.

The Kabul government now came under the direct control of supporters of Babrak Karmal, and they began to reinforce the defenses of the city by bringing troops in from northern Kabul, drawn from groups with whom they had reached a compromise over the formation of a coalition government. Directives were also issued to all government employees and military forces in the provinces to join with mujahideen elements with whom they had reached an agreement. At the same time, they were urged to surrender to the weakest mujahideen groups where the Islamic Party was the strongest element, and under no circumstances were they to surrender to the Islamic Party. The coalition consisted of the Islamist Movement of Burhanuddin Rabbani, the Uzbeks under Dostum, the Ismai'li faction of Sayed Jafar Nadari, and supporters of Babrak Karmal.

Under the terms of the coalition agreement, control of the cities and highways would reside with the military forces of the Communist government, and all political parties would be fused into the civil administration of a new coalition government. However, Hekmatyar's Islamic Party was pushing for the formation of a transitional government acceptable to all parties, transfer of power to an interim government, and the holding of a general election six moths after the interim government came into being. It was the aim of the Islamic Party to persuade mujahideen leaders not to form a coalition government with the Communist government but to combine together to form an interim government that would be subjected to elections and the endorsement of the people.

All of the parties concerned about the establishment of an Islamic government in Afghanistan by the mujahideen supported the formation of either a coalition government with the Communists or a coalition of nationalist movements and figures acceptable to the Western powers. This approach was rejected by the Islamic Party, which proposed that:

- Najibullah should resign
- Mujahideen groups should agree on the formation of an interim government acceptable to all the groups
- Communist militia forces should be disbanded and their weapons transferred to the army
- Responsibility for the security of the city of Kabul should be transferred to the police force
- Power should be transferred peacefully to the interim administration
- General elections should be held within a six-month time frame

These proposals were accepted by all of the mujahideen except for Abdul Rasul Sayyaf, a member of the Islamic Alliance for the Liberation of Afghanistan and the Islamic Party of Yunis Khales. The draft plan was submitted to the UN special envoy for Afghanistan and was to pave the way for an interim administration to replace the Communist regime, with a peaceful transition of power. The plan appeared to have received endorsement by Rabbani's Islamist Movement when leaders of that group agreed to sign the agreement on 4 April 1992, but they reversed their stand on 30 April after the Communist generals put their support behind the movement.

Leaders of the Islamist Movement insisted on the establishment of an interim government made up of mujahideen leaders, as this would lead them into a coalition with elements of the Communist government. However, Najibullah attempted to counter these developments by proposing that the Islamic Party under Hekmatyar should have a larger share of the government and should link with the Watan (Homeland Party), formerly known at the PDPA. This proposal was rejected because Hekmatyar saw no need for a compromise with the Communists and responded by demanding that power be peaceably transferred and that the Communists take advantage of the amnesty being offered by the mujahideen. Even up to the last few days of his regime, Najibullah was still trying to form an alliance between the Islamic Party and Watan and warning that a further refusal would mean the transfer of power to other elements, such as the former king, which could lead to another major crisis in the country.

On 17 April, Hekmatyar left Peshawar, Pakistan, for Afghanistan to counter the movement of militia forces into Kabul and the arrival of the mujahideen forces of Ahmad Shah Masood, who was a supporter of Rabbani's Islamist Movement. Hekmatyar issued a directive to all of his forces to take control of cities from the Communists and to move on Kabul in order to force the Communist regime to give up the idea of a coalition government and concede power to the mujahideen. On 24 April, the Kabul government attempted last-minute negotiations with Hekmatyar to try to agree on a coalition, but the eventual outcome was a recommendation to the executive council of the government that Hekmatyar's proposals be accepted in order to prevent bloodshed in Kabul.

Mujahideen Coalition Government and Collapse

Early in 1992, the Tajik forces of Masood, the Uzbek forces of General Dostum, and the Hazara forces of the Islamic Unity Party joined together in a coalition called the Northern Alliance; the coalition was at odds with the Islamic Party of Hekmatyar as well as the Najibullah government. On 15 April 1992, a non-Pashtun mujahideen group allied with the government mutinied and took control of the Kabul airport, preventing Najibullah from leaving Afghanistan and preempting a transfer of power under the auspices of the United Nations. Najibullah was forced to seek refuge in the UN compound in Kabul, remaining for a period of four years, until he was murdered by the Taliban in September 1996. On 25 April 1992, Masood entered Kabul with his forces, and on the following day, the Northern Alliance reached an agreement on a coalition government that excluded the Islamic Party of Hekmatyar, who had received the backing of Pakistan.

The first leader of the coalition was President Sabghatullah Mujaddidi, but he stood down in June 1992 and was replaced by Burhanuddin Rabbani, the leader of the Islamist Movement, who was elected by the Shura (Council) for a period of four

months. These moves resulted in the forces of Hekmatyar launching intensive and indiscriminate rocket attacks on Kabul from their bases to the south of the city. The mujahideen coalition elsewhere did not last, as there was also fierce fighting between the Hazara-dominated Islamic Unity Party and the Islamic Alliance for the Liberation of Afghanistan, which resulted in the deaths of hundreds of civilians. In December 1992, Rabbani, who had had his period of office extended by two months, was again elected president after ensuring that the governing council had been filled with his supporters; this only intensified the struggle with Hekmatyar, whose forces continued their attacks on Kabul, killing hundreds of civilians. Rabbani's government changed the name of the Republic of Afghanistan to the Islamic State of Afghanistan; introduced Shari'a as the only source of Afghan law; transformed coeducational schools and colleges into single-sex institutions; and issued decrees banning alcohol, gambling, and nightclubs and requiring women to wear veils. But these measures had little impact on society in Kabul and its environs because the government did not have the power or will to enforce its policies. The Kabul government was soon to become embroiled in a bitter civil war fueled by long-standing rivalries between leaders of the various factions and of the four main ethnic groups.

Largely as a result of the years of fighting following the Soviet intervention of 1979, there had been a large internal displacement of the population, in addition to the millions who had fled to Iran and Pakistan. As a result, the population of Kabul had swelled to 2 million, almost a third of whom were Hazaras and located in the western sections of the city, which were loyal to the Islamic Unity Party headed by Abdul Ali Mazari. Tajik, Uzbek, and Hazara fighters now controlled Kabul, and they were not prepared to allow Pashtun hegemony—which dated back to 1747—to reassert itself, as was the declared intention of Hekmatyar. In August 1992, Kabul came under a series of onslaughts from Hekmatyar's forces, with the city being defended by the fighters allied with Dostum, Masood, and Mazari. A cease-fire was reached toward the end of the month, but by then, at least 2,500 people were dead and some 50,000 Afghanis were displaced. At the same time, Hekmatyar continued to support Islamic fundamentalists in Tajikistan, partially for ideological reasons but also to prevent the Tajiks from offering support to their counterparts in Afghanistan.

The Islamic Unity Party had boycotted the council that extended Rabbani's presidency by two years, and party members joined the forces of Hekmatyar in assaults on Kabul, particularly the Tajik strongholds in the northern suburbs. During these assaults, Dostum remained neutral as the city was pounded, with suburbs in the south and west being reduced to rubble. The result was yet a further outpouring of refugees into the eastern provinces and across the border into Pakistan, complete with harrowing tales of murder, mutilation, abduction, and rape at the hands of both government forces and the rebels. The outcome was not just a breakdown of law and order but also a total disintegration of Afghan society; interethnic atrocities on both sides traumatized the civilian population.

The prime minister of Pakistan, Muhammad Nawaz Sharif, offered to mediate between the opposing factions, and a meeting was held in Islamabad in March 1993 between the mujahideen coalition, the Islamic Party, and the Islamic Unity Party. The meeting resulted in an accord, which gave Hekmatyar the premiership and confirmed Rabbani's presidency for a period of eighteen months, commencing in December 1992. At the end of this period, parliamentary elections were to have been held under a new constitution, which was to be drafted by the signatories to the accord. Under pressure from Hekmatyar, Dostum was denied any role in the Leadership Council or in the Constitutional Committee established to draw up the new constitution on the grounds that he was an unreconstructed Communist. Sharif then traveled with Hekmatyar to Mecca, where King Fahd cosigned the agreement, and then to Tehran, where it was cosigned by President Ali Akbar Rafsanjani.

Afghanistan was again a divided nation, with Dostum, as the self-styled "president of the Northern Alliance," controlling six provinces extending from the Central Asian borders to the outskirts of Kabul. Dostum's capital was Mazar-i Sharif. He controlled the gas fields near Sheberghan and a large chemical plant at Mazar-i Sharif, and the region under him had its own effective bureaucracy, complete with the power to collect taxes and customs. The population of Mazar-i Sharif had swelled to 500,000, but the city had electricity, drinking water, and public transportation, in marked contrast to the destruction and disorder in Kabul, whose population had shrunk from 2 million to 500,000. In addition, Dostum's military force was the most powerful in Afghanistan, with Soviet tanks, fighter aircraft, helicopter gunships, and transport planes, and it was manned by Uzbeks, Tajiks, and Turkomans together with former Communist Pashtun officers.

In Kabul, the Constitutional Committee became embroiled in controversy over the relative status of the Shi'a Jaafari and the Sunni Hanafi codes of law, leading to a rift between the Islamic Alliance for the Liberation of Afghanistan, represented by Sayyaf, and the Islamic Unity Party, represented by Mazari. This major disagreement threw the election timetable into disarray, as it had been conditional on the adoption of a new constitution, and led to fighting between the two factions in Kabul in October 1993. This conflict was followed by clashes between the forces of Rabbani and Hekmatyar in November, during which Dostum maintained his neutrality. The two sides agreed to a truce in December, largely to replenish their ammunition, but on 1 January 1994, Dostum suddenly launched an attack on Rabbani's forces in the center of Kabul, and in the fashion of Afghan politics, his hitherto sworn enemies—Hekmatyar and Mazari—joined him.

The first assault lasted for a week without respite, and at the end, there was a brief truce that allowed foreign diplomats to leave Kabul, with Tajik residents fleeing to the Tajik districts in the north of the city. Fighting then broke out again and lasted, with brief respites, for almost two months, during which the city experienced frequent power cuts and breakdowns in the water supply; hospitals were shelled by rockets, bakeries were abandoned, and half of the residential areas were destroyed. The establishment of the Supreme Coordination Council, chaired by Hekmatyar, formalized the alliance. On 28 June 1994, Rabbani refused to step down as required under the terms of the Islamabad Accord, and the civil war intensified. The Tajik forces of Rabbani performed well and routed Hekmatyar's troops in southeastern Kabul and seized control of the Kabul airport from Dostum. The efforts of the United Nations and other countries in the region to secure peace were to no avail, for the Afghan factions were no longer influenced by the foreign powers that had originally backed them. The United States and Russia were content to see the internecine violence continue, fearing that a stable Islamic Afghanistan would assist Islamic militant forces in Tajikistan and elsewhere in Central Asia and damage their own interests in the region.

Afghanistan was now in a state of total anarchy, with no semblance of a government or law and order. A great deal of suffering and starvation was inflicted on the civilian population, many of whom were only kept alive by relief provided by the United Nations and nongovernment organizations (NGOs). Outside of Kabul and the area controlled by Dostum, the rest of the country had been carved up among a number of mujahideen commanders who had set themselves up as local warlords. The civilian population had no security from murder, rape, looting, or extortion, and even humanitarian agencies found their offices ransacked, their vehicles hijacked, and their staff members threatened. It was against this background that the Taliban movement emerged and gained ascendancy.

Military Successes of the Taliban

The nucleus of the embryonic movement that would become the Taliban was composed of former mujahideen leaders who had been disillusioned with the chaos following the mujahideen victory. They joined with a number of Pashtun mullahs, who were veterans of the war against the Soviet Union and wished to see an end to the civil war. The movement began to center on a former mujahideen commander, Mullah Muhammad Omar, who was the village mullah of Singesar in Kandahar Province and head of the local *madrasa* (religious school). He and others in the movement were soon to be joined by commanders from other Pashtun parties, Khalq PDPA members, and students from the Afghan madrasas. The movement became known as the Taliban—referring to students who pursue religious learning—due to the relationship with the religious schools in Afghanistan and Pakistan and the young people in the refugee camps. The Taliban was formed with a three-point program: restoring peace; disarming civilians; and fully applying Shari'a, with its strict interpretation and application of Islamic law.

In the spring of 1994, Mullah Omar was elected leader of the Taliban, and one of his first moves was to act against the commander of a military camp near Singesar who had abducted two teenage girls;

the girls had then been raped. Omar took a party of Taliban to the camp, freed the captives, seized arms and ammunition, and hanged the commander from the barrel of a tank. In July 1994, he intervened in a public argument between two commanders in Kandahar over a young boy wanted as a homosexual partner, and he freed the captive. His reputation grew as a result of these interventions, and Omar was then approached by truckers from Pakistan who were being subjected to harassment and extortion by local warlords. The warlords had erected some 200 roadblocks on the road from Quetta in Pakistan to Iran, via Herat. The truckers offered the Taliban leader payment to clear the highway for their trucks, which he did. This action also resulted in the Taliban receiving support from Pakistan, as they were seen as able to secure the trade routes to Central Asia and form a government in Kabul sympathetic to Pakistan's interests.

The first military operation of the Taliban was the seizure of the munitions depot and the town of Spin Boldak on the border with Pakistan, which had been held by Islamic Party forces. This operation provided them with a large quantity of material, including rockets, artillery, small arms, and ammunition. In addition, in October 1994, the Pakistan government sent a convoy of trucks loaded with medical supplies on a trial run; it was stopped by local warlords, who were then attacked by Taliban forces called on by Pakistan's Inter-Services Intelligence (ISI) officers. The Taliban then moved on Kandahar and took the city, with the local commander, loyal to the Rabbani government, having ordered his troops not to resist. This action allowed the Taliban to acquire heavy weapons, fighter aircraft, and tanks, and they saw their ranks swelled by volunteer fighters from Pakistan who had crossed the border at Spin Boldak with the knowledge of the Pakistan authorities. The Taliban then spread north and east to the outskirts of Kabul and west toward Herat, receiving strong financial backing from Pakistan traders anxious to sell their goods to Central Asia.

In January 1995, the Taliban advanced on Kabul and squeezed the forces of Hekmatyar between their lines and those of Masood, inducing Hekmatyar to abandon Charasyab and leave behind a large store of weaponry for the Taliban forces. However, after Masood had reached an accommodation with the fighters of the Islamic Unity Party, he launched an attack on the Taliban positions and threw them out of Charasyab. Fighting flared up again in the summer of 1995, with the Taliban occupying the Shindand military base in Herat Province and seizing aircraft and helicopters; they then moved on to take the city of Herat and end the rule of Isma'il Khan, an ally of Rabbani, while also cutting the road connecting Rabbani's government with Iran.

The area of Herat was primarily populated by Shi'a Muslims who were held in low esteem by the Taliban, and that attitude turned Iran into a strongly anti-Taliban regime. Leaders in Tehran therefore increased their assistance to Rabbani and advised him to settle his differences with other anti-Taliban factions in order to overcome the Taliban threat. Meetings were held with Hekmatyar, Dostum, and Karim Khalili, and a committee to stand against the Taliban, who were still laying siege to Kabul, was set up. Iran's attempts to put together an effective anti-Taliban alliance were countered by Pakistan, with an increase in its material support for the movement. The Pakistan government repaired roads and restored electricity to the south of the country held by the Taliban and, significantly, improved the Kandahar airport to maintain a steady supply of food and arms and ammunition, which were also trucked in from Spin Boldak. The Taliban were provided with a telephone and wireless network as well and given full access to intelligence data through the ISI. Aid was also received from Saudi Arabia in the form of finance, fuel, and pickup trucks that were used extensively in the fighting. At the same time, Pakistan was professing its neutrality and a policy of nonintervention in Afghan politics.

In May 1996, Osama bin Laden arrived in Afghanistan, having been expelled from Sudan, together with followers who were veteran fighters from the jihad against the Soviet Union. These individuals formed the backbone of the al-Qaeda terrorist organization. Bin Laden set up training camps in the area controlled by the Taliban and in the North-West Frontier Province of Pakistan. Meanwhile, fighting in Afghanistan had shifted to the eastern portion of the country. On 26 June, Hekmatyar arrived with some of his forces to take up the premiership in Kabul, and Dostum raised the siege of the capital to the north. On 25 August, the Taliban attacked Jalalabad and laid siege to the city, an operation that lasted two weeks, with the city only

being taken after the local commander, Haji Abdul Qadir, had been promised safe passage to Pakistan and a bribe of $10 million.

Immediately after the fall of Kandahar, the Taliban enjoyed rapid success in Nangarhar, Laghman, and Kunar Provinces, all of which fell in the course of ten days and which had been under the control of the Eastern Shura Council that was operating independently of Kabul. This action was followed on 24 September by the capture of Sarobi, which was the stronghold of Hekmatyar. An advance followed up this action on Kabul from the east and the south, with a third group of Taliban forces progressing north to neutralize any threat from the Bagram air base. Kabul fell on the night of 26 September, and the speed of its fall was a surprise to many observers, except for Pakistan, which had heavily backed the Taliban. The occupation was orderly, with no looting or a breakdown in discipline, unlike the occupation by the mujahideen in 1992. However, prior to the Taliban arrival, Ahmad Shah Masood had already evacuated the city and moved his troops north, together with most of their artillery and tanks.

Northern Alliance Reverses

The Northern Alliance forces of Masood were forced to withdraw to the north and the Tajik stronghold in the Panjshir Valley and part of the eastern mountains. By this time, the Taliban had control of about 65 percent of Afghanistan, and its forces had been joined by members of al-Qaeda, who were all seasoned fighters from the war against the Soviet Union or actions in Bosnia, Chechnya, and Kashmir. One of the first actions of the new regime was to storm the UN compound in Kabul and forcibly remove former president Muhammad Najibullah from his refuge and to submit him to Taliban justice: he was castrated, dragged behind a jeep around the presidential palace, shot by Taliban militia, and then hung from a traffic control post with his brother in Ariana Square on 27 September. Death sentences were also passed on Dostum, Masood, and Rabbani but not on Hekmatyar, who was also a Pashtun whereas the other opposition leaders were Tajik and Uzbek.

The Taliban established a six-man shura headed by Mullah Mohammad Rabbani (no relation to the Afghan president) as prime minister of an interim government. The new regime then issued a number of decrees that imposed a strict interpretation of Shari'a law on all areas controlled by the Taliban, together with a demand that civilians and non-Taliban militia disarm. The victory of the Taliban alarmed Iran and the Central Asian republics, especially when the military commander, Muhammad Shoiab, declared that after defeating Masood in the Panjshir Valley, they would move into Tajikistan and Uzbekistan to rout out Communists. Thus, the region became divided into the pro-Taliban states of Saudi Arabia and Pakistan and the anti-Taliban group of Iran, Central Asia, and Russia, a coalition that was to be significant in events after 11 September 2001. During this initial period, bin Laden became closely associated with the Taliban and voiced opposition to the United States and U.S. interests elsewhere in the region.

At the beginning of 1997, Mullah Omar determined to rid the rest of Afghanistan of anti-Taliban forces who had centered themselves on Mazar-i Sharif, where President Rabbani had joined General Dostum. On 1 August, the Taliban began an offensive against Sheberghan, Dostum's major military base; the area was taken, largely as a result of Hekmatyar's Islamic Party fighters colluding with the Taliban. Dostum, however, maintained that the fall of his base was due to the participation of the Pakistan air force and 1,500 commandos who had taken part in the assault. Further groups of Hekmatyar's forces in the countryside also defected to join the Taliban, which enabled them to march on Mazar-i Sharif on 8 August. During the attack on the city, the Taliban went on the rampage in revenge for the massacre of 3,000 Taliban fighters by Hazaras early in 1997, slaughtering some 4,000 Hazaras. At the same time, ten Iranian diplomats and an Iranian journalist also disappeared from the Iranian consulate. Iran maintained that they had been moved to Kandahar as hostages, but the Taliban authorities contended that they had been killed in the fighting or had fled with opposition forces. This time, the Taliban stayed in the city and followed up their success by taking Hariatan, on the Uzbekistan border, and Taloqan, the headquarters of President Rabbani. These successes led to further increases in the strength of the Taliban militias, with the addition of thousands of madrasa students from Pakistan, and by this stage, the Taliban controlled 85 percent of Afghanistan.

The advance of the Taliban on Northern Alliance positions then slowed, largely because of the onset of winter, but in 1998, with summer approaching, the Taliban took control of five more provinces and completely ousted the forces of General Dostum. This move worsened already strained relations with Iran, which massed troops along the border, but the Taliban were not distracted and moved on to Bamian Province, which fell in mid-September. Consequently, the Taliban now controlled 90 percent of the country, and Northern Alliance forces were penned in the Panjshir Valley and capable of no action beyond resisting further Taliban advances on their territory (though even this was uncertain).

The civil war as a major conflict had really ceased, as the situation in the Panjshir was, by and large, a stalemate and meaningful resistance had ceased elsewhere. It was events outside Afghanistan that were to determine the future. The attacks on the U.S. embassies in Kenya and Tanzania and their attribution to Osama bin Laden and al-Qaeda led to greater cooperation between U.S. intelligence services and Masood in an endeavor to track down bin Laden and bring him to account. The outcome was a U.S. Cruise missile attack on 20 August 1998 on al-Qaeda terrorist training camps near Khost in Paktia Province. The strike was unsuccessful in terms of damaging al-Qaeda or bin Laden, but the reputation of the latter rose within the Islamic world as a result of the embassy attacks and his survival of the U.S. assaults. Yet again, the fate of Afghanistan and its civil war was to be affected by external forces with the aftermath of the 11 September 2001 attacks on the World Trade Center and the Pentagon.

See also Amin, Hafizullah; Dostum, Gen. Abdul Rashid; Geneva Accords; Hazaras; Hekmatyar, Gulbuddin; Inter-Services Intelligence Service; Karmal, Babrak; KHAD; Khales, Yunis; Masood, Ahmad Shah; Mazar-i Sharif; Mujahideen; Najibullah, Muhammad; Northern Alliance; People's Democratic Party of Afghanistan; Rabbani, Burhanuddin; Taliban

References

Gohari, M. J. 2000. *The Taliban: Ascent to Power.* Karachi, Pakistan: Oxford University Press.

Goodson, Larry P. 2001. *Afghanistan's Endless War: State Failure, Regional Politics, and the Rise of the Taliban.* Seattle: University of Washington Press.

Hiro, Dilip. 2002. *War without End: The Rise of Islamist Terrorism and Global Response.* London and New York: Routledge.

Magnus, Ralph H., and Eden Naby. 1998. *Afghanistan, Mullah, Marx and Mujahid.* Boulder, CO: Westview Press.

Maley, William. 1999. *Fundamentalism Reborn? Afghanistan and the Taliban.* London: Hurst.

Marsden, Peter. 1998. *The Taliban: War, Religion and the New Order in Afghanistan.* London: Zed Books.

Rashid, Ahmed. 2001. *Taliban: The Story of the Afghan Warlords.* London: Pan.

CLIMATE

The climate in Afghanistan varies with geographic zones and ranges, from subarctic conditions in the northwest and Hindu Kush mountains to a semi-arid steppes climate in low-lying areas and mild, moist weather in the areas bordering Pakistan. The estimated annual rainfall is between 11 and 15 inches.

The Wakhan-Pamir area, 83 percent of which is above 10,000 feet and the remainder between 6,000–10,000 feet, has perpetual snow cover in the mountains above 12,000 feet, and most of the passes closed during the winter months, from December to March. The yak and the Bactrian camel are the main forms of transport for both people and goods.

The central mountains region has a similar climate. This area covers most of central and eastern Hazarajat and the Hindu Kush ranges, extending from the Shibar Pass through the Koh-i-Baba in the west, which is crossed by the strategically important Salang Pass and Salang Tunnel at an altitude of some 11,000 feet. The climatic conditions allow for some agriculture in the valleys, with the foothills being seasonally grazed by the flocks of the nomads. The eastern mountains include four major valleys: Kabul, Kuhistan/Panjshir, Ghorband, and Nuristan, with the latter being extremely inaccessible. In the winter, temperatures fall below zero; summer temperatures vary according to altitude.

The southwest is a region of stony deserts, which extend to the Iranian border, and the Registan, or "Country of Sand," which extends south of the Helmand River and eastward as far as Sharawak, thus forming an almost impregnable boundary with Pakistan. Only at the edges of the desert is there any vegetation, usually bushes and seasonal vegetation following any rain. The edges of the Registan are seasonally grazed by Baluch and Brahui nomads.

The main agricultural areas of Pakistan are confined to the valleys watered by the Amu Daria and the Turkestan plains, in the northwest the Hari Rud–Murghab system, the Helmand-Argharbad system, and the Kabul River system. Much of the water flow in spring is dependent on the melting mountain snows, which supply the irrigation systems.

The climate and resultant topography of Afghanistan have had a direct impact on conflicts in the country, especially when outside forces are involved, as was evidenced during the Soviet occupation. In the winter, nearly all the mountain passes are inaccessible, as are some of the valley areas in the north, and transportation can only be accomplished on foot or by camel or yak. These conditions have also adversely affected the distribution of humanitarian aid during the recent conflicts, as access to certain areas in winter is almost impossible due to the adverse weather conditions.

References

Amin, Hamidullah, and Gordon B. Schiltz. 1976. *A Geography of Afghanistan.* Omaha, NE: University of Omaha, Center for Afghan Studies.

COALITION AIR CAMPAIGN AGAINST THE TALIBAN

The United States provided the bulk of the input to the air strikes on Afghanistan that began on 7 October 2001, with the dual objectives of destroying Taliban installations and infrastructure and attacking al-Qaeda training camps. Secondary objectives were to prepare the ground for further operations involving conventional ground forces and to aid the anti-Taliban Afghan forces. Intelligence for the air campaign was provided by Northern Alliance forces and by U.S. and UK Special Forces operating independently within Afghanistan or as advisers to the Northern Alliance. Strikes were mounted by aircraft operating from U.S. naval task forces and by B-52 bombers operating flying out of the Diego Garcia base in the Indian Ocean, as well as bases in Europe and Turkey.

The air strikes provided the trigger for the Northern Alliance and its allies in the United Front to open up offensive operations against the Taliban. As a consequence, the U.S. strategy changed to providing air support for these forces by targeting the frontline positions of the Taliban, though the Northern Alliance was somewhat frustrated by the delay in implementing the new tactics. The attacks against Taliban positions were initially centered on northern Afghanistan, with this change having taken place toward the end of October 2001.

The attacks were run from a sophisticated operations center at the Prince Sultan Air Base, near

Riyadh in Saudi Arabia, where target lists were prepared and all warplane movements over Afghanistan were controlled. The logistics were complex, for U.S. Navy jets were flying 500-mile round-trips from carriers based in the Arabian Sea and bombers were flying six-hour missions from Diego Garcia in the Indian Ocean. The operation was a major undertaking, the extent of which was made possible by the cooperation of states bordering Afghanistan. Forces had to be deployed from 267 bases and operated from 30 locations in 15 countries, with over 46 nations being overflown during the course of operations.

From 7 October to 23 October 2001, U.S. Air Force B-2, B-1, and B-52 bombers flew over 600 sorties and dropped more than 80 percent of the tonnage dropped on Afghanistan during the entire Operation Enduring Freedom. Initially, targets included early-warning radar installations, ground forces, command-and-control facilities, al-Qaeda infrastructure, and airfields and aircraft. By 20 November 2001, more than 10,000 bombs or missiles had been dropped or fired into Afghanistan, of which over 60 percent were precision-guided munitions. As of December 2001, C-130 and C-17 cargo aircraft were maintaining a nightly air bridge to the U.S. base south of Kandahar, with the C-130s averaging ten flights in and out every night. In addition to key personnel, the C-17s delivered 1,450 tons of heavy equipment, including graders, earthmovers, and bulldozers. As part of the same operation, the Central Command, based in Germany, also flew some 162 humanitarian sorties and dropped 2.5 million individual, specially prepared rations for the Afghan people.

The main operation lasted from 7 October to 23 December 2001, when the action slowed down. During that period, about 6,500 strike missions were flown over Afghanistan. Roughly 17,500 munitions were expended against 120 fixed-target complexes and over 400 vehicles and artillery guns. Naval forces flew about 75 percent of the sorties; the air force flew the remaining 25 percent but delivered over 70 percent of the ordnance. By the end of December 2001, some 24,000 bombs and missiles had been dropped on Afghanistan.

The scale of the air support was aptly demonstrated during Operation Anaconda, launched against Taliban and al-Qaeda positions near Gardez in eastern Afghanistan on 1 March 2002. The ground attack was supported, on a daily basis, by 10 long-range bombers, 30 to 40 fighter jets, and two to four AC-130 gunships. By the end of the operation in late March, some 3,500 bombs had been dropped on enemy positions. This level of air support was also in place for the subsequent Tora Bora campaign, in which cave complexes sheltering Taliban and al-Qaeda fighters were attacked by U.S. and Afghan tribal forces.

Air Support for Anti-Taliban Forces

As part of a change in strategy, the emphasis of the air campaign was switched to assaults on Taliban frontline positions, designed to aid Afghan opposition forces in their advances on major cities. The Northern Alliance, however, wanted the bombardments to cover a wider area in order to break Taliban and al-Qaeda resistance.

On 21 October 2001, the U.S. Air Force pounded Taliban frontline positions outside Kabul and, on the following day, at Mazar-i Sharif in northern Afghanistan, indicative of an increased level of activity on behalf of the northern-based opposition forces. The air activity continued at Kabul on 24 October after the Taliban again refused to hand over Osama bin Laden; this attack was the most intense launched against Taliban positions and included a night of heavy bombing on the city itself. The operation was intensified by resumed attacks on the frontline positions outside Kabul on 25 October, with one objective being to relieve pressure on the Bagram air base to enable it to be used by Northern Alliance forces to bring in supplies and reinforcements. At the same time, air strikes continued on Taliban positions at Mazar-i Sharif and Herat.

On 28 October, the United States also bombed Taliban positions near the border with Tajikistan, as Taliban artillery was threatening a crucial Northern Alliance supply line near the Kakala River. The crossing point of the river had no bridge, and the Northern Alliance had to operate a small ferry to carry vehicles and supplies across the water. It had also been reported by alliance commanders that the Taliban artillery was protected by a large number of Arab and other foreign fighters, thought to be from the Islamic Movement of Uzbekistan. The bombing of Taliban positions at Mazar-i Sharif, Kabul, Herat, and Kandahar was ongoing, with raids by seventy fighters and bombers on eighteen targets in these areas. However, the Northern Alliance complained about the use of limited-precision attacks by U.S. warplanes instead of an all-out air assault on Taliban positions at Mazar-i Sharif and Kabul.

To secure the supply lines of alliance forces and to bolster their defenses, the United States began a series of air operations in the areas bordering Tajikistan and Uzbekistan. As an aid to the stalled opposition advance on Mazar-i Sharif, bombing raids were also made on Taliban positions at Dara-i-Suf and in areas of Balkh Province to the north of the city. In addition, attacks were targeted on the airport of Kunduz Province and on Taliban positions in northern Jozjan Province, on which alliance forces were advancing. Aircraft were also used to drop weapons, ammunition, and food to Northern Alliance forces, and the number of special forces advisers was increased to establish supply routes, to improve communications with Coalition command centers, and to target specific Taliban positions for air strikes against the front lines.

The U.S. operation became even more sophisticated at the start of November 2001 with the deployment of Joint Surveillance Target Attack Radar System (JSTARS) aircraft, designed to provide continuous surveillance of moving ground targets over a wide area; they were supplemented by the use of Global Hawk high-altitude drones. The U.S. defense secretary, Donald Rumsfeld, also indicated that the number of special forces aiding the Northern Alliance was to be tripled or quadrupled. The bombing of Taliban positions to the north of Kabul was also intensified with the use of B-52 bombers, which Northern Alliance commanders described as very effective; at least fifteen Taliban tanks were destroyed. The logistical problems faced by the U.S. command and control were somewhat alleviated when Azerbaijan and Armenia granted overflight rights for U.S. military planes operating from bases in Europe and Turkey.

A decision was taken not to stop the air strikes during the holy month of Ramadan, which commenced in mid-November, to maintain the momentum of the campaign and deny the Taliban an opportunity to repair some of the damage inflicted on their positions. Although attacks continued on Kabul, Kandahar, and Mazar-i Sharif and U.S. forces maintained that B-52 bombers were having some effect on the situation, the frontline position had not changed. Efforts on the ground in northern Afghanistan were hampered by fog, sandstorms, 100-mile-an-hour winds, and subzero temperatures that had grounded helicopters and delayed planned deployments of special forces.

On 5 November, the air campaign was intensified to help the anti-Taliban forces gain ground and seize strategic targets before the onset of winter. Heavy raids were mounted in the provinces of Samangan and Balkh to assist the advance of the alliance forces on Mazar-i Sharif, but an opposition attack launched on 4 November had already faltered. Raids also continued near the border with Tajikistan on Taliban targets northeast and east of Taloqan, which had been the opposition's northern capital until September 2000. Further B-52 attacks were also launched on enemy positions north of Kabul, and bombing resumed against Kandahar after a four-day lull.

In addition to air assaults on Taliban front lines, attacks were also made on caves and tunnels identified as arms stores and command centers. Among the ordnance used in these attacks were 5,000-pound bunker-busters and a 15,000-pound, full-air explosion bomb known as a "Daisy Cutter." The raids were informed by intelligence from special forces operating behind enemy lines, from defectors, and from the Russian military, based on knowledge acquired during the Soviet war against the mujahideen. On 6 November, further intensive bombing on Taliban positions near Mazar-i Sharif enabled alliance forces to advance under cover of the attack, and they seized the town of Ogapruk and a number of small villages about 45 miles south of the city. By the following day, the Taliban had been forced to withdraw from the Shol Gar district, 24 miles from the city, and by 9 November, the city had fallen to Northern Alliance forces; Herat followed after final assaults aided by U.S. air strikes.

Meanwhile, Kabul was still being subjected to air strikes, with alliance commanders reporting more destruction of tanks and antiaircraft gun emplacements. This action continued until 13 November, when Northern Alliance troops advanced and took Kabul after the bulk of the Taliban and al-Qaeda forces withdrew overnight toward Kandahar, having first emptied the National Bank and the contents of Kabul's money market. A few Arab and other non-Afghan fighters discovered during the search of the city by alliance forces were summarily executed. Alliance forces also moved toward the city of Jalalabad, and the Kandahar airport was captured. U.S. aircraft continued to attack armored vehicles and pickup trucks used by the Taliban as they fled their positions. An airfield in southern Tajikistan was being used by at least fifty warplanes to intensify attacks on retreating Taliban forces and to increase the deliveries of food and other supplies to Northern Alliance forces and the civilian population. In the main, bombing raids were concentrated to the southwest of Taliban-held Kunduz in the northeast of the country and Kandahar in the south. The aerial pounding of Kandahar continued on a daily basis until 7 December 2001, when Taliban forces fled the city and headed for the mountainous areas in eastern Afghanistan, bordering Pakistan. The action then was switched to attacks on the fleeing forces and in the White Mountains on the Pakistan border.

The air campaign then entered into the phase of supporting assaults on Taliban and al-Qaeda positions in the mountains under Operation Tora Bora and Operation Anaconda. All action was concentrated on destroying the remaining elements of Taliban and al-Qaeda that were largely based in the mountainous region of eastern Afghanistan, intending either to mount guerrilla warfare from prepared hideouts or to cross into the tribal borderlands of Pakistan.

See also Coalition Land Campaign against the Taliban; Mazar-i Sharif; Operation Enduring Freedom; Taliban; UK Special Forces; U.S. Special Forces

References

Hiro, Dilip. 2002. *War without End: The Rise of Islamist Terrorism and Global Response.* Rev. ed. London: Routledge.

Ratnesar, Romesh, Hannah Beech, Anthony Davis, Michael Fathers, Terry McCarthy, Alex Perry, Johanna McGeary, and Rahimullah Yusufzai. 2001. "The Afghan Way of War." *Time Atlantic* 158, no. 21: 28–37.

Ratnesar, Romesh, Massimo Calabresi, James Carney, Mark Thompson, Karen Tumulty, J. F. O. McAllister, Hannah Beech, Anthony Davis, Alex Perry, Johanna McGeary, and Rahimullah Yusufzai. 2001. "Bombs Away." *Time Atlantic* 158, no. 20: 22–28.

http://www.bbc.co.uk/news/southasia
http://www.cnn.worldnews.com
http://www.gulf-news.com
http://www.nytimes.com
http://www.time.com
http://www.washingtonpost.com
http://www.whitehouse.gov/news/releases

COALITION LAND CAMPAIGN AGAINST THE TALIBAN

The Coalition land campaign in Afghanistan was prefaced by U.S. air attacks on Taliban and al-Qaeda installations and infrastructure and the use of U.S. and UK Special Forces in operations behind enemy lines, with Northern Alliance forces to provide intelligence for Operation Enduring Freedom. This action was launched in October 2001 as a direct response to the 11 September terrorist attacks in the United States and the failure of the Taliban regime to hand over the leader of al-Qaeda, Osama bin Laden, to face trial for being responsible for the attacks on the World Trade Center and a number of other atrocities. The bulk of the ground forces and the special forces were drawn from the United States and the United Kingdom, with special force contributions made by Australia, France, Germany, and New Zealand as well. These ground operations were completely divorced from the International Security Assistance Force (ISAF) that was to be deployed in Kabul under the auspices of the United Nations. The air operation began on 7 October and was designed to destroy Taliban and al-Qaeda installations and infrastructure in preparation for a ground campaign by the Northern Alliance and Coalition forces. Initially, the Coalition presence was in the form of special forces working behind enemy lines or with anti-Taliban forces providing advice and intelligence while at the same time guiding the U.S. Cruise missile and bombing attacks. The first major Coalition action in Afghanistan was mounted by 100 U.S. Army Rangers and small groups of Delta Force commandos against the compound of Mullah Muhammad Omar at Kandahar and the nearby airfield. The attack was launched from Black Hawk helicopters and C-130 transport planes backed by heavily armed AC-130 gunships, and although twenty fighters of the opposition were killed, there were no Taliban leaders at the site. The forces destroyed a bridge near the home of Mullah Omar, a Taliban command-and-control center, and a large cache of weapons (including rocket-propelled grenade launchers) discovered at the airport.

This raid was seen as part of a campaign to destabilize the Taliban and to generate intelligence on the whereabouts of Osama bin Laden and his al-Qaeda fighters. Additionally, small groups of Coalition special forces were still operating in southern Afghanistan in a campaign to split the Taliban, while other groups were working with Central Intelligence Agency (CIA) specialists and the Inter-Services Intelligence (ISI) of Pakistan in trying to bribe or persuade local Afghan warlords to turn against the Taliban. In eastern Afghanistan, CIA operatives, Delta Force commandos, and the UK Special Air Service (SAS) were reconnoitering the area in search of al-Qaeda targets, and it is believed that the Revolutionary Warfare Wing of the SAS was also in the area working with potential anti-Taliban groups and was staffed by individuals who spoke Pashtun, the majority language in Afghanistan.

Providing Coalition support for the Northern Alliance was a calculated strategy to accelerate the collapse of the Taliban by ensuring that it was being attacked from all sides, with alliance forces pressuring the Taliban in the north while special forces kept up the pressure in southern Afghanistan. However, it should be noted that the Northern Alliance was the only credible military force on the ground because, despite pressures from the U.S. government, the CIA, and ISI, there was no matching Pashtun resistance in the southern part of Afghanistan. Although some opposition in the south had been stirred up through the activities of Abdul al-Haq (who was later executed by the Taliban) and Hamid Karzai, there was no coordination between any of the groups, and a formal resistance movement was not really in place.

Having the Northern Alliance as a Coalition ally was seen as problematic because Pashtuns in the south distrusted the alliance. That distrust was only tempered by the alliance leaders' announcement that the organization would refrain from taking Kabul, for there was much resentment and fear arising from the mujahideen rule between 1992 and 1996. This apprehension was illustrated in a meeting of Afghan exiles in Peshawar, Pakistan, headed by Sayyed Ahmad Gailani, which called for a halt to U.S. bombing and the formation of a southern alliance to back the former king, Zahir Shah, with such an alliance including any dissident Taliban who changed sides. Gailani was voicing a need to find a nonviolent solution by persuading the Taliban to give up power and to concentrate on the reconstruction of Afghanistan. The meeting was held on 23 October 2001, but significantly, the former king had no representatives at the meeting.

The Coalition ground war took a new turn on 26 November when a force of U.S. Marines landed by helicopter near Kandahar, the last Taliban stronghold in the south, since Kabul had already fallen to the Northern Alliance. Tribal leaders had been trying to negotiate a handover of the city for just over a week but without success, though talks were ongoing with Taliban leaders about individual defections to the Northern Alliance. Meanwhile, anti-Taliban forces were still being supported by U.S. air strikes, and the marines were establishing a forward operating base to enable them to interdict all Taliban lines of communication out of Kandahar. Thousands of refugees fled from the city to Pakistan and south to Kabul as it became clear that the backbone of the city's defense were the al-Qaeda fighters who had prevented the Taliban from surrendering. However, by 6 December, Taliban forces were fleeing from the city, and U.S. Marines killed seven Taliban and al-Qaeda fighters fleeing Kandahar as part of their first combat mission.

Tora Bora Campaign

The defeat of the Taliban throughout Afghanistan on the ground largely came at the hands of the Northern Alliance and other anti-Taliban forces in

A U.S. B-52H bombing raid in Afghanistan in support of the Coalition land campaign against the Taliban and al-Qaeda (Reuters NewMedia Inc./CORBIS)

southern Afghanistan. However, it is obvious that this outcome would not have been achieved without the massive U.S. bombing campaign and the support of Coalition special forces on the ground. Because of this effort from the air and on the ground, U.S. and UK ground troops, together with the special forces, could concentrate on their main target after bringing down the Taliban—the forces of Osama bin Laden and al-Qaeda. Intelligence reports indicated that these forces had withdrawn to the caves in the Tora Bora hills area, some 30 miles to the south of Kandahar. Both sides of Tora Bora had a network of caves, with Milawa on the southwest side said to house the main concentration of al-Qaeda. The use of the caves dated back to the 1980s, when they were excavated to protect mujahideen fighters from Soviet forces. It soon became evident that the network had been extended and improved by the al-Qaeda fighters.

On 7 December, 200 U.S. troops arrived in the vicinity of Milawa and the nearby city of Jalalabad to supplement the small groups of U.S. and UK Special Forces in the area. (Logistical supplies had been flown into the Jalalabad airport by cargo planes and helicopters.) Meanwhile, the U.S. Air Force began a sustained bombing attack on the cave complexes in support of an offensive by Afghan mujahideen, but advances in the area were slow, resistance was fierce, and, at times, fighting came down to hand-to-hand combat. Air support was directed by Afghan commanders using satellite phones to indicate the caves thought to be occupied by al-Qaeda fighters; these targets were then attacked by combinations of 500-, 1,000-, and 2,000-pound precision-guided bombs directed into the cave openings.

A major attack was launched on Tora Bora on 10 December. Afghan troops, backed by tanks and U.S. warplanes, hit positions occupied by about 1,000 al-Qaeda fighters while U.S. Marines with armored personnel carriers set up a staging ground in the south to cut off escape routes and to hunt for fleeing Taliban and al-Qaeda fighters. The U.S. Air Force continued to bomb the complex of caves at Tora Bora but without effecting total destruction, for after the bombardments, fighters would emerge from the caves to mortar-bomb advancing Afghan troops with their Soviet T-55 tanks. However, by the end of the day, Afghan tribal forces had captured a ridge on the Milawa Valley adjacent to the Tora Bora Valley.

In the area to the south of Kandahar and Jalalabad, U.S. Marine convoys reinforced patrols hunting for fleeing Taliban and al-Qaeda fighters, with a holding facility set up at the main U.S. Marine camp for any prisoners of war. On 11 December, negotiations between Afghan tribal forces and al-Qaeda resulted in a truce, while al-Qaeda considered terms for surrender and a deadline for disarming. However, the deadline passed without any signs of an al-Qaeda surrender, and the truce was broken on 12 December when tribal eastern alliance forces opened fire on the cave complex in the canyon. A heavy bombing raid followed as B-52s and other U.S. warplanes hammered al-Qaeda positions in the canyon and in the Milawa and Tora Bora Valleys. It was reported in Pakistan that the al-Qaeda fighters had been demanding that their surrender be witnessed by diplomats from their home countries and by the United Nations; further, the al-Qaeda group was said to consist of Chechens, Egyptians, Iraqis, Libyans, Saudi Arabians, Sudanese, Yemenis, and Arabs from Arab gulf states. It was also reported that Osama bin Laden was in the Tora Bora area, but it was unclear as to whether Mullah Omar was with the group, though it was known that he was on the run in southern Afghanistan.

In the days following the failed truce, the Afghan tribal forces were joined by Coalition special forces on a search-and-destroy mission against the enemy, whose room for maneuver was becoming restricted: snow-covered peaks stood on two sides, Afghan and U.S. forces were on the third side, and Pakistani troops patrolled the border that made up the fourth, though it was impossible to guarantee security along the 1,510-mile border (particularly that along the semiautonomous tribal belt in Pakistan, where many inhabitants were sympathetic to the Taliban).

Afghan tribal fighters and special forces eventually took the complex of caves and tunnels, and fleeing al-Qaeda fighters were pursued by alliance forces. In an action that had lasted about nine weeks, it is estimated that some 200 fighters were killed, hundreds more were on the run in the mountains, and several dozen were taken prisoner. But there was no sign of Osama bin Laden and his close associates. In the search of the caves complex, significant caches of arms, munitions, and stores were discovered, evidence of the forward planning undertaken by the al-Qaeda network. The caves at Tora Bora had been the network's last stronghold in Afghanistan; however, despite the successes of the operation, at least 2,000 of the fighters were on the run in eastern Afghanistan.

As was to be expected, large numbers of Taliban and al-Qaeda fighters had fled across the border into Pakistan, with the latter being mostly Arab and other non-Afghan fighters. Many were arrested by Pakistani troops, but some of them rose up against their captors, resulting in fierce fighting before a number were killed and others recaptured. Pakistan had put thousands of troops into the area with helicopter support, and checkpoints were set up in an endeavor to cut off the escape routes from Tora Bora; some 108 fighters were arrested, including at least 60 non-Afghan fighters. It was reported that al-Qaeda troops, including two top commanders, were allowed to escape by leaders of the Afghan eastern alliance who had been involved in the assault on Tora Bora. Intelligence officers interrogated captured al-Qaeda fighters before they were transferred to the holding camp at Guantanamo Bay, Cuba. A great deal was discovered in searches of the caves, including maps and training manuals, information on positions, and ammunition and arms. Five prisoners were sent to the USS *Peleliu* for questioning, among them an American caught fighting with the Taliban, an Australian citizen, and a Saudi Arabian member of a group accused of ties with terrorists.

The fall of the Taliban and the defeat of al-Qaeda had not extinguished the threat posed by the survivors, as the whereabouts of at least 2,000 of these troops was unknown. A large number had moved across the eastern and southern borders into Pakistan, while others had fled west into Iran. Many hundreds remained in Afghanistan but proved difficult to detect, having merged back into Afghan society or gone to areas where support for the Taliban still existed. In addition, the major Coalition targets—Osama bin Laden and Mullah Omar—had eluded all attempts at capture; the former bought safe passage across the border into Pakistan, and the latter was still thought to be hiding in Afghanistan. The searches conducted by U.S. and Afghan forces went on, but returns were sparse, though fourteen al-Qaeda were captured by U.S. commandos at Zhawar, near Khost, in the middle of January 2002 following a U.S. bombing raid on yet another cave complex.

Searches of caves and bunkers in eastern Afghanistan had uncovered computer files and videotapes that yielded intelligence about al-Qaeda cells operating outside Afghanistan, and one such group was broken up in Singapore on the basis of this intelligence. However, pockets of al-Qaeda fighters were still thought to be present in areas north of Mazar-i Sharif and in the mountains of Helmand Province. Significantly, local officials in Khost had reported that at least 2,000 fighters regularly moved across the border and rested and resupplied in Pakistan before returning to positions in the mountains of Khost, Paktia, and Paktika Provinces, using the mountain tracks rather than the patrolled main roads. Such reports would prove to be indicative of the future instability.

Operation Anaconda

Operation Anaconda was mounted on 1 March 2002 by U.S. Army forces and Afghan allies, with the objective of ousting al-Qaeda and Taliban fighters from their refuge in Paktia Province. The allied troops succeeded in killing between 350 and 550 of the enemy, with the loss of 11 lives among their own ranks.

Operation Anaconda took place some 100 miles south of Kabul in the mountainous region near Gardez, in Paktia Province. The U.S. forces involved in the operation numbered about 1,200, and they were aided by local Afghans and backed by helicopter support. Allied intelligence indicated that a mixed force of al-Qaeda and Taliban fighters had gathered in the area, preparing to mount attacks against the Afghan Interim Government. However, after a week of intensive action, about half of the estimated enemy force had been killed and a few taken prisoner, with eleven allied troops killed and seventy wounded.

The battle took place in the Shah-i-Kot Valley. Afghan forces, aided by special forces, targeted al-Qaeda positions in hopes of flushing them toward the exits from the valley where U.S. troops were waiting. However, after two days of fierce combat, the al-Qaeda fighters were still in their positions, and on 2 March 2002, two U.S. Chinook helicopters were attacked as they prepared to set down at one of the battle positions; they were forced to take off again, leaving behind a rear gunner who had fallen from the aircraft as it made an evasive maneuver. U.S. commanders at the Bagram air base granted permission for a rescue team to be landed, and six U.S. Rangers were sent in to search for the missing

U.S. Navy Seal. Some three hours later, two more Chinooks set off to insert more troops into the battle position, code-named Ginger, and to pull out the rescue team. One of the Chinooks was downed by heavy machine-gun fire and crash-landed near the site of the first incident, and the troops on board came under heavy al-Qaeda fire. The United States used AC-130 gunships to provide cover, but the enemy pressure was such that a rescue attempt was impossible in the daylight, and it was not until midnight that the troops could be evacuated, including the first team of U.S. Rangers that had been landed to effect the rescue of the U.S. Navy Seal. The United States had seven men killed and eleven wounded in the operation, including the Seal, who was killed by his pursuers.

Fighting was intense for some time, with Taliban and al-Qaeda forces making hit-and-run attacks on the U.S. and Afghan tribal force of some 1,500 that had laid siege to their caves and bunkers. The opposition forces were using guerrilla tactics and darting back into the caves after each attack, using their knowledge of the area to full effect. The rebel forces were well armed with rockets, mortars, and heavy machine guns, but ammunition soon began to run low, enabling the besieging forces to get within 300 feet of the caves; at that point, side arms became the order of the day. The caves had originally been developed as defensive positions against the Soviet troops in the 1980s, and the Coalition forces were intent on making them unsuitable for future military use by blocking the entrances, using shoulder-launched rockets.

It was evident that the Coalition forces were engaging hardened fighters intent on fighting to the death from their complex of caves and bunkers. At one point, the opposition forces were being reinforced with fighters who had traveled to the caves through the mountain passes, but Afghan forces then formed an outer ring around the area to stop the infiltration. Meanwhile, U.S. and other Afghan forces closed in on the al-Qaeda positions that were being defended by non-Afghan professional soldiers; few, if any, Taliban fighters were present.

It was thought that some of the top al-Qaeda or Taliban leaders might have been in the complex, which would have explained, in part, the ferocity of the al-Qaeda fighters. Intelligence reports seemed to support this assumption, as hundreds of sympathizers had been detected streaming toward the front

line from within Pakistan. And yet again, the situation on the ground had been complicated by infighting among the local warlords, which allowed al-Qaeda to mass in the area. This, together with misinformation, accounted for the fact that the U.S. forces expected to face about 200 fighters whereas the real total was closer to 900. The battle ended on 13 March when U.S., Canadian, and Afghan forces stormed the caves and bunkers, which were then blown up to prevent their reuse. The aftermath of Operation Anaconda was a mopping-up operation, particularly around Khost and Gardez, the capital of Paktia Province.

Although Anaconda can be classified as a major success, the nature of the terrain meant that many of the surviving enemy were able to filter across the border into northern Pakistan. The operation was difficult for U.S. forces because much of the fighting was at altitudes where the air was thin, breathing was difficult, and most of the supporting helicopters reached their operational limit. Action on the ground was hampered by the nature of the terrain, the enemy's knowledge of the country, and the need to avoid civilian casualties. Consequently, patience had to be exercised before engaging targets, and careful exploration of the area was essential due to the presence of caves that could be used as refuges and the possibility of encountering booby traps. In essence, Anaconda was a major, high-profile operation by U.S. and Afghan forces that dealt a severe blow to al-Qaeda and Taliban forces.

The threat posed by the survivors of Operation Anaconda was illustrated on 20 March when U.S. and other Coalition troops at Khost came under attack from al-Qaeda forces. The attackers used rocket-propelled grenades, mortars, and machine guns in an attack that lasted several hours. An AC-130 gunship was called up to bolster the defenses. This attack had been preceded on 17 March by a U.S. assault on a convoy of four vehicles leaving Shah-i-Kot for what was known to be a location of fleeing al-Qaeda fighters, resulting in a number of them being killed and one taken prisoner.

Operation Snipe

Operation Snipe, mounted by UK commandos and local Afghan troops, was to be a secret search-and-destroy mission targeting southeastern Afghanistan, with the objective of clearing and destroying any terrorist infrastructure and making the area safe for subsequent humanitarian operations. The force of 1,000 commandos was supplemented by 500 local Afghan troops and backed by Royal Air Force (RAF) Chinook helicopters. The operation began in the middle of April and lasted just over two weeks.

Operation Snipe succeeded in capturing a significant amount of weaponry and supplies but failed to locate any groups of Taliban or al-Qaeda, with only two suspected Taliban having been taken to the Bagram air base for interrogation. Among the weapons discovered were over 100 mortars, 100 recoilless antitank guns, hundreds of rocket-propelled grenades, 200 antipersonnel mines, hundreds of artillery rounds and rockets, and thousands of small arms and light antiaircraft ammunition. Coalition commanders gauged the operation a success because the area had not previously been investigated and the commandos had succeeded in denying territory to the enemy. However, the action was further confirmation that the remnants of al-Qaeda were elusive and highly mobile enemies, probably operating in small groups in the mountain areas, with well-planned lines of retreat into Pakistan or Iran.

Operation Mountain Lion

Operation Mountain Lion began on 15 April 2002 and was coordinated with the UK-led Operation Ptarmigan, which was launched the following day. Both operations were designed to find enemy fighters in the Gardez and Khost regions, to deny the enemy control of the area, and to prevent al-Qaeda from reorganizing their forces to attack Coalition or government forces.

Mountain Lion involved Coalition special forces, as well as conventional ground forces, with helicopter gunship backup. It resulted in a number of small but fierce engagements with the enemy, who had been infiltrating across the Pakistan border. The operation tailed off on 16 May 2002, but the Coalition commander, Maj. Gen. Franklin L. Hagenbeck, warned that al-Qaeda still possessed much of its leadership and an effective command-and-control structure.

Operation Ptarmigan

This UK-led operation was launched on 16 April 2002 and was coordinated with the U.S.-led Operation Mountain Lion. Both actions were designed to search areas suspected of being occupied by al-Qaeda and Taliban forces, but no opposition forces

were discovered. The Ptarmigan force consisted of commando reconnaissance troops and Royal Marine commandos supported by Chinook helicopters of the Royal Air Force. The operation was concluded on 18 April with the return of the force to the Bagram air base.

Operation Buzzard

The UK-led Operation Buzzard was launched on 29 May 2002 with forty-five Royal Marine commandos and local Afghan fighters undertaking a series of patrols in the Khost region of southeast Afghanistan. This period of sustained patrolling was seen as an indication that the opposition had been forced to abandon a large-scale presence in the region. The patrols also engaged in humanitarian aid work, particularly a wide-ranging program of medical assistance in the rural areas. The operation came to an end on 9 July 2002.

Evidence that the Taliban and al-Qaeda were not spent came on 27 January 2003 with the engagement of U.S. and Afghan forces against some eighty rebels in the mountains of southern Afghanistan, near the border town of Spin Boldak. It is thought that the group was composed of fighters loyal to Gulbuddin Hekmatyar, who had been trying for several months to consolidate with remnants of the Taliban and al-Qaeda to form one anti-Coalition force. As such, the action would be part of the jihad declared by Hekmatyar against U.S. forces and their Afghan allies.

The operation began when U.S. Special Forces searching a compound near Spin Boldak came under fire; the U.S. soldiers killed one attacker, wounded another, and took one prisoner, who divulged the whereabouts of eighty fighters hiding in the mountains. Apache helicopters, which were fired on, located the enemy positions, and B-1 bombers, F-16 warplanes, AC-130 gunships, and Apache helicopters launched an attack before troops moved in. At least eighteen rebels were killed in the engagement, which was the largest since Operation Anaconda.

Operations Viper and Eagle Fury

On 10 February 2003, U.S. troops from the Eighty-Second Airborne Division launched an operation against suspected Taliban forces in Helmand Province. The operation was targeted along a mountain ridge in the Baghran district, where Taliban fighters had been seen taking up offensive positions by a U.S. patrol. The troops called up air support, and the ridge was pounded for eight hours with smart bombs dropped by B-52 and B-1 bombers. On the following day, twelve armed men suspected to be Taliban were arrested near the village of Lejay in the Baghran Valley. U.S. troops found abandoned ammunition cases and rocket-launcher tubes, indicating that Taliban fighters were still active in the area. It was estimated that there were between 30 and 100 rebels in the area, and although 25 suspects had been detained, there was no confirmation as to the number of rebels killed. U.S. troops mounted a systematic search of villages in the area, which was considered to now be the heartland of the Taliban but had not been comprehensively searched before this operation. They seized concealed weapons but met no resistance.

The operations were marred by claims that seventeen Afghan civilians, including women and children, had been killed in the bombing raids, though the deputy governor of the province stated that he had seen dead bodies but was unable to determine whether they were civilians or Taliban. The U.S. commander maintained that only an eight-year-old boy, the son of a suspected Taliban fighter, had been injured and taken to Kandahar for treatment. The Afghan authorities announced an investigation into the alleged incident, and the commander of U.S. forces in Afghanistan, Gen. Dan McNeill, met with President Hamid Karzai to discuss the alleged outcomes. The president called on U.S. forces to take special care to avoid civilian casualties, but at the same time, he asked Afghans to help U.S. soldiers track down suspected terrorists in southern Afghanistan.

Clashes were reported elsewhere in the country during the same period. For example, an attack took place at a compound near Tarin Kot in the province of Oruzgan on 24 February 2003. One terrorist was killed and another wounded, and Coalition forces lost one Afghan soldier and had another severely wounded. On the same day, at Wazir in Nangarhar Province, a U.S. military convoy was assaulted by a small number of terrorists, but no casualties were reported on either side.

On 3 March 2003, the U.S. military stated that it had extended the search for fugitive Taliban into a second valley in Helmand Province. The operation would comprise a search of other villages thought to have connections with the Taliban, based on specific intelligence reports. The new search in Baghni Valley resulted in twelve arrests and the seizure of sixty rifles in the first thirty-six hours. Since the start of the operation three weeks before, forty people had been arrested, twenty Taliban had been killed, and caches of weapons were seized.

The war is now being fought on several fronts, and it includes the use of misinformation, propaganda, and terror tactics. In addition to the anti-American leaflet campaign undertaken in towns such as Spin Boldak, leaflets urging resistance to U.S. forces have appeared in a number of villages along the border with Pakistan. In cities patrolled by Coalition forces, such as Kandahar, land mines and booby traps have been laid to kill U.S. forces, but in many cases, they kill innocent Afghans instead, instilling fear in the population. Planners in the U.S. headquarters at the Bagram air base are also trying to counter "disinformation" campaigns in which civilian casualties from U.S. bombings are being exaggerated. Reports on the alleged incident in Helmand Province, for instance, first said there were seventeen dead, but the number soon rose to twenty and then finally to hundreds, despite the fact there was no evidence for any civilian deaths at all.

Ongoing Situation 2003

It soon became clear that the remnants of the Taliban and al Qaeda were not a spent force, especially after they joined up with the fighters of Gulbuddin Hekmatyar following his declaration of a jihad against Coalition troops and their Afghan supporters. Actions continued in southern and eastern Afghanistan to counter enemy activity of a sporadic, small-scale nature, particularly in Kandahar Province. There, intelligence reports and intercepted radio signals indicated that Taliban and al-Qaeda forces were regrouping and planning raids against Coalition and Afghan government targets. As a response, Operation Valiant Strike was launched at the end of March 2003 in the Marif district of the province, with the objective of tracking down groups of enemy fighters. The operation involved some 1,000 U.S. troops and 3,000 Afghan government forces, backed by U.S. Apache helicopters and gunships. It began with a series of house-to-house searches in the district, resulting in the arrest of a number of suspects. The action in the area continued into April, and on 4 April, a Taliban base near Spin Boldak in the mountainous area of Kandahar was captured, with eight Taliban killed and another fifteen taken prisoner.

A further offensive was launched on 1 April in Badghis Province by Afghan security forces, in a search for Taliban and Hekmatyar fighters suspected of conducting a number of attacks in the region. A series of villages were targeted, based on lists of Taliban fighters found in the pockets of Taliban commanders captured during earlier fighting. The lists showed that 500 Taliban fighters were active in the area. As a result of the operation, 150 were killed, 50 were taken prisoner, and the remainder fled into the mountains. Among those taken prisoner was Mullah Badar, who had been governor of the province under the Taliban regime.

On 2 April, U.S. Green Berets and Afghan security forces attacked Taliban fighters in the Tora Ghar Mountain region in southern Afghanistan, forcing them to retreat into the hills, where they were attacked by U.S. air support from the Bagram air base. A new Taliban base was also identified in the Haba Mountains north of Kandahar after the interrogation of captured Taliban fighters. In the resultant action, twenty Taliban fighters were killed, with the loss of three Afghan soldiers. Also in April 2003, U.S. troops mounted further operations in the Sangeen district of Kandahar Province, where it was thought that former Taliban commanders, including Mullah Akhtar Mohammed, were hiding.

Throughout the ensuing months up to the time of writing in June 2003, this type of action has continued with some success, but there is no evidence that the combination of Taliban, al-Qaeda, and Hekmatyar fighters are being defeated. Sporadic actions continue, and there is much evidence of continued attacks on Coalition and Afghan government forces, government officials, and aid workers. Attacks tend to be small-scale strikes on limited or opportune targets, with rocket attacks on military bases. Evidence has emerged that guerrillas are paying poor Afghans $10 to fire crude rockets on military bases, and it is thought that an attack on a military base at Asadabad in Kunar Province on 31 May fit this pattern. In most cases, probably due to inexperience, the majority of these rockets fall short of their targets, but there is little doubt that the security situation in Afghanistan remains critical. Taliban and other antigovernment activity is creating continued instability, delaying development, and weakening the position of the Karzai government.

Joint Regional Team Program

On 13 January 2003, General McNeill, the Coalition commander, announced a change in strategy that would extend security beyond Kabul and improve stability in Afghanistan. The general has established a joint regional team (JRT)—composed of seventy soldiers, civil affairs officers, engineers, medical staffers, and other officials—that began operations in Gardez, eastern Afghanistan, in February 2003, in an attempt to expand the authority of the Kabul government. The team is to pursue a program of reconstruction that will pull security improvements along with it, as reconstruction will make people feel more secure and blunt the impact and propaganda of the remnants of al-Qaeda and the Taliban. A further JRT was established in Kunduz in northern Afghanistan and began operations in April 2003 after an advance team had started preliminary work in February and after the Bamian JRT began operations in March 2003.

The concept of the JRT was first raised in November 2002, and detailed consultations took place with a number of interested bodies, including the United Nations, nongovernmental organizations (NGOs), officials from members of the Coalition, the ISAF, and the government in Kabul. The objective is to provide a reasonable degree of stability and security in a short span of time. The move is, in part, an answer to criticism from a number of Afghan and Western aid agencies that the United States is not doing enough to help the Karzai government extend its authority, combat the power of the regional warlords, and begin the essential reconstruction of the country.

It was intended that by the summer of 2003, JRTs would also be operating in Mazar-i Sharif, Herat, Jalalabad, and Kandahar (with more to follow if they were successful), but these were awaiting a review of the effectiveness of operational JRTs. The JRTs will also receive full backing, including, if conditions become dangerous, the rapid deployment of troops, air cover, and airlift operations. JRTs will work with local authorities, UN agencies, and NGOs as they begin spending $300 million in aid earmarked for the reconstruction of rural areas. However, NGOs have warned that the members of the JRTs will need to understand that aid is ecumenical and cannot just be directed to communities that support the United States or U.S. positions. Although local commanders will have flexibility in dealing with regional warlords, General McNeill has made it clear that the central government must take the dominant role in controlling local friction. It is thought that the JRT project will aid stability, but critics maintain that it falls short of a full solution and cannot be a substitute for an expansion of the ISAF.

See also Coalition Air Campaign against the Taliban; Mazar-i Sharif; Northern Alliance; Operation Enduring Freedom; Taliban; UK Special Forces; U.S. Special Forces

References

Hiro, Dilip. 2002. *War without End: The Rise of Islamist Terrorism and Global Response.* Rev. ed. London: Routledge.

http://www.bbc.co.uk/news/southasia

http://www.cnn.worldnews.com

http://www.gulf-news.com

http://www.institute-for-afghan-studies.org

http://www.nytimes.com

http://www.time.com

http://www.washingtonpost.com

http://www.whitehouse.gov/news/releases

DARI LANGUAGE

The Dari language is spoken by about a third of the Afghani population and also serves as a means of communication between speakers of different languages in Afghanistan. It is a member of the Iranian branch of the Indo-Iranian family of languages and is the Afghan version of Farsi, spoken in Iran, with some minor variations in the vowel system and additional consonants. The Hazara, Tajik, Turkoman, and Uzbek tribes, as well as some Pashtuns, speak Dari.

See also Hazaras; Languages; Pashtuns; Tajiks; Turkomans; Uzbeks
References
Foreign Service Institute. 1957. *Spoken Afghan Persian.* Kabul: U.S. Embassy.
Miran, M. Alan. 1977. *The Functions of National Languages in Afghanistan.* New York: Afghanistan Council, Asia Society.

DARULAMAN

Darulaman was a new capital city built by King Amanullah in the early 1920s, 6 miles from the city of Kabul and linked to it by a narrow-gauge railway. The king constructed a number of government buildings, including a prestigious parliament and a municipality building. In addition, members of the court and government officials built villas in the new capital. However, it ceased to be the capital after the downfall of the king. It was renamed Bar-al-Habib (meaning "Abode of Habib") after Habibullah Kalakani and in 1930 Dar-al-Funun (or "Abode of the Arts"). In 1947, the city again reverted to its original name, but all of the major administrative offices were transferred to Kabul. The municipality building was converted into Kabul Museum, which housed archaeological treasures from the Hellenistic, Greco-Buddhist, and Ghaznavid periods. However, as a result of the civil war and the Taliban regime, the museum has been almost completely looted. The old parliament building was seriously damaged by fire in 1969 and then restored to house the Ministry of Defense. It was again damaged during the Tanai coup of March 1990 and the subsequent civil war between the mujahideen groups.

See also Amanullah, King
References
Dupree, Nancy Hatch. 1977. *An Historical Guide to Kabul.* Kabul: Afghan Tourist Organization.

DAUD, SARDAR MUHAMMAD (1909–1978)

Sardar Muhammad Daud was born in Kabul in 1909, the son of Sardar Muhammad Aziz Khan, half brother to King Nadir Shah. He was educated at the Amania School in Kabul and spent seven years in France, where his father was in charge of Afghan student affairs and his uncle, Nadir Shah, was ambassador to Paris. He returned to Kabul in 1930 and attended a year's course for infantry officers in 1931. A year later, he was promoted to major general and appointed commander of the eastern provinces, becoming governor in addition to his military post in February 1934. In 1934, he also married the younger daughter of King Nadir Shah, and he was transferred in July to Kandahar as governor and general commanding officer, to include the divisions in the provinces of Farah and Chakhansur.

During his period in Kandahar, he encouraged the adoption of Pashtu as the only national language. In 1939, he was made commander of the Central Forces, a post he held until 1947, during which he subdued the Safi Revolt of 1945. He became defense minister in 1947 but disagreed with Prime Minister Shah Muhammad and was sent to the Paris embassy from 1948 to 1949. He returned to serve as minister of the interior from 1949 to 1950 and, at the same time, president of tribal affairs.

Daud became prime minister in 1953 and held the post for ten years, during which some advances were made in the state infrastructure. He was responsible for the adoption of the First Five-Year Plan in 1956, which resulted in the construction of paved highways and other improvements in public services, with financial support from the United States, and in 1959, he also encouraged and protected efforts to abolish the requirement that women wear veils, or *chadaris,* though the benefits were mainly restricted to women in Kabul. Daud also aspired to enhance the role and power of the military in order to sustain the state and the reform movement, but he was unsuccessful in attempts to obtain support from the United States and was forced to turn to the Soviet Union for assistance and technical expertise. On the international scene, he also represented Afghanistan at the Belgrade summit of nonaligned countries in September 1961. Daud was a protagonist of the Pashtunistan question—that is, he supported the creation of a Pashtun state, or Pashtunistan—but the pursuit of this policy had caused a serious deterioration in relations with Pakistan. Moreover, Daud's autocratic rule also caused unease at home, to the point that he became a liability to the ruling elite. The king demanded—and received—his resignation in 1963. He opposed parts of the newly drafted constitution, which was adopted by the Loya Jirga (Great Council) in 1964.

Daud was in retirement from 1963 to 1973 but mounted a coup against the monarchy, with Marxist support, on 17 July 1973 and deposed King Zahir, who went into exile in Rome. Thereupon, Daud proclaimed the Democratic Republic of Afghanistan and nominated himself as president. However, following the secret founding of the Afghan Communist Party, known as the People's Democratic Party of Afghanistan (PDPA), a number of sleepers had been placed in the military and the bureaucracy, and after the coup, they emerged in positions of authority, even in the president's own retinue, though some remained covert.

Daud was keen to divest himself of his Communist backers, and in the first two years of the republic, he steadily removed his Marxist supporters from office. In 1977, he introduced a new constitution that called for socioeconomic reforms and an end to the exploitation of the ordinary Afghan citizen. A program of land reform was also promised, together with proposals to nationalize key industries and regulate business to eliminate exploitation. Daud also declared, within the proposals, that power was to be exercised by the people, the majority of whom were identified as farmers, workers, enlightened individuals, and youths, and that the proposed new legislature would be required to draw half of its members from among the farmers and workers. In addition, a political role was accorded to the military through the High Council of the Armed Forces, and the rights already given to women were incorporated into the constitution for approval by a *loya jirga.*

Daud still attempted to found a one-party state through his creation of the National Revolutionary Party in 1975, which excluded his former backers in the PDPA and was charged with approving all candidates for the forthcoming elections under the new constitution. However, the Central Committee of the party was appointed by Daud, without any consultation, in 1977 and was immediately criticized for its composition, which was deemed too full of corrupt officials or cronies of the president; this alienated all sectors of the community, turning his former Marxist supporters into the opposition.

In April 1977, Daud visited Moscow for high-level negotiations, which became acrimonious because of his refusal to change the policy of employing foreign experts from countries other than the Soviet Union. Meanwhile, back in Afghanistan, the Khalq and Parchami wings of the PDPA were holding reunification talks, and they succeeded in sorting out their differences by July 1977. Although Daud wished to retain good relations with the Soviet Union, he also wanted to ensure that Afghanistan remained a nonaligned state. By this time, the Soviets were unwilling to risk losing their considerable investment in Afghanistan and their sleepers in the military and the bureaucracy, only to be replaced by the Arab oil-rich states and Iran, which had agreed to fund Daud's reformist program. Moscow therefore instructed the PDPA to plan a coup to oust the Daud regime.

On 27 April 1978, the PDPA mounted the Saur Revolt, after which the Communists rose to power. The Marxists had attained a considerable measure of support within the armed forces through a targeted recruiting program, particularly by the Khalq faction led by Hafizullah Amin and, in secret, the Parchami faction using Mir Akbar Khaibar. Daud and his family were killed in fighting during the revolt after a bitter defense of the royal palace; his supporters were unable to resist the armor of the opposing forces led by Maj. Muhammad Aslam Watanjar, a prominent officer in Daud's own coup of 1973. The leaders of the PDPA feared Daud's execution had become a specific objective of the coup.

See also Amin, Hafizullah; People's Democratic Party of Afghanistan; Taraki, Nur Muhammad

References

Kaker, Hasan. 1978. "The Fall of the Afghan Monarch in 1973." *International Journal of Middle Eastern Studies* 9, no. 2: 195–225.

Magnus, Ralph H., and Eden Naby. 2000. *Afghanistan: Mullah, Marx and Mujahid.* Boulder, CO: Westview Press.

DA'UD SHAH (1832–?)

Da'ud Shah was a general in the Kabul army who sided with Amir Shir Ali during the civil wars (1863–1866), and at the time of the Battle of Saidabad in May 1866, he was a prisoner in Afzal Khan's camp but managed to escape and rejoined Shir Ali's forces. In June 1869, he was dispatched to Turkestan where, with Governor Mir Alam Khan, he put down a rebellion raised by Ishaq Khan. Following these military actions, he remained in Turkestan as military commander. However, his relations with the governor were not good, and he was suspected of instigating a mutiny among his troops in April 1870, designed to disgrace Mir Alam Khan.

It was recommended by the commander-in-chief of the Kabul army that Da'ud be recalled with his four regiments due to the complete breakdown in relations with the governor. In July 1870, he was imprisoned by the amir in Kabul, but Commander-in-Chief Faramuz Khan pleaded for leniency, and in September 1870, Da'ud Shah and his officers were released. In June 1871, Ramauz Khan was murdered, and Da'ud was appointed commander-in-chief but removed from his post after complaints from his second in command. He was put in charge of raising recruits and held no power within the military administration.

After the arrest of Herat's governor, Yaqub Khan, Da'ud was sent to Herat in November 1874 to join Mustaufi Habibullah, who had replaced Yaqub Khan. After the rebellion of Muhammad Ayub Khan—who was the brother of Yaqub Khan and would be the victor against the British at the Battle of Maiwand in 1880—Da'ud entered Herat with his troops but again held no power within the military administration. On his return to Kabul, he was made commander-in-chief once more, but after the massacre of the staff of the British mission at Kabul in September 1879, he was deported to India.

References

Khaflin, N. A. 1958. "The Rising of Ishaq Shah in Southern Turkestan." *Central Asian Review* 6, no. 2: 253–263.

Malleson, G. B. 1984. *History of Afghanistan, from the Earliest Period to the Outbreak of the War of 1878.* Peshawar, Pakistan: Saeed Book Bank.

DESTRUCTION OF PRE-ISLAMIC HERITAGE

On 26 February 2001, the Taliban leader, Mullah Muhammad Omar, announced that, on the basis of consultations between the religious leaders, religious judgments of the *ulama* (Islamic scholars and clergymen), and rulings of the Supreme Court, all non-Islamic shrines were to be destroyed. The action was deemed necessary because the statues were considered shrines of infidels and were still worshiped and respected by infidels; as false shrines, they needed to be destroyed, for Allah was the only real shrine.

Taliban troops were spread out around the country on 1 March, equipped with tanks, rocket launchers, and explosives to destroy all statues, including the two fifth-century statues of Buddha carved into the mountainside at Bamian. The authorities ignored the international outcry that followed Omar's decree, and troops began to demolish pre-Islamic images in the capital, Kabul, as well as in Bamian, Ghazni, Herat, Jalalabad, and Kandahar; the actions were strongly defended by the information minister, Qadradullah Jamal.

On 2 March, the United Nations sent a representative to plead with the Taliban to call off the destruction, which faced mounting international criticism due to the historical significance of the artifacts. This message was reinforced by pressure from United Nations Educational, Scientific, and Cultural Organization (UNESCO), which asked other Islamic nations to apply pressure on the Taliban regime to halt the program; meanwhile, museums, such as the Metropolitan Museum in New York, pleaded for the statues to be given or sold to foreign museums in order to preserve Afghanistan's cultural heritage.

UNESCO also sent a special envoy, Pierre Lafrance (a former French ambassador to Pakistan), to deliver a message to the Taliban authorities.

A giant stone Buddha from the fourth or fifth century was a testament to Afghanistan's long and rich history. It was destroyed by the fundamentalist Taliban regime in March 2001. (UNESCO/F. Riviere)

Lafrance met with the Taliban ambassador to Pakistan, Abdul Salam Zaeef, who stated that the decree had not been implemented. However, this information was dated, as large-scale destruction had already taken place. On the very day the meeting was taking place, Jamal announced that troops had completed the destruction of two-thirds of all the pre-Islamic statues in Afghanistan and had begun the destruction of the two statues of Buddha at Bamian. International pressures mounted to try to preserve these statues, but on 3 March, the Taliban reported that most of the ancient statues had been destroyed. Troops had used rockets and mortars to destroy the heads and legs of the sandstone statues,

and by the following day, with the use of antiaircraft weapons, tanks, and mortars, the remainder of the statues were destroyed.

The Taliban foreign minister brushed aside criticism and rejected offers from foreign museums to house the artifacts, arguing that the relics were against Islamic belief and that Afghanistan was capable of maintaining its own history and heritage. The action was regarded by Mullah Omar as a tribute to Islam and to the Afghan nation, and it was directly stated that no response would be made to international pressure.

Contrary to the claims of the Taliban authorities, it became clear that the destruction of the statues of the Buddha had not been completed, and on 6 March, the operation was suspended to enable troops to celebrate the feast of Eid al-Adha, though it was confirmed that the operation would resume when the holiday was over. The delay allowed the international community to mount further attempts to halt the destruction, with representations being made by Egyptian president Hosni Mubarak. The Japanese parliament also dispatched a delegation to Kandahar to express the concerns of the Japanese people about reports of damage to the statues of Buddha. An offer was made by the Sri Lankan government to finance an international operation to save the statues as part of a UNESCO mission. However, the UNESCO representative stated that the Taliban leaders had shown no interest in reversing their decision and that the figures had not been damaged to the extent claimed by the Taliban militia.

On 9 March, the Taliban foreign minister, Wakil Ahmad Muttawali, issued a statement declaring that the international campaign would not succeed in preserving the Bamian statues. Despite this pronouncement, efforts persisted over the next few days. The three-member team from Japan arrived in Kandahar to try to reverse the decree, and UNESCO's special envoy Pierre Lafrance announced his intention to return to Afghanistan; the Pakistan prime minister, Moinuddin Haider, failed to have the decision reversed at a meeting held in Kandahar. Egypt also sent a leading authority on Islam in order to get the operation canceled by arguing that the presence of the Bamian Buddhas did not represent an affront to Islam.

The secretary-general of the United Nations, Kofi Annan, had been told by the Taliban authorities that virtually all the pre-Islamic statues had been destroyed and that the operation at Bamian was well under way. Meanwhile, the Taliban religious leaders rejected the arguments of international Islamic scholars sent by the Organization of the Islamic Conference (OIC) to Kandahar on the grounds that they were un-Islamic. Taliban leaders contended that the OIC scholars had not provided any religious justification for preserving the statues and had only argued about the timing of the operation.

On 13 March, an Afghan freelance photographer provided Cable News Network (CNN) with photographs from the scene showing that the statues had been destroyed, and as expected, the international community reacted with anger and sadness. A Taliban soldier told a reporter that there were over 4,000 troops involved in the operation to destroy the statues, which were 123 feet and 178 feet high, utilizing artillery fire, tanks, explosives, and land mines. The scope and duration of the operation was clearly an embarrassment to the Taliban authorities. The operation had lasted some two weeks, and Mullah Omar was so upset by the delay that he ordered the sacrifice of 100 cows in atonement for the delay, with the meat being distributed to the poor and needy.

References

Institute for Afghan Studies. "How the Precious Statues of Afghanistan Got Destroyed?" http://www.institute-for-afghan-studies.org (cited 26 April 2001).

DIN MUHAMMAD, MASHK-IL-ALAM (1790–1886)

Mashk-il-Alam Din Muhammad is considered a national hero by Afghans because of his hostility toward British India and its interference in the affairs of Afghanistan in the nineteenth century. He was a mullah in the frontier area between India, where his family originated, and Afghanistan. The name Mashk-il-Alam (meaning "Scent of the World") was given to him by one of his teachers because of his exceptional intellect. Din Muhammad was a militant mullah who gained considerable influence among the Ghilzais, and he opened up a *madrasa* (religious school) for the training of mullahs. He was provided with an allowance by Amir Shir Ali and preached jihad, or holy war, against the British during the Second Anglo-Afghan War (1878–1879). Although Amir Abdur Rahman attempted to curb his influence and to restrict his activities, Din Muhammad successfully incited the Mangals and Ghilzais to revolt against the amir. The opposition to the amir continued after Din Muhammad's death in 1886, with his son, Mullah Abdul Karim, leading another Ghilzai revolt that was only suppressed with great difficulty.

References

Martin, Frank A. 2000. *Under the Absolute Amir of Afghanistan.* New Delhi: Bhavana Books and Prints.

DISARMAMENT PROGRAM

Security in post-Taliban Afghanistan remains a major problem for the government of President Hamid Karzai, whose authority still does not extend much beyond Kabul even in his second year of office. The situation is a legacy of twenty-three years of war, interethnic conflict, and tribal rivalry, with regional warlords maintaining their own private militias and the country awash with weapons. The main objective is the creation of an effective national army and police force, both built on multiethnic foundations, as a means of establishing security and stability throughout the country.

In the summer of 2002, an attempt was made to introduce a disarmament program in northern Afghanistan, but it merely ended with smaller groups being forced to surrender their arms to more powerful commanders. Due to the absence of a national security or police force, the militias had assumed responsibility for filling the security vacuum in about 90 percent of the country. Estimates vary, with the government indicating that between 100,000 and 150,000 individuals need to be disarmed, whereas aid agencies put the figure in excess of 200,000. The scale of the problem is suggested by the fact that there are some 8 million guns in circulation as well as significant caches of sophisticated weaponry hidden by Taliban and al-Qaeda fighters.

On 27 February 2003, a conference was held in Tokyo to discuss the question of demobilization and disarmament, since the process is crucial to improvements in security and the development process. The U.S. and Japanese governments pledged $95 million to fund the process of demobilization, disarmament, and reintegration of fighters into a civil economy. In a separate deal, the Japanese government pledged $35 million to fund Afghanistan's New Beginnings Program (ANBP), which is seen as crucial for the integration of demobilized fighters into normal civilian society and the peacetime economy. President Karzai indicated that ANBP funding could be used to provide jobs for former fighters in the construction of highways, bridges, and dams, with others being absorbed into the new Afghan national army. The objective would be to complete this process before the elections scheduled for the summer of 2004.

Attempts to disarm in Afghanistan have been slow and in some areas have ceased altogether because of outbreaks of fighting between rival warlords, particularly in the north of the country and in Paktia Province in the southeast. The ANBP is expected to offer cash payments and microcredit programs to start up new businesses in order to wean fighters away from depending on middle-ranking militia commanders for their financial survival. This approach is seen as a means of preventing village communities from having to rely on militia commanders to provide economic opportunities.

At the Tokyo conference, President Karzai stated that the process of disarmament would take about three years, with the first year largely devoted to the registration of all warlords by special government committees. Following the conference, the Afghan government committed itself to work with the United Nations to produce a disarmament strategy for UN consideration, which was announced to the Afghan nation by President Karzai on 21 March 2003.

The situation in northern Afghanistan illustrates the problems faced by the Kabul government and the Coalition forces in trying to disarm the various regional warlords and their militias. On 28 February 2003, the chief of the UN Refugee Agency, Rudd Lubbers, convened a meeting at Mazar-i Sharif with the regional leaders, Gen. Abdul Rashid Dostum, Gen. Ustad Atta Mohammad, and Saradar Saeedi, to consider the problems of ethnic violence and the issue of persons displaced by the conflict, as some 50,000 Pashtuns had fled the region to live in camps in southern Afghanistan.

After the meeting, an accord was issued, with the leaders having agreed to improve security and to work to end ethnic conflicts in order to assist the return of refugees and displaced persons. At the meeting, the leaders were firmly told by the UN representative that "return is about today and the future, it should not be about the past." The three leaders also promised to take measures against any of their local commanders who breached the accord. However, the situation is a delicate one and illustrates the gravity of the situation in Afghanistan.

See also Afghan Army; Bonn Conference; Reconstruction Program

References

"Karzai Says It Will Take Years to Disarm Afghan Warlords; Donors Pledge US50.7 Million to Help." 2003. http://story.news.yahoo.com/news?tmpl=story&u=/ap/20030222/ap_wo_en_ge/as_gen_japan_afghan_donors_5 (cited 22 February 2003).

Pitman, Todd. 2003. "Joint UN, Afghan Government Team to Present Disarmament Strategy to Karzai Next Month." http://www.story.news.yahoo.com/news?tmpl=story2&cid=506&u=ap/20030227/ap_wo_en (cited 28 February 2003).

DOBBS, SIR HENRY

Sir Henry Dobbs was the British envoy to Afghanistan in 1921 and in charge of the mission to Kabul that negotiated the Anglo-Afghan Treaty of 1921, which reestablished Anglo-Afghan relations after the Third Anglo-Afghan War (1919). He had also been the head of the British negotiating team at the Mussoorie Conference, held from 17 April to 18 July 1920, which had failed to normalize Anglo-Afghan relations. Dobbs had first served in Afghanistan in 1903 as a political officer in charge of a team sent to restore and repair boundary pillars along the Afghan-Russia border.

See also Mussoorie Conference
References
Heathcote, T. A. 1980. *The Afghan Wars, 1839–1919.*
    London: Osprey.

DOST, SHAH MUHAMMAD (1928–)

Shah Muhammad Dost's career was entirely devoted to government service. He was in the Ministry of Foreign Affairs in various posts from 1956 before becoming a member of the Directorate of United Nations Affairs in 1957 and going on to serve in embassies in Washington, Islamabad, and Peshawar. He was born in 1929, the son of Dost Muhammad, and gained a diploma from the Faculty of Law at Kabul University, where he is reputed to have become a friend of Babrak Karmal, a leading member of the People's Democratic Party of Afghanistan (PDPA) who later became secretary-general of the party and then president of Afghanistan from 1979 to 1986. Dost was secretly a member of the PDPA and became deputy foreign minister in 1978 and foreign minister in 1980. He was also a member of the Central Committee and Revolutionary Council of the PDPA.

See also People's Democratic Party of Afghanistan

DOST MUHAMMAD, AMIR (1792–1863)

Amir Dost Muhammad, also known as the "Great Amir" (Amir-i-Kabir), took the throne of Afghanistan in 1826 and ruled, initially, until 1838 before being ousted by Britain at the start of the First Anglo-Afghan War. He was born in Kandahar in 1792, the son of Painda Khan, who was killed when Dost Muhammad was eight years old. He became acting governor of Ghazni and then established

British depiction of the surrender of Afghan ruler Dost Muhammad to the British in 1840 during the Anglo-Afghan Wars. (Library of Congress)

himself as ruler of Kabul after the death of Muhammad Azam in 1824. His next major success was the defeat of his primary rival, Shah Shuja, at Kandahar in 1834, which enabled him to extend his control through the rest of Afghanistan. He also defeated the Sikhs at the Battle of Jamrud in 1837 and took on himself the title "Commander of the Faithful."

However, Britain had turned against Dost Muhammad after he was suspected of having opened negotiations with Russia, a view reinforced by the arrival in Kabul of a Russian emissary, Capt. Ivan Vitkevich. Dost Muhammad was anxious to regain territory lost to the Sikhs under Ranjit Singh and was willing to ally himself with Britain, but he was advised by the British to make peace with the Sikhs. Britain then decided to support Shah Shuja in his attempt to regain the throne, and they invaded Afghanistan, taking Kabul on 23 July 1839. On 2 November 1840, Dost Muhammad surrendered to the British and was exiled to India until 1842.

The British army in Afghanistan found its lines of communication being disrupted, and garrisons in the outlying areas were expelled by Afghan tribesmen. The army in Kabul was forced to negotiate conditions for a withdrawal, which resulted in a massacre of all of the troops on the retreat to the frontier. As a result, the British government allowed Dost Muhammad to return to Afghanistan to put an end to the chaos that had ensued. However, it took him some time to reestablish his power over the whole of the kingdom; Kandahar was not retaken until 1855 and Herat in 1863. Dost Muhammad died of natural causes a few days after the capture of Herat, to be succeeded by Shir Ali.

See also Burnes, Alexander; First Anglo-Afghan War;
  Vitkevich, Capt. Ivan

References

Noelle, Christin. 1997. *State and Tribe in Nineteenth-Century Afghanistan: The Reign of Amir Dost Muhammad Khan.* London: Curzon Press.

DOSTUM, GEN. ABDUL RASHID (1954–)

Abdul Rashid Dostum, born in 1954 in Jozjan Province in northern Afghanistan, is one of the most controversial figures in contemporary Afghan politics. An Uzbek, he heads the National Islamic Front of Afghanistan and is supported by Uzbekistan, whose leaders see him as a guarantor of the integrity of their border with Afghanistan and a bulwark against Islamic unrest on the lines of the insurgency in Turkestan. In 1985, Dostum's militia numbered some 20,000 men, based in the northern provinces.

Dostum joined with the government of Muhammad Najibullah and fought against the mujahideen, receiving the "Hero of the Republic of Afghanistan" award for his efforts. He was a member of the Homeland Party, formerly called the People's Democratic Party of Afghanistan (PDPA). Seeing that the government of Najibullah was in a terminal state, he distanced himself from it and allied himself with the mujahideen during the transfer of power in 1992. This action was largely responsible for Najibullah's downfall, and Dostum and his allies seized Mazar-i Sharif and the surrounding area. However, this was not a settled period, for Dostum, a master of intrigue, had a habit of establishing alliances of convenience and then stabbing his allies in the back. He moved in and out of alliances with Ahmad Shah Masood, commander of the Islamist Movement; with the Islamic radical Gulbuddin Hekmatyar; and finally with the fundamentalist Taliban movement, whose members were the enemies of both Masood and Hekmatyar. Even within his own organization, dissent or rivalry was harshly resolved, with Dostum's rivals being involved in helicopter crashes and other fatal incidents.

Dostum soon disassociated himself from the central power struggle in Kabul and succeeded in establishing autonomous control over the northern provinces. However, in 1997, he was driven out by the Taliban and after a brief return was forced to flee again in 1998, when he sought refuge in Turkey. The Taliban took temporary control of Mazar-i Sharif at that point, and the population suffered from a period of savage rule, massacres, and violations of human rights. During Dostum's absence, the Islamist Movement's commander, Ustad Atta Mohammad, led anti-Taliban forces in the hills south of Mazar-i Sharif and succeeded in ousting the Taliban, being joined by Dostum on his return from Turkey in May 1999. Thereafter, Mazar-i Sharif's schools and university were able to reopen, and women could work and study outside of the home, a marked contrast to the situation in areas under Taliban control.

Mazar-i Sharif is seen as a key stronghold because it is the most important city in northern Afghanistan and is vital to the region's economic wealth in agriculture, oil, and natural gas. However,

Gen. Abdul Rashid Dostum, Uzbek warlord, deputy defense minister, and security advisor, with President Hamid Karzai at a ceremony to mark the Afghan new year on 21 March 2002 at Rosa Sharif Azrat Ali shrine, Mazar-i Sharif. (AFP/Corbis)

tension soon rose between Dostum and Ustad Atta Mohammad, with Dostum resenting the Islamist Movement's increasing influence in the area, and there were a number of armed clashes between the Uzbek forces of Dostum and those of Atta Moham-mad. The Afghan Interim Government, established at the UN-sponsored talks in December 2001, ex-cluded Dostum from its membership, but after he refused to recognize the administration, he was given the post of deputy defense minister.

Dostum regained a great deal of control in his old area in northern Afghanistan, largely with the aid of U.S. Special Forces and quickly became an anti-Taliban spokesman; he was transformed from warlord to politician, while at the same time con-trolling a force of some 7,000 men. He now controls the Uzbek and Turkoman provinces of Fariab and Jozjan and has formed an unlikely alliance with President Karzai, who has appointed Dostum his special representative in the north. He has also formed links with the former king, Mohammed Zahir Shah.

However, his power in the north is challenged by the Tajik-dominated Islamist Movement, and Atta Mohammad is supported by Defense Minister Mohammad Fahim, who made him a full general without consulting his deputy, Dostum. Fahim also approved the movement of troops and armor to support Atta, and in April 2002, a full-scale fight nearly occurred after Atta moved tanks into Mazar-i Sharif for a parade to mark the fall of the Communist government in 1992. His move was matched by Dostum, and clashes broke out in the area south of the city. The United Nations brokered a deal, signed on 5 May 2002, under which both sides agreed to withdraw their armor, and security in the city was turned over to a 600-man police force, consisting of troops from the two main factions and three smaller Shi'a groups. The peace is, however, shaky and uncertain, with the power struggle seeming certain to continue due to the nature of the two leaders.

Dostum is attempting to re-create his image by dressing as a political leader and attempting to sell himself as a democratic politician and servant of the people. His speeches are full of anti-Taliban rhetoric and espouse a future in which the defense of Afghanistan is accomplished by the rule of law and political parties. He has relaunched his old political party, the National Islamic Movement, with a platform of secular democracy and respect for minority rights, implying a federalist agenda, and opposition to extremism and fundamentalism, which relates to the politics of the Islamist Movement. However, there is grave doubt as to whether there has been a change in his outlook, for he is still seen by many observers as an autocratic, patriarchal ruler who does not understand or embrace the give-and-take of democratic politics.

See also Hekmatyar, Gulbuddin; Masood, Ahmad Shah; Najibullah, Muhammad; National Islamic Front of Afghanistan; Taliban

References

Davis, Anthony. 2002. "Makeover for a Warlord." Time Atlantic 159, no. 22: 60–63.
Maley, William. 1999. Fundamentalism Reborn? Afghanistan and the Taliban. London: Hurst.
Rashid, Ahmed. 2001. Taliban: The Story of the Afghan Warlords. London: Pan.

DRUG TRADE

Afghanistan has been involved in the drug trade for centuries, with opium having been planted as a cash crop as far back as the sixteenth century. As such, the country has become embroiled in terror networks and international crime syndicates. Given the nature of the Afghani agricultural economy, the incidence of drought, and the subsistence existence of the majority of farmers, opium has been an effective solution for many farmers over the centuries and a lucrative source of revenue for the various warlords. The 2002 crop was scheduled to reach record levels, despite the efforts of President Hamid Karzai's government, which banned production in January 2002, for the government's authority does not extend much beyond Kabul.

In recent years, the opium trade has been of major significance in Afghanistan, and all sides in the conflicts have been involved in the trade, with the Northern Alliance, particularly the Islamic Revolutionary Movement, regarded as corrupt and heavily involved in the drug trade. During the Taliban regime, the drug trade was a major source of revenue and helped fund the ongoing war against the Northern Alliance. The trade was originally ignored by the United States, as it was thought that the Taliban would bring in controls and also because UNOCAL, an American oil company, was involved in talks to build a pipeline from Turkmenistan to Pakistan.

In 1995, about 2,000 tons of dried opium was produced in Afghanistan, and this volume increased to 2,300 tons in 1996 and 2,800 tons in 1997. Production fell to 2,100 tons in 1998, but only because of bad weather, not control measures. By 1999, production had risen to 4,600 tons, boosted by high prices on the world drug market, which meant that Afghanistan was producing 75 percent of the total world production, with a street value, at that time, of $80 billion. It is worth noting that in 1978, before the Soviet occupation, the crop was only 200 tons.

The opium crop is mainly grown in the provinces of Helmand and Nangarhar, which at that time were Taliban-controlled areas. The harvested crop is refined in small laboratories on and across the Pakistan border and is shipped out via Karachi and the Central Asian republics. The trade

Afghan workers cut open poppy bulbs. Despite UN and Afghan government efforts, poppy cultivation and the drug trade still flourish. (AFP/Corbis)

is very much in the hands of international crime syndicates, such as the Russian mafia, and it is also known that the Kurdistan Workers Party (PKK) in Turkey is heavily involved in the trade as a means of financing its terror campaign against the Turkish state. The rising tide of production caused concern among neighboring countries, with the Iranian police, on 2 March 2000, calling for a concerted international effort to reinforce borders around Afghanistan to stop the flow of drugs to adjacent countries and the West. This appeal was followed by a gun battle between the police in eastern Iran and Afghan drug traffickers on 7 March, resulting in the deaths of seven traffickers.

In face of mounting international pressure, the Taliban announced that it was going to cut the 1999 production level by a third. In 2000, Mullah Muhammad Omar issued an edict banning production but said that international assistance would be needed to halt the trade. The UN International Drug Control Program agreed on a four-year plan with the Afghan authorities and funding of $16.4 million, but the agreement had little effect due to incompetence on the part of the Afghan authorities and insufficient funds. It is also not clear how effec-

tive the Taliban wished the program to be, as producing opium had become an economic necessity for small farmers. In addition, between 10 and 20 percent of the taxes paid to village mullahs on agricultural products went directly to the Taliban, as did levies imposed on transportation. Income to the Taliban from opium production ranged from $60 million to $300 million a year, which made it a crucial source of funding for the war in Afghanistan against the Northern Alliance. However, it is clear that some efforts were made to fulfill the edict because on 5 April 2000, the governor of Nangarhar Province, Maulvi Abdul Kabir, began an operation, which lasted until 15 April, to destroy poppy fields alongside the road from Jalalabad to the Pakistan border, with tractors plowing up the fields and the poppy crop.

The move by the Taliban authorities was welcomed by the UN Drug Control Program for Pakistan and Afghanistan, which estimated that 3,500 tons of opium had been destroyed. However, UN officials pointed out that it was premature to state that production had been wiped out, since it was not known how much opium was stockpiled within Afghanistan. And both the UN and the Taliban stressed that international aid for farmers was essential if farmers were to make the transition to legitimate crops, but at the time of the report of the UN Drug Control Program, such aid had not been forthcoming, though in 2001 the crop was only estimated to be some 280 tons.

The downfall of the Taliban did little to change the trade, and, indeed, the prevailing economic climate made the opium crop even more of a necessity for small farmers. In January 2002, President Karzai banned the planting of poppies, but he was unable to enforce the decree; in May 2002, the interim administration announced that it had destroyed opium worth $5 million, which, although encouraging, has done little to impact on the trade. The opium crop is thirty-one times more profitable per hectare than wheat, and farmers had no hesitation in tearing up grain seedlings to replace them with poppies. Moreover, a farmer can turn in two poppy crops in a year, and with seeds being provided free and the crop showing an immediate cash return at harvest, it is understandable that poppy growing is an attractive proposition.

The situation is causing much consternation in Iran, which wants the Afghan authorities to be harder on drugs and to halt their export to Iran, primarily from Helmand Province, to satisfy the needs of its 2 million addicts. Iranian authorities have strengthened already heavy security on the border and have seized large quantities of drugs and killed a number of drug smugglers, but there is little doubt that large quantities of opium are still getting through. Although the price has remained high in the border areas because of the increased military presence, prices have fallen heavily in Tehran, following a sharp rise after the Taliban ban on poppy growing was put in place.

It is also evident that heroin laboratories are being reestablished in eastern Afghanistan and across the border in the North-West Frontier Province of Pakistan. In Afghanistan, laboratories are operating in the mountain areas near Jalalabad and in the province of Nangarhar, with each refining lab having a capacity to produce some 220 pounds of refined heroin per day. The refineries are said to be operating in broad daylight and are capable of boosting production if the supply of raw poppies should increase. The revitalization of the trade has caused concern at the prospect of further destabilization in Afghanistan, with many violent incidents now being linked to drug-related feuds, the most notable being the assassination of Vice-President Abdul Qadir in Kabul on 14 July 2002.

Prices of heroin in eastern Afghanistan are relatively low because of the stocks of opium held by the warlords and because of the anticipated increase in production, and heroin and heroin-refining chemicals are openly traded in the markets. The growth of refining in the country is also a reflection of the fact that the refined product is easier to smuggle across the borders than raw opium. The United Nations and its various agencies recognize that the drug problem needs to be resolved if all of the work in Afghanistan is not to have been in vain. However, the involvement of local warlords in production and in taking the largest share of the profits, together with the involvement of international criminal organizations and terror networks, will be more difficult to resolve.

It will be vital for reconstruction and development programs funded by the international community to be effective in removing the need for farmers to grow the crop. This message has been reinforced by estimates of a 2002 crop of some 2,700 tons, largely because the authority of the Kabul administration does not run to the provinces, leaving the local warlords and the drug trade to exploit the economic plight of the farmers; a further increase is expected in the 2003 crop, despite the antidrug strategy. The United States and other nations are even considering buying the raw opium from farmers and then destroying it, but it is difficult to see how farmers can be induced to switch crops in future years and to cope with the effects of droughts and lower returns. The drug trade can only be effectively controlled once security is assured throughout Afghanistan, with the government in Kabul having enforcement capabilities in all of the provinces, with the power of local warlords contained, and with a degree of sustained economic activity.

The situation in Afghanistan has improved, according to findings of the U.S. Department of State's Bureau of International Narcotics and Law Enforcement annual certification process, released on 31 January 2003. Although Afghanistan is said to still present concerns as a drug-producing and drug-transiting country, the bureau recognized the efforts of the Karzai government to address these problems, in partnership with the international community. Farmers in Afghanistan have increased poppy cultivation as a result of the economic incentive to grow the crop, which was well adapted to the climate and yielded an excellent profit in a country ravaged by war and drought. However, the government has taken actions to tackle the problem, including a ban on poppy cultivation and production, sale of the crop, and its transportation. The United States and the United Kingdom have worked together to promote an antidrug strategy, with the prime objective of steering farmers toward alternative crops. The strategy, backed by the Kabul government and U.S. funding of $17 million, rests on the principle of promoting alternative crops and strengthening Afghan law enforcement agencies, eradication of the industry, and interdiction.

The bureau has acknowledged the commitment of the Afghan government but stressed that the campaign will still be a long-term effort due to the low base from which the initial institutions have to work. It is recognized that the actual situation on the ground is serious and still a matter of concern for the international community, for the illicit profits are massive and have been used to fuel a war economy. It is essential that the drug economy not regain its former proportions.

See also Afghan-Iranian Relations; Taliban

References
Bokhari, Farhan. 2003. "Poverty Fuels Afghanistan's Drug Trade." http://www.japantimes.co.ip/cgi-bin/getedp/5?eo2003024b.htm (cited 17 February 2003).
Cooley, John K. 2000. *Unholy Wars: Afghanistan, America and International Terrorism.* London and Sterling, VA: Pluto Press, 126–160.
Galeotti, Mark. 2001. "Business as Usual for Afghan Drugs." http://www.theworldtoday.org (cited 12 December 2001).
Goodhand, Jonathan. 2000. "From Holy War to Opium War? A Case Study of the Opium Economy in North Eastern Afghanistan." *Central Asian Survey* 19, no. 2: 265–280.
Porter, Charlene. 2003. "Afghanistan Improves Performance in International Anti-Drug Cooperation." http://www.washingtonpost.com (cited 3 February 2003).

DURAND AGREEMENT (1893)

The Durand Agreement, signed on 12 November 1893 at Kabul, was intended to define the frontier between Afghanistan and British India, subsequently known as the Durand Line. The agreement was signed by Sir Henry Mortimer Durand, foreign secretary of the government of India, and Amir Abdul Rahman, with the latter maintaining that he signed under duress.

The boundary was drawn without any consideration of the ethnic composition of the population. One consequence was the severance of the Pashtuns into two different countries, Afghanistan and British India, the latter subsequently becoming part of Pakistan. The Durand Line was never completely demarcated because of tribal hostility on both sides of the border.

Afghanistan received an increase in its subsidy from Britain and a renewed guarantee of protection against unprovoked Russian aggression. This guarantee was dependent on Afghanistan unreservedly following British "advice" with regard to external relations. The establishment of Pakistan in 1947 led the Afghan government to demand that the Pashtuns be given the right to decide whether they wanted an independent state or union with Afghanistan or Pakistan. The resultant plebiscite only allowed for union with India or Pakistan, and as a result, the question of the Pashtuns has remained an issue between Afghanistan and Pakistan. In 1979, the Afghan government repudiated the Durand Agreement.

References
Alder, G. 1963. *British India's Northern Frontier, 1869–95: A Study in Imperial Policy.* London: Longman.
Durand, Algeron George Arnold. 1974. *The Making of a Frontier.* Graz, Austria: Akademische Druck-u Verlagsansalt. (Reprint of 1899 edition, London: John Murray).
Gregorian, Vartan.1969. *The Emergence of Modern Afghanistan: Politics of Reform and Modernization, 1880–1946.* Stanford, CA: Stanford University Press.

DURRANI, AHMAD SHAH ABDALI
(1722–1772)

Ahmad Shah Abdali Durrani was the king of Afghanistan from 1747 to 1772 and the founder of the Sadozai dynasty of the Abdali tribe. He was born in 1722 in Herat and was the son of the governor of Herat, Muhammad Zaman Khan. After Nadir Shah of Iran had captured Kandahar in 1736, Ahmad Shah was exiled to Mazandoran in northern Iran, but he was subsequently appointed governor of that province. On Nadir Shah's death in 1747, he was

Ahmad Shah Abdali Durrani was the founder of modern Afghanistan. (UCSB Davidson Library)

commander of an Afghan contingent of the Persian army based at Kandahar, and in that role, he captured a caravan with booty from India, which assured him of election to the throne at an assembly of Pashtun chiefs in October 1747. As a result, the Pashtun tribesmen rallied to his cause, and he led them on eight campaigns into India in search of plunder and territory. The campaigns added Kashmir, Sind, and Western Punjab to his Ahmad Shah's territory. His kingdom now stretched from eastern Persia to northern India and from the Amu Daria River in the east to the Indian Ocean, thus founding the kingdom of Afghanistan. He appointed his son, Timur Shah, as his successor. Ahmad Shah died of natural causes on 14 April 1772 and was buried at Kandahar, which had been the capital of Afghanistan until Timur Shah made Kabul his capital.

See also Durrani Dynasty; Durrani Tribe
References
Ahmad, N. D. 1990. *The Survival of Afghanistan,
    1747–1979: A Diplomatic History with an Analytic
    and Reflective Approach.* Lahore, Pakistan: Institute of
    Islamic Culture.
Singh, G. 1959. *Ahmad Shah Durrani, Father of Modern
    Afghanistan.* Bombay, India: Asian Publishing House.

DURRANI DYNASTY

The Durrani dynasty, founded in 1747 by Ahmad Shah Durrani, ruled Afghanistan until the assassination of President Muhammad Daud in 1978. Ahmad Shah was a direct descendant of Sado, an Abdali chief at the court of Shah Abbas the Great, a Savafid who ruled from 1588 to 1629. The Durrani are divided into two main branches, the Sadozai and the Muhammadzai, though the dynasty did not always rule over the whole of Afghanistan and on other occasions the country was split between two rulers. The dynasty ruled Afghanistan from 1747 to 1817, but from 1817 to 1863, the country was ruled from Herat, Kabul, and Kandahar by different parts of the tribe. However, from 1863 to 1978, the dynasty again ruled Afghanistan as a single entity.

The Durrani had been granted land in Kandahar by Nadir Shah as a military fief, with divisions of land, or *qulba*, being granted in return for providing a quota of horsemen for military service. The quotas were based on the number of qulba held, calculated at one horseman per division. At the time of Nadir Shah, about 100,000 families had received this allocation of land, and the area of land held was greatly increased during the reign of Ahmad Shah Durrani.

See also Durrani, Ahmad Shah Abdali
References
Dupree, Louise. 1980. *Afghanistan.* Princeton, NJ:
    Princeton University Press.

DURRANI TRIBE

The Durrani was the dominant tribe among the Afghans, and the ruling family had been drawn from this tribe until the Saur Revolt of 27 April 1978, in which the Communists seized power.

The tribe was known as the Abdalis until the time of Ahmad Shah Durrani, who changed the name as a result of a dream. The origins of these people are unknown, but it is thought that they may have come from the mountains of either Toba or, more probably, Ghor. The tribe is divided into the Zurak and Panjpai branches, and it forms the bulk of the population of Farah and Kandahar Provinces and the Sabzawar district of Herat Province.

The tribe's form of government differs from that of other tribes largely because of the Durranis' direct link to the amir and the fact that their lands were given to them in return for military service. Each of the clans is ruled by a *sardar* (chief) chosen from the head family, and subdivisions are ruled by chiefs known as *khans,* also taken from the head families, but power, though effectively administered, is limited. The tribe is largely engaged in pastoral activities, with some cultivation of land, and the women also weave cloth. Crops are mainly wheat, barley, melons, cucumbers, and forage; stock includes bullocks, sheep, and mules. Horses are also bred, and camels are used for long journeys and hired out to merchants.

The more affluent Durranis do not cultivate their own land but have the work done by *buzgars* (farm managers), with labor being provided by Tajik casual day laborers. Poorer Durranis may take employment as buzgars but never as laborers. All villages tend to be built around the house of the khan, which has, traditionally, been fortified. Durranis are all religious, and every village or camp has a mullah who tends to be moderate in terms of politics and more concerned with the spiritual welfare of the communities.

Hospitality is a feature of the tribe's culture, and every settlement has arrangements for the reception of guests; in the largest settlements, such arrangements are usually based on the mosque. Members of the tribe are also distinguished by their sense of superiority and national dignity, with a reverence for Kandahar, which contains the tombs of their ancestors.

See also Durrani, Ahmad Shah Abdali; Durrani Dynasty

References

Clifford, Mary Louise. 1973. *The Land and People of Afghanistan.* Philadelphia: Lippincott.

ELPHINSTONE, MAJ. GEN. WILLIAM (1782–1842)

William Elphinstone was the British commander in Afghanistan in 1841 and has been held largely responsible for the British defeat in the First Anglo-Afghan War (1838–1842). Among charges levied against him were: failing to be decisive after Alexander Burnes, the assistant British envoy in Kabul, was killed, together with his staff; setting up camp in an area overlooked by nearby hills instead of using a fortified position that was close by; and failing to recognize the strength and deployment of the opposing forces. The British were compelled to negotiate terms for a withdrawal from Kabul to India, which ended in disaster, as most of the 16,000 troops and camp followers as well were killed by tribal forces or by the freezing cold or disease. Elphinstone died in captivity on 23 April 1842; in his late sixties at the time, he succumbed to exhaustion and sickness.

See also First Anglo-Afghan War

References

Jones, A. 1967. *The First Anglo-Afghan War, 1838–42.* London: Cambridge University Press.

ELPHINSTONE, MOUNTSTUART (1779–1859)

Mountstuart Elphinstone's significance lies in the fact that he was the envoy of the British East India Company to the court of Shah Shiya in 1808 and 1809, concluding the first agreement between Britain and Afghanistan. He succeeded in negotiating an agreement of eternal friendship, which allowed for joint action in the event of Franco-Persian aggression in Afghanistan. He also used his time in Afghanistan to learn as much as possible about the history and culture of the country, writing a book entitled *An Account of the Kingdom of Caubul* that appeared in 1815 and was the first comprehensive study on Afghan society to appear in English.

E

References

Elphinstone, Mountstuart. 1815. *An Account of the Kingdom of Caubul, and Its Dependencies in Persia, Tartary and India.* London: Longman.

ENAYATULLAH, SARDAR (1888–1946)

Sardar Enayatullah became king of Afghanistan following King Amanullah's abdication on 14 January 1925, but he, too, was forced to abdicate and after only three days on the throne; Habibullah Kalakani succeeded him. Enayatullah was born on 20 October 1888 and was the eldest son of Amir Habibullah and accorded the title "Supporter of the State" (Muin al-Sultanat). In 1905, he was appointed as marshal (an honorific title), and he became minister of education in 1916. He was a friend of Sardar Nasrullah, and both of them were in close contact with the Hentig-Niedermayer Expedition in Kabul, a German expedition designed to foment unrest in British India during World War I. It is thought that Enayatullah was in favor of Afghanistan's intervention in the war against Britain. After the assassination of Amir Habibullah, Nasrullah offered Enayatullah the throne, but he declined and recognized Nasrullah as king. However, the army refused to recognize the proclamation of Nasrullah as king and revolted to support Amanullah, who was in Kabul at the time; Amanullah came to power in 1919. During his rule, Enayatullah remained in virtual retirement. But on 14 December 1928, prior to his resignation, Amanullah appointed Enayatullah to be his successor. However, as mentioned, Enayatullah was forced to surrender to Kalakani after only three days on the throne, and on 18 January 1929, he was evacuated, together with his family, to Peshawar by the British air force. He then went to Tehran as a guest of the ruler of Persia and remained there until his death on 12 August 1946.

See also Amanullah, King
References
Adamec, Ludwig W. 1967. *Afghanistan, 1900–1923: A Diplomatic History.* Berkeley: University of California Press.

F

FARAH PROVINCE

Farah is the second largest province in Afghanistan. Located in the western part of the country, it has an area of 21,666 square miles and a population of some 356,000. The provincial capital is the town of the same name and has a population of about 19,000 inhabitants. The province is traversed by the Farah, the Khash, and the Herut Rivers and contains the major mountain ranges of the Khak-i-Safid, the Siyah Kuh, the Malmand, Kuh-i-Afghan, and the Reg-Rawan. The economy of the province is totally dependent on agriculture and the breeding of livestock. The major crops are barley, cotton, and wheat, and livestock herds include sheep, goats, cattle, camels, and donkeys. The town of Farah was an important junction in the trade between India and Persia in the seventeenth century. It was destroyed by fire in 1837 and remained a small, walled town until the early part of the twentieth century, when a new town was gradually developed; by 1934, the population was about 6,000 inhabitants. However, in 1965, a new Kandahar-to-Herat highway was opened, thus bypassing Farah and sending it into a period of decline. In 1972, the town was devastated by floods, and the administration had to move to Farah Rud until 1974. Although the population of the province is largely Pashtun, there is a significant Tajik community, and other ethnic communities are also present.

References

Adamec, Ludwig W. 1972–1985. *Historical and Political Gazetteer of Afghanistan.* 6 vols. Graz, Austria: Akademische Druck-u Verlagsansalt.

FARHAD, GHULAM MUHAMMAD (?–1984)

Ghulam Muhammad Farhad was an Afghan nationalist, a Pashtun, and an ardent supporter of Pashtunistan, in company with many Pashtuns who wanted to be reunified with their tribal brothers in Pakistan or at least to secure independence or autonomy for the region. He was the founder of the Afghan Social Democratic Party, more popularly known as Afghan Nation. He was educated in Kabul and Germany, earning a degree in engineering. On returning to Afghanistan, he became president of the Afghan Electric Company, a position he held from 1939 to 1966, and mayor of Kabul from 1948 to 1954. As mayor, he was responsible for the building of Maiwand Street as a major avenue through the old town, with displaced residents being relocated. As a nationalist, he sought the restoration of "Greater Afghanistan," to include Pakistan's North-West Frontier Province and Baluchistan. He was pro-German and was accused by his opponents of giving preference to German technology and consultancy when allocating government contracts. In 1968, he was elected to parliament, but he resigned his seat two years later. In 1978, he was arrested by the Khalq regime, with his party being accused of attempting a coup, but he was freed in 1980 following a general amnesty decreed by Babrak Karmal. He died in 1984 in Kabul.

References

Arnold, Anthony. 1983. *Afghanistan's Two-Party Communism: Parcham and Khalq.* Stanford, CA: Hoover Institution Press.

FARIAB PROVINCE

Fariab Province is located in north-central Afghanistan and has an area of 8,226 square miles and a population of about 547,000. The province borders on Turkmenistan in the north, Badghis Province in the south, and Jozjan in the east. Fariab is famous for horse breeding, and Karakul sheep are bred for the export of skins. Carpet weaving is an important industry, and melons, nuts, cereals, and cotton are the major agricultural products. The capital of the province is the town of Maimana, which has about

38,000 inhabitants (mainly Uzbeks) and was at one time the capital of a semi-independent fiefdom and a dependency of the ruler of Kabul. The town had only about 17,000 inhabitants in 1973, but it and the surrounding district have grown as a result of internal migration and industrial development. Today, the town has a modern road system with bungalow-style housing, but it has obviously suffered as a result of the civil war in Afghanistan (1989–2001). This area is controlled by the forces of Gen. Abdul Rashid Dostum.

References
Adamec, Ludwig W. 1972–1985. *Historical and Political Gazetteer of Afghanistan*. Graz, Austria: Akademische Druck-u Verlagsansalt.

FARSIWAN

The Farsiwan are an ethnic group of Farsi-speaking Shi'a Muslims. Numbering around 100,000, they live primarily near the Iranian border in Ghazni, Herat, and Kandahar Provinces. Some are also scattered in towns in southern and western Afghanistan. Most Farsiwan, of Mediterranean origin, are engaged in agriculture.

References
Clifford, Mary Louise. 1973. *The Land and People of Afghanistan*. Philadelphia: Lippincott.

FATEH KHAN (1777–1818)

Fateh Khan, also known as Fath, was the eldest son of Painda Khan and was born in Kandahar in 1777. A skillful politician and an accomplished soldier, he helped Shah Mahmud gain the Afghan throne, having captured Farah and Kandahar from the forces of Zaman Shah in 1800. He was given the post of *grand wazir* (personal or chief adviser), established law and order, and deftly handled the affairs of Mahmud's government. However, when Shah Shuja came to the throne in 1803, Fath was again appointed grand wazir but remained loyal to Mahmud, assisting his return to the throne six years later. Afghan control over Kashmir was consolidated by Fateh Khan, and order was established in Herat. However, Kamran, the son of Shah Mahmud, was jealous of his position and had Fateh Khan blinded and then had him killed in 1818. As a consequence, the Barakzai chiefs rebelled against the regime in a conflict that led to the overthrow of the Sadozai dynasty and its replacement by the Barakzai-Muhammadzai branch of the Durrani tribe.

See also Mahmud Shah
References
Griffiths, John C. 1967. *Afghanistan*. London: Pall Mall Press.

FIRST ANGLO-AFGHAN WAR (1839–1842)

Britain's policy with regard to Afghanistan in the nineteenth century was determined by a desire to keep its Indian empire secure from the perceived threats posed by French and Russian aspirations in the region. These concerns were highlighted by the Napoleonic invasion of Egypt in 1798 and by the spread of Russian influence to the banks of the Amu Daria River in Afghanistan. By that time, Britain had also moved north into the Punjab to provide a secure frontier for its possessions in India.

In Afghanistan, internecine warfare had resulted in the deposing of Shah Shuja of the Sadozai dynasty in 1826, who was replaced by Dost Muhammad, the first Muhammadzai ruler. Dost Muhammad was keen to form an alliance with India and wanted to regain Peshawar, which had been lost to the Sikh nation under Ranjit Singh in 1818. The British view of the situation was also affected by the Persian siege of Herat in 1838, which caused the governor-general of India, Lord Auckland, to become increasingly worried about the position of Afghanistan and the possible threat to India. As a result, Lord Auckland determined to restore Shah Shuja to the throne by forming an alliance with the Sikh ruler, Ranjit Singh, but Singh was unwilling to use his troops to effect the restoration. This policy was contained within the Simla Manifesto, signed by the British India government, Ranjit Singh, and Shah Shuja; it was concluded in July 1838.

The catalyst for the outbreak of the First Anglo-Afghan War was the arrival in Kabul of a Russian, Capt. Ivan Vitkevich, who was accused of being an agent of the czar, coupled with the open hostility of Dost Muhammad toward Ranjit Singh. Because the Sikh ruler was reluctant to commit troops, it was left to the British Army of the Indus to invade Afghanistan but without the approval of the Board of Directors of the British East India Company. Initially, the British met with little resistance, taking Ghazni on 23 July 1839 and completing the occupation of Kabul on 7 August; Shah Shuja was restored to the throne, and Dost Muhammad was sent into exile in India.

Although the bulk of the British army had left Afghanistan by 18 September 1839, a force had to be left behind to maintain Shah Shuja in power, and in effect, it became an army of occupation. Families of British officers went to Kabul, together with thousands of Indian camp followers who were making a good living by providing for the needs of the army and the families. However, on 2 November 1841, a crowd of Kabuli citizens stormed the British mission and killed the British representative, Alexander Burnes, and all of his staff. At the same time, other Kabulis raided some £17,000 from the treasury adjacent to the mission and plundered the army stores that were held in a number of forts outside the mission emplacements.

Muhammad Akbar, a son of Dost Muhammad, and a number of other tribal chiefs used these incidents to rally their forces and to threaten the occupying army. The dangers inherent in this situation were realized by the British commander, Maj. Gen. William Elphinstone, who withdrew his troops to the cantonment that was commanded from nearby hills; he also decided to withdraw forces under Gen. Sir Robert Henry Sale from Gandomak and Gen. William Nott from Kandahar. However, routes were blocked due to the advent of winter weather and because of the activities of the *lashkars* (tribal forces) operating in the area, which prevented the reinforcement of the garrison at Kabul.

A sortie designed to put the Afghan guns out of action was badly mauled, and the position throughout was critical, with both Gandomak and Kandahar also under siege. As a result, the British forces had to negotiate an orderly retreat back to India, through an agreement known as the Treaty of Capitulation. The whole retreating body amounted to some 16,500 people, comprising some 3,500 British and Indian infantry, 970 cavalry, and over 12,000 camp followers (including a large number of women and children). The retreat began on 6 January 1842, but the column covered only 6 miles on the first day, with the roads becoming jammed and much of the baggage abandoned. Progress was no better on the second day: when the group reached the Khund Kabul Pass, just 5 more miles had been covered.

At that point, the cavalry of Shah Shuja deserted the column, and it was soon discovered that a number of the remaining troops and camp followers had frozen to death. On day three, the British rear guard was attacked by Ghilzai *ghazis* (holy warriors), and it

proved impossible to separate troops from camp followers in order to organize an orderly defense. Consequently, some 500 troops and 2,500 camp followers were killed. British officers and women and children were surrendered as hostages to Muhammad Akbar and thus survived the debacle. The retreat soon developed into a rout, and on the fifth day, a stand was made at Jagdalak, but by then, about 12,000 of the retreating column had perished. It is suggested that at that point, Muhammad Akbar tried to stop the Ghilzais' attacks by buying them off with 200,000 rupees, but this effort was spurned because the driving force behind the attacks was revenge.

On the eighth day of the retreat, two British officers and seven or eight wounded were taken prisoner, leaving only one man, Dr. William Brydon, to reach the safety of Jalalabad. The First Anglo-Afghan War was a disaster for Britain's reputation and to the British economy, particularly in India: the total cost of the war was some £20 million, and it took the lives of roughly 15,000 troops and camp followers. It also resulted in disgrace for Lord Auckland, who had to face a court of inquiry of the East India Company. Ultimately, he was recalled to London. Britain sought retribution for the debacle by sending a force back into Afghanistan under Gen. George Pollock in September 1842. Pollock captured Kabul, burning down the covered bazaar and allowing troops to plunder and destroy much of the rest of the city. The siege at Jalalabad was lifted, and the British force withdrew, leaving the way open for Dost Muhammad to return to Afghanistan to rule, with British recognition, until his death through natural causes in 1862.

See also Akbar, Sardar Muhammad; Auckland, Lord George Eden; Burnes, Alexander; Capitulation, Treaty of; Dost Muhammad, Amir; Elphinstone, Maj. Gen. William; Pollock, Field Marshal Sir George; Shuja, Shah; Simla Manifesto; Vitkevich, Capt. Ivan

References
Jones, A. 1967. *The First Afghan War, 1838–42.* London: Cambridge University Press.
Richards, Donald Sydney. 1990. *The Savage Frontier: A History of the Anglo-Afghan Wars.* London: Macmillan.

FIRUZKUHI TRIBE

The Firuzkuhis, one of the Sunni Chahar Aimaq tribes, live in eastern Badghis Province and northern

Ghor Province. They number about 1 million and are Farsi-speakers, having originally come from Iran in the fourteenth century when they were relocated to Herat by Timur-i-Lang, the founder of the Timurid dynasty who led successful campaigns against the Ottomans, Russia, and India and was responsible for the splendor of Samarkand in the late 1300s. Subsequently, they migrated further east into their present location. The descendants of the Firuz in Herat were initially small chiefs under the Taimani Khans, but they eventually took over most of the Taimani territory southeast of Herat.

References

Ali, Mohammed. 1964. *A Cultural History of Afghanistan.* Lahore, Pakistan: Punjab Educational Press.

G

GAILANI, SAYYED AHMAD (1932–)

Sayyed Ahmad Gailani is the hereditary head of the Qadiri Sufi fraternity, succeeding to the position following the death of his elder brother, Sayyid Ali, in 1964. He was born in 1932 in Kabul and was educated at the Abu Hanifa College and the Faculty of Theology at the University of Kabul. After the Saur Revolt of April 1978, which brought the Communists to power, he left for Peshawar and founded the National Islamic Front of Afghanistan (Mahaz-i Milli-yi Afghanistan), which was part of the seven-member mujahideen alliance that formed the Afghan Interim Government in 1989. Although he did not seek a position in the Interim Government, he later accepted the post of supreme justice. His son, Ishaq Gailani, was also a commander of moderate mujahideen groups.

References
Kaplan, Robert D. 1990. *Soldiers of God: With the Mujahideen in Afghanistan.* Boston: Houghton Mifflin.

GAILANI, SAYYID HASAN (1862–1941)

Sayyid Hasan Gailani was born in Baghdad in 1862 and was a descendant of Caliph Ali and a member of the Naqib-al-Asraf family. He arrived in Afghanistan in 1905, motivated by his wish to get married (despite opposition from his brother, who was head of the family); to avoid being sent back to Baghdad, it was essential for him to leave the Ottoman Empire. On arrival, he was warmly received by Amir Habibullah, who provided him with a residence at Chaharbagh, near Jalalabad, and an allowance of 3,500 rupees a month. He then became known as the Naqib Shah of Chaharbagh, as well as the Pi Naqib of Baghdad, the location of the tomb of his ancestors.

As a member of the Qadiri, a Sufi order, he was well received in Afghanistan, which was a Hanafite country with many Qadiri families; his father, Abdul Qadir Gailani, was revered as a saint in the Muslim world. He had been told about the goodwill of Afghans toward him by visitors to the mausoleum of Sheikh Abdul Qadir Gailani in Baghdad. Given his reception by the amir and the goodwill of the Afghans, he was persuaded to accept Afghan citizenship and to stay in the country. He came to be greatly respected by the Afghans, who looked to him as an example of Qadiri life, and was well regarded by Habibullah, Nasrullah Khan, and King Nadir Shah. He had two sons from his four marriages; Sayyid Ali became head of the Qadiri after his father's death, and Sayyd Ahmad became the founder of the National Islamic Front of Afghanistan.

See also Gailani, Sayyed Ahmad
References
Dupree, Louise. 1980. *Afghanistan.* Princeton, NJ: Princeton University Press.

GANDOMAK, TREATY OF (1879)

The Treaty of Gandomak, concluded between the British government and Amir Yaqub Khan, was signed by the amir and by Pierre Louis Cavagnari, on behalf of the British government, on 26 May 1879. The viceroy of India, Lord Lytton, ratified it four days later. The treaty was designed to restore friendly relations between the two countries following the Second Anglo-Afghan War (1878–1879). It also provided for an amnesty for all Afghans who had collaborated with the British army of occupation, and the amir agreed to conduct his foreign policy in accordance with the advice and wishes of the British government. Britain also agreed to support the amir with money, arms, or troops in the event of an unprovoked aggression, a move designed to counter Russian aspirations in the region.

The treaty also provided for a British representative to be based at Kabul, together with a suitable military escort and an appropriate residence, whereas an Afghan envoy was to be sent to the court of the viceroy of India. The Khyber and Michni Passes were to be controlled by Britain, and the towns of Kurram, Pishin, and Sibi were also to be under British control but not permanently taken from the kingdom of Afghanistan. Kandahar and Jalalabad were, however, restored to the control of the amir. Afghans have largely regarded this treaty as a capitulation to Britain and believe that by signing the treaty, the amir had committed an act of treason.

See also Cavagnari, Sir Pierre Louis; Second Anglo-Afghan War

References
Hanna, Henry B. 1910. *The Second Afghan War, 1878–1880: Its Causes, Its Conduct, and Its Consequences.* 3 vols. London: Constable.

GENEVA ACCORDS

The Geneva Accords were the outcome of talks between Afghanistan and Pakistan, conducted in the 1980s under the auspices of the United Nations and aimed at ending external interference in the war in Afghanistan. The talks also involved the United States and the Soviet Union and were held between 1982 and 1988. One accord was a bilateral agreement between Pakistan and the Communist government of Afghanistan on the principles of multilateral relations, particularly noninterference and nonintervention in each other's affairs. A second accord was an agreement between the United States and the Soviet Union promising nonintervention in Afghanistan and an agreement to act as guarantors of the accords. These accords eventually resulted in the withdrawal of Soviet troops from Afghanistan in February 1989.

However, the accords were a total failure, primarily because the mujahideen were not represented at Geneva but also because the Soviet-backed regime in Afghanistan did not immediately collapse. The Soviets had left a considerable supply of weaponry behind and promised to supply more under the 1978 Treaty of Friendship, whereas the United States was obliged to cease military support for the mujahideen. After a great deal of haggling, the two powers agreed informally to a position of "positive symmetry"—reserving the right to send arms in response to any shipments made by the other side.

The outcome was that both sides continued to provide support to the parties involved in the conflict and Pakistan continued to allow weapons to pass through its territory. The war continued apace, and the superpower guarantees of noninterference proved meaningless.

See also Afghan-Pakistani Relations; Soviet War in Afghanistan

References
Chopra, V. D. 1988. *Afghanistan, Geneva Accord and After.* New Delhi: Patriot Publishers on Behalf of Indian Centre for Regional Affairs.
"Geneva Accords of 1998 (Afghanistan)." 1998. http://www.institute-for-afghan-studies.org/Accords%20Treaties/geneva_accords_1998_pakistan_afghanistan.htm (cited 12 February 2003).
Klass, Rusanne, and Theodore L. Elits. 1989. "The Geneva Accords: Excerpts and Short Commentaries." *Defence Journal* 15, nos. 1–2: 49–57.
United Nations. 1988. *Geneva Accords.* New York: United Nations.

GEOGRAPHY AND ENVIRONMENT

Afghanistan is a mountainous, landlocked country covering some 251,000 square miles. It has a population of about 15.5 million, though this figure is an estimate due to twenty-three years of war and a large refugee problem. It is bounded by China, Iran, Pakistan, Tajikistan, Turkmenistan, and Uzbekistan. The Hindu Kush mountains form a real barrier between the northern provinces and the rest of the country, and the range has divided Afghanistan into three vastly different geographic regions known as the Central Highlands, the Northern Plains, and the Southwestern Plains. The geography of Afghanistan has had a direct bearing on its people and its history, with altitude, climate, and environment varying greatly according to region.

The Central Highlands region covers an area of some 160,000 square miles. Its high mountains, in excess of 11,000 feet, and steep narrow valleys have proved to be historically important to the defense of the country. The most famous of these valleys contains the Khyber Pass, a strategic route to the Indian subcontinent. The climate is usually dry, with summer temperatures around 80° Fahrenheit, and the winters are very cold. Many of the valleys are impassable during the winter months. The soil in the region varies from desert-steppe type to meadow-steppe type. The area of

The Hindu Raj Mountains and Panjshir Valley stretch toward the Pamir Mountain Range, which separates Tajikistan from Afghanistan. (Reza/Webistan/Corbis)

the Hindu Kush is also susceptible to severe earthquake activity.

The Northern Plains cover an area of about 40,000 square miles of very fertile foothills and plains. The Amu Daria River runs through the edge of the foothills, and the average elevation of the region is some 2,000 feet. This region is an important center for the agricultural industry of Afghanistan due to its rich soils and mild climate. It also contains the bulk of the country's mineral resources, including oil and gas, though many of these resources have not truly been exploited.

The Southwestern Plains covers an area of about 50,000 square miles and consists of high plateaus and sandy deserts. It is a largely desolate region crossed by several large rivers, including the Helmand. The average elevation of the region is about 3,000 feet, though the city of Kandahar is some 3,500 feet above sea level and enjoys a dry, mild climate. In the arid plains of the region, sandstorms are a common feature of the climate.

The mineral resources of Afghanistan are mainly located in the Northern Plains, with coal being the only resource that has been widely exploited. The deposits of oil and natural gas have the potential to be of great significance to the economy of Afghanistan, but outside expertise would be essential to exploit them fully. The remainder of the mineral resources have only been exploited in small amounts, and the following are to be found in varying quantities: chrome, copper, gold, iron ore, lapis, rubies, salt, silver, sulfur, uranium, and zinc.

Afghanistan is watered by the Amu Daria (formerly known as the Oxus River), the Hari Rud–Murghab system, the Helmand-Argharbad system, and the Kabul River system, all of which rely on melting snow in the spring. These river systems also provide the bulk of the water used for irrigation. The water available has been badly affected by four years of drought conditions. In terms of usage, about 12 percent of the land is arable, 46 percent is meadows and pasture land, 3 percent is woodland, and 39 percent is desert or mountains.

The environment of Afghanistan has been severely devastated by over two decades of conflict, compounded by four years of drought and the impact of hundreds of thousands of returning refugees and internally displaced persons. The UN

Environmental Program has undertaken a post-conflict survey, which was released on 29 January 2003 and was produced in conjunction with the Afghan Transitional Authority, with twenty Afghan and foreign scientists visiting thirty-nine urban sites in four cities and thirty-five rural sites.

In remote mountain areas, inspectors found rampant deforestation, parched aquifers, soil erosion, and pesticide pollution, which could set back rehabilitation of the agricultural sector for decades. The environmental degradation in rural areas is critical, as over 80 percent of Afghans normally live in these areas; these people have now seen their basic resources lost in one generation. Deforestation has been extremely severe: satellite imagery shows that conifer forests in Nangarhar, Kunar, and Nuristan Provinces have shrunk by half since 1978. The situation is even worse in Badghis and Takhar Provinces, which had 55 percent and 37 percent of their land, respectively, covered by forests in 1977, whereas in 2002, almost no trees were discernible. Pressures on wildlife have increased because of this process and also because returning refugees and displaced persons have increased the demands on the land and the environment.

The situation in the urban areas is equally bad, with only one in ten people drinking safe water in Kabul and with 60 percent of that city's freshwater supply lost through illegal use and leakage. In the city of Herat, there were just 150 water taps but at the time of the scientists' visit, only 15 were working. The situation is worsening because of the breakdown of the infrastructure and the almost total collapse of public services. The city rubbish dump in Kabul, for example, is located upstream of the city and the Kabul River, allowing rain to flush poisons into the water system. A similar situation exists in Herat and Kandahar, and tests showed high levels of the E. coli bacteria in the water system emanating from the sewage systems.

The inspectors also found that medical wastes from hospitals, including human organs and syringes, were being dumped in the streets in Kabul, Kandahar, and Mazar-i Sharif, so that disease epidemics remain a constant threat. Further pollution is coming from industrial sites, with dangerous environmental and health risks being identified. One particular example was a plastics recycling factory in Kabul where inspectors found children working twelve-hour shifts and sleeping at their machines or elsewhere in the factory, having no protection from toxic chemicals.

Clearly, environmental restoration must be a major part of Afghanistan's reconstruction program. If the issues identified in the report are not dealt with, the country is in danger of facing a future without water, forests, wildlife, and clean air, but the solutions proposed will require a significant amount of foreign aid and investment.

See also Climate; Khyber Pass; Registan Desert

References

Amin, Hamidullah, and Gordon B. Schiltz. 1976. *A Geography of Afghanistan.* Omaha: University of Nebraska, Center for Afghan Studies.

Formoli, Tareq A., Afzal Rashid, and James P. Du Bruille. 1994. *An Overview and Assessment of Afghanistan's Environment.* Sacramento, CA: Afghanistan Horizon.

UN Environment Program. 2003. *Afghanistan: Post-Conflict Environmental Assessment.* Geneva, Switzerland: UNEP.

GHANI, ABDUL (1864–1945)

Abdul Ghani was an Indian Muslim who graduated from Lahore Medical School in 1883 before going to London to continue his studies. There, he met Nasrullah, son of Amir Abdur Rahman, who arranged for the amir to award Ghani a study scholarship. In 1891, Ghani returned to India and then went to Kabul to become secretary to the amir before going back to Lahore again, where he became principal of the Islamia College. He returned to Afghanistan around 1984 and served under Amir Habibullah as chief medical officer and principal of Habibia School. There, he began to champion the causes of political and social reform. He helped form a secret society, Secret of the Nation, and he recruited a number of students to its membership. In 1909, he was one of a number of members of the society arrested on suspicion of plotting to assassinate Amir Habibullah. He remained in prison until King Amanullah assumed the throne in 1919. The king appointed him a member of the delegation to the Rawalpindi Peace Conference in August 1919, which was the forerunner of the Anglo-Afghan Peace Treaty of 1919. He subsequently returned to India and wrote about his experiences and the region.

References

Ghani, Abdul. 1989. *A Brief Political History of Afghanistan.* Edited by Abdul Jaleel Nafji. Lahore, Pakistan: Najaf Publishers.

GHAUS, ABDUL SAMAD (1928–)

Ghaus was director of the UN Affairs Department and served under President Muhammad Daud as director-general of political affairs in the Ministry of Foreign Affairs in 1974. He served as deputy minister of foreign affairs from June 1977 until the April 1978 Saur Revolt of April 1978, and the advent of Communist rule. He was imprisoned following the revolt and was not released until 1980; he left for the United States in 1981.

Ghaus was born in Rome in 1928 and was educated at Istiqal High School and in Switzerland before embarking on a career in foreign affairs in 1956. He also wrote a book on Afghanistan, which covered President Daud's negotiations with various heads of state, including critical negotiations with Leonid Brezhnev of the Soviet Union.

References

Ghaus, Abdul Samad. 1988. *The Fall of Afghanistan.*
    Washington, DC: Pergamon-Brassey.

GHAZI

The term *Ghazi* was originally used to describe Arab Bedouin raiders who would strike from their desert territory to raid adjacent tribes for booty and captives. However, after the arrival of Islam, the word was used to describe a holy warrior fighting against a non-Muslim enemy; it was similar to the term *mujahideen,* used to describe the Afghan resistance to the Soviet occupation in the 1980s. In the Anglo-Afghan wars, the ghazi were the irregular troops who often engaged in suicidal attacks against British forces, having taken vows to die in battle against the unbelievers and thus secure entry to Paradise. These forces were particularly effective in the wars, especially at the Battle of Maiwand in 1880. Traditionally, the appellation *ghazi* was accorded to victorious Afghan commanders, such as Mahmud Shah of Ghazi, though others, such as King Amanullah, Habibullah Kalakani, and Nadir Shah, also claimed the honor. The sons of Mahmud Shah adopted the title as a family name.

References

Forbes, A. 1892. *The Afghan Wars, 1839–42 and*
    1878–80. London: Seeley.

GHAZI, SHAH MAHMUD (1896–1959)

Shah Mahmud Ghazi was the Afghan minister of war and commander-in-chief from 1929 until 1946. He then became prime minister, holding the post until 1953. He was born in 1896, the youngest son of Muhammad Yusif, and his early career was dedicated to the military. He was made a colonel in 1917 and became civil and military governor of Paktia Province in September 1919. He was named as the general commanding officer in Badakhshan and Kataghan from 1922 to 1925, then governor of the Eastern Province in April 1926. He was transferred from Jalalabad to Kabul in February 1928 and appointed deputy interior minister in March 1928. In 1929, he was sent as an emissary of Habibullah Kalakani (who ruled Afghanistan from January to October of that year) to the tribes of the eastern and southern provinces. He joined his brother Nadir Khan at Khost in March 1929 and helped him defeat Habibullah Kalakani. Thereafter, he served as his brother's minister of war and commander-in-chief from November 1929 to 1946. He left Kabul for the northern provinces and in January 1931 was appointed *rais-i-tanzimieh* (regional governor) for northern Afghanistan.

He succeeded in driving Ibrahim Beg across the Soviet border and returned to Kabul in August 1931, receiving the title of marshal in September 1931. (Beg was an Uzbek Bashmati who led raids from Afghanistan across the Soviet border; after these activities were stopped by Afghan authorities, he conducted raids inside Afghanistan until he was expelled across the border and captured by the Soviets.) Ghazi became prime minister in 1946 and was present at the assassination of Nadir Shah in Kabul. He nominated Zahir Shah as king and swore allegiance to him, continuing as prime minister until 1953. Ghazi visited the United States between 1950 and 1951 and accepted U.S. cooperation in the development of the Helmand Valley. His government also launched a campaign in favor of Pashtunistan and self-determination for the Pashtuns in the frontier area. He resigned in 1953, allowing Sardar Muhammad Daud to become prime minister. At the beginning of his period in office, he had allowed freedom of speech and of the press, but when these liberal policies led to criticism of his government, he reverted to a more totalitarian form of rule. He died in retirement in 1959. His sons were also active in public life, with Zalmay Mahmud serving as ambassador to Paris, London, Tehran, and Cairo; Sultan Mahmud serving as president of civil aviation and tourism from 1971 to 1976, and Abdul Azim serving as military attaché to the Afghan embassy in Moscow.

See also Habibullah Kalakani; Zahir Shah, Mohammed
References

Shahrani, M. Nazif, and Robert L. Caufield, eds. 1984.
    Revolutions and Rebellions in Afghanistan. Berkeley:
    Institute of International Relations, University of
    California.

GHAZNI PROVINCE

This province is located in eastern Afghanistan, occupies an area of 12,663 square miles, has a population of about 700,000, and is subdivided into twenty-
four districts. The Tajiks inhabit the north of the
province, there are Ghilzais in the center and south,
and Hazaras are in the west; in addition, some Durrani Pashtuns are scattered throughout the province.
Ghazni is a major agricultural and industrial area, famous for its sheepskin coats but also for corn, fruit,
and sheep's wool and camel hair cloth. The town of
the same name is strategically located on the road
from Kabul to Kandahar, some 80 miles southeast of
Kabul and 7,000 feet above sea level. Its fame is derived from the fact that it was the capital of the Ghaznaid dynasty from 977 to 1186; the old town is
walled and guarded by a citadel. Because of its strategic location, it was the scene of severe fighting between Afghan and British forces in the first two
Anglo-Afghan wars, with a British force in the first
war being wiped out in December 1841. The citadel
in the old town was garrisoned by Afghan troops but
was then seized and held by the mujahideen. The
town has a population of about 30,000 and has the
same population mix as the rest of the province, with
the addition of a few Hindu shopkeepers.

References

Bosworth, Clifford E. 1963. *The Gaznavids: Their Empire
    in Afghanistan and Eastern Iran, 944–1040.*
    Edinburgh: Edinburgh University Press.
Elliot, H. M., and J. Dowson. 1953. *History of Ghazni.*
    Calcutta, India: Sasil Gupta.

GHILZAI TRIBE

The Ghilzai is a major Pashtu-speaking tribe, occupying an area roughly bounded by Kalat-i-Ghilzai in
the south, the Gal-Kaul range in the west, the Sulaiman range in the east, and the Kabul River in the
north. The Ghilzais call themselves Ghaljais and
claim to be descendants of Ghalzoe, son of Sha Husain, a Tajik or Turk, and of Bibi Mato, who descended from Sheikh Baitan, second son of Qais, the
progenitor of the Afghan nationality. The origin of
the name comes from *Ghal Zoe* (meaning "thief's
son"), *Khilzi* (Turki for "swordsman"), or the name
of the Khilji Turks, who entered the region in the
tenth century. The tribe has two main divisions, the
Turan and the Burham Ibrahim. The Sulaiman Khel
comprise the most important branch of the tribe as
a whole, and the Ali Khel are the most important of
the Burham Ibrahim. In the nineteenth century, the
tribe numbered about 10,000 families and could
raise an armed force of between 30,000 and 50,000
fighters. These people were largely nomadic and
often traveled deep into India, earning a living as
nomadic merchants.

The Hotaki Ghilzais achieved fame for liberating
Kandahar from Safavid control, and they were the
leading force in the invasion of Iran and the destruction of the Persian Empire in 1722. Mir Wais, who
was taken hostage to Tehran but permitted to return,
raised a revolt against the Kandahar governor and
ruled over the province from 1709 to 1715. His son
led the invasion of Iran and defeated the Safavid
armies at the Battle of Galnabad in 1722. However,
the Afghan victory was short-lived, as Nadir Khan
reunited the Persian Empire and invaded Afghanistan. Following the death of Nadir Shah, the Ghilzais
lost their power and influence and were unable to resist the emergence of the Durrani dynasty.

The Ghilzais fought the British during the Anglo-
Afghan wars and continued to be the main rivals of
the Durrani. As a tribe, they repeatedly rebelled
against Muhammadzai rule, with revolts taking place
in 1801,1803, 1883, 1886, and 1937; each was put
down only with great difficulty. However, in recent
times, Ghilzais in urban areas have intermarried with
Muhammadzai. The Ghilzais were strongly represented in the Marxist government through Nur
Muhammad Taraki, Dr. Muhammad Najibullah, and
Hafizullah Amin, among others, but also in the resistance movement, through Gulbuddin Hekmatyar
and Abdul Rasul Sayyaf, which in itself represented a
power shift from the Durrani to the Ghilzais.

See also Durrani Tribe
References

Clifford, M. L.1973. *The Land and People of Afghanistan.*
    Philadelphia: Lippincott.

GHOBAR, MIR GHULAM MUHAMMAD
(1897–1978)

Mir Ghulam Muhammad Ghobar was a historian,
writer, and poet, noted for a critical analysis of

Afghan history published in 1968. He was born in 1897 in Kabul of a Sayyid family, and he was initially in the service of King Amanullah, being editor of the newspaper *Sitare-yi-Afghan* from 1919 to 1920 and chief of police from 1920 to 1921. He also served as secretary at the Afghan embassies in Paris (in 1926) and Berlin (in 1930). Just prior to Amanullah's downfall, he was also a participant in the Pagham Loya Jirga (Great Council). Ghobar then returned to his academic pursuits, becoming a prominent member of the Afghan Literary Society and the Afghan Historical Society before serving as a literary adviser to the Department of Press in 1948. He was imprisoned from 1933 to 1935 and again from 1952 to 1956 for his opposition to the government and also served as a member of parliament, representing Kabul, in 1948 and again from 1949 to 1951. Ghobar was a founding member of the Watan Party and editor of its newspaper of the same name in 1951. He died on 5 February 1978 in Germany.

References

Ghobar, G. 1968. *Afghanistan dar masir-i tarikh.* (Afghanistan in the path of history). Kabul: Government Press.

Poullada, Leon B. 1973. *Reform and Rebellion in Afghanistan, 1919–1929.* Ithaca, NY: Cornell University Press.

GHOR PROVINCE

Ghor Province lies in west-central Afghanistan, occupies an area of 13,808 square miles, and has a population of about 341,000, with the capital being the town of Chaghcharan. The province is mainly mountainous, but there is some cultivation of wheat and barley in the Farah, Hari Rud, and Murghat Valleys. The main mountain ranges in the province are the Firuzhak Sujahkan and the Band-i Bayan.

The people of the province are primarily of Taimani origin, a part of the Chahar Aimaq ethnic group, and they tend to be seminomadic, living in conical felt yurts. At times in the past, they were independent or allied with the Durrani rulers of Herat, but their power was severely curbed by Amir Abdur Rahman.

References

Adamec, Ludwig W. 1972–1985. *Historical and Political Gazetteer of Afghanistan.* 6 vols. Graz, Austria: Akademische Druck-u Verlagsansalt.

GHULAM, JILANI CHARKHI (1886–1933)

Jilani Charkhi Ghulam served as a major general under Amir Habibullah and led several victorious campaigns against rebellious tribes, securing the amir's power base in Afghanistan. Ghulam was born in 1886, and his first military appointment was as superintendent of the military college in Kabul in 1962. He also served King Amanullah as governor and military commander in various provinces before being appointed minister at Ankara in 1925. He was recalled to Kandahar by Amanullah in April 1929 in a vain attempt to secure the king's position; he was unable to defeat the forces of Habibullah Kalakani, and Amanullah was forced to abdicate. Ghulam fled to India with the deposed monarch and also accompanied him to exile in Rome. He returned to Afghanistan in August 1930 but was imprisoned and executed in 1933.

References

Poullada, Leon B. *Reform and Rebellion in Afghanistan, 1919–1929.* Ithaca, NY: Cornell University Press.

GOLDSMID AWARD

The Goldsmid Award was a result of the 1872 Sistan boundary arbitration, which drew the line between Afghanistan and Iran. Persia had occupied Sistan, which was also claimed by Afghanistan, and the British government offered to provide an arbitration service, carried out by General Sir Frederic Goldsmid. The arbitration determined that the majority of Sistan should become part of Persia but should have no land rights in the Helmand area nor interfere with the water supply from the Helmand River. Neither country was satisfied with the arbitration, and the issue of water was a continuing source of conflict that was not resolved until the Helmand Water Treaty of 1973, ratified by Afghanistan in 1979.

References

Aitchinson, C. U. 1933. *A Collection of Treaties, Engagements and Sanads Relating to India and Neighbouring Countries.* Vol. 13, *Persia and Afghanistan.* Calcutta, India: Superintendent of Government Printing.

GRANVILLE-GORCHAKOFF AGREEMENT (1873)

The Granville-Gorchakoff Agreement, struck between the British and Russian foreign ministers in an exchange of letters, sought to define the boundaries between Russia and Afghanistan. Only in the west was the issue not resolved completely, which allowed Russia to subsequently annex Panjdeh. Russia also agreed that Afghanistan was not within its sphere of influence. The agreement was used by the British government in 1876 to remind Russia's leaders that they had agreed to cease interfering in the affairs of Afghanistan and to halt any negotiations with Shir Ali, the ruler of Afghanistan from 1863 to 1866 and again from 1868 to 1879. However, there is some doubt as to whether these negotiations constituted a breach of the agreement or whether the incident was used by the British Indian government to increase political pressure on the two states, for the British saw the agreement defining the borders of Afghanistan as critical to their policy of using it as a buffer state between Russia and British India.

References

Adamec, Ludwig W. 1974. *Afghanistan's Foreign Affairs to the Mid-Twentieth Century: Relations with the USSR, Germany and Britain.* Tucson: University of Arizona Press.

GROMOV, GEN. BORIS V. (1943–)

Boris Gromov was commander of the Fortieth Army, which represented the limited contingent of Soviet forces in Afghanistan from 1979 to 1989, and he spent three tours of duty in the country. In January 1988, he was responsible for raising the siege of Khost when he led a force of 10,000 Soviet and Afghan troops from Gardez in what was to be the last major Soviet operation against the mujahideen. However, it was Gromov's strategic view that the role of the Soviet forces should have been to guarantee stability, establish garrisons, and refrain from counterinsurgency actions, which he believed should have been left to the forces of the Democratic Republic of Afghanistan.

The strategy could never be fully implemented, and at best, only about one-third of the Soviet forces were devoted to the defense and security of fixed sites, with the remainder being drawn into the counterinsurgency operations. Gromov himself accepted that this outcome was inevitable, given the circumstances, and admitted that the Afghan operations were the perfect example of the difference between theory and practice.

On his final tour of duty, Gromov was responsible for organizing the withdrawal of the last remaining contingent of Soviet forces, numbering some 1,400 men and 450 armored vehicles. On 14 February 1989, he became the last Soviet soldier to cross the "Friendship Bridge" back into the Soviet Union, maintaining that the Soviet forces had fulfilled their duty. In 1990, Gromov was made minister of the interior for the USSR, and he became commander of all Russian ground forces two years later.

See also Soviet War in Afghanistan

References

Cordovez, Diego, and Selig S. Harrison. 1995. *Out of Afghanistan: The Inside Story of the Soviet Withdrawal.* New York: Oxford University Press.

GUARDIANS OF THE ISLAMIC REVOLUTION (PASDARAN-I-JIHAD-I-ISLAMI)

The Guardians of the Islamic Revolution was established in the Hazarajat region in 1983 as a radical Shi'a group, drawing its inspiration from the Guardians of the Iranian Revolution in Iran, from whom it received arms and financial support. The original membership was recruited from Hazaras living in Iran and militants in the Hazarajat region; this younger generation of Islamic radicals usurped the traditional leaders who had emerged to oppose the Soviet invasion in 1979. The group allied itself with Haijjat al-Islam Mir Hussain Sadeqi of Nasr, a prominent Shi'a mujahideen leader, in a successful campaign to rid the region of the Shura (Council) led by Sayyid Ali Beheshti.

The Guardians follow the teachings of Ayatollah Khomeini—the former spiritual leader and president of Iran, who had led the Islamic revolution against the shah in 1979—with respect to relations with the United States and the Soviet Union and with regard to the creation of an Islamic state in Afghanistan. But throughout the 1980s, they were more concerned with factional infighting than opposing the Soviet presence. As a result, they were always peripheral to the mainstream mujahideen opposition in Afghanistan.

See also Beheshti, Sayyid Ali; Shi'a Mujahideen Groups

References

Oleson, A. 1995. *Islam and Politics in Afghanistan.* London: Curzon Press.

General Boris Gromov looks back and waves as he crosses the border at Termez as the last of the Soviet soldiers leaves Afghanistan. (Reuters NewMedia Inc./CORBIS)

GULBAZOI, LT. GEN. SAYYID MUHAMMAD (1945–)

Sayyid Muhammad Gulbazoi began his career in the military, and after the Saur Revolt of 27 April 1978, which brought the Communists to power, he was appointed aide-de-camp to President Nur Muhammad Taraki, becoming minister of communications that same year. He was born in 1945 in Paktia Province, the son of Gulab Shah. After his elementary and secondary education, he attended air force courses, and in 1966, he became a military officer in Mazar-i Sharif. He served at Khwaja Rawasl Military Airport in 1969, and he was a Pashtun nationalist, later becoming a populist with a Marxist slant. He participated in the coup led by Muhammad Daud in 1973, which overthrew the monarchy, and was appointed as an aide to the commander of the air force. In 1976, he went to the Soviet Union for higher education and further military training.

He was dismissed as minister of communication in September 1979 and disappeared until the Parchami regime came to power in December of that year; he was appointed minister of the interior on 11 January 1980. He was a member of the Central Committee and Revolutionary Council of the People's Democratic Party of Afghanistan.

See also People's Democratic Party of Afghanistan

References
Bradsher, Henry St. Amant. 1999. *Afghan Communism and Soviet Intervention.* London and New York: Oxford University Press.

GULNABAD, BATTLE OF (1772)

The Battle of Gulnabad took place on 8 March 1772 between Afghanistan and Iran. The Afghan forces were led by Mahmud, son of the Ghilzai chief Mir Wais, and they decisively defeated a far superior Iranian army, marking the end of the Safavid Empire of Iran. The Afghans then besieged Isfahan for a period of six months before taking the capital of the Iranian Empire. However, the Ghilzai army was unable to hold on to the Iranian conquests and was compelled to fall back before the forces of Nadir Shah Afshar, crossing the border back into Afghanistan. Following this action, the Ghilzais' position in Afghanistan was weakened, and they were eventually replaced as the dominant tribe by the Durranis.

References
Lockhart, Laurence. 1958. *The Fall of the Safavi Dynasty and the Afghan Occupation of Persia.* Cambridge: Cambridge University Press.
Malleson, George B. 1879. *History of Afghanistan from the Earliest Period to the Outbreak of the War of 1878.* London: W. H. Allen.

H

HABIBULLAH, AMIR (1871–1919)

Amir Habibullah was a son of Amir Abdur Rahman and was born during the his father's period of exile in Samarkand on 21 April 1871. During the reign of his father, he was actively involved in the administration and was generally popular due to his competence and because he was thought to be more lenient than his father.

He took the throne on 3 October 1901 and began his rule with some positive actions, which included raising the pay of the army, recalling exiles, promising reforms, and releasing prisoners. However, this approach was short-lived, as he soon resorted to his father's policy of severe punishments and confiscation of property and he became less interested in the affairs of state. The British government tried to renegotiate some of the agreements reached with Amir Abdur Rahman and attempted to maintain that these had been personal agreements, not accords reached with the state of Afghanistan. Under extreme pressure from the British India government, Habibullah refused to yield, and after two years of stalemate, the foreign secretary of the government of India, Louis W. Dane, went to Kabul to negotiate and eventually had to accept the amir's position. As a result, the agreements were renewed, and Britain agreed to recognize Habibullah as king of Afghanistan and its dependencies.

Habibullah was a good Muslim but began to adopt Western ways following a visit to India in 1907. This change, together with his adoption of freemasonry, led to a sharp decline in his popularity. During his visit to India, the amir found out about the Anglo-Russian Convention of 1907, which divided Iran and Afghanistan into spheres of influence between the two states, but Habibullah refused to ratify the convention, which was never implemented. Some reforms were effected during his reign, including the establishment of modern schools, the import of cars, a road-building program, and the introduction of electricity in Kabul.

The outbreak of World War I caused a further strain in Anglo-Afghan relations. In defiance of the wishes of the viceroy of India, Habibullah received the Hentig-Niedermayer Expedition at Kabul—a German expedition designed to foment unrest in British India during the war. A secret treaty of friendship and military assistance was concluded with Germany, in the event of an Allied defeat in the war, but Germany could not fulfill its part of the bargain, and Britain promised the amir a substantial reward if Afghanistan remained neutral. As a result, the amir decided to keep Afghanistan out of the war, but Britain did not fully respect his actions and endeavored to reassert its control over Afghanistan at the conclusion of hostilities with Germany.

However, certain factions in the amir's court felt that he had failed Afghanistan. They believed World War I had provided an ideal opportunity to secure complete independence from Britain—an opportunity he failed to exploit. As a consequence, conspiracies were formed to remove him from power, and he was assassinated on 20 February 1919 in Kala Gosh, Laghman Province, while on a hunting trip.

See also Anglo-Russian Convention; Hentig-
   Niedermayer Expedition

References

Gregorian, Vartan. 1969. *The Emergence of Modern
   Afghanistan: Politics of Reform and Modernization,
   1880–1946.* Stanford, CA: Stanford University Press.

HABIBULLAH KALAKANI (C. 1890–1929)

Habibullah Kalakani was born about 1890 in Kalakan village in Kohdaman, a Tajik and son of a water carrier; hence, he was also known as Bacha-i-Saqqau ("son of a water carrier"). He held several menial positions before joining Jemal Pasha's

Ottoman Turkey regiment in Kabul in 1919. However, he deserted from the army because of his sympathies with the Mangals during the 1924 Mangal Rebellion against the reform program of King Amanullah, and he fled to Peshawar in India, where he worked as a tea vendor before moving to Parachinar, India. There, he was sentenced to eleven months of imprisonment for breaking into a house. During the Nangarhar Rebellion of 1928, launched by a coalition of tribes opposed to the legal and social reforms of the king, he offered his services to King Amanullah but then defected and joined the Kohistani forces fighting the ruler.

On 14 December 1928, with a loose coalition of Kohistani forces, Kalakani took advantage of a tribal revolt by the Shinwaris and other Pashtun tribes to attack Kabul. As a charismatic figure, he became the leader of the antireformist action against King Amanullah. The attack was repelled but only after nine days of fierce fighting, and Kalakani retired toward Pagham. But on 7 January 1929, he again went on the offensive and took Kabul, forcing King Amanullah to abdicate on 18 January. He proclaimed himself amir of Afghanistan but only had a tenuous hold on parts of the country. His aspirations to become accepted as the ruler were hindered by the fact that he was a Tajik, rather than a member of the dominant Pashtun tribe, and because of his background as a brigand; only his Kohistani supporters regarded him as a hero. The tribes on either side of the Durand Line (which was determined by Britain in 1893 to demarcate the boundary between Afghanistan and British India) were shocked at his success, but the forces of Shah Wali Khan, brother of the future king Nadir Shah, eventually defeated him. He surrendered to the opposing forces and was executed on 1 November 1929.

Habibullah was considered by his Kohistani supporters to be an outlaw hero because he preyed on government officials and the wealthy after the failure of the Mangal Rebellion. However, to his opponents, he was regarded as a bandit and a common criminal. In his purported autobiography, *My Life from Brigand to King,* he depicted himself as a bandit who managed to come to power during a period of civil war. He has also been regarded by some as a mujahideen acting against an infidel king.

See also Amanullah, King; Khost Rebellion

References

Gregorian, Vartan. 1969. *The Emergence of Modern Afghanistan: Politics of Reform and Modernization, 1880–1946.* Stanford, CA: Stanford University Press.

Habibullah, Amir. 1990. *My Life: From Brigand to King—Autobiography of Amir Habibullah.* London: Octagon Press.

HAMAD, ABDUL SANAD (1929–)

Abdul Sanad Hamad was born in Jalalabad on 8 January 1929 and graduated from Nejat School in 1948. He then went to Switzerland for further study, obtaining a Ph.D. in law in 1957. In his early career in law, he was an associate professor in the Faculty of Law and Political Science at Kabul University from 1957 to 1965 and legal adviser to the Afghan parliament. He then moved into education, becoming deputy president of secondary education in the Ministry of Education from 1959 to 1960 and president from 1960 to 1963. Hamad was governor of Parwan Province from 1963 to 1964 and president of Kabul University from 1964 to 1965. During 1964, he was also a member of the drafting committee for the new constitution and a member of the Loya Jirga (Great Council) that approved its adoption in the same year. He held a number of other significant government appointments before becoming deputy prime minister and minister for tribal affairs from 1971 to 1972. He was a political prisoner in Pul-i Charkhi from November 1978 to 11 January 1980, accused of opposing the government, and on 15 March 1980, he left Afghanistan for exile in Germany.

References

Grover, Verinder. 2000. *Afghanistan: Government and Politics.* New Delhi: Deep and Deep Publications.

HAQ, ABDUL (1958–2001)

Abdul Haq was a Ahmadzai Pashtun from Nangarhar Province in southeast Afghanistan, from an affluent background, and would become a renowned mujahideen commander. As a student, he had affiliated with the Organization of Muslim Youth, which had opposed the reforming regime of President Muhammad Daud. He was imprisoned in 1975 for his activities and only freed after the Saur Revolt of April 1978, which brought the Communists to power. As a mujahideen commander, he was affiliated with the Islamic Party of Yunis Khales and operated in the area south of Kabul, from where he

Abdul Haq, renowned Pashtun mujahideen leader, captured by Taliban troops on 26 October 2001 while on a mission to foment opposition to the Taliban regime. Executed as an enemy of the state. (Reuters NewMedia Inc./CORBIS)

organized attacks on the capital. However, in 1987, he received injuries to a foot, which severely curtailed his participation in guerrilla raids. After the fall of the Marxist government in April 1992, he was appointed chief of police and security and commander of the gendarmerie, but he resigned from all his posts at the outbreak of civil war between the various mujahideen groups. Abdul Haq adopted a neutral position in the initial struggle between the Taliban and the forces of Burhanuddin Rabbani, turning his attention to trade with the Arabian gulf states. However, on 11 September 1992, Taliban forces captured Jalalabad, and he was forced to flee the country for Dubai and thence to London, from where he ran a successful import-export business.

In 1998, Abdul Haq became a UN peace mediator and helped to design the intra-Afghan dialogue process under the auspices of the U.S. Afghanistan Foundation. In the following year, his first wife and one of his sons were assassinated in Peshawar, Pakistan; it is claimed that the assassination was authorized by the Taliban. It was Haq's view that the Taliban could never be defeated by the Northern Alliance on its own and that it was necessary to secure support from the Pashtuns and to convene a *loya jirga* to secure a democratic future for Afghanistan. In October 2001, he returned secretly to Afghanistan as an emissary of the exiled king, Zahir Shah, in order to inform tribal elders about the peace process being mounted from Rome. He was captured by the Taliban with twenty of his followers and was executed on 26 October for treason and being a spy for Great Britain and the United States.

References
Joffe, Lawrence. "Abdul Haq: Veteran Afghan Leader Seeking Post-Taliban Consensus Rule." http://www.guardian.co.uk (cited 26 October 2001).

HAQANI, MAULAWI JAJALUDDIN (1930–)
Maulawi Jajaluddin Haqani was the deputy chief of the Islamic Party and joined the faction led by Yunis Khales after the break with Gulbuddin Hekmatyar in 1979. He drew support from his own Jadran tribe, and in 1979, he controlled large areas of Urgun in Paktia Province. Together with his brothers Abdul Haq and Abdul Qadir, he effectively controlled the Jalalabad Shura (council) that ruled Nangarhar Province, but after Jalalabad was captured by the Taliban in 1996, Haqani joined their ranks. He was born in 1930 in Paktia Province and educated in a private *madrasa* (religious school), before completing his studies in Peshawar, Pakistan.

See also Haq, Abdul; Khales, Yunis
References
Roy, Olivier. 1994. *From Holy War to Civil War.* Princeton, NJ: Princeton University Press.

HASHIM KHAN, MUHAMMAD (1886–1953)
Muhammad Hashim Khan was born in 1886, the son of Yaqub Khan and uncle of the former king Zahir; he also was a half brother of Nadir Shah. As commander of Amir Habibullah's bodyguard, he accompanied the amir on his visit to India in 1907. In 1916, he was appointed to a post in Herat Province. He became governor of Jalalabad in December 1919 and of the Eastern Province in 1920. He stood in for Gen. Nadir Khan at the Ministry of War in 1922 and was appointed ambassador to Moscow in 1924, holding the post for two years. On 9 November 1929, he was appointed prime minister and minister of the interior and was on a tour in the

northern provinces when Nadir Shah was assassinated. He retained the post of prime minister until 1946, having maintained Afghanistan's neutrality during World War II. He was regarded as a good administrator, but he was strict in his dealings with people, and he led an austere personal life. He died on 26 October 1953.

References

Dupree, Louis. 1980. *Afghanistan.* Princeton, NJ: Princeton University Press.

HASHT-NAFARI

Historically, the rulers of Afghanistan had always relied on support in the form of armed troops from the tribes to supplement their small forces in any major military campaign. Amir Abdul Rahman introduced this system of imposed recruitment within the frontier tribes in 1896 as a means of guaranteeing an adequate supply of soldiers. Under the system, tribes were required to provide one able-bodied man in eight for military service, hence the title of the system (*hasht* meaning "eight" and *nafar* meaning "persons"); chiefs or tribal elders were required to make the selection and to provide those selected with all their requirements. The system was accepted by the tribes during emergencies but was met with resistance at other times, often resulting in revolts against the recruitment. It was discontinued because of opposition from the tribes but was reintroduced in 1922 and was a factor in the growing opposition to King Amanullah. The system fell into disuse with the advent of a centrally recruited and paid armed force, which gradually developed into a modern corps with a regular army and air force. However, as was evidenced during the war against the Soviet occupation from 1979 to 1989, the civil war from 1989 to 2001, and the campaign against the Taliban from 1996 to 2001, the tradition among the tribes has remained active and effective, particularly in light of the breakdown of the kingdom into provinces and districts controlled by local warlords.

HATEF, ABDUR RAHIM (1926–)

Abdur Rahim Hatef was born in Kandahar in 1926 and is a member of the Takhi tribe. He was educated at Ahmad Shah Baba School, Habibia School, and the College of Letters at Kabul University. During Zahir Shah's reign (1933 to 1973), he was the head of the Kandahar Municipality, and he also held a variety of posts during President Muhammad Daud's rule (1973 to 1978). In 1985, he became president of the Loya Jirga (Great Council) in Kabul, and although not a party member, he became a member of the Revolutionary Council of the People's Democratic Party of Afghanistan (PDPA) in December 1985.

References

Ghani, Abdul. 1989. *A Brief Political History of Afghanistan.* Edited by Abdul Jaleel Nafji. Lahore, Pakistan: Najaf Publishers.

HAZARAJAT

The Hazarajat is a mountainous region in central Afghanistan that is predominantly inhabited by the Hazara people. The region incorporates the provinces of Bamian, Ghor, and Oruzgan and parts of the adjoining provinces. It became fully integrated into Afghanistan following a series of wars instigated by Amir Abdur Rahman from 1881 to 1883. However, it was not until 1893 that the region was fully subdued and under the total control of the Kabul government, which pursued a policy of repression to ensure that the Hazaras did not again revolt against the government. Large numbers of the population fled to Iran or Pakistan, and many hundreds were enslaved and forcibly removed to Kabul.

The region is dominated by the Koh-i-Baba range of mountains and its branches, with the peaks rising to altitudes from 9,000 to 16,500 feet and passes crossing the mountains at 8,000 to 10,000 feet. Roads capable of handling modern forms of transport are few in number. The main road from Kabul to Herat skirts the region, and the route from Kabul to Bamian and then east to Chaghcharan can only be negotiated by four-wheel-drive vehicles in the summer months.

The climate of the region is harsh, with long, cold winters that last from late September to April; heavy snowfall occurs from December to the onset of spring. The snows fill the reservoirs for the various rivers that rise in the Hazarajat and irrigate the rest of the country, and the summer months of July and August are dry and extremely hot. Although the region is rich in mineral deposits, most of these resources are in the inaccessible mountain areas and therefore not economically viable. During the history of Afghanistan, the region has been the scene of a great deal of conflict, and during the recent struggles against the Taliban, it was the scene of massacres perpetrated by Hazaras and Taliban alike.

See also Hazaras; Human Rights Violations
References
Amin, Hamidullah, and Gordon B. Schiltz. 1976. *A Geography of Afghanistan.* Omaha: University of Nebraska, Center for Afghan Studies.

HAZARAS

The Hazaras are Afghans with predominantly Mongoloid features who were originally Sunni Muslims until they were converted to the Shi'a Islam faith in the sixteenth century under the Safavid dynasty of Iran. A small number of them are Isma'ilis, and a number of Hazaras in the Panjshir district are still Sunni Muslims. Estimates as to the size of the Hazara population are difficult. The official estimates indicate a population of 1 million, but the Hazaras themselves claim to be 2 million in number in Afghanistan with an equal number living in adjacent lands, such as Iran and Pakistan.

The Hazara heartland is known as the Hazarajat, but the Hazaras are also found in the major cities of Afghanistan, where they take up employment as seasonal workers or day laborers. They speak a Farsi dialect called Hazaragi, which includes some Turkic and Mongol vocabulary. The Hazaras are largely a settled community and are no longer organized on tribal lines but are divided into groups. One such group, the Kala Nai Hazaras, are Sunni Muslims who claim descent from the hordes of Genghis Khan; they settled in Kala Nau, now Badghis Province, having been moved into the area under the Persian ruler Nadir Shah Afshar. As such, they were heavily involved in the struggle for Herat Province, collaborating with the rulers of Herat. However, their power in the province was broken by Wazir Yar Muhammad in 1847.

In 1856, the Persians invaded Herat Province and laid siege to the city of Herat, and after its fall, they forcibly relocated the Hazaras to Khorasan in Persia. After a fourteen-year exile, most of the tribe returned to Herat, but some 2,000 families remained in the Isfarayin area in present-day Iran. The tribe members supported the governor of Herat against Amir Dost Muhammad, and they were constantly in conflict with the Jamshidis and the Firuzkuhis. The Dai Mirdad Hazaras inhabit the area of Dara-i-Suf, which is now part of Samangan Province, and they are more like Pashtuns than Hazaras and dress like

Thousands of ethnic minority Afghanistan Hazaras attend a rally to welcome Hazara leader Karim Khalili in the capital of Kabul, 27 December 2001. (Reuters NewMedia Inc./CORBIS)

Tajiks or Uzbeks. Other groups include the Dai Kundi, the Dai Zangi, and the Ghazni Hazaras.

After the founding of the modern state of Afghanistan in 1747, the Hazaras were gradually incorporated into the state and paid taxes to the government in Kabul. However, they continued to live under independent or autonomous control of their tribal *mirs* (chiefs). It was not until the reign of Amir Abdur Rahman that the Hazaras were brought under the complete authority of the Kabul government following an intermittent war lasting from 1890 to 1893 and successfully waged by the amir's forces under Gen. Abdul Quddus.

The region of the Hazarajat suffered badly from this war and subsequent occupation. There was widespread destruction of the infrastructure and annexation of the territory by the Pashtun tribes. Many of the Hazaras were taken back to Kabul as slaves, with others fleeing from Afghanistan to Iran or India. Despite an amnesty that was declared when Amir Habibullah came to power, not all of the refugees were prepared to return, and many remained abroad, particularly in India; a large community still exists in Quetta, Pakistan. The accession of King Amanullah in 1919 brought an end to enslavement in Afghanistan, which won him support from the Hazara community. The people repaid the king by supporting him in his fight with Habibullah Kalakani in 1929.

In the first half of the twentieth century, the Hazarajat region was a neglected area in which public services and infrastructure were practically nonexistent. Today, no industry exists in the region, and the sole economic activity is farming and animal husbandry. For these economic reasons, the Hazaras have sought seasonal employment as low-grade civil servants, shopkeepers, artisans, factory workers, and unskilled laborers. It is estimated that in the 1960s, some 30 to 50 percent of the male population migrated to urban areas to seek employment, where they were considered to be on the lowest rung of the social order.

During the period of the Soviet occupation (1979–1989), the region was largely independent of Kabul. An elected *Shura* (council) was established under the leadership of Sayyid Ali Beheshti, and it effectively assumed all of the functions of the Kabul government. Beheshti levied taxes on the population, set up his own bureaucracy, and raised his own force of mujahideen. However, his authority was

challenged by the Islamists of Nasr and Parsdaran, who took over most of the region. In 1988, the Kabul government attempted to satisfy the aspirations of Hazara nationalism by creating the Hazara province of Sar-i-Pul, taking the districts of Charkant, Keshandekh, and Sozma Kala from Balkh Province and the district of Kohestant from Jozjan Province.

During the period of resistance to the Soviet presence and in the 1989–2001 civil war, the region was under the control of the Islamic Unity Party, which was supported by Iran but only to a modest degree due to the financial problems caused by the 1980–1988 Iraq-Iran War. Because of the breakdown in relations between Iran and the United States, no international aid reached the Hazara Shi'a mujahideen groups, particularly the Guardians of the Islamic Revolution. The result of Iranian funding meant that by 1982, Iranian influence had encouraged a younger generation of Islamic radicals, trained in Iran, who usurped the traditional leadership that had emerged to challenge the Soviet invasion in 1979. However, due to Iran's ideological policy in viewing loyalty to Tehran as more important than unity among the Hazaras, the various mujahideen groups fought more among themselves than with the Soviets.

However, by 1988, when a Soviet withdrawal appeared imminent, Iran recognized the need to strengthen its support for the Hazaras and brokered the union of seven mujahideen groups into the Islamic Unity Party (Hizb-i Wahdat). Iran also began to press for the Islamic Unity Party's inclusion in international talks to form a new mujahideen government. Further, although a small minority, the Iranians demanded a 50 percent share of the government for the Hazaras, subsequently reduced to 25 percent. The situation was complicated by the fact that rivalry with Saudi Arabia intensified, with the latter funding the spread of Wahhabism and anti-Shi'ism within Afghanistan.

The rivalry intensified further after the Soviet withdrawal when Iran recognized that the Kabul regime was the only force capable of resisting a Sunni Pashtun takeover of Afghanistan. As a consequence, Iran heavily rearmed the Islamic Unity Party, and by the time the mujahideen took over Kabul in 1992, the group had total control of the Hazarajat region and a significant section of western Kabul. The Iranian-backed group was further strengthened by the split between Gulbuddin Hekmatyar and Abdul Rasul Sayyaf, with Hekmatyar opposing the Kabul regime and joining with the Hazaras bombarding the city. The civil war between the mujahideen groups, which ran from 1992 to 1995, saw the rivalry between Iran and Saudi Arabia intensify, and although Saudi Arabia and Pakistan tried to maintain cohesion between the groups, they also tried to exclude Iran and the Hazaras from any potential agreements. Consequently, these groups were sidelined from the Islamabad and Jalalabad Accords.

In 1995, the Taliban appeared on the scene and gradually began to take over Afghanistan and were soon in a position to threaten Kabul. The forces of Ahmad Shah Masood in Kabul were being threatened by the Taliban and the Hazaras who occupied the southern suburbs, and Masood determined to remove the Hazara threat by launching an attack on 6 March 1995 with heavy armor, forcing them to retreat from Kabul. During the withdrawal, the Hazaras opened negotiations with the Taliban and agreed to hand over their positions and heavy weapons, but in the process, the Hazara leader Abdul Ali Mazari died while in Taliban custody. It was subsequently claimed by the Hazaras that Ali Mazari had been pushed out of a helicopter as he was resisting transfer to prison in Kandahar. Regardless of whether the death of their leader was accidental or deliberate, the event condemned the Taliban in the eyes of the Hazaras and of Iran. The incident was never forgotten or forgiven by the Hazaras and was to impact on future Hazara-Taliban relations.

After the fall of Kabul and the extension of Taliban control to the remainder of western Afghanistan, attention turned towards the north, which was the last stronghold of the anti-Taliban alliance. The main assault was to be against Mazar-i Sharif, which was under the control of Uzbek forces under Gen. Abdul Rashid Dostum but with a large Hazara population and mujahideen presence. The city had been relatively untouched by the conflict in Afghanistan, and it had become a secure haven for thousands of refugees who had fled the capital, Kabul, from 1992 onward. However, there was a bitter feud between Dostum and his second in command, Gen. Malik Pahlawan, and on 29 May 1987, Malik called for the assistance of the Taliban to oust Dostum.

After the Taliban had taken Mazar-i Sharif, they refused to share power with Malik and began to disarm the Uzbek and Hazara troops. They also imposed Shari'a law, shut down schools and the university, and drove women off the streets. In a city with a mix of religious and ethnic groups that had been the most open and liberal in Afghanistan, the Taliban actions were a prelude to disaster. On 28 May 1997, a group of Hazara troops refused to be disarmed, and the Hazara population in the city rose in revolt. The Taliban were not used to street fighting and lost some 600 troops killed in the streets and over 1,000 taken prisoner. The Hazaras also raised the siege on the Hazarajat, and Taliban forces at the mouth of the Bamian Valley were pushed back south. Other actions initiated by the forces of Ahmad Shah Masood also inflicted heavy defeats on the Taliban, marking the worst period of their history since they began the takeover of Afghanistan

The series of military attacks and counterattacks also unleashed other hatreds and the desire for revenge, with the Taliban massacring some seventy Shi'a Hazaras in the village of Qazil Abad on their retreat from Mazar-i Sharif, though the figure could have been much higher. Evidence also exists of massacres of Taliban prisoners by Hazara forces, with the discovery of mass graves at Sheberghan in Jozjan Province containing some 2,000 bodies. This incident was confirmed by UN investigators, who also found that the prisoners had been starved and tortured before being killed. The whole struggle in the north of Afghanistan was marked by ethnic cleansing and religious persecution, and no group was innocent.

As mentioned, the Hazarajat region of central Afghanistan, the country of the Hazaras, had been under siege by the Taliban, and by 1998, the majority of the people were starving due to crop failures and the Taliban siege; the Taliban had closed the roads leading north and were refusing to allow the World Food Program (WFP) to deliver aid. Relief could not be delivered from the north, as roads and winter snows blocked mountain passes. As Shi'as, the Hazaras were considered by the Taliban to be hypocrites and beyond redemption as followers of the true Islam. This attitude was further reinforced by the fact that Hazara women were playing a significant role in the politics, economy, social life, and defense of the region. However, the Hazaras had overstretched themselves, and interfactional disputes also broke out with other groups, such as the fighting between the Hazaras and the forces of General Dostum in February 1998.

The Taliban waited while the forces of the anti-Taliban alliance fought among themselves, and in March 1989, they launched an offensive against the north with the backing of Pakistan and Saudi Arabia. As far as the Hazaras were concerned, the major engagement came on 8 August 1989 when Uzbek commanders guarding the road to Mazar-i Sharif accepted bribes to let Taliban forces through. The Hazara forces found themselves surrounded. Out of a total of 1,500, only 100 Hazaras survived, having fought until their ammunition ran out. The Taliban forces then embarked on an orgy of violence to take revenge for their losses of the previous year.

The massacre was initially indiscriminate, with pickup trucks driving up and down the streets and killing everything that moved. Bodies were left where they had fallen, and no burials were allowed for six days. However, the genocide soon became targeted against the Hazaras. Pashtun guides were used to target Hazara households, whose occupants were then massacred; women were raped, and thousands were taken to the Mazar jail, locked into containers, and left to suffocate. In all, it is estimated that some 5,000 to 6,000 Hazaras were killed, with the objective of cleansing northern Afghanistan of the Shi'a population.

Further instances of actions directed against the Hazara population included an incident at Robatak Pass on the road between the towns of Tashqurgham and Pul-i-Khumri, which took place in May 2000. No final figure exists of the number massacred, but twenty-six bodies were identified as Hazara civilians from Baghlan Province. At least three other burial sites have been identified, and it is thought that these contained the bodies of prisoners taken in January 2000 by the Taliban commander Mullah Shahzad Kandahari. A Human Rights Watch investigation was unable to confirm the number of dead, for it looked as if some of the evidence had been removed.

Another massacre took place at Yakaolang in January 2001 when Taliban forces advanced from Bamian, using Feroz Bahar as a base for a three-pronged assault. After anti-Taliban forces retreated, the Taliban began a systematic search of the district in an effort to kill Hazaras, including two occasions on which Hazara elders who were trying to negotiate security for their villages were slain. Some of those killed were workers from a local relief agency and staffers from the local hospital and a leprosy clinic. Other Hazara civilians were slaughtered when the Taliban troops were forced to retreat by Shi'a mujahideen fighters.

The ethnic cleansing of the Hazaras by the Taliban was a more intensive action than previous incidents in Afghanistan's history, but it is another chapter in the persecution of the Hazara population. However, in the post-Taliban era, there are reports that the Hazaras themselves are engaged in ethnic cleansing through the expulsion of Pashtun families who had moved into the Hazarajat.

See also Beheshti, Sayyid Ali; Guardians of the Islamic Revolution; Hazarajat; Human Rights Violations; Jamshidi Tribe; Quddus, Abdul

References

Canfield, Robert Leroy.1977. *Hazara Integration into the Afghan Nation: Some Changing Relations between Hazaras and Afghan Officials*. New York: Afghan Council of Asia Society.

"Hazaras of Afghanistan." 2002. http://www.afghan-network.net/Ethnic-Groups/hazaras.html (cited 7 February 2002).

Mousavi, Sayed Askar. 1998. *The Hazaras of Afghanistan: An Historical, Cultural, Economic, and Political Study*. London: Curzon.

Poladi, Hassan. 1989. *The Hazaras*. Stockton, CA: Mughal Publishing.

HEKMATYAR, GULBUDDIN (1947–)

Gulbuddin Hekmatyar is of Khoroti Ghilzai origin and was a student at the Engineering Faculty of Kabul University, where he was active in student affairs between 1970 and 1972. He was imprisoned in the Dehmazang jail from 1972 to 1973 for opposition to the government. Following the coup staged by Muhammad Daud on 17 July 1973, he was released from prison, but in May of the next year, he was accused of leading a coup himself and was forced to go into hiding. In 1975, he became a member of the Islamic Party mujahideen group, and he was made secretary-general and then leader of the group in December 1978.

During the battles against the Soviets and the Afghan government from 1979 to 1989, he was the most powerful warlord and received the bulk of the support from the United States, channeled through Pakistan. Hekmatyar was favored by the Inter-Services Intelligence Service of Pakistan, which controlled the distribution of resources. His mujahideen group was the most destructive and antisocial unit, carrying out a number of terrorist attacks in Afghanistan. After the mujahideen took control of Kabul in 1992, Hekmatyar began to attack the government of Burhanuddin Rabbani and the forces of Ahmad Shah Masood. However, in March 1996, he reached an agreement with Rabbani to jointly defend Kabul against the Taliban. A peace accord was agreed to between the two leaders on 24 May, which called for new elections and the creation of a real Islamic government.

On 26 June 1996, Hekmatyar became prime minister in Rabbani's government and introduced Islamic measures, such as the banning of cinemas and the requirement that women dress modestly. However, the moves did not mirror the Taliban program of work and educational restrictions for women or the forcing of men to grow beards to secure employment and receive government services. After the fall of Kabul to the Taliban in 1996, Hekmatyar fled to Iran and called for a jihad against the United States in November 2001. The Iranians closed his offices in February 2002, and he was compelled to leave for Afghanistan by way of Pakistan.

Hekmatyar is considered a ruthless extremist, and he has opposed both the Northern Alliance and the Taliban. However, some conjecture that he might be trying to form an alliance with the remnants of the Taliban and al-Qaeda. He has now become overtly hostile to the United States, which he views as an enemy of Islam, and vehemently opposes the U.S. role in Afghanistan. It is reported that in May 2002, the Central Intelligence Agency (CIA) attempted his assassination, using a missile fired from an unmanned Predator aircraft in an attack near Kabul. The mission failed because Hekmatyar was not located, but a number of his key aides were killed.

The attack has been justified on the basis of intelligence that showed Hekmatyar had planned to strike against the Interim Government and possibly President Hamid Karzai himself. In March 2002, Hekmatyar's party announced that it had sent representatives to Kabul to try to resolve differences with the Karzai administration, but in the following month, hundreds of Hekmatyar's supporters were arrested in Kabul because of an alleged plot to overthrow Karzai and to mount a bombing campaign in the capital. Hekmatyar's continuing involvement in actions against the Karzai government and the U.S. presence in Afghanistan was confirmed by the fighting that began on 28 January 2003 between U.S. and

Afghan forces and about eighty fighters allied to Hekmatyar near Spin Boldak in southeastern Afghanistan, close to the Pakistan border. These fighters were thought to be part of an alliance between the followers of Hekmatyar and vestiges of the Taliban known as the Islamic Martyrs Brigade, who were being trained as suicide squads to act against U.S. and Karzai government targets in Afghanistan. In the fighting, eighteen of the rebel forces were reported as killed, with no Coalition casualties. U.S. airpower was also called up to attack cave complexes in the area being used by the rebel forces.

On 19 February 2003, Hekmatyar was designated as a global terrorist by the United States. He responded in a signed statement released by an officer from his Islamic Party in Afghanistan in which he expressed pride at being branded a terrorist. At the same time, he advocated suicide attacks against Americans by Muslims throughout the world. It is thought that Hekmatyar is constantly on the move between the provinces of Kapsia, Nangarhar, Laghman, and Kunar, all of which border Pakistan. It is also clear that he still has support from members of Islamic political parties in Pakistan, particularly the Islamist Movement that controls the North-West Frontier Province. Also, many of the intelligence officers within Pakistan's Inter-Services Intelligence unit sympathize with Hekmatyar, having befriended and supported him during the mujahideen war against the Soviets.

See also Civil War; Inter-Services Intelligence Service; Islamic Society of Afghanistan; Rabbani, Burhanuddin

References
Hekmatyar, Gulbuddin. 1998. *Clues to the Solution of the Afghan Crisis.* Peshawar, Pakistan: Directorate of International Affairs.

HELMAND PROVINCE

Helmand is the largest of the Afghan provinces, with a population of some 570,000 and an area of 23,058 square miles in southwestern Afghanistan. The population is largely Pashtun, though there are some Baluchs in the south of the province and Hazaras in the north. The capital is Lashkargal, which has a population of just under 22,000. The economy of the province is based on agriculture—growing cereals, cotton, and fruit and raising a variety of livestock. The area is irrigated by the Helmand River, which is also used to provide hydroelectric power.

The river and its course have been, in the past, a source of conflict with Iran, and the change of channels, to improve irrigation for Afghan farmers in the province, called earlier agreements with Iran into question. The situation was not resolved until the Helmand Water Treaty of 1973 with Iran, ratified by Afghanistan in 1979.

The irrigation and electrification project in the Helmand Valley was established using the Tennessee Valley Authority in the United States as a model; it is run by the Helmand Valley Authority. The authority worked closely with the Morrison Knudsen Afghanistan construction company from Boise, Idaho, which, from 1946 to 1959, built the Arghandab and Kajakai Dams, together with a network of canals to increase cultivation in the Helmand Valley.

However, the project consumed so much of Afghanistan's hard-currency resources that the government had to apply for loans of $21 million in 1951 and $18 million in 1953 from the U.S. Import-Export Bank, followed by Point Four Assistance aid. The project was completed in 1959 at a cost of $100 million, but it netted only modest gains for the country. The lack of a comprehensive soil survey of the area brought subsequent problems, with some areas becoming waterlogged and others experiencing increased levels of salination. The shortcomings of the scheme also caused displacement of about 1,300 nomads and peasant farmers that had been settled in the Nad-i-Ali area. The authority had to take remedial measures to alleviate the problems, and these efforts were given further financial support from the United States in order to restore its prestige in the country, which had been damaged by the project.

See also Goldsmid Award

References

Adamec, Ludwig W. 1972–1985. *Historical and Political Gazetteer of Afghanistan.* 6 vols. Graz, Austria: Akademische Druck-u Verlagsansalt.

Stevens, I. M., and K. Tarzi. 1965. *Economies of Agricultural Production in Helmand Valley, Afghanistan.* Denver, CO: U.S. Department of Interior, Bureau of Reclamation.

HENTIG-NIEDERMAYER EXPEDITION (1915–1916)

The Hentig-Niedermayer Expedition was planned by the German General Staff in August 1914, with the objectives of stirring up a revolution in British India, encouraging Afghanistan to attack India, and securing Iran as a link between the Ottoman Empire and Afghanistan. Werner Otto von Hentig was a diplomat who had served in Iran, and Oskar von Niedermayer was a captain in the German army; the rest of the expeditionary group comprised a Turkish officer, two Indian revolutionaries, and a number of Pashtuns released from a prisoner-of-war camp. Hentig was charged with forming an alliance with Afghanistan and establishing diplomatic relations, whereas Niedermayer was to pursue military cooperation backed by messages from the Sultan Caliph and the Ottoman government. The Indian revolutionaries were present to obtain Amir Habibullah's support for a fight against the British in India.

The expedition arrived overland from Iran, reaching Kabul in September 1915. The amir, although loyal to the Sultan Caliph, was well aware of the British position in India and unwilling to risk an all-out confrontation with no guarantee of success, so he initialed an agreement whose military and financial demands could only be met if Germany won World War I. In May 1916, the expedition came to an end. Hentig returned to Germany through China and the United States, and Niedermayer returned through Iran and the Ottoman Empire and resumed his service in the German army. Although the expedition did not achieve its real objectives, it marked the first diplomatic contact between Afghanistan and Germany and the end of the British monopoly over Afghanistan's external affairs.

See also Habibullah, Amir

References

Vogel, Renate. 1976. *Die Persien und Afghanistan expedition: Oskar Ritter Von Niedermayer, 1915–16.* (The Persian and Afghanistan expedition: Oskar Ritter Von Niedermayer, 1915–16). Osnabruck, Germany: Biblio-Verlag.

HERAT PROVINCE

Herat Province, in northwestern Afghanistan, has a population of about 650,000 and occupies an area of 16,603 square miles. The capital is Herat, which is the third largest city in Afghanistan and has about 140,000 inhabitants. The economy is largely based on arable and pastoral agriculture, and the presence of four rivers and underground water channels enables extensive irrigation to be carried out.

The city of Herat is the major commercial center of western Afghanistan and also of great strategic importance; as such, it has been a fortified town since its early history around 1500 B.C. The city has always played a leading role in conflict in Afghanistan, having been on the route of the armies of Darius, Alexander the Great, and Genghis Khan. As a consequence, the city has often been destroyed and the population decimated. After each destruction, the city has been rebuilt, seen periods of great prosperity, and been regarded as a renowned center for literature and art in the central and western Asian region.

Herat was at the core of conflicts in the region from the sixteenth through eighteenth centuries, and in the latter part of the nineteenth century, it was ruled by a number of princes whose constant struggles so weakened the province that it became a target for Persian attack. In 1837, the city was besieged by the Safavid ruler Muhammad Shah, but the resistance of the inhabitants and British counteraction in the Persian Gulf caused the siege to be abandoned after nine months. The province was only brought under total control of the Afghan government during the reign of Amir Abdul Rahman (1880 to 1901), and at that time, Herat was a walled city with some 20,000 inhabitants. Construction of a new town began in 1925 under King Amanullah, and the population steadily grew to its present size. The civil war in Afghanistan caused considerable destruction in the capital and in the province as a whole following a popular revolt against the government in March 1979. Thereafter, the city remained under government control, but large areas of the province were dominated by the mujahideen until the Taliban seized power in 1995.

See also Hazaras; Human Rights Violations; Isma'il Khan

References
Adamec, Ludwig W. 1972–1985. *Historical and Political Gazetteer of Afghanistan*. 6 vols. Graz, Austria: Akademische Druck-u Verlagsansalt.
Matthai, James. 1966. *A Geographical Introduction to Herat Province*. Kabul: Faculty of Education, University of Kabul.

HIJRAT MOVEMENT

The Hijrat Movement, also known as the Khilafat Movement, was an emigration drive that emerged in the North-West Frontier Province of India among Indian Muslims in 1920. The movement was a reaction to the breakup of the Ottoman Empire following World War I as Indian Muslims recognized the sultan of Turkey's office of caliph and his spiritual leadership of the Sunni Islamic world. The leader of the movement, Muhammad Ali, preached that it was the Islamic duty of Indian Muslims to leave a country administered by a sacrilegious government and to move to an Islamic state. King Amanullah encouraged the movement, for he hoped to attract professionals and skilled workers to assist with his modernization program. Some 18,000 Indian Muslims crossed into Afghanistan, but the bulk of them were poor and unskilled workers who found it difficult to settle there. Some immigrants established themselves in the areas around Kunduz and Balkh and some made their way to the Soviet Union and Europe, but the majority returned to India.

References
Gregorian, Vartan. 1969. *The Emergence of Modern Afghanistan: Politics of Reform and Modernization, 1880–1946*. Stanford, CA: Stanford University Press.

HINDU KUSH

The Hindu Kush is a major mountain massif that originates in the southwest corner of the Pamirs and runs the entire length of central Afghanistan before becoming the Koh-i-Baba. Mountains in the range generally rise between 14,500 and 17,000 feet, but many peaks exceed 20,000 feet. Although it is crossed by passes at altitudes of 12,000 feet, the Hindu Kush still constitutes a formidable obstacle between the north and the south of the country. The range is divided into three major sections: in the east from the Pamirs to the Darah Pass, in the center from the Darah Pass to the Khawak Pass, and in the west from the Khawak Pass to where the range terminates at the Shibar Pass. The term *Hindu Kush*, of uncertain origin, is not generally used by Afghans, who instead prefer local names for the area in which they live.

In the winter, heavy snowfall on the mountains seals off northern Afghanistan from the rest of the country. The nature of the terrain has led to small populations surviving in remote, marginal valleys with subsistence levels of agricultural activity. Due to poor communications and the lack of a government presence in the area, these groups enjoyed a measure of autonomy, and there was extensive linguistic and cultural diversity. However, the construction of an all-weather highway and the Salang Tunnel in 1964 led to more centralized control over

Travelers on a highway near Hindu Kush (Carl and Ann Purcel/Corbis)

northern Afghanistan. Together, the tunnel and the highway became a strategic artery for the Soviet Union in supplying the Marxist government in Kabul and its own forces between 1979 and 1989, and as a result, the route was subjected to frequent attacks by the mujahideen, especially the forces of Ahmad Shah Masood.

References

Amin, Hamidullah, and Gordon B. Schiltz. 1976. *A Geography of Afghanistan.* Omaha: University of Nebraska at Omaha, Center for Afghan Studies.

HOSHIMIAN, SAYYID KALILULLAH (1929–)

An academic at Kabul University, Sayyid Kalilullah Hoshimian was involved with, among others, Muhammad Kakar and Faze Rabbi Pazhwak in the translation of "night letters" into English. These letters were being distributed to Russians, Afghan Communists, and Third World embassies and contained threats to destabilize the regime from elements who opposed the Marxist government in Kabul and the Soviet occupation. They were always delivered at night, hence their name.

Hoshimian was born in Kabul in 1929, a son of Sayyid Muhammad Sarwar, who was a Kunari, and

his Muhammadzai wife. He was educated in the fields of language and literature, obtaining a B.A. degree in the Dari language at Kabul University in 1964 and both an M.A. in linguistics and a Ph.D. in education from Indiana State University. He entered the Afghan foreign service in 1947 and became second secretary at the Afghan embassy in London in 1951 but resigned his position after marrying a British citizen two years later. He then became traffic manager for Ariana Airlines, from 1955 to 1957, and then returned to his academic career in Afghanistan.

In 1964, he became a lecturer in the Faculty of Letters at Kabul University. Six years later, he was elected to the Kabul University Commission, with a view to suing the government for police assaults that took place at the university in that year. Hoshimian became a professor of linguistics in 1979 and was coordinator of the linguistics section from 1979 to 1980. His work on the "night letters" spanned the period from 1979 to 1981, but, fearing discovery of his covert activities, he resigned from the university in 1981 and left for the United States in 1982.

See also Pazhwak, Faze Rabbi

References
Roy, Olivier. 1986. *Islam and Resistance in Afghanistan.*
London and New York: Cambridge University Press.

HUMAN RIGHTS VIOLATIONS

The twenty-three years of war in Afghanistan (from 1979 to 2002) were marked by human rights violations, with all participants in the conflicts being guilty to a greater or lesser degree. In the period of the Soviet occupation from 1979 to 1989, both sides set aside the normal rules of war, with Soviet and government forces pursuing a scorched-earth policy and collective punishments and the mujahideen guilty of torturing Soviet prisoners of war.

However, by far the worst period of atrocities began with the outbreak of the civil war between the mujahideen groups in 1992 after the fall of the Communist government. In this period, all parties were responsible for egregious violations of human rights. Such violations continued throughout the civil war, through the period of Taliban rule, and, to a lesser degree, in the period following the defeat of the Taliban. A large number of incidents were interrelated or interdependent, but for ease of considerations, these will be treated here according to the record of the two main antagonists.

Northern Alliance–United Front

The inhabitants of the city of Kabul suffered badly during the period of mujahideen rule and the struggle between mujahideen groups for control of the capital. Among the recorded atrocities was the assault of the forces of Abdul Rasul Sayyaf and Burhanuddin Rabbani on 11 February 1993 in the western area of Kabul, which resulted in the killing or "disappearance" of ethnic Hazara civilians and widespread rape and looting. Accurate figures are not possible to obtain, but the estimated number of deaths ranges from 70 to more than 100. In the following year, at least 25,000 civilians were killed in Kabul as a result of rocket and artillery attacks, with the rule of law having ceased to exist. In the city, all the warring factions were guilty of summary executions, arbitrary arrests, torture, "disappearances," and rape.

In March 1995, the forces of Ahmad Shah Masood captured the district of Karte Seh in Kabul, an area primarily inhabited by Hazaras; they systematically looted the area and raped indiscriminately. Further abuses in Kabul were also noted in January 1997 when forces of Gen. Abdul Rashid Dostum dropped cluster bombs on the residential area of Kabul, causing widespread civilian casualties. A similar incident occurred between 20 and 21 September 1988 when the forces of Masood fired several volleys of rockets into the northern part of Kabul, with one hitting a busy night market. Accurate casualty figures are not available, but it has been estimated that between 76 and 180 civilians were killed.

In northern Afghanistan, some 3,000 Taliban soldiers were summarily executed in and around the city of Mazar-i Sharif in May 1997 by the forces of General Dostum. This incident followed Uzbek Gen. Abdul Malik's withdrawal from an alliance with the Taliban and the subsequent capture of Taliban forces trapped in the city. A number of Taliban prisoners were transported into the desert, shot, and buried in mass graves; others were thrown down wells, which were then blown up with grenades.

Toward the end of 1999 and in early 2000, internally displaced Afghans from the district of Sangcharak, which had been held by United Front forces for some four months, related accounts of summary executions, the burning of houses and villages, and widespread beatings and looting. In the main, the victims were ethic Pashtuns who were suspected of being sympathetic to the Taliban. Since the fall of the Taliban, there have also been reports of Tajiks and Uzbeks conducting ethnic cleansing of the Pashtun minority in areas of northern Afghanistan controlled by Uzbek and Tajik warlords. This violence against Pashtun communities in northern Afghanistan has been cited by the U.S.-based group Human Rights Watch, whose report on the subject was issued on 8 April 2002. The Northern Alliance forces had been wreaking vengeance on the minority Pashtun communities in return for Taliban atrocities committed against non-Pashtuns in the north between 1997 and 2001. The report details cases of beatings, abductions, looting, summary executions, and rape between November 2001, when the Northern Alliance regained control over the area, and March 2002. Although it has been acknowledged that President Hamid Karzai wants to improve human rights in Afghanistan, the capacity of the central government to act is limited because of the power of the regional warlords.

Taliban

The Taliban regime in Afghanistan was based on a strict interpretation of Shari'a law, and this impacted on the non-Taliban population, especially women. An early indication of the nature of Taliban rule came in September 1996 following the capture of Kabul. The former president Muhammad Najibullah was dragged from the UN compound, where he had sought refuge in 1992, and was castrated, dragged behind a pickup truck around the royal palace, and then shot. His brother was also tortured and throttled to death, and both bodies were hung in public. Severe repressive measures were imposed against women: they were banned from working, banned from schools, forbidden to leave home unless accompanied by a close male relative, and forced to cover themselves from head to foot when not in their homes. As a result of these actions, many more women who had been widowed by the war and had dependent children became destitute. It was also more difficult for aid workers to assist the population because male aid workers were forbidden from making contact with women and female workers were banned from working with the aid agencies. Beatings were also meted out to men for failing to grow beards or for possession of music cassettes, videos, and televisions, all of which had been banned by the Taliban.

A number of atrocities were recorded during the Taliban campaign to conquer the remainder of Afghanistan after the fall of Kabul in 1996. In January 1998 in Fariab Province, the Taliban massacred around 600 Uzbek villagers, who were dragged from their homes, lined up, and gunned down. In August 1998, there was an even worse massacre at Mazar-i Sharif after the city was retaken by the Taliban, with between 2,000 and 5,000 men, women, and children murdered. The Taliban had carried out a systematic search of the city for male members of the ethnic Hazara, Tajik, and Uzbek communities, and hundreds (mainly Hazaras) were summarily executed, almost certainly in revenge for the massacre of Taliban forces in 1997. Other reports detailed the rape or abduction of women and girls during the taking of the city.

The Taliban were guilty of two other atrocities in 1999. In the first incident, summary executions were carried out when Bamian was captured. Hundreds of men and some women and children were separated from their families, taken away, and executed; all of them were noncombatants. In addition, houses were razed to the ground, and some detainees were used for forced labor. The second incident took place in July 1999 in the Shomali Plains, when summary executions, the abduction of women, and the destruction of homes, property, and the orchards of the farmers marked the Taliban assault. In these and other actions, the Taliban did not distinguish between combatants and civilians.

The Shi'a of the north, who were Hazaras, were regarded by the Sunni Taliban as inferior, and this was reflected in their treatment. In May 2000, a massacre took place at Robatak Pass in the Hazarajat region, with 31 bodies found in one mass grave, 26 of whom were positively identified as civilians. In August 2000, prisoners of war were executed in the streets of Herat as an example to the local population. Another massacre of the Hazaras took place at Yearling, beginning on 8 January 2001 and lasting four days. At least 300 male civilians were detained by the Taliban, including staff of local humanitarian agencies; they were taken to assembly points and executed by firing squads in full public view. At least 170 of those detained were confirmed killed. Taliban soldiers also killed at least 70 women, children, and elderly men who had taken shelter in a mosque that was deliberately destroyed by rocket fire. In June of the same year, the administrative center of the town was also bombed, resulting in the decimation of the district hospital and an aid agency office.

Other reports detailed the atrocities committed during the Taliban's fourteen-month occupation of Taloqan, former headquarters of the Northern Alliance; there, mutilations, beatings, summary executions, and the torture of children for the sins of their parents were carried out. Other reports cited beatings of civilians who refused to parade in the streets to demonstrate against the U.S. bombings of Kabul. In Kunduz on 18 November 2001, just before its fall, 8 boys were shot dead for daring to laugh at Taliban soldiers, and at least 300 Taliban soldiers were killed by non-Afghan fighters from their own side because they wished to surrender. Additionally, Tajik and Uzbek men in Taloqan were shot on suspicion of trying to escape to territory held by the Northern Alliance.

However, it must be noted that the Afghan ideas as to how people should behave toward each other often clash with Western concepts of human rights. Afghan society does have codes of behavior, which represent a fusion of Islam and tribal values. But for Afghanistan to develop a code of human rights in the Western sense, several factors must be present: a fair and efficient judicial system must be in place, a police system must be established, and an Afghan national army with respect for human rights must be set up; the latter would necessarily exclude commanders.

See also Civil War; Hazaras; Mazar-i Sharif; Taliban

References

Coalition Information Centre. 2001. "Fact Sheet: Al-Qaeda and Taliban Atrocities." http://www.usinfo.state.gov/regional/nea/sasia/afghan/fact/1123tlbn (cited 22 November 2001).

"Examination of Human Rights Violations." 2000. http://www.ishr.ch/About%20UN/Reports%20 Analysis/Sub%2053%20.%20examination.htm (cited 12 February 2002).

"Genocide in Afghanistan." 1991. http://www.members.tripod.com/MillateHazara/ (cited 12 February 2002).

Human Rights Watch. 1991. Afghanistan, the Forgotten War: Human Rights Abuses and Violation of the Laws of War since the Soviet Withdrawal. New York: Human Rights Watch.

Krushelnycky, Askold. 2002. "Afghanistan: Human Rights Abuses Threaten Peace Process." http://www/rferl.org/nca/features/2002/04/11042002083542.asp (cited 11 April 2002).

"Repeated Massacres of Hazaras." 2002. http://www.members.tripod.com/MillateHazara (cited 11 February 2003).

Samad, Omar. 1999. "UN Rapporteur Tells of 'Evidence of Widespread Human Rights Violations' by Taliban; Accuses 'External Forces' of Interference and Calls for Total Comprehensive Solution." http://www.afghanvoice.org/ARTICLES/SAMAD.shtml (cited 12 February 2003).

http://www.rferl.org

HUMANITARIAN AIRDROPS

At the time of the Coalition action against Afghanistan in 2001, the humanitarian situation was critical as a result of war, drought, and the internal displacement of the population. The situation inside Afghanistan was not helped by the fact that the Taliban–Northern Alliance war and Operation Enduring Freedom made aid distribution difficult, as the UN World Food Program and the nongovernmental organizations (NGOs) were unable to arrange safe passage for their vehicles and personnel. The approach of winter also impacted adversely on the relief operations.

U.S. president George Bush decided that the Department of Defense should organize airdrops of humanitarian rations to refugees inside Afghanistan. The rations packs were to be mostly vegetarian, with added vitamins, and provide enough calories for one adult for one day. The rations had been developed following the U.S. experience in providing for Kurdish refugees in Iraq after the Gulf War and for displaced populations in Somalia. The rations were wrapped in plastic packaging that allowed them to float down, thus avoiding the need to drop pallets by parachute. The goals were to allow for a wide distribution of the brightly colored ration packs and to avoid fights among recipients over pallets of food.

The airdrops were organized from U.S. air bases in Germany using C-17 Globemaster III aircraft. The first drop took place on 7 October 2001 and delivered 35,000 daily ration packs. The flights were made under combat conditions, following U.S. bombing raids of Taliban and terrorist targets inside Afghanistan. They represented a major logistical effort, as the missions lasted twenty-two hours, entailed multiple refuelings in the air, and were made over a war zone. The rations were dropped over northern and eastern Afghanistan, with the drop zones determined by the needs of the people in the area while also taking into account potential threats and the weather conditions to try to ensure accuracy and minimize the risk to the recipients. Each load was released using specially made container systems that were tied to static lines that tightened and turned the containers over once they were clear of the aircraft. The containers then opened, and the rations were spread over the drop zone. The individual packs each contained 2,200-calorie, ready-to-eat rations; a typical pack consisted of two vegetarian meals, based on lentils and beans or rice, together with bread, a fruit bar, a biscuit, peanut butter, and spices.

The packages were all marked with the legend "Food gift from the people of the United States of America" in the hope that this would persuade the Afghan population that the war was being waged against the Taliban and terrorists, not the ordinary citizen. The case, however, proved difficult to make because U.S. bombing raids had almost destroyed a residential area on the outskirts of Kabul and because, on two separate occasions, a warehouse used by the International Red Cross in Kabul had been bombed in error. The program was also criticized by some relief organizations as confusing to the Afghan people and, in a country where 7.5 million people

A group of Afghan children collecting packets of food aid after a U.S. aircraft completed a night time air drop over a refugee camp in Kumkishlyak in Northern Afghanistan, 25 October 2001. (Reuters NewMedia Inc./CORBIS)

were at risk of starvation, totally inadequate. The groups argued for the suspension of bombing raids to allow distribution of food, medicine, and other supplies on the ground before the onset of the Afghan winter, which would close many of the roads and all of the high passes in the mountains.

The whole operation for each drop was an extremely complex affair, for the United States had to obtain permission to overfly a group of countries, such as Georgia, Turkmenistan, and Uzbekistan, for the Globemaster aircraft and their fighter escorts. In addition, refueling operations had to be put in place, and airborne warning and control system (AWACS) missions had to be flown to provide the command and control needed to direct each mission. Due to problems over Afghanistan, aircraft had to fly at 25,000 feet to avoid Taliban antiaircraft fire, which caused health risks to the crews who were exposed to decompression sickness during the process of dropping the supplies; thus, medical staff had to be dispatched with all air crews.

Despite the difficulties and shortcomings of the program, operations continued on a daily basis,

and between 7 and 24 October 2001, 785,000 ration packages were delivered. The whole project was threatened by intelligence reports indicating that the Taliban were prepared to poison the packages and to lay the blame on the United States. However, the operations continued, and by 16 November, nearly 1.6 million packages had been dropped, with daily deliveries varying between 35,000 and 75,000 packages. The total effectiveness of the program had been questioned by the various aid agencies, as mentioned. Moreover, television coverage has shown packages being collected by groups of fighters in pickup trucks, as well as packages being offered for sale in local markets, though this says more about the situation in Afghanistan than about the motives of the United States. The airdrop operations ceased on 21 December 2001 due to the ability of the Coalition, the United Nations, and the NGOs to get relief into Afghanistan by road, rail, and river.

References

United Nations. 2002. "Immediate and Transitional Assistance for the Afghan People, 2002: Updated

Financial Requirements." http://www.reliefweb.int (cited 12 March 2002).

HUMANITARIAN RELIEF

The humanitarian crisis in Afghanistan developed rapidly after the Soviet invasion in 1979 and the rise of the mujahideen opposition, swelling the ranks of refugees and internally displaced persons. However, there was a lack of international interest in Afghanistan's social problems and an ignorance of how the country was coping with the complete collapse of society and the infrastructure of the state. Initially, thousands of aid workers were attracted to Afghanistan and were prepared to endure hardship and danger in order to bring aid to embattled communities, with the emphasis on medical aid. In the first few years of the Soviet occupation, there seems to have been an innocence among the aid workers who went to Afghanistan for altruistic reasons without any knowledge of the political realities of the situation there, but this gradually disappeared as the 1980s wore on and aid became less a gesture of solidarity with the Afghan people and more a matter of politics.

It is also questionable whether the administration in Afghanistan had ever seen providing for the social welfare of the population as part of its role, notwithstanding Islamic rules and tradition in this regard. Throughout the struggle against the Soviets, the mujahideen were never noted for giving social issues a priority, and the burgeoning aid community seemed to soak up funds without showing much evidence of a deliverable service. It is also clear that funding for the various nongovernmental organizations (NGOs) owed a great deal to the West's political objective of supporting the mujahideen guerrillas in order to eject the Soviets from Afghanistan. In addition, the period of the Soviet occupation was characterized by widespread corruption and the diversion of aid to local mujahideen commanders. Aid workers also queried why greater pressure was not brought to bear on Afghanistan's neighbors to create the external conditions necessary for peace, especially as many of them were paying a high price for the disintegration of Afghanistan: smuggling, corruption, drug addiction, and terrorism were also affecting their own states.

In the early 1990s, the delivery of aid was also beset by problems, especially after the collapse of the mujahideen government in 1992 and the subsequent resumption of fighting among the various factions. The aid agencies tried to reassert principles of impartiality and neutrality, but the breakdown of security in Afghanistan made it difficult for them to establish space for humanitarian programs in the midst of widespread anarchy. The problems were exacerbated by the insecurity of road communications, with various mujahideen groups fighting over control of sections of road in order to extort tolls from travelers, including representatives of aid agencies. The humanitarian agencies also attempted to develop programs that were longer-term in nature and based on reconstruction and development, with the aim of facilitating the return of refugees from Iran and Pakistan. As a result, programs came to rely less on handouts to mujahideen commanders and more on improved connections with local communities, which led to a better aid program, though it was often tinged with a Western human rights agenda that was objectionable to radical Islamic mujahideen parties; nevertheless, they were willing to cooperate with the aid agencies.

The rise of the Taliban in 1994 and their strict interpretation of Shari'a law caused even more problems for aid agencies, especially with the edicts against female education, employment, and movement. Yet only Save the Children and the UN Children's Fund (UNICEF) suspended operations in this period. However, due to the Taliban's relationship with the international community, humanitarian aid was never able to achieve the aim of saving lives through short-term humanitarian assistance while at the same time facilitating a transfer from a state of internal conflict to a sustainable peace. Although food aid and other short-term assistance certainly saved lives, they also had the effect of destabilizing communities, creating dependencies, and failing to help the people cope with disaster in an intensifying environment of despair.

To develop a coherent approach to aid in Afghanistan, the Strategic Framework for Afghanistan (SFA) was developed throughout 1996 and 1997 and adopted in September 1998, two years after the Taliban had captured Kabul and established the Islamic Emirate of Afghanistan. The concept was to get the United Nations, donors, and aid agencies to work collaboratively in providing direction to the overall aid mission, based on the following seven common principles:

1. Life-sustaining humanitarian assistance shall be provided in accordance with the principles of humanity, universality, impartiality, and neutrality.
2. Assistance shall be provided as part of an overall effort to achieve peace.
3. International assistance will be provided on the basis of need; it cannot be subjected to any form of discrimination, including gender.
4. Rehabilitation and development assistance shall be provided only when it can be reasonably determined that no direct political or military advantage will accrue to the warring parties in Afghanistan.
5. Institution and capacity-building activities must advance human rights and will not seek to provide support to any presumptive state authority that does not fully subscribe to the principles contained in the founding instruments of the United Nations, the Universal Declaration of Human Rights, the Convention on the Rights of the Child, the Convention on the Elimination of Discrimination against Women and International Human Law.
6. Assistance activities must be designed to ensure increasing indigenous ownership at the village, community, and national levels and to build the country as a whole.
7. Assistance activities must attain high standards of transparency and accountability and must be approved, monitored, measured, and evaluated against clear policy and programmatic objectives.

These common principles were backed by five strategic objectives, which were regarded as being mutually reinforcing:

1. The alleviation of human suffering
2. The protection and advancement of human rights
3. The provision of basic social services
4. The building of sustainable livelihoods by empowering Afghans
5. The supporting of the return of refugees

Some have asserted that the attempts by the West to isolate the Taliban were largely responsible for reinforcing the prejudices of the hard-liners who most distrusted the West. It has been argued that the international community failed to take advantage of opportunities to influence the Taliban, which caused the moderates who sought to gain legitimacy in the international community to lose out to the hard-liners. This situation was illustrated by the reactions of the international community to the Taliban's policy regarding opium production when, after years of complaints from the international community, the Taliban banned poppy growing in 2000; by 2001, 90 percent of the poppy crop had been destroyed. However, the West did nothing to reward the Taliban, resulting in a further loss of credibility for the moderates who had argued in favor of complying with the demands of the international community.

Aid in the era of the Taliban was consistently underfunded and concentrated on short-term, life-saving emergency assistance, often against the advice of aid workers in the field who warned against creating dependencies, undermining local coping mechanisms, and drawing the rural population away from their villages to displacement camps. These short-term emergency programs did little to help Afghanis reestablish long-term livelihoods and to wean them away from dependence on aid. However, military activity by the Taliban also exacerbated the situation. Although food aid was getting into Afghanistan, many districts were not receiving any assistance at all, and in other areas, deliveries were erratic due to the lack of security and attacks on aid workers. The military action by the U.S. and Coalition forces in support of the anti-Taliban opposition also worsened the situation, as the whole food pipeline was almost completely blocked during September and October 2001. However, because of the work of the United Nations and the NGOs, famine was averted, though there was still widespread starvation. In addition, a general lack of rain suggested that drought conditions would continue.

The overthrow of the Taliban still posed problems for the humanitarian relief program. The general level of insecurity was marked by bandits preying on food convoys, warlords extorting tolls and bribes from aid agencies, and many remote areas still having trouble receiving food. Because the mandate of the Karzai government does not extend very far past Kabul, NGOs are now being forced to combine emergency relief with actions to improve people's access to education, health care, jobs, and security, though it is clear that they need to take a subordinate role in supporting fledgling government departments. The aid agencies will have to put to one side their experience of autonomous operations in order to help Afghanistan get back on its feet by facilitating the process of moving toward stabilization and peace.

Afghanistan, after twenty-three years of conflict, is one of the world's poorest nations. Child and maternal mortality rates are the highest in Asia. One child in four does not reach the age of five, and all children are vulnerable to measles, pneumonia, and parasitic diseases. Only 39 percent of boys and 3 percent of girls attend school, and adult literacy is low—about 47 percent for men and 15 percent for women. The situation is made worse by endemic unemployment, subsistence farming ravaged by drought, and the fact that fighting has been the only growth industry. Aid agencies, some with over a decade of experience in Afghanistan, have learned from the past and are now careful to engage local residents in relief efforts working through the traditional local structures, thus strengthening these institutions instead of undermining their authority. Groups are now only giving food aid to people with no other means of support in order to avoid creating a dependency culture or fostering internal migration to food distribution sites. Various charities, such as Cooperative for Assistance and Relief Everywhere (CARE), are now offering their assistance in return for work in order to promote self-respect and to minimize dependency. One project in Kabul has engaged 3,000 residents to clean up the streets and to transport rubbish to the city dump in return for enough money to buy food in the local market. Another two projects involve women in sewing school uniforms for poor families or teaching other women basic hygiene measures for their families.

The aid agencies are now pursuing policies that strengthen local institutions, with the intention of building a structure whose management, coordination, and regulation can be transferred to state institutions and Afghan civil society. However, this will not be an easy transition, as everyone involved in Afghanistan carries institutional, political, and ethnic baggage. Short-term humanitarian aid is still needed, especially for returning refugees and internally displaced persons. But development is also a priority, as is the need to clear areas of land mines, unexploded bombs, and ammunition before people can return to their homes. It will also be necessary to reconstruct irrigation systems to restore agricultural production and to develop schools and health centers as part of a daunting task that will require a long-term commitment from donors. However, relief and reconstruction will only succeed if security can be improved and the country prevented from fragmenting into a state of chaos.

See also Afghanistan Peace Association; Reconstruction Program; Refugee Problem; Revolutionary Association of Women of Afghanistan

References

Duffield, Mark, and Patricia Grossman. 2001. *Review of the Strategic Framework for Afghanistan (Final Draft): Report Commissioned by the Strategic Monitoring Unit Afghanistan.* Islamabad: UNOCHA.

Marsden, Peter. 2000. *The Taliban: War, Religion and the New Order in Afghanistan.* London: Zed Books.

Newberg, Paula R. 1999. "Politics at the Heart: The Architecture of Humanitarian Assistance to Afghanistan." http://www.ceip.org/files/Publications/wp2.asp?from=pubauthor (cited 3 January 2000).

Oxfam. 2000. "Crisis in Afghanistan: Humanitarian Situation." http://www.oxfam.org.uk/atwork/emerg/afghanprogramme.html (cited 7 February 2002).

United Nations. 2002. "Immediate and Transitional Assistance for the Afghan People, 2002: Updated Financial Requirements." http://www.reliefweb.int (cited 1 March 2002).

INTERNATIONAL SECURITY ASSISTANCE FORCE (ISAF)

On 20 December 2001, the UN Security Council approved a multinational force to help provide security in Afghanistan, giving it a mandate of six months, subject to renewal. The International Security Assistance Force (ISAF) was initially headed by Britain and comprised contingents from nineteen countries with authorization to provide security for Kabul and its immediate environs. Turkey led the force from June 2002; Germany took over in December and was followed by the Netherlands. Although the ISAF mandate is restricted to Kabul, there are now plans to install security in key areas elsewhere in the country to counter the regional conflicts between warlords that are now prevalent in the provinces; at the time of writing, however, these had yet to come to fruition, and security operation are being conducted only by the U.S. military in certain areas.

The ISAF was charged with three principal tasks:

1. Aiding the Interim Government in developing national security structures
2. Assisting with the country's reconstruction
3. Assisting with the development and training of future Afghan security forces

Under the agreement with the Afghan Interim Government, the ISAF was granted complete and unimpeded freedom of movement throughout the territory and airspace of Afghanistan, though its area of responsibility was restricted to Kabul. However, from the outset, President Hamid Karzai indicated that many Afghans would wish to see international peacekeepers throughout Afghanistan. This expansion was resisted by the United States, which felt that would be an inappropriate move while the military campaign was ongoing. Such a development would have needed approval by the UN Security Council before it could be implemented.

Initially, the ISAF consisted of a contingent of UK Royal Marines who had landed at the Bagram air base just as the UN Security Council voted to approve the force. The marines were charged with providing security at the inauguration of the new Interim Government on 22 December 2001. At the same time, the Afghan Ministry of Defense ordered all Northern Alliance soldiers and police officers to lay down their weapons and to withdraw from the city. Although most of the commanders agreed to obey the instruction in the interests of security and stability, many troops remained in the city with their guns.

The rules of engagement were determined by a military-technical agreement between the UK commander, Maj. Gen. John McColl, and the Interim Government, which was reached on 31 December 2001. Under the agreement, the ISAF committed itself to the tasks detailed in the UN Security Council resolution while at the same time agreeing to establish liaison, as necessary, with political, social, and religious leaders to ensure that the ISAF respects the religious, ethnic, and cultural sensitivities in Afghanistan. This step was particularly significant given that the force, with the exception of troops from Turkey, was non-Muslim in composition. In return, the Afghan Interim Government accepted that the Bonn Agreement of December 2001 required a major contribution on its part in terms of cooperating with the ISAF and the organizations and agencies assisting it. The Afghan administration also agreed to ensure that all Afghan military units came under the ISAF's command and control and would be returned to their barracks, as detailed under an annex to the agreement. The Interim administration also consented

Briefing of a Turkish contingent of the ISAF prior to a night patrol in Kabul (AFP/Corbis)

to refrain from any offensive action in the area controlled by the ISAF, and both sides agreed to participate in a joint coordinating body to discuss current and forthcoming issues and to resolve any dispute that might arise.

The ISAF was to total some 5,000 personnel, drawn from Austria, Belgium, Bulgaria, Czechoslovakia, Denmark, Finland, France, Germany, Greece, Italy, New Zealand, the Netherlands, Norway, Portugal, Romania, Spain, Sweden, Turkey, and the United Kingdom, with the last providing the largest single contingent. The force comprised a variety of units, including two infantry battle groups, a reconnaissance squadron, engineers, ordnance disposal teams, and military police, in addition to logistical support, helicopters, and air transport support.

Initially, the ISAF was involved in a number of incidents, most of which involved suspected Taliban or al-Qaeda fighters, and there were a small number of accidental deaths and injuries. In June 2002, as planned, Turkey took over the leadership of the ISAF from the United Kingdom and boosted the number of personnel significantly. In June 2002, the UN Security Council extended the authorization by a further six months, and in December 2002, it was extended again for a twelve-month period because

the Security Council thought the situation in Afghanistan still presented a threat to international peace and security. However, the presence of the force was not able to prevent the murder of the minister of air transport and tourism at Kabul's airport on 14 February 2002 by angry pilgrims delayed on their journey to the hajj.

Negotiations have been ongoing for some time about the expansion of the ISAF's role in Afghanistan, with the cities of Mazar-i Sharif, Kandahar, Herat, and Jalalabad seen as priority areas. It is believed that the expansion of the force's area of responsibility would help President Hamid Karzai's government extend its authority throughout the country, would aid the process of reconstruction, and would give time for an Afghan army and police force to be established. The plan only envisages a small presence of possibly 400 troops in each location and, although the United States would not provide peacekeepers, it would give intelligence and logistical support. However, as of February 2003, this development of the role of the ISAF had not been agreed to, and the international community was not addressing the security issues in the provinces.

Nonetheless, some moves have been made by the Coalition commander, Gen. Dan McNeill. After protracted negotiations, he established joint regional teams (JRTs) composed of soldiers, civil affairs officers, engineers, medical teams, and U.S. State Department officials in order to improve security outside Kabul and to aid reconstruction. The first deployment, agreed to on 13 January 2003, was for the city of Gardez in eastern Afghanistan, which had been the scene of bitter struggles between rival warlords during 2002. The concept was first discussed in November 2002 and is the result of negotiations with the Afghan government, Coalition partners, the United Nations, and nongovernmental organizations (NGOs). The move also came after a great deal of criticism from Afghan and Western aid agencies, who charged that the U.S. government was not doing enough to cope with the power of the warlords in the provinces or to help Karzai's government with the reconstruction program.

The JRTs are designed to improve stability and to increase security in Afghanistan while at the same time beginning reconstruction projects, with the objective of foiling the residue of al-Qaeda, the Taliban, and their supporters. JRT operations are to be expanded to Kunduz, Bamian, Mazar-i Sharif, Herat, Jalalabad, and Kandahar. Critics maintain that although these JRTs will undoubtedly improve stability, they fall short of a full solution and cannot be seen as a substitute for the expansion of the ISAF. JRT commanders will have flexibility in dealing with regional warlords, but the dominating role will still rest with the central government. JRTs have been promised full backup, with air support, rapid deployment of support troops, and airlifts, if necessary.

References

Elliott, Michael, Mike Billips, Tim McGirk, Michael Ware, Sean Scully, and Mark Thompson. 2002. "The Battle over Peacekeeping." *Time Atlantic* 158, no. 9: 33–34.

McGirk, Tim. 2002. "Murder in the Airport." *Time Atlantic* 159, no. 8: 25.

UN Security Council. 2001. *Resolution 1386.* New York: United Nations.

———. 2002. *Resolution 1413.* New York: United Nations.

———. 2002. *Resolution 1444.* New York: United Nations.

INTER-SERVICES INTELLIGENCE SERVICE (ISI)

The Inter-Services Intelligence Service (ISI) had been used by Pakistan as an agency to keep watch on querulous politicians since its founding by Gen. Ayub Khan in the 1950s. When he seized power in 1958, it became the political arm of the military. The organization was used by Pakistan as a means of controlling the mujahideen in the war against the Soviet forces in Afghanistan and the Communist government in Kabul from 1979 to 1989. In 1994, it was active in supporting the Taliban movement in its struggle against the mujahideen, and it has remained active since the movement's downfall, though it is not clear whether it is operating according to its own objectives or those of the Pakistan government.

Gen. Zia al Haq assigned the task of arming, training, and funding the Afghan mujahideen to the ISI, and Gen. Akhtar Abdul Rahman Khan was appointed to head an organization with a staff of 100 military officers and a network of internal and external agents and freelance spies. Due to its enhanced role and funding, the ISI expanded its operations and engaged Pakistan agents fluent in Persian and Pashtu, together with hundreds of Afghan agents who were given promises of money and refuge in Pakistan. By 1988, the directorate had grown to 100,000 employees.

The ISI was used by Pakistan to control the mujahideen and directing its objectives while distributing the funds and weaponry being supplied by the U.S. Central Intelligence Agency (CIA). Distribution was initially governed by the number of refugees registered with the Pakistan government, all of whom had to declare an allegiance to one party or another. It is estimated that from 1984 to 1986, over 80,000 mujahideen had passed through ISI-sponsored training camps, together with hundreds of thousands of tons of weapons and ammunition. To direct operations in the eastern and southern provinces of Afghanistan, the ISI used its position by only releasing weapons for use at particular times and for specific operations at predetermined locations. Officers of the ISI participated in meetings of mujahideen leaders and played an important role in the council set up to establish the Afghan Interim Government in Peshawar.

It was the ISI that favored Gulbuddin Hekmatyar and his Islamic Party as the representative of a malleable regime in Kabul and as a counter to Afghan claims to Pakistan's Pashtun northwest province. A disproportionate share of the weaponry and funds were provided to Hekmatyar, with the ISI having persuaded the United States that his disciplined forces represented the best tools for success. This policy caused resentment from the other groups, especially, for example, when the ISI tried to dictate the order of battle in February 1989 at Jalalabad to enable Hekmatyar to claim that it was his troops that had captured the city. The mujahideen within Afghanistan saw the ISI control over the alliance as ensuring that the Peshawar group was a tool of the policies of the Pakistan government.

The Kabul government's strategy was designed to cut off the supply lines of the mujahideen from Pakistan, and to combat this, the CIA and the ISI constructed a tunnel complex at Zhawar Killi, near Khost and close to the Pakistan border, which housed a training center, a weapons store, and a clinic, with electricity, piped water, and a holding area for prisoners of war. The project was overseen by Osama bin Laden, who also set up a training camp close to the complex; at that time, he was supported by the United States as a brave, resourceful mujahideen commander. In August 1998, Gen. Zia al Haq and his military chief of staff, Gen. Akhtar Khan, former head of the ISI, were killed in a midair helicopter explosion, but this did not change the policy, as the director of the ISI, Gen. Hamid Gul, was even more committed to the mujahideen and an ardent supporter of Hekmatyar.

The Soviet government completed its withdrawal from Afghanistan in February 1989, and the ISI and the Saudi Intelligence Service together pressured and bribed the members of the Islamic Alliance of Afghan Mujahideen to meet in Rawalpindi, Pakistan, with the aim of establishing an interim government. On 19 February 1989, the Afghan delegates elected an interim government, with Sabghatullah Mujaddidi and Abdul Rasul Sayyaf as chair and deputy chair and Hekmatyar, Yunis Khales, and Burhanuddin Rabbani, respectively, as foreign, defense, and interior ministers. The ISI continued its involvement in the affairs of the mujahideen and their seizure of power in 1992 when Kabul fell to the forces of the Northern Alliance.

The rule of the mujahideen in Afghanistan soon disintegrated into civil war, for the fragile coalition did not last once the government of Muhammad Najibullah had fallen: opposition to the Communist regime was the one factor that held the coalition together. The period from 1992 to 1994 saw the disintegration of the coalition and the formation of the Islamist Taliban movement in Kandahar in 1994. The Taliban regime was seen by the ISI as a more acceptable form of government in Kabul in terms of the interests of Pakistan, and it was given considerable backing. Assistance for the Taliban from Pakistan was also secured by close contacts with Pakistani fundamentalists who, at that time, were in coalition with Prime Minister Benazir Bhutto.

The ISI would again be the main agent of the support for the Taliban, with this policy having been partially dictated by the crucial role that Afghanistan played in Pakistan's commercial trading interests with the Central Asian republics. This arrangement was exemplified, among other things, by Pakistan's support for the Taliban in clearing the toll barriers erected by warlords on the road from Quetta to Herat in order to further trade with the Central Asian republics. The ISI was also involved with the Saudi Intelligence Service in secret meetings with the Taliban over plans to capture Kabul before the winter of 1996. The relationship between Pakistan and the Taliban continued to grow and deepen, and by 1998, the presence of Pakistani intelligence agents and military advisers was known to most foreign observers in Kabul. Indeed, Gen. Abdul Rashid Dostum claimed that the Pakistan air force and 1,500 commandos had been involved in the Taliban assault on his military base at Sheberghan on 1 August 1998.

In 1999, after the Taliban scored further military successes, there was a slight change in ISI policy with respect to the presence in Afghanistan of Osama bin Laden and al-Qaeda, resulting from a secret deal between U.S. president Bill Clinton and Pakistan's prime minister Nawaz Sharif. Pakistan promised active participation in attempts to capture bin Laden, one manifestation of which was the training of sixty ISI operatives by the CIA to seize or assassinate bin Laden. But this development ceased when Gen. Pervez Musharraf overthrew the Sharif government on 12 October 1999. Pakistan continued to provide support for the Taliban, and in June 2000, the Taliban launched what was intended to be a crucial attack on the Northern Alliance; it was backed by material and technical support provided by the ISI, together with 10,000 non-Afghan troops consisting of al-Qaeda fighters and Pakistani irregulars. However, the United States continued to maintain pressure on Pakistan to withdraw support for the Taliban, warning that severe consequences would follow any refusal to back the international community.

The terrorist attacks of 11 September 2001 completely changed the situation. The Pakistan government tried to distance itself from the Taliban after the atrocity, with the ISI warning the Taliban of the military consequences of a refusal to cooperate over Osama bin Laden. The overtures were rejected, and the U.S.-led coalition laid plans to attack Afghanistan in order to overthrow the Taliban and capture or kill bin Laden. The Northern Alliance accused the ISI of continuing to supply the Taliban and providing military advisers to help prepare defenses against a U.S. attack, but it is thought that only a small number of operatives were involved, probably working independently.

Pakistan's current president, Pervez Musharraf, has been engaged in a struggle to gain control over the ISI, which has been described as a kingdom within a state, and this struggle is seen as a high-stakes one for the president. If the ISI is to pursue a meaningful role in the War on Terror, a major shift in attitudes will be needed, since, prior to 11 September, the service was mainly concerned with keeping the Taliban in power and, by default, protecting al-Qaeda. Some indications exist that ISI is cooperating with the United States, particularly in respect to al-Qaeda fighters sheltering in Pakistan, and some 300 suspects were taken in 2002, mostly Yemenis, Saudis, and Palestinians, all of whom were sent to the U.S. holding facility at Guantanamo Bay. The ISI was also instrumental in providing the intelligence that led to the capture of bin Laden's chief of operations, Abu Zubaydah. However, the ISI is operating in difficult circumstances, as the tribal borderlands with Afghanistan are sympathetic to the Taliban and prepared to take U.S. dollars to enable al-Qaeda fugitives to escape the checkpoints and to reach the major cities in Pakistan.

The loyalty of the ISI is also crucial to Musharraf's own survival, as the population in Pakistan is angered over the U.S. bombing of Afghanistan. However, the new director of the organization, Lt. Gen. Ehansul Haq, a trusted head of military intelligence, is more sympathetic to Musharraf's views. A major reshuffling was also instigated to weed out Islamic extremists from the organization and to make the directorate more obedient to the will of the president. But it should be noted that the ISI has been involved with militants in Kashmir, some of whom have also been al-Qaeda fighters, and although links with the Taliban may have been broken, those with Kashmir persist. Meanwhile, President Musharraf has attempted to bring the organization under control by replacing its head, Gen. Mohammad Ahmad, with the moderate head of military intelligence, Lt. Gen. Ehansul Haq, who has been charged with purging the ISI of its fundamentalist supporters. This move has deprived the ISI of backing from the leaders of the military officers corps, and the directorate has also had its political and economic lifelines severed due to the policies of the new ISI head in getting rid of the fundamentalist elements.

See also Afghan-Pakistani Relations; Central Intelligence Agency and Its Support for the Mujahideen; Civil War; Hekmatyar, Gulbuddin; Islamic Alliance for the Liberation of Afghanistan; Mujahideen; Taliban

References

Hiro, Dilip. 2002. *War without End: The Rise of Islamic Terrorism and Global Response.* Rev. ed. London and New York: Routledge.

McGirk, Tim, Hannah Bloch, and Massimo Calabresi. 2002. "Has Pakistan Tamed Its Spies? *Time Atlantic* 159, no. 18: 54–57.

Rashid, Ahmed. 2001. *Taliban: The Story of the Afghan Warlords.* London: Pan.

ISHAQ, MUHAMMAD (1851–1888)

Muhammad Ishaq, the son of Amir Muhammad Azam Khan, had an Armenian mother and was a cousin of Abdur Rahman, the amir of Afghanistan from 1880 to 1901. In 1869, he was commander of Rahman's forces in Afghan Turkestan, where he attacked the troops of Shir Ali, who was amir of Afghanistan from 1863 to 1866 and again from 1868 to 1869. Initially successful due to the desertion of Turkestan troops, he was later defeated and fled across the Amu Daria River to Bukhara, where he was stripped of his allowance and banned from Abdur Rahman's court. He remained in Samarkand and later shared Rahman's exile but was not well respected by the amir of Bukhara.

In 1871, he made overtures to the British government for asylum, and in May 1872, he requested asylum for himself and 300 followers, but the exodus was obstructed by the amir of Bukhara, who instructed the governor of Afghan Turkestan to only allow Ishaq and some five or six followers to cross back over the Oxus River. The offer of asylum was refused by Ishaq, and he was apprehended on his way to Kakand by Russian forces. But in November 1872, he left Samarkand with some eighty followers, arriving in Badakhshan with the objective of fomenting unrest there.

On Abdur Rahman's return to Afghanistan in 1879, he again had military success in Afghan Turkestan, and when Rahman became king, Ishaq was made governor of Mazar-i Sharif, which at that time was a northern province of Afghanistan. He was regarded as a capable administrator and was well liked by the army. He ruled Mazar-i Sharif as if it were independent and sought full autonomy for the northern province before extending his control over the province of Herat. His relations with Amir Abdur Rahman had deteriorated, and it is thought that the king was fearful of the power that Ishaq had gained. In 1888, Abdur Rahman was ill, and Ishaq proclaimed himself king. However, the amir recovered, and his army, under Gen. Ghulam Haidar, defeated the forces of Muhammad Ishaq on 29 September 1888 at Tashqurgham, forcing Ishaq to flee to Russian Turkestan, where he died in exile.

See also Rahman, Amir Abdur

References

Khalfin, N. A. 1958. "The Rising of Ishaq Khan in Southern Turkestan (1888)." *Central Asian Review* 6, no. 2: 253–263.

ISLAMABAD ACCORD (1993)

The Islamabad Accord, also known as the Afghan Peace Accord, was signed on 7 March 1993 in Islamabad, Pakistan, and was designed to produce a broad-based Islamic government following the Soviet withdrawal from Afghanistan in 1989. The accord provided for the establishment of a government for a period of eighteen months, with Burhanuddin Rabbani remaining as president and with Engineer Gulbuddin Hekmatyar or his nominee as prime minister. The cabinet was to be formed by the prime minister in consultation with the president and the leaders of the mujahideen parties within two weeks of signing the agreement.

An electoral process was also agreed to, which had to be implemented within eighteen months from 29 December 1992. The timing was designed to accommodate elections for a grand constituent assembly charged with formulating a constitution, under which general elections would be held for a president and a parliament. In addition, the accord provided for a defense council charged with forming a national army, disarming all parties of heavy weapons, and removing them from Kabul and all other cities to preserve the security of the capital. The council was also to take responsibility for operational control of the armed forces, ensuring that state funds were not used for private armies, and seeing that all roads in Afghanistan were kept open for normal use.

In addition, the accord provided for the immediate and unconditional release of all Afghan detainees held by the government and all other mujahideen groups as a result of recent atrocities. Further, all properties seized by armed groups were to be returned to their original owners, and steps were to be taken to return all displaced persons to their former homes and locations. A cease-fire was to take immediate effect, and a complete cessation of hostilities was to go into force once a cabinet had been formed. The overall position of the cease-fire was to be monitored by a joint commission formed by representatives from the Organization of the Islamic Conference and from all Afghan parties.

An annex to the accord detailed the division of powers between the president and prime minister and was also signed by all the participants. However, it should be noted that two of the signatories signed with reservations concerning the length of the president's term.

References

"Afghan Peace Accord or the Islamabad Accord of March 1993." 1993. http://www.forisb.org.afghan_docs/15islbad/htm (cited 11 February 2003).

"Islamabad Accord." 1993. http://.www.ariaye.com/islamabad.html (cited 11 February 2003).

ISLAMIC ALLIANCE FOR THE LIBERATION OF AFGHANISTAN

The Islamic Alliance for the Liberation of Afghanistan was a short-lived coalition of five mujahideen groups formed on 27 January 1980. With headquarters in Peshawar, Pakistan, the alliance's objectives were to obtain recognition as a government in exile and to secure support from the Islamic Foreign Ministers Conference held in Islamabad in May 1980. The group was chaired by Abdul Rasul Sayyaf, who had no forces of his own, and it did not include the faction led by Gulbuddin Hekmatyar because of a dispute over its position within the alliance. The alliance disintegrated in December 1980 due to internal rivalries and a failure to agree on a common program.

In 1981, the Pakistan government decided that it would only officially recognize six groups (later increased to seven) and that all aid to the mujahideen and refugees would be channeled through these groups, which meant that all refugees had to register as members of a group. In 1985, the alliance was reconstituted as the Islamic Unity of Afghan Mujahideen, comprising three moderate and seven radical groups, the latter being constantly at odds with one another, especially those led by Burhanuddin Rabbani and Hekmatyar.

In 1988, the alliance declared the formation of an Afghan Interim Government (AIG), with Engineer Ahmad Shah as prime minister. There were to be elections among the mujahideen and refugees after three months, but these were not held because the groups could not agree on the distribution of seats in a proposed 520-member assembly. On 20 February 1989, a new AIG was formed, with Abdul Rasul Sayyaf as prime minister, but again, internal dissent caused its collapse. Gulbuddin Hekmatyar withdrew from the alliance once more. The AIG never became a viable proposition due to internal disputes, sectarian divisions, and rifts along ethnic lines, as exemplified by the actions of Hekmatyar, who followed an independent line regardless of the impact on Afghan unity.

See also Hekmatyar, Gulbuddin; Sayyaf, Abdul Rasul
References
Khalilzad, Zalmy. 1991. *Prospects for the Afghan Interim Government*. Santa Monica, CA: Rand Corporation.

ISLAMIC FRONT (JUMBESH-I-MILLI ISLAMI)

The Islamic Front is the party of Gen. Abdul Rashid Dostum and is in control of large stretches of northern Afghanistan, using Uzbek or Turkoman nationalist rhetoric as its basis, though it does draw support from large numbers of ethnic Tajiks. Dostum's forces had fought the mujahideen almost to the end because the front's membership is drawn from former Communist cadres and militants from northern Afghanistan. The Islamic Front is not recognized as a legitimate movement by other mujahideen groups due to its policy of allowing supporters of the former Communist government to become members and because it is rooted in secularism rather than Islam (which lies at the foundation of all other groups).

The Islamic Front's only real hope for survival as a party is to continue to exploit the divisions between the mujahideen parties. Dostum has successfully used this ploy to the weaken the strongest party, at any given moment, to prevent the formation of a dominant coalition. A variant of this policy was used by Dostum to ensure his presence in the Afghan Interim Government, from which he had been excluded.

Dostum's revived party has the following objectives:

- Putting an end to fratricide and bloody wars
- Establishing a comprehensive Islamic state and ensuring broad peace
- Guaranteeing the rights and recognition of all communities living in the country
- Resurrecting the national army
- Recovering territorial integrity, independence, and the rule of national will
- Formulating the political order of the country so that all segments of the society can contribute
- Restructuring Afghanistan by way of foreign assistance and investment by the private sector
- Reviving the original cultures and traditions of people living in Afghanistan
- Enabling women's contribution in all political and social activities in accordance with the religion of Islam
- Reviving Afghanistan's international status and enhancing the national economy

The party has laid particular stress on its role in providing the functions of government offices in the areas controlled by General Dostum, including the opening of schools, colleges, hospitals, and social and cultural institutions, but also restoring the devastated infrastructure, particularly in Mazar-i Sharif and Sheberghan. However, Dostum's main power base is his army and his position among the Uzbek population.

See also Dostum, Gen. Abdul Rashid
References
"National Islamic Movement of Afghanistan and Its Indispensable Duties at Present." 2001. http://www. angelfire.com/ny/Chapandaz/index.html (cited 12 December 2001).

ISLAMIC PARTY—HEKMATYAR
(HIZB-I-ISLAMI—HEKMATYAR)

Islamic Party—Hekmatyar, led by Gulbuddin Hekmatyar, is the largest of the two mujahideen movements of the same root name, the other being led by Yunis Khales. Its origin actually dates back to the 1960s and the creation of the Organization of Muslim Youth, which had been formed to oppose secularization in Afghanistan and the growth of Marxism among the students at Kabul University. The Islamic Party was forced to operate as an underground movement during the rule of President Muhammad Daud from 1973 to 1978, and Hekmatyar had to take refuge in Pakistan, from where he mounted small raids into Afghanistan.

However, the movement became engaged in full-scale guerrilla activity following the Saur Revolt of April 1978, during which the Communists rose to power. The Islamic Party followed the patterns of the Muslim Brotherhood, with a centralized command structure, secret membership, a cell structure, infiltration of government and state institutions, and the intent to be an Islamic vanguard in Afghanistan. Its fighters have been largely recruited from the *madrasas* (religious schools) established by the party. Voting rights within the party, which is primarily Pashtun in membership, are restricted to those who joined before 1975, and membership is stratified, with other classes being those who joined between 1975 and 1978 and those who joined after the Marxists seized power.

The Islamic Party received considerable support from the Pakistan government and from Islamist groups in Pakistan and the Arab gulf states. It is clear that the Inter-Services Intelligence Service of Pakistan favored Hekmatyar's Islamic Party when distributing arms and equipment supplied by the Central Intelligence Agency, giving them to the mujahideen groups. The party favors the creation of an Islamic state based on Shari'a law and the enforcement of Islamic obligations, which would mean restrictions on the participation of women in public life, the banning of alcohol, and the eradication of Western influences.

Under Hekmatyar, the party has pursued radical policies and has been at odds with other mujahideen groups forming the Islamic Alliance for Afghanistan, based in Peshawar, Pakistan. After the capture of Kabul by the mujahideen in 1992, the Islamic Party turned against President Burhanuddin Rabbani and the forces of Ahmad Shah Masood, and bitter fighting ensued between the opposing groups, accompanied by the usual switching of allegiances as the fighting became more violent and acrimonious. It was not until May 1996 that the party made peace with Rabbani's government and Hekmatyar became prime minister. However, his tenure in that position was short-lived, as the mujahideen government was overthrown in September 1996 when the Taliban took Kabul.

Hekmatyar fled to Iran, where he called for a jihad against the United States, and in February 2002, the offices of the Islamic Party where closed by the Iranian government and Hekmatyar was forced to flee for Afghanistan via Pakistan. The party has become overtly hostile to the United States and its presence in Afghanistan, regarding it as an enemy of Islam. The party also planned to strike against the Interim Government of Hamid Karzai, and in April 2002, hundreds of party members and supporters were arrested in Kabul because of an alleged plot to mount a bombing campaign in the capital and to overthrow the Interim Government. Members of Hekmatyar's party are now thought to have allied themselves with vestiges of the Taliban and al-Qaeda, and it is believed they were involved in fighting against U.S. and Afghan forces at Spin Boldak, near the Pakistan border, on 28 January 2003. About eighty fighters were involved in a battle with Coalition forces, eighteen of the rebel fighters were killed, and U.S. airpower was used to attack the cave complexes in which they were thought to be sheltering. Many believe the fighters at Spin Boldak might have been part of the Islamic Martyrs Brigade formed by Hekmatyar, the Taliban, and al-Qaeda to mount suicide attacks against U.S. and government forces in Afghanistan. In February 2003, Hekmatyar was designated a global terrorist by the United States.

See also Hekmatyar, Gulbuddin; Inter-Services Intelligence Service; Islamic Alliance for the Liberation of Afghanistan

References

Hekmatyar, Gulbuddin. 1988. *Clues to the Solution of the Afghan Crisis*. Peshawar, Pakistan: Directorate of International Affairs.

Maley, William, ed. 1988. *Fundamentalism Reborn? Afghanistan and the Taliban*. London: Hurst.

ISLAMIC PARTY—KHALES
(HIZB-I-ISLAMI—KHALES)

The Islamic Party—Khales was founded by Yunis Khales, a former theology teacher, as a breakaway faction of the Islamic Party led by Gulbuddin Hekmatyar. Although the group is small, it is heavily armed. The members are primarily Pashtuns from eastern Afghanistan, an area that has been undergoing a process of destabilization in the absence of strong central government. The movement is strongest in the provinces of Kabul, Nangarhar, and Paktia. The Kabul branch was formerly led by Abdul Haq, who was killed by the Taliban on 26 October 2001 while on a mission for the former king Zahir.

As a result of tribal fragmentation in the region, political affinities based on clan have emerged, and tribal leaders have no desire to influence the future of the state; political factors, such as party membership and ideology, are less significant. Tribal leaders prefer to maintain tribal authority, which would be threatened by the creation of a centralized state. The group draws members from Khales's own tribe, the Khugiani, and from the Jadran. The Khales group is ideologically the same as that led by Hekmatyar, save that it favors cooperation with the other mujahideen groups. As such, the group was initially a strong supporter of the Afghan Interim Government (AIG), which was established by the mujahideen leaders in Peshawar, Pakistan. Khales had been appointed minister of the interior in that government, but he resigned his position in May 1991.

The party is opposed to the concept of universal suffrage, the emancipation of women, and Shi'a participation in the AIG. After the fall of the Marxist government in April 1992, Khales and his various commanders became the dominant powers in the Shura (council), which ruled Jalalabad and most of Nangarhar Province. The group was not represented in the tribal civil war after 1992; rather, commanders acted independently on regional interests. However, Khales's power base was destroyed when the Taliban took Jalalabad in September 1996. Khales took up residence in Pakistan.

See also Haq, Abdul; Khales, Yunis
References
Oleson, A. 1995. *Islam and Politics in Afghanistan.* London: Curzon Press.

ISLAMIC REVOLUTIONARY MOVEMENT (HARAKAT-I-INQLIAB-I-ISLAMI)

The Islamic Revolutionary Movement was one of the early mujahideen organizations that resulted from a merger of various Islamist groups in the 1960s. It is traditional in outlook and considered to be moderate. The group was originally headed by Muhammad Nabi Muhammadi and based on a network of clergy and *madrasa* (religious school) students, with some Pashtun tribal support in southern Afghanistan. In the early 1980s, it was the largest and most influential of the mujahideen groups, but it lost some of its power and significance when the Islamists of Burhanuddin Rabbani and Gulbuddin Hekmatyar left its ranks and formed their own parties. The movement favors the establishment of a state based on Shari'a law and is strongly opposed to self-determination for Afghanistan's ethnic or religious minorities.

See also Hekmatyar, Gulbuddin; Muhammadi, Maulawi Muhammad Nabi; Rabbani, Burhanuddin
References
O'Ballance, Edgar. 2002. Afghan Wars: Battles in a Hostile Land. New York: Brassey's.

ISLAMIC SOCIETY OF AFGHANISTAN (JAM'IAT-I ISLAMI-YI AFGHANISTAN)

Burhanuddin Rabbani has led the Islamic Society of Afghanistan since 1971. In 1978, the organization became a mujahideen force engaged in activities against the Marxist regime in Kabul. The group was one of those accorded recognition by Pakistan, was based in Peshawar, and was largely non-Pashtun in membership. Rabbani had a number of alliances with other factions, including those led by Ahmad Shah Masood in northern Afghanistan and Isma'il Khan in Herat Province. The movement also drew support in the west and south of Kandahar Province and had strong representation in the cities of Kabul, Herat, and Kandahar but not in Jalalabad or Mazar-i Sharif.

The movement is composed mainly of Sunni Muslim Tajiks, the second largest ethnic group in Afghanistan. It favors the construction of a centralized state to forward its ideological project, and during the struggle against the Soviet occupation (from 1979 to 1989), it had established embryonic regional states in Herat and the northwest region of Afghanistan controlled by Ahmad Shah Masood. The movement is Islamist in nature and supports the establishment of an Islamic state. It has been constantly at odds with the Islamist group led by Gulbuddin Hekmatyar, and at times, bloody conflict has ensued. For example, several of Rabbani's military commanders were killed on 9 July 1989 after clashes with Hekmatyar's group, some after being taken prisoner. Reconciliation was reached in October 1990 in Peshawar through the arbitration efforts of Masood, but the truce that evolved was always a fragile peace.

The movement was bolstered when Rabbani was elected president of Afghanistan in 1993. But after the rise of the Taliban, the movement withdrew to northern Afghanistan in 1996 and became a leading player in the Northern Alliance.

See also Masood, Ahmad Shah; Rabbani, Burhanuddin
References
Maley, William. 1999. *Fundamentalism Reborn? Afghanistan and the Taliban.* London: Hurst.

ISLAMIC UNION FOR THE LIBERATION OF AFGHANISTAN (ITTIHAD-I-ISLAMI BARAYI AZADI-Y-AFGHANISTAN)

The Islamic Union for the Liberation of Afghanistan supports the concept of a strong state and is largely funded by Wahhabi networks in Saudi Arabia. It draws the bulk of its membership from Pashtuns west of Kabul and in Kunduz Province. Given that the Wahhabi networks finance the group, the Islamic Union is of course opposed to the Shi'a in Afghanistan, who are supported and financed by Iran. The social base of the party, composed of Pashtuns and clerics, subscribe to anti-Shi'ite sentiments, specifically directed against members of the Hazara ethic group, who have traditionally opposed the power of the Pashtuns. To demonstrate its Islamic credentials, the group has backed symbolic measures, such as the elimination of female television hosts.

The movement was founded in 1980 by Abdul Rasul Sayyaf following his period as chair of the Islamic Alliance and was part of the loose grouping of the Islamic Unity of Afghan Mujahideen. Sayyef and his followers are now part of the Northern Alliance.

See also Mujahideen; Northern Alliance; Sayyaf, Abdul Rasul
References
Fuller, Graham E. 1991. *Islamic Fundamentalism in Afghanistan: Its Character and Prospects.* Santa Monica, CA: Rand Corporation.

ISLAMIC UNITY PARTY (HIZB-I WAHDAT)

The Islamic Unity Party is primarily a regrouping of the various Hazara organizations who opposed the power of the ruling Pashtuns and who were, in turn, despised by the Pashtuns. This group of eight previously separate mujahideen groups espouses an ideology based on the beliefs of Ayatollah Khomeini of Iran and was formed at the instigation of the Iranian government. It has held itself aloof from the state and the parties dominated by the Sunni Muslims, viewing a centralized state, which would be Sunni-dominated, as a threat to Hazara independence. The leadership refused to join the Afghan Interim Government formed in Peshawar, Pakistan, in 1989 because it felt that it was not being accorded appropriate representation. The party is trapped between the desire to be involved in government with guarantees (for example, a federal system) and the desire to oppose the state in order to maintain its independence.

See also Shi'a Mujahideen Groups
References
"Hizb-i Wahdat (The Unity Party)." 2000. http://www.fas.org/irp/world/para/hizbi_wahdat.htm (cited 10 December 2001).
Oleson, A. 1995. *Islam and Politics in Afghanistan.* London: Curzon Press.

ISLAMIST MOVEMENT (JAMI'AT-I ISLAMI)

The Islamist Movement was born in the 1950s as a reaction to the influence of Westernization and the growth of secularism in Afghanistan, particularly among young people. With leaders including Burhanuddin Rabbani, the movement was modeled on the Muslim Brotherhood, which had been founded in Egypt. The Islamist Movement was initially intellectual in nature, studying the works of Islamic scholars while it developed an ideological base and drew heavily from the student population for support. It became political during the premiership of Sardar Daud (from 1953 to 1963), with students staging demonstrations against government policies and international causes such as Zionism and the Vietnam War.

In 1970, the student members formed the Islamic Youth Movement, winning power in the university elections and alarming the Marxist government. The movement was formally organized in 1971, with Rabbani as Chair, Abdul Rasul Sayyaf as his deputy, and a council that was assigned political and cultural tasks; it called itself the Islamic Society (Jam'iat-i Islami). Following the coup by Muhammad Daud on 17 July 1973, the movement was forced underground. Members prepared for armed struggle, but this effort was thwarted by government

Toppled Afghan president and leader of the Islamist Movement, Burhanuddin Rabbani, in Faizabad, Badakhshan Province, on 3 July 2001. Faizabad was the administrative capital of the 5 percent of Afghanistan then controlled by the Northern Alliance. (AFP/Corbis)

action; a number of the leaders of the movement were arrested, though Rabbani and Gulbuddin Hekmatyar managed to escape to Pakistan.

Hekmatyar began to make sporadic but unsuccessful raids into Afghanistan, which led to a public rift with Rabbani. Following the Saur Revolt of April 1978 and the advent of Communist rule, attempts were made at a reconciliation with the formation of a twenty-one-member committee, but the organization was still split along ethnic and ideological lines. In terms of policy, Hekmatyar favored immediate armed struggle, whereas the Tajik supporters of Rabbani favored a period of consolidation and preparation before taking action. By 1979, the group had again fragmented, largely because of a dispute over the distribution of foreign donations. Thereafter, each leader organized his own movement.

As a group, members of the Islamist Movement were reformist. They supported the type of political activism advocated by Jamaluddin Afghani, known as the father of the concept of pan-Islam (which was designed to stem the tide of Western imperialism and was propagated in the late nineteenth century). And they opposed Western influences, secularism, and the lack of respect for traditional values. Although they also wished to impose Islamic law on

Afghan society, they were not fundamentalist, and they were critical of the clergy, who, in turn, criticized the movement. After going underground and operating in small cells, the movement was accused of using political assassination as a weapon, but it was also victimized by such assassinations.

The aims of the movement were:

- The elimination of poverty, deprivation, unemployment, oppression, colonialism, and injustice
- The spread of Islamic teaching to bring about conditions under which the basic needs of people would be met
- The attainment of peace and prosperity, the safeguarding of dignity, the preservation of human rights, and the protection of property from looting and arson
- The distribution of uncultivated land to landless farmers and owners of small plots and greater cooperation between landowners and farmers, with income distribution based on equity and justice

Members of the movement also expressed a wish to end linguistic and regional prejudices and to promote unity among all the races and tribes of Afghanistan. They sought to back all religious schools and to use the media to propagate the rich culture and heritage of Islamic values. Finally, they believed they had a duty to promote the spirit of jihad to wipe out the criminal enemies of Islam.

See also Hekmatyar, Gulbuddin; Rabbani, Burhanuddin

References
Jamiat-i-Islami Afghanistan. 1961. *Aims and Goals of Jamiat-i-Islami Afghanistan*. Peshawar, Pakistan: Jamiat-i-Islami Afghanistan.

ISMA'IL KHAN (1946–)

Isma'il Khan, more properly known as Muhammad Isma'il, is the Tajik governor of the western province of Herat and has become the de facto ruler of western Afghanistan. He occupied this post prior to the arrival of the Taliban in the area in 1997, when he was forced to flee to Iran. He was a mujahideen commander in the war against the Soviets, continued the struggle against the Communist government in Kabul and then against the Taliban, and now rules Herat without any real recourse to the government in Kabul. He has been aided in his consolidation of power by Iran. Indeed, shops in Herat are filled with Iranian goods, the Iranian currency is accepted alongside the Afghani, and Iran has financed a road to link the city of Herat with the Iranian border.

During the ten-year Soviet occupation, from 1979 to 1989, Isma'il Khan was a guerrilla fighter operating in western Afghanistan and an officer in the national army rising up against the Soviets months after they arrived in Herat. His initial attack against Soviet forces resulted in the deaths of hundreds of Soviet soldiers, though 20,000 Heratis lost their lives in one day of retaliation. Isma'il Khan was a successful mujahideen leader and was one of the first to be supplied with Stinger missiles by the United States, through the Central Intelligence Agency, and he maintained his opposition to the Soviets until their withdrawal in 1989. His resistance continued against the Communist regime in Kabul until its collapse in 1992, when he became governor of Herat.

As governor, he instigated a process of reconstruction and oversaw a period of relative peace (though his regime was accused of corruption) until the Taliban captured the province in 1995 and he was forced to take temporary refuge in Iran. Isma'il Khan returned to Afghanistan after a brief period of exile and began to organize resistance to the Taliban. However, in 1997, while building a resistance movement in Badghis Province, he was betrayed by opponents and handed over to the Taliban. They imprisoned him, with other opposition leaders, in Kandahar under extremely harsh conditions. In March 2002, Isma'il Khan and other jailed opposition leaders managed to escape, and he made his way back to freedom in Mashad in western Iran.

By May 2001, Isma'il Khan had returned to Afghanistan and was establishing anti-Taliban movements in the provinces of Badghis, Herat, and Ghor in support of sporadic actions conducted elsewhere in northern Afghanistan by the United Front. Initially, actions against the Taliban were of a hit-and-run nature, avoiding major confrontation with Taliban forces bolstered by Pakistani, Arab, and Central Asian fighters. The resistance faced a variety of obstacles—among them drought, road blockades, shortages of logistics, and inadequate transportation between the various regions in which the groups were operating.

Little was achieved until the U.S. air campaign began on 7 October 2001 in response to the 11 September terrorist attacks in the United States. Isma'il Khan had tried to put himself forward as the successor to Ahmad Shah Masood, the military leader of the Northern Alliance who had been assassinated, but although he commanded the loyalty of ethnic Tajiks in western Afghanistan, he had little support in the northeastern part of the country, the stronghold of the Northern Alliance. In late October, forces loyal to Isma'il Khan took control of Chaghcharan, the capital of Ghor Province, and then moved on Taliban positions in Herat. The assault on the Taliban was supported by heavy U.S. bombing raids on frontline positions, with special forces providing intelligence to the anti-Taliban fighters and guiding the bombing raids.

After the fall of the Taliban forces in northern Afghanistan, Isma'il Khan again became governor of Herat, and he now commands a force of some 25,000 men. Although he has pledged allegiance to Hamid Karzai's government in Kabul, he has operated independently of the central government, and many observers feel that he regards the Herat region as his personal fiefdom, being known locally as emir, rather than governor. The location of the province near the borders with Iran and Turkmenistan ensures millions of dollars in tax revenues every month because of its significance as a transit route for trade to the Central Asian republics, with very little of this going to the Kabul administration. Isma'il Khan has been accused by human rights groups of running a corrupt, repressive ministate with only nominal allegiance to the central government. The U.S.-based Human Rights Watch has accused his administration of being responsible for widespread intimidation, arrests, beatings, and torture.

Herat has been described as a province whose society allows little dissent, no criticism of the administration, no independent newspapers, no freedom to hold meetings, and no respect for the rule of law. However, some observers feel that international scrutiny and pressure from Kabul has caused some relaxation in restrictions; for example, women are now allowed to work for foreign aid groups. Some residents resent Isma'il Khan's fundamentalism, which grew following his exile in Iran, resulting in restrictions on music, liquor, and social life in a society that is more sophisticated than some and that

values individual liberties. Many also resent the close links with Iran in terms of political influence, despite the cultural ties that exist between the two peoples.

In economic terms, Herat is well provided for because of its strategic location in relation to Iran and Turkmenistan. It has been estimated that Isma'il Khan collects $600,000 a day in taxes on goods entering Herat Province and sends less than $50,000 a day to the central government in Kabul, which has estimated his daily revenue at $1 million. It has been reported by the Central Bank in Kabul that only 30 percent of the revenue kept by Herat is spent on reconstruction, with the rest being retained by Isma'il Khan and spent on a life of opulence and lavish presents for friends and relatives. The administration maintains that it has built parks, roads, a sewage system in Herat, and a library and has opened schools and medical facilities. However, the city of Herat has no central power plant, and many of its streets are shattered and only paved with gravel. The point has also been made by some residents that although schools have been reopened, the children have nowhere to sit and no books; similarly, they contend, the hospital is open but has no doctors.

Some residents, however, credit Isma'il Khan with bringing peace and prosperity to Herat Province, making the commercial and cultural hub the safest and most prosperous in Afghanistan. They see the forces at his disposal as essential to the maintenance of peace in a region cut off from Kabul by impassable roads and an intermittent telephone service; further, it still faces dangers from renegade Taliban supporters. Many perceive the administration as a benevolent dictatorship and regard support for it as a small price to pay for security and a guarantee of peace and stability. For ethnic Pashtuns, life has become hard in the region controlled by Isma'il Khan, as they are associated with the despised Taliban by many Tajiks, and there have been reports of torture, looting, and rape perpetrated against Pashtuns by forces loyal to the governor.

Isma'il Khan functions as the virtual ruler of Herat, and other regional warlords occupy similar positions. This situation is seen as a major problem for the central government in Kabul and the future sustainability of Afghanistan as a unified state. Some criticism is also being leveled against the United States for supporting regional warlords and for making it more difficult for Afghanistan to build a strong, central regional government.

See also Civil War; Coalition Land Campaign against the Taliban; Islamist Movement; Taliban

References

Daraghai, Borzov. 2002. "Afghan Governor Spurns Instability Fears." http://www.washingtontimes.com (cited 13 April 2002).

Oleson, A. 1995. *Islam and Politics in Afghanistan.* London: Curzon Press.

Samad, Omar. 2001. "Ismail Khan Opens Up New Front." http://www.afghan-info.com (cited 6 November 2001).

Stone, Andrea. 2002. "Afghan Governor De Facto Ruler in West." http://story.news.yahoo.com/news?templ:story2&sid=675&u=ustoday/20021219/ts (cited 19 December 2002).

ISMA'ILIS

The Isma'ilis are members of a Shi'a Islamic sect established in A.D. 765, after the death of Imam Isma'il, who was believed by his followers to have been the Seventh Imam and due to return on the Day of Judgment. The present leader of the Isma'ili community is Karim, Aga Khan IV, who leads some 300,000 people living in Africa, India, Iran, Pakistan, Tajikistan, and northwestern Afghanistan. The Isma'ilis believe in an esoteric interpretation of the Koran, with stages of initiation based on the believer's level of understanding; they also pay a tax to support the poor of their community. They are a small group in Afghanistan, and during the struggle against the Marxist government and the Soviet forces (from 1979 to 1989), they refused to cooperate with any mujahideen groups operating in their territory. They did, however, ally themselves with Gen. Abdul Rashid Dostum following the capture of Kabul by the Taliban in 1996.

References

Goodson, Larry P. 2001. *Afghanistan's Endless War: State Failure, Regional Politics, and the Rise of the Taliban.* Seattle: University of Washington Press.

Olsen, A. 1995. *Islam and Politics in Afghanistan.* London: Curzon Press.

JADRAN TRIBE

The Jadran tribe occupies the eastern slopes of the Sulaiman mountain range to the east of Zurmat in Paktia Province. Members of this tribe are closely related to the Shasta Pashtuns. They tend to live in very small villages and cultivate a little land, but they rely on their flocks to provide a subsistence living. Their main trading center is Gardez, to which they take wool and cheese to sell and in return purchase corn and cloth. They are regarded as excellent warriors and were active in the war against the Afghan government from 1979, having expelled government troops from the Organ region of the province.

References
Clifford, Mary Louise. 1973. *The Land and People of Afghanistan*. Philadelphia: Lippincott.

JAGRAN, SAYYID MUHAMMAD HASAN (1949–)

Jagran is the nom de guerre of Sayyid Hasan, the commander of the Hazara front, which operated in Behsud in Ghazni Province. He was an extremely successful military commander in actions against government forces in the 1980s and, as such, was able to administer his area as an autonomous district. He was affiliated with the mujahideen group led by Sayyid Ali Beheshti, which had been the only Shi'a mujahideen force represented at the conference of mujahideen leaders held in Rawalpindi, Pakistan, in February 1989. However, Jagran's relations with the other Shi'a mujahideen groups were always poor, and he fought several engagements against the Nasr and Pasdaran groups.

See also Beheshti, Sayyid Ali; Shi'a Mujahideen Groups
References
Roy, Olivier. 1988. "Has Islamism a Future in Afghanistan?" In *Fundamentalism Reborn? Afghanistan and the Taliban*, edited by William Maley, 199–211. London: Hurst.

J

JAJI TRIBE

The Jajis are a Sunni Muslim tribe in Paktia Province, residing mainly in the valley of the Hariab River and the immediate vicinity. Reputed to be excellent fighters, they have been involved in numerous internal conflicts in Afghanistan. They helped the Sulaiman Khel, a division of the Ghilzai tribe, to oust King Amanullah in 1929, and they assisted Nadir Shah in becoming ruler when he defeated Habibullah Kalakani, who had seized the throne, at Kabul on 13 October 1929. However, they have weakened their position over the centuries by the pusuit of internal feuds. Indeed, the ways in which their villages are built suggest the tensions between parts of the tribe, and their houses are designed with defenses that reflect a life of contention. Traditionally, they have been involved in agriculture, but their pasture and soil are poor and the land provides only a subsistence level of crops through extensive irrigation. Goats are their primary stock. In recent times, the Jajis have been prominent in the trucking business in Afghanistan. During the civil war (from 1989 to 2001), they allied themselves with the National Islamic Front of Afghanistan.

References
Bellew, H. W. 1880. *The Races of Afghanistan: Being a Brief Account of the Principal Nations Inhabiting That Country*. London: Thaker.

JAM'IAT-I-'ULAMA

Jam'iat-i-'Ulama was a consultative body of *ulama* (Islamic scholars and clergymen) that was founded in 1931 by Nadir Shah and charged with the responsibility for judging the constitutionality of laws. As a body, it wielded considerable power, for all new laws had to be submitted to it for consideration. But

Prime Minister Muhammad Daud removed most of its executive power in 1953, and it effectively became a "rubber stamp" body for the Afghan government. After the Saur Revolt of April 1978, which brought the Communists to power, it issued fatwas, or legal decisions, recognizing Nur Muhammad Taraki as the legitimate head of state and authorizing a jihad against Islamist mujahideen groups.

References

Huquqi, Walid A. 1971. *Judicial Organization in Afghanistan.* Kabul: Government Press.

JAMILURRAHMAN, MAULAWI HUSAIN (1933–1992?)

Maulawi Husain Jamilurrahman was a leader of an Islamic revivalist movement whose members became popularly known as Wahhabis because of similarities with the movement in Saudi Arabia. He ruled Kunar Province as an Islamic amirate from 1990 to 1991, having ousted all other mujahideen groups from the province; he also imposed an Islamic regime that only allowed bearded men into the amirate and banned all forms of tobacco.

Jamilurrahman had been a member of the Islamic Society of Afghanistan and was active in attacks against the government of President Muhammad Daud. After the Saur Revolt of 1978 and the assumption of power by the Communists, he joined the Islamic Party of Gulbuddin Hekmatyar and acted as his amir in Kunar Province. After breaking with the party in 1982, he ousted all other groups and assumed sole power in the province. In February 1991, he formed a cabinet, but the upper echelons of the group were decimated by a bomb attack on his headquarters on 20 April 1991. As a consequence, Hekmatyar and other groups were able to capture the town of Asadabad and expel most of the Wahhabis from the province. Jamilurrahman fled to Pakistan, where he was assassinated by an Egyptian.

See also Hekmatyar, Gulbuddin; Islamic Society of Afghanistan

References

Fuller, Graham E. 1991. *Islamic Fundamentalism in Afghanistan: Its Character and Prospects.* Santa Monica, CA: Rand Corporation.

JAMSHIDI TRIBE

The Jamshidis are one of four tribes that are collectively known as Chahar Aimaq; tribal members are Dari-speaking Hanifa Sunni Muslims. The tribe numbers between 60,000 to 80,000 people, concentrated mainly in the central area of Badghis Province, with smaller communities in the northwest of the province and in the provinces of Herat and southern Fariab. The origins of the tribe are uncertain, but members claim to be descendants of the legendary pre-Islamic kings of Sistan (located in present-day Iran) who migrated to Afghanistan centuries ago.

In 1842, because of persecution and unrest in Herat Province, a number of tribal members went to Panjdeh and some went to Persia. In 1857, after an occupation of Herat, Persia withdrew from the province, and the Jamshidis submitted to the rulers of Afghanistan. But in 1862, they were attacked by Sultan Ahmad Khan, and the tribe moved to the Kushk district. For a period, they enjoyed a relatively stable existence, but ten years later, they were attacked by the Turkomans. The initial assaults were successfully repelled, but in 1889, after a further series of Turkoman encroachments, they withdrew to Herat. On their return to Kushk district, they found that their land had been appropriated by district officials, and they were forced to become tenant farmers.

See also Chahar Aimaqs; Taimaris

References

Clifford, Mary Louise. 1973. *The Land and People of Afghanistan.* Philadelphia: Lippincott.

JIRGA

The *jirga* is a tribal council that exercises legislative and judicial authority in the name of the tribe. The council is elected by tribal members and may be composed of the tribe's notables or all its main members. The jirga can consider social issues and controversies, and a meeting of the body can be called at the request of the tribal elders or by a member of the council. The jirga is governed by its own rules, regulations, and formalities, and outcomes of its discussions are determined by consensus and are binding on all of the members of the tribe. The jirga is particularly common among the Pashtun tribes in the border areas, which has always been permitted by the Afghan government despite its claim to national jurisdiction. In a national emergency, a *loya jirga* (great council), representing all of the tribal communities, can be convened to determine a national consensus.

See also Loya Jirga

Candidates elected in the first phase of Loya Jirga from the four districts of Parwan Province, North of Kabul, raise their hands before a vote during a meeting to elect a leader among themselves for the second phase of Loya Jirga, in Kabul, 31 May 2002. (AFP/Corbis)

References

Mehreban, Abdullah. 1982. "National Jirgahs (Assemblies) and Their Role in the Socio-Political Life of the People of Afghanistan." *Afghanistan Quarterly* 35, no. 2: 50–58.

JOZJAN PROVINCE

Jozjan Province is located in north-central Afghanistan and has an area of 10,126 square miles and a population of about 642,000. The administrative capital, Sheberghan, has about 19,000 inhabitants. The province is naturally rich in mineral resources, with significant quantities of oil and natural gas having been discovered at Khwaja, Gugudak, and Jarquduq; natural gas reserves are estimated to exceed 500 trillion cubic feet. In 1968, a pipeline was constructed to transport the natural gas to the Soviet Union, built with financial and technical assistance from the Soviet government. Supplies were sold at prices below world market rates, but in essence, the Soviet Union was the only practical partner. A small amount of gas was also used locally for the production of fertilizer.

The Jozjanis also provided forces for a militia of some 3,000 to 4,000 Uzbek troops, which served the Kabul government in the 1980s. They were an extremely reliable and effective group in southern and western Afghanistan and replaced Soviet troops in Kandahar, where they provided the protective force for the airport. After the mujahideen captured Kabul in April 1992, they merged with the forces of Gen.Abdul Rashid Dostum, becoming involved in the struggle for control over sections of the city. The force pulled out of Kabul at the insistence of Gulbuddin Hekmatyar after a deal with President Burhanuddin Rabbani, but they joined the opposing forces after Dostum was refused a role in the government by Rabbani. The Jozjanis were assimilated into General Dostum's army in northern Afghanistan and are now seen as defenders of Uzbek ethnic interests.

References

Adamec, Ludwig W. 1972–1985. *Historical and Political Gazetteer of Afghanistan.* 6 vols. Graz, Austria: Akademische Druck-u Verlagsansalt.

KABUL CITY

The city of Kabul has suffered badly from twenty-three years of invasions and civil war. Almost half of the city has been leveled, and at least 90 percent of the surviving buildings having been damaged by mortars, rockets, and gunfire. The problems of Kabul have also been complicated by the presence of at least 500,000 refugees or internally displaced persons, many of whom come from rural environments and have no family connections to the city. The problems facing the government and the municipal authorities in Kabul, the capital of Afghanistan, are immense and will not be solved in the immediate future.

Kabul has existed as a center of population for over 3,000 years and was mentioned in Indian scriptures back to 1500 B.C. Herodotus (484–424 B.C.) detailed its trading links with Greece and Rome and its significance as a trading center at the time of Alexander the Great. It is also in a strategic location on the main route to India through the Khyber Pass, to the north through the Hindu Kush, and to the south through Ghazni and Gardez.

Kabul became the capital of Afghanistan in 1773 under the reign of Timur Shah, who made this move to weaken the power of the Durrani chiefs in Kandahar Province. Thus, Kabul would become the dominant urban center in Afghanistan, making it the best-equipped city in the country in terms of schools, paved roads, telephones, and commercial activity. All international connections were also centered on Kabul, which helped contribute to a rapid growth in the population; by 1982, 40 percent of the nation's urban dwellers lived there. As a result of this rapid expansion in population, the infrastructure of the city showed signs of strain, including lack of access to good running water and a modern sewage system. In the old part of the city, the sewage system was open and therefore affected the health of the urban poor. In 1878, the city had a population of about 70,000, but by 1970, this number had grown to 500,000. The first secular secondary school—the Habibia School—was opened in 1904; by 1967, the city had ninety-seven secondary schools, technical and vocational schools, and a university. In 1908, the first telephone line was installed between Kabul and Jalalabad, and Kabul was also the first city to have electricity; in addition, work had commenced on a hydroelectric plant, which was completed in 1913.

Some 90 percent of the housing in Kabul consists of low buildings, one or two stories high and largely constructed of adobe bricks. A good 40 percent of the people rent their homes, but there was a severe shortage of housing even before the damage inflicted on residential areas during the civil war (1989 to 2001). In the Communist era (from 1978 to 1992), the government tried to alleviate the housing problem by building apartment blocks, with assistance from the Soviet Union. Each block had its own water supply, sewage system and treatment plant, hot water, and heating system. However, the city was devastated during the civil war, and much of the housing and the infrastructure was destroyed, making a major reconstruction program a priority for the new government and the international community.

On 20 September 2002, an international conference was held in Kabul, tasked with planning the reconstruction of the city and drawing up a list of priorities to ensure that the planning was rational. The conference was sponsored by the Afghan Ministry of Urban Development and Housing, together with the UN Habitat for Humanity program and the American Society of Afghan Engineers. The ministry hoped that the conference would enable Afghanistan leaders to learn from foreign experts on reconstruction and

Snow-capped mountains of the Hindu Kush range surround the Afghan capital of Kabul. (Patrick Robert/Corbis)

in particular from the experiences of Germany, Japan, and the Balkans, all of which had expertise in postwar rebuilding.

Funds for reconstruction have been scarce relative to the size of the task, and there has been some dispute as to the order of priorities, whether it be sewage and wastewater, roads, telecommunications, or drinking water. The refugee problem has also received uneven emphasis, with some experts favoring returning the refugees to their villages but others accepting the fact that some will have grown to like city life and will have no wish to return to their former homes. If the latter is the correct interpretation, Kabul will need to provide housing for a much larger population. The former mayor of Kabul, Anwar Zakdalek, advised the conference that the first priority for reconstruction should be getting the population, whether permanent residents or refugees, under roof before the onset of winter. The scale of the problem is such that many experts feel it will take Kabul twenty years to get back to where it was in 1979, prior to the Soviet invasion.

In November 2002, work on rebuilding Kabul began under the supervision of Yusef Pashtoon, minister for housing and city planning. Housing was the immediate problem addressed. Kabul has an acute shortage of housing, with a minimum of 50,000 and ideally 100,000 units needing to be built by the end of 2004. The focus is on housing for the permanent residents whose homes were destroyed or damaged during the conflict and the housing of hundreds of thousands of refugees and internally displaced persons. The situation has been further complicated by the fact that some people have just moved into empty houses and others have built illegal houses, with the latter probably accounting for 40 percent of the housing stock.

Many of the illegal houses are sited on hillsides and therefore were not constructed securely enough to deal with the harsh winter weather. However, the authorities will not evict the squatters in empty houses or demolish the illegal houses but will concentrate construction on the edges of the city, with five suburban areas being planned. The project calls for these "satellite towns" to have a mix of low-, middle-, and high-income housing to accommodate some 500,000 people. Another top priority is the rebuilding of Kabul's power system: only about two-thirds of the city receives electricity (on an irregular basis), and the remainder gets no power at all. In addition, the water and sewage systems need to be completely reconstructed, and in many areas of the city, there is a desperate need for potable water.

The rebuilding plans have not attracted sufficient funding from international aid organizations, and the Ministry of Urban Development and Housing has admitted that private enterprise will be the key to the city's development. International aid tends to concentrate on long-term projects that bring large-scale economic development or on humanitarian relief. Although the city has started to revive, this major reconstruction project will take decades to show any long-lasting results—results that will be crucial to the health and sustainability of the country as a whole.

References

Adamec, Ludwig W. 1985. *Kabul and Southeastern Afghanistan*. Graz, Austria: Akademische Druck-u Verlagsansalt.

"Afghanistan Starts Arduous Task of Rebuilding Kabul." 2002. http://www.afgha.com/article.php?sid=17391 (cited 11 November 2002).

Sofi, Lutfullah. 1982. "Historical Development of Cities in Afghanistan." *Afghanistan* 34, no. 1: 54–69.

KAFIR WAR (1895)

The question of Kafiristan was a matter of great concern to Amir Abdur Rahman because of the activities of his powerful neighbors, British India and Russia, on the borders of Afghanistan. The Russians had penetrated into the Pamirs region, and Britain had taken control of eastern Kafiristan. The amir was concerned that an independent Kafiristan would be subject to annexation by either of the two powers, which could lead to claims to Panjshir, Laghman, and Jalalabad, areas that had belonged to the Kafirs in the past. Additionally, the Kafirs were seen as a threat to the amir, for when Afghan troops were fighting elsewhere, they continually raided Afghan provinces.

In 1895, Abdur Rahman decided to resolve the problem once and for all by taking control of the Kafiristan region. He selected the winter for the start of his campaign. The timing was deliberate, as the snows would prevent the Kafirs from using the high passes to retreat into Russian territory for protection; moreover, the amir wanted a brief campaign so that his neighbors would not have time to react and Christian missionaries would not be able to foment trouble.

Afghan forces were split into four sections, with one force under Capt. Muhammad Ali Khan proceeding through Panjshir to Kulam, while a second force under Gen. Ghulam Haidar Charkhi moved from Asmor and Chitral. The other forces moved from Badakhshan and Laghman Provinces. However, since all the troop movements were near the Afghan border, they did not arouse any suspicion, and the four armies, supplemented by tribal levies, attacked simultaneously and conquered Kafiristan in forty days. The Kafirs had no hope of defending themselves, as they were armed mainly with bows and arrows and only a few rifles and faced an Afghan army with infantry, cavalry, and artillery. Some of the defeated Kafirs were resettled in Paghman Province and converted to Islam, and many of the young males trained for military service. Within a short period, all the Kafirs were converted to Islam. In 1906, Amir Habibullah changed the name of the region to Nuristan, or the "Country Enlightened by the Light of Islam."

See also Kafiri Tribe

References

Robertson, George Scott. 1974. *The Kafirs of the Hindu Kush*. Karachi, Pakistan, and New York: Oxford University Press.

KAFIRI TRIBE

The Kafiris are thought to be the original inhabitants of the plains country of Afghanistan in what is now Nuristan. They were driven back into the mountain areas by the arrival of Islam in the country about A.D. 700. They are thought to be the descendants of the old Indian population that used to occupy the region, and they did not convert to Islam with the rest of the population, remaining pagan for several more centuries. Their language is very much akin to ancient Sanskrit, and the family is the most significant element of the Kafiri society. Intertribal disputes have been quite common over the centuries; indeed, some have been ongoing for hundreds of years. The Kafiris are considered to be skilled in many trades, including shoemaking, ropemaking, pottery, silver and brassware, wood carving, and leather crafts. The Kafiris were largely independent until the late nineteenth century, when the region was attacked by the forces of Abdur Rahman and the population was more or less forcibly converted to Islam. The name of the province was then changed from Kafiristan to

Nuristan. A large number of Kafiris were also forced to resettle in the Kohdaman, north of Kabul.

References

Robertson, George Scott. 1974. *The Kafirs of the Hindu Kush.* Karachi, Pakistan, and New York: Oxford University Press.

KALAKANI, ABDUL MAJID (1939–1980)

Abdul Majid Kalakani had established a reputation as a poet and writer by 1953, but from 1958 to 1963, he was in hiding due to his political activities as a supporter of the democratic movements in the second part of the 1950s. He was one of the founders of the Marxist Shala-yi Javid (Eternal Flame) party in 1968 and was forced into hiding again that same year. During the period of Muhammad Daud's rule (1973 to 1978), a price of 1 million Afghanis was placed on his head, but he avoided capture. After the Marxist coup of 27 April 1978, he helped found the Organization for the Liberation of the Afghan People (SAMA) and the United National Front of Afghanistan. He was arrested on 27 February 1980 for opposing the PDPA and executed.

See also Poya, Nadir Ali

References

Hammond, Thomas Taylor. 1984. *Red Flag over Afghanistan: The Communist Coup, the Soviet Invasion and the Consequences.* Boulder, CO: Westview Press.

KAM

KAM, the acronym for the Workers' Intelligence Institute (Da Kargaron Amniyyati Mu'assan), was established by President Hafizullah Amin (1978–1979) and was the successor to the security service set up by President Nur Muhammad Taraki. The security service was headed by Aziz Ahmad Akbari from August to September 1979, but Akbari was replaced by Asadullah Amin, the nephew of President Hafizullah Amin. Both Asadullah Amin and the president were killed on 27 December 1979 by Soviet special forces.

See also Afghan Security Service; KHAD

References

Rubin, Barnett R. 2002. *The Fragmentation of Afghanistan.* 2nd ed. New Haven, CT: Yale University Press.

KANDAHAR PROVINCE

Kandahar Province is located in south-central Afghanistan and is bounded on the west by Helmand Province, in the north by Oruzgan Province, in the northeast by Zabul Province, and in the south and southeast by Pakistan. The city of Kandahar is the only major settlement in the province. Most of the people of Kandahar are Durranis, but there are Ghilzais and Hazaras (mainly in the urban areas), and in the city, there are Hindus who are traders and bankers. The province is watered by the Arghastan, Tarnak, and Arghandab Rivers, which lie between 3,000 and 7,000 feet above sea level; the city of Kandahar is some 2,462 feet above sea level.

The city is the second largest in Afghanistan, of ancient origin, and significant because of its strategic location on the trade and invasion route to the Indian subcontinent. It is also famous in Afghanistan because it is the site of the tomb of Ahmad Shah Durrani—the man who is credited with being the founder of modern Afghanistan and ruled as its king from 1747 to 1773. Business in the city manufacture silks, felt for coats, and rosaries made from silicate of magnesia. Kandahar has also been involved in the opium trade since the beginning of the twentieth century. It was the capital of Afghanistan until Timur Shah moved the capital to Kabul in order to weaken the power of the Durrani chiefs. In recent years, the city has been the center of power for the Taliban.

The city of Kandahar is surrounded by fertile land and renowned for the cultivation of fruit, especially grapes and pomegranates. Kandahar is connected by a tarmac highway with Kabul, Herat, and Chaman on the border with Pakistan, and it became an important trade and commercial center because it was a key location on the route to Iran and Pakistan. The city also has a major airport. It is dominated by the Durranis, who have tended to support the former king Zahir. On 5 November 1994, the city was captured by the Taliban, who made it their provincial capital, and it was the base for Mullah Muhammad Omar, the leader of the Taliban movement, until it fell to anti-Taliban forces in 2001. Although the Taliban had promised to defend Kandahar to the death, the city was abandoned after a short siege and U.S. bombing raids. The control of both the city and province of Kandahar is critical to the continued success of the central government in Kabul.

References

Adamec, Ludwig W. 1972–1985. *Historical and Political Gazetteer of Afghanistan.* 6 vols. Graz, Austria: Akademische Druck-u Verlagsansalt.

Interior of the City of Kandahar. Engraving from Scenery, Inhabitants and Costumes of Afghanistan *(Stapleton Collection/Corbis)*

KARMAL, BABRAK (1929–1996)

Babrak Karmal was said to have been a liberal democrat activist who became a Marxist, as demonstrated by his adoption of the pen name Karmal (meaning "son of labor") in 1954. He was born in 1929 in Kabul, the son of Maj. Gen. Muhammad Husain, former governor of Paktia Province. He was educated at Nejat High School, from which he graduated in 1948, but was refused entry to the Faculty of Law and Political Science at Kabul University because of his student union activities. However, he attended another institution, the College of Law and Political Science, from 1951 to 1953, when he was imprisoned, again because of his political activities among the student body.

He was released from prison in 1956 by President Muhammad Daud and obtained employment as a translator of English and German before going on to military training in 1957. Karmal graduated from the College of Law and Political Science in 1960 and one year later joined the Compilation and Translation Department of the Ministry of Education. He moved to the Ministry of Planning, where he

worked from 1961 to 1963, all the while increasing his involvement in political activities. In 1965 and again in 1969, he was elected to the Wolesi Jirga (House of the People) as a representative of Kabul, a position he held until 1973.

In 1974, Karmal became a member of the founding congress of the People's Democratic Party of Afghanistan (PDPA) and was elected as a member and secretary of the party's Central Committee. From 1965 to 1977, he led the Parcham faction of the PDPA, which reunited with the Khalq in 1977. He was a member of the Secretariat and of the Political Bureau of the Central Committee of the PDPA in 1977 but was arrested again in the following year after the funeral of Mir Akbar Khaibar. (Khaibar was the editor of *Parcham*, the newspaper of the Parchami faction of the PDPA, and had been assassinated, it was claimed, by Khalq supporters.) Karmal was released after the Saur Revolt of 27 April 1978, which brought the Communists to power, and he was elected vice-chair of the Revolutionary Council and deputy prime minister of Afghanistan. Karmal was an eloquent orator, an expert propagandist, and one of the most able of the Marxist leaders.

In July 1978, he was appointed Afghan's ambassador to Czechoslovakia but was dismissed a month later after being accused of plotting against the revolutionary government; thereafter, he was deprived of his party membership and all his positions. He returned to Kabul and succeeded Hafizullah Amin on 27 December 1929, becoming president and secretary-general of the PDPA, posts he held until 1986, when he was replaced by Dr. Muhammad Najibullah. He then left Afghanistan for Moscow until the fall of the Marxist regime in his homeland in April 1992; he returned to Mazar-i Sharif, which was held by his friend Gen. Abdul Rashid Dostum. He later went back to Moscow, where he died of cancer in December 1996.

See also People's Democratic Party of Afghanistan
References
Hammond, Thomas Taylor. 1984. *Red Flag over Afghanistan: The Communist Coup, the Soviet Invasion, and the Consequences.* Boulder, CO: Westview Press.

KARZAI, HAMID (1959–)

Hamid Karzai was appointed head of the Afghan Interim Government in December 2001 and confirmed as president of Afghanistan for a further period of two years by the Loya Jirga (Grand Council) held in June 2002. As such, he is responsible for bringing peace to a troubled nation, resolving issues related to the power of the warlords, and trying to rebuild the infrastructure and economy of Afghanistan utilizing international aid. Karzai is a powerful Pashtun tribal leader from Kandahar, the power base of the Taliban, and is a member of the same clan as the former king, Mohammed Zahir Shah.

Karzai received part of his education in India and speaks fluent English and six other languages. Unusually for an Afghan, he was a bachelor until the age of forty; in1999, he married an obstetrician-gynecologist who has been active in assisting refugees in Pakistan. His lateness in marrying was due to his dedication to the cause of Afghanistan; personal considerations were not a priority for him until his mother contracted a fatal illness and expressed a desire to see him settled before she died.

Following the Soviet invasion of Afghanistan in 1979, Karzai fled to Pakistan, where he set up supply routes between the mujahideen guerrillas in Af-

ghanistan and their U.S. backers. After the mujahideen defeated the Marxist government in 1992, Karzai returned to Afghanistan and became deputy foreign minister in the government of President Burhanuddin Rabbani until 1994. However, he grew disillusioned with the infighting of the mujahideen leaders and left the government. He briefly joined the Taliban, who once tried to make him their representative to the United Nations, a post he declined. An Islamic moderate, Karzai soon turned against the excesses of the Taliban regime, being particularly opposed to its brutal restrictions on women. He also became concerned that the movement had been infiltrated and was being controlled by foreigners, including Pakistanis, Chechens, and militant Arab radicals from Egypt, Saudi Arabia, and the gulf states.

Karzai again left Afghanistan for Pakistan with his father, who had been a deputy in the Afghan government; the elder Karzai was assassinated at age 75 in Quetta, probably by Taliban agents. As a result of this act, Hamid Karzai became an implacable foe of the Taliban, and he approached Washington with plans for leading a resistance to the extremist movement. His opposition to the Taliban was also due to the destruction being caused in Afghanistan by radical Arab elements and other foreign fighters who wantonly destroyed houses, orchards, and vineyards. He has also accused Taliban members of killing Afghans without cause, other than the desire to impose their will on the population.

The 11 September 2001 terrorist attacks in the United States persuaded Karzai that it was time to act, and on 7 October, he slipped across the border into Afghanistan. He first went to his ancestral village of Karz, near Kandahar, before setting off into the mountains of Oruzgan Province, where he started to recruit other tribal leaders to join the anti-Taliban cause. However, he soon became a target for the Taliban, and he only avoided death or at least capture in a Taliban ambush by calling on U.S. forces to mount a helicopter rescue operation in November 2001. He soon returned to the mountains and continued his recruitment drive to oppose the Taliban, which grew in popularity as Northern Alliance forces continued their advance toward Kabul, backed by U.S. air strikes. In December 2001, Karzai was instrumental in securing the negotiated surrender of the city of Kandahar, the Taliban stronghold that Mullah Muhammad

Secretary of Defense Donald H. Rumsfeld (left) escorts Chairman of the Afghan Interim Administration Hamid Karzai through an honor cordon and into the Pentagon on 28 January 2002. (R. D. Ward/Department of Defense)

Omar, the leader of the Taliban movement, had promised to defend to the death. The Taliban fled into the mountains before the handover could take place.

Also in December 2001, Karzai was nominated as leader of the Afghan Interim Government by the UN-sponsored Bonn Conference; he was supposed to hold the post for six months until a loya jirga could be convened. A transitional government was then appointed for a period of two years, pending the holding of new elections, under a newly drafted constitution. Some Afghan leaders are skeptical of Karzai, as they feel Afghanistan can only be ruled by a battle-hardened fighter, but others—and the international community—feel that someone with his leadership qualities, astute diplomacy, and the manner and judgment of a civilian is well placed to counter the misrule of the various warlords.

After the fall of Kandahar, Karzai set off to Kabul to formally take up his post as leader of the Afghan government on 22 December 2001. His thirty-member cabinet included two women, occupying the posts of minister of public health and minister of women's affairs. Karzai's position was not an enviable one, for he was beset by problems even before he assumed control, primarily because the new government had not included the regional warlords, who had been sidelined by the Bonn Conference. Opposition came from a variety of sources, with Gen. Abdul Rashid Dostum being the most angry and problematic opponent, due to his having been ignored and key defense and security posts having gone to rivals in the Northern Alliance. As leader of the Uzbek minority and controller of a large part of northern Afghanistan, with an army of 7,000 men, Dostum is a formidable player in Afghan politics. The former president, Burhanuddin Rabbani, was also considered to be a possible center of opposition, with some Pakistani intelligence officers reporting that Rabbani supporters had been buying allegiance among Pashtun leaders in eastern Afghanistan to oppose both Karzai and the return of the former king using funds that were possibly supplied by Iran.

Karzai calls himself "a pauper king" and follows a relatively austere lifestyle, maintaining a simply furnished office and infrastructure to reflect the suffering of the majority of the Afghan population. His strength derives from several facts: that he was not involved in the civil war between the mujahideen groups, that he opposed the Taliban when the excesses of the regime became apparent, and that he is a respected tribal leader who considers himself an Afghan first and a Pashtun second. However, the weakness of the new government was illustrated on 14 February 2002 when the tourism minister, Abdul Rahman, was murdered at the Kabul airport. First reports indicated that he was killed by an angry mob of pilgrims who were waiting to go on the hajj. They had experienced long delays because of the lack of aircraft and were supposedly incensed that the minister was boarding a plane to New Delhi. However, subsequent statements from Karzai's office indicated that the killing was really an assassination, and key members of the Northern Alliance were named as being involved in the murder. There is some speculation that the original version is correct and that the official version of events is being used to counter factional opposition. Five officials were arrested in Afghanistan and three in Mecca, Saudi Arabia—Gen. Abdullah Jan Tawhidi, head of intelligence, Qalander Bed, a senior defense official, and Sananwal Haleem, a senior prosecutor in the Ministry of Justice.

The Loya Jirga, which was opened by the former king Zahir on 11 June 2002, elected Hamid Karzai as president by a landslide vote, though this was aided by the king's announcement that he did not wish to become involved in Afghan politics, the withdrawal from the contest of former president Rabbani and the support of a number of powerful Tajik leaders, including Mohammad Qasin Fahim, the defense minister, and Younis Qanooni, another Tajik minister. In his acceptance address, Karzai called for reconciliation in the post-Taliban era and stated that ordinary members of the religious militia should not be prosecuted. He also said that a prime concern had to be the reconstruction of the devastated country, with foreign aid being spent with transparency and precision and protected from plundering and looting, as it would be the only chance that Afghanistan would have to receive aid for its reconstruction. The newly elected president added that the Afghan people desired peace, stability, and disarmament and that the existing peace needed to be strengthened.

The administration of President Karzai is beset with difficulties. At present, his authority is, by and large, limited to Kabul, and the power of the regional warlords has yet to be challenged. A further concern is that the Taliban and al-Qaeda have not been eradicated and pose a real threat to future stability, especially as Mullah Omar, former leader of the Taliban, is still at large. The regime also faces major problems over the return and resettlement of refugees and the slow arrival of reconstruction aid promised by the international community. A great deal of the credibility of the new regime rests on the ability of the president to deliver on two fronts—stability and reconstruction—with both being somewhat tenuous as of July 2003.

The problem of stability was again highlighted in September 2002 when a car bomb in Kabul killed at least ten people, followed a few hours later by an assassination attack on President Karzai in Kandahar. These incidents were not totally isolated: there had been eight explosions in Kabul in less than a month; Karzai's deputy, Haji Abdul Qadir, had been assassinated in July; and there had been a number of bombings and ambushes of U.S. forces throughout the summer. These events demonstrated the fragility of the regime, which was under attack by the Taliban, al-Qaeda, and other dissident elements, some of whom were former mujahideen leaders. One of these was Gulbuddin Hekmatyar, who had declared a jihad against foreign forces in Afghanistan and who, it is thought, might still be receiving support from Iran despite being expelled by the Iranian regime.

The countryside is firmly in the hands of the warlords, and there is also a great deal of suspicion among the Pashtuns, who previously had dominated the country's politics, in regard to the large number of ethnic Tajiks in the government. This suspicion has been exploited by opposition forces anxious to use this rivalry to foment a new jihad against President Karzai. The rivalry among local warlords has also helped Karzai's opponents, especially since many of the regional chieftains have been recognized by the new government or financed and armed by the United States to aid in the hunt for Osama bin Laden's fighters. This instability is best illustrated by events in Gardez in January 2002, where factional fighting between rival warlords resulted in a number of deaths and injuries to fighters and civilians alike. The struggle between the Karzai-appointed governor of Paktia Province, Badsha Khan, and the tribal leader of Gardez City, Hajji Sayfullah, threatened the stability of the government, especially because forces loyal to the administration were told to remain neutral, despite the governor's defeat, and because U.S. soldiers in the area made it plain that they were not taking sides. Most civilians were bitter at the actions of both factions and fervently wished the government to bring peace and security. Kabul's response was to set up a commission under the border affairs minister, Amanullah Zadran, to investigate the situation and determine whether there had been interference from Pakistan, Iran, the Taliban, or al-Qaeda.

The Karzai regime is seen as deriving power from the presence of foreign forces, comprising U.S. troops, Coalition special forces backed by U.S. airpower, and the International Security Assistance Force (ISAF) in Kabul, provided by European nations and headed by Turkey. For some time, Karzai had been requesting an expansion of the ISAF's mandate, but such a move was consistently opposed by the United States, which wanted to speed the extraction of troops from Afghanistan. However, toward the end of 2002, the Bush administration began to relax its opposition to a more extensive ISAF, although the United States made no commitment in terms of troops or funding. At this point, it seems evident that the Karzai government will only be kept in power by expanding the present authority of Coalition troops, especially with the threat of the Taliban and al-Qaeda still to be resolved and reconstruction still to materialize.

See also Afghanistan Interim Government; Coalition Land Campaign against the Taliban; Dostum, Gen. Abdul Rashid; International Security Assistance Force; UK Special Forces; U.S. Special Forces

References
"Insecure and Suddenly Even the Capital Is Dangerous." 2002. *Economist* (London) 364, no. 8289: 42–43.
McGirk, Tim. 2002. "Lonely at the Top." *Time Atlantic* 159, no. 9: 36–38.
McGirk, Tim, Massimo Calabresi, Mark Thompson, Ron Stodgill II, and Charles P. Wallace. 2001. "The Great New Afghan Hope." *Time Atlantic* 158, no. 25: 41–42.
Quinn-Judge, Paul. 2001. "So Many Warlords, So Little Time." *Time Atlantic* 159, no. 4: 23.

KATAWAZI, KHILGAL MUHAMMAD (1948–)

Khilgal Muhammad Katawazi was a founding member of the Khalq faction of the People's Democratic Party of Afghanistan (PDPA). He had been a producer for Radio Afghanistan before undergoing military training in 1972 and rejoined the radio station in 1973. He was used by the PDPA as a messenger to take instructions to the armed forces to begin the Saur Revolt on 27 April 1978, ushering in the Communist regime. He was born in 1948 in Sharno-Katawaz in Paktia Province and entered a career in journalism after receiving a degree from the Faculty of Letters at Kabul University in 1970. Following the Saur Revolt, he became deputy minister of radio and television and then minister of information and Culture in April 1979. He was a member of the Central Committee and Revolutionary Council of the PDPA and trained under Nur Muhammad Taraki, the prime minister of Afghanistan from 1978 to 1979. However, on the fall of the Khalq government led by Hafizullah Amin in December 1979, he was arrested and jailed in the Pul-i Charkhi prison.

See also People's Democratic Party of Afghanistan

References
Arnold, Anthony. 1983. *Afghan's Two-Party Communism: Parcham and Khalq.* Stanford, CA: Hoover Institution Press.

KESHTMAND, SULTAN ALI (1935–)

Sultan Ali Keshtmand stood for election to the lower house of the Meshrano Jirga (Upper House of Parliament) in 1965 but was not voted in, and he secretly became a member of the Central Committee of the People's Democratic Party of Afghanistan (PDPA). He was born in 1935, son of Njaf Ali, a Hazara, and graduated in economics from Kabul University. He became director of the Economic Section of the Ministry of Mines and Industries in 1967. After the Saur Revolt of 27 April 1978 and the advent of Communist rule, he became minister of planning, but he was arrested in August 1978 and accused of plotting against the Khalq government. He was sentenced to death, but on 7 October 1979, his sentence was commuted to fifteen years of imprisonment. After the downfall of Hafizullah Amin, the Khalq leader, on 27 December 1979, Keshtmand was appointed deputy prime minister, vice-president of the Revolutionary Council, and minister of planning. He was also a member of the

Politburo and president of the Revolutionary Council and became prime minister in June 1981. He was prime minister from 1981 to 1988. In May 1990, he was appointed first vice-president of Afghanistan, but in February 1991, he was ousted from all his positions and left for Moscow, returning to Kabul in July 1991. After the fall of Kabul to the mujahideen, he left Afghanistan. He remains in exile.

References
Arnold, Anthony. 1983. *Afghanistan's Two-Party Communism: Parcham and Khalq*. Stanford, CA: Hoover Institution Press.

KHAD

KHAD is the acronym for the State Security Service (Khedamat-i Ettela'at-i Daulati) that was set up by Babrak Karmal. The organization was initially headed by Dr. Muhammad Najibullah, before he became secretary-general of the People's Democratic Party of Afghanistan (PDPA) and then president of Afghanistan. Under Najibullah, the organization was upgraded to a ministry and became known as Wazarat-i Ettela'at-i Daulati (WAD). Najibullah was replaced by Gen. Ghulam Faruq Yaqubi. The organization had several thousand operatives as well as informers in all branches of the military and in the National Guard. The State Security Service was well trained, disciplined, well armed, well paid, and a major source of President Najibullah's power. Control of the security forces rested with the Parchami faction, which provided a balance to the Khalq influences in the military (which KHAD had also penetrated).

See also Afghan Security Service; KAM
References
Rubin, Barnett R. 2002. *The Fragmentation of Afghanistan*. 2nd ed. New Haven, CT: Yale University Press.

KHAIBAR, MIR AKBAR (1925–1978)

Mir Akbar Khaibar was born in 1925 in Logar and attended Kabul Military School, graduating in 1947. In 1950, he was arrested and sentenced to six years of imprisonment, and during that period, he met Babrak Karmal, a leading member of the People's Democratic Party of Afghanistan (PDPA) who would become secretary-general of the party and then president of Afghanistan from 1979 to 1986. Khaibar served as an officer in the Ministry of the Interior from 1955 to 1965 but was banished to Paktia Province from 1965 to 1975. He was one of the founding members of the PDPA and a member of its Central Committee. He became editor of *Parcham*, the party's weekly newspaper, and was in charge of the party's recruitment activities within the armed forces. He was assassinated on 17 April 1978 following a visit to the Bagram air base. According to Parchami sources, the assassins were supporters of the Khalq faction led by Hafizullah Amin, but other sources pointed to Daudists (Muhammad Daud's supporters). However, his death and the arrest of members of both factions of the party provided the trigger for the Saur Revolt of 27 April 1978, which brought the Communists to power.

See also People's Democratic Party of Afghanistan
References
Arnold, Anthony. 1983. *Afghanistan's Two-Party Communism: Parcham and Khalq*. Stanford, CA: Hoover Institution Press.

KHALES, YUNIS (1919–)

Yunis Khales is the leader of a group called the Islamic Party—Khales, having left Gulbuddin Hekmatyar's group of the same root name. Khales was born in 1919 in Gandomak and was educated in Islamic law and theology after graduating from the Shah Mahmud High School in Faizabad and teaching in a Yaftal primary school. An Islamist and fervent anti-Communist, he was forced to flee to Pakistan following the coup staged by Muhammad Daud in 1973. He joined Hekmatyar's resistance movement in 1979, fighting in Badakhshan Province and commanding the group operating in the Upper Yuftasl region. His breakaway group was active in armed raids on the Marxist government in Kabul, particularly in the Khugiana area. Khales was a member of the Afghan Interim Government (AIG) and was appointed minister of the interior; he resigned from this post in May 1991, though he was originally one of the AIG's strongest supporters. As a radical, Khales is opposed to the concept of universal suffrage, the emancipation of women, and Shi'a participation in the AIG.

See also Hekmatyar, Gulbuddin; Islamic Party—Khales
References
Rashid, Ahmed. 2001. *Taliban: The Story of the Afghan Warlords*. London: Pan.

KHOST   147

KHALILULLAH, LIEUTENANT GENERAL (1944–)

The son of a farmer, Khalilullah was born in 1944 in Shiwaki and attended Ghazi High School before going to military school for a one-year course in 1963. His career was marked by a series of military appointments and postings, and he played a significant role in the delivery of military support for the coup staged by Muhammad Daud in 1973 and the Saur Revolt of 27 April 1978 (which ushered in Communists rule), through his position as chief of staff of the Eighty-Eighth Corps from 1973 to 1978. As a result of the factional infighting within the PDPA, he was imprisoned from July 1978 until the downfall of the Khalq regime under Hafizullah Amin on 27 December 1979. On his release, he was made commander of the Central Forces and of the Kabul garrison. He was a member of the Central Committee and Revolutionary Council of the PDPA and served as deputy minister of defense until January 1984, when he became governor of Herat and commander of the Western Zone.

See also People's Democratic Party of Afghanistan
References
Arnold, Anthony. 1983. *Afghanistan's Two-Part Communism: Parcham and Khalq.* Stanford, CA: Hoover Institution Press.

KHALQ

The Khalq was a faction of the People's Democratic Party of Afghanistan (PDPA), which was led from April 1978 to September 1979 by Nur Muhammad Taraki and by Hafizullah Amin from September to December 1979. The faction was named after its newspaper, *Khalq* (meaning "people"). Prior to this, Khalq had been reunited with the Parcham faction of the PDPA, led by Babrak Karmal. Together, the two factions staged the Saur Revolt on 27 April 1978, which brought the Communists to power. However, Taraki's faction achieved dominance, and Parcham members were purged from the leadership. Karmal was able to return to power in December 1979 with Soviet backing, and Parcham became the dominant element in the PDPA. Rivalry between the two factions continued, and eventually a number of Khalqis were expelled from the party, forming themselves into the Islamic Unity Party (Hizb-i Wahdat).

See also People's Democratic Party of Afghanistan

References
Rubin, Barnett R. 1988. "Soviet Militarism, Islamic Resistance and Peace in Afghanistan." Typescript. Afghan Research Center, University of Nebraska, Omaha.

KHAN, KHAN ABDUL GHAFFAR (1890–1988?)

Khan Abdul Ghaffar Khan was a Pashtun nationalist who advocated nonviolent means for gaining independence from Britain for Afghans living in the frontier areas of British India and later Pakistan. He was the founder of a number of organizations, including the Red Shirts, or Servants of God, and enjoyed enormous popularity in Afghanistan and the North-West Frontier Province of India.

Khan was born in 1890 in the North-West Frontier Province and educated in a village school in Utmanzai prior to going to high school in Peshawar. Due to his Pashtun nationalist activities, especially his founding of the Red Shirts, he was imprisoned several times by the British Indian and Pakistan governments, but he still attracted a large following and was acclaimed as "the Frontier Ghandi." His organization was allied with the Congress Party of Mahatma Gandhi, divided into cells, and represented in most villages in the frontier region.

Due to his political activities, Khan was always welcomed in Kabul, as the Afghan governments strongly supported the Pashtunistan issue (calling for the return of Pastun tribal territory in Pakistan to Afghan control or at least the granting of independence or autonomy for the region). Indeed, King Amanullah bestowed on Khan the title "Pride of the Afghans" (Fakhri-i Afghan). Khan often lived in Kabul as the guest of all governments—royal, republican, and Marxist. He died in Peshawar in the late 1980s and was buried in Jalalabad.

See also Red Shirts
References
Jannson, Eland. 1981. *India, Pakistan or Pakhunistan?* Uppsala, Sweden: Almquist.

KHOST

Khost is a town and an administrative district in Paktia Province, which occupies the upper portion of the valley of the Shamil and Kaitu Rivers. The valley is 40 miles long and is watered by three streams. Given the good water supply, the district is largely agricultural, and the primary crop is rice; cows and goats are the chief stock. The upper part of the valley is occupied by Khostwalis and the lower part by Waziris. The town and district saw severe fighting during the Afghan civil war (1989 to 2001) due to their strategic location on the supply lines of the mujahideen forces, being some 18 miles from Pakistan. Many of the leaders of the Marxist regime in Kabul originally came from the district and were supported by the population. The town was besieged by mujahideen forces in 1986 and finally fell to them on 31 March 1991, after which about 2,000 residents fled to Pakistan because of concerns about their security under the mujahideen. The economy of the area has largely survived because of the illegal export of timber into Pakistan, but this business has caused severe environmental damage to the district.

During the period of Taliban rule (1996 to 2001), Khost, as a predominately Pashtun area, was strongly pro-Taliban. The city and surrounding area became an important trading and logistic center for the Taliban, providing a link with Pakistan and aiding in the movement of foreign fighters supporting the Taliban. Since the fall of the Taliban, the area has become a base for Coalition forces hunting remnants of the Taliban and al-Qaeda. Throughout 2002, there were a series of actions in the area around Khost, with numerous small-scale raids made on Coalition forces by fighters using the steep mountain paths to cross and recross the border with Pakistan.

In April 2002, U.S. Special Forces began to train Afghans to fight against the Taliban and al-Qaeda, and troops loyal to Badsha Khan, who had been removed as governor of Khost by President Karzai, fought alongside U.S. forces in Operation Anaconda in May 2002. However, the factional disputes in the region were not resolved, and on 8 September, Badsha Khan was ousted from his stronghold at Khost by troops loyal to the new governor, Hakim Taniwal, who was a supporter of President Karzai. Two days later, Badsha Khan launched a counterattack but was unsuccessful, and many civilians were injured and some killed in rocket attacks on the city. The action was monitored by Coalition forces, but they were under instructions to maintain their distance and to refrain from fighting unless directly challenged. However, more fighting ensued between the rival factions themselves, with Badsha Khan attempting to take control of the city of Gardez, the capital of Paktia Province. Thereafter, the U.S. forces severed all links with Badsha Khan.

The strategic significance of Khost has been recognized by the U.S. military, which maintains a special forces presence at the nearby airfield and ground troops based near the city. However, these soldiers have been subjected to guerrilla attacks since their arrival and have used fighter jets to strike suspected enemy positions launching rocket attacks on Coalition positions.

The ability of Coalition forces and their allies to hunt down al-Qaeda and Taliban fighters has been hindered by the factional infighting and the inability of the Karzai government to impose its authority on the region, though moves were made in that direction, with government troops taking control of Gardez in February 2003. Due to its location in relation to Pakistan, the Khost area must be made secure by the Kabul government if peace and stability is to come to Afghanistan.

See also Coalition Land Campaign against the Taliban; Paktia Province

References

Adamec, Ludwig W. 1972–1985. *Historical and Political Gazetteer of Afghanistan.* 6 vols. Graz, Austria: Akademische Druck-u Verlagsansalt.

Krushelnycky, Askold. 2002. "Afghanistan: Khost Region Is Focus of Fighting, Training." http://www.rferl.org/nca/features/2002/04/08042002 090002.asp (cited 8 April 2002).

Marsden, Peter. 1998. *The Taliban: War, Religion and the New Order in Afghanistan.* London and New York: Zed Books.

KHOST REBELLION

The Khost Rebellion began in March 1924 as a response to the reform program of King Amanullah and was led by the Mangal tribe, under Abdullah Kan and Mulla-i-Lang. The rebels were beaten by the king's forces the next month but not routed, and they were then joined by the Sulaiman Khel and Ali Khel tribes. In August 1924, the king declared a holy war against the rebels, but the revolt lasted until January 1925, ending with the rebels' defeat; the leaders were taken prisoner and executed. The revolt caused the king to slow the process of Westernization, and reforms were not resumed until 1928.

See also Amanullah, King

References

Poullada, Leon B. 1973. *Reform and Rebellion in Afghanistan, 1919–1929.* Ithaca, NY: Cornell University Press.

KHUGIANI TRIBE

The Khugiani tribe is a branch of the Durrani tribe, coming primarily from the Jalalabad area but also from the provinces of Laghman and Kandahar. The Khugianis are organized into three clans. The tribe played a leading role in the revolt that led to the downfall of King Amanullah in 1928. Over the centuries, the Khugianis have been at odds with the neighboring tribes of the Ghilzais, on one side, and the Shinwaris, on the other. The Khugianis are now part of the mujahideen forces led by Yunis Khales.

See also Amanullah, King

References

Clifford, Mary Louis. 1973. *The Land and People of Afghanistan*. Philadelphia: Lippincott.

KHURRAM, ALI AHMAD (1931–1977)

Ali Ahmad Khurram had begun his career in the Ministry of Planning in 1956 and served as minister of that office from 1974 until he was assassinated in 1977. He had graduated from Kabul University in 1957 with a B.A. in economics, and he obtained his M.A. in 1965 at the University of Pittsburgh, remaining in the United States until 1968 for postgraduate studies. In 1958, he had been made director of the Plan Formulation and Coordination Department, and he later became director of the Trade Department and president of planning from 1956 to 1971. He served as deputy minister and then minister of planning from 1971 to 1977. During this period, Prime Minister Muhammad Daud had decided to reduce his country's reliance on Soviet aid and to accept development funds from Arab states and Iran. As a consequence, Khurram was instructed to accept no more Soviet aid and to expedite the completion of all projects already in process. On 16 November 1977, he was assassinated by Muhammad Marjan, who claimed that he was acting in the name of the Islamic revolution but was also suspected of having allegiances to Khalq, a faction of the People's Democratic Party of Afghanistan. Marjan was sentenced to life imprisonment but was later released under a general amnesty.

References

Dupree, Louis, and Linette Albert, eds. 1974. *Afghanistan in the 1970s.* New York: Praeger.

KHYBER PASS

Steeped in the violent history of the region, the Khyber Pass runs through a gorge and high hills from the border of Afghanistan to Peshawar in Pakistan. The entrance to the pass in Pakistan is at Ali Masjid village, some 10 miles from Peshawar; the pass then narrows to some 200 yards in width and runs to a height of 3,518 feet before widening out at Tarkham, the frontier post shared with Afghanistan.

The area occupied by the pass is largely populated by the Afridis, members of a Pashtun-speaking tribe who had always seen themselves as the protectors of the gateway to India (now Pakistan). At times, they have entered into military service with rulers of Afghanistan, serving as bodyguards or militia, and they fought in campaigns against British India. The Khyber Pass has had a bloody history, as evidenced by the struggles that took place in the three Anglo-Afghan wars, particularly during the British retreat in the first of those wars. The pass was critical for the transport of men and munitions during the mujahideen struggle against the Soviets (1979 to 1989), and the Afridis levied tolls on all convoys passing through their territory into Afghanistan.

Such was the strategic significance of the pass to the British India government that a narrow-gauge railway was built at the end of the nineteenth century to link the pass with the railway terminal at Peshawar. Control of the pass went to Britain in 1879 under the terms of the Treaty of Gandomak following the Second Anglo-Afghan War. In 1893, Britain concluded the Durand Agreement with Amir Abdur Rahman in an attempt to demarcate the frontier between Afghanistan and British India; the border that was decided on placed the Khyber Pass within British India (in the area that became Pakistan in 1947), though Afghanistan has always disputed the agreement, maintaining that it was signed under duress.

The whole region around the Khyber Pass is part of the tribal area of Pakistan but is only loosely controlled by Islamabad. As a consequence, the region and the pass have continued to be a center for the smuggling of foreign-made goods, arms, and drugs. The trade is focused on the town of Landi Kotal, which is a few miles within the pass. Although the Pakistan government has tried to suppress the trade, its successes have been minimal, and given the nature of the terrain and the tribal society, such efforts are unlikely to succeed in the future.

See also Afridi Tribe; Durand Agreement; First Anglo-Afghan War; Second Anglo-Afghan War

Trucks negotiate the winding road leading through the Khyber Pass in northwestern Pakistan. (Ric Erginbright/Corbis)

References

Alder, G. 1963. *British India's Northern Frontier 1869–95: A Study in Imperial Policy*. London: Longman.

Forbes, A. 1982. *The Afghan Wars, 1839–42 and 1879–80*. London: Seeley.

Storr, Lilian A. 1920. *Frontier Folk of the Afghan Border and Beyond*. London: Church Missionary Society.

KUNAR PROVINCE

Kunar Province, located in northeastern Afghanistan, covers some 3,742 square miles and has a population of about 250,000. It is dominated by Nuristanis in the north and west and Pashtuns in the south and east. The two ethnic groups have always been in conflict with each other, largely because of Pashtun incursions into traditional Nuristan territory. The territorial integrity of the province was altered by the Kabul government in 1970 when it was absorbed into Nangarhar, but Kunar was again designated as a province in 1977. Following the Soviet withdrawal in 1989, the Kabul government created Nuristan from parts of Kunar and Laghman Provinces, with the residue again being incorporated into Nangarhar Province.

The revolt of the mujahideen began in Kunar Province in 1978. Nearly all of the mujahideen groups were present in Kunar, and the bulk of the government bases in the province were captured. However, the two main groups at the beginning of the revolt were those led by Gulbuddin Hekmatyar and the Wahhabis led by Maulawi Husain Jamilurrahman. The latter declared an Islamic amirate after a break with Hekmatyar. However, an explosion in Jamilurrahman's headquarters at Asadabad decimated the leadership and enabled an alliance of mujahideen forces to expel the Wahhabis, who were backed by volunteer fighters from Arab states.

The province's economy is based on subsistence agriculture (which is, in turn, reliant on irrigation) and timber, being one of only two wooded provinces in the country, the other being Paktia. Kunar shares a border with Pakistan, and its administrative center, Asadabad, is renowned as the birthplace of Sayyid Jamaluddin Afghani, the founder of the concept of pan-Islam propagated as a counter to Western imperialism at the end of the nineteenth century.

References
Adamec, Ludwig W. 1972–1985. *Historical and Political Gazetteer of Afghanistan.* 6 vols. Graz, Austria: Akademische Druck-u Verlagsansalt.
Emadi, Hajizullah. 1990. *State, Revolution, and Superpowers in Afghanistan.* New York: Praeger.

KUNDUZ PROVINCE

Kunduz Province is situated in northern Afghanistan, in the northwestern part of what used to be Kataghan Province, and occupies an area of 2,876 square miles. The provincial population is roughly 57,000, of whom about 53,000 live in the administrative capital of the same name. The province is well watered, with the major rivers being the Amu Daria, Khanabad, and Kunduz. The main economic activity is agriculture; cotton, beets, cane sugar, and melons are the primary crops. The province is one of the few industrial areas in Afghanistan, a sector based on cotton, silk weaving, vegetable oil, soap, and carpets. The population is largely Uzbek, but there are some Pashtuns and other ethnic minorities in the province.

References
Adamec, Ludwig W. 1972–1985. *Historical and Political Gazetteer of Afghanistan.* 6 vols. Graz, Austria: Akademische Druck-u Verlagsansalt.

KUSHANI, MAHBUBULLAH (1944–)

Mahbubullah Kushani had worked in the Department of Water and Power in Kabul before serving in the Ministry of Planning from 1980 to 1987, becoming deputy prime minister in 1987 and again beginning on 27 May 1990. He had also served as first secretary of the Organization of Revolutionary Toilers of Afghanistan.

References
Magnus, Ralph H., and Eden Naby. 2000. *Afghanistan: Mullah, Marx and Mujahid.* Rev. ed. Boulder, CO: Westview Press.

LADEN, OSAMA BIN (1955–)

Osama bin Laden, one of the most internationally notorious Islamic fundamentalists, is the leader of the al-Qaeda terrorist network and is charged with responsibility for the abortive attack on the World Trade Center in 1993, the bombing of the U.S. embassies in Kenya and Tanzania in 1998, and the suicide attack on the USS *Cole* in Aden in October 2000. There is also strong suspicion that he was behind operations against the United States in Somalia and bomb attacks on U.S. military facilities in Saudi Arabia. Worldwide condemnation came when he was deemed responsible for the terrorist attacks on the World Trade Center in New York and the Pentagon building in Washington on 11 September 2001.

Bin Laden became involved in Afghanistan as a mujahideen leader fighting against the Soviet occupation forces and the Marxist government in Kabul and later as a supporter of the Taliban regime. The seventeenth son of a Saudi who ran an extremely successful construction business, he received a degree in public administration from King Abdul-Aziz University, Jeddah, in 1981, before joining the family firm. He became extremely religious when he was involved in the reconstruction of the holy mosques in Mecca and Medina, which was done by his father's company. However, his political outlook and his fervent Islamic fundamentalism was largely shaped by his move to Afghanistan in 1979 to help the Afghans in their struggle against the Soviets and the Marxist government in Kabul. Largely as a result of his fervor and the funds at his disposal, he was able to recruit a large number of Arab fighters to go with him to Afghanistan, and he also attracted some recruits from students at Pakistani *madrasas* (religious schools).

He spent ten years in Afghanistan as a successful mujahideen leader and, ironically, received U.S. military aid arranged by the Central Intelligence Agency (CIA) and channeled through the Inter-Services Intelligence Service of Pakistan. However, he left Afghanistan in 1989 after the Soviet withdrawal and returned to Saudi Arabia, where he founded an organization to help fighters returning from Afghanistan, many of whom then went to fight in Bosnia: this was the embryonic al-Qaeda organization. Bin Laden also continued his studies with Islamic radical thinkers and became incensed by Saudi Arabia's willingness to allow U.S. military forces to be stationed on its soil during the Gulf War against Iraq, which was sparked by Iraq's invasion of Kuwait. He was expelled by the Saudi administration in 1991 for his antigovernment activities and went to Sudan.

Bin Laden remained active in extremist Islamic causes in Sudan. At the same time, he was providing funding to Islamic humanitarian organizations, to other Islamic groups, and to militant Islamic publications. In 1994, he was stripped of his Saudi citizenship and disowned by his family; the Saudi government also froze his assets in the kingdom, but he had removed the bulk of his funds when he left for Sudan. In 1995, it was reported that he was behind the formation of the "Gulf Battalion" organized by the Guardians of the Iranian Revolution, and it was thought that the Yemeni fundamentalist Abd-al-Majid-al-Zandai housed some of these fighters in his training camps. A year later, bin Laden was behind attacks on U.S. personnel and facilities in Riyadh and Khobar in Saudi Arabia, justifying these attacks on the grounds that infidel soldiers should not be present in the holy land of Islam.

In 1996, bin Laden was expelled from Sudan. His expulsion was the result of pressure applied on the Sudanese government by the United States and Saudi Arabia as well as the threat of UN sanctions that resulted from Sudan's alleged complicity in the attempted assassination of President Hosni Mubarak of Egypt while on a visit to Ethiopia. After his expulsion, bin Laden returned to Afghanistan, where he continued to support extremist Islamic activities. His base was at the Taliban-held town of Jalalabad, where he was accompanied by about fifty family members and followers. In February 1997, the new Taliban government in Kabul refused a U.S. request to expel bin Laden, turning down an offer from the West to grant the Taliban international recognition and an opportunity to take Afghanistan's seat in international organizations. On 19 March 1997, an attempt was made to assassinate bin Laden in Jalalabad: an explosion destroyed the police station, killed more than 50 people, and wounded another 150. As a result of this attack, bin Laden moved his base to Kandahar, which was the Taliban stronghold and the home of the Taliban's leader, Mullah Muhammad Omar. The Taliban have since claimed that they had moved his location in order to place him under house arrest and to prevent his use of Afghan soil to harm any country, including Saudi Arabia.

In February 1998, bin Laden announced the formation of a new alliance of terrorist organizations entitled the World Islamic Front for the Jihad against Jews and Crusaders, which included a number of militant groups, particularly in Egypt. The main plank of the front's policy was the declared intention to attack America and its allies, including civilians, anywhere in the world. By May 1998, the front had effectively merged with bin Laden's al-Qaeda network. During all of this activity, bin Laden continued to be sheltered by the Taliban regime, which resisted international efforts to secure his expulsion from Afghanistan. On 20 August 1998, the United States attacked al-Qaeda training camps set up by bin Laden, but the assault had limited effect and no real military value. At the same time, President Bill Clinton froze all of bin Laden's assets in the United States, which included property and bank accounts.

On 15 October 1999, the UN Security Council demanded that the Taliban regime hand over Osama bin Laden to authorities in a country where he could be brought to justice for indicted crimes. This demand was backed by a threat to impose sanctions. After further Taliban intransigence, these sanctions were imposed on 14 November: all Taliban funds were ordered frozen, and Taliban-owned aircraft were prohibited from taking off or landing. Despite this international pressure, the Taliban refused to budge, insisting that under Islamic law, bin Laden was a guest and that he was no longer in communication with his followers. However, it is clear that followers of bin Laden were active in Chechnya, Tajikistan, Uzbekistan, and Kashmir and probably linked with Islamic militants in Indonesia and the Philippines, using funds supplied by bin Laden. His finances are spread around the world through companies involved in property management, maritime transport, aircraft rental, construction, and a range of other commercial activities. He has major construction and agricultural investments in Sudan and commercial interests in Somalia, Luxembourg, and Switzerland, making it difficult to track down and neutralize many of his financial transactions.

The terrorist attack on the World Trade Center in New York and the Pentagon in Washington on 11 September 2001 radically changed the attitude of the international community toward Osama bin Laden, al-Qaeda, and the Taliban regime in Afghanistan. The United States and the United Kingdom quickly laid the responsibility for the atrocities at bin Laden's door, and, in response, he released a video, transmitted by the al-Jazeera satellite television station in Qatar, applauding the attacks as legitimate strikes against an infidel nation. Subsequent investigations also began to produce evidence linking the hijackers of the aircraft involved in the September attacks to Osama bin Laden and the al-Qaeda network, which clearly had followers in Europe. The loss of nearly 4,000 lives in the terrorist attacks shook the world and led George W. Bush's administration to declare that the United States was now involved in a "War on Terror." The U.S. policy was immediately backed by the United Kingdom.

It was determined that military action was needed to overthrow the Taliban regime in Afghanistan, to destroy al-Qaeda, and to capture and bring to justice Osama bin Laden. This effort was to be undertaken under the terms of the UN Charter, which allows nations to act in self-defense. An operation entitled Enduring Freedom was launched by the United States and the United Kingdom in October 2001 with Cruise missile attacks on strategic interests of the Taliban regime, on suspected al-Qaeda training camps, and on possible hideouts of Osama bin Laden and his immediate entourage. In addition, support was provided for the forces opposing the Taliban, largely through the supply of military equipment and intelligence and the deployment of U.S. and UK Special Forces. Action was then intensified through bombing raids by the U.S. Air Force, designed to destroy the Taliban's infrastructure and to weaken their resistance so that opposition forces would be able to oust the regime. The military resistance of the Taliban soon crumbled, and the opposition forces quickly gained control over the bulk of Afghanistan. The remnants of the Taliban and al-Qaeda fighters withdrew to the mountain regions close to the Pakistan border.

The United States and United Kingdom finally deployed conventional ground troops in an endeavor to eliminate the Taliban and al-Qaeda, with specific operations being mounted to achieve this objective. In December 2001, a major U.S. action was mounted in the Tora Bora region, where it was thought that some 4,000 to 5,000 fighters were hiding in the mountains amid a complex of caves and bunkers; bin Laden was thought to be with that force. A bombing campaign was begun, followed by an assault by U.S. ground forces and Afghan allies. Crucially, however, a snowy track to the south was left open, and it is reported that this was used as an escape route by a large number of al-Qaeda fighters. Some observers and U.S. intelligence officials felt that the U.S. military force had been too small and that too much reliance had been placed on Afghan warlords who were more interested in receiving U.S. payments than capturing al-Qaeda fighters. Some thought that bin Laden may have been killed or injured during the U.S. bombardments, but it was subsequently reported that he had escaped from the Tora Bora region in the first two weeks of December, fleeing into Afghanistan under the escort of Pakistani frontier tribesmen in return for a large sum of money. The Indian press reported that bin Laden had paid $15 million for safe conduct across the border and that he was certainly accompanied by his deputy Ayman Muhammad al-Zawahiri, who was also treating bin Laden for his kidney ailment.

It is clear that a large number of bin Laden's followers escaped from Afghanistan into Iran and Pakistan, with some having made their way to Kashmir, Yemen, Chechnya, Indonesia, and the Philippines. Bin Laden was allegedly seen in Shah-i-Kot and Waziristan in February 2002, but since that time, no substantive news has emerged. In fact, there is no real knowledge as to whether he is dead or alive. Although a number of al-Qaeda members have been captured, no intelligence on the whereabouts of bin Laden has been forthcoming. But his network is still in existence, as evidenced by terrorist activity in Indonesia, the Philippines, and Yemen and continued operations against the Interim Government in Afghanistan. Speculation is also mounting that Osama bin Laden's son, Saad bin Laden, is now heavily involved in operations, and he is suspected of being implicated in the bombing of a Tunisian synagogue on 11 April 2002 that killed nineteen people, most of whom were German tourists.

It now seems likely that bin Laden is still alive. Experts have examined an audiocassette featuring him that was handed to the al-Jazeera television station, and they believe the tape is genuine. The bombing attack in Bali and the attack in Tunisia were mentioned on the tape, so the currency of the information is not in question. And on the tape, further action against America and its allies was threatened, with the United Kingdom seen as a likely target. This prospect has been reinforced by another audiotape broadcast by al-Jazeera on 11 February 2003, which Western intelligence services deem to be genuine; on this tape, bin Laden mentioned the Tora Bora battle, offered support for the Iraqi people, and advocated further attacks on the United States and Israel.

See also Coalition Land Campaign against the Taliban; al-Qaeda; 11 September 2001; Taliban; UN Sanctions

References

Abu Khalil, A. 2002. *Bin Laden, Islam and America's New "War on Terrorism."* Washington, DC: Seven Stories Press.

Bergen, Peter, and Rachel Klayman, eds. 2001. *Holy War Inc.: Inside the Secret World of Osama bin Laden.* New York: Free Press.

Bodansky, Yossef, and Helen Deliel Bentley. 1999. *Bin Laden: The Man Who Declared War on America.* Rocklin, CA: Forum.

Cooley, John K. 1999. *Unholy Wars: Afghanistan, America and International Terrorism.* Sterling, VA: Pluto Press.

Reeve, Simon. 1999. *The New Jackals: Ramzi Yousef, Osma bin Laden and the Future of Terrorism.* Boston: Northeastern University Press.

Reid, Robert H. 2003. "Man Thought to Be Osama bin Laden Urges Followers to Back Saddam; US Says It Shows Iraqi Ties to al Qaeda." http://story.nes. yahoo.com/news (cited 15 April 2003).

LAGHMAN PROVINCE

Laghman Province in eastern Afghanistan comprises an area of 2,790 square miles and has a population of about 387,000; Mehtarlam is its administrative center. It is bordered by the provinces of Kunar in the east, Kabul in the southwest, Nangarhar in the south, and Badakhshan in the north. The eastern boundary is a chain of spurs from the Kashmund range and consists of sandy hillocks with no vegetation. The northern part of the province is extremely attractive, and the area is irrigated by the Kabul and Alishang Rivers. The province used to be Kafiri territory but is now populated by Ghilzais, Tajiks, and some Hindus. According to local mythology, Noah's Ark landed on Kund Mountain; the province was originally named Larnech after Noah's father.

References

Adamec, Ludwig W. 1972–1985. *Historical and Political Gazetteer of Afghanistan.* 6 vols. Graz, Austria: Akademische Druck-u Verlagsansalt.

Data Collection for Afghan Repatriation Project. 1989. *Laghman Province.* Islamabad: UN High Commissioner for Refugees.

LALA PIR

Lala Pir, also known as Sayyid Lal Shah, was a mullah from Khost who was summoned to Kabul in 1906 and appointed by Nasrullah Khan as his agent to work among the Khostwalis, Waziris, and Mahsuds. In 1907, Lala Pir was extremely active in dealing with the mullahs of the various tribes, and he secured the allegiance of Mullah Powinda and Mullah Hamzullah against the British government in the eastern provinces.

However, Lala Pir was most active in his struggles against the British in the northwest frontier provinces, and in March 1908, he brought together *lashkars* (tribal armies) in Khost with the intent to strike against the British but was dissuaded from action by the governor of Khost Province. In 1912, he received a substantial reward from the amir for his services in suppressing the Mangal and Ahmadzai Rebellions that year. Seven years later, he was again involved in the raising of lashkars in Khost in actions against the British during the Third Anglo-Afghan War.

References

Poullada, Leon B. 1973. *Reform and Rebellion in Afghanistan, 1919–1929,* Ithaca, NY: Cornell University Press.

LANGUAGES

Afghanistan has three main languages—Pashtu, Dari, and Turki—and a number of dialects and minority languages. Pashtu-speakers are the dominant group. Dari is the second most widely spoken language, largely used by the Hazaras, and it also the main language of education. Pashtu and Dari are the official languages of Afghanistan, and most Afghans are bilingual. The Turki language is spoken by the Uzbeks, and dialects of it are used by Turkomans and other ethnic groups. A number of smaller language groups exist, including Baluchi, Brahui, and Nuristani; Nuristani had, at one time, been recognized by the Marxist government as the national language. Language divisions based on ethnicity contribute to instability and mistrust among the tribal groups.

See also Dari Language; Pashtu Language

References

Miran, M. Alan. 1977. *The Functions of National Language in Afghanistan.* New York: Afghanistan Council, Asia Society.

Morgenstierne, G. 1967. "The Language of Afghanistan." *Afghanistan* 20, no. 3: 81–90.

LAYEQ, SULAIMAN (1930–)

Sulaiman Layeq was a founding member of the People's Democratic Party of Afghanistan (PDPA) and editor in chief of the party newspaper, *Parcham.* He was born on 7 October 1930, the son of Maulawi Abdul Ghani, who was a devotee of Sheikh Ahmed Sarkindi. Prior to his general state schooling, Layeq received a mosque education, studying Dari verse books and elementary Arabic. In 1941, he was enrolled at the Habibia High School and then transferred to the Pagham School of Islamic Law, graduating in 1952. He then entered the College of Islamic Law at Kabul University but was expelled in 1954 for his political activities and for voicing opposition to the government. He did, however, gain entry to the Faculty of Letters at the university and graduated in 1957. He then began work in the media on newspapers and at Radio Afghanistan before joining the Ministry of Information and Culture. It was in 1965 that he became publisher and editor in chief of *Parcham.*

In 1964, Layeq participated in the twenty-seven-man congress that established the PDPA and became a founding member of the party. He was a candidate for the PDPA from Pul-i-Khumri, in

Baghlan Province, in 1965 and 1969 but was defeated on both occasions. He was forced to resign his positions as editor in chief of *Parcham* and member of the PDPA Central Committee in December 1978, was arrested in February 1979, and was removed from the Central Committee by Hafizullah Amin, leader of the group's Khalq faction, on 23 October 1979. However, after Babrak Karmal was installed as prime minister, Layeq was appointed president of the Academy of Sciences on 13 April 1980 and made minister of foreign affairs in 1981. He also recovered his status within the party and became vice-chair of the National Fatherland Front. In addition, he composed the national anthem of the Democratic Republic of Afghanistan.

See also National Fatherland Front; People's Democratic
    Party of Afghanistan

References
Emadi, Hafizullah. 1990. *State, Revolution and
    Superpowers in Afghanistan.* New York: Praeger.

LOGAR PROVINCE

Logar Province lies south of Kabul and occupies an area of 1,702 square miles with a population of about 424,000. But as a result of the civil war (from 1989 to 2001), nearly half of that population became refugees in Pakistan. The area is bounded by the provinces of Maidan in the west, Kabul in the north, Nangarhar in the east, and Paktia in the south. The administrative capital is Pul-i-Alam. The province is completely shut in by high, barren hills laced with bridle roads through the passes. The population is predominantly Pashtun, but there are some Tajiks in the region of Kashmir. Almost the entire workforce is engaged in agriculture, with fruit, vegetables, rice, wheat, and barley being the major crops and Kabul the main market. Clover is also grown as grazing for cattle.

References
Adamec, Ludwig W. 1972–1985. *Historical and Political
    Gazetteer of Afghanistan.* 6 vols. Graz, Austria:
    Akademische Druck-u Verlagsansalt.
Data Collection for Afghan Repatriation Project. 1989.
    Logar Province. Islamabad: UN High Commissioner
    for Refugees.

LOYA JIRGA

The Loya Jirga is the Great (or National) Council at which all matters of national importance are discussed. All communities in Afghanistan are represented in this body. The first Loya Jirga was held in 1709, and others have been convened at times of national importance ever since; for this reason, representation is based on both geography and ethnicity, with some members elected and others appointed. Both the Marxist government in Kabul and the mujahideen groups have convened Loya Jirgas to further their causes, but the validity of these councils has always been disputed because neither was considered representative of the Afghan people.

The concept of the Loya Jirga is considered crucial to the establishment of representative and stable government in Afghanistan after the fall of the Taliban. The agreement setting up the Afghan Interim Government, signed at Bonn, Germany, on 5 December 2001, provided for a special commission to be appointed to organize the calling of an emergency Loya Jirga that would be able to revise the appointed interim cabinet and create a two-year transitional government. To ensure that a consensus acceptable to the Afghan people is reached, the agreement also laid out details of representation to encompasses Afghan refugees, people in the Afghan diaspora, Islamic scholars and intellectuals, and women.

The Loya Jirga specified under the Bonn Agreement was set for 10–16 June 2002 at Kabul. Procedures for the elections of the members and for the observance of the elections were set up by the Interim administration in March 2002, as was the membership of the Independent Commission charged with calling the meeting. The Independent Commission consisted of twenty-one members, led by Chair Ismael Qaimyar, a Qizilbash from Hera and an expert in constitutional law. The commission also had two vice-chairs: Mrs. Mahbooba Hoquqmal, a Tajik and a professor of law and political science at the University of Kabul and the Afghan university in Peshawar, and Abdul-Aziz al-Haj, a Pashtun from Laghman and a professor of Shari'a law at the University of Kabul.

The commission also included the Relations Committee, headed by Ahang Mohammad Kazim, a Tajik from Kabul and head of the Faculty of Journalism at Kabul University, as well as the Drafting Committee, headed by Mohammed Taher, an Akmedzai and a lecturer in law and science at Kabul University. The remainder of the commission was selected to provide a range of appropriate expertise and to reflect the ethnic communities in

07 كابل
Kabul

Masooda Jalal, 34, an Afghan medical doctor and the only female candidate, votes during the traditional Afghan grand assembly, or Loya Jirga, in Kabul, 13 June 2002. (AFP/Corbis)

Afghanistan. A series of procedures were also set up to provide for observation of the elections to the body and to deal with any complaints arising from the election process. The observation of the elections and the adjudication over complaints was the responsibility of constituency observer teams and regional observer teams, and the specific responsibilities of these teams were also determined.

Election to the Loya Jirga was to take place in two stages. The first was the election itself, using traditional methods of selecting the representatives from each constituency, on the basis of an allocated number between twenty and sixty, according to the size of the constituency. The representatives selected by the people then formed the panel from which the quota for election to the Loya Jirga was to be made, with the final membership selected from the panel in a secret election. All of these processes were overseen by the constituency observation team and then submitted to the regional observation team for final approval.

The regional centers from which the elections were to be run were to be based on eight cities, and the provision of the logistical services (including salaries, transportation, security, and all of the necessary infrastructure) was to be the responsibility of the United Nations. All proposals had to be approved by the Independent Commission before they could go into effect. The composition of the Independent Commission was determined on 2 May 2002 and was announced by the United Nations at Kabul.

The procedures for the election were also published by the Interim administration through the United Nations, and they reiterated the intention of the Bonn Agreement, stipulating that the Loya Jirga should be representative of all ethnic and religious groups in Afghanistan and that women should be able to participate in the election process. A set of formulaic tables were also set up, which determined the representation from each constituency and other specified representation covering refugees, civil society institutions, and selected individuals such as intellectuals, scholars, religious leaders, and women. The United Nations was to assist in the organization of elections from among the refugees, both internal and external, and the nomads, according to their predetermined quotas. The Independent Commission was charged with the selection of representatives from civil society institutions, religious scholars, and credible individuals and intellectuals, from both home and abroad, again based on predetermined quotas.

The commission was also to approve the representatives of women, who were drawn from among community members, women's educational institutions, and associations. The representatives of traders were to be the responsibility of the Chambers of Commerce and similar bodies, again endorsed by the commission according to predetermined formulas, and through the cooperation of the United Nations. Representatives from the religious minorities were to be selected by their organizations, again according to a predetermined table.

The Interim Government also established terms and conditions for both candidates and voters. Voters had to be:

- Citizens of Afghanistan by birth
- At least eighteen years old
- Capable of exercising their full legal rights

Candidates had to:

- Be at least twenty years old
- Subscribe to the principles and values of the Bonn Agreement
- Have no links with terrorist organization
- Not have been involved in spreading and smuggling narcotics, any abuse of human rights, war crimes, looting of public property, smuggling of cultural and archaeological heritage, or, in the eyes of the electorate, directly or indirectly in the killing of innocent people
- Be able to read and write at least one of the official languages

As a general condition, all forms of coercion, intimidation, bribery, corruption, use of force, and weapons were banned during the election. Additionally, anyone in government service wishing to stand as a candidate had to resign his or her official position before 10 April 2002 to be eligible for selection. The Loya Jirga began on 12 June 2002, and its first acts were to elect a chair and to reelect Hamid Karzai as president of Afghanistan and leader of the new Transitional Government.

After a week of debate, Karzai presented a new cabinet to the delegates for their approval, but submission of that list was delayed until 19 June due to the need to reach a compromise with the various factions wanting a role in the new government. In the meeting of 1,600 delegates, many participants saw an opportunity to carve out a position for themselves in order to secure their financial future. The cabinet announcement was seen as a test of Karzai's political acumen and the depth of his support. Although he favored a small cabinet to cut down on the costs of government, President Karzai also had to please as many factions as possible by giving jobs to representatives of their groups. It was also evident that the Loya Jirga was marked by intimidation and rifts between various factions; some delegates reportedly even received death threats.

The Karzai cabinet that was finally approved by the Loya Jirga represented a compromise between the ethnic Tajiks and Uzbeks of the Northern Alliance and members of the majority Pashtun ethnic group, who had felt sidelined by the Interim Government set up in December 2001.

See also Afghanistan Transitional Government

References

Mehreban, Abdullah. 1982. "National Jirgahs (Assemblies) and Their Role in the Socio-Political Life of the People of Afghanistan." *Afghanistan Quarterly* 35, no. 2: 50–58.

Rasham, G. Rauf. 2001. *Loya Jirga: One of the Last Political Tools for Bringing Peace to Afghanistan.* http://www.institute-for-afghan-studies.org (cited 8 June 2002).

Salahuddin, Sayed. 2002. "Karzai Arrives at Loya Jirga for Inauguration." http://www.afghan.com/aop/yest.html (cited 20 June 2002).

MACNAGHTEN, SIR WILLIAM (1793–1839)

William Macnaghten was the British chief secretary to the Indian government and was appointed as an envoy to the court of Shah Shuja following the British occupation of Kabul on 7 August 1839 during the First Anglo-Afghan War. Shah Shuja's position as the ruler of Afghanistan was insecure, and he could not survive without British support. Macnaghten became the real power behind the throne, using gold to buy the loyalty of tribal chiefs and directing Afghan affairs to protect British interests in the region. He assumed that the strategy he was following had succeeded in stabilizing Afghanistan and therefore allowed families of British officers to join the troops encamped at Kabul.

However, Afghan forces began to harass British lines of communication, and a mob attacked the residence of the British mission, killing all of the inhabitants. In light of this unrest, Macnaghten reached an agreement with the major tribal chiefs to secure a British withdrawal of outlying forces to Kabul and then withdrawal from the capital itself. But he played a game of duplicity by simultaneously holding talks with Sardar Muhammad Akbar, son of the former amir Dost Muhammad and commander of the Afghan forces. On learning of the other negotiations, Akbar killed Macnaghten in a fit of anger. Only a few British troops survived the retreat to Kabul; ironically, some of those who did survive were saved by the protection Akbar provided while they were in his charge, with their families as hostages to guarantee the British withdrawal.

See also First Anglo-Afghan War

References

Norris, James A. 1967. *The First Afghan War, 1838–42.* London: Cambridge University Press.

MAHMUD PACHA, SAYYID

Sayyid Mahmud Pacha, also known as Babu Jan, was a spiritual leader who was given an endowment of land in the Kunar Valley by Amir Shir Ali. In 1868, he revolted against Azam Khan, the nominal amir who ruled from 1867 to 1869. However, when Amir Shir Ali returned to power, Mahmud Pacha was appointed a member of the newly formed advisory council at Kabul, a position confirmed by Amir Abdur Rahman when he came to power in 1880. But Abdur Rahman removed his independence by making his administration in Kunar subject to central control, and Mahmud Pacha was compelled to remit tax revenues to Kabul. As a consequence, he rebelled against the amir but failed and was forced to go into exile in India. His descendants, known as the Sayyids of Kunar, have held important positions in Afghanistan, and Afghan historians claim that the pan-Islamist Sayyid Jamaluddin Afghani was a descendant of the Kunari Sayyids.

See also Rahman, Amir Abdur

References

Griffiths, John C. 1967. *Afghanistan.* London: Pall Mall Press.

MAHMUD SHAH (?–1829)

Mahmud Shah spent his life engaged in an internecine struggle for power in Afghanistan, using his position as governor of Herat to conduct a struggle against his brother Zaman Shah. He became the Afghan king in 1800 but delegated most of the responsibility for state affairs to his ministers. However, internal strife continued, and in 1803, Kabul was captured by Shah Shuja (the amir of Afghanistan from 1803 to 1809 and again, with British support, from 1839 to 1842), and Mahmud was imprisoned. He escaped, and with the aid of a former minister, he attacked Kandahar in 1809 before moving on to Kabul, regaining his throne in 1813. Soon thereafter, he was again driven out of Kabul. Mahmud returned to Herat, where he retained all the

Mahmud Shah, Amir of Afghanistan from 1800 to 1803 and again from 1813 to 1829, when he was poisoned by his son (Perry-Castaneda Library)

trappings of a ruler while his son Kamran held all the executive power. His son poisoned him in 1829.

References

Habib, Mohammad. 1951. *Sultan Mahmud of Ghaznin.* Delhi, India: G. S. Sharma.

Nazim, M. 1931. *The Life and Times of Sultan Mahmud of Ghazne.* Cambridge: Cambridge University Press.

MAIMANA

Maimana, the capital of Fariab Province, rests in a valley among low hills. The city's population is almost totally Uzbek. Maimana originally came into being as a power base for an Uzbek named Haji Khan following the 1747 death of Nadir Shah, the ruler of Iran whose death created an opportunity for the Afghans to expel the Iranians from their territory. Haji Khan was also a comrade of Ahmad Shah Durrani, who ruled from 1747 to 1772 and is regarded as the founder of modern Afghanistan. On assuming control of Afghanistan, Ahmad Shah made his former comrade the *wali* (governor) of Maimana and Balkh in return for a promise to supply military aid if called on.

In the last quarter of the nineteenth century, the city suffered considerable damage as a result of a siege by the forces of Abdur Rahman, and about 15,000 of the inhabitants were slaughtered. The city was also involved in further unrest in 1891, following a revolt by soldiers ordered to Herat by the amir. But the rebellion was soon crushed, and some 4,000 rebels crossed the border into Russia. This displacement of rebel soldiers caused friction between Russia, Afghanistan, and the British India government. The city and the province also saw bitter fighting between forces of the government of Burhanuddin Rabbani and the opposition during the civil war between 1992 and 1996 and between differing factions within the opposition, resulting in many deaths and injuries.

References

Adamec, Ludwig W. 1972–1985. *Historical and Political Gazetteer of Afghanistan.* 6 vols. Graz, Austria: Akademische Druck-u Verlagsansalt.

MAIWAND, BATTLE OF (1880)

The Battle of Maiwand took place on 17 July 1880, during the Second Anglo-Afghan War. Near the village of Maiwand, close to Kandahar, the forces of Muhammad Ayub Khan wiped out Britain's entire Sixty-Sixth Regiment. The British had attempted to forestall the troops of Ayub Khan but were caught in a ravine and subjected to an artillery attack that was far more effective that the British response, as the Afghans had thirty guns to the Britons' twelve. The barrage killed about 14 percent of the British cavalry attached to the regiment and killed or maimed about 50 percent of their horses. The British were then attacked by *ghazis* (holy warriors), and most of the demoralized sepoys were slaughtered while British officers were picked off by Afghan marksmen. On the field of battle, the British lost about 1,000 dead, most of their artillery, and the complete baggage train that accompanied the regiment. The few survivors fled to Kandahar and were harried by Afghan villagers all along their route. Meanwhile, Gen. J. M. Primrose, the commander at Kandahar, panicked and withdrew all his troops into the city, where they came under siege. The nature of the defeat was such that the British forces realized their position in Afghanistan was untenable, leading to their recognition of Abdur Rahman as the new ruler of Afghanistan.

See also Second Anglo-Afghan War

References

Ali, Mohammad. 1955. "Battle of Maiwand." *Afghanistan* 10, no. 2: 26–38.
Maxwell, Leigh. 1979. *My God—Maiwand.* London: Leo Cooper.

MAIWANDAL, MUHAMMAD HASHEM (1919–1973)

Muhammad Hashim Maiwandal was founder of the Progressive Demoratic Movement (PDM) and prime minister of Afghanistan from 1965 to 1967. His prior career was in journalism, and he was the editor of the magazine *Agreement of Islam* from 1942 to 1945 in Herat and then editor of the daily newspaper *Anis.* The PDM advocated the principles of Islam, based on a constitutional monarchy, nationalism, democracy, and socialism, together with the reform of economic, social, cultural, and moral spheres of Afghan life. Maiwandal's ideas were propagated through a weekly newspaper, *Musawat,* launched in January 1967 and published in Persian and Dari. But he was forced to resign as prime minister in the same year due to continued ill health.

Maiwandal had also served in various ambassadorial posts before becoming prime minister, including two terms in Pakistan. In 1973, he was imprisoned when Muhammad Daud came to power in Kabul. He was killed in prison, allegedly under torture, though the government maintained he committed suicide. He was posthumously sentenced to death in December 1973.

References

Newell, Richard S. *The Politics of Afghanistan.* Ithaca, NY: Cornell University Press.

MAJID, ABDUL (C. 1875–?)

Abdul Majid was a Muhammadzai, born about 1875, who lived at Mashed. He left Afghanistan for Russia and then went to Constantinople (Istanbul), Turkey. However, in 1905, he returned to Afghanistan and became governor of Laghman Province one year later. In 1907, he was appointed civil commander of Kabul, but he was dismissed in March 1908 and began a period of prolonged unemployment. It was not until 1916 that he reemerged into public service, becoming the governor of Sheberghan in October 1916; there, he saw the safe departure of the Hentig-Niedermayer Expedition, which had been sent to Afghanistan with the objective of fomenting unrest in British India during World War I. The next period of Majid's life is cloaked in some mystery, as he left Afghanistan for Baghdad and then Constantinople with a mission to conclude a treaty with Turkey on behalf of King Amanullah. To disguise his true intentions, his departure from Afghanistan was covered by a story of desertion.

The Turkish government agreed to the conditions laid down by Amanullah, but the proposed treaty was conditional on Afghanistan opening up hostilities on the side of the Axis powers in World War I. While in Turkey, Majid discovered that he had strong anti-German feelings and that there was a powerful movement in Constantinople opposed to the pro-German stance of the party of Enver Pasha; as a result, he refused to go on to Berlin to conclude the negotiations or to take back the reply to Amanullah. He was forbidden to return to Afghanistan by the king and was detained by the British authorities until the end of hostilities in 1919.

References

Kakar, M. Hasan. 1979. *Government and Society in Afghanistan: The Reign of Amir Abd-al-Rahman.* Austin: University of Texas Press.

MAJRUH, SAYYID BAHA'UDDIN (1928–1988)

Sayyid Baha'uddin Majruh was a professor at Kabul University who fled from Afghanistan after the Saur Revolt of April 1978 and the advent of Communist rule in Kabul. He founded the Afghan Information Center in Peshawar and the *Monthly Bulletin,* a periodical that reported on events in the Afghan war. He was born in Kunar, the son of Sayyid Shamsuddin, and graduated from Istiqal High School in 1951 before going to the Universities of Paris and Montpellier and the University of London in 1955, studying English language and literature. He then went to Marburg and Munich Universities in 1957 to study German language and literature. In 1962, he became a professor of philosophy and sociology at Kabul University and was dean of the Faculty of Literature from 1961 to 1964. From 1965 to 1968, he served as president of the Afghan Cultural Office in Munich, Germany, and he was president of the Afghan Historical Society in 1972. Majruh was also a member of the Pashto Academy and published in Pashtu, Dari, French, English, and German. His best-known works are *The Dialectics of Freedom and Determination,* published in 1962, and *Danger of Selfishness,* published in 1972 in Dari and Pashtu. In 1982, he became head of the Afghan Information Center in Peshawar. A moderate in terms of Afghan politics, he was assassinated by unknown opponents in February 1988 in Peshawar.

References

Guistozzi, Antonio. 2000. *War, Politics and Society in Afghanistan, 1978–1992.* Washington, DC: Georgetown University Press.

MANGAL TRIBE

The Mangals are members of a Pashtun tribe and inhabit the southern and upper portion of the Kurram Valley in Paktia Province. They are fiercely independent and have supported the mujahideen forces in recent decades. Throughout the years, they have fought against various Afghan rulers and against the British during the Anglo-Afghan wars. In the Second Anglo-Afghan War, they followed Mullah Din Muhammad when he declared a jihad against the British. They were also involved, with the Ghazais, in uprisings against Amir Abdur Rahman, who was trying to curb the activities and influence of Din Muhammad. The Mangal tribe was the leading force in the Khost Rebellion of 1924 and 1925, which had attempted to oust King Amanullah. It has always been in a state of rebellion with the governors of Khost.

See also Din Muhammad, Mashk-il-Alam; Khost Rebellion

References

Poullada, Leon, B. 1973. *Reform and Rebellion in Afghanistan, 1919–1929.* Ithaca, NY: Cornell University Press.

MAQSUDI, ABDUL HUSAIN (1933–)

Abdul Husain Maqsudi was born in Maqsud Burjagi in Ghazni Province and is a Hazara. He was privately educated and was a bazaar inspector before becoming the representative in the parliament of Nowar from 1965 to 1973; there, he was a member of the conservative faction. During the period of President Muhammad Daud, from 1973 to 1978, he was unemployed. He left Afghanistan in 1978 for Saudi Arabia but returned after four months to Kabul, leaving Afghanistan once again toward the end of the year. He founded the Islamic Union for the Liberation of Afghanistan, a Hazara group based in Quetta, Pakistan. The mujahideen group was formed in 1979 and was heavily involved in arranging the transportation of supplies from Pakistan to the Hazarajat, a mountainous region in central Afghanistan. He also became a member of the Shura (Council) of Ayatollah Beheshti in the Hazarajat.

See also Islamic Union for the Liberation of Afghanistan; Shi'a Mujahideen Groups

References

Kaplan, Robert D. 1990. *Soldiers of God: With the Mujahideen in Afghanistan.* Boston: Houghton Mifflin.

MASOOD, AHMAD SHAH (1953–2001)

Ahmad Shah Masood was a charismatic leader of the mujahideen, or freedom fighters, in the struggle waged against the Soviet Union from 1979 to 1988. He was a prime mover in the formation of the Northern Alliance and a dedicated opponent of the Taliban. He controlled the northeast region of Afghanistan and was assassinated on 9 September 2001.

Masood was born in 1953 and graduated from the Afghan Military Academy in 1973. He was one of the most successful of the mujahideen leaders and controlled the Panjshir Valley north of Kabul, part of the province of Parwan. He successfully repelled a number of Soviet incursions into his territory following the Soviet occupation of 1979. In this capacity, he earned the title "Lion of Panjshir." Masood was a member of the Afghanistan Islamic Society (Jam'iat-i Islami-yi Afghanistan), led by Burhanuddin Rabbani, which drew its support from the non-Pashtun tribes in the north of Afghanistan, an area largely populated by Tajiks.

In 1983, after a number of actions against Soviet forces in the Panjshir Valley, Masood concluded a truce with the Soviet commander, but this did not prevent the forces that Masood controlled from operating elsewhere in Afghanistan. Following the Soviet withdrawal in 1988, Masood increased the territory under his control and set up his headquarters at Taloqan. However, the departure of the Soviet forces allowed old conflicts to reopen, and clashes soon erupted between Masood's forces and those led by Gulbuddin Hekmatyar of the Islamic Party (Hizb-i-Islami), with large numbers of casualties on both sides. Nonetheless, an attempt at reconciliation seemed to have succeeded at a meeting of mujahideen leaders held in Pakistan in October 1990. Masood's control actually extended over a wide area of territory through his establishment of the Supervisory Council (Shura-yi-Najar), whose objective was the coordination of all the resistance forces in the area. Effectively, this gave Masood control over the provinces of Badakhshan, Baghlan, Parwan, and Takhar.

Many observers believed that the withdrawal of the Soviet forces would herald the immediate collapse of the Communist government in Kabul, but this did not prove to be the case. However, at the end of 1991, President Muhammad Najibullah's militia forces in the north of the country rebelled against

Ahmad Shah Masood, charismatic military leader of the Northern Alliance, assassinated by al-Qaeda agents on 9 September 2001. (AFP/Corbis)

the regime, under the leadership of Gen. Abdul Rashid Dostum, and Dostum was soon joined by other militia leaders in the area. Masood seized this opportunity to form an alliance with the rebels to overthrow the Najibullah government in northern Afghanistan. At this time, Iran also began to exert influence behind the scenes, using ethnic and linguistic allegiances to persuade Masood, Dostum, and members of the Islamic Unity Party (Hizb-i Wahdat), a pro-Shi'a party, to enter into a politico-military confederation, the outcome of which was the Northern Alliance.

The new coalition was instrumental in bringing down Najibullah's government in April 1992, and through the collusion of some of the Parcham faction in the government, it was able to seize Kabul and thwart the establishment of a Pakistani-engineered administration. The state was renamed the Islamic Republic of Afghanistan, and an agreement was reached between the mujahideen leaders whereby there was to be a rotating presidency, commencing with Burhanuddin Rabbani. However, disputes soon broke out over the distribution of other posts within the new government, and fighting flared up again between the various groups. Mujahideen control of Kabul was a disaster for the citizens, as rape, pillage, and murder went largely unchecked because the commanders had little control over their troops. The conflict all but decimated the city, it seriously crippled the infrastructure, and it resulted in much loss of life, with many of the casualties being civilians.

As a result, the fragile coalition collapsed at the end of 1993, and there was great concern among the Pashtun leaders, who had held power in Afghanistan for some 250 years, about control passing to other ethnic groups. Afghanistan proceeded to disintegrate into areas run by competing groups with constantly shifting alliances. The government of President Rabbani, backed by the forces of Masood, held Kabul and the northeastern portion of the country, whereas the northern provinces were under the control of General Dostum, from the Uzbek tribe. The western provinces around Herat were ruled by another warlord, Isma'il Khan, and the areas to the south and east of Kabul were in the hands of Gulbuddin Hekmatyar. Meanwhile, the central provinces were dominated by the Hazaras, and the eastern border with Pakistan was governed by a council of mujahideen leaders who effectively prospered by extorting tolls from the cross-border trade.

In 1994, the Taliban appeared on the scene in the south, largely backed by the Pashtuns but with support from Pakistan, particularly through its Inter-Services Intelligence Service. After a series of military actions around Kandahar and Herat, the Taliban took Kabul from Masood. The government of President Rabbani was forced to flee, and Masood withdrew to his power base in the northeast. This reverse, however, also provided the motivation for the other warring factions to come together again as the Northern Alliance. With further military successes by the Taliban, the territory controlled by the Northern Alliance shrank to about 10 percent of the country, mainly in its Tajik heartland in the northeast, and by the end of 1999, the Taliban exercised firm control over the rest of the nation.

In the territory that he controlled, Masood made some attempt to set up a civil administration and to instill a sense of military discipline in his forces. The infrastructure was frail, but Masood's declared aim was to create a sort of democratic framework in the northeast, and plans were drawn up for elections. He also understood the importance of education and was trying to establish a system of schooling, including opportunities for girls, but he was careful in the way he introduced his modernization policies in what was still a traditional society. However, Masood's reputation and skill at public relations was such that he was able to deal with a number of external agencies and to bring funds into his territory.

As part of his public relations campaign, Masood always made himself accessible to the media from the outside world: he realized the impact that publicity could have on his cause in terms of garnering support and financing from neighboring states. In the end, this approach would turn out to be his downfall, as the two pseudo-Arab journalists to whom he granted an interview on 9 September 2001 were suicide assassins whose cameras were actually bombs. Masood was fatally injured when the bombs exploded. At the time, there was speculation that Osama bin Laden was behind the assassination. This supposition has since been reinforced by statements made by the Taliban's former deputy interior minister, Mullah Mohammed Khaksar, who maintained that the Arab assassins had been diverted by bin Laden from a mission to Indonesia to make the attack on Masood. Khaksar, who left the Taliban after Kabul was captured by Northern Alliance forces, also maintained that the Taliban leadership knew of this mission; in fact, it had further endeared bin Laden to the Taliban, thus making his expulsion by Mullah Mohammed Omar an impossibility.

See also Afghan-Pakistani Relations; Afghan-Soviet Relations; Hazaras; Hekmatyar, Gulbuddin; Islamic Society of Afghanistan; Islamic Unity Party; Mujahideen; Najibullah, Muhammad; Pashtuns; Rabbani, Burhanuddin; Tajiks

References

Astute, J. Brice. 1986. *Afghanistan: The First Five Years of Soviet Occupation.* Washington, DC: National Defense University.

Brigot, Andre, and Roy Olivier. 1988. *The War in Afghanistan.* New York: Harvester-Wheatsheaf.

Institute for Afghan Studies. "Masoud's Role as a Political Leader Questioned." http://www.institute-for-afghan-studies.org (cited 28 November 2001).

Kaplan, Robert D. 1990. *Soldiers of God: With the Mujahideen in Afghanistan.* Boston: Houghton Mifflin.

MAZARI, ALI (1935–)

Ali Mazari was born in Kandahar Province in 1935 and educated at a Shi'a university in Iraq. In 1980, he was elected chair of the Afghan Shi'a Alliance, which was an umbrella organization of Shi'a mujahideen groups that received support from the Iranian government and was initially based in Iran. It later relocated to Quetta in Pakistan, and in June 1990, a new organization of Shi'a groups, the Unity Party (Hizb-i Wahdat), was formed. This group was headed by Mazari once the mujahideen came to power in 1992, but two years later, he was killed in a conspiracy by Pashtun mujahideens. The alliance had been involved in many clashes with Pashtun mujahideen groups, especially those led by Gulbuddin Hekmatyar. Hekmatyar was replaced by Karim Khalili, and the group has cooperated with the forces of Gen. Abdul Rashid Dostum.

See also Shi'a Mujahideen Groups

References

Kaplan, Robert D. 1990. *Soldiers of God: With the Mujahideen in Afghanistan.* Boston: Houghton Mifflin.

MAZAR-I SHARIF

Mazar-i Sharif is a strategic town in northern Afghanistan that was the site of bitter fighting between the Hazara mujahideen and the Taliban in 1998, with atrocities committed by both sides. Still the stronghold of Gen. Abdul Rashid Dostum and his Uzbek forces today, it was a key objective of the opposition forces in the advance against the Taliban in October 2001.

Strategic Significance

The town of Mazar-i Sharif is the capital of Balkh Province and has an estimated population of 20,000. By the 1930s, it had become the major commercial center in northern Afghanistan. It had a strategic significance due to its proximity to the border area of the former Soviet Union that is now Uzbekistan, and since it is sited on flat terrain, it was an easily defended location. It was also a crucial town on the main route to northern Afghanistan, and it has a major air base. The town is some 270 miles northwest of Kabul, to which it is linked by an all-weather highway, and it was a stronghold of the Marxist regime based in Kabul from 1979.

The Fall to the Mujahideen

The fall of Mazar-i Sharif to the mujahideen took place in March 1992 and was a vital factor in the demise of the Marxist government of President Muhammad Najibullah. The collapse of Marxist control in the town was an outcome of a power struggle within the Marxist leadership. The town was under the command of a Tajik, General Mumin, who commanded the garrison and the major weapons and ammunition store in the northern province. President Najibullah wanted to replace him with General Rasul, a Pashtun commander. However, Mumin refused to accept dismissal and formed an alliance with General Dostum, commander of the militia in Jozjan Province, and Sayyid Mansur Nadiri, head of the Shi'a forces that controlled the area north of the Salang Pass. This gave the mujahideen access to a major supply of weaponry, an air base, and an easily traveled route to Kabul. The new coalition cooperated with the forces of Ahmad Shah Masood, the military commander of the Northern Alliance, and helped him to capture Kabul on 25 April 1992.

Capture by Taliban

In the spring of 1997, the Taliban was preparing for an offensive in the north of Afghanistan. This engagement was prefaced by a blockade of the last Northern Alliance stronghold, resulting in a severe shortage of food and fuel supplies. Mazar-i Sharif was to be a key objective, as the northern part of Afghanistan had 60 percent of the country's agricultural resources and 80 percent of its mineral and gas wealth, as well as industrial potential. It was therefore crucial that the Taliban crush resistance in northern Afghanistan if they were to keep the country unified. The Taliban advance came in May 1997 and was marked by a series of betrayals and counterbetrayals and interethnic bloodshed that was extreme even by Afghan standards.

The city and surrounding region was the stronghold of General Dostum and his Uzbek followers. Dostum had managed to protect Mazar-i Sharif from the ravages of the eighteen-year war. Indeed, the city had prospered as a vital staging post in the massive smuggling trade between Pakistan, Central Asia, and Iran. The trade's magnitude was so great that Dostum set up his own airline to bring smuggled goods in from Dubai, which were then trucked out to provide the general with a lucrative income.

This business enabled Dostum to operate an efficient administration with functioning public services, including health and education; the education system still allowed girls to attend school and the Balkh University, which was the only university still operational in Afghanistan.

However, there was a bitter feud between Dostum and his second in command, Gen. Malik Pahlawan, with the latter being persuaded to betray his leader through promises of bribes and the prospect of sharing power with the Taliban. Malik was joined by three other senior Uzbek generals, aided by the fact that Dostum had not paid his troops for some months. The Taliban moved north from Herat and Kabul and allied themselves with Malik's forces from Fariab, so that Dostum and just over a hundred officers and men were forced to flee to Uzbekistan and thence to Turkey. As a result, the city was left open to the advancing Taliban forces, led by Mullah Abdul Razaq, an inflexible hard-liner who had ordered the murder of Najibullah. He led 2,500 heavily armed Taliban into the city and refused to share power with Malik, who was offered an insignificant post in the Kabul government.

The city previously had a healthy ethnic mix and was one of the most open and liberal centers in Afghanistan, but the Taliban remained politically inflexible and insisted on the strict imposition of Shari'a law. All schools were shut down, the university was closed, women were banned from the streets, and a process of disarming Uzbek and Hazara troops was begun. The agreement with Malik and his forces was already showing signs of disintegration, and Pakistani diplomats and Inter-Services Intelligence officers arrived from Islamabad to try to renegotiate the agreement. However, the situation within Mazar-i Sharif was further aggravated by Pakistan's recognition of the Taliban as the official government of Afghanistan, which showed the Uzbeks that the agreement for power sharing was meaningless; instead, it effectively laid the groundwork for a Taliban takeover. Malik's betrayal of Dostum was also aggravated by his betrayal of Isma'il Khan, who had been resisting the Taliban in Fariab Province and was made a prisoner of the Taliban.

The situation inside Mazar-i Sharif was extremely tense, and only one incident was needed to trigger bloodshed. The trigger came on 28 May 1997 when a group of Hazara militia refused to be disarmed. The Hazaras and the rest of the population of the city rose up in revolt. The Taliban had no experience in street fighting and no knowledge of the layout of the maze of streets and alleys in the city; thus, they became easy targets in their pickup trucks for opponents watching from houses and sharpshooters on rooftops. The fighting was intense and bloody, and after fifteen hours of nonstop combat, at least 600 Taliban troops had been massacred in the streets, with some 1,000 captured at the airport as they sought to flee the city. At least 10 top Taliban commanders were killed or captured, among them Mullah Razaq and Foreign Minister Mullah Mohammad Ghaus. Malik's troops then proceeded on an orgy of looting, including the ransacking of the UN offices, whose staffers were forced to abandon the city.

The recapture of the city led to further outbreaks of anti-Taliban activity throughout the north, with the Hazaras raising the Taliban blockade of the Hazarajat, Malik's troops retaking four northern provinces, and Ahmad Shah Masood recapturing several towns in northeastern Afghanistan, blowing up the entrance to the Salang Tunnel, and trapping Taliban forces in the north. In the course of all of these actions, the Taliban had some 3,000 troops killed or wounded and some 3,600 taken prisoner. Much to Pakistan's embarrassment, about 250 Pakistanis were killed and nearly 600 others were captured during these engagements.

Ultimately, the city would be retaken by the Taliban in August 1998 in a particularly violent battle with tragic consequences for the non-Pashtun population, especially the Hazaras.

Atrocities in Mazar-i Sharif and the Surrounding Area

In the fighting within the city in May 1997, no quarter was given in the battles with the Taliban, but worse was to happen elsewhere as hundreds of Taliban and Pakistani prisoners were captured or shot dead and buried in mass graves. General Malik has been accused of the slaughter of some 2,000 Taliban prisoners, who were buried in mass graves near Sheberghan, and subsequent UN investigations revealed that they had been tortured and starved before being killed. Other reports indicated that Taliban prisoners were taken to wells on the pretext of being exchanged for opposition prisoners; then, instead of being exchanged, they were thrown into the wells, and the wells were blown up with hand grenades. As various eyewitness reports emerged, it became clear that vicious ethnic cleansing had taken place, with Taliban prisoners being shot and buried or else held in containers where they died from the heat and lack of oxygen, a method of killing that was used by both sides. One of Malik's generals admitted that 1,250 Taliban prisoners had died in this manner.

The Taliban were also guilty of atrocities when they retook the city in August 1998. In the process, they shot and killed both combatants and civilians indiscriminately. The assault took place on 8 August, and on the following day, the Taliban began a systematic search of the city for male members of the Hazara, Tajik, and Uzbek communities, often using information supplied by local informers or local Pashtun forces. In a number of cases, male members of suspect families were beaten or shot on the spot, and some had their throats cut. In other cases, they were beaten and trucked to the city jail. Although most of them were Hazaras, there were Tajik and Uzbek prisoners among them, and most of these were noncombatants. A number of eyewitness accounts mentioned meaningless and unjustified killings and bodies left lying in the streets, with the Taliban refusing to let them be buried.

The actions of the Taliban were a harsh revenge for their defeat in 1997 at the hands of the Hazaras and Uzbeks in Mazar-i Sharif, when they suffered one of their worst reverses. The central jail in the city was so crowded that there was no room for anyone to lie down, and many prisoners were transferred to other jails in Sheberghan, Herat, and Kandahar in large metal container trucks, each holding between 100 and 150 individuals. It has been reported that at least two trucks delivered dead prisoners who had succumbed to asphyxiation due to the crowded conditions and the desert heat; in one case, there were only three survivors in a container truck. It is not clear whether these outcomes were intentional or the unanticipated result of the cruel and inhumane methods that characterized the treatment of prisoners by both sides.

Recapture by Northern Alliance

In October 2001, the United States was engaged in an action in Afghanistan to overthrow the Taliban and to hunt down al-Qaeda terrorists and their leader, Osama bin Laden. As part of this action, the United States and the United Kingdom were sup-porting the Northern Alliance with special forces on the ground and with U.S. bombing attacks from the air, targeting strategic locations and Taliban front lines. On 31 October 2001, anti-Taliban forces were moving on Mazar-i Sharif, and U.S. jets zeroed in on the Taliban positions in a series of raids in Samangan and Balkh Provinces, as well as in the city itself. The air assault was intended to coordinate with the actions of Northern Alliance troops, who were being aided by special forces providing intelligence and directing the bombing raids and Cruise missile attacks. Yet again, the recapture of Mazar-i Sharif was a key objective, as it would enable the Northern Alliance and Coalition forces to open up supply routes from Tajikistan and Uzbekistan.

On 5 November 2001, the Northern Alliance forces had moved to within 45 miles of Mazar-i Sharif and had taken the town of Ogapruk and two nearby villages, having advanced under cover of a U.S. bombing raid. The Taliban had reinforced their front lines with 400 fresh troops composed of Arab and Pakistani volunteers, but they were under intense bombardment from the U.S. Air Force. It was reported on 7 November that Northern Alliance troops had forced a Taliban withdrawal from the Shol Gar area some 24 miles from the city and that 500 Taliban soldiers had changed sides and joined the opposition. Fighting around the city was fluid and totally disorganized, with Northern Alliance forces even attacking Taliban tanks and armored personnel vehicles on horseback.

The Northern Alliance forces continued to advance on the city, and the Taliban front lines were now being subjected to round-the-clock bombing. In a series of attacks, 3,500 men serving under Dostum pushed the Taliban out of Kishindi, killing 200 Taliban, while in the west, forces loyal to Ustad Atta Mohammad had seized the outlying village of Aq Kuprick. Some Taliban soldiers ran in the face of Northern Alliance troops, and others changed sides and allowed access through their lines. The city had fallen by 9 November, but as they retreated, the Taliban torched villages, and many ethnic Uzbeks, Tajiks, and Hazaras lost their lives in their burning houses as Taliban troops streamed out of the city and the surrounding area.

This defeat marked the end of the Taliban presence in northern Afghanistan, though some small pockets of resistance survived. In military terms, it was a good strategic victory, as the airfield could be used as an advance base for Coalition air activity. Further, the capture of the city meant an opening up of a land route from Uzbekistan, enabling ground troops to enter the area; equally important, essential humanitarian aid could now be delivered to the starving population and the refugees. Significantly, Mazar-i Sharif was again the stronghold of General Dostum.

Qala-i-Jangi Uprising

On Saturday 24 November 2001, some 300 Taliban fighters, who had fled Kunduz following U.S. bombing strikes, surrendered to Northern Alliance forces under General Dostum. The Taliban fighters were transported to the nineteenth-century fortress of Qala-i-Jangi in Mazar-i Sharif. However, they had not been searched by Dostum's troops for fear that fighting would break out. Dostum had been preaching reconciliation, and Afghans eventually were freed to return to their homes and foreigners were handed over to the United Nations. The prisoners were transferred by flatbed truck through the city and were greeted with open hatred by the local people, who had suffered under the Taliban occupation.

However, the whole operation began to go wrong when prisoners were asked to turn out their pockets. One soldier waited for the Northern Alliance commander, Nadir Ali, to pass before taking out a grenade, pulling the pin, and killing himself and the commander. Another prisoner committed a similar act, killing himself and Saeed Asa, a senior Hazara commander. The rest of the prisoners were then taken to underground cells to join other captured Taliban, but despite these incidents, the levels of security were not raised. On the following day, two Central Intelligence Agency (CIA) agents went to the prison to try to identify any al-Qaeda members within the captives, but they mistakenly conducted interviews with groups of prisoners in the compound. The agents were attacked by the prisoners, and only one escaped: Johnny Michael Spann was killed by the Taliban prisoners, who then overpowered their Northern Alliance guards and took their weapons.

The group then went back into the jail and released the remainder of the prisoners, three of whom escaped through a drain underneath a wall only to be shot by Northern Alliance guards outside the fort. The remainder stormed a nearby armory, obtaining AK-47s, grenades, mines, rocket launchers, mortars,

and ammunition. Northern Alliance troops held the southeastern quarter of the fort and the north wall, from where they opened fire on the Taliban, as did two tanks by the north wall, and a fierce gun battle ensued. In the afternoon, U.S. and UK Special Forces arrived and established communications with U.S. air command to obtain support, and more Northern Alliance troops arrived from the northeast battlefields to join the attack. The battle raged throughout the afternoon, and the U.S. Special Forces called up a missile strike on a building inside the Taliban-held area, which was duly destroyed.

Fighting continued to rage throughout the night, and it was not until nightfall that the surviving CIA agent and some trapped journalists managed to escape over the north wall, making their way into the city. By Monday morning, a new Northern Alliance command post had been established at the northeast tower, and mortar and rocket fire was ranged on the Taliban positions. More special forces arrived, as did members of the Tenth Mountain Division, who took up positions some 300 yards to the northeast of the fort; other spotters inside the fort called up more air strikes. Despite warnings from the pilots about the location of Northern Alliance troops in the fort, the attack proceeded, and heavy casualties were inflicted on Coalition forces in close proximity to the strike. Reports stated that five U.S. Special Forces were wounded, as were four UK Special Forces, with Northern Alliance troops suffering thirty dead and at least fifty wounded.

Once darkness fell on Monday evening, an AC-130 gunship flew over the fort five times and strafed the area, setting off explosions in stocks of ammunition, which continued throughout the night. On Tuesday morning, Taliban resistance was beginning to weaken, as these soldiers were running out of ammunition, water, and food, and in the afternoon, Northern Alliance troops moved in on the Taliban positions, advancing through the hundreds of dead and dying in the courtyard. Northern Alliance troops shot the wounded and looted the bodies, particularly for footwear, and a number of the bodies were identified as foreign fighters, including Arabs, Pakistanis, and Chechens. Five Taliban trapped in the basement of a building were killed by grenades, and a tank used to demolish the stable block in which Taliban were thought to be hidden. However, fighting still continued, with Taliban fighters trapped in the basements underneath the fort, and it was not until Saturday that the basements were flooded to force the Taliban out. Some eighty-six prisoners emerged, one of whom was an American citizen who had converted to Islam and gone to Afghanistan from a *madrasa* (religious school) in Pakistan. An accurate death toll is difficult to establish, but it is thought that at least 500 Taliban fighters died and that many of these were foreigners who had been determined to fight to the death.

After the incident, much of which was captured on video by journalists and broadcast to the world, Amnesty International demanded an investigation, but the U.S. and UK governments declined, maintaining that their forces had acted within the rules of engagement and in accordance with international law.

Historical Significance

Mazar-i Sharif is held sacred by Afghans as the burial place of Caliph Ali, who ruled from 656 to 661 (though the majority of scholars believe he is buried in Najaf), and a shrine and great mosque have been built on this site of pilgrimage. Once a year, on 21 March, a fair is held, during which crowds camp around the shrine of the caliph in hopes that the saint will cure them of their ills or disabilities. At one time, Mazar-i Sharif was a province in its own right, but the area was reorganized, and the three provinces of Balkh, Jozjan, and Samangan were created. During the 1970s, the town had developed into a small urban area constructed in accordance with some concept of modern town planning, complete with good roads, modern shops, and a thriving commercial center important for the export of skins from Karakul sheep, carpets, and melons; it was also a major producer of textiles and fertilizer.

See also Dostum, Gen. Abdul Rashid; Hazaras; Taliban

References

Adamec, Ludwig W. 1972–1985. *Historical and Political Gazetteer of Afghanistan.*6 vols. Graz, Austria: Akademische Druck-u Verlagsansalt.

Maley, William. 1999. *Fundamentalism Reborn? Afghanistan and the Taliban.* London: Hurst.

Perry, Alex, and Johnny Michael Spann. 2001. "Inside the Battle at Qala-i-Jangi." *Time Atlantic* 158, no. 24: 28–35.

MESHRANO JIRGA

The Meshrano Jirga is the Pashtun name for the Upper House of Parliament, which was established under the terms of the 1931 and 1964 Constitutions. It is also known in the Dari language as the House of Notables. The 1931 Constitution provided for all of the members of the Upper House to be appointed, but in 1964, the new constitution allowed for two-thirds of the membership to be elected. On 26 August 1965, elections were held for the Meshrano Jirga and its 28 elective seats and for the Wolesi Jirga (House of the People) with 216 seats. Three members of the People's Democratic Party of Afghanistan were elected, including Babrak Karmal. On 12 October, King Zahir appointed Abdul Hadi Dawai president of the Meshrano Jirga, and the appointed members of the House of Notables were announced on the following day.

On 4 May 1966, the Meshrano Jirga debated the publication of *Khalq,* a newspaper that was owned by Nur Muhammad Taraki, and determined that any publication against the values of Islam should be stopped. Consequently, publication was banned on 23 May under the government's press laws. The parliament ceased to have any real significance under the presidency of Muhammad Daud (1973 to 1978) and in the subsequent Communist regime (1978 to 1996).

See also Loya Jirga

MISAQ, ABDUL KARIM (1937–)

Abdul Karim Misaq is a Hazara who was a member of the Khalq faction of the People's Democratic Party of Afghanistan (PDPA) and served as minister of finance from May to December 1979. He was born in Jaghatun in Ghazni Province in 1937, the son of Safar Ali, and was self-educated. He started his career in the Ministry of Agriculture and was then employed in the Demographic Department of the Ministry of the Interior from 1956 to 1958. He was dismissed from his post and became a bookkeeper before training as a mechanic and working in offices, factories, and at the Kabul airport. He was director of transport at the airport from 1960 to 1963 and then director of personnel in the General Transport Department. Between 1965 and 1975, he was employed in various departments in the Ministry of Mines. Misaq also had a literary side to his career, publishing *Seven Stories* in 1973, *Smile of the Mother* in 1974, and *Bach Melodies* in 1975. These works also appeared as *Path* in Dari and Pashtu, under the pseudonym Koh-i-Baba. Misaq was minister of finance after the Saur Revolt of April 1978, which brought the Communists to power, and was imprisoned when the Parchami faction assumed power in late 1979. He did not appear in public life again until August 1989, when he became mayor of Kabul. Although a Khalq, he continued to serve in Dr. Muhammad Najibullah's Central Committee but ultimately defected to Germany in 1990.

See also People's Democratic Party of Afghanistan
References
Astute, J. Brice. 1986. *Afghanistan: The First Five Years of Soviet Occupation.* Washington, DC: National Defense University.

MOHMAND TRIBE

The Mohmand tribe is of Pashtun origin and migrated from the Kandahar area to Peshawar. The tribe's territory was dissected by the 1893 Durand Line (delineated by Britain as the boundary between Afghanistan and British India), with one division living in the southwest corner of the Peshawar district and the other in the network of hills between the Kabul and Swet Rivers, which connect the Sufed Koh with the Hindu Kush. The Mohmands moved before the Mongol and Hazara invasions and successfully subdued the Shinwaris or expelled them from the Shilman Valley and the low-lying country south of the Kabul River. The Mohmand tribe has four main divisions—the Tarokzai, Halimzai, Baezai, and Khwaezai—together with a string of affiliated clans.

The tribe's relations with Britain were poor, due to the existence of the Durand Line, and the Mohmands constantly conducted raids from Afghanistan into British India. One example occurred in March 1870, when 3,000 Mohmands led by Mullah Khalil crossed the border at Kam Dakka and were expelled by British forces only with difficulty. Unrest continued in the 1880s, and the tribe was exploited by Dost Muhammad (who ruled from 1826 to 1838) and Shir Ali (who ruled from 1863 to 1878) to act against the British and the Sikhs. As a powerful tribal force, the Mohmands have been significant players in the politics of both Afghanistan and Pakistan. They have been involved in conflicts throughout Afghanistan's history, having joined the revolt against King Amanullah in 1928 and seen action against British forces on the frontier in 1930 and again in 1935. In the Afghan civil war (1989 to 2001), they maintained a neutral position and protected the autonomy of their region from both warring states.

See also Khost Rebellion
References
Mark, William Rudolph Henry. 1984. *The Mohmands.* Lahore, Pakistan: Vanguard Books.

MUHAMMAD, ISHAQ (1952–)

Muhammad Ishaq was born in Panjshir in 1952 and graduated from the Faculty of Engineering at Kabul University, where he was influenced by student politics and became a member of the Islamist Movement. In 1982, he became the political officer in the movement and was a regular contributor to its newspaper, the biweekly *AFGHANews*. In 1975, he had cooperated with Ahmad Shah Masood, the military commander of the Northern Alliance, when he started to raid the military outposts of the regime of Muhammad Daud. After the Saur Revolt of April 1978 and the beginning of Communist rule, he joined with Masood's forces in concerted action against the Marxist government in Kabul.

References
Kaplan, Robert D. 1990. *Soldiers of God: With the Mujahideen in Afghanistan.* Boston: Houghton Mifflin.

MUHAMMADI, MAULAWI MUHAMMAD NABI (1921–)

Maulawi Muhammadi was born in 1921 in Logar and educated in local *madrasas* (religious schools) before becoming a teacher in Abbas village, Logar, Maimana, and Jozjan. After a pilgrimage to Mecca in 1954, he returned to teaching at Abbas but began preaching against communism around the region. Four years later, he returned to Jozjan, where he continued to preach against communism and began to attract a circle of followers. His campaign convinced the local authorities that Communists had infiltrated the Afghan education systems and that action was demanded from the Kabul government.

Between 1963 and 1967, he was active in Logar and was a representative in the Wolesi Jirga (House of the People) in 1963, becoming a member of the right-wing faction in the parliament. He also traveled to Helmand and Kandahar to try to persuade other *maulawis* (senior mullahs) to enter parliament in 1973. But after the coup launched by Muhammad Daud in 1973, he was arrested, interrogated for three days, and then freed. In 1974, he founded a madrasa at Marja, but after the Marxist takeover in 1978 following the Saur Revolt, he fled to Quetta, Pakistan. He linked up with about thirty to forty maulawis and formed a group, for which he needed to purchase arms. While in Peshawar, he encountered Gulbuddin Hekmatyar, whom he had met earlier in Kabul, and was then linked into the network of Burhanuddin Rabbani.

After a short period, a meeting of the forces of Rabbani and Hekmatyar elected him leader of their united group, and the Islamic Society of Afghanistan was born. However, the group split up when Sabghatullah Mujaddidi returned from Denmark to form his own group and Hekmatyar and Rabbani moved apart. A jihad was proclaimed on 27 November 1975. Muhammadi bought weapons on credit in Pakistan, and with Wazir and Mahsud tribal support, he was able to start a military action. In 1981, he united the groups of Mujaddidi and Sayyed Ahmad Gailani in a loose federation, which was short-lived due to rivalry between the factions.

See also Gailani, Sayyed Ahmad; Hekmatyar, Gulbuddin; Islamic Society of Afghanistan; Rabbani, Burhanuddin

References
Farr, Grant M., and John G. Merrian, eds. 1987. *Afghan Resistance: The Politics of Survival.* Boulder, CO: Westview Press.

MUHSINI, AYATOLLAH MUHAMMED ASEF (1935–)

Ayatollah Muhammed Asef Muhsini is a Hazara from Kandahar noted for his involvement in the Islamic Movement of Afghanistan, which grew out of a cultural organization called Dawn of Science. This mujahideen group is a rural-based Shi'a movement, but Muhsini has not received any support from the Iranian regime. In 1980, he became chair of the Afghan Shi'a Alliance, which was an umbrella organization of mujahideen groups based in Iran, but he left the alliance and moved to Quetta in Pakistan. Muhsini's group was a powerful body and expelled rival groups from the Hazarajat region, working in alliance with Sazman Nasr. The Shi'a groups joined together as the Unity Party in June 1990 in order to protect Shi'a interests; Muhsini refused to join the party, but some of his regional commanders cooperated with the coalition.

See also Shi'a Mujahideen Groups

References
Farr, Grant M., and John G. Merrian, eds. 1987. *Afghan Resistance: The Politics of Survival.* Boulder, CO: Westview Press.

MUJADDIDI

Mujaddidi is the name of a family of religious leaders descended from the Sufi reformer Sheikh Ahmed Sirhindi, who is thought to have been born in Kabul in 1564 and buried in India when he died in 1624. In the early nineteenth century, one of his descendants, Qayyum Jan Agha, went to Afghanistan and founded a *madrasa* (religious school) and Sufi center in the Shor Bazaar area of Kabul. Succession continued through several generations of the family. The family also established itself in Herat and other towns in Afghanistan, led the Naqshbandi Sufi order in southern Afghanistan, and was always involved in politics.

The family was actively opposed to the British influence in Afghanistan; in fact, it declared a jihad against Britain sometime during 1919, at the time of the Third Anglo-Afghan War. Family members were also actively opposed to the secular reforms introduced by King Amanullah and President Muhammad Daud. They were instrumental in encouraging tribal revolts against these reforms to restore their own view of Islamic orthodoxy. Although some members of the family have held government positions throughout their period in Afghanistan, others have lived in exile in India because of their activities. In January 1979, Muhammad Ibrahim, "the Light of Sheikhs," and some ninety-six male members of the family were arrested and executed during the Khalq regime.

References
Fuller, Graham E. 1991. *Islamic Fundamentalism in Afghanistan: Its Character and Prospects.* Santa Monica, CA: Rand Corporation.

MUJADDIDI, SABGHATULLAH (1925–)

Sabghatullah Mujaddidi is the leader of the largely Pashtun National Liberation Front of Afghanistan, which he founded in 1978. He was responsible for a number of attacks on the Marxist government and Soviet forces in Afghanistan from 1980 forward. He had been a teacher of Islamic studies in schools and colleges in Kabul but was imprisoned from 1959 to 1964 for his public statements denouncing unbelievers and Communists. Following his release from prison, he left Afghanistan for two years. He returned and eventually formed the Organization of Muslim Clergy in 1972, but he was again forced to flee because of his political activism. Between 1974 and 1978, he was head of the Islamic Center in Copenhagen, only returning to Pakistan after the Saur Revolt to form his mujahideen group. He is considered to be a moderate and draws support from the Pashtun communities in the provinces of Paktia and Kunar.

See also National Liberation Front of Afghanistan
References
Farr, Grant M., and John G. Merrian, eds. 1987. *Afghan Resistance: The Politics of Survival.* Boulder, CO: Westview Press.

MUJAHIDEEN

The mujahideen are fighters in a jihad—a holy war that can only be waged against non-Muslims and apostates. The designation was adopted by Afghan resistance fighters in 1979 to show that they were engaged in a lawful war against an infidel government backed by the Communist regime of the Soviet Union. The mujahideen were never a unified force: in fact, there was a major split between the Sunni and Shi'a groups and within the Sunni groups between the moderates and the Islamic radicals.

The Sunni mujahideen were organized into a tenuous alliance of seven groups, based in Peshawar, Pakistan. Leaders included the moderates Sayyed Ahmad Gailani, Muhammad Nabi Muhammad, and Sabghatullah Mujaddidi and the Islamist radicals Gulbuddin Hekmatyar, Muhammad Yunis Khales, Burhanuddin Rabbani, and Abdul Rasul Sayyaf. It was this group that, in 1989, formed the Afghan Interim Government (AIG), with Mujaddidi as the president. At the same time, the Shi'a groups, some of them small and inactive, formed an umbrella organization of eight groups in Iran called the Islamic Unity Party (Hizb-i Wahdat). The Shi'a groups refused to join the AIG because they felt that they were being offered too small a presence.

The mujahideen groups in Peshawar relied on the goodwill of the Pakistan government, which decreed that it would only recognize seven mujahideen groups to receive assistance and that all refugees had to be affiliated with one of the groups in order to get help. Control was exercised through the Inter-Services Intelligence (ISI) Service of the Pakistani military, which helped to organize and approve operations in Afghanistan and to determine who received assistance and weaponry. The ISI gave priority to the Islamist groups rather than the moderates and particularly the mujahideen group led by Gulbuddin Hekmatyar when allocating funds and equipment, including that being covertly supplied by the U.S. Central Intelligence Agency.

However, there was always a state of flux in terms of group membership, as allegiances were often switched in order to obtain funds and supplies. In addition to the divisions on religious lines, individual groups also reflected their regional, tribal, or ethnic origins. The party of Burhanuddin Rabbani, for example, was largely non-Pashtun in ethnic composition and was active and strongly represented in northern Afghanistan, and though it was Islamist, it did not share the ideology of the Islamist group of Hekmatyar. A further illustration of the shifting allegiances was the alliance made in March 1990 between Hekmatyar, a radical Islamist, and Shanawaz Tanai, a Khalq hard-liner from the Marxist regime.

One month after the fall of the regime of President Muhammad Najibullah in March 1992, the mujahideen took Kabul and then proceeded to wage war among themselves for control of the capital and its environs. In particular, there was a bitter struggle between the forces of Rabbani and Hekmatyar that was only resolved in 1996 when a peace agreement was reached between the two leaders, with Hekmatyar becoming prime minister in Rabbani's government. Another major player, General Abdul Rashid Dostum, head of the Uzbek-based mujahideen, had withdrawn from Kabul to the north of Afghanistan, which he controlled from Mazar-i Sharif. However, the mujahideen groups in Kabul were defeated by the Taliban and forced to withdraw to their traditional ethnic or tribal strongholds. The various groups were equally as active against the Taliban regime, which was overthrown in December 2001, and the new Afghan Interim Government was established with UN backing. However, recent events, such as the assassination of the minister of public works, Haji Abdul Qadir, on 6 July 2002, demonstrate the fragility of the post-Taliban alliance between the various power brokers in Afghanistan.

See also Afghanistan Interim Government; Gailani, Sayyed Ahmad; Hekmatyar, Gulbuddin; Inter-Services Intelligence Service; Khales, Yunis; Muhammadi,

Mujahideen at Kabul Airport (Patrick Robert/Corbis)

Maulawi Muhammad Nabi; Mujaddidi, Sabghatullah; Rabbani, Burhanuddin; Sayyaf, Abdul Rasul; individual entries for mujahideen groups

References
Kaplan, Robert D. 1990. *Soldiers of God: With the Mujahideen in Afghanistan.* Boston: Houghton Mifflin.
Magnus, Ralph H., and Eden Naby. 2002. *Afghanistan: Mullah, Marx and Mujahid.* Rev. ed. Boulder, CO: Westview Press.

MUSLIM BROTHERHOOD

The Muslim Brotherhood, formally known as the Society of Muslim Brethren, was founded in Egypt in 1928 by Hassan al-Banna as a youth club committed to pursuing moral and social reform through propaganda and an information program. However, in 1939, in response to popular movements in Egypt and Palestine, the society transformed itself into a political entity and spread throughout the Islamic world as a religio-political organization. The movement aims at imposing Islamic law on all aspects of a Muslim state and is pan-Islamic in nature. Its strength has always been drawn from the urban poor and the rural population, and its message was spread in Afghanistan by Afghans who had been studying in Egypt. The ideology was spread by these intellectuals to students in Afghan schools and colleges, and the students formed the basis of the Islamist Movement in Afghanistan and were recruited as fighters by the Islamic Party of Gulbuddin Hekmatyar. All of the various movements owe their origins to the Muslim Brotherhood in Egypt and share common principles, but they operate as separate entities within the various countries in which they have a presence. Hekmatyar modeled the infrastructure of his Islamic Party after that of the Muslim Brotherhood.

See also Islamist Movement

References
Mitchell, Richard P. 1969. *The Society of the Muslim Brothers.* London: Oxford University Press.

MUSSOORIE CONFERENCE

The Mussoorie Conference between representatives of Afghanistan and the British government in India was held from 17 April to 18 July 1920 at Mussoorie, north of Delhi. The objective of the conference was to restore friendly relations following the 1919

Third Anglo-Afghan War. It was essentially a failure, as the Afghan foreign minister, Mahmud Tarzi, and the Indian government foreign secretary, Sir Henry Dobbs, failed to reach agreement on a treaty, though some economic assistance was promised by Britain. Consideration of the main objective—treaty negotiations—was postponed to a future conference, which was held in Kabul in 1921. On that occasion, agreement was reached.

See also Anglo-Afghan Treaty of 1921

References

Adamec, Ludwig W. 1967. *Afghanistan, 1900–1923: A Diplomatic History.* Berkeley: University of California Press.

NADIR, SHAH MUHAMMAD (1888–1933)

Muhammad Nadir was the son of Sardar Muhammad Yusuf Khan and was king of Afghanistan from 1929 to 1933 following a successful military career. In 1912, he was active in the suppression of the Mangal Revolt and was promoted to lieutenant general. Implicated in the killing of Amir Habibullah in 1919, he was arrested but was exonerated by King Amanullah and given command of the forces in Khost Province. He was active in the 1919 Third Anglo-Afghan War, crossing the border into Waziristan and attacking British forces at Thal. The result of this and other actions led the British to recognize Afghanistan's independence.

In 1919, Nadir was appointed minister of war, and he held the post until 1924, when he was made ambassador to France. He resigned from this position two years later on the grounds of ill health but remained in France, where he was joined by relatives. After King Amanullah abdicated in January 1929, Nadir left for India and established himself in the frontier region. Then, with tribal support from Waziristan and the acquiescence of the British, he returned to Afghanistan and defeated Habibullah Kalakani (the amir of Afghanistan from 18 January to 29 October 1929), taking Kabul on 13 October 1929. He was proclaimed king two days later. Kalakani was taken prisoner and hanged, together with a large number of his followers.

Muhammad Nadir Shah's rule was a contradiction. He reversed many of Amanullah's modernization programs and courted favor with the religious extremists. Yet at the same time, he put in place a restructuring program, which included the provision of schooling, and in 1932, he founded the Faculty of Medicine in Kabul University. A new constitution was drafted in 1931, which provided for a parliament, a national council, a senate, and an advisory council. Nadir Shah struggled against elements that sought to restore Amanullah to the throne, and he executed his main opponent, Ghulam Nabi, in 1932. As part of the campaign to defeat the opposition, he also set ethnic groups against each other, with Tajiks and Pashtuns, for example, destroying the Shamali area north of Kabul. Thus, for many Afghans, his rule was regarded as oppressive, and in 1933, he was assassinated by a Hazara who was the adopted son of Ghulam Nabi Charkhi.

See also Amanullah, King; Habibullah Kalakani; Third Anglo-Afghan War

References

Lockhart, L. 1988. *Nadir Shah: A Critical Study Based Mainly on Contemporary Sources.* London: Luzac.

King of Afghanistan Nadir Shah (Hulton-Deutsch Collection/Corbis)

NAJIBULLAH, MUHAMMAD (1947–1996)

Muhammad Najibullah was president of the Republic of Afghanistan and general secretary of the People's Democratic Party of Afghanistan (PDPA) from 1986 to 1992. He was born in 1947 in Kabul of an Ahmadzai Ghilzai Pashtun family; his father was an Afghan trade agent in Peshawar. Najibullah was educated at Habibia High School and Kabul University, graduating from the College of Medicine in 1975. He had joined the Parcham faction of the PDPA in 1965 and was repeatedly arrested for his political activities. After the Saur Revolt of April 1978, which brought the Communists to power, he was appointed ambassador to Tehran in July 1978 as part of a move to get leading Parchamis out of the country. He was dismissed in October 1978 by the government of Nur Muhammad Taraki when the Parchami faction was suspected of plotting a coup.

Najibullah initially remained in Iran but returned to Kabul with Babrak Karmal (a leading member of the PDPA who would be president of Afghanistan from 1979 to 1986) after Hafizullah Amin was ousted in December 1979. (Amin served as president of Afghanistan from September 1979 until his assassination by Soviet special forces on 27 December of that year.) Najibullah's next appointment was as general president of KHAD, the Afghan Security Service (also known as the State Information Service), a post he held from 1980 to 1986. In 1986, he replaced Karmal as general secretary of the PDPA. He then purged the Central Committee, brought in new members, and ultimately became president in 1987. Government reorganizations followed in 1988 and 1990, and in March 1990, he withstood an attempted coup from the Khalq faction of the PDPA, headed by Minister of Defense Shanawaz Tanai.

In an attempt to sustain himself in power, he downplayed Marxist ideology and annulled most of the early reforms instigated by the Communist regime. Najibullah tried to declare a national policy of reconciliation in order to form a broad-based Afghan national government, but the mujahideen, who regarded him as a puppet of the Soviet Union, rejected these overtures. To gain support for his proposals, he traveled to several European capitals, warning that Afghanistan was in danger of becoming a haven for drug dealers and that civil war would ensue between the various mujahideen groups. He attempted to achieve some reconciliation by offering Ahmad Shah Masood, the leader of the Northern Alliance, the post of minister of defense in his final government, but that offer was rejected.

Najibullah resigned in 1992 as part of a plan by the United Nations to form a broad-based Afghan government, and the mujahideen assumed power that year. However, by 1994, fierce fighting among the various mujahideen groups had devastated Kabul, and Najibullah took refuge in the UN compound in the city. When the Taliban captured Kabul two years later, he was forcibly removed from the UN compound, killed, and then hung in public by the Taliban forces.

See also People's Democratic Party of Afghanistan;
Tanai, Lt. Gen. Shanawaz

References
Brigot, Andre, and Olivier Roy. 1988. *The War in Afghanistan: An Account and Analysis of the Country, Its People, Soviet Intervention and the Resistance.* New York: Harvester-Wheatsheaf.

NANGARHAR PROVINCE

Nangarhar Province is located in eastern Afghanistan. Its capital is the important city of Jalalabad, whose earlier population of about 57,000 has been swelled to about 200,000 by refugees (roughly between 1998 and 2002). The province occupies an area of 7,195 square miles and has a population of about 740,000; at present, some 400,000 are being accommodated in refugee camps elsewhere in Afghanistan as internally displaced persons. The population is predominantly Pashtun, but other ethnic groups live in the capital.

Jalalabad grew in importance when it became the winter capital of Afghan kings after Kabul was established as the seat of government. Agriculture is the mainstay of the economy, with irrigation being aided by the Darunta Dam on the River Kabul (which also provides hydroelectric power). Timber is found in the mountain areas but is smuggled into Pakistan because of higher prices paid for it across the border. The province and particularly Jalalabad were held by the government against the mujahideen and were also a stronghold of the Taliban regime when it came to power in 1996.

References
Adamec, Ludwig W. 1972–1985. *Historical and Political Gazetteer of Afghanistan.* 6 vols. Graz, Austria: Akademische Druck-u Verlagsansalt.

Data Collection for Afghan Repatriation Project. 1989. *Nangarhar Province.* Islamabad: UN High Commissioner for Refugees.

NARANJAN DAS (1853–?)

An Afghan Hindu who served as finance minister during the reigns of Amir Habibullah and King Amanullah, Naranjan Das was well respected by Amanullah, and no funds could be released without his signature as *diwan* (head of civil service). In 1906, he was granted the rank of civil colonel. He became subordinate to Mir Ahmad Shah, head of the Revenue Department, in November 1906, and in 1912, he took charge of the collection of tools and *octroi* (toll or tax on goods brought into a city) throughout the country from Mustafi Muhammad Husain Khan. He was part of the Afghan delegation that produced the Anglo-Afghan Treaty of 1919 and was also involved in the Mussoorie Conference of 1920, which eventually led to the Anglo-Afghan Treaty of 1921. He became a civil brigadier in February 1920.

See also Amanullah, King; Anglo-Afghan Treaty of 1919; Anglo-Afghan Treaty of 1921; Mussoorie Conference

References

Wild, Roland. 1933. *Amanullah: Ex-King of Afghanistan.* London.: Hurst and Blackett.

NASIR TRIBE

The Nasir tribe is an affluent Pashtun tribe whose wealth is in its flocks and herds. Sheep and camels provide for the Nasirs' immediate needs, with the excess produce being sold or traded to meet their other requirements. A nomadic people, they used to winter in India and were in constant conflict with the Waziris, whose territory they passed through on route to their winter quarters. The structure of the Nasir tribe is democratic and not dominated by their chiefs, in line with the normal nomadic social structure. During the reign of Amir Abdur Rahman, who ruled from 1880 to 1901, attempts were made to settle the members of the tribe in Herat Province, but they agreed to pay taxes in order to protect their traditional way of life.

References

Hammerton, J. A. 1984. *Tribes, Races and Cultures of India and Neighbouring Countries: Afghanistan, Bhutan, Burma, Ceylon, Nepal, and Tibet.* Delhi, India: Mittal.

NASRULLAH KHAN (?–1919)

Nasrullah Khan was the second son of Amir Abdur Rahman and effectively controlled the government administration while his brother, Habibullah, was amir. He was also president of the amir's advisory council and commander-in-chief of the armed forces. In terms of policy, he was a conservative who was an ardent supporter of the religious establishment and a committed foe of the British. The enmity toward Britain was reinforced in 1895 when he was sent by Amir Abdur Rahman to London to obtain consent for an Afghan embassy in London but the British government refused approval. On Amir Habibullah's assassination in February 1919, Nasrullah Khan was proclaimed king in Peshawar, Pakistan, but the army gave its support to Amanullah Khan, who controlled Kabul palace and the treasury. Nasrullah was arrested and assassinated while in custody.

See also Amanullah, King; Habibullah, Amir

References

Gregorian, Vartan. 1969. *The Emergence of Modern Afghanistan: Politics of Reform and Modernization, 1880–1946.* Stanford, CA: Stanford University Press.

NATIONAL FATHERLAND FRONT (JABHA-YI-MILLI-YI PADAR WATAN)

The National Fatherland Front (NFF) was established in 1980 by Babrak Karmal to unite all the progressive forces of Afghanistan. The People's Democratic Party of Afghanistan (PDPA) was the driving force behind the association. The move was endorsed by a *loya jirga* (great council) attended by 940 delegates and was inaugurated on 15 June 1981 in Kabul. The organization's membership included all trade unions, guilds, women's organizations, and professional bodies. With about 55,000 members by 1984, the NFF was designed to encourage the solidarity of the working people and to direct their struggles against those who did not want revolution.

The objectives of the NFF were:

- To lead the revolution to its final victory
- To promote the revolutionary process
- To facilitate extensive participation of people in the administration of the affairs of state, and
- To promote unity without discrimination and distinction and to work to build a new, just, progressive, free, and independent revolution in Afghanistan

Unlike other Communist regimes, the NFF never mobilized the masses under party control, and in

1987, it was renamed the National Front of the Republic of Afghanistan. It did not survive the fall of the Marxist regime as a cohesive organization.

See also Karmal, Babrak; People's Democratic Party of Afghanistan

References

Arnold, Anthony. 1983. *Afghanistan's Two-Party Communism: Parcham and Khalq.* Stanford, CA: Hoover Institution Press.

NATIONAL ISLAMIC FRONT OF AFGHANISTAN (MAHAZ-I MILLI-YI AFGHANISTAN)

The National Islamic Front of Afghanistan was founded in Peshawar, Pakistan, in 1979 by Sayyed Ahmad Gailani as an armed resistance movement, part of a loose confederation of moderate mujahideen groups. The front is a liberal, nationalist Islamic party supporting a free and elected government. The group is extremely supportive of the Afghanistan Interim Government (AIG) and advocates a strong and unified mujahideen movement.

Portrait of Pir Sayyed Ahmad Gailani, leader of the National Islamic Front of Afghanistan, at a peace summit in Peshawar, Pakistan. (LE SEGRETAIN PASCAL/CORBIS SYGMA)

The movement also campaigns for the fundamental rights of freedom of speech, protection of private property, and social justice, which includes providing education and health care for all Afghans. The movement supports the principles of the UN Charter, the Declaration of Human Rights, and the Islamic Organization Conference but favors nonalignment and respect for Afghanistan's neighbors.

See also Gailani, Sayyed Ahmad

References

Roy, Olivier. 1986. *Islam and Resistance in Afghanistan.* London and New York: Cambridge University Press.

NATIONAL LIBERATION FRONT OF AFGHANISTAN (JABHA-YI-NAJAT-YI MILLI-YI AFGHANISTAN)

The National Liberation Front of Afghanistan was founded in 1978 by Sabghatullah Mujaddidi and was one of seven mujahideen movements with headquarters in Pakistan. The front is a small and moderate group, which was formed with the objective of overthrowing the Marxist regime in Kabul in 1979 and replacing it with an Islamic state based on parliamentary democracy. The movement is largely Pashtun in terms of membership.

See also Mujaddidi, Sabghatullah

References

Oleson, A. 1995. *Islam and Politics in Afghanistan.* London: Curzon Press.

NATIONAL REVOLUTIONARY PARTY (HIZB-I INQILAB-I MILLI)

The National Revolutionary Party (NRP) was founded by Afghanistan president Muhammad Daud in 1975 to garner support and grassroots backing for his republican regime. The NRP was also founded in an attempt to limit the influence of the Communist supporters of Daud, who had helped him to gain power, and it was to be the only permitted political party. The party was designed to be an umbrella organization representing all of the progressive forces within Afghanistan. It was run by a central council comprising Gen. Ghulam Haidar Rasuli, the minister of defense; Sayyid Abdullah, the minister of finance; Dr. Abdul Majid; and Professor Abdul Qayyum. The party did not survive the Saur Revolt of April 1978.

See also Daud, Sardar Muhammad; Rasuli, Maj. Gen. Ghulam Haidar

References
Ahmad, N. D. 1990. *The Survival of Afghanistan,
1747–1979: A Diplomatic History with an Analytic
and Reflective Approach.* Lahore, Pakistan: Institute of
Islamic Culture.

NAZAR, LT. GEN. MUHAMMAD (1935–)

Muhammad Nazar was a member of the Khalq faction of the People's Democratic Party of Afghanistan (PDPA) who joined the party in 1974. Five years later, he was involved in the Homeland High Defense Council, founded as a result of increasing mujahideen activity. A Durrani Pashtun, he was educated at the Afghan Military Academy and received further training at the USSR Military Academy before returning to the Afghan air force. His position was used to full effect during the Saur Revolt of April 1978, which led to the installation of a Communist regime. The coming to power of the PDPA saw Nazar as chief of staff of the armed forces and minister of defense from 1984 to 1986. In 1990. he joined Defense Minister Shanawaz Tanai in a plot against the regime of Muhammad Najibullah, and he was arrested and stripped of all his positions following the failure of the coup.

See also People's Democratic Party of Afghanistan; Saur Revolt; Tanai, Lt. Gen. Shanawaz

References
Arnold, Anthony. 1983. *Afghanistan's Two-Party
Communism: Parcham and Khalq.* Stanford, CA:
Hoover Institution Press.

NIAZI, GHULAM MUHAMMAD (?–1978)

Ghulam Muhammad Niazi was one of the founders of the Organization of Muslim Youth, which was affiliated with the Islamic Society in Pakistan before becoming the nucleus of the Islamist Movement. He was born in Ghazni Province and educated at Abu Hanifa Theological School in Kabul before going to al-Azhar University in Egypt, where he absorbed the teachings of the Muslim Brotherhood. On returning to Afghanistan, Niazi taught at Kabul University, eventually becoming dean of the Faculty of Theology. Burhanuddin Rabbani, the leader of the Islamist Movement and the president of Afghanistan from 1992 to 1996, and Abdul Rasul Sayyaf, leader of the Islamic Union for the Liberation of Afghanistan, were among his students. He was succeeded as leader of the organization in 1972 by Rabbani. He was arrested two years later and was executed in 1978 during the Khalq regime.

See also Islamist Movement

References
Oleson, A. 1995. *Islam and Politics in Afghanistan.*
London: Curzon Press.

NIMRUZ PROVINCE

Nimruz Province is located in southwestern Afghanistan and has an area of 20,980 square miles but a population of only 112,000. Until 1968, the province was called Chakhansur. It was part of ancient Sistan and the site of earlier civilizations destroyed by the Mongol invasions. The capital of the province, Zaranj, was built in the 1960s. The economy is based on agriculture in the well-watered Helmand Valley and animal husbandry, with nomadic groups living in the deserts. The strong winds in this area are harnessed by windmills throughout the province. Baluchs, Brahuis, Pashtuns, and Tajiks comprise the ethnic makeup of the Sunni population of Nimruz, in order of size.

References
Adamec, Ludwig W. 1972–1985. *Historical and Political
Gazetteer of Afghanistan.* 6 vols. Graz, Austria:
Akademische Druck-u Verlagsansalt.

NIZAMNAMA

The Nizamnama was a code of regulations enacted during the reign of King Amanullah and embodied all of his reforms, including the Constitution of 1923. Incorporated were regulations relating to the organization of the state, payment of taxes, engagements and marriages, and the establishment of schools for women. These regulations and the modernization process were opposed by traditionalists, who believed they were at variance with Islamic law. Consequently, the traditionalists enlisted tribal support to oust King Amanullah.

See also Amanullah, King

References
Wild, Roland. 1933. *Amanullah: Ex-King of Afghanistan.*
London: Hurst and Blackett.

NORTHERN ALLIANCE

The Northern Alliance evolved from the power struggle that ensued after the Soviet withdrawal from Afghanistan was completed on 14 February 1989. The alliance was a grouping of disparate mujahideen groups united against the Communist

Afghanistan Northern Alliance troops move from the northern part of the country to Kabul across the Kukcha River in Takhar Province, 14 November 2001. (Reuters NewMedia Inc./CORBIS)

government of President Muhammad Najibullah. It came into being in 1992, disintegrated in 1993, and was resurrected in 1996 with the coming to power of the Taliban.

The Soviet withdrawal did not lead to the immediate collapse of the Najibullah government as many observers had expected, which set into motion a struggle for control of a post-Communist Afghanistan. The situation was complicated by the role played by countries in the region, each of which wanted to see a regime installed in Kabul that would meet its own short- and long-term interests in Afghanistan and the region as a whole. Inside Afghanistan, the various factions and political parties began to form both political and military alliances in order to secure control—or at least a significant presence—in any future government.

At the time of the Soviet withdrawal, the main power brokers were Ahmad Shah Masood and Gulbuddin Hekmatyar, two men who had been fighting each other for military and political power since the Soviet invasion of 1979. Immediately after the Soviets withdrew, Masood had considerable control over

large areas of Afghanistan through the Shura-yi-Najar (Supervisory Council), which coordinated all of the resistance forces under his authority. He was also quick to seize the opportunities presented by the Soviet departure, and by the middle of 1991, he had extended his control to most of the northeast provinces of Afghanistan.

However, toward the end of 1991, a new politico-military situation arose in northern Afghanistan as Gen. Abdul Rashid Dostum, head of President Najibullah's northern militia, rebelled against the Kabul regime and Monsaur Naderi, whose group controlled the northern part of the Salang highway, joined him. Masood immediately invited Dostum to league with him in opposition to Najibullah's government and to free northern Afghanistan from the Kabul regime. Additionally, with support from Iran, the Shi'a Islamic Unity Party, largely based in Herat, joined the alliance struck between Masood and Dostum, thus creating the Northern Alliance.

The Northern Alliance was successful in bringing about the downfall of Najibullah's government in April 1992, partially as a result of secret negotiations with members of the Parcham faction in the government. Thus, alliance forces were able to occupy Kabul and thwart the efforts of other Afghan leaders based in exile in Peshawar, Pakistan. However, the unity of the alliance was short-lived, as a power struggle soon ensued between Masood, Dostum, and Gulbuddin Hekmatyar, and the whole structure disintegrated. Afghanistan sank into a state of total anarchy, and the power struggle soon developed into an all-out civil war. The new government headed by President Burhanuddin Rabbani, who was backed by Masood, had no power other than in Kabul, which was less than secure, and in the Panjshir Valley.

In essence, Afghanistan's government had ceased to exist, and areas were controlled by various mujahideen warlords whose allegiances and alliances constantly shifted in their attempts to secure overall control of Kabul in order to try to establish control over Afghanistan and secure recognition as the new national government. It was in this period of anarchy that the Taliban movement came into being, formed in Kandahar in 1994 under the leadership of Mullah Muhammad Omar. The movement attracted support from Islamic militants in the *madrasas* (religious schools) of Pakistan and from other parts of the Muslim world, including Egypt, the Arab gulf states, Saudi Arabia, and Chechnya. Such was the state of disarray among the various mujahideen groups that the Taliban at once began to enjoy considerable military success, and by 1996, it had taken Kabul and most of southern and western Afghanistan. In some cases, the Taliban troops were joined by mujahideen groups, and they were often welcomed by the people, who were weary of the civil war and the excesses of the fighting mujahideen groups.

The forces of the Northern Alliance were forced to withdraw northward, and President Rabbani declared Mazar-i Sharif to be the new capital of the country. But Taliban forces ousted the alliance in 1997, with much bloodshed. Eventually, the Northern Alliance was left in control of only about 10 percent of northern Afghanistan, centered on Masood's stronghold in the Panjshir Valley and a small mountainous area in the northeast. However, it was still recognized by the outside world as the legitimate government of Afghanistan, with Burhanuddin Rabbani as president. The military force consisted of some 10,000 troops, equipped with tanks, fighter jets, and helicopter gunships left over from the Soviet era.

The alliance was dealt a severe blow on 9 September 2001 when Ahmad Shah Masood was fatally wounded by assassins posing as Arab journalists, possibly agents of the Taliban or al-Qaeda. Masood's former head of intelligence, Gen. Mohammad Fahim, assumed control of the military wing of the movement. The Northern Alliance, which then became known as the United Front, represented the last opposition to the Taliban.

In fact, that opposition against a common enemy was the only unifying element in the movement, whose composition was ethnically and religiously disparate and primarily non-Pashtun. The essence of its military strength was drawn from the Tajik and Uzbek populations, and the alliance was also backed by Iran, Russia, Tajikistan, and Uzbekistan. At the time of Masood's death, the alliance was unable to do much more than hold its own against the Taliban advances.

The Northern Alliance's nominal head was still President Rabbani, who was the most senior figure in the movement, an ethnic Tajik, and a former professor at Kabul University; he was still recognized by the United Nations and within Afghanistan's embassies in thirty-three countries. His seat of government was in Faizabad, but the location was rather insecure and almost totally dependent on goods smuggled in from territory controlled by the Taliban. Rabbani's concept of an Islamic state was less strict than that of the Taliban, and in alliance-held areas, women and girls were able to work and receive an education. However, the Northern Alliance, like the Taliban, was not noted for its respect for human rights.

The terrorist attacks on the World Trade Center and the Pentagon on 11 September 2001 proved to be a morale booster for the Northern Alliance due to the declared intent of the United States to take action against the Taliban regime, al-Qaeda, and Osama bin Laden. Alliance leaders took the view that the Taliban would be doomed, and they immediately announced that they would be willing to fight with the United States against the Taliban forces, thus providing a reason for the fragile alliance to continue to hold together. However, as a portent for the future, the Islamic Unity Party led by Gulbuddin Hekmatyar was opposed to U.S. involvement in Afghanistan, and Hekmatyar warned that he would take action against American troops. After the U.S. ground forces arrived in Afghanistan in October 2001, Hekmatyar declared a jihad against their presence in the country.

Initially, U.S. support for the Northern Alliance action against the Taliban was restricted to providing technical assistance, intelligence data, and funding, but this was later boosted by the presence of U.S. and UK Special Forces, who began operating with Northern Alliance troops. Both Iran and Russia were ready suppliers of arms, ammunition, and military equipment for alliance forces, whom they saw as furthering their own interests in the region; such support was justified by the fact that Rabbani was still recognized as the legitimate head of state. It is clear that the conflict in Afghanistan continued to have a regional dimension. Russia had supported Masood as a counter to Taliban expansionism in the region, whereas Uzbekistan had supported the Uzbek leader, Gen.Abdul Rashid Dostum, to provide a buffer against the spread of Islamic militancy from Afghanistan. Tajikistan has been engaged in a civil war against Islamic fundamentalists within its own borders and supported the Tajiks led by Rabbani for the same reasons as Uzbekistan, though some Afghan Tajiks also favored linking their territory with Tajikistan.

The U.S. bombing raids on Taliban and al-Qaeda installations and then against Taliban frontline positions assisted the Northern Alliance in its efforts against the Taliban. In fact, it was airpower that enabled alliance forces to make rapid gains against Taliban positions. The opposition soon disintegrated, with some warlords changing sides, Taliban fighters laying down their arms and melting into the countryside, and alliance forces advancing on Kabul with the backing of U.S. and UK ground forces. However, after the fall of Kabul and the Taliban stronghold of Kandahar to the Northern Alliance, the hard-core elements among the Taliban fighters and al-Qaeda, including a large number of foreign fighters, moved into the mountainous areas of eastern Afghanistan or across the border into the North-West Frontier Province of Pakistan. These several thousand hard-core elements were pursued by Coalition special forces and conventional troops, with the backing of local warlords in a series of actions.

The UN-sponsored conference held in Bonn, Germany, in December 2001 led to the formation of an interim government in Afghanistan in which the Northern Alliance was heavily represented, though the new president, Hamid Karzai, was a Pashtun. Even with this agreement, however, the fragility of the Northern Alliance was revealed: General Dostum had been excluded from the administration, and as a result, he rejected the Bonn Agreement, especially as he saw rivals being given portfolios in the government. The situation was only defused by President Karzai appointing Dostum as deputy defense minister and his special representative in northern Afghanistan. The current situation in Afghanistan is fraught with problems and tensions, for President Karzai's authority is essentially limited to Kabul, where he is backed by the International Security Assistance Force (ISAF) and where warlords still wield power in the majority of the provinces while at the same time declaring their support for the Karzai government. At present, the alliance is still holding, but the situation is delicate, with traditional rivalries and enmities simmering just below the surface. In many cases, these old hatreds are manifesting themselves through action, such as the ethnic cleansing of Pashtuns in Herat and Mazar-i-Sharif. Frequently, such actions are responses to atrocities committed during the Taliban regime, but the rivalries often go back through generations: for many, it is a question of settling old scores.

Conditions in Afghanistan are largely affected by the presence of Coalition forces, the provision of humanitarian aid by the UN agencies and nongovernmental organizations (NGOs), promises of restructuring aid, and, for many, an overwhelming war-weariness. However, security is far from assured, especially since Taliban and al-Qaeda elements are still active, opium production and the drug trade are on the increase, and warlords are vying for control in the provinces. The allegiances that held together against the Taliban as the common enemy will be sorely tested in the post-Taliban era.

See also Civil War; Coalition Air Campaign against the Taliban; Coalition Land Campaign against the Taliban; Dostum, Gen. Abdul Rashid; Hekmatyar, Gulbuddin; Laden, Osama bin; Masood, Ahmad Shah; Rabbani, Burhanuddin; Taliban

References
Carew, Tom. 2000. *Jihad: The Secret War in Afghanistan.* Edinburgh: Mainstream.
Goodson, Larry P. 2001. *Afghanistan's Endless War: State Failure, Regional Politics, and the Rise of the Taliban.* Seattle: University of Washington Press.

Guistozzi, Antonio. 2000. *War, Politics and Society in Afghanistan, 1978–1992.* Washington, DC: Georgetown University Press.

Marsden, Peter. 1998. *The Taliban: War, Religion and the New Order in Afghanistan.* London and New York: Zed Books.

NUR, NUR AHMAD (1937–)

Nur Ahmad Nur was a member of the Parcham faction of the People's Democratic Party of Afghanistan (PDPA). He embarked on a career in the foreign ministry after graduating from Kabul University. Following the April 1978 Saur Revolt and the Communists' rise to power, Nur became minister of the interior but in August was sent to Washington as ambassador. However, he was purged with other Parcham leaders suspected of plotting a coup, and he went to Eastern Europe. He only returned to Afghanistan after Babrak Karmal took the reins of power in December 1979. In 1981, he became a member of the Politburo and Central Committee of the PDPA. Among his posts were ambassador to Warsaw in 1988, representative at the United Nations in 1989, and, in January 1991, ambassador to Havana.

See also People's Democratic Party of Afghanistan; Saur Revolt

References

People's Democratic Party of Afghanistan. 1980. *Fundamental Principles, Democratic Republic of Afghanistan.* Kabul: Ministry of Information and Culture.

NURISTAN PROVINCE

Prior to 1990, the 1,409-square-mile area that is now Nuristan Province was a district of Laghman Province. The area was part of the ancient Karifstan, or Land of the Infidels, and its people became converted to Sunni Islam after being conquered by Amir Abdur Rahman in 1895 and 1896. The territory was then renamed Nuristan, or Land of Light. Nuristanis number some 100,000 and also predominate in Kunar and Laghman Provinces. Their languages are Indo-Iranian in origin and have a number of dialects that have developed in isolation from other Indian and Iranian languages.

The Nuristanis allied with the Safi Pashtuns to rise up against the People's Democratic Party of Afghanistan in October 1978. The Marxist regime was unable to fully suppress the rebellion, and Nuristan almost became an autonomous region. It was a vital base for mujahideen groups during the civil war from 1989 to 2001.

References

Adamec, Ludwig W. 1972–1985. *Historical and Political Gazetteer of Afghanistan.* 6 vols. Graz, Austria: Akademische Druck-u Verlagsansalt.

"Other Ethnic Groups of Afghanistan." 2002. http://www.afghan-network.net/Ethnic-Groups/other-groups/html (cited 7 February 2002).

NURISTANI, ABDUL WAKIL (?–1929)

Abdul Wakil Nuristani was an attendant to Amir Abdur Rahman, ruler of Afghanistan from 1880 to 1901, and on 5 June 1913, he took control of the garrison at Kandahar. Three years later, he was recalled to Kabul and appointed to command the gendarmerie, Ghud-i-Khotwali, and he was promoted to major general by the king in March 1919. During the Third Anglo-Afghan War in 1919, he commanded the Afghan forces at Kunar in June 1919 and was on the Chitral front in October 1920. His military career continued as he served as the officiating commander, Jalalabad, in October 1920 and returned to Kabul in the following month. In November 1923, he was commander of the Kabul Corps. He became Naib Sular of Badakhshan and Qatagham in August 1925.

In December 1928, Nuristani was called to Jalalabad during the rebellion against the king and was said to be fighting for Ali Ahmad Khan, the governor of Herat, in January 1929. He was reported to have been arrested and killed while in command of the pacification of Kohdaman after the execution of Habibullah Kalakani, who ruled Afghanistan from 18 January to 19 October 1929.

See also Third Anglo-Afghan War

References

Khan, Sultan Muhammad. 1980. *The Life of Abdur Rahman, Amir of Afghanistan.* Karachi, Pakistan: Oxford University Press.

NURZAI, ABDUL QAYYUM (1942–)

Abdul Qayyum Nurzai was born in Farah Province and entered a career in teaching, rising to the post of deputy minister of education in April 1978 and then deputy minister of information and culture. He is a Khalqi (a member of the Khalq faction of the People's Democratic Party of Afghanistan, or PDPA), and in March 1979, he became editor of

Khalq, the faction's newspaper. He then became editor of *Dehqan,* which was the organ of the PDPA's Central Committee. In May 1990, he was made deputy prime minister in the government of Fazl Haq Khaliqyar.

See also Khalq; People's Democratic Party of Afghanistan

References
Arnold, Anthony. 1983. *Afghanistan's Two-Party Communism: Parcham and Khalq.* Stanford, CA: Hoover Institution Press.

NURZAI TRIBE

The Nurzais are members of a significant and prosperous Durrani tribe. Though renowned for their prowess as warriors, they have an agriculturally based economy. They live primarily in Kandahar, Farah, and Herat Provinces, and they tend to be settled rather than nomadic.

References
Bellew, H. W. 1880. *The Races of Afghanistan: Being a Brief Account of the Principal Nations Inhabiting That Country.* London: Thaker.

OFUQ, MUHAMMAD ZAHIR

Muhammad Zahir Ofuq was the head of a small, left-wing group known as the Revolutionary Society of Afghan Toilers, which joined with the People's Democratic Party of Afghanistan (PDPA) in July 1986. He was one of the founding members of the PDPA and a supporter of its Khalq faction before forming his own group. In 1986, he also became vice-president and scientific secretary of the Academy of Science, but his career came to an end with his arrest in 1991, likely for opposition to the government.

See also People's Democratic Party of Afghanistan
References
Arnold, Anthony. 1983. *Afghanistan's Two-Party Communism: Parcham and Khalq.* Stanford, CA: Hoover Institution Press.

OMAR, MULLAH MUHAMMAD (1959–)

Mullah Muhammad Omar was the leader of the Taliban. Because of his association with Osama bin Laden and the human rights violations of the Taliban regime, he is at the head of the most-wanted list of the Coalition force put together at the instigation of President George W. Bush as part of Operation Enduring Freedom. As supreme leader of the Taliban, he became virtual ruler of much of Afghanistan once his forces had defeated the mujahideen, which had come to power after the fall of the Marxist regime in 1992. Omar had been a fighter in the mujahideen group led by Muhammad Nabi Muhammadi; in time, he became a deputy chief commander of the group and was actively involved in raids against Soviet and government forces from 1989 to 1992. He was reputed to have destroyed several Soviet tanks and was wounded four times in action; despite losing sight in one eye, he is still said to be an expert marksman.

Mullah Omar has been described by diplomats as extremely shy. He is untalkative with foreigners, has given very few interviews, rarely meets with non-Muslims, and seems to have been photographed

only once, as a young man. He is not regarded as a great orator; for his followers, the strength of his leadership lies in his piety and the force of his beliefs. In April 1996, he was elected *amirul momineen* (commander of the faithful) by a *shura* (council) of about 1,000 members of *ulamas* (Islamic scholars and clergymen). He was the first Muslim since the Fourth Caliph to publicly accept the title.

The son of a peasant farmer, he grew up in the village of Singesar, near Kandahar, and was educated in a village *madrasa* (religious school) before going to Pakistan to further his Islamic education at a fundamentalist religious school. That education was not completed due to the Soviet occupation of Afghanistan in 1979. This lack of a full education has always been acknowledged by Omar, who has described himself as a seeker of knowledge rather than a mullah who imparts knowledge (though at one time, he actually was a mullah in a village *madrasa* near Kandahar). He was relatively unknown in Afghanistan until 1994, when he started the Taliban movement and rose to power. Observers maintain that he was reluctant to assume a position of power, but Omar has said that his leadership was the result of a dream in which Allah came to him, in the form of a man, and asked him to lead the faithful.

Omar is said to have been horrified by the behavior of the mujahideen (of which he had been a part until 1992) toward the Soviets and the Marxist government in Kabul. The country had descended into anarchy at that point, with some mujahideen fighters kidnapping and raping boys and girls, robbing travelers on the roads, and driving international aid workers from Kandahar. Omar and some thirty Pashtun followers took up arms to deal with four mujahideen who had been raping women near Omar's village, and from this small beginning, the Taliban movement was born. Recruits to the Taliban came from the Pashtun majority in southern Afghanistan, but the movement also attracted volunteers from the religious schools in Afghanistan and foreign fighters who had been involved in the mujahideen campaign against the Marxist regime.

The ultimate goal of the Taliban and Mullah Omar was the establishment of a Muslim state that would function according to a strict interpretation of the Koran, based on the tenets taught by the fundamentalist schools in Pakistan. In the two years following its founding in 1994, the Taliban succeeded in capturing about 90 percent of Afghanistan, with only the area of the Panjshir Valley, controlled by Ahmad Shah Masood, resisting their advance. Taliban forces had also been swollen by fundamentalist fighters from other Muslim states, particularly Pakistan, Saudi Arabia, Egypt, and the gulf states, some of whom were seasoned combatants, having already served with the mujahideen. The climax of the campaign came in September 1996 with the fall of Kabul to the Taliban, and it was then that Omar became commander of the faithful in a ceremony held at Kandahar. After his election, Omar appeared before his supporters wearing a cloak said to have belonged to the prophet Muhammad, which had lain in a Kandahar shrine for sixty years.

Taliban rule in Afghanistan was marked by oppression, a strict interpretation of the Koran and Shari'a law, and violations of human rights, particularly against women. It was also Taliban policy to eradicate all Western influences from the country: accordingly, television sets and videocassette recorders were confiscated, music was banned, men were forced to grow beards, and women were forbidden to work or receive an education. The result was that many cultured and educated Afghans fled from the country to escape the oppression of the regime. Others accepted the excesses of the Taliban as the price of peace.

The Taliban regime under Omar never really had a functioning government, and Omar himself never left Kandahar to go to Kabul, the nation's capital, to assume power. All decisions were made in private by Omar and a small group of elders, and funds were distributed to Taliban leaders from a large, tin box full of U.S. dollars, which was held by Omar. The Council of the Taliban itself was buffeted by pressures from a variety of sources, including Pakistan and the radical Arab elements operating within Afghanistan, many of whom were part of Osama bin Laden's al-Qaeda network. Omar had originally been supported by Pakistan, through its Inter-Services Intelligence Service, but the regime had received international recognition only from Pakistan, Saudi Arabia, and the United Arab Emirates. The Taliban soon came into conflict with the international community for providing a safe haven for Osama bin Laden in 1996, following his expulsion from Sudan. Despite UN demands that bin Laden be expelled to answer charges of involvement in a number of terrorist incidents, such as the abortive attack on the World Trade Center in 1993, Omar refused to act, arguing that bin Laden was a guest of Afghanistan and protected by Islamic law. In response, UN sanctions against the Taliban regime were imposed, including the freezing of overseas assets and the refusal of takeoff and landing rights to the Afghan national airline.

International opinion was further incensed by Mullah Omar's declared policy of destroying Afghanistan's pre-Islamic heritage. One egregious example was the regime's destruction of the statues of Buddha at Bamian in 2001. Despite pressure from a number of governments, including Egypt, and international bodies such as the UN Educational, Scientific, and Cultural Organization (UNESCO), Omar refused to abandon or relax this policy, and the destruction proceeded throughout Afghanistan. It also seems that, as a result of a drought in Afghanistan, military problems with the opposition, sanctions, and international isolation, Mullah Omar became increasingly isolated in Kandahar. Observers have indicated that this isolation led him to fall under the influence of radical Arab militants—in particular, Ayman al-Zawahiri, Osama bin Laden's deputy—as was demonstrated by the fact that Omar's rhetoric changed from speeches on the rebuilding of Afghanistan to pan-Islamic addresses marked by radical Islamism in which he reflected the thoughts of militant Islamic radicals from Egypt and Saudi Arabia.

Omar maintained to the rest of the world that Osama bin Laden had been placed under house arrest by the regime in Kandahar, barred from access to his communications facility, and forbidden to use Afghan soil for actions against other countries. However, the 11 September 2001 attacks on the World Trade Center and the Pentagon and their attribution to bin Laden and al-Qaeda would have a dramatic impact on the future of the Taliban and Afghanistan. Omar's continued refusal to expel bin Laden led U.S. President George W. Bush to declare a "War on Terror," with the initial objectives being the overthrow of the Taliban regime and the capture of Osama bin Laden and the leaders of al-Qaeda. At first, covert support for forces opposing the Taliban was provided through the supply of arms and equipment, as well as the infiltration of special forces to assist with training and intelligence activities.

The real campaign was prefaced by Cruise missile attacks on Taliban strongholds and al-Qaeda training camps by the United Kingdom and the United States, followed by U.S. air strikes on Taliban frontline positions using B-52 bombers. The Taliban resistance soon collapsed under the air strikes and the advance of the opposition forces, supported by U.S. ground troops, and the conflict was rapidly transformed into a search-and-destroy mission to mop up the last of the Taliban and al-Qaeda fighters. During the advance of the Coalition forces, Mullah Omar had remained in the Taliban stronghold of Kandahar, but by the time the town fell to the Coalition forces, he and his advisers had disappeared, as had Osama bin Laden and his immediate entourage, though they did not necessarily flee together.

The hunt for Taliban and al-Qaeda fighters was largely taking place in Paktia Province in eastern Afghanistan, near the Pakistan border, but the hunt for Mullah Omar and the Taliban leaders was centered on the Oruzgan Province in southern Afghanistan, which had been Omar's home base. The area was raided several times between March and May 2002 by U.S. Special Forces, resulting in a few deaths and some arrests, but there was no sign of Mullah Omar or Mullah Dadullah, a brutal commander who had escaped capture following the surrender of Kunduz in November 2001. It was then reported that Mullah Omar had taken shelter in the remote mountain area west of Char Chine, in Helmand Province, a heavily forested region riddled with narrow valleys that are difficult to penetrate and not easy to survey from the air.

The hunt for Mullah Omar and his close associates goes on. It seems obvious that these individuals are either taking refuge in areas of Afghanistan where geography as well as tribal and family allegiances are

to their advantage or hiding out in the lawless frontier districts of Pakistan. A remarkable piece of intelligence—or an outright betrayal—will be required for the Taliban leaders to be given up to the Afghan government or the Coalition armed forces, as there is still a great deal of sympathy for the Taliban in parts of Afghanistan and Pakistan. On 17 February 2003, in a statement released to the press and purportedly from Mullah Omar, Afghans were instructed to wage a jihad against U.S. forces in their country and against the government of Hamid Karzai. Afghans who failed to distance themselves from either the U.S. forces or the Karzai administration were to be considered allies of the enemies of Islam and dealt with accordingly. The statement was issued in Mullah Omar's name and title, but the document was not signed and gave no indication as to his location.

See also Coalition Air Campaign against the Taliban; Coalition Land Campaign against the Taliban; Destruction of Pre-Islamic Heritage; Laden, Osama bin; Taliban

References

Goodson, Larry P. 2001. *Afghanistan's Endless War: State Failure, Regional Politics, and the Rise of the Taliban.* Seattle: University of Washington Press.

Magnus, Ralph H., and Eden Naby. 2002. *Afghanistan: Mullah, Marx and Mujahid.* Rev. ed. Boulder, CO: Westview Press.

Maley, William. 1999. *Fundamentalism Reborn? Afghanistan and the Taliban.* London: Hurst.

Matinnusin, Karmal. 1999. *The Taliban Phenomenon: Afghanistan, 1994–1997.* Karachi, Pakistan: Oxford University Press.

Rashid, Ahmed. 2001. *Taliban: The Story of the Afghan Warlords.* London: Pan.

OPERATION ENDURING FREEDOM

Following the 11 September 2001 terrorist attacks on the World Trade Center and the Pentagon, U.S. President George W. Bush announced the beginning of Operation Enduring Freedom on 20 September in an address to a joint session of Congress. Originally known as Operation Infinite Justice, the mission's main objectives were the destruction of terrorist training camps and infrastructure within Afghanistan, the capture of al-Qaeda leaders, and the dismantling of all terrorist activities in Afghanistan.

The U.S. objectives were further defined on 7 October 2001 in a speech by Secretary of Defense Donald Rumsfeld: to make clear to the Taliban that the sheltering of terrorists was unacceptable to the

Members of VFA-37's Ordnance Control manually load an AIM-120 AMRAAM Missile onto an FA-18 Hornet on the flight deck of the USS Harry S. Truman *on March 1, 2003. (Department of Defense)*

international community, to gather information on al-Qaeda and Taliban resources, to build up relations with groups opposed to the Taliban, to stop Afghanistan from being a safe haven for terrorists, and to destroy the Taliban military so that the anti-Taliban forces would be successful in their operations. Further, U.S. military forces would help to facilitate the delivery of humanitarian aid to the Afghan people.

The UK government immediately joined the Coalition, using the code name Operation Veritas for the British mission, and it defined its objectives on 16 October 2001. The short-term goals of the operation were the capture of Osama bin Laden and other al-Qaeda leaders, the prevention of further al-Qaeda terrorist attacks, the destruction of terrorist training camps and Afghanistan's role in providing a safe haven for al-Qaeda, and the removal of the Taliban regime. Longer-term objectives included ending terrorism, deterring state sponsorship of terrorism, and reintegrating Afghanistan into the international community.

U.S. Forces

Navy and Marine Corps. The naval contribution to the operation in Afghanistan was significant and in-

cluded as many as three carrier battle groups operating in the region with strike aircraft, as follows:

- *Enterprise* battle group
  Composed of eight ships and submarines, together with an amphibious ready group of three ships and a Marine Corps component
- *Carl Vinson* battle group
  Composed of nine ships and submarines, together with an amphibious ready group of three ships and a marine component to provide security at the airfields in Pakistan being used by U.S. forces; subsequently, these ships were redeployed to southern Afghanistan
- *Theodore Roosevelt* battle group
  Composed of nine ships and two submarines and stationed in the Arabian Sea
- *Kitty Hawk* battle group
  This battle group was operational in the area until 16 December 2001 and had flown about 100 strike missions in Afghanistan since 7 October 2001. It also

U.S. marines walk with their battle gear to a forward position at the U.S. Marines operations base in southern Afghanistan, 4 December 2001. (AFP/Corbis)

deployed special forces, including the Special Operations Aviation Regiment, the Navy Seals, and the Air Force Special Operations forces, together with Blackhawk, Chinook, and Pave Low helicopters.

Air Force.   The initial deployment for the operation included some 150 aircraft, including 24 bombers and support aircraft. Also deployed were an unspecified number of B-52 bombers, using the Indian Ocean base of Diego Garcia. Uzbekistan allowed the United States to use a former Soviet airfield near Tashkent for C-130 cargo planes, followed by three AC-130 gunships, with an additional three special forces gunships arriving in late November 2001. In December 2001, a squadron of 24 fighter aircraft were dispatched to Kyrgyzstan, later followed by six French Mirage multipurpose bombers and refueling aircraft.

Reinforcements to these deployments were made in March 2002, with the transfer of A-10 ground attack planes from their base in Kuwait to Pakistan. The sorties from Pakistan marked the first time that the A-10s had been used in the war.

Army.   The first contingent of army forces dispatched to Afghanistan included an unspecified number of special forces, among them Rangers, Delta Force commandos, and Navy Seals.

The main army contingent was drawn from the 101st Airborne Division, together with troops from the Tenth Mountain Division from bases in Uzbekistan. These troops were also supported by AH-64 Apache attack helicopters, in addition to the AC-130 gunships. U.S. Marines who had been redeployed from their airfield security role in Pakistan supported these units. In December 2001, the command of ground forces in Afghanistan was transferred to Kuwait.

UK Forces

Naval Forces.   A Royal Navy task force had been present in the Afghan area since September 2001, on a rotational basis. The original task group consisted of an aircraft carrier and an assault ship, together

U.S. Defense Secretary Donald Rumsfeld (left) and Joint Chiefs of Staff chairman Gen. Richard B. Myers (right) brief the press on the war with Iraq on 28 March 2003. The defense secretary took a hard stance on reports of weapons entering Iraq from Syria, declaring, "We consider such trafficking as hostile acts and will hold the Syrian government accountable for such shipments." (Department of Defense)

with three nuclear submarines. Early in 2002, the aircraft carrier was replaced with a helicopter carrier with a contingent of Royal Marines. Initially, the nuclear submarines based in the area were used to mount Tomahawk missile attacks on Taliban positions in October 2001. Although these ships have since been withdrawn, an unspecified submarine presence has been maintained in the area.

Air Force. The commitment from the Royal Air Force took the form of Tristar and VC-10 tanker aircraft, together with E-3D Sentry AEWI surveillance and control aircraft, Nimrod R-1 surveillance aircraft, Nimrod R-2 marine surveillance aircraft, Canberra PR-9 reconnaissance aircraft, and Chinook helicopters.

Army. The first army commitment to Afghanistan was in the form of an unspecified number of special forces, including units from the Special Air Service (SAS). However, the Ministry of Defense never releases any data on deployment or operations in respect to these units.

The main contingent included 45 Commando Royal Marines as well as 7 Commando Battery Royal Artillery, 59 Independent Commando Squadrons of the Royal Engineers, and a detachment from the Commando Logistics Regiment. The force totaled some 1,700 personnel, excluding special forces.

In addition, the United Kingdom made a significant contribution to the International Security Assistance Force (ISAF), with some 1,800 personnel including an infantry battle group, sixteen Air Assault Brigades, the Parachute Regiment, and a company of Ghurkhas. The contingent also included Royal Engineers, a Signals Regiment, and the Royal Army Medical Corps. A short-term deployment was also made to repair and operate the Kabul airport.

Other Coalition Forces

Australia. Australian Special Forces were operating in Afghanistan together with other troops totaling 1,500 personnel. Additional commitments included maritime surveillance aircraft, fighter-bomber strike aircraft, and a guided missile frigate.

Canada. The Canadian government deployed a frigate to the Persian Gulf and promised an additional six ships, surveillance aircraft, and transport planes. In January 2002, 750 troops from a light infantry battle group were deployed to Kandahar, with the objective of joining combat operations with the U.S. task force and security operations to facilitate the delivery of humanitarian aid.

France. France provided a naval task force made up of an aircraft carrier, three frigates, a submarine, and a supply tanker. The aircraft carrier was equipped with Super-Etandard reconnaissance and assault aircraft and two Hawkeye surveillance aircraft. In addition, six Mirage 2000 combat aircraft were deployed to Kyrgyzstan in January 2002. On 17 November 2001, France also deployed troops from the Twenty-First Marine Infantry Regiment to repair and secure the airfield at Mazar-i Sharif.

Germany. In addition to a unit of 100 troops from the Special Commando Forces, Germany supplied naval support to patrol the area between the Arabian Peninsula and East Africa, surveillance aircraft, and search-and-rescue units. Some 500 air crew were also dispatched to the U.S. Air Force base at Incilik, Turkey, to assist with shipments being carried by C-160 transport planes.

Italy. A naval task force consisting of one aircraft carrier, two frigates, and a supply ship was deployed, together with 1,400 troops. In addition, Tornado reconnaissance aircraft, transport planes, helicopters, and eight Harriers were also dispatched.

Japan. The Japanese provided a naval task force of five vessels, based at Diego Garcia in the Indian Ocean, to monitor shipping lanes. This deployment ceased at the end of March 2002.

Other Forces

On 1 October 2001, a trinational detachment of Danish, Dutch, and Norwegian fighter aircraft replaced the French Mirages in Kyrgyzstan and were tasked with providing day and night air support to U.S. and Coalition forces inside Afghanistan. The detachment of eighteen fighter aircraft was also available to support the ISAF in Kabul.

See also Coalition Air Campaign against the Taliban; Coalition Land Campaign against the Taliban; International Security Assistance Force; Northern Alliance; Taliban

References

http://www.globalspecops.com/oefportal.html.

http: www.operations.mod.uk/veritas

http://www.whitehouse.gov/response/military.response.html

ORUZGAN PROVINCE

Oruzgan Province is located in central Afghanistan, covers an area of 11,169 square miles, and has a population of about 483,000. It is bordered by the provinces of Helmand on the west, Ghor and Bamian in the northwest and north, Ghazni in the east, and Kandahar and Zabul in the south. The people are mainly Hazaras, but the southern part of the province is home to some Pashtuns and other ethnic minorities. The province is part of the Hazarajat region, and in the nineteenth century, it was part of Kandahar Province, becoming a province in its own right in March 1964. Oruzgan is mountainous and accessible only from the south. With the valleys watered by the Helmand River complex, it has a moderate climate in summer and cold winters. The economy is largely based on agriculture, with the main crops being wheat, barley, maize, chickpeas, millet, and sesame; the province is also renowned for its woven carpets.

References

Adamec, Ludwig W. 1972–1985. *Historical and Political Gazetteer of Afghanistan.* 6 vols. Graz, Austria: Akademische Druck-u Verlagsansalt.

PAGHMAN

The town of Paghman lies in the foothills some 12 miles northwest of Kabul. The modern town was built by King Amanullah around 1921, together with a royal palace. This royal endorsement induced many members of the upper class to construct luxury villas in the new town. An open-air theater was built to cater to the citizens of Kabul who visited the town on weekends during the hot summer months, and the town also houses a triumphal arch to honor the dead of the Anglo-Afghan wars.

The town lies on the eastern slopes of the Paghman range of mountains about 8,000 feet above sea level and is surrounded by woods and mountains. A reservoir and a pipeline in this area provide the city of Kabul with drinking water. During the war against the Marxist regime (from 1979 to 1989), Paghman served as a stronghold and a shelter for the mujahideen, and in the civil war (from 1989 to 2001), it was the scene of bitter struggles between mujahideen groups. It also saw intense fighting when the forces of Burhanuddin Rabbani were ousted by the Taliban in 1996. Much of the town was destroyed in the various military actions. The town was the birthplace of President Hafizullah Amin and the Islamist mujahideen leader Abdul Rasul Sayyaf.

References
Adamec, Ludwig W. 1972–1985. *Historical and Political Gazetteer of Afghanistan.* 6 vols. Graz, Austria: Akademische Druck-u Verlagsansalt.

PAGHMANI, TAJ MUHAMMAD (?–1929)

Taj Muhammad Paghmani was the son of Ali Mohammed Paghmani. A Baluch who was with Amir Abdur Rahman in Bukhara, he subsequently became a government official. He was arrested after Abdur Rahman Lodin attempted to assassinate Amir Habibullah in 1918 and spent sixteen months in jail, suspected of being involved in the plot. Habibullah was assassinated in 1919 on the night before Paghmani and Lodin were due to be sentenced, and all the prisoners were released by King Amanullah. Paghmani became head of the Foreign Affairs Department, Qataghan, Herat, and governor of Chakhansur. He returned to take up a post promised by Afghanistan's amir, Nadir Shah, in 1929 but was accused of helping to foment the second Kol Daman Rebellion and was executed by being fired from a cannon.

References
Adamec, Ludwig W. 1967. *Afghanistan, 1900–1923: A Diplomatic History.* Berkeley: University of California Press.

PAKTIA PROVINCE

Paktia Province is located in eastern Afghanistan and occupies an area of 3,860 square miles. Its population is about 484,000, although the majority of the people are still refugees in Pakistan (with whom it shares a border) due to insecurity in the area, especially around Gardez. The size of the province was reduced during the rule of President Muhammad Daud (1973–1978) when it lost territory to Paktika and Ghazni Provinces. The economy is based on agriculture: the area is well watered and supports cereal and rice crops, together with some animal husbandry. The province also has timber, but the forest area has been decimated by illegal felling and smuggling into Pakistan because of the higher market price offered there.

The people of Paktia are largely Pashtuns from the Ghilzai tribe, but the Jadran tribe is found in the south and west of the province, and the Mangal, Waziri, Jaji, and Tari tribes are in the east. The province has strategic importance because of its shared border with Pakistan and its location on the route to Kabul. It was the scene of bitter fighting

195

during the civil war (1989 to 2001) due to its importance to the mujahideen, but resistance was strong, as many of the leaders of the People's Democratic Party of Afghanistan (PDPA) came from the Ghilzai tribe in Paktia. The area fell under mujahideen control in March 1991 with the capture of Khost, and many of the PDPA supporters fled to Pakistan because of fears over their security. The province fell to the Taliban after the collapse of mujahideen rule in Kabul. Because of all the conflict experienced in this area, Paktia has more of its population living as refugees than any other province in the country.

The most important town in the province is the capital, Gardez, which has a largely Tajik and Ghilzai population. It is at the heart of an agricultural area and previously had a thriving commercial center, supplying grain and *ghi* (clarified butter) to Kabul markets, as well as flocks of sheep. Horse breeding is also carried out in the area, using Waziri stock. The city commands a strategic pass south of Kabul and has been the scene of recent factional fighting. Badsha Khan and his brothers have ruled the provinces of Khost, Paktia, and Paktika since the fall of the Taliban in 2001, and they are supporters of the former king Zahir Shah. They have an uneasy alliance with the U.S. military and are grudgingly recognized by the government of Hamid Karzai, the president of Afghanistan.

However, the people of Gardez defied the authority of Badsha Khan and put control of the city in the hands of a local council headed by Saif Ullah, a tribal leader from the region. Heavy fighting broke out on 1 February 2002 when Bala Hisar, the city's fortress, was approached by Khan's men to assert his right as governor. Khan's forces deployed tanks and artillery and subjected the city to rocket attacks, causing a number of deaths and injuries. The intense fighting was an affront to Karzai's authority, but even so, troops loyal to the government stayed neutral, as did a small detachment of U.S. forces. On the following day, Khan's troops were forced to retreat from positions around Gardez after being attacked by fighters supporting Saif Ullah, who was, in turn, loyal to Burhanuddin Rabbani. (Rabbani was president of Afghanistan from 1992 and was still recognized as such by international bodies during the period of Taliban rule.)

Khan had a letter from President Karzai naming him as governor, but the local leaders of Gardez voiced their support for Saif Ullah. In the initial fighting, at least eighty people were killed, including some twenty civilians, and a number of Khan's troops were taken prisoner. This incident has been seen as a real blow to the authority of President Karzai and a reinforcement of the view that his authority does not extend beyond Kabul. Khan's forces resumed their attacks on 3 February, and further fierce fighting broke out between the rival warlords. A special nine-member commission was established under Border Affairs Minister Amanullah Zadran to investigate the factional violence and to coordinate an exchange of prisoners. This incident reinforced the pleas of the Kabul government for the mandate of the International Security Assistance Force to be extended to other key cities in Afghanistan.

A number of U.S. forces are still operating in the region, mounting actions against remnants of al-Qaeda and Taliban, but they have refrained from taking sides in factional violence. This lack of intervention has led to some resentment from many in the civilian population, who are sick of the fighting and had hoped for a period of peace and stability. The local council of Gardez still professes loyalty to the Karzai government but wants a new governor, accusing Badsha Khan of being a smuggler and tyrant and requesting UN mediation.

UN officials have been trying to negotiate a way out of the situation, as Badsha Khan has been steadily losing support in eastern Afghanistan while still railing against the Karzai administration and demanding the return of King Zahir. His continued opposition has been a problem for President Karzai because Khan continues to insist that he be reinstated as ruler of Paktia, Khost, and Paktika, as originally promised by Karzai. However, support for Karzai appears to be growing in eastern Afghanistan, and tribal leaders and local commanders have voiced support for the central administration, probably in the expectation of receiving reconstruction funds.

In September 2002, Badsha Khan's troops began to cause problems for U.S. forces, despite their previous support in the war against the Taliban and al-Qaeda. The troops occupied positions overlooking a special forces camp at Gardez and trained their guns on U.S. supply helicopters, forcing the U.S. commander, General Dan McNeill, to lodge a protest with Khan Within hours, government troops under a local commander, Atiqullah Lindin, pushed

Khan's forces out of Gardez and Khost, leaving the government troops in control.

The forces of Khan are now reduced to manning roadblocks between Khost and Gardez, and they remain an irritant to soldiers and officials loyal to the government who try to use the road. Despite previous levels of cooperation, U.S. forces have severed all links with the regional warlord, and nephews of Badsha Khan operating out of the U.S. base at Khost were arrested by government troops in December 2002. The spokesman for the president admitted in January 2003 that talks had been held with Badsha Khan to try to restore peace and stability, but he made it clear that the government reserved the right to change governors in provinces where people were facing hardship and complaining about a worse law-and-order situation.

See also Khost

References

Adamec, Ludwig W. 1972–1985. *Historical and Political Gazetteer of Afghanistan.* 6 vols. Graz, Austria: Akademische Druck-u Verlagsansalt.

Baldauf, Scott. 2003. "Once Powerful Warlord Is Shunted Aside." http://www.afgha.com/?af=article&sid=29422 (cited 22 January 2003).

Gall, Carlotta. 2003. "Holdout Afghan Warlord May Join Karzai Camp." http://www.iht.com/articles/83722.html (cited 18 January 2003).

PAKTIKA PROVINCE

Paktika Province is located in eastern Afghanistan on the border with Pakistan and occupies an area of 7,336 square miles. It has a population of about 245,000, but some 75,000 are refugees in Pakistan. Paktika was created from the southeastern districts of Paktia and Ghazni Provinces during the period of President Muhammad Daud (1973–1978). The inhabitants are mainly Ghilzais, but there are Tajiks and Waziri Pashtuns as well. The provincial capital is Sharan.

Paktika was ravaged by the civil war (from 1989 to 2001), and the agricultural mainstay of the economy has been severely damaged by the destruction of the traditional irrigation system. The environment has also been adversely affected by unrestricted felling of timber, much of which has found its way illegally into Pakistan, where it fetches a much higher price. During the civil war, the province was firmly under mujahideen control, but it was captured by the Taliban on their move to Kabul in 1995.

References

Adamec, Ludwig W. 1972–1985. *Historical and Political Gazetteer of Afghanistan.* 6 vols. Graz, Austria: Akademische Druck-u Verlagsansalt.

PANIPAT, BATTLE OF (1761)

The Battle of Panipat on 14 January 1761 saw the defeat of the Maratha tribal confederation by Ahmad Shah Durrani, near the town of the same name some 50 miles north of Delhi. Members of the Maratha Confederation were the champions of Hinduism and posed a threat to Afghanistan when they occupied the Punjab. Durrani crossed the River Jumna with a force of some 60,000 men to counter this threat and to challenge the Maratha army commanded by Sadashiv Bhau. The first two months of confrontation were a series of feints and skirmishes by the opposing forces, with varying degrees of success for both sides, until the Afghan army succeeded in blocking the supply routes of the Indian army.

The Maratha army was outnumbered, as they were fielding only some 45,000 troops, and they were also hampered by the fact that their camp followers, families, and supplies were in the town, which affected their mobility. In recognition of this, Sadashiv Bhau tried to negotiate with Durrani, but the amir rejected his overtures and the Maratha were forced to engage in battle. The Afghans had a further advantage in that their artillery was lighter and more mobile than the heavier guns of the Indians, and although the Maratha attacked the Afghan center with some initial success, the latter troops were able to reinforce their positions and hem the Indian troops in on three sides.

The Afghans loosed volley after volley at the Indian ranks, who were unable to group their forces to withstand the assaults. The Marathas were completely routed, and Sadashiv Bhau and Wishwas Rao, the nominal head of the Marathas, were killed. The defeat ended the Marathas' dream of becoming rulers of India but also dimmed the ambitions of Durrani, for his troops hated the heat of the Indian plains and only wished to return home with their booty. As a result, Durrani had no choice but to withdraw his forces back across the border.

See also Durrani, Ahmad Shah Abdali

References

Sing, G. 1989. *Ahmad Shah Durrani, Father of Modern Afghanistan.* Bombay, India: Asian Publishing House.

PANJDEH INCIDENT

In 1885, a Russian force annexed the Panjdeh district north of Herat Province, which now forms part of Turkmenistan. Afghani rulers had claimed the region on the grounds that the population had been occasional tributaries; the Russians argued that they were part of the Turkoman nation of Khiva and Mir, which had been annexed by Russia in 1881 and 1884, respectively. The Afghan forces under General Ghausuddin numbered about 500, and the vastly superior Russian forces overwhelmed them. The dispute was supposed to have been resolved by an Anglo-Russian commission, but the battle took place before the negotiators arrived on the scene. The action occurred while Amir Abdur Rahman was on an official visit to India, and the viceroy of India, Lord Dufferin, coerced him into accepting the situation as a fait accompli. Britain's failure to aid Afghanistan against the Russian aggression, as required by treaty, reaffirmed the amir's belief that he could not rely on British support in the event of external aggression.

References
Ganjoo, Satish. 1990. *Soviet Afghan Relations*. Delhi, India: Akashdeep Publishing House.
Khan, Sultan Muhammad. 1980. *The Life of Abdur Rahman, Amir of Afghanistan*. Karachi, Pakistan: Oxford University Press.

PANJSHIR

The Panjshir region is an inaccessible administrative district in Kaspia Province and comprises an area of 273 square miles, with a largely Tajik population of some 30,000. The economy is based on agriculture, and the valley is traversed by the Panjshir River, which rises in the Hindu Kush. Historically, the area was often autonomous or independent due to its geography, and although the people paid allegiance to the rulers of Afghanistan, they rarely paid taxes to the central government. Only since the time of Amir Abdur Rahman (probably beginning in 1881, when he took the northern provinces under his direct control) has Kabul asserted sovereignty over the district.

Due to the region's geography, the Marxist government and the Soviet forces of occupation were unable to bring the area under government control, which was of strategic significance because of the location of the Salang highway that links Kabul to the northern provinces and passes through the valley.

The Panjshir Valley became a major center of activity for mujahideen forces led by Ahmad Shah Masood—also known as "the Lion of Panjshir" by his followers—who withstood all Soviet attempts to remove him from the valley. Masood was one of the most successful and charismatic leaders of the mujahideen and the Northern Alliance. Arab militants assassinated him on 9 September 2001.

See also Masood, Ahmad Shah
References
Amin, Hamidullah, and Gordon B. Schiltz. 1976. *A Geography of Afghanistan*. Omaha: University of Nebraska, Center for Afghan Studies.
Kaplan, Robert D. 1990. *Soldiers of God: With the Mujahideen in Afghanistan*. Boston: Houghton Mifflin.

PANJSHIRI, DASTAGI (1933–)

Dastagi Panjshiri was one of the founding members of the Khalq faction of the People's Democratic Party of Afghanistan (PDPA) and served in a variety of ministerial posts in the Khalq government. He was born in 1933 in Panjshir, the son of Malik Dad Muhammad, and educated in primary school in Herat; he then attended the Teacher Training College in Kabul and obtained a B.A. degree at Kabul University. During his early career, he served in a variety of public service posts, including as director of research and study "Anis" from 1955 to 1959; as deputy director of libraries in the Ministry of Information and Culture; and as a teacher of literature at Kabul Teacher's College from 1959 to 1960. In 1963, he became director of liaison at the Ministry of Information and Culture, a post he held until the following year while also serving as director of censorship for Radio Afghanistan in 1963. From 1964 to 1969, he was in charge of the manuscript section at the Ministry of Information and Culture.

Panjshiri ran for election to parliament in 1969 but was arrested, accused of causing a political disturbance, and imprisoned until 1972. After the Saur Revolt of April 1978, which brought the Communists to power, he became minister of education, holding the post in May and June of that year before moving on to become minister of public works. He was imprisoned again for a short time in 1979 but returned to power after the fall of Hafizullah Amin on 27 December 1979 and became a member of the Politburo. In January 1980, he became a member of the Central Committee and Revolutionary Council of the PDPA and chair of the Union of Writers and Poets. He asked to give up his membership in the Central Committee and Politburo in 1985 because of ill health.

See also People's Democratic Party of Afghanistan
References
Bradsher, Henry St. Amant. 1999. *Afghan Communism and Soviet Intervention.* London and New York: Oxford University Press.

PARCHAM

The weekly newspaper *Parcham* was founded in March 1968 by the Parcham faction of the People's Democratic Party of Afghanistan (PDPA) but was closed down in July 1969 because of its opposition to the government. The paper was edited by Sulaiman Layeq and Mir Akbar Khaibar, the faction's theorist. A faction of the PDPA led by Babrak Karmal adopted the title of the paper.

See also People's Democratic Party of Afghanistan
References
Yunas, S. Frida. 1977. *History of People's Democratic Party of Afghanistan (PDPA) Watan Party of Afghanistan.* Peshawar, Pakistan: University of Peshawar.

PARWAN PROVINCE

Parwan Province is located north of Kabul, has an area of 2,282 square miles, and is home to a population of about 418,000. Parwan is of strategic importance because it is traversed by the Salang highway, which links Kabul to the northern provinces and the Hindu Kush. The capital of the province is Charikar, which lies 49 miles north of Kabul at the mouth of the Ghorband Valley and has a population of some 23,000. The province has some industrialization, with a cement factory, a textile industry, and a hydroelectric plant that services Kabul, but these activities have been adversely affected by the ravages of war in the area. Traditionally, the province is noted for its grapes, which are also dried and exported as raisins.

References
Adamec, Ludwig W. 1972–1985. *Historical and Political Gazetteer of Afghanistan.* 6 vols. Graz, Austria: Akademische Druck-u Verlagsansalt.

PASHTU LANGUAGE

The Pashtu language is spoken by the largest ethnic group in Afghanistan, the Pashtuns, and also by large sections of the population in neighboring Baluchistan and the North-West Frontier Province in Pakistan. The language is Indo-Iranian in origin and is related to Dari, the other main language in Afghanistan, but the two are not mutually intelligible. Two main dialects are spoken—Pakhto and Pashtu—with the former being spoken in the north and east of the country and the latter in the south and west. A considerable amount of literature exists in Pashtu, mainly histories and love poems dating back to the fifteenth century, and the Pashtu Academy has conducted research into this body of literature. Afghan governments have promoted Pashtu as the national language, but Dari remains the language of education and the educated, with many Pashtuns using it as their first tongue. Under the Afghan constitution, both Pashtu and Dari are classed as official languages.

See also Dari Language
References
Chavaria-Aquiler, Oscar Luis. 1962. *A Short Introduction to the Writing System of Pashto.* Ann Arbor: University of Michigan Press.

PASHTUNISTAN DISPUTE

The Pashtunistan dispute between Afghanistan and Pakistan arose over the status of the Pashtun tribes that were split in 1893 by the Durand Line. This line, a political boundary drawn up as a by-product of colonial imperialism, is still causing problems in the twenty-first century because it arbitrarily divides the Pashtun tribes. The Afghan government argued that a case could be made for granting self-determination to the Pashtuns in Pakistan, but it also stressed that the dispute should be peaceably resolved. However, Afghanistan has also denied that government support for this cause meant that it had territorial aspirations on the Pashtun lands in Pakistan. The government maintained that the Durand Agreement had been made under duress, whereas Pakistan maintained that the self-determination issue was resolved in 1947 by plebiscite and a 90 percent vote in favor of joining Pakistan. The decision was also approved at tribal *loya jirgas* (grand councils), but Afghanistan held that the results were invalid because the only questions asked were whether the Pashtuns wished to unite with India or Pakistan and no consultation took place over possible independence.

See also Durand Agreement

References

Durand, Algernon George Arnold. 1974. *The Making of a Frontier*. Graz, Austria: Akademische Druck-u Verlagsansalt (Reprint of 1899 edition, London: John Murray)

Poullada, Leon B. 1969. "Some International Legal Aspects of Pashtunistan Dispute." *Afghanistan* 21, no. 4: 10–36.

PASHTUNS

The Pashtun people, known in India as Pathans, constituted a significant minority before 1979, forming some 47 percent of the population of Afghanistan. After the formation of the Afghan state in 1747 by Ahmad Shah Durrani, the Pashtuns dominated the country's government. From 1994 on, they offered support to the Taliban. A critical element in regional conflicts is the fact that some 7 million Pashtuns live in Pakistan on the other side of the Durand Line, by which Britain in 1893 had demarcated the frontier between Afghanistan and British India.

Pashtuns are organized into tribes and owe their loyalty to tribal and subtribal groups. These loyalties have been a source of conflict throughout their history. The tribes are ruled by consensus through the *jirga* (council), which determines the welfare of the tribe and arbitrates disputes. The Pashtuns primarily live off animal husbandry, trade, and some agriculture, and they are also renowned as extremely capable soldiers. The majority of the people speak the Pashtu language, though some who reside in Kabul speak Dari.

The Soviet invasion of Afghanistan in 1979 caused a major shift in the balance of the Afghan population. Because nearly 85 percent of the 6.2 million refugees who fled the country at that time were Pashtuns, this lowered their percentage of the population so that they no longer formed the majority ethnic group. This exodus suited the Soviets, as Pashtun soldiers were a major force in the jihad against the occupying forces. The balance has been slightly redressed since 1990, with returning refugees increasing the Pashtun presence to 38 percent of the population.

Despite their diminished numbers, the Pashtuns were still a dominant political force after the Soviet occupation. Until 1991, for example, the national government was controlled by various factions of the People's Democratic Party of Afghanistan (PDPA), which was dominated by Pashtuns, and all other factions allied themselves either with or against the PDPA; some of those opposing the PDPA were Pashtuns. Alliances were constantly shifting both between the government and opposition and within each camp, with all factions in ceaseless competition with each other. The population movement that occurred as a result of the Soviet invasion weakened the tribal power of the Pashtuns and allowed other ethnic groups to become involved in the government.

In 1994, the Taliban became a major force in Afghanistan, and its power base was in the southern territory of the Pashtuns, particularly in Kandahar Province. The movement had primarily emanated from the religious schools in Pakistan, established by President Mohammad Zia al Haq and guided by Pakistan's Inter-Service Intelligence unit. Support from Pakistan appeared to have two main objectives: first, to direct Pashtun militancy toward Afghan affairs and thereby marginalize the cause of Pashtun self-determination in Pakistan and second, to enable Pakistan to become the dominant foreign power in terms of influencing affairs within Afghanistan. This policy reflected the fragility of the Pakistan state, with its large Pashtun population, its fear of Indian expansionism, and its dispute with India over Kashmir.

Today, however, after the overthrow of the Taliban, it is essential that the Pashtuns have a political role: otherwise, there cannot be a lasting peace in Afghanistan. The Pashtuns would not be able to reconcile themselves to not having a major role in government after some 250 years of dominance. Consequently, the Northern Alliance, as the other major faction and buoyed as it is by military success, will need to recognize and accommodate the needs of the Pashtun community.

See also Afghan-Pakistani Relations; Dari Language; Durand Agreement; Durrani, Ahmad Shah Abdali; Inter-Services Intelligence Service; Northern Alliance; Pashtu Language; People's Democratic Party of Afghanistan

References

Afghan Network. 2001. " Pashtuns." http://www.afghan-network.net/ethnic-groups/pashtuns.html (cited 28 November, 2001).

Clifford, Mary Louise. 1973. *The Land and People of Afghanistan*. Philadelphia: Lippincott.

Jannson, Eland. 1981. *India, Pakistan or Pakhunistan?* Uppsala, Sweden: Almquist.

Spain, J. W. 1962. *The Way of the Pathans*. London: Hale.

PASHTUNWALI

Pashtunwali is the traditional code of behavior of the Pashtun people and is divided into three main sections: mediation and protection (*nanawati*); retaliation (*badal*); and hospitality (*melmastia*). However, the strength of the traditional codes of behavior has been weakened as a result of Islamization, sedentarization (the settling of nomadic or seminomadic peoples in communities), and a loosening of the tightly knit tribal community. Nanawati is the obligation to give protection to anyone seeking asylum; badal is that which must be exacted to redress personal insults, damage to property, or blood feuds; and melmastia is the sacred duty of hospitality, with each village maintaining a guest house or space in the mosque to accommodate visitors. Violations of the code brought dishonor not only to the violator but also to the entire community or, in extreme cases, the whole tribe.

References
Clifford, Mary Louise. 1973. *The Land and People of Afghanistan.* Philadelphia: Lippincott.
Spain, J. W. 1962. *The Way of the Pathans.* London: Hale.

PAZHWAK, FAZE RABBI (1929–)

As a professor of the Faculty of Law and Political Science at Kabul University, Faze Rabbi Pazhwak opposed the Soviet occupation of Afghanistan (from 1979 to 1989) and was arrested as a member of the Underground Union of University Professors. It was this organization that wrote and translated the famous "night letters"—a series of antigovernment and threatening messages that were delivered at night to Russians, members of the government, and Third World embassies. The tone of the letters was particularly hostile during the regime of President Muhammad Daud (1973 to 1978), but the letters were also directed against the post-1978 Marxist government in Kabul. Further, they expressed concern about the presence of Soviet troops and also attempted to persuade Soviet troops to disobey orders from their commanders.

Born in 1929 in Kaja, Khugiana, Pazhwak graduated from Habibia High School in 1947 and from the Faculty of Political Science at Kabul University in 1950. He studied extensively abroad through fellowship schemes and was president of Kabul University from 1967 to 1969. He convened the General Assembly of University Teachers to condemn police raids on Kabul University and cooperated with a commission set up to sue the government for injuries inflicted on students during the police actions. He was governor of Lashkargal in 1973 and served in the Planning and Interior Ministries between 1975 and 1977 before being reinstated as professor in the Faculty of Law and Political Science in 1979. He was later imprisoned, almost certainly for opposition to the Marxist government, but was released in 1983 because of ill health.

See also Hoshimian, Sayyid Kalilullah
References
Rubin, Barnett R. 1988. "Soviet Militarism, Islamic Resistance and Peace in Afghanistan." Typescript. University of Nebraska, Center for Afghan Studies.

PAZHWAK, NE'MUTALLAH (1928–)

Ne'mutallah Pazhwak was one of five deputy prime ministers appointed in Prime Minister Fazl Haq Khaliqyar's government in 1990, following a career in education and in the administration of various governments. He was born in Nangarhar Province in 1928 and educated in Kabul and the United States, returning to become head of the Teacher Training and Habibia Schools. In 1970, he was appointed governor of Bamian and of Kabul in 1971, before serving as minister of interior from 1972 to 1973 in the government of Musa Shafiq and minister of education under President Muhammad Daud in 1973. After the Saur Revolt of April 1978, which brought the Communists to power, he became minister without portfolio in 1980, despite the fact that he was not a member of the People's Democratic Party of Afghanistan (PDPA).

References
Barnett, R. 1995. *The Fragmentation of Afghanistan: State Formation and Collapse in the International System.* New Haven, CT: Yale University Press.

PEOPLE'S DEMOCRATIC PARTY OF AFGHANISTAN (PDPA)

The PDPA was established in January 1964 at its first congress, which was instigated by Nur Muhammad Taraki, a politician with Marxist leanings. The congress set up a central committee to control its affairs, and Taraki was elected its first general secretary. The party also established a weekly newspaper, *Khalq* (meaning "people"), but it was banned by King Zahir after only six editions. The PDPA was active in organizing public demonstrations; put forward candidates at every election; and exposed what it saw as treachery, corruption, and the decaying nature of the ruling class in Afghanistan.

After the 1973 coup led by Muhammad Daud, which ousted the king and established the Democratic Republic of Afghanistan, the PDPA maintained its independence and identity, while backing the democratic values of the government's aims (though the coup had been aided by many of the members of a competing faction within the PDPA, the Parcham). The party worked particularly hard to recruit members, and the faction led by Hafizullah Amin was especially active in promoting Marxism-Leninism through the armed forces, for which it received a large measure of support. In time, the PDPA was attacked by President Daud, who feared its growing power. His fears proved to be justified when the PDPA, through the armed forces, launched a revolt on 27 April 1978, which became known as the Saur Revolt (after the Afghan name for the month of April).

The PDPA was split into two factions, and it was always a strained alliance. The faction headed by Taraki was called Khalq and appealed mainly to the rural Pashtun middle class but also recruited among the student population because of its policy of employment for the educated. In the mid-1970s, the faction began to recruit members from the armed forces through the efforts of Hafizullah Amin, who was always prepared to use force as a means of achieving power.

The second faction was the Parcham (meaning "flag"), which was less Pashtun-oriented and recruited students and teachers from the schools of the wealthy and from Kabul University. It drew support from the urban areas and the mainly non-Pashtun northern provinces. The faction backed Daud in the 1973 coup, but he perceived that support to be based on personal loyalty, having nothing to do with the ideology of the PDPA. However, he saw the dangers of factional support and broke links with the Parcham in 1977, thus leaving the way clear for the Saur Revolt.

The two factions split apart in 1967 but reunited again in 1977 in time for the Saur Revolt and the formation of a new government under Nur Muhammad Taraki, who was a charismatic figure and seen as a great leader by party members. However, by the end of 1978, the alliance ruptured again, and the Parchamis were purged from the government by the dominant Khalq faction, with many of their leaders being sent into diplomatic exile as ambassadors or officials in overseas embassies. However, the Parchamis returned to power on 27 December 1979 with the backing of the Soviet Union, and the Khalq leader Hafizullah Amin was killed by Russian Special Forces.

The post of president was then taken by Babrak Karmal, a Marxist backed by the Soviets, and he held power until 1986, throughout the period of Soviet occupation and the early years of the resistance campaign mounted by the mujahideen. However, in 1986, he was replaced by Dr. Muhammad Najibullah, who remained in office until 1992 and attempted to dispense with some of the worst excesses of the Marxist regime. Najibullah tried to broaden the appeal of his government by expanding its base, but the mujahideen rejected this effort. Najibullah was eventually persuaded to stand down, partially as a result of pressure from the United Nations, which endeavored, unsuccessfully, to form a broadly based government.

The program of the PDPA incorporated the following concepts:

1. A national democratic government
2. An administration and social system based on principles of communism and socialism
3. The end of a capitalistic economic system and the nationalization of all foreign trading interests in Afghanistan
4. The instigation of a process of speedy industrialization
5. A land reform program with a view to distributing land among tenants
6. A reformed economic policy that reflected national interests
7. A program to improve the welfare of workers and peasants and enable them to share in the national wealth
8. An end to unemployment
9. Provision of irrigation facilities and self-sufficiency in food
10. Price controls
11. The constitution to be adhered to properly and the state to have only a constitutional monarchy
12. Freedom of press and speech, the right to form parties and worker/student organizations, and the right to demonstrate/strike

13. Establishment of elected Jirgas (Councils) in each province, increased membership in the Wolesi Jirga (House of the People), and an increase in people's representation in the Meshrano Jirga (Parliament)
14. Provision of free education, medical aid, and other basic necessities
15. Political and social freedom for women
16. An end to repression and injustice in civil administration
17. Settlement of all Kuchis (seasonal migrants) as soon as possible and an end to the tribal system
18. A peaceful and permanent foreign policy based on:

- No participation in military pacts
- No participation in trade and military pacts that benefit imperialism
- Sympathizing with and providing help for all nations struggling to secure independence from imperialism and colonialism
- Helping people in Pashtunistan to secure freedom
- Good relations with all socialist countries and countries that are well-wishers of Afghanistan
- Denouncement of all countries out to disrupt the peace of the world for selfish motives

As part of Najibullah's efforts to form an acceptable government, the PDPA had renamed itself the Watan (Homeland Party) in 1990. This change was designed to broaden the appeal of the party by moving away from its Marxist base and introducing some aspects of Islamic principles. It was an attempt to defuse opposition from Islamic groups and to distance the party from its association with the Soviet occupation, in the hope that, in the process, the regime's chances of survival would be enhanced.

See also Amin, Hafizullah; Daud, Sardar Muhammad; Najibullah, Muhammad; Saur Revolt; Taraki, Nur Muhammad

References

People's Democratic Party of Afghanistan. 1980. *Fundamental Principles, Democratic Republic of Afghanistan.* Kabul: Ministry of Information and Culture.
Shahrani, M. Nazif, and Robert L. Caufield. 1984. *Revolutions and Rebellions in Afghanistan.* Berkeley, CA: Institute of International Studies.
Yunas, S. Frida. 1977. *History of People's Democratic Party of Afghanistan (PDPA) Watan Party of Afghanistan.* Peshawar, Pakistan: University of Peshawar.

PESHAWAR, TREATY OF (1856)

The Treaty of Peshawar, for which negotiations began in 1885, was concluded in 1856 and opened diplomatic relations between Britain and Afghanistan and stated that perpetual peace and friendship would exist between the two countries. Under the treaty, the British government agreed to respect the territories under the control of the Afghan amir, and Afghanistan, in turn, agreed to respect the territories of the British government. The treaty also stipulated that Britain would assist Afghanistan against its enemies "if they thought fit to do so"—a stipulation that became a matter of contention with Amir Dost Muhammad, who considered the guarantee worthless.

References

Noelle, Christin. 1987. *State and Tribe in Nineteenth-Century Afghanistan: The Reign of Amir Dost Muhammad Khan.* London: Curzon Press.

PESHAWAR ACCORD

The Peshawar Accord was signed by the mujahideen political party groups in March 1993 and was designed to lay the groundwork for the formation of an Islamic state of Afghanistan but was a failure from the outset.

The agreement provided for a fifty-one-member body to take over in Kabul for a period of two months under the leadership of Hazrat Sahib Sabghatullah Mujaddidi; it would also represent the presidency of the state during the initial period. The body would then become an interim Islamic council, which would endure for a period of four months with Burhanuddin Rabbani as president of the state. The period of the council and the presidency would not be extended even by a day. Provision was also made for a premiership and various key ministries, to be allocated among the various political parties. The newly formed national government was to last for two years.

Cabinet posts and ministries were to be distributed as follows:

Prime ministership—Islamic Party
Deputy prime ministership and Ministry of the
    Interior—Islamic Union for the Liberation of
    Afghanistan
Deputy prime ministership and Ministry of
    Education—Islamic Party
Deputy prime ministership and Ministry of
    Foreign Affairs—National Islamic Front
Deputy prime ministership and Ministry of
    Defense—Islamist Movement
Supreme Court—Islamic Revolutionary Movement

See also Mujaddidi, Sabghatullah
References
Maley, William. 1992. *Political Order in Post-Communist
    Afghanistan.* Boulder, CO: Lynne Rienner.
"The Peshawar Accord (March 1993)." 1993.
    http://www.institute-for-afghan-
    studies.org/Accords%20Treaties/peshawar_accord_1
    993.htm (cited 11 February 2003).

POLLOCK, FIELD MARSHAL SIR GEORGE (1786–1872)

Following the rout of the British army in the First
Anglo-Afghan War (1839 to 1842), George Pollock
commanded an army of retribution, which entered
the Khyber Pass on 5 April 1842 and consisted of
about 8,000 troops arrayed in eight infantry regiments, three troops of cavalry, a troop of mounted
Jazailchis (known as such because of their long-bar-
reled muskets), and two batteries of artillery. Pollock initially resisted an attack by Afridi tribesmen
and marched on Jalalabad, where he rescued the
British garrison, which was close to surrender due to
starvation. He then defeated Akbar Khan at the Battle of Tezin before entering Kabul on 16 September
1842, where he destroyed the fortifications of Bala
Hisar and the Kabul bazaar. Pollock allowed his
troops to plunder the city, resulting in wholesale destruction; hundreds of the citizens were killed or executed. He then negotiated, through Maj. Eldred
Pottinger, the release of British hostages by granting
their guardian, Sahel Muhammad, a gift of 20,000
rupees and a pension of 12,000 rupees per annum
for life. Before leaving Afghanistan on 12 October
1842, Pollock's forces destroyed the towns of Istalif
and Charikar.

See also First Anglo-Afghan War; Pottinger, Maj. Eldred
References
Norris, James A. 1967. *The First Afghan War, 1838–42.*
    London: Cambridge University Press.

POTTINGER, MAJ. ELDRED (1811–1843)

British officer Eldred Pottinger had been sent from
India to explore Central Asia, and he ventured into
Kabul in the guise of a horse dealer. In 1837, he
reached Herat and became involved in the defense of
the city when it came under siege from the Persian
army between 1837 and 1838. In recognition of his
efforts, he was appointed political officer to Prince
Kamran, the ruler of Herat. During the First Anglo-
Afghan War (1839 to 1842), he was one of only two
survivors of a British outpost at Charikar when it
was captured in November 1841 and the Fourth Infantry was wiped out. One month later, he was the
senior surviving officer at Kabul and was responsible
for negotiating the Treaty of Capitulation with the
Afghan tribal chiefs. He was among the British officers taken into protective custody by Sardar Muhammad Akbar, the leader of the Afghan forces attacking
Kabul, and thus survived the massacre of the British
troops on their retreat from Kabul. He was involved
in the negotiations for the release of the British
hostages held by Saleh Muhammad Khan when
Field Marshal Sir George Pollock returned to Kabul
in September 1842 with his army of retribution. On
his return to India, Pottinger faced a court of inquiry,
which accused him of signing the Treaty of Capitulation without authority and drawing bills of money
(putting in claims for cash against promissory notes
or invoices) in favor of the Afghans. Although exonerated, he did not receive his back pay for the time he
spent as a hostage, and he was refused a medal for his
services in Afghanistan, despite the fact that the
viceroy of India called him the "Hero of Herat" during the Persian siege. He died of typhus in 1843 in
Hong Kong.

See also Capitulation, Treaty of; First Anglo-Afghan War;
    Herat Province
References
Pottinger, George. 1983. *The Afghan Connection: The
    Extraordinary Adventure of Major Eldred Pottinger.*
    Edinburgh: Scottish Academic Press.

POWINDAHS

Also known as the Kuchis, the Powindahs were the
merchant-nomads who seasonally migrated between Afghanistan and India. The majority being
Sulaiman Khel Pashtuns, members of one of the
largest of the Ghilzai tribes, they led a pastoral life
and followed a number of occupations, some
being nomad shepherds, some being merchants,

and some owning camel trains and trade between the two countries. A few of the tribe traveled without their families and earned a living as day laborers or moneylenders. The Powindahs were often scattered across northern India, and some of the merchants traveled as far as Nepal and Burma. The tribespeople are Sunni Muslims of the Hanafi School and adhere to a Sufi fraternity, leading their lives according to a combination of tribal code and Shari'a law.

The creation of Pakistan in 1947 meant that limits were imposed on their migrations across the Afghanistan-Pakistan border, which was reinforced when the border was closed because of the Pashtunistan dispute. Consequently, the Powindahs had to redirect their migrations, and the Afghan government had only limited success in persuading them to adopt a sedentary lifestyle. However, the nomads have adapted to the modern aspects of trade by investing in motorized transport services, and they now control much of the transportation of goods from the port of Karachi in Pakistan and Afghanistan.

References

Pedersen, G. 1994. *Afghan Nomads in Transition.* London: Thames and Hudson.

POYA, NADIR ALI (C. 1940S–1982)

Nadir Ali Poya was second in command of the Organization for the Liberation of the Afghan People (Sazman-i-Azadibakhshi-i-Mardin-i-Afghanistan, or SAMA), a left-wing, anti-Pashtun movement that was opposed to the Marxist government in Kabul. He succeeded Mujid Kalakani as leader of the SAMA in 1979. He was born in the vicinity of Mazar-i Sharif in the 1940s and educated there before going to the Polytechnic Institute at Kabul. In the 1960s, he was imprisoned for two years because of his involvement with the opposition, and on release, he became a member of SAMA, where he acquired a reputation as an organizer and an agitator. He was arrested again in 1981 for opposing the government and executed one year later.

References

Astute, J. Brice. 1986. *Afghanistan: The First Five Years of Soviet Occupation.* Washington, DC: National Defense University.

PUL-I CHARKHI PRISON

The village of Pul-i Charkhi on the Kabul River, east of Kabul, is the site of a modern but now infamous prison, built in the time of President Muhammad Daud (completed around 1975) and heavily utilized by subsequent regimes. The prison was built with a capacity of 5,000 prisoners, but during the Khalq regime, it housed double that number. The prison has special wings for foreigners, political prisoners, and women, and in the year immediately following the Saur Revolt of April 1978, large numbers of prisoners were executed; in 1979, the government of Hafizullah Amin produced a list of some 12,000 Afghan prisoners who had been executed. In 1980, Babrak Karmal, secretary-general of the People's Democratic Party of Afghanistan and president of Afghanistan from 1980 to 1986, disassociated himself from the excesses of the Khalq regime, and most of the remaining prisoners were freed under an amnesty. In the civil war (from 1989 to 2001) parts of the prison were destroyed, but it was still in use during the regime of Burhanuddin Rabbani (1992 to 1996) and was subsequently used by the Taliban regime after it captured the prison in September 1996.

References

Rostar, Mohammed Osman. 1991. *The Pul-i-Charkhi Prison: A Communist Inferno in Afghanistan,* Translated and edited by Ehsonullah Azari. Peshawar, Pakistan: Writers' Union of Free Afghanistan.

PUZAMOV, ALEXANDR

Alexandr Puzamov was the Soviet ambassador to Kabul in 1972 and was a political activist who was probably involved in the reunification of the People's Democratic Party of Afghanistan in 1977. He was closely tied to internal Afghan politics and supported Nur Muhammad Taraki in his struggle against Hafizullah Amin. However, an ambush on Amin on 14 September 1979 failed, and Amin demanded his recall to Moscow. Puzamov left Kabul on 19 November 1979.

See also Taraki, Nur Muhammad

References

Ashitov, Vladimir, Karen Gevorkian, and Vladimir Svetozarov. 1986. *The Truth about Afghanistan.* Moscow: Novasti Press Agency Publishing House.

QADIR, MAJ. GEN. ABDUL (1944–)

Abdul Qadir was a Parchami member of the People's Democratic Party of Afghanistan (PDPA) and was commander of the country's air defense forces in 1973. He used his position to support Muhammad Daud in his coup against Zahir Shah in that same year. And in April 1978, he actively participated in the Saur Revolt, which brought the Communists to power, and became head of the Revolutionary Council until the civilian government of Nur Muhammad Taraki was in place. In May 1978, Qadir became minister of defense, but in August, he was sentenced to death for plotting against the Khalq regime. The sentence was commuted to fifteen years of imprisonment, but he was released when Babrak Karmal took power in December 1979. He was restored to his positions within the PDPA and again served as minister of defense from 1982 to 1985, before resigning from the Politburo on the grounds of ill health. He was appointed ambassador to Warsaw in November 1986 and recalled to Afghanistan in 1988 when he was elected as an ordinary member of parliament. He is thought to have fled to Bulgaria in 1989 and sought political asylum on the fall of the Marxist government.

Qadir was born in Herat Province of a Tajik family and attended military school in Kabul before going to the Soviet Union for pilot training and a course at Staff College.

References

Guistozzi, Antonio. 2000. *War, Politics and Society in Afghanistan, 1978–1992.* Washington, DC: Georgetown University Press.

AL-QAEDA (THE BASE)

Al-Qaeda was founded in 1988 or 1989 by Osama bin Laden and Muhammad Atef. It is renowned for a number of terrorist attacks in Saudi Arabia, Somalia, Kenya, and Tanzania but mainly for the attack on the twin towers of the World Trade Center in New York and the Pentagon in Washington on 11 September 2001.

The organization is multinational and formed into loosely linked cells, which are thought to cooperate but also function as separate, independent entities. Primarily, al-Qaeda seeks to radicalize existing Islamic groups with the goals of overthrowing Muslim governments, which it sees as corrupt; driving Western influences from Muslim states; and abolishing boundaries between Muslim states.

The driving force of al-Qaeda was Osama bin Laden, who may or may not have been killed in fighting against Coalition forces in Afghanistan sometime after October 2001; media evidence in the form of audiotapes seems to indicate that he is still alive. The first contact between bin Laden and Afghanistan occurred when he went to that country in 1979 to fight against the Soviets. He funded and led groups of Arab fighters in mujahideen actions against Soviet and Afghan Marxist government forces. He remained in Afghanistan until the Soviet withdrawal in 1989, when he founded al-Qaeda and returned to Jeddah in Saudi Arabia

Arrival in Afghanistan

In May 1996, bin Laden was expelled from Sudan, which was under pressure from Saudi Arabia and the United States and faced the threat of having sanctions imposed by the United Nations. He returned to Afghanistan, where he renewed his support for Islamic extremist activities through the al-Qaeda organization. During the period of Burhanuddin Rabbani's rule in Kabul (1980 to 1986, bin Laden and his followers were moving freely around the country, but their base was in Jalalabad, where bin Laden had about fifty family members and bodyguards. Camps were established by al-Qaeda to train terrorists to support extreme

This undated photo shows Saudi-born dissident Osama Bin Laden (C) and top deputies Ayman Al-Zawahiri (L), a physician and the founder of the Egyptian Islamic Jihad, and Muhammad Atef (R), who has been indicted in the United States for his alleged involvement in the 1998 bombings of U.S. embassies in Tanzania and Kenya. (AFP/Corbis)

Islamic organizations and actions throughout the Islamic world.

Relations with the Taliban

The Taliban took power in Afghanistan in 1996, having defeated the forces of Rabbani, Ahmad Shah Masood, and the Northern Alliance. It is clear that al-Qaeda fighters assisted the Taliban in their actions against the mujahideen forces and enabled them to gain control over about 90 percent of the country in the period after the 1996 capture of Kabul. In February 1997, the Taliban regime rejected a demand from the United States to hand over bin Laden in return for international recognition and assuming the country's seat in international organizations. The Taliban refusal to take action eventually led to the imposition of UN sanctions against Afghanistan, as well as the U.S. Cruise missile attacks against al-Qaeda terrorist training camps on 28 August 1998. Previously, in early 1997, two bombs had been detonated in Jalalabad and were thought to have been an assassina-

tion attempt on bin Laden; this event led him to move his main al-Qaeda base to Kandahar, which was the stronghold of the Taliban and its leader, Mullah Muhammad Omar. The Taliban claimed that bin Laden had been moved to Kandahar to control his activities and to prevent his organization from using Afghan soil to harm any country.

In 1998, bin Laden began to increase the influence of al-Qaeda throughout the Islamic world by creating a new alliance of terrorist organizations called the World Islamic Front for the Jihad against Jews and Crusaders. The alliance included a number of militant organizations in Egypt, and the Egyptian Islamic Jihad merged with al-Qaeda. During all of this activity, the Taliban continued to protect bin Laden and al-Qaeda and ignored resolutions of the UN Security Council on 15 October 1999, which resulted in the imposition of sanctions. The Taliban argued that bin Laden was a guest in Afghanistan and that he no longer had contact with his followers, even though al-Qaeda announced that it had sent fighters to Chechnya, was present in Kashmir, and was possibly active in Tajikistan and Uzbek-istan. Today, it is also thought that al-Qaeda is active in Algeria, Eritrea, the Philippines, Somalia, and Yemen. It is unclear whether all activities are insti-gated and directed by bin Laden or whether these groups operate independently but with funding by al-Qaeda.

War against the Taliban

Though the Taliban controlled 90 percent of Af-ghanistan by 2001, opposition to the regime was al-ways present. The main opposition, under Ahmad Shah Masood, was bottled up in the Panjshir Valley in the northeast portion of the country. The Taliban were pursuing a harsh policy in terms of oppressing all things deemed un-Islamic; they also committed egregious human rights violations, particularly in relation to women and ethnic minorities, including Shi'a Muslims. The situation changed radically after the 11 September 2001 attacks in the United States on the World Trade Center and the Pentagon, which were laid at the door of al-Qaeda and Osama bin Laden.

In October 2001, the United States began a cam-paign, with the support of Britain, to overthrow the Taliban regime and al-Qaeda and to bring bin Laden and other al-Qaeda leaders to justice. Ini-tially, the United States and its allies provided sup-port to the Northern Alliance, to enable then to move out of the Panjshir Valley and engage the Tal-iban, and to Gen. Abdul Rashid Dostum, leader of the Uzbeks in Mazar-i Sharif. The opposition suf-fered a setback on 9 September 2001 when two Arab journalists assassinated Masood, and there is specu-lation that this killing was organized and funded by al-Qaeda. Additionally, Cruise missile attacks were launched on key Taliban and al-Qaeda strongholds and on the regime's infrastructure. The early fight-ing between the opposition forces and the Taliban was spasmodic and often conducted at long range, but as the fighting intensified, Arab and other for-eign fighters of al-Qaeda were the mainstay of the Taliban resistance.

However, the opposition to the Taliban soon gained momentum, particularly in the north of the country, and the regime began to lose territory. Mazar-i Sharif was taken after bitter fighting, with the support of Coalition special forces and air at-tacks, and al-Qaeda fighters were at the heart of the Taliban defense. Indeed, following the battle for Mazar-i Sharif, al-Qaeda prisoners led an uprising against their captors, and a bloody battle ensued, with much loss of life, including the death of an op-erative of the Central Intelligence Agency (CIA). Kabul itself was taken with very little resistance, and elsewhere, the Taliban crumbled as forces changed sides, fighters melted away, and limited resistance was put up against Coalition advances. The main re-sistance always occurred where the Taliban forces were bolstered by committed, dedicated al-Qaeda and other foreign fighters. The United States and Britain determined to try to oust the Taliban and al-Qaeda, a move that was seen as critical to securing peace in Afghanistan, and to strike a blow against the perceived worldwide terror network.

Taliban and al-Qaeda forces initially withdrew to their stronghold in Kandahar, but they were soon under siege from opposition forces. However, a major battle did not take place, as the fighters chose to leave the area and withdraw into the mountain-ous regions to regroup.

U.S. ground forces, supported by air strikes and helicopter gunships, mounted a series of operations in the mountains, at a cave complex in Tora Bora and in the mountainous region of Shah-i-Kot in Paktia Province. These operations succeeded in killing large numbers of Taliban and al-Qaeda fight-ers, capturing a few prisoners, and destroying arms dumps and other caches of supplies. In all of these engagements, al-Qaeda fighters fought to the death, partially because of their dedication but also be-cause they had no other recourse when cornered. But inevitably, because of the nature of the terrain, many of them were able to escape the Coalition forces.

Some major successes have been achieved in the struggle against al-Qaeda. Their military comman-der, Muhammad Atef, was killed in a U.S. air raid in November 2001, and another top member, Abu Zubaydah, was captured in March 2002 in Pakistan. However, the fate of Osama bin Laden is unknown. It is clear, however, that his deputy, Ayman al-Za-wahiri, an Egyptian surgeon, is alive and function-ing in the region, as evidenced by videotapes re-leased to the Qatari satellite television station al-Jazeera. It is also evident that large numbers of al-Qaeda and Taliban troops crossed the borders into Pakistan and Iran following the Coalition opera-tions at Tora Bora and Operation Anaconda in the Shah-i-Kot Mountains. Intelligence units in the CIA and Pakistan estimated that some 3,500 fighters have crossed into the frontier provinces and cities of Pakistan.

Many of the al-Qaeda fighters have sought refuge in Waziristan in Pakistan, which borders Afghanistan, and although Pakistani forces have waged battles against them, many are still on the loose. A number are also thought to be in Peshawar, which was a breeding ground for the Taliban, and some hundreds of fighters of Arab origin have vanished into Karachi. Pakistani intelligence officials also believe that al-Qaeda has established close working links with banned extremist groups of Pakistani origin and may have been the driving force behind the murder of U.S. journalist Daniel Pearl in 2002, the bombing of a bus carrying French technicians in Karachi in May 2002, and the June 2002 bombing of the U.S. consulate in the city.

Clearly, the al-Qaeda operation is still alive and flourishing, with small groups present in Afghanistan and larger elements across the borders in Pakistan and Iran. It is also thought that significant numbers of al-Qaeda fighters escaped to Yemen, the Persian Gulf, and Indonesia, where they remain active and are recruiting new members. The organization is a worldwide network, which has been weakened but not defeated by operations in Afghanistan and Pakistan. It has connections with other militant Islamic organizations in countries such as the Philippines, Indonesia, and Yemen, as evidenced by the attack on a French oil tanker off the coast of Yemen and the bombing in Bali on 12 October 2002, which may have been backed and financed by al-Qaeda. However, some successes have been achieved against the organization, as demonstrated by the CIA-led missile attack, using an unmanned drone, that killed one of bin Laden's chief followers, Salim Sinan al-Harethi, in the Yemeni desert. Al-Harethi had been tracked for some months and was wanted by the United States for involvement in the suicide bombing attack on the USS *Cole* in Aden harbor in October 2000.

A further major breakthrough took place on 1 March 2003 with the arrest of a Kuwaiti, Khalid Sheikh Mohammad, who was reputed to be the number three man in the al-Qaeda hierarchy, at Rawalpindi, Pakistan, together with two other suspected members of the group. The raid that snared these men was a coordinated operation between Pakistani intelligence and CIA agents. The arrest took place at the house of a member of Pakistan's Islamist Party. Mohammad is thought to have been the planner for al-Qaeda and responsible for a number of atrocities, including the 11 September 2001 attacks in the United States; after that event, he was responsible for the movement of al-Qaeda funds and recruitment. He is now in U.S. custody and being questioned by U.S. and Pakistani officials and is regarded as a major capture in the ongoing operation against the Taliban and al-Qaeda. The Pakistan authorities also regard his apprehension as a clear demonstration of their effectiveness and role in the War on Terror.

See also Coalition Air Campaign against the Taliban; Coalition Land Campaign against the Taliban; Laden, Osama bin; Taliban

References

Gunaratna, Roham. 2001. *Inside al-Qaeda: Global Network of Terror.* New Delhi: Roli Publishers.

Yonak, Alexander. 2001. *Usama bin Laden's al-Qaida: Profile of a Terrorist Network.* New York: Transnational Publishers.

QUDDUS, ABDUL (1842–1921?)

Abdul Quddus was a nephew of Amir Dost Muhammad and a general in the Afghanistan army who was in exile with Amir Abdur Rahman in Bukhara and Samarkand. In 1866, he returned with the amir to Afghanistan and worked to extend Rahman's power over the whole country. In 1881, he led a small force of 400 cavalry and 400 infantry troops in an attack on Herat, which he captured from Ayub Khan, the son of Amir Shir Ali. In a campaign lasting from 1890 to 1893, he conquered the Hazarajat region and was awarded the title of "Confidence of the State" by Amir Habibullah, who appointed him prime minister, a position later confirmed by King Amanullah. In the Third Anglo-Afghan War of 1919, he was placed in command of the Kandahar front and was viewed by the opposing British officers as a true apostle of "Afghanistan for the Afghans."

References

Tate, George Passman. 1975. *The Kingdom of Afghanistan: A Historical Sketch.* New York: AMS Press.

R

RABBANI, BURHANUDDIN (1940–)

Burhanuddin Rabbani became president of Afghanistan on 28 June 1992 following the downfall of the government of Muhammad Najibullah two months earlier. Power had been handed over to a leadership council made up of top mujahideen leaders under the interim president Sabghatullah Mujaddidi. The council agreed to Rabbani's appointment as president, though Mujaddidi was reluctant to relinquish power. This reluctance boded ill for the future.

Rabbani was born in 1940 in Faizabad and was educated at a local primary school before moving to Kabul to attend the Abu Hanifa School, where he graduated in 1959. After Abu Hanifa, he went to the Faculty of Shari'a at Kabul University, graduating in 1963 and then teaching in the faculty from 1963 to 1966. He obtained an M.A. degree from the al-Azhar University in Egypt in 1968. On his return to Afghanistan, he became a professor of philosophy in the Faculty of Shari'a at Kabul University and a member of the University Research Department.

After returning from Egypt in 1968, Rabbani began to recruit his students into the Organization of Young Muslims, which developed into the Islamist Movement in 1972; Rabbani was elected as leader of the movement by the fifteen-member council that year. In 1974, he was forced to flee from Kabul to avoid arrest for opposition to the government of President Daud, and he ended up hiding in the tribal territory in the mountains. Following the Saur Revolt of April 1978 and the advent of the Communist regime, Rabbani traveled extensively abroad. In 1980, he delivered an address to the Islamic Foreign Ministers Conference at Islamabad, Pakistan.

Rabbani's term as president of Afghanistan ran from 1992 to 1996 but was never secure, as the consensus among the various mujahideen groups soon disintegrated. Even Kabul was not secure; in fact, it was said that there was a different government on each street of the city as the groups vied for power. Foremost of these was the Islamic Party of Gulbuddin Hekmatyar, the fundamentalist mujahideen leader who had aspirations to lead Afghanistan but had been ejected from Kabul by government troops. Hekmatyar was engaged in sporadic shelling of Kabul by rockets from his bases to the south of the city. In July 1992, some of his troops moved back into the capital, and fierce fighting ensued.

Some doubt existed as to Rabbani's ability to bring order to Kabul due to his policy of using consensus and gradualism as means of achieving an Islamic state rather than the coercion favored by others, such as Hekmatyar. However, Rabbani did have the backing of the renowned mujahideen leader Ahmad Shah Masood from the Panjshir Valley area of northern Afghanistan, (Ironically, both Rabbani and Masood were Tajiks in the largely Pashtun-dominated area of southern Afghanistan.) The rivalry between the various groups soon developed into a civil war, with alliances being made and broken and the balance of power continually shifting from one group to another. As a result, Afghanistan descended into a state of anarchy, though Rabbani was still recognized as president by the international community.

Meanwhile, in 1994, the Taliban movement was founded in Kandahar, and it soon grew in power with the backing of foreign fighters from the Muslim world. Soon, it began to challenge the mujahideen warlords throughout Afghanistan with its brand of Islamic fundamentalism. In 1996, the Taliban took Kabul, and the forces of Masood and Rabbani were forced to withdraw to northern Afghanistan. Rabbani then declared Mazar-i Sharif to be the new capital, but following further Taliban

Burhanuddin Rabbani, ousted as Afghan president by the Taliban, attends a news conference in Dushanbe, 11 October 2001. (Reuters NewMedia Inc./CORBIS)

advances, he was forced to withdraw with Masood back to the Panjshir Valley.

During the period of Taliban rule, Rabbani remained in Masood's stronghold and was still recognized by the international community as the legitimate president of Afghanistan. After the rout of the Taliban at the end of 2001 and the fall of Kabul to the Northern Alliance, Rabbani attempted to reassert his position as president in Kabul, but this move was thwarted by the UN-sponsored Bonn Conference in December 2001, which formed an interim government with Hamid Karzai as president. Rabbani's hold on power was finally relinquished in July 2002 when, before the meeting of the Loya Jirga (Great Council), he withdrew his candidacy for president, thus leaving the way open for Karzai to be reelected as president of the Interim administration.

References

Maley, William. 1998. *Fundamentalism Reborn? Afghanistan and the Taliban.* London: Hurst.

Rashid, Ahmed. 2001. *Taliban: The Story of the Afghan Warlords.* London: Pan Books.

RAHMAN, AMIR ABDUR (?–1901)

Abdur Rahman was amir of Afghanistan from 1880 to 1901, assuming the throne at the end of the Second Anglo-Afghan War. He was reluctantly recognized by the British occupation forces because of the support that he was accorded by the populace, despite the fact that he had the backing of Russia.

Abdur Rahman had been involved in a conflict with his uncle, Amir Shir Ali, in 1864 and had been forced to flee Afghanistan. He returned two years later to defeat his uncle and recognize his father, Afzal Khan, as king. However, Amir Shir Ali regained his throne in 1869, and Abdur Rahman was again forced into exile. On the amir's death in February 1879, Abdur Rahman returned to Afghanistan, raising a large army on his journey south. British recognition came on 22 July 1880, and in the following year, Rahman took possession of Kandahar and Herat, thus becoming the undisputed ruler of Afghanistan.

Amir Abdur Rahman concluded an agreement with Britain to protect Afghanistan from Russian aggression; in return, Britain was given responsibility for Afghanistan's external affairs. He also received a subsidy from Britain to bolster his defenses, particularly along the northern borders, but without giving Britain any real influence in Afghanistan's internal affairs. In 1893, Afghanistan's northern and eastern borders were demarcated, and this effort included the Durand Line agreement with the British over the border with India, an agreement that was accepted by Afghanistan under duress. During his reign, the amir also built fortifications in Khulm, Mazar-i-Sharif, and Kabul to ensure stability and control over the kingdom. He died in 1901 and was buried in the capital city.

References

Kakar, M. Hasan. 1979. *Government and Society in Afghanistan: The Reign of Amir Abd al-Rahman Khan.* Austin: University of Texas Press.

Khan, Sultan Mohamed. 1980. *The Life of Abdur Rahman, Amir of Afghanistan.* Karachi, Pakistan: Oxford University Press.

Martin, Frank A. 2000. *Under the Absolute Amir of Afghanistan.* New Delhi: Bhavana Books and Prints.

RASULI, MAJ. GEN. GHULAM HAIDAR (1919–1978)

Ghulam Haidar Rasuli was a supporter of Muhammad Daud and was placed in charge of the Central

Forces of Afghanistan in 1973; he became chief of the General Staff two years later. He was made minister of defense in 1977 but was killed during the April 1978 Saur Revolt, which brought the Communist regime to power.

Rasuli was born in 1919 in Rustaq, the son of Ghulam Rasul, a Muhammadzai of Kandahar. His received his early education at the Military High School, graduating in 1933, before receiving military training in India from 1956 to 1958. He then occupied a number of military posts in Afghanistan: in charge of the cavalry at Kabul from 1946 to 1954; in Jalalabad from 1954 to 1956; and serving as chief of staff at Mazar-i Sharif from 1958 to 1960, at Pul-i-Khumri from 1960–1964, and at Gardez from 1964 to 1966. He finally became a lieutenant colonel and director of recruitment in the Ministry of National Defense in 1966. He backed Muhammad Daud while in retirement and was active in organizing political support for him and was brought back to active service in 1973 after the coup that ousted King Mohammed Zahir.

References

Ahmad, N. D. 1990. *The Survival of Afghanistan, 1747–1979: A Diplomatic History with an Analytic and Reflective Approach.* Lahore, Pakistan: Institute of Islamic Culture.

RATEBZAD, ANAHITA (1931–)

Anahita Ratebzad holds the distinction of having been the highest-ranking woman in the People's Democratic Party of Afghanistan (PDPA) as a member of the Parcham faction. She was elected to parliament in 1965 and founded the PDPA-sponsored Democratic Women's Organization. Previously, she had been educated in Chicago and at Kabul University, graduating as the first woman doctor in Afghanistan. In the government of Nur Muhammad Taraki, formed after the April 1978 Saur Revolt, she was appointed minister of social affairs and tourism, and two months later, she was made ambassador to Belgrade. However, she was a victim of the purge of the Parchami in 1979, having been accused of plotting against the Khalq regime, and she remained outside the country until Babrak Karmal assumed power in 1980. In Karmal's first administration, she served as minister of education from 1980 to 1981 and became a member of the PDPA Politburo and also oversaw the Ministries of Information and Culture, Higher and Vocational Education, and Public Health. She relinquished all of these government posts and became a member of the Presidium of the Revolutionary Council from 1981 to 1988. Since the fall of the Marxist government in 1992, she has held no official position in Afghanistan.

See also People's Democratic Party of Afghanistan
References
Bradsher, Henry St. Amant. 1999. *Afghan Communism and Soviet Intervention.* London and New York: Oxford University Press.

RECONSTRUCTION PROGRAM

After twenty-three years of war, almost the entire vital infrastructure in Afghanistan was destroyed, and initiating a rebuilding program represented a major challenge for the international community. In addition, some 6 million citizens were suffering from hunger, and the scarcity of food and water led to widespread malnutrition, leaving large numbers of children vulnerable to life-threatening diseases. Among the priorities identified by the UN Development Program in December 2001 were mine-clearing operations; the demobilization of former soldiers and militia; the reconstruction of public institutions; and the restoration of health, education, and agriculture. However, a prerequisite for reconstruction is security, and in Afghanistan, insecurity, lawlessness, and continued unrest are making the distribution of aid difficult.

Although large-scale fighting seemed to have ended by the beginning of 2003, significant elements of the Taliban and al-Qaeda are still at large, and significant threats are still posed by dissident elements, such as Gulbuddin Hekmatyar and his Iranian-backed Islamic Party. In addition, the authority of the government of President Hamid Karzai does not really extend beyond Kabul, and in the provinces, local warlords are vying for control in a manner reminiscent of the chaos following the Soviet withdrawal in 1989. In the main, the assistance provided to Afghanistan up to the end of 2002 came in the form of short-term humanitarian aid, totaling some $1.8 billion. However, the infrastructure needs to be rebuilt to provide a welcoming environment for private investment and to create jobs for the millions of unemployed. International support is desperately needed, but it must be part of a sustained program that will continue long after Afghanistan has faded from the headlines.

The absence of a strong central government presents problems for reconstruction. But Afghans have, throughout their history, rejected the concept of a strong central state, and this situation is unlikely to change in the immediate future. As a result and because of the breakdown in interethnic links, a grassroots approach is vital, with links to local communities and local organizations. Many observers have also made the point that the lofty pledges of the international community have been received with some skepticism within the country, for Afghans have been abandoned in the past with support being channeled only to military groups, not the broader society. Planners estimate that something in the region of $25 billion will be needed over a period of ten years in order to create a stable country with security, a government based on consent, and an administrative structure capable of handling the reconstruction program.

In considering the implementation of a program of reconstruction, bodies such as the International Crisis Group, based in Brussels, have advocated the use of nongovernmental organizations (NGOs) with proven track records in Afghanistan to deliver immediate aid and provide a bridge to the more effective work of reconstruction and development. In a report on the situation in Afghanistan, published in November 2001, the International Crisis Group determined that reconstruction efforts should be driven by the following standards:

- Aid commitments should be considerable, coordinated, and long-term.
- Aid should be delivered in a decentralized way that recognizes the political realities in Afghanistan and the likely weakness of the central government.
- Local communities should have an important stake in projects, and the provision of assistance should be a vehicle to promote civil organization.
- Small, fast-disbursing, and flexible community improvement programs, rather than slow-moving infrastructure projects, should be implemented as a more effective means of preventing future conflict.
- Conflict prevention should be considered in the design of projects in order to ensure equitable distribution and reduce local tensions. Priorities should include

employment and training for demobilized fighters and support and education for conflict resolution.
- Consideration should also be given to the needs of Afghanistan's neighbors in Iran, Pakistan, and the Central Asian republics.

It is clear that Afghanistan is a difficult case, and an unrealistic Western reconstruction program, based on the goal of creating a democratic secular state, is seen by many experts as an impossibility due to the extreme fragmentation and militarization of Afghan society. Thus, it is felt that aid must be provided on a regional basis and, wherever possible, to local organizations and village communities. At the same time, however, some point out that it will be impossible to completely bypass local warlords and tribal leaders; experience in other countries has shown that armed groups and powerful individuals always influence how aid is used within their spheres of influence. Some organizations, such as the Carnegie Endowment for International Peace, advocate the following key principles:

- Discarding assessments of what help Afghanistan needs to become a modern democratic state and replacing them with a sober evaluation of the minimum a central administration needs to foster a measure of normal life, economic activity and, most important, trade
- Working directly with regional leaders whose power is well established but closely monitoring their behavior, using liaison officers, especially with respect to the leaders' treatment of local ethnic minorities and their relations with other regions and ethnic groups. They should also be prevented from providing shelter to any terrorist groups.
- Instructing liaison officers to work with international and domestic NGOs to ensure that they can function unhindered and that they do not become entangled in local politics.
- Considering seriously the standards to be met by local leaders in exchange for aid and ensuring that they are realistic. All parties involved should recognize that

incremental change is more likely to be sustainable.

The road construction program to be financed by the Asian Development Bank aptly illustrates the problems faced by Afghanistan and by the funding and donor agencies. The bank initially agreed to take on the reconstruction of the Kabul-to-Kandahar highway, a critical artery, at an estimated cost of $150 million, making it the largest single infrastructure investment since the fall of the Taliban. However, in July 2002, the deal fell apart when the government refused the bank's request to have the government accept loans to finance the project as it could not meet the conditions. The Asian Development Bank maintained that there was a misunderstanding, for the bank had $200 million for projects in Afghanistan, of which $150 million was to be in the form of loans, and $50 million in grants from the Japanese government that could only be used to improve secondary roads and therefore could not be spent on the Kabul-to-Kandahar project.

The outcome infuriated the Afghan government because of the arbitrary conditions, and officials questioned how donors could talk about secondary roads when there are only 2,000 miles of tarmac roads in the whole country, of which about 80 percent are in an appalling condition. At a conference in Tokyo in January 2002, donors had promised to deliver $4.5 billion of aid over five years, yet little has been forthcoming. Indeed, despite the critical needs in this area of basic communication, only one road project has been undertaken since the fall of the Taliban and that is a road between Herat and Islam Qala on the Iranian border, funded by the Iranian government. The issue has become a critical one for the Karzai government, as highways are politically important in integrating the country and linking Afghanistan with its neighbors.

The situation in Afghanistan has also been highlighted by NGOs such as the Cooperative for Assistance and Relief Everywhere (CARE), which, in September 2002, asserted that only 5 percent of the aid pledged at Tokyo had been forthcoming, with the result that no large highway or other infrastructure projects had been started. The World Health Organization (WHO), which stated that it had only received 7 percent of the $60 million it needed to begin implementation of a health care reconstruction plan, has reinforced this view. Many areas have never had any health care provision at all, and 6 million Afghans currently having no access to health care facilities, and even in major cities such as Kabul and Kandahar, hospitals are in dire shape.

At a conference held in Oslo on 18 December 2002, donor nations promised to provide $1.24 billion to help rebuild Afghanistan in 2003 through a series of projects ranging from road reconstruction to the provision of education for girls. However, it was not clear how much of the pledges from twenty-three nations were new funds or, instead, part of the aid promised at Tokyo. Among the projects identified by Afghan Finance Minister Ahmadzai were: providing education for girls, improving water and sanitation systems, rebuilding the shattered infrastructure, training bureaucrats, and creating a new army. Additionally, work needed to start on 1,800 miles of roads and on reconstruction in Kabul and Kandahar. At the conference, President Karzai urged donors to shift away from short-term humanitarian aid, of which there has been a great deal, and focus on the longer-term investment needed to rebuild Afghanistan. This approach is seen as politically important to the credibility and survival of the fledgling central government and to the success of elections scheduled to take place at the end of the current government's mandate.

However, it must be recognized that reconstruction and long-term funding efforts are threatened by the growing insecurity in Afghanistan, which also affects neighboring countries such as Pakistan, Iran, and Tajikistan. The lack of security outside of Kabul is a major constraint to reconstruction, as is the power of the regional warlords, corruption in provincial regimes, and tension along Afghanistan's borders because of the continued threat from the Taliban, al-Qaeda, and other Islamic militants, among them Gulbuddin Hekmatyar. The situation is further compounded by the problem of returning refugees: since the fall of the Taliban, some 1.6 million have returned to Afghanistan, mostly to urban areas; the population of Kabul alone has risen from 1.2 to 2.3 million. This ongoing issue will test the resolve of the international community and determine whether it has the will to be in Afghanistan for the long haul.

In January 2003, after months of negotiations, the Coalition commander, General Dan McNeill, announced the formation of joint regional teams (JRTs) in an endeavor to improve stability and security in

Afghanistan while at the same time beginning reconstruction programs. Each team will consist of seventy soldiers, civil affairs officers, engineers, medical personnel, and U.S. State Department officials. The JRT initiative—a result of negotiations with the Afghan government, Coalition partners, the United Nations, and NGOs—came after months of criticism from Afghan and Western aid agencies that the United States was doing little to help the Karzai government deal with the regional warlords or begin reconstruction of the country.

The decision to form the JRTs was also shaped by the belief that involvement in reconstruction projects would improve security and stability, while speeding up economic activity in the country. The main objective is to help local authorities, UN agencies, and NGOs pave the way for the expenditure of $300 million in aid designated for the reconstruction of rural areas. The first JRT was destined for Gardez in eastern Afghanistan, which had been the scene of bitter fighting between rival warlords throughout 2002. According to plans, JRTs would also be operating in Kunduz, Bamian, Mazar-i Sharif, Herat, Jalalabad, and Kandahar by the summer of 2003, with more to follow if the initial deployment proves successful. A further JRT began operations in Bamian in March 2003, followed a month later by one in Kunduz and then a British-led JRT in Mazar-i Sharif in July. Additional JRTs are planned for Herat, Jalalabad, and Kandahar, but these are awaiting a review of the effectiveness of operational JRTs.

Some small examples of efforts that offer real hope do emerge. One example is in the village of Farza, two hours north of Kabul, which has been devastated by war and is to be rebuilt by a group from the University of Colorado. The project will operate under the auspices of a group known as Engineers without Borders and is regarded by the university as a long-term commitment to the village. An initial survey took place in March 2003 to scope out the area, locate a source of water, and assess the available manpower and equipment. The group returned in the spring to begin work and to aid the Afghans in their rebuilding efforts using new techniques designed to repair war damage. It is hoped that gestures such as this will keep Afghanistan from sliding back into anarchy and again becoming a safe haven for terrorists.

See also Humanitarian Airdrops; Humanitarian Relief; Kabul City; Refugee Problem

References
International Crisis Group. 2001. *Afghanistan and Central Asia: Priorities for Reconstruction and Development.* Asia Report no. 26. Brussels: ICG.
Ottaway, Marian, and Anatol Lieven. 2002. "Rebuilding Afghanistan: Fantasy versus Reality." http://www.ceip.org/pubs (cited January 2002).

RED SHIRTS

Khan Abdul Ghaffar Khan founded the Red Shirts in 1921 as a Pashtun independence movement among the tribes in the North-West Frontier Province of India. The Red Shirts were mistrusted by the British government in India because of their demands for autonomy and their philosophy, based on freeing the oppressed, feeding the poor, and clothing the naked, all of which aroused suspicions that they had Communist leanings (an impression that was, of course, reinforced by their red uniforms). The movement was allied with the Congress Party of Mahatma Gandhi and organized in cells, with a presence in most villages in the tribal borderland. The movement had seven basic tenets: opening admission to all adults; rejecting the Indian caste system; wearing national dress; being ready to serve the people; dedicating one's life to the interests of the people; recognizing all members as brothers; and obeying the orders of the party. The question of Pashtunistan has concerned the governments of Afghanistan and Pakistan since the creation of the Pakistan state in 1947, and at the very least, the Pashtun independence movement wants autonomy for the province and a change of name to reflect the makeup of the majority population.

See also Pashtunistan Dispute

References
Jannson, Eland. 1981. *India, Pakistan or Pakhunistan?* Uppsala, Sweden: Almquist.

REFUGEE PROBLEM

The problem of refugees fleeing from Afghanistan began in the early 1980s after the Soviet occupation was under way and the mujahideen launched their war against the Soviets and the Communist government in Kabul. The size of the problem, which was caused both by war and by the severe and prolonged drought in Afghanistan, is immense and poses major problems for the government of Hamid Karzai, for refugees have begun to return home following the defeat of the Taliban. The returning

Afghan refugees sit among their belongings in a truck on their way back to Afghanistan from Chaman, 20 May 2003. Part of a UNHCR-sponsored repatriation program from Iran and Pakistan. (AFP/Corbis)

communities have expectations that the government is finding difficult to meet due to the slow pace of reconstruction, high rates of unemployment, and reliance on international aid agencies for food and other supplies.

At one stage, estimates indicated there were some 5 million Afghan refugees—mainly in Iran and Pakistan but with smaller numbers in the Central Asian republics, India, and Europe—as well as many displaced Afghans remaining within Afghanistan. In Pakistan, some 2 million refugees were spread over the country, though most were in the North-West Frontier Province around Peshawar and Quetta. The bulk of these refugees were living in camps, and it was from this population that the various mujahideen groups drew their recruits. The UN High Commission for Refugees (UNHCR) supported the refugees, and the camps consisted mainly of fixed housing. with water, sanitation, electricity, and health services.

In early 2000, the number of refugees in Iran and Pakistan grew rapidly, largely as a result of the military successes of the Taliban but also because of

drought and abject poverty. Most of the new refugees were Tajiks and Turkomans, with a smaller percentage of Uzbeks and Pashtuns. They had to be accommodated in tents, with makeshift facilities provided through support from the UNHCR and food distributed by nongovernmental organizations (NGOs). In the new camps, environmental conditions were conducive to the spread of epidemics of communicable diseases. Although the UNHCR personnel had been trying to provide basic services and health facilities, they were working in difficult circumstances and without the cooperation of the Pakistan government that would have allowed them to function systematically and in an official capacity.

The influx of new refugees caused Pakistan to close its borders to new arrivals, and more than 600,000 were living outside the official camps. The situation was beyond the capacity of the Pakistani government to handle. But the position of refugees in Iran was even worse, as the only support they received came from the Iranian government. Further, as a consequence of Pakistan closing its borders, tented camps grew up in the Taliban-held territory of eastern Afghanistan, relying solely on support from NGOs, operating with dwindling supplies, and receiving no support from the Kabul regime.

Inside Afghanistan, there was also the problem of the many people who were displaced by war or by ethnic cleansing. In the middle of 1999, for example, the Taliban launched a major offensive into the Shomali Plains, north of Kabul, forcing back Northern Alliance forces but also causing more than 150,000 civilians to flee either to the alliance stronghold in the Panjshir Valley or to Kabul. Although some of the displaced Afghans returned home in 2000, at least 60,000 remained in the Panjshir Valley, which continued to experience sporadic violence, and others remained in Kabul. The internal displacement continued throughout July, August, and September 2000 in the face of further Taliban advances, which reached almost as far as the Tajikistan border. This military action in Bangi and Taloqan displaced tens of thousands of civilians, the majority of whom were trapped in Afghanistan due to the closure of the border with Pakistan. These refugees fared worse than those in neighboring countries, for the United Nations had only received 48 percent of the funding needed to provide support; this situation was exacerbated by the most severe drought that Afghanistan had experienced in thirty years, affecting the whole country. Tens of thousands of Afghans were forced to leave their homes in search of food.

In June 2000, more refugees moved into Pakistan, and this process accelerated in October as a result of additional fierce fighting in northern Afghanistan. Their numbers probably totaled around 172,000. During the year, the UNHCR did repatriate some 76,000 Afghans to Afghanistan, providing them with a six-month supply of food, seeds, and materials to rebuild their homes, but the figure was lower than hoped for, largely because of the drought situation. The UNHCR also provided returning children with schoolbooks, helped communities build wells, and funded income-generation projects for returning women, but the operation lacked sufficient international support. An agreement was reached with Iran over the repatriation of undocumented refugees from Iran, in return for Iran agreeing to allow Afghans who claimed to be refugees to apply for asylum and, if classed as refugees, to remain legally in Iran. But before repatriation could begin, hundreds of Afghans were arrested and deported from Tehran, a move criticized by the UNHCR and the Afghan opposition.

Some suggest that the deportation from Iran might have been intended to encourage other Afghans to participate in the voluntary repatriation efforts, and between April and December, some 133,600 Afghans were repatriated from Iran under the UNHCR program. The UNHCR and the World Food Program (WFP) gave refugees cash grants, a quantity of wheat, and items such as agricultural tools. Approximately half of the returnees originally came from Herat Province. However, the UNHCR had only limited funds to implement the program and could only aid a finite number of refugees back in their home environments. A U.S. NGO, the International Rescue Committee, and the International Red Cross provided some aid, but only a small number of refugees were able to benefit from these programs. During the remainder of 2000, a further 50,000 refugees were repatriated from Iran, but it is not clear how many of them did so voluntarily and how many were forcibly removed by overstretched Iranian authorities. Despite this, some 1.4 million Afghan refugees remained in Iran at the end of 2000.

During the year, hundreds of thousands of Afghans became displaced (though the true number is unknown), mainly due to the Taliban offensives throughout northern Afghanistan. Accurate records are not available, as many of the displacements were temporary, with the population returning home once the lines of battle shifted to other areas. A survey carried out in Kabul in 1999 by the International Red Cross revealed that 83 percent of those interviewed had been displaced from their homes on at least one occasion. A minimum of 250,000 Afghans were displaced, though many were able to return home later in the year, but the United Nations recorded that 100,000 remained displaced in Takhar and Badakhshan Provinces, 100,00 in Mazar-i Sharif and the immediate environs, and 46,000 in Kunduz and Baghlan Provinces. In Takhar Province, some 10,000 people were stranded on islands in a river along the border with Tajikistan; being refused entry by Tajikistan, they were subject to sporadic attacks by Taliban forces and could receive little aid, as access was only available from Tajikistan.

Forced migration was also fueled by the drought, with more than 70,000 displaced in southern Afghanistan and a similar number in and around the city of Herat. Because these refugees were displaced by drought, they were not included in the UNHCR figures for displaced persons. The situation in Herat was particularly bad, largely due to the lack of funds: in December 2000, WFP warned that it only had enough food in the area to last until the following February. The Taliban did little to provide aid to communities displaced by war or drought, preferring to concentrate its resources on the war effort and leave humanitarian relief to the international community.

The situation deteriorated further in 2001. The UNHCR estimated that some 4.5 million Afghans were living as refugees, mainly in Iran and Pakistan, and the U.S. Committee for Refugees estimated that there were also some 1 million displaced persons in Afghanistan. During 2001, more than 200,000 Afghans fled to Pakistan. Others fled to Iran; the number is unknown but is thought to be tens of thousands. Repatriation programs also continued, with 21,000 returning from Pakistan under a UNHCR program, a further 45,000 of their own volition, and 3,000 expelled. About 144,000 Afghans were expatriated from Iran because they received no assistance and were not allowed to work, and a further 120,000 were forcibly repatriated.

In early 2001, NGOs described the situation in Afghanistan as "apocalyptic" and assessed the need for some $3.5 million for food, shelter, and blankets. Yet only $200,000 was forthcoming. The situation of displaced persons in Herat was particularly serious, as many of them lacked food and shelter; in January 2001, over 100 died because of cold temperatures and lack of shelter and blankets. Only an emergency airlift by the United States helped to ease the situation, and the Europeans and Japanese committed further resources. The Hazaras also suffered because of the Taliban siege of the region and because aid agencies were prohibited from providing assistance. In other areas, such as Ghor Province, relief operations were halted because of continued fighting and attacks on aid workers by armed groups. On 6 September 2000, the WFP estimated that more than 5.5 million Afghans were dependent on food aid and that in some areas, people were eating grass, locusts, and bread crumbs.

The start of the U.S. bombing campaign against the Taliban and al-Qaeda on 7 October caused thousands of Afghans to move from their homes, especially in the large cities. By November, there were 500,000 displaced persons in the Mazar-i Sharif area, and 160,000 managed to enter Pakistan despite the closure of the borders, having paid smugglers to guide them through the high mountain passes. The Iranians attempted to prevent an influx by establishing two camps just inside the Afghan border, accommodating about 11,000 refugees in inadequate conditions. However, as Taliban control in western Afghanistan collapsed, fighting broke out in one of the camps between Taliban and opposition supporters. The U.S. bombing raids seriously disrupted relief work for the refugee communities, and these efforts were further hampered by the Taliban seizure of two UN food compounds and by the accidental U.S. bombing, on two occasions, of International Red Cross warehouses in Kabul.

With the collapse of the Taliban, the end of the U.S. bombing campaign, and the arrival of the International Security Assistance Force (ISAF), hundreds of thousands of displaced persons and tens of thousands from Iran and Pakistan returned home to northern and western Afghanistan. However, in southern Afghanistan, another refugee problem was created by the campaign waged by Coalition and Afghan forces against Kandahar, with tens of thousands of civilians fleeing the fighting. Pakistan imposed severe restrictions on this new wave of refugees, allowing access only to the truly vulnerable, so that most of these people were displaced into villages in the mountains or makeshift camps near Spin Boldak, close to the border with Pakistan, where they lived in extremely poor conditions.

Despite the establishment of a new government in Kabul and the arrival of the ISAF, the UNHCR believed that at the end of 2001, there were still 1 million displaced people in Afghanistan. Delivery of food improved, and the WFP was satisfied with the level of aid (though this assessment was disputed by some NGOs), but some areas were still suffering due to adverse weather or poor security conditions. Meanwhile, in northern Afghanistan, yet another problem arose when tens of thousands of Pashtuns were forced to leave their homes because of ethnic tensions with Tajiks and Uzbeks following the collapse of the Pashtun-dominated Taliban. The United Nations had to open up a new refugee camp in Zhare Dasht, a desert area in the border region of Pakistan. The camp was to house about 60,000 refugees who had been denied admittance by Pakistan on the grounds that the country no longer had the capacity to support them. Also in the camp were nomadic shepherds left destitute by the four-year drought who had nowhere else to go. The situation in the camp was poor because of the environment and the fact that it was adjacent to a huge minefield laid by the Soviets and the mujahideen in the 1980s.

The repatriation programs continued, and 2002 saw the largest numbers of returnees from Iran, Pakistan, and the Central Asian republics. The UNHCR assisted 1,603,000 to return between March and August, and a further 1,600,000 were sent back by asylum countries. As part of the ongoing repatriation, the UNHCR operates thirty offices in Afghanistan to coordinate protection and assistance activities in what will be a multiyear program needing strong donor support. The UNHCR had also experienced some problems with refugees receiving their repatriation assistance packages and then not returning to Afghanistan, so recipients are now screened before being accepted into the program. In 2002 in Pakistan, some 68,000 families were refused assistance after the screening process because agency staff were not satisfied that they intended to return to Afghanistan.

Toward the end of 2002 and in the beginning of 2003, figures for returning refugees dropped significantly due to the onset of winter and concerns about the security situation, given the ongoing struggles between regional warlords in Paktia and other provinces. In some areas, the situation remained critical because of minimal rainfall and a depleted water table; the provinces of Oruzgan, Bamian, and Wardak were badly affected. However, the WFP mounted a large-scale operation in December 2002 to move food into Afghanistan through a variety of routes from adjacent countries, thus preventing a return of famine to the nation, though the situation in some areas was difficult because of continued fighting. The program was largely made possible by $320 million in supplemental aid from the United States and further assistance from the European Union and Japan, together with increased activity on the part of NGOs.

The emphasis now is on the need to strengthen ties between humanitarian relief and rehabilitation and reconstruction programs; thus far, the work of the UNHCR and the NGOs has been concentrated on the initial stages of reintegrating returning refugees and displaced persons. The efforts of all these group now must be linked into a reconstruction program incorporating the provision of schools, medical facilities, irrigation systems, and employment to secure long-term sustainability. Clearly, this situation is a major challenge for the Karzai government and the international community alike.

See also Humanitarian Airdrops; Humanitarian Relief

References

Hussain, Syed Shabbir. 1982. *Afghan Refugees in Pakistan: The Long Wait.* Islamabad: Kamran Publishing House.

"Internal Displacement in Afghanistan: New Challenges." 2001. http://www.hspl.harvard.edu/hpct (cited 28 March 2002).

Migration and Refugee Services. 1984. *Refugees from Afghanistan: A Look at History, Culture and the Refugee Crisis.* Washington, DC: United States Catholic Conference.

Miller, Georgi Boris. 1985. *Refugees from Afghanistan.* London: Cleveland Press.

Shalinsky, Audrey. 1994. *Long Years in Exile: Central Asian Refugees in Afghanistan and Pakistan.* Lanham, MD: University Press of America.

http://www.hsph.harvard.edu/hpct.

http://www.un.org.pk/unhcr.

http://www.unhcr.ch.

REGISTAN DESERT

The Registan is a desert area covering the southern parts of Kandahar, Helmand, and Nimruz Provinces and is known as "the Country of Sand." The desert is higher than the surrounding alluvial plains—the sand hills can be 200 to 300 feet high—and resembles the deserts of Saudi Arabia. It is a large area of ridges and hillocks of loose red sand, and it has proved a major natural barrier to conventional armed forces where it is bordered by Pakistan. The desert hosts a sparse coverage of bushes and vegetation on its edges, with alluvial soils in the hollows being cultivated by Baluch and Brahui nomads. The desert is also home to broken clans or outcast robbers.

References

Amin, Hamidullah, and Gordon B. Schiltz. *A Geography of Afghanistan.* Omaha: University of Nebraska, Center for Afghan Studies.

REVOLUTIONARY ASSOCIATION OF WOMEN OF AFGHANISTAN (RAWA)

The Revolutionary Association of Women of Afghanistan was founded in 1977 in Kabul as an independent organization of Afghan women committed to the fight for human rights and social justice. The founders were women intellectuals, and their objective was to involve Afghan women in social and political activities aimed at acquiring human rights for women; establishing a democratic government based on secular values; and increasing women's presence in the arenas of education, health, income generation, and political agitation.

After the Soviet intervention in the country in 1979, RAWA became heavily involved in the resistance movement. A number of members were sent to work among refugee women in Pakistan, where they established schools, hostels for children, and a hospital for refugee women and children in Quetta. RAWA also introduced nursing and literacy courses and provided vocational training for women. During the Soviet occupation, members of RAWA were responsible for distributing antigovernment leaflets, staging demonstrations, and organizing strikes in schools and universities. A number of members were arrested and tortured, and many of them were imprisoned for eight years in the Kabul prison; the founding leader, Meena, and two of her associates were murdered in 1987 in Quetta, with the association accusing agents of Gulbuddin Hekmatyar of committing the deed. The movement has been opposed by the mujahideen fundamentalists operating from Peshawar, Pakistan, and by similar groups in Afghanistan.

At the time of the fall of Muhammad Najibullah's government in 1992 and the rise of the mujahideen government, RAWA began to focus more on women's rights, human rights, and the exposure of the barbaric policies of the fundamentalist groups. The organization continues to be active in both Pakistan and Afghanistan.

Pakistan

RAWA's work among women in the refugee camps has been difficult because of the group's stand against fundamentalism and its lack of financial resources to provide significant material help. Despite pressure from the fundamentalists, however, Afghan women refugees have approached the group for help, even though, in most cases, only moral support can be provided. RAWA also tries to attract the support of aid agencies, especially for their health and education projects, in order to compensate for their shortage of funds.

The group is active in the following areas:

- Education: RAWA runs primary and secondary schools for refugee girls and boys and literacy courses for women, as well as five orphanages for boys and girls.
- Health care: RAWA has mobile health teams operating in the refugee camps at Peshawar and Quetta and also runs Malalai Hospital in Rawalpindi and a clinic in Quetta.
- Human rights: The organization is providing human rights groups with details of violations committed by fundamentalists, such as stoning, amputation, torture, beating, lashing, killing, and imprisonment.
- Propaganda and political activity: RAWA organizes demonstrations and other functions and uses the press and events of Pakistani political parties or women's groups to expose actions of the Islamic fundamentalists. Members also provide assistance to the widows and families of prisoners in both Afghanistan and Pakistan and to women being treated badly by their male relatives.
- Sustainability: The organization runs workshops in handicrafts, carpet making, tailoring, and bead knitting; it also operates chicken and fish farms and produces jams and pickles.

Afghanistan

RAWA's activities within Afghanistan are mainly directed to the support of female victims of war and atrocities committed by the various belligerent groups, particularly the Islamic fundamentalists. Among the range of activities are: transferring victims to Pakistan for medical treatment, transferring traumatized children to Pakistan for rehabilitation, tracing missing females, and assisting families in evacuating from battlefield areas. Food is also distributed to poor and needy families in areas affected by drought, earthquake, and war. In addition, RAWA is passing on information about human rights violations to organizations such as Amnesty International and through the publication of pamphlets and reports.

The group is active in the following specific areas as well:

- Education: Activities in this area have, until recently, been mainly underground because of the restrictions imposed by the Taliban and, since the fall of the Taliban, by some of the regional warlords (for example, in Herat). However, the group has had success in running home-based schools and literacy courses for women. At the same time, members have been organizing discussion groups covering concepts such as women's rights, social participation, concepts of democracy and civic freedoms, the right to education, and the maintenance of human rights for women.
- Health: RAWA operates eight mobile health teams in eight provinces, providing treatment for women who cannot afford to go to a doctor, as well as midwifery. The teams also run first-aid courses for young girls and literate women. In 2001, the teams carried out the polio vaccination program in their areas.
- Sustainability: RAWA operates chicken farms; small carpet-weaving, embroidery, knitting, handicrafts, and tailoring workshops; and bee-keeping projects. Women are also provided with short-term loans to launch such projects, which are designed to help them feed their families, for many of the participants having been widowed by the various conflicts.

RAWA has plans for future development in all these areas of activity, but as an antifundamentalist, feminist organization, it has not received any support from the United Nations or from nongovernmental organizations (NGOs) working for Afghanistan. The group relies almost entirely on individual supporters from around the world and from income-generating projects such as the various workshops and the sale of publications, cassettes of folk songs, and posters. In terms of the current situation in Afghanistan, the leader of RAWA, Saima Khan, at a meeting of Afghan elders held in Peshawar on 28 January 2003, argued for the disarming of regional warlords as a prerequi-

site for the restoration of peace and prosperity and the bringing to justice of the warlords through a judicial commission.

See also Human Rights Violations
References
http://www.rawa.org

ROBERTS, GEN. SIR FREDERICK (1832–1914)

Frederick Roberts was commander of the Khurran Field Force in the Second Anglo-Afghan War (1878–1880) and was infamous in Afghanistan for his indiscriminate execution of prisoners. Roberts led the invasion of Afghanistan through the Kurram Valley, reaching Kabul on 12 October 1879, which he then controlled after the forced abdication of Yaqub Khan and his exile to India. Following the assassination of the British envoy to the court at Kabul, Sir Pierre Louis Cavagnari, on 3 September 1879, Roberts took command of the Kabul Field Force. He engaged in a number of actions at Charasia, Sharpur, Maiwand, and Kandahar and followed a policy of retribution for aggressive acts committed against British forces or British interests in Afghanistan. He destroyed villages, ordered that no prisoners should be taken, and tried Afghans before a military commission for the attack on the British mission at Kabul, with the result that eighty of the accused were executed for a variety of offenses. These actions were reported by the British press, but Roberts defended himself in official telegrams and accounts of the campaign. Although Ayub Khan had been defeated at Kandahar, the Indian government withdrew its forces from Afghanistan in April 1881 to avoid a repeat of the First Anglo-Afghan War disaster.

See also Second Anglo-Afghan War
References
Forbes, A. 1982. *The Afghan Wars, 1839–42 and 1878–80.* London: Seeley.

ROSHAN

Roshan is a district in northern Badakhshan Province on the left bank of the upper Amu Daria River, with an area of 1,413 square miles and a population of some 6,500 people who are engaged primarily in agriculture. In 1973, the Granville-Gorchakoff Agreement defined the Amu Daria as the northern boundary of Afghanistan, but at the same time, it was not known that Roshan and Shignan included territory on both sides of the Amu Daria

River. The original size of Roshan was reduced as a result of the Durand Agreement of 1893, which brought a compromise, with Afghanistan gaining territory on its side of the river to compensate for land lost across the river. The district lies at a height of 6,000 feet above sea level, has a moderate climate, and contains significant deposits of iron and copper, some of which are mined by the inhabitants. The district is populated by Ghilzais, Pashtuns, Tajiks, and Isma'ilis.

See also Durand Agreement; Granville-Gorchakoff Agreement

References

Adamec, Ludwig W. 1972–1985. Historical and Political Gazetteer of Afghanistan. 6 vols. Graz, Austria: Akademische Druck-u Verlagsansalt.

S

SAADABAD PACT

The Saadabad Pact was concluded in 1937 between Afghanistan, Iran, Iraq, and Turkey. Renewed in 1943, it is also known as the Oriental Entente. The pact was more a gesture acknowledging common interests rather than a treaty with real political significance, though it was seen by the Soviet Union as part of a British plot because Iraq, though independent, was still under British control.

SAFRONCHUK, VASILY S.

Vasily Safronchuk was a Soviet economist and diplomat who was based in Kabul from 25 May 1979 until 1982. Officially, he held the position of counselor envoy of the Soviet embassy in Kabul, but unofficially, he was an adviser to the Afghan Foreign Ministry. He tried, unsuccessfully, to prevent the rift between Nur Muhammad Taraki and Hafizullah Amin (both members of the Khalq faction of the People's Democratic Party of Afghanistan), seeing the solution as the formation of a broad-based national government, which was to include non-Communists. He suggested Nur Ahmed Etemadi, who was in the Pul-i Charkhi prison, as prime minister, but Amin rejected the suggestion, and Etemadi was executed in his cell. After the Soviet withdrawal from Afghanistan in 1989, Safronchuk published articles denying his role and maintaining that his advice was limited to matters relating to the United Nations and international relations.

References
Astute, J. Brice. 1986. *Afghanistan: The First Five Years of Soviet Occupation.* Washington, DC: National Defense University.

SALANG TUNNEL

The Salang Tunnel was opened in 1964, together with an all-weather road over the Hindu Kush range linking Kabul to northern Afghanistan. The tunnel is 1.7 miles long and at an altitude of 11,000 feet; like the highway, it was built by Soviet experts. The highway was one of the routes used by Soviet forces to occupy Afghanistan in December 1978 and was a vital supply line for the Soviet forces and the government in Kabul. As such , it was a constant target for attacks by mujahideen fighters, particularly those led by Ahmad Shah Masood. Masood's forces mounted numerous ambushes along the road, the most notable being the destruction of 70 fuel tankers en route to Kabul in March 1984 and an explosion in the tunnel that killed some 700 Soviet troops and 300 Afghan government forces in October 1984. The Soviets launched a series of unsuccessful attacks against Masood's stronghold in the Panjshir Valley in attempts to undercut the mujahideen leader and secure this vital route to Kabul.

References
Galeotti, Mark. 1995. *Afghanistan, the Soviet Union's Last War.* Portland, OR: Frank Cass.

SALE, GEN. SIR ROBERT HENRY (1782–1845)

Robert Henry Sale was commander of the First Brigade of the Infantry Division of the Bengal Column of the Army of the Indus during the First Anglo-Afghan War (1839 to 1842). He led the advance brigade to Kandahar in April 1839 and captured Ghazni, though not without difficulty. Sale's forces defeated Amir Dost Muhammad at Parwan Darra on 2 November 1840 and forced passage through Khurd Kabul, reaching Jalalabad on 12 November 1841. However, he was unable to withdraw to Kabul when ordered to do so by Gen. Mountstuart Elphinstone, and he remained besieged in Jalalabad until 7 April 1842, when he was relieved by Gen. George Pollock's army of retribution. His command abilities were questionable, and it is clear that he would have surrendered Jalalabad if it had not been for the intervention of two of his officers.

A local Afghan appears at the north entrance after coming out of the Salang Tunnel, 160 kilometers (99.5 miles) north of Kabul, 29 December 2001. The Salang Tunnel, which links Kabul to the northern city of Mazar-i Sharif, was blown up by mujahideen commander Ahmad Shah Masood in 1998 to prevent the Taliban from coming to the north. (AFP/Corbis)

His sally from the town in April 1842 against the forces of Akbar Khan was the result of pressure applied by his officers and was against his better judgment. Sale was a severe disciplinarian and an advocate of harsh floggings for any transgressions by his troops. He returned to India in September 1842.

See also First Anglo-Afghan War; Pollock, Field Marshal Sir George

References
Norris, James A. 1967. *The First Anglo-Afghan War, 1838–42.* London: Cambridge University Press.

SAMANGAN PROVINCE

Samangan Province, in north-central Afghanistan, occupies an area of some 14,640 square miles and has a population of about 180,000 inhabitants. The province is bordered on the west by Jozjan and Balkh Provinces, in the north by the former Soviet Union, in the east by Kunduz and Baghlan, and in the south by Bamian Province. A mainly agricultural region, Samangan relies heavily on irrigation and has suffered badly during recent droughts.

References
Adamec, Ludwig W. 1972–1985. *Political and Historical Gazetteer of Afghanistan.* 6 vols. Graz, Austria: Akademische Druck-u Verlagsansalt.

SARABI, ABDUL WAHID (1926–)

Abdul Wahid Sarabi (or Sorabi) was vice-president of Afghanistan in 1988 and became deputy prime minister and minister of planning in the Khaliqyar government of May 1990. He became vice-president again in May 1991. Sarabi is a Hazara from Ghazni Province and taught economics at Kabul University, where he was dean of the faculty in 1960 and from 1965 to 1966 and deputy rector of the university in 1963. In 1967, he entered government service as minister without portfolio before occupying the post of minister of planning from 1969 to 1973. Sarabi was arrested in 1974 (presumably suspected of plotting against the government) and was out of office and favor until the Saur Revolt of April 1978, which brought the Communists to power. He became minister of irrigation in 1982, minister without portfolio in 1985, and minister of higher education in 1987. He is also a member of the Academy of Sciences and deputy chair of the Committee of Hazara Nationality. However, he has claimed that he was not a member of the People's Democratic Party of Afghanistan (PDPA).

References
Arnold, Anthony. 1983. *Afghanistan's Two-Party Communism: Parcham and Khalq.* Stanford, CA: Hoover Institution Press.

SARAIS

Sarais are man-made structures that were once used as fortifications but are now resting places for travelers. Surrounded by high walls for protection, which are maintained in the frontier areas by tribal chiefs, sarais have watchtowers for use in local skirmishes. The advent of aerial and mechanized warfare has rendered them obsolete as fortifications, and they largely remain to shelter travelers in areas inaccessible to motorized transport. Initially, the sarais existed for garrisons of troops and storage of ammunition, being built at roughly 12-mile intervals along main roads and in major towns. They varied in size, with some of them capable of housing 300 troops and their equipment. The average area occupied by the sarai was from 80 to 100 square yards, and their walls were 20 feet high, 3 feet thick, and equipped with firing platforms. Each sarai had its own potable water supply and was the residence for governors and military officials; it was also used to provide hospitality for distinguished visitors.

References
Szabo, Albert, and Brenda Dyer Szabo. 1991. *Afghanistan: An Atlas of Indigenous Architecture.* Austin: University of Texas Press.

SARWARI, ASADULLAH (1930–)

Asadullah Sarwari was a member of the Khalq faction of the People's Democratic Party of Afghanistan (PDPA) and initially the head of the Afghan Security Service set up by Nur Muhammad Taraki, before being replaced by Asadullah Amin, the nephew of Hafizullah Amin, in October 1979. After Babrak Karmal came to power in December 1979, Sarwari was appointed vice-president and deputy prime minister, but he was quickly made ambassador to Ulan Bator, Mongolia, where he served from 1980 to 1986. In 1981, he was stripped of membership in the PDPA Politburo, and he was ex-

pelled from its Central Committee five years later. Muhammad Najibullah appointed him ambassador to Berlin until 1988 and then to South Yemen in 1989. At the time of the attempted coup by Shanawaz Tanai, the commander-in-chief, against Najibullah, Sarwari was in India, where he was arrested, but Afghanistan's request for extradition was refused. Sarwari was trained in the Soviet Union as a helicopter pilot and was a participant in the 1973 coup staged by Muhammed Daud. After the Saur Revolt of April 1978, he was appointed first deputy prime minister and vice-president of the Revolutionary Council.

See also Afghan Security Service; KHAD
References
Guistozzi, Antonio. 2000. *War, Politics and Society in Afghanistan, 1978–1992.* Washington, DC: Georgetown University Press.

SAUR REVOLT

The Marxist coup of 27 April 1978 was called the Saur Revolt after the Afghan month in which it took place. It brought the Communists to power and heralded eleven years of rule by the People's Democratic Party of Afghanistan (PDPA). Preparations for the revolt had been under way for a number of years after the secret formation of the party in 1965, with sleepers being placed within the bureaucracy and the military. The Khalq faction of the PDPA, under Hafizullah Amin, organized further infiltration within the military, though the Parchami faction also operated in the military through Mir Akbar Khaibar.

Although President Muhammad Daud had repeatedly affirmed his policy of maintaining good relations with the Soviet Union, he also wished for Afghanistan to be a truly nonaligned state. Relations became strained when, on a visit to Moscow in April 1977, Daud refused to alter his policy of employing experts from countries other than the Soviet Union. At the same time, the two wings of the PDPA were having unification talks, which were concluded in July 1977. The Soviet Union was now concerned about the situation in Afghanistan and unwilling to risk losing its investment there, both in terms of finances and in terms of the area's potential as a springboard for future incursions in the Middle East and South Asia. As a result, the PDPA was instructed by Moscow to plan a coup to depose the Daud regime.

The spark for the revolt was the assassination of the Parcham strategist Mir Akbar Khaibar. The killing was thought to have been initiated by the PDPA's Khalq faction, whose members resented Parcham attempts to recruit support in the army, but the PDPA accused the government of responsibility. Khaibar's funeral was followed by a procession that turned into a public demonstration against the government, with a crowd numbering some 15,000. The government arrested the leaders of the demonstration, but three days later, a coup was staged by the military, resulting in the death of President Daud and the members of his family during the storming of the royal palace. The leaders of the PDPA feared Daud, and his execution had been a prime objective of the coup.

The coup resulted in the installation of a Marxist government and a total dependence on the Soviet Union for the next decade. Leaders of the PDPA and members from within the military led the coup, but neither faction of the party had been aware that there were also sleepers within the military and the bureaucracy who were already under the direct control of the Soviet Union; these sleepers only revealed themselves at the time of the coup. Such was the degree of infiltration that the coup was a complete success and met with minimal resistance. Members of the Central Committee of the PDPA were operating under the illusion that they were in control of the relationship with the Soviet Union and that they would be allowed freedom to reconstruct Afghan society. However, the Soviets were not concerned with socioeconomic change. They only sought control over Afghanistan as a reward for their patience and investment over decades.

See also Amin, Hafizullah; Daud, Sardar Muhammad; People's Democratic Party of Afghanistan; Taraki, Nur Muhammad

References

Hammond, Thomas Taylor. 1984. *Red Flag over Afghanistan: The Communist Coup, the Soviet Invasion, and the Consequences.* Boulder, CO: Westview Press.

Ministry of Foreign Affairs. 1984. *Achievements of the April Revolution in Afghanistan.* Kabul: Democratic Republic of Afghanistan, Ministry of Foreign Affairs.

Shahrani, M. Nazif, and Robert L. Caufield. 1984. *Revolutions and Rebellions in Afghanistan.* Berkeley, CA: Institute of International Relations.

SAYYAF, ABDUL RASUL (1946–)

Abdul Rasul Sayyaf was a member of the Islamic Alliance for the Liberation of Afghanistan and was elected as its president in 1980. He was born at Pagham, near Kabul, and graduated from the Hanifa Theological School in 1963 and from the Islamic College of Kabul University in 1967. He then took a post as a teaching assistant at the Shari'a College before going to al-Azhar University in Egypt, where he obtained an M.A. degree in 1972. On his return to Afghanistan, he became an assistant professor at Kabul University. He was arrested in 1974 for political activities and sentenced to five years of imprisonment. He was freed under a general amnesty in 1980 and joined the mujahideen on his release. He did not have a group of his own, which paved the way for his presidency of the alliance of seven mujahideen groups based in Pakistan and recognized by the Pakistan government to receive financial and military support from the United States.

See also Islamic Alliance for the Liberation of Afghanistan

References

Kaplan, Robert D. *Soldiers of God: With the Mujahideen in Afghanistan.* Boston: Houghton Mifflin.

SECOND ANGLO-AFGHAN WAR (1878–1879)

After the debacle of the First Anglo-Afghan War (1839–1842), British policy toward Afghanistan became characterized by inactivity and an ethic of "leaving Afghanistan to the Afghans." However, the situation ultimately changed, largely because of pressure from some quarters to counter Russian moves in Central Asia. Since the first conflict, British influence had extended to the passes leading into Afghanistan and was accompanied by the construction of railway lines and telegraph lines. In addition, the British India army had been reequipped with breech-loading rifles, whereas the Afghan army was still equipped with muzzle-loading rifles.

The ruler of Afghanistan from 1863 was Shir Ali, a son of Amir Dost Muhammad. Shir Ali had succeeded to the throne after a bitter struggle with his rivals, but it was not until 1869 that he gained British recognition. He was invited to meet Lord Mayo, the viceroy of India, at Ambala in the same year, and at that meeting, the amir raised his concerns about Russian advances in Central Asia. Shir Ali wanted British guarantees of help in the event of Russian aggression; further, in order to secure the future of his dynasty, he sought Britain's recognition of his son Abdullah Jan as crown prince and his successor. However, the amir's requests were not acceded to, and Shir Ali was merely given a gift of 600,000 rupees and a few pieces of artillery.

Tensions rose between Afghanistan and Britain when the Russian governor of Tashkent, Gen. Konstantin Petrovich Kaufman, made overtures to the amir and again when these tentative contacts were followed up with the uninvited arrival of General Stolietoff at Kabul on 22 July 1878, charged with concluding a treaty with Afghanistan. The British India government viewed these developments with alarm, and a decision was taken to send Gen. Neville Chamberlain on a military mission to Kabul. He was to be accompanied by 1,000 troops supplied by the autonomous frontier tribes, but the mission was prevented from crossing the border into Afghanistan by Afghan forces.

The move by the Afghans prompted the India government to issue an ultimatum, and this was followed up by the dispatch of a British force under Gen. Frederick Roberts, which arrived at Kabul on 24 July 1878. The amir fled to northern Afghanistan to seek support from the Russians, but no assistance was forthcoming, and he died of natural causes in Mazar-i Sharif on 21 February 1879. In the amir's absence, Britain had recognized his son Yaqub Khan as the new ruler, with the price of this support being the signing of the Treaty of Gandomak on 26 May 1879. This document restored friendly relations between the two countries, but Afghanistan had to agree that its foreign policy would not be at variance with British interests. Consequently, many Afghans regarded this treaty as a capitulation. The British Indian government appointed Pierre Louis Cavagnari as envoy to Kabul, but he was assassinated, together with all of his staff, by mutinous Afghan troops on 3 September 1879.

This move was a signal for armed resistance to break out at other locations where British troops were stationed, and despite British attempts to put down these uprisings, the action intensified. The critical event in the war was the Battle of Maiwand on 27 July 1880, during which a British force under Gen. G. R. S. Burrows was totally routed by Afghan troops and tribal forces. The survivors withdrew to Kandahar to join the garrison there, which then came under siege and was not relieved until 1 September 1879 when British forces defeated the Afghan army under Ayub Khan.

However, the British India government regarded the Battle of Maiwand as a sound reason for disentangling itself from conflict in Afghanistan, fearing a debacle similar to the First Anglo-Afghan War. It therefore recognized Abdur Rahman as amir of Afghanistan and was able to withdraw its forces across the border into India. The war could not, in any way, be counted as a British success: casualties were high, with about 40,000 dead or wounded, including camp followers, and at least 1,000 troops were lost at Maiwand. In addition, the operation represented a significant economic burden for the Indian government, for the cost of the operation was £19.5 million and the British taxpayers picked up only the costs of the original estimate, £5 million. The action was not supported by a significant number of the viceroy's advisers and ministers, who saw it as an economic drain and a serious depletion of the troops needed to guarantee the peace in India.

See also Ambala Conference; Gandomak, Treaty of; Maiwand, Battle of; Shir Ali, Amir; Yaqub Khan, Amir Muhammad

References
Cardew, F. G. 1908. *The Second Afghan War, 1878–80.* London: J. Murray.
Heathcote, T. A. *The Afghan Wars, 1839–1919.* London: Osprey.

SECRET OF THE NATION (SIRR-I-MILLI)

Secret of the Nation was a covert organization that was involved in a plot to mount a coup against Amir Habibullah in 1909, with the objective of setting up a republican government. The campaign was waged largely through letters to the amir, which threatened retribution unless his style of government was changed. It is thought that the organization was headed by Maulawi Muhammad Sarwar Wasif, a native of Kandahar, and Dr. Abdul Ghani, an Indian Muslim and head of Habibia School in Kabul. Habibia was an Islamic institution of higher education, and the students proved to be willing recruits to the organization. Abdul Ghani was arrested, accused of implication in the plot to assassinate Amir Habibullah, and remained in prison until 1919 when King Amanullah became ruler of Afghanistan.

See also Habibullah, Amir

References

Adamec, Ludwig, W. *Afghanistan 1900–1923: A Diplomatic History.* Berkeley: University of California Press.

11 SEPTEMBER 2001

On 11 September 2001, groups of terrorists hijacked four passenger jets on domestic flights in the United States, crashing two of them into the twin towers of the World Trade Center in New York City and one into the Pentagon building in Washington, D.C. The fourth hijacked aircraft failed in its objective and crashed in Pennsylvania—a crash that was later discovered to have been caused by a struggle between the passengers and the terrorists. The death toll of the multiple attacks was just under 4,000, and the site of the World Trade Center was so badly destroyed that it became known as Ground Zero.

The victims of the attack were mainly Americans, including emergency personnel trying to rescue trapped victims, but there were a large number of British nationals among the victims as well; in fact, an estimated eighty countries lost nationals as a result of these attacks. The whole sequence of events was captured by tourist camcorders and broadcast around the world, giving the tragedy a global dimension. The world was shocked at the scale and the impact of the hijackings, and there was a general sense that the world would never be the same again. The United States also had to come to terms with the fact that it was not immune to terrorist attacks, as had been experienced elsewhere in the world.

The tragedy of 11 September and its immediate aftermath was played out before the world's media, and it was to have a major impact within the United States and throughout the world. However, the main concern in the present context is the relationship of the events to the situation in Afghanistan and, in particular, the role played by Osama bin Laden and the al-Qaeda network. The nature of the atrocity and the nationality of the hijackers led to an immediate suspicion that bin Laden and his followers were behind the operation. Initially, this belief was bolstered by bin Laden's involvement in previous attacks against the United States and U.S. interests abroad, particularly the abortive attack on the World Trade Center in 1993, the bombing of the U.S. embassies in Kenya and Tanzania in 1998, and the attack on the USS *Cole* in Aden in October 2000. There is also strong evidence that al-Qaeda was behind operations against U.S. forces in Somalia, as well as bomb attacks on U.S. military facilities in Saudi Arabia.

Evidence for al-Qaeda's involvement was largely based on statements made by Osama bin Laden prior to and immediately after the attacks. In June 2001, he had told supporters that it was time to assault America and Israel where it would hurt them the most, and this pronouncement was followed by a report by the Middle East Broadcasting Center quoting al-Qaeda supporters as forecasting a severe blow to U.S. and Israeli forces in the immediate future. A warning had also been issued to leading al-Qaeda members around the world to return to Afghanistan by 10 September 2001, and rumors circulated among bin Laden's supporters that 11 September was to be a major day of action.

The impact of the terrorist attack on the United States and the sheer magnitude of the atrocity led President George W. Bush to declare the War on Terror. As investigations proceeded into the hijackings, more evidence of the involvement of bin Laden and al-Qaeda surfaced. It became clear that the detailed planning for the attacks had been undertaken by close associates of bin Laden, that al-Qaeda personnel in Europe had been activated, and that the flight training for the hijackers, which took place in the United States, was funded by al-Qaeda, as were all other aspects of the operation. Dossiers were produced by the U.S. administration and the British government, largely based on intelligence reports, demonstrating the involvement of bin Laden and his followers. Evidence was also presented by the U.S. administration to the North Atlantic Treaty Organization (NATO), which found the information compelling; in response, NATO invoked Article 5 of its founding treaty, which declared the attack on the United States to be an attack on NATO itself.

As a result of previous terrorist attacks against the United States, Osama bin Laden had already been placed on the list of the ten most wanted fugitives of the Federal Bureau of Investigation (FBI), with a reward of $5 million offered for his arrest or conviction. Meanwhile, the U.S. Congress had given President Bush powers to pursue the parties behind the atrocity, including the use of military force, and the administration began to take measures against the al-Qaeda network. However, the administration was extremely careful to try to ensure that public reaction was directed not against Arab Americans and

The site of the World Trade Towers in New York, destroyed in an attack on 11 September 2001 (US Air Force)

Muslims in general but specifically against the real perpetrators, wherever they might be.

The administration invoked a number of security measures, particularly at airports, but in terms of al-Qaeda, the first actions were directed against its access to funds. On 24 September 2001, the U.S. government announced a series of measures aimed at trying to cut off al-Qaeda's access to funds for its operations. A freeze was immediately placed on the U.S.-based assets and transactions of individuals and groups with alleged links to terrorist activities, and international banks were advised that assets and transactions would be frozen if they refused to cooperate in the antiterrorist campaign. A prohibition order was also made on transactions with groups believed to be linked to bin Laden and the al-Qaeda network and on donations to nonprofit organizations suspected of providing funds to terrorist organizations. The Foreign Terrorist Asset Tracking Center was also established to track down sources of funding for terrorist organizations. However, such moves would not cut off funds entirely but only re-

strict them and cause al-Qaeda to rely more heavily on cash transactions, which would be almost impossible to trace.

The Bush administration had stated that its response would be directed not only against the terrorists responsible for the 11 September attacks but also against states that harbored them. Attention therefore centered on Afghanistan and specifically the Taliban regime because of its close links with Osama bin Laden and al-Qaeda fighters operating in Afghanistan. The United States had already attempted to destroy al-Qaeda training camps in 1998 through the use of Cruise missiles, but those sorties were considered to have been of little military value. Further, the United Nations had also been putting pressure on the Taliban regime, passing resolutions demanding that it cease providing sanctuary and training facilities for terrorists and that Osama bin Laden be handed over for due judicial process in a country where he had been indicted. The failure of the Taliban to respond to these resolutions had already led to the imposition of a range of sanctions beginning on 14 November 1999, which included a freeze on the funds of bin Laden and his associates.

In the immediate aftermath of 11 September, it was evident that the Bush administration was committing itself to a long-term, open-ended campaign against international terrorism, and the nature of the conflict, the initial military targets, and its objectives became the subject of debate within the administration. Two contrasting views manifested themselves within the administration. On one hand, the Department of Defense and Deputy Defense Secretary Paul Wolfowitz advocated a broad campaign, including the overthrow of regimes suspected of harboring and supporting terrorists, with the Taliban and Iraqi regimes identified as possible targets. It was argued that such a policy would ensure that terrorists were denied any safe haven, and it would deliver a message that would deter other regimes that might consider sponsoring terrorism. On the other hand, the State Department, under Secretary of State Colin Powell, adopted a more cautious approach and advocated a limited and targeted use of force, with an emphasis on the need to build a broad-based international coalition. It was argued that the removal of the Taliban regime as a military objective could entangle the United States in the internal strife of Afghanistan, with no guarantee as to the final outcome.

The Bush administration made it clear that initial military action would be restricted to the capture of Osama bin Laden and the defeat of the al-Qaeda network. This policy was announced by the president to a joint session of Congress on 20 September 2001, but Bush made it plain that the operation would not end until every global terrorist group had been stopped and defeated. The Pentagon code-named the military campaign against terrorism Operation Enduring Freedom, and Congress voted $40 billion of extra funding to cover any military response to the attacks of 11 September, as well as national security needs. At a press briefing on 25 September 2001, the U.S. secretary of defense, Donald Rumsfeld, made it plain that the campaign would involve a sustained effort over a long period of time.

Initially, it was thought that actions against Afghanistan would consist of selective air and missile strikes, together with raids by U.S. and UK Special Forces. However, a major problem regarding the use of such strikes was the difficulty in identifying really worthwhile military targets in a country denigrated by ten years of Soviet occupation and civil war. Obvious targets would be air bases housing the small air force of the Taliban at Kabul and Kandahar in the south of Afghanistan, Shindand and Herat in the west, and Mazar-i Sharif and Kunduz in the north and northeast. Other targets would be the army bases and training camps at Qargah and Rishkor just outside Kabul and Deh Dadi near Mazar-i Sharif. The U.S. decision to remove the Taliban regime and to destroy the al-Qaeda network in Afghanistan was supported by the United Kingdom, both politically and militarily, and also by the Pakistan government, which had broken with the Taliban and indicated its support for the War on Terror. As an outcome, the United States and United Kingdom formed the mainstay of a coalition designed to overthrow the Taliban regime, destroy al Qaeda, and bring Osama bin Laden to justice.

See also Coalition Air Campaign against the Taliban; Coalition Land Campaign against the Taliban; Laden, Osama bin; al-Qaeda; Taliban

References
"Blowback." 2001. *Jane's Intelligence Review* (August): 42–49.
http://www.bbc.co.uk/news, 20 September 2001
http://www.defenselink.mil
http://www.pm.gov.uk/news-asp?NewsId=2601
http://www.whitehouse.gov

SEWWUM-I-AQRAB

Sewwum-i-Aqrab is the Afghan date for a series of demonstrations held on 25 October 1965, mounted by a leftist group of students protesting against a secret session of parliament considering a vote of confidence in the government of Muhammad Yusuf. The troops lost control of the crowds when the students started throwing stones and opened fire, killing three students and wounding countless more. This incident brought about the resignation of the Yusuf government and became a rallying cry of the Left in Afghanistan.

References
Dupree, Louise. 1980. *Afghanistan.* Princeton, NJ: Princeton University Press.

SHAFIQ, MUHAMMAD MUSA (1930–1978)

Muhammad Musa Shafiq had a distinguished legal career in Afghanistan, becoming director-general of the Legislative Department in the Ministry of Justice and teaching at the College of Law and Political Science at Kabul University. He also opened the first private law firm in Afghanistan, in 1961. He had been born in 1930 in Kabul and was educated at an elementary *madrasa* (Islamic school) and a state primary school in Kabul before going to Egypt, then to Columbia University in New York City, where he studied Islamic law and comparative law.

Between 1963 and 1966, he served as deputy minister in the Ministry of Justice, had a major role in the drafting of a new constitution, and participated in the Loya Jirga (Great Council) that adopted it. He was also an adviser to the Ministry of Foreign Affairs from 1966 to 1968 and then became ambassador to Cairo. In the period between 1970 and 1973, he was an active lobbyist for drought relief from abroad, while occupying the post of foreign minister in 1971 and prime minister from 1971 to the time of the coup led by Muhammad Daud in 1973. In that year, he was the leading figure in the negotiations to secure the Helmand Water Agreement with Iran. He was arrested in July 1973 for opposing President Daud and placed under house arrest until 1976.

Shafiq was also a writer in Dari and Pashtu, producing numerous short stories and poems for various newspapers and journals. It was reported that he was executed in May 1978.

References

Ahmad, N. D. 1990. *The Survival of Afghanistan: A Diplomatic History with an Analytic and Reflective Approach.* Lahore, Pakistan: Institute of Islamic Culture.

SHI'A MUJAHIDEEN GROUPS

The majority of the Shi'a people of Afghanistan live in the Hazarajat region, and in February 1979, they rose against the Marxist regime in Kabul. By the end of the year, control of the region had passed to the mujahideen under the Revolutionary Council of Islamic Unity of Afghanistan, which established a government in the region, set up an administration, and levied taxes on the population. The dominant group in the administration was the Shura (Council), but in 1983, the emergent radical Islamist groups challenged its supremacy. The main opposition was led by the Guardians of the Islamic Revolution, whose adherents followed the teaching of the Iranian Ayatollah Khomeini, and they allied themselves with Sheikh Mir Husain

Sadeqi of Nasr to rid the Hazarajat of the Shura. A number of other radical Shi'a groups were also active in the region, such as the Union of Islamic Fighters, which controlled small enclaves within the area. In 1987, the various groups came together as the Council of Islamic Alliance, joined by the Shura in 1988; the alliance reformed in 1990 as the Party of Islamic Unity of Afghanistan, led by Abdul Ali Mazari and then, following his assassination, by Karim Khalili. However, unity was impossible to achieve, and there was ongoing rivalry between the traditionalists, the Islamic groups, and the radical Islamists, all competing for the leadership. With the rise of the Taliban in September 1996, the Islamic Unity Party and the Uzbeks led by Gen. Abdul Rashid Dostum were the only real opposition to the new regime, but initially, Dostum supported the Taliban government.

See also Dostum, Gen. Abdul Rashid; Guardians of the Islamic Revolution

References

Roy, Olivier. 1998. "Has Islamism a Future in Afghanistan?" In *Fundamentalism Reborn? Afghanistan and the Taliban,* edited by William Maley, 199–211. London: Hurst.

SHINWARI TRIBE

The Shinwaris are members of a Pashtun tribe who migrated to the Nangarhar area in the sixteenth century. The tribe has a reputation for its fighting capabilities, and members of one of its four divisions, the Alisher Khel, live in Pakistan, having been separated from the rest of the tribe by the Durand Line (drawn up by Britain to demarcate the frontier between Afghanistan and British India). The tribespeople have been intimately involved in conflicts in the region for centuries. They accompanied Mahmud of Ghazni in his invasions of India in the eleventh century, fought against the British in three Anglo-Afghan wars, and were active in rebellions against Amir Abdur Rahman in 1882 over management of the road that passed through their territory to British-controlled Dakka. In 1883, Ghilan Haidar Khan was sent to quell the tribe, having successfully defeated the Mangals. However, in 1888, their raiding commenced again, and sporadic operations continued throughout 1889. They also formed part of the coalition that overthrew King Amanullah in 1928. In a manifesto released by the Shinwari leaders

Muhammad Alam and Muhammad Afzal in November 1928, known as the Shinwari Manifesto, they detailed their grievances against King Amanullah. In effect, this pronouncement amounted to a declaration of war and was an attack on the legal and social reforms of Amanullah, which included recommending monogamy, eliminating the purdah, and allowing cinemas and theaters in Kabul. The military actions of the Shinwaris enabled Habibullah Kalakani to capture and claim the Afghan throne. The tribe inhabits the area between the Khugianis of Jalalabad and the Afridis of the Khyber range.

See also Amanullah, King

References

Bellew, H. W. 1880. *The Races of Afghanistan: Being a Brief Account of the Principal Nations Inhabiting That Country.* London: Thaker.

Wild, Roland. 1933. *Amanullah: Ex-King of Afghanistan.* London: Hurst and Blackett.

SHIR ALI, AMIR (?–1879)

Shir Ali was one of the sons of Amir Dost Muhammad and ruled Afghanistan from 1863 to 1866 and again from 1868 to 1869. However, his periods of rule were characterized by a constant power struggle with his brothers, who held positions as governors of provinces in the country. His position was not really secured until 1869 when he traveled to India to obtain guarantees from the British of protection against Russian aggression and recognition of succession for his son. However, the viceroy of India was not prepared to meet his requests and instead gave Shir Ali a gift of money and some pieces of artillery but no promises of military or political support. As a direct consequence of this rejection, the amir decided to listen to overtures from Russia, which sent General Stolietoff to Kabul on 22 July 1878 to provide backing for the Afghan state. The moves alarmed the British Indian government. Britain tried to send a representative to Kabul, but he was refused entry; an ultimatum was then issued by the British Indian government, followed by the invasion of a British army. The resultant conflict was the Second Anglo-Afghan War.

The amir had left Kabul for the north, leaving his son Yaqub in charge to try to seek support from the Russians. But the amir was advised by the Russians to make peace with Britain. Shir Ali died of natural causes at Mazar-i Sharif on 21 February 1879 and was succeeded by Yaqub, who was defeated by the British. Abdur Rahman was recognized by Britain as the new amir. During his short period of rule, Shir Ali had initiated a modest program of reforms. He had established an advisory council to assist with the governance of the state, tried to model his army along European lines, set up a state postal system, abolished the feudal system of tax farming, and published the first newspaper in Afghanistan, called *Sun of the Day* (*Shams al-Nahar*).

See also Second Anglo-Afghan War

References

Gregorian, Vartan. 1969. *The Emergence of Modern Afghanistan: Politics, Reform and Modernization, 1880–1946.* Stanford, CA: Stanford University Press.

SHUJA, SHAH (C. 1792–1842)

Shah Shuja-ul-Mulk was the seventh son of Timur Shah and was born around 1792, becoming governor of Peshawar in 1801 during the reign of his brother, Shah Zaman. In 1802, he captured Kabul, imprisoned his brother Mahmud, and seized the throne, proclaiming himself amir. However, Mahmud effected his escape with the assistance of Dost Muhammad, the amir of Afghanistan from 1820 to 1838 and again from 1842 to 1863.

In 1809, Shah Shuja received a British mission under Mountstuart Elphinstone and secured British support for his position as amir. He also concluded a treaty of alliance, which guaranteed British intervention in the event Afghanistan was subjected to an unprovoked attack, particularly from France or Persia. In the same year, Fath Khan and Mahmud captured Kandahar and moved on Kabul, defeating Shah Shuja at Gandomak. The following year, he was forced to flee to India, where he spent nearly thirty years in exile. On his journey to India, he had to pass through the Sikh territory controlled by Ranjit Singh, who took from him the Koh-Nur diamond, now part of the British crown jewels.

Internal unrest within Afghanistan saw the Sadozai princes locked in an internecine struggle that allowed Dost Muhammad, the first Muhammadzai ruler, to come to power, marking the end of the Sadozai dynasty. In 1839, British India was still concerned about its northern frontiers and wanted to ensure that a friendly regime controlled Afghanistan; it was concerned as well about the apparent negotiations between the Russians and Dost

Muhammad, who was also unwilling to drop his claim to Peshawar. The viceroy of India, Lord Auckland, decided to strike an alliance with the leader of the Sikhs, the aforementioned Ranjit Singh, and wanted to restore Shah Shuja to the throne. However, the Sikhs were unwilling to risk troops in any venture into Afghanistan, and it was left to the British to invade the country in 1839, thus beginning the First Anglo-Afghan War.

The British returned Shah Shuja to the throne, but he was never supported by the Afghan people and was only able to rule with British protection. However, the British presence in Afghanistan was itself tenuous, and an uprising in Kabul led to the death of British representative Alexander Burnes, the ignominious retreat of the British army, and its total destruction during the retreat from Kabul. Shah Shuja himself was captured by Afghan militia forces and killed by Shiya-ud-Daula, a leader of a Barakzai clan, on 3 April 1842. Thereafter, the throne was again assumed by Amir Dost Muhammad, who was recognized by the British as ruler.

See also Burnes, Alexander; First Anglo-Afghan War
References
Heathcote, T. A. 1980. *The Afghan Wars, 1839–1919*. London: Osprey.
Poullada, Leon B. *Reform and Rebellion in Afghanistan, 1929–1973*. Omaha: University of Nebraska, Omaha.

SIMLA MANIFESTO (1838)

Also known as the Tripartite Agreement or the Treaty of Simla, the Simla Manifesto was signed on 16 July 1838 between Ranjit Singh, ruler of the Sikh nation in the Punjab; Shah Shuja, the exiled king of Afghanistan; and the British government. The agreement was reached in order to determine future relations between the parties once Shah Shuja had been restored to the throne as a result of this alliance, which also required the Afghans to recognize the independence of the Sikh nation from Afghanistan. This agreement was, in effect, a declaration of war against Amir Dost Muhammad, who did not respond to the manifesto. Afghanistan was invaded in 1839 by the British army. The Sikh ruler had not committed any forces to the operation and thus avoided the disaster that faced the British in the conflict that ensued—the First Anglo-Afghan War.

See also Dost Muhammad, Amir; First Anglo-Afghan War

References
Noelle, Christin. 1997. *State and Tribe in Nineteenth-Century Afghanistan: The Reign of Amir Dost Muhammad Khan*. London: Curzon.

SOVIET WAR IN AFGHANISTAN

The Soviet military intervention in Afghanistan in the 1970s and 1980s was aimed at supporting the Marxist government in Kabul, which, under Hafizullah Amin, was crumbling and in danger of collapse. The intervention began on 25 December 1979, lasted for ten years, and proved to be a disaster for the Soviet forces, who found themselves drawn into a guerrilla war that they were not equipped to wage. Ultimately, they were forced to withdraw, having sustained heavy casualties and failed in their mission.

The Communists had come to power in Afghanistan on 27 April 1978 following the Saur Revolt, which had been led by left-wing politicians and backed by sympathetic military personnel, most of whom had received training in the Soviet Union. The coup resulted in the assassination of President Muhammad Daud and his family and the rise to power of Nur Muhammad Taraki. The new government introduced a program of land distribution, the dismantling of the traditional Afghan social structure, and the emancipation of women, but it ran into immediate opposition and armed resistance. A revolt had already broken out in Herat and was savagely put down, with the loss of some 5,000 lives, including about 100 Soviet advisers, and the army began to disintegrate as the regime purged the officer corps.

In September 1979, Hafizullah Amin, the Afghan prime minister, seized power, and Taraki was summarily executed. However, the leadership change did not bring stability; indeed, opposition to the regime intensified. Large sections of the armed forces defected to the resistance, and by the end of 1979, the army's strength had been reduced from 90,000 to 40,000, brought about by the combination of defections, desertions, purges, and executions. The result was that the new regime was spinning out of control: it was in danger of complete collapse and of falling out of the Soviet sphere of influence. Taraki had already appealed for Soviet assistance in March 1979, but his pleas went unanswered, and it was not until near the end of the year that the Soviet Politburo approved intervention as a temporary

A young Soviet soldier carries an AK-47 rifle on a busy shopping street in Kabul. (Patrick Robert/Corbis)

measure to stabilize the Kabul regime and to prevent its defeat by the mujahideen.

The Soviets followed an improved version of an invasion plan that had been successfully used in other stability operations within the Soviet bloc, as in Czechoslovakia in 1968. The plan involved the establishment of an in-country presence to assist the invasion force. In August 1979, prior to the actual intervention, Gen. Ivan G. Pavloski led a group of sixty officers on a reconnaissance tour of Afghanistan to assess the situation and to conclude invasion plans. The initial Soviet objective was to capture strategic targets such as major airfields, key government buildings, and communication facilities and to win control of the major towns and lines of communication.

Soviet forces began moving into Afghanistan on 24 December 1979, Christmas Eve, which meant that Western governments were not geared up for an immediate reaction. Soviet advisers who had been brought in after the Saur Revolt disabled equipment, blocked arms stores, and sabotaged any attempts at a coordinated response from the Afghan military. The Salang Pass and Salang Tunnel were seized by the Spetsnaz, or special forces, to protect the route for Soviet troops, and airborne troops seized airfields (such as the Bagram air base) and critical government facilities in Kabul. Spetsnaz forces killed Hafizullah Amin, the leader of the Khalq faction of the People's Democratic Party of Afghanistan and president of Afghanistan in 1979, in order to set up a puppet government under Babrak Karmal, and the invading Soviet troops very quickly subdued small pockets of Afghan military resistance. The initial aspects of the occupation were a complete success, and the government in Moscow expected resistance to end at that point.

However, like previous invaders, the Soviets had rashly miscalculated the situation in Afghanistan. They did not foresee that the Afghans' traditional values, their Islamic faith, and their love of freedom—even from central control in Kabul—would only intensify the resistance to the Soviet incursion. It had been expected that the Soviet military would prevail: after all, they must have had extensive knowledge of Afghanistan, since they had had a presence in the country from the 1950s, had built many of the airfields, and had constructed the road network and the Salang Tunnel. The occupation was based on the concept of stabilizing the country by occupying and holding key objectives, while allowing Afghan forces to mount counterinsurgency measures. The Soviets planned to provide logistic, air, artillery, and intelligence support for Afghan forces operating in the countryside but have only minimal contact with the local population themselves. A further prime objective was to keep Soviet casualties to a minimum and to strengthen the Afghan military to defeat the mujahideen in order to allow for a prompt Soviet withdrawal.

The occupation was expected to last a few months, but in the end, it endured for ten years. In the process, the Soviets probably had about 40,000 men killed in action, and a further number were murdered, committed suicide, became dependent on drugs, or suffered from a variety of diseases. Afghan casualties were between 1.5 and 2 million dead, with 5 million fleeing Afghanistan as refugees and another 2 million becoming internal refugees. In purely economic terms, it was estimated that the war cost the Soviet economy some $8 billion a year for each of the ten years.

The Soviet military had been prepared to fight a conventional war, using tactics and operational plans that a modern army would have used elsewhere in the world. These tactics involved the use of massive firepower from fixed-wing aircraft, helicopter gunships, and artillery, with rocket attacks and tanks preceding any infantry advances. The Soviets believed that such assaults would either destroy their ill-equipped opponents or cause them to flee in terror across the borders with Iran or Pakistan. However, the mujahideen came from a traditional warrior society and proved to be a highly resourceful and implacable enemy. They were adept at temporarily withdrawing in the face of Soviet assaults and returning later to strike at exposed units of the enemy. The harsh and inhospitable terrain and the reaction of the people who opposed and obstructed the Soviets at every turn did not help the position of the Soviet military on the ground.

Despite the size of the Soviet commitment, which varied in strength from 90,000 to 104,000 troops operating on a rotational basis, the invading force was strained to provide some level of security throughout the main towns in the twenty-nine provinces and could not extend its control to the thousands of villages or any but the main lines of communication. In addition, Soviet forces found it extremely difficult to develop a methodology to cope with guerrilla warfare. The inability to win the war condemned the force to a slow process of bloodletting, which adversely affected the morale of the troops. Officially, the number of Soviet deaths was put at 15,000 but could have been as high as 40,000, and beyond that, some 400,000 troops were wounded or contracted diseases such as hepatitis and typhoid.

The Soviets were extremely slow to adopt new tactics to cope with the terrain and the strategies of the mujahideen, and by the time the command decided to use troops for close combat and mopping-up operations, it was too late. The soldiers preferred to stay with the relative safety of their armored carriers and to call on air strikes and artillery rather than fight an enemy that did not seem to know the meaning of defeat. The situation was not helped by the fact that the mujahideen refused to fight a conventional war and continued to deploy their effective guerrilla tactics. One such tactic was to disrupt the roads and pipelines essential to the supply chain of Soviet forces; despite destroying villages and adopting a scorched-earth policy, the Soviet forces could not break the morale of the mujahideen.

The mujahideen forces improved their sources of supplies from Iran and Pakistan, and the latter also channeled covert aid from the U.S. Central Intelligence Agency (CIA). In addition, they captured equipment from Soviet and Afghan government forces and from a steady stream of Afghan deserters. The Soviets used helicopter gunships to great advantage, but the guerrillas soon adapted by operating at night or by using intelligence reports to provide air defense ambushes and setting up protective bunkers. Eventually, the mujahideen received Stinger missiles through the CIA, and these were deployed to great effect by the resistance forces, such that the Afghans began to win the war against the Soviets and the government forces of Babrak Karmal. The toll on Soviet equipment was also high, with estimates showing the loss of some 118 jets, 330 helicopters, 147 tanks, large numbers of armored personnel carriers, and, significantly, some 12,000 supply trucks.

The Soviet military was never able to field full-strength forces because disease cut heavily into troop numbers, largely due to poor sanitation in the field and a poor diet. Even when they were able to mount a well-resourced operation, the Soviets were never completely successful, as evidenced by a least ten major assaults on the stronghold of Ahmad Shah Masood in the Panjshir Valley, which never succeeded in dislodging the guerrillas from their stronghold. Moreover, the Soviet uniforms and equipment were designed for a European theater of war and did not suit the terrain, so the troops were never as agile as their mujahideen opposition and were unable to catch opposition forces in the mountainous terrain.

It was evident that the morale of the Soviet forces had deteriorated with the length of the occupation, even as that of the mujahideen continued to grow. In addition, soldiers, particularly in the noncombat areas, were exposed to the narcotics trade, and a great deal of Soviet equipment ended up in mujahideen hands, having been sold by troops to fund their drug habits. Soviet effectiveness was also hampered by political and domestic problems within the Soviet Union and the attitude of the population at home to an unpopular war. The casualties inflicted, the problem of narcotics, and the stories relayed by rotating troops led to draft dodging, and returning troops were spurned by the population rather than being welcomed as heroes.

The Soviet Union had intimated in 1982 that it would consider a withdrawal from Afghanistan under certain conditions, and UN-sponsored talks were held at Geneva, lasting until 1988. The talks were primarily between Afghanistan and Pakistan and focused on ending interference in the internal affairs of Afghanistan, but they also involved the United States and the Soviet Union. An accord was signed between Afghanistan and Pakistan, guaranteeing noninterference and nonintervention in each other's affairs; a similar agreement was signed between the United States and the Soviet Union, both of which promised nonintervention in Afghanistan and consented to act as guarantors of the accords. These accords paved the way for a Soviet withdrawal from Afghanistan, which was completed in February 1989.

However, the accords failed because the mujahideen had not been represented at Geneva, and the Soviet-backed regime in Afghanistan did not immediately collapse. The Soviets left behind a considerable supply of weaponry and promised to continue providing supplies under the 1978 Treaty of Friendship. Although the United States was supposed to cease supplying the mujahideen, the agreement eventually reached between the two superpowers was that each reserved the right to send supplies in response to shipments made by the other side. The outcome was that both powers continued to supply arms to the opposing sides, and Pakistan continued to allow the passage of arms through its territory. Consequently, a civil war continued in Afghanistan, although the Soviets had succeeded in disentangling themselves from a campaign that was causing a financial drain, political unrest at home, and heavy casualties without any success in stabilizing the Kabul regime.

See also Afghan-Soviet Relations; Amin, Hafizullah; Central Intelligence Agency and Its Support for the Mujahideen; Geneva Accords; Inter-Services Intelligence Service; Masood, Ahmad Shah; Mujahideen; Saur Revolt; Taraki, Nur Muhammad

References
Alexiev, Alexander. 1988. *Inside the Soviet Army in Afghanistan.* Santa Monica, CA: Rand Corporation.
Bocharov, G. 1990. *Russian Roulette: Afghanistan through Russian Eyes.* New York: Hamish Hamilton.
Brigot, Andre, and Olivier Roy. 1988. *The War in Afghanistan: An Account and Analysis of the Country, Its People, Soviet Intervention and the Resistance.* New York: Harvester-Wheatsheaf.
Cordovez, Diego, and Selig S. Harrison. 1995. *Out of Afghanistan: The Inside Story of the Soviet Withdrawal.* New York: Oxford University Press.
Galeotti, Mark. 1995. *Afghanistan, the Soviet Union's Last War.* Portland, OR: Frank Cass.
Rogers, Tom. 1992. *The Soviet Withdrawal from Afghanistan: Analysis and Chronology.* Westport, CT: Greenwood Press.
Saikal, Amin, and William Maley. 1989. *The Soviet Withdrawal from Afghanistan.* Cambridge and New York: Cambridge University Press.

T

TAIMARIS

The Taimaris are the largest of the Chahar Aimaq tribes in Afghanistan and occupy the hilly regions in the southeast of Herat, an area of some 12,000 square miles. The tribe has a large nucleus of Pathan origin, and at one point in the eighteenth century, the Taimaris controlled Farah and Sabzawar, a move made possible by the breakup of the Safavid monarchy. However, this independence ended in 1730 when Nadir Shah's forces defeated the Taimaris but granted Jafir Kali the governorship of the lands that he had held. Some 12,000 families were deported to Persia, the majority of whom returned after Nadir Shah was assassinated in 1747.

The tribe members are mainly involved in agriculture, raising cattle and sheep, and there tends to be an absence of real conflict between them and other tribes in the area, including the nomads who use the hills for grazing. However, following the rule of Ahmad Shah Durrani, the tribe came under closer government control, and the Afghans began to interface with Taimari politics. They took little interest in the general politics of Afghanistan, with their concerns being centered on the situation in Herat and Farah, but their power and presence waned toward the end of the nineteenth century as more and more Afghanis settled in their territory and took their lands, causing extensive migration of families into Persia.

See also Chahar Aimaqs; Jamshidi Tribe
References
Clifford, Mary Louis. 1973. *The Land and People of Afghanistan*. Philadelphia: Lippincott.

TAJIKS

The Tajiks are the second largest ethnic group in Afghanistan, are generally Dari-speakers, and number about 5 million; most are Sunni Muslims, but there are some members of the Isma'ilis Shi'a sect, living in the mountainous areas of Badakhshan Province. The Tajiks are from the ancient population of Khorasan and Sistan, whose economy was based on trade. Although found all over Afghanistan, the Tajiks are concentrated in western, northern, and northeastern Afghanistan. The stronghold of the Tajiks is the Panjshir Valley region north of Kabul, but they are also found to the north in the country of Tajikistan, formerly part of the Soviet Union. Tajik society is not organized on a tribal basis; instead, communities usually take on themselves the name of the valley or region in which they live, such as Panjshiris. The economies of Tajik communities are largely based on agriculture, with families being farmers or herders, and the valley communities often move to the mountains in the summer to harvest crops such as wheat and melons.

The Tajiks have frequently migrated to the cities, especially Kabul until it was declared a Pashtun capital in 1776 by Amir Timur. As a community in urban areas, they tend to be better educated, more responsive to change, and often engaged in government service or business, forming a significant section of the upper middle class. The urban Tajiks maintain close links with their kin in the rural areas, who in the off-season often become temporary workers in factories in urban areas.

Despite being the second largest ethnic group in Afghanistan, they only held real political power in 1928, under Bacha-i-Saqqau, because the country has traditionally been ruled by the Pashtuns. However, the Tajiks have dominated the mujahideen of the Northern Alliance, and one of their leaders, Burhanuddin Rabbani, served as president of Afghanistan from 1992 until 1996 until overthrown by the Taliban. Tajiks were given a number of significant posts in the Afghan Interim Government established after the Bonn Agreement of 27 December 2001, which attempted to represent the major factions in the country. They continued to be well represented in the Afghan Transitional Government approved by the Loya Jirga (Great Council) in June 2002.

See also Masood, Ahmad Shah; Rabbani, Burhanuddin

References

Jawad, Nassim. 1992. *Afghanistan: A Nation of Minorities.* London: Minority Rights Group.

"Tajiks of Afghanistan." 2002. http://afghan-network. net/Ethnic-Groups/tajiks.html (cited 7 February 2002).

TALIBAN

The Taliban regime of radical and extreme Muslims governed most of Afghanistan from 1996 until 2002 and was regarded by many governments and opposition forces as representing a police state based on religion. The regime, which was infamous for its extensive human rights violations, particularly against women, and which harbored the al-Qaeda terrorist organization and its leader Osama bin Laden, was viewed by many observers throughout the world as being synonymous with the conflict in Afghanistan at the turn of the twenty-first century.

The Taliban derived its name from the *talibs* (students) who were studying at the *madrasas* (religious schools) in large numbers throughout Pakistan. For many of those students, studying in Pakistan was a way of improving their lot and avoiding the despondency and misery of life in Afghanistan. The main support base for the Taliban was drawn from the leaders of the various madrasas. Early on, important support was provided by Fezlu Rahman from Baluchistan, who organized the military training of students in camps close to the border with Afghanistan. Another major source of recruits was the madrasa run by Maulana Mohammed Yusuf Binnori in Karachi, where Mullah Muhammad Omar, the subsequent leader of the Taliban, was believed to have studied. However, it also important to note that the madrasas had students from all over the Muslim world, and the Karachi school had some 8,000 students

Creation of the Taliban

The Taliban grew out of a battle within Pakistan between the Interior Ministry and the Inter-Services Intelligence (ISI) division. The ISI had controlled mujahideen operations in Afghanistan since the Soviet intervention in 1979, and it was not in favor of the Taliban, having put its faith in the Islamic Party led by Gulbuddin Hekmatyar as the instrument for toppling the government of Burhanuddin Rabbani in Kabul. Throughout the operation, the ISI had consistently favored Hekmatyar when it came to the allocation of funds and arms, including covert supplies provided by the U.S. Central Intelligence Agency (CIA). However, the Interior Ministry, following the instructions of Pakistan Prime Minister Benazir Bhutto, had used the Taliban in November 1994 to rescue a trade caravan seized by a warlord in Kandahar, although this action was viewed by the ISI as a ploy by Bhutto to reduce its influence in Afghan affairs.

However, Bhutto persisted with a policy of supporting the Taliban and appointed a retired major general, Nasrullah Babar, to pursue the Taliban option as a means of developing another track, which might provide new options within Afghanistan. With their organization having begun in 1993 within the madrasas, Taliban members soon found themselves being trained and guided by the ISI, which was forced to recognize their success and to support the movement if it wished to retain its hold over Pakistan's policy toward Afghanistan. The ranks of the Taliban were also swelled by a few thousand mujahideen troops who were disillusioned by the internecine fighting between the various mujahideen groups after the Soviet withdrawal and the downfall of Muhammad Najibullah's government. Babar was instrumental in identifying the madrasa as fertile ground for the indoctrination of Afghan students to establish a new order in Afghanistan, with the objective of cleansing the country of the corrupt mujahideen leaders.

Support for the Taliban

It is clear that the Taliban had been created, trained, and equipped by Interior Ministry special forces and the ISI in Pakistan. Funding came from supporters in the Arab world, including Saudi Arabia and the Arab gulf states; from proceeds collected at illegal tax checkpoints on the trade routes linking Pakistan to the Central Asian republics; and from Pakistan itself. This funding enabled the Taliban to equip itself with state-of-the-art weaponry and air support, thus turning it into a cohesive fighting force.

The growth of the Taliban ran parallel to the growth of the madrasas in Pakistan, illustrated by the fact that there were fewer than 900 schools in 1975 but since 1987, the figure has grown to some 2,500. As such, the madrasas have extended their influence throughout Pakistan, with support for the Taliban permeating the religious schools and the political infrastructure. Support from Pakistan was also encouraged by the realization that the mujahideen forces within Afghanistan were incapable of retaining their fighters, whose loyalty was only being maintained through money. This situation had manifested itself during the period of Najibullah's rule after the Soviet withdrawal, during which desertions and loyalty changes by local commanders became commonplace. The tact was used to great effect in 1992 when mujahideen attacks on Jalalabad, backed by Pakistan, were repulsed by government forces following a series of defections from the local mujahideen forces.

Rise to Power in Afghanistan

The Talibs moved into Afghanistan with a force of probably around 2,500 and began their campaign with the capture of a small town called Doorahi, near Kandahar, before moving on Spin Boldak, which was controlled by forces led by Mullah Akhtar Jan and loyal to Gulbuddin Hekmatyar. From there, the Taliban moved on toward the outskirts of Kabul, taking control of ten provinces on the way but without any real military action. Success was achieved by bribery in most cases, with mujahideen groups switching sides and either joining with the Taliban or agreeing to cease resistance against Taliban rule over their particular area. The successes led the leadership to seek more recruits from the madrasas and volunteers from other Muslim countries, so that by the end of 1995, their strength had increased from 2,500 to about 30,000, with a large number of non-Afghans in their ranks.

In the struggle against the mujahideen forces near Kabul, they were forced into real military action in order to capture Farah and Nimruz Provinces, but they were less successful against the battle-hardened forces of Ahmad Shah Masood, who held the perimeter around Kabul until December 1996; they also experienced defeat against the forces of Rabbani at Zabul and in areas of Helmand Province. Kabul was eventually taken due to a variety of factors. The first was the desertion of the Pashtun mujahideen, who switched their allegiance to the Taliban. But most significant was the failure of

Gen. Abdul Rashid Dostum to ally himself with Masood instead of the Taliban, which would have relieved pressure to the northwest of Kabul. The Taliban were able to make slow advances on Kabul, and they inflicted large-scale damage on the city, including rocket attacks on residential areas designed to destroy morale. At the same time, they were also cutting Masood's links with Jalalabad, and the largely Tajik-based militia was forced to withdraw from Kabul toward their stronghold in the Panjshir Valley.

Following the capture of Kabul in September 1996, the Taliban pushed farther north and achieved instant successes at Jabul-us-Sivaq, Gubahar, and Bagram, which gave them control of the Bagram air base. However, the advance came to a grinding halt at the Salang Pass, near the Salang Tunnel, when they suffered a comprehensive defeat at the hands of the Northern Alliance forces. This defeat caused the Taliban to revert to the strategy of subverting the opposition through defections prior to launching any advances. In February 1997, Taliban forces moved into the Ghorband Valley, adjacent to Masood's stronghold in the Panjshir Valley—but only after bribing several opposition commanders to switch sides and to bring with them their men and equipment, a move that severely weakened Masood's position.

In March 1997, the Taliban pushed farther through the Ghorband Valley and were able to effect a split in the Islamic Unity Party by arranging for the desertion of two key commanders from the Khalili faction. This advance opened up the route to Mazar-i Sharif and was accompanied by the desertion of two of Masood's commanders, resulting in a weakening of the Masood-Khalili alliance. At the same time, Taliban leaders were also negotiating with members of the Uzbek community, particularly those belonging to the Rasul Pahalwan faction, and they succeeded in attracting the support of Gul Mohammad and Abdul Malik Pahalwan, the latter no doubt encouraged by a payment of $200 million. At one stroke, most of General Dostum's field commanders deserted him, forcing him to flee from Mazar-i Sharif and leaving the way open for a Taliban occupation. However, counterattacks followed from the forces of Abdul Malik and Karim Khalili, largely as a result of the Taliban's failure to understand the nature of the Shi'a and Uzbek populations of the region, and both sides committed a number of atrocities during these actions. Despite these reverses, the Taliban controlled 95 percent of the country by 1999, with opposition troops being forced to withdraw to an enclave in the northeast of the country.

Taliban Ideology

As noted, the Taliban originated on the Afghan scene as a militia drawn from the madrasas in Pakistan, with its ranks swollen by disenchanted mujahideen leaders. However, following the capture of Kandahar, the true Islamic ideology of the Taliban was revealed. Prior to this event, the ISI had secured tacit support from the United States, solely based on the Taliban's attempts to curb poppy growing and heroin production, an approach that seemed to succeed where former programs had failed. The Islamic ideology of the Taliban found favor with the main financial backers—the Saudi Arabians, who were backing the madrasas in Pakistan and providing funds for the Taliban. The main dissent was expressed by the minority groups in Afghanistan, especially the Tajiks, the Uzbeks, and the Shi'a Hazaras, backed by Iran, all of whom perceived the Taliban as a movement aimed at restoring Pashtun hegemony at the expense of the plural character of Afghan society.

The Taliban proceeded to impose a very narrow interpretation of Shari'a law in the territory that they controlled, and draconian measures were introduced. Many Western influences—such as TVs, videocassette recorders, music, films, and photography—were banned, with items being seized and destroyed and owners punished. Enforcement was administered by the Department of Promoting Virtue and Preventing Vice, which searched houses for evidence of infractions of the religiously based decrees. Individuals were beaten on the streets by the militia for breaking rules concerning dress, hair length, and facial hair and for violating the restriction that forbade women from appearing in public unless in the company of men. Edicts were issued requiring men to grow beards of a certain length, and public servants were threatened with dismissal for any infraction or failure to grow acceptable beards following the issuing of the edict. Capital punishment and amputations were widely used, with punishments often administered in public—for example, during halftime at football matches held in the Kabul stadium.

The Taliban's greatest impact, however, was on the role and status of women within Afghan society. Under the regime, women were obliged to be totally covered, from head to foot, by a garment known as a *chadari* when in public, and they were forbidden to work, attend school, or pursue higher education. Infringement of the codes of dress and other aspects of Shari'a law were met by severe beatings or other punitive measures. Such restrictions had serious effects on an already depressed economy and infrastructure, and they crippled the education system and health services, which were heavily reliant on female employees. Restrictions on health services were later relaxed to allow women doctors and nurses to work in female-only facilities, but many women were afraid to return to work because of the nature of the regime. The general ban on employment also caused immense hardship to women who had been widowed as a result of the conflicts that had been going on since 1979, and many were forced to rely on aid from UN agencies or nongovernmental organizations (NGOs) to support themselves and their families. Some women continued to hold clandestine classes in their homes and to provide health services for other women and children, but they did so at great risk to themselves.

The ideology of the Taliban led to the regime being recognized only by Pakistan, Saudi Arabia, and the United Arab Emirates, with the Rabbani government still being acknowledged as the legitimate representative to the United Nations. International opinion was even more inflamed by the Taliban's destruction of Afghanistan's pre-Islamic heritage, particularly the destruction of the statues of the Buddha at Bamian in March 2001. The Taliban, under Mullah Omar, ignored all external pressures to halt this destruction: the pleas of the United Nations, the UN Educational, Scientific, and Cultural Organization (UNESCO), and other Muslim countries such as Egypt were totally dismissed. As a consequence of these actions, coupled with documented human rights violations, the Taliban regime was largely isolated, and their society was regarded by many governments and oppositions forces as nothing more than a police state based on religion.

The Taliban's Foreign Policy

The Taliban's isolation in international terms has largely stemmed from its strict imposition of Shari'a law (particularly the measures aimed at women), which were at variance with trends elsewhere in the international community. The regime's lack of experience, sophistication, and knowledge of world affairs also caused its recognition to be limited to Saudi Arabia, Pakistan and the United Arab Emirates. Russian enmity was assured when the Taliban chose to recognize the government of an independent Chechnya, which existed only in name. In terms of a moral stance against Russia's treatment of fellow Muslims, the Taliban's expressions of support would have been understandable, but recognition of a state not recognized by any other country in the world fostered Russian animosity and increased the amount of aid supplied by Moscow to the forces of Ahmad Shah Masood.

Relations with Iran were also difficult because of the Taliban's treatment of the Shi'a minority in the Hazarajat region. A tense situation was further inflamed by the killing of nine Iranian consulate workers and a journalist during the Taliban seizure of Mazar-i Sharif in 1997, an incident that almost resulted in an Iranian invasion of western Afghanistan. India had been at odds with the Taliban as well, over accusations that the regime had been aiding Islamic insurgents in Indian-administered Kashmir. However, the Taliban's weakness also resulted from efforts by neighboring states, including Tajikistan and Uzbekistan, to isolate and undercut the regime, primarily because of the treatment their minorities received in Afghanistan. Opposition from Tajikistan was also spawned by of its own internal Islamist insurgency, which the authorities believed was supported by the Taliban.

However, the most significant factor affecting the international standing of the Taliban was the regime's position on Osama bin Laden, who was granted refuge in Afghanistan following his expulsion from Sudan, where he had been accused of various acts of terrorism. Subsequently, the leader of the al-Qaeda terrorist organization was charged with being involved in operations against the United States in Somalia in 1993; the bombing of the World Trade Center in 1993; bomb attacks against American personnel in Dhahran, Saudi Arabia, in 1997; and attacks on the U.S. embassies in Kenya and Tanzania in 1999. In Afghanistan, the al-Qaeda worked closely with the Taliban, providing their best fighters, and the regime allowed terrorist training camps to be set up; these camps were subjected to U.S. Cruise missile attacks on 20 August 1998. The UN Security Council had also passed a resolution imposing sanctions on Afghanistan if the Taliban failed to hand over bin Laden to face trial and answer the various charges levied against him. The Taliban refused on the grounds that he was a guest in their country, but they advised that he had been placed under house arrest and that his communications and activities were restricted. This response failed to satisfy the United Nations, and sanctions were imposed.

All of this paled into insignificance when the suicide attacks on the twin towers of the World Trade Center and the Pentagon took place on 11 September 2001, with the loss of almost 4,000 lives. Osama bin Laden and al-Qaeda were implicated in this atrocity by the U.S. and UK governments, and the attack was publicly welcomed by bin Laden and his supporters. The Taliban regime still vacillated over taking action, though Saudi Arabia, the United Arab Emirates, and Pakistan withdrew recognition from the regime. As a consequence of the Taliban's decision, the United States, backed by the United Kingdom, launched bombing attacks against Afghanistan, with the expressed aim of dealing with Osama bin Laden and al-Qaeda and toppling the Taliban regime.

This action was followed by the landing in Afghanistan of U.S. and UK Special Forces in October 2001, primarily to assist the opposition forces and to provide intelligence for subsequent military operations in Afghanistan under Operation Enduring Freedom, part of the War on Terror. Initially, action was directed toward supplying and training the opposition forces and supporting their military operations as they moved out of their northern enclaves to advance on Kabul. The efforts were largely successful, and the Taliban were soon forced to withdraw to their stronghold in Kandahar before fleeing into the mountains and the North-West Frontier Province of Pakistan. Significant territorial gains were made by the Northern Alliance and its supporters without much resistance from the Taliban, except from its foreign fighters or when the Taliban followed the Afghan expedient of persuading opponents to change sides.

At the time of this writing, the Taliban still represent a distinct threat to the Afghan government of President Hamid Karzai, as they have not been comprehensively defeated militarily, and al-Qaeda also remains a potent threat within and without Afghanistan. Despite military action by allied forces and

Afghan troops in the mountains of eastern Afghanistan, it is clear that large numbers of Taliban and al-Qaeda members are still at large in the mountains and across the border in Pakistan. Neither Mullah Omar, leader of the Taliban, nor Osama bin Laden have been located.

Evidence of the continuing Taliban and al-Qaeda activity came on 31 January 2003 when eighteen people were killed on a bus crossing the Rambasi Bridge, some 6 miles south of Kandahar. A bomb destroyed the bridge, and there were only two survivors. It was thought that the attack was directed against Afghan soldiers, loyal to the governor of Kandahar, who regularly patrol the road. Reports indicated that the Taliban and al-Qaeda were responsible, but intelligence sources also think that fighters aligned with Gulbuddin Hekmatyar may have joined them. This band may have been linked with another band that had come under attack from U.S. and Afghan forces on 27–28 January in the mountains near Spin Boldak.

Ongoing Taliban activity is demonstrated by the numerous attacks against U.S. and Coalition forces and bases throughout southern Afghanistan. Taliban sources are said to have faxed a report to the Afghan Islamic Press, based in Peshawar, Pakistan, on 3 March 2003, claiming responsibility for at least fifty attacks across the country. Most of the assaults had been limited to ineffective rocket fire on Coalition bases, but in Kandahar Province, at least twenty Afghan civilians had been killed since the start of the year, and attacks had been made on Afghan officials in adjoining provinces. The fax also warned that any Afghan helping the United States would be treated as a collaborator and an infidel in the ongoing jihad against the United States.

Structure of the Taliban

The Taliban was headed by Mullah Omar, who was elected as leader by Islamist clerics forming the Shura (council) that controlled the movement, and after the capture of Kabul in September 1996, the infrastructure of the government was established. However, there were divisions within the movement, with moderate and hard-line elements—the former represented by Mullah Mohammad Ghaus and Mullah Ehsan Ehsanullah and the latter by Mullah Khairullah and Mullah Mohammad Rabbani (no relation to President Rabbani)—supported by Mullah Omar. Further divisions were also apparent following the incorporation into the movement of mujahideen leaders, often with their own agendas. Despite the apparent monolithic structure under Mullah Omar, the Taliban was never able to produce a cohesive fighting force capable of crushing its opponents; indeed, most of its successes were based on bribery and shifting loyalties, rather than military prowess.

See also Civil War; Coalition Air Campaign against the Taliban; Coalition Land Campaign against the Taliban; Destruction of Pre-Islamic Heritage; Hazaras; Hekmatyar, Gulbuddin; Human Rights Violations; Inter-Services Intelligence Service; Laden, Osama bin; Masood, Ahmad Shah; Omar, Mullah Muhammad; al-Qaeda

References
Griffin, Michael. 2001. *Reaping the Whirlwind: The Taliban Movement in Afghanistan.* London and Sterling, VA: Pluto Press.
Maley, William, ed. 1998. *Fundamentalism Reborn? Afghanistan and the Taliban.* London: Hurst.
Marsden, Peter. 1998. *The Taliban: War, Religion and the New Order in Afghanistan.* London and New York. Zed Books.
Nejumi, Neamatallah. 2002. *The Rise of the Taliban in Afghanistan: Mass Mobilization, Civil War and the Future of the Region.* New York: Palgrave.
Rashid, Ahmed. 2001. *Taliban: The Story of the Afghan Warlords.* London: Pan.

TANAI, LT. GEN. SHANAWAZ

Shanawaz Tanai was a member of the Khalq faction of the People's Democratic Party of Afghanistan (PDPA), chief of the General Staff from 1986, and minister of defense from 1988 to 1990. He is a Pashtun from the small Tani tribe in Paktia Province and was considered to have a real future within the party but became disillusioned by the policies of the government of Muhammad Najibullah. On 6 March 1990, he joined with other Khalq officers in an attempted coup to topple the government. It was mounted from the Bagram air force base, and attacks were made on key government installations in Kabul and on the presidential palace. But the loyalty of the air force and control over communications ensured the survival of the regime. Tanai and other Khalq officers escaped by military aircraft from Bagram and flew to Parachinar in Pakistan, where they received support from Gulbuddin Hekmatyar, leader of one of the most radical of the mujahideen groups—the Islamic Party of Afghanistan (Hizb-i-Islami-yi Afghanistan).

The alliance between the Khalq officers and the Islamic Party of Afghanistan was seen as a serious threat in Afghanistan, as it demonstrated that various factions were prepared to shelve ideological differences in an attempt to gain power. On 16 March 1990, Tanai resurfaced in Logar Province in Afghanistan in one of Hekmatyar's bases, where he planned to continue the campaign against the Najibullah government, while maintaining his loyalty to the PDPA. After the fall of Najibullah's government in April 1992, other Khalq officers also joined the Hekmatyar group, but it is thought that Tanai joined with the Taliban in 1995.

See also Najibullah, Muhammad; People's Democratic Party of Afghanistan

References

Guistozzi, Antonio. 2000. *War, Politics and Society in Afghanistan, 1978–1992.* Washington, DC: Georgetown University Press.

TARAKI, NUR MUHAMMAD (1917–1979)

Nur Muhammad Taraki was a member of the Khalq faction of the People's Democratic Party of Afghanistan (PDPA), and after the Saur Revolt of April 1978, which brought the Communists to power, he became president of the Revolutionary Council and prime minister of the Democratic Republic of Afghanistan. He had converted to communism in the early 1960s and convened the founding congress of the PDPA on 1 January 1965. The congress elected him as secretary-general of the PDPA in a competition with Babrak Karmal, who was elected as secretary of the Central Committee. In April 1966, Taraki began to publish *Khalq,* the party newspaper, which then became the name of his faction of the PDPA. The party split into two factions in 1967 in disputes over leadership, policies, and tactics, only to be reunited in 1978 prior to the April coup.

After the Saur Revolt, Taraki was the object of a leadership cult, becoming known as "the Great Leader," and a propaganda campaign was mounted to legitimize his rule and his leadership of the Communist movement in Afghanistan. Possible opposition was removed by purging the leading Parchami (members of the Parcham faction) from the government, and the Khalq faction reigned supreme. However, a split developed within the Khalqi, with Hafizullah Amin attacking his former leader as unfit to rule. The Taraki faction became known as the "red Khalqis" and that of Hafizullah Amin the "black Khalqis." The faction led by Hafizullah eventually gained dominance, and on 9 October 1979, Taraki was executed in secret.

Taraki was from a Ghilzai nomad family and was born on 15 July 1917 in Ghazni Province. His education was at a village school, followed by college credits in Kabul before he gained employment in the Pashtun Trading Company in Kandahar and then in Bombay. Due to his command of English, he held various posts in Afghan ministries and worked at the Bakhtrar News Agency. He became known as a journalist and author, and in 1953, he served briefly as press attaché in the Afghan embassy in Washington. On his return to Kabul, he opened the New Translation Bureau, which translated material from Dari and Pashtu for various foreign embassies and missions in Kabul.

See also Khalq; People's Democratic Party of Afghanistan

References

Hammond, Thomas Taylor. 1984. *Red Flag over Afghanistan: The Communist Coup, the Soviet Invasion and the Consequences.* Boulder, CO: Westview Press.

People's Democratic Party of Afghanistan. 1978. *A Short Biography of Noor Mohammad Taraki: Secretary General of the Central Committee of the People's Democratic Party of Afghanistan, President of the Revolutionary Council and Prime Minister of the Democratic Republic of Afghanistan.* Kabul: Political Department of the People's Democratic Party of Afghanistan.

TASHKENT DECLARATION

The Tashkent Declaration was signed on 17 July 1999 by representatives of China, Iran, Pakistan, Tajikistan, Turkmenistan, Uzbekistan, the Russian Federation, and the United States, as well as a UN observer. The declaration was issued because of the concerns of the signatory states regarding the conflict in Afghanistan and the threat it posed to regional security.

The declaration confirmed the commitment of the signatory states to the resolutions of the United Nations, the body's role as an intermediary, and the position of the special envoy of the UN secretary-general to Afghanistan. It also committed the signatories to supporting the independence, territorial integrity, and national unity of Afghanistan. Concern was expressed about violations of human rights, particularly of ethnic minorities and women, as well as violations of international humanitarian laws. Deep concern was also expressed about the use of Afghan territory, particularly areas controlled by the Taliban, to harbor terrorists and provide training facilities for them, with consequences for the internal conflict in Afghanistan, its neighbors, and other states. The increase in drug trafficking and its impact on the region and the rest of the world was also deemed a matter of grave import.

The deputy foreign ministers of the signatory states came to the following conclusions:

1. The Afghan conflict had to be settled through peaceful political negotiations in order to establish a broad-based, multiethnic, and fully representative government.
2. No further military support would be provided to any Afghan party, and their territories were not to be used for such purposes. An appeal was also issued to the international community to support this objective.
3. The readiness of the group to promote direct negotiations under the auspices of the United Nations and in line with General Assembly and Security Council resolutions was also affirmed. Negotiations were to take place in two stages:

Stage 1.
The signing of an immediate, unconditional cease-fire with no preconditions. Direct negotiations between representatives of the United Front and the Taliban on the exchange of prisoners of war and the lifting of internal blockades to facilitate trade and humanitarian assistance.

Stage 2.
The Afghans themselves were to draw up basic principles for the future of the state, with the objective of establishing a broad-based, multiethnic, fully representative government.

1. Signatory states with a common border with Afghanistan agreed to bilateral and multilateral measures designed to combat illegal drug trafficking in accordance with the UN Drug Program.

2. The Taliban was urged to fully investigate the killings of diplomatic staff of Iran in Mazir-i Sharif as well as a correspondent of the Islamic Republic News Agency and to bring the guilty to justice.
3. Afghan parties, especially the Taliban, were urged to stop providing refuge and training facilities for international terrorists and to bring such individuals to justice.

The remainder of the conclusions referred to support for the Afghan government that was to be formed as a result of the proposals, to aid the return of Afghan refugees to their homes, and to provide support for the reconstruction of Afghanistan through relevant UN agencies and other international programs. A call was also made to the international community to support humanitarian relief for Afghanistan and all other proposals in the declaration.

The declaration was not well received in Afghanistan, as many of the states that described themselves as friends of Afghanistan were regarded as having been party to the destruction of the country and continuing to fuel the current hostilities.

See also Drug Trade; Taliban
References
"Tashkent Declaration on Fundamental Principles for a Peaceful Settlement of the Conflict in Afghanistan." 1999. http://www.institute-for-afghan-studies. org/Accords%20Treaties/tashkent_declaration_1999. htm (cited 28 June 2002).

TAWANA, SAYYID MUSA

Sayyid Musa Tawana was one of the founding members of the Islamist Movement in Afghanistan, working from his position as a professor at the Faculty of Shari'a at Kabul University. He had studied at al-Azhar University in Egypt, where he had been exposed to the teachings of the Muslim Brotherhood; those teachings influenced his philosophy. Prior to graduating from Kabul University in 1963, Tawana had been a member of a group of students who were reacting against a growing secularism among their fellow students and who formed a group to combat this trend with a three-pronged plan of action:

• Refute the claims of secularists on questions of Islam

- Write and translate articles to propagate the teachings of Islamist scholars
- Study communism and European history in order to understand the enemy

On becoming a professor at Kabul in 1972, he was part of a group of academics who formed the Organization of Muslim Youth, later to become the Islamist Movement (Jami'at-i-Islami) headed by Burhanuddin Rabbani with Engineer Habiburraham as secretary and in charge of military affairs. The movement was supported by Gulbuddin Hekmatyar, who was in the Kabul prison at the time it was founded. After the coup staged by Muhammad Daud on 17 July 1973, the movement was forced to go underground.

References
Carew, Tom. 2000. *Jihad: The Secret War in Afghanistan.* Edinburgh: Mainstream.

THIRD ANGLO-AFGHAN WAR (1919)

The Third Anglo-Afghan War was the shortest of the conflicts between Britain and Afghanistan, lasting from 4 May 1919 until a cease-fire was agreed to on 3 June 1919. During World War I, Afghanistan had remained neutral (although some members of the government had favored an invasion of India), and Amir Habibullah had anticipated receiving a financial reward from Britain and a recognition of Afghanistan's status as an independent nation. However, Britain was not prepared to relinquish its hold over Afghanistan, and Habibullah was assassinated in February 1919 without any progress having been made.

His son, Amanullah, succeeded Habibullah and immediately demanded that the British negotiate a treaty that would secure recognition of Afghanistan's independence and restore normal relations between the two states. However, the viceroy of India, Lord Chelmsford, insisted that no new treaty was necessary—a position that was at total variance with earlier British arguments, which consistently maintained that agreements with Afghan rulers were personal and had to be renegotiated with each new ruler. Lord Chelmsford would only recognize Amanullah as ruler of Kabul and its immediate surroundings, maintaining that the amir did not have total control of the country. As a consequence, the subsidy paid to former Afghan rulers was withdrawn.

Amanullah began to assert his independence, and on 13 April 1919, he announced to an assembly of dignitaries that Afghanistan was a free and independent state and would resist any attempt by a foreign power to interfere in either its internal or external affairs. His words were reinforced by action when the amir sent three of his generals to the border with British India: Sahel Muhammad, the commander-in-chief, went to Dakka on the border on 3 May 1919, and two days later, Abdul Quddus, the prime minister, moved to the region of Qalat-i-Ghilzai; the third general, Muhammad Nadir, who later became king of Afghanistan, moved to Khost on 6 May with several thousand *lashkars* (tribal forces) in addition to his regular forces.

The British government in India responded by halting the post–World War I demobilization of all forces in India and initiated a recall of all British officers, with the intention of facing Afghanistan with a superior force that would intimidate the Afghans and cause them to withdraw from the border regions. Although the British army viewed the Afghan troops as understrength, poorly trained, and badly paid, they were aware of the power of the tribal forces on both sides of the border, who were noted for their aggression and had intimate knowledge of the terrain. The position was complicated by the fact that the Pashtun members of the British Khyber Rifles were unwilling to fight against fellow Pashtuns, and the units had to be disbanded after 600 soldiers of the 700-man force chose to be discharged rather than serve against their Afghan brothers.

The first aggressive action came from the Afghan forces, who cut the water supply to Landi Kotal on the Indian side of the frontier; Britain responding by closing the Khyber Pass. The Afghans hoped to strengthen their position by causing the frontier tribes to take up arms against the British, particularly in Peshawar. The situation in Peshawar was contained when the British forces cut off supplies of water, food, and electricity to the city, but the entire frontier area was seething with unrest. Although Sahel Muhammad's forces had lost ground to the British forces, the Afghans were able to break through in Waziristan and lay siege to the British base at Thal. On the southern front, British forces captured the town of Spin Boldak but were unable to advance farther, and in the area around Chitral, no actions took place.

The siege of Thal prevented British forces from moving on Jalalabad because of a shortage of mechanized transport, which meant that two offensives could not take place simultaneously. The government in India allowed the Afghan envoy in India to return to Kabul to attempt to persuade Amanullah to cease hostilities, and a cease-fire was agreed to. Peace negotiations were protracted, with negotiations taking place at Rawalpindi and Mussoorie, before a treaty was concluded at Kabul in 1921. The treaty led to British India's recognition of King Amanullah as ruler of an independent state, and neighborly relations were established between the two countries.

See also Anglo-Afghan Treaty of 1921; Mussoorie Conference

References
Heathcote, T. A. 1980. *The Afghan Wars, 1839–1919.* London: Osprey.
Molesworth, George Noble. 1962. *Afghanistan, 1919: An Account of Operations in the Third Afghan War.* London and New York: Asia Publishing House.

TIMUR SHAH (1742–1793)

Timur Shah was one of Ahmad Shah's six surviving sons. He served as governor of Herat and was named as his father's successor prior to his death in 1772. He was opposed by his brother, Sulaiman Mirza, who was soon defeated, and Timur Shah was acknowledged as successor to the throne at Kandahar. To weaken the power of the Durrani chiefs, he moved his capital to Kabul, where he continued the alliance with the Barakzais, further strengthened alliances through marriage, and secured his own position by creating a personal bodyguard of non-Pashtun soldiers. Despite these alliances, he never realized the goal of creating a truly centralized state; he was assessed as a humane ruler who was more of a scholar than a soldier. On his death in 1793, his five sons, who had been appointed governors of various Afghan provinces, started an internecine struggle for power, which eventually lost the family the throne.

References
Dupree, Louis. 1980. *Afghanistan.* Princeton, NJ: Princeton University Press.

TURI TRIBE

The Turis are members of a Shi'a Pashtun tribe who have been living in Kurram Valley since the sixteenth century. Until 1880, the area was part of Afghanistan, but in that year, the Turis rebelled against Afghan rule and were accorded British protection in 1882, with the region then coming into the orbit of British India. The Kurram Valley was an important supply route for the mujahideen forces operating in the Kabul area against the Communist government (1979 to 1992), and there was a great deal of friction between the mujahideen and the local population.

References
Bellew, H. W. *The Races of Afghanistan: Being a Brief Account of the Principal Nations Inhabiting That Country.* London: Thacker.

TURKOMANS

The Turkomans are a Sunni Muslim Turki people who number between 125,000 and 400,000 and inhabit the northwestern part of Afghanistan. The majority of the Turkomans had fled from the Soviet Union, having been driven from their pastures by the Soviet troops who were attempting to stop the flow of Chinese armaments through the Wakhan Corridor. The tribes speak an archaic form of Turkish and Persian, with the nomadic tribes still living in the yurt, a dome-shaped felt tent on a collapsible wooden frame found throughout Central Asia. They have contributed significantly to the traditional Afghan economy through the breeding of Karakul sheep and the weaving of Turkoman carpets. The Turkomans are recognized by their distinctive dress, with the men wearing belted cloaks, turbans, and soft leather boots and the women wearing long dresses in bright floral patterns over leggings. At one time, the Turkomans were courted by the Marxist government in its endeavor to win minority support, with Turkami being declared a national language and newspapers and radio broadcasts being allowed in the same language.

References
Clifford, Mary Louise. 1973. *The Land and People of Afghanistan.* Philadelphia: Lippincott.
Jarring, Gunnar. 1939. *On the Distribution of Turki Tribes in Afghanistan: An Attempt at a Preliminary Classification.* Lund, Sweden: Gleerup.
"Uzbeks and Turkoman of Afghanistan." 2002. http://www.afghan-network.net/Ethnic-Groups/uzbeks-turkmen.html (cited 7 February 2002).

TWELVER (ITHNA 'ASHARIYA)

The Twelvers make up the predominant category among the Shi'a peoples, deriving their name from a belief in twelve Imams. They believe that Muhammad al-Qasim, the infant son of the Eleventh Imam, went into a state of occulation, or hiding, in A.D. 873, leaving four special assistants. The last of the assistants failed to name a successor, and the line of divinely inspired Imams was deemed to have become extinct in A.D. 940. The Twelvers believe that the last Imam will end his occulation at the end of time and will return to deliver the last judgment and justice for mankind. Most of the Hazaras, the Qizilbash, and the population of Herat are members of this sect. They are a religious minority within Afghanistan and, as such, have been persecuted for their beliefs, particularly by the Taliban, who declared then to be un-Islamic and indeed forcibly converted a number to the Sunni sect of Islam.

References

Oleson, A. 1995. *Islam and Politics in Afghanistan.* London: Curzon Press.

ULAMA

The *ulama* are doctors of Islamic sciences who traditionally were organized into a hierarchy by the Afghan rulers. They were headed by the chief of the ulama, judges, canon lawyers, and mullahs, and during the reign of Amir Abdur Rahman (1880 to 1901), they were accorded status through membership in the Royal Council. The ulama did not wield any real political power, but they have always exercised a great deal of influence among the population. This influence was evidenced by their mobilization of the masses against King Amanullah in 1929 and against the Marxist regime in Kabul after the Saur Revolt of April 1978, which brought the Communists to power. The traditional ulama were threatened by the arrival of the Taliban, who established their own hierarchy of ulama and Islamic students.

References

Ghani, Ashraf. 1978. "Islam and State Building in a Tribal Society." *Modern Asian Studies* 12, no. 2: 269–284.

ULFAT, AZIZURRAHMAN (1936–1983)

Azizurrahman Ulfat was born in 1936 in Kuhastan, Kapisa Province, and graduated from the Law Faculty of Kabul University in 1960. He then became a government official in a number of provinces, including Kandahar, Jalalabad, Bagram, and Herat. He went to the United States in 1964 and earned an M.A. from the University of Indiana two years later. After the Marxist takeover in 1978 following the Saur Revolt, he wrote extensively in support of the cause of the mujahideen but was also extremely critical of abuses of human rights, which were being carried out in the name of a jihad. An unknown assailant assassinated Ulfat on 19 September 1983 in Peshawar, Pakistan.

References

Magnus, Ralph H., and Eden Naby. 2002. *Afghanistan: Mullah, Marx and Mujahid.* Rev. ed. Boulder, CO: Westview Press.

U

UK SPECIAL FORCES

Naturally enough, detail as to the size and nature of the operations of the United Kingdom's Special Forces is difficult to ascertain, but it is clear that they have been involved in operations against the Taliban and al-Qaeda from the outset in autumn 2001. The involvement of the Special Air Service (SAS) and the Special Boat Service (SBS) was initially intended to collect intelligence in preparation for subsequent military action and to provide covert support and assistance for the forces opposed to the Taliban regime, in an operation code-named Infinite Justice.

Authorization was obtained from President Pervez Musharraf of Pakistan for these forces to operate from bases within his country, with the initial objective being to make contact with opposition forces in northern Afghanistan. Predator unmanned aircraft were used to provide round-the-clock surveillance, but they were also armed with Hellfire antitank missiles, allowing the ground operators to launch attacks on any potential targets. The SAS and the SBS had experience operating inside Afghanistan at the time of the Soviet occupation, when they had been involved in the training of the mujahideen. The special forces operated in small units, planned to link up with troops opposing the Taliban, and had access to close air support in case of danger or when potential targets had been pinpointed.

In October 2001, it was announced by President George W. Bush that U.S. and UK Special Forces were operating in Afghanistan against al-Qaeda terrorists and in the hunt for Osama bin Laden. Although the countries two forces tend to function separately because of their different modes of operation, there was coordination between the various units. This was especially the case in November 2001 when UK and U.S. Special Forces were engaged in actions against the Taliban and al-Qaeda while conventional ground forces were built up by the United States. Special forces were heavily involved in the area around Kandahar, the stronghold of the Taliban, stopping travelers to gather intelligence and plotting Taliban and al-Qaeda positions. The teams then cut off areas containing opposition forces, disrupted supply lines, and called in U.S. air strikes to destroy the enemy positions. Once these actions had been successfully concluded, local tribal leaders were appointed to control the freed pocket of land.

A further example of an SAS operation was an assault on mountain caves near Kandahar during the last week of November 2001, in an area where al-Qaeda fighters were thought to be hiding. In a four-hour battle, eighteen al-Qaeda fighters were killed, four SAS soldiers were wounded, and dozens of terrorists were wounded and captured, though none were high in the al-Qaeda leadership. The details of this operation, which would normally be kept secret, were released in an endeavor to show that British troops were involved in ground operations in Afghanistan. In general, however, the UK Ministry of Defense has banned discussion of special forces operations in Afghanistan, and only small, often unconfirmed snippets of information emerge.

Further evidence of SAS involvement in covert operations came with the riot by Taliban and al-Qaeda prisoners at the Mazar-i Sharif fort in November 2001, with the incident being filmed by an Afghan cameraman. Soldiers thought to be from the SAS were shown firing assault weapons and sniper rifles in an action in which hundreds of armed Taliban and al-Qaeda were killed during furious exchanges of fire. All the Ministry of Defense would confirm was that British troops were in the vicinity of Mazar-i Sharif, had acted in accordance with domestic and international law, and had followed their own rules of engagement.

The SAS and SBS were also engaged with U.S. and Australian Special Forces in the action on the Tora Bora ridges to oust what was thought to be a large contingent of Taliban and al-Qaeda fighters holed up in a complex of caves and bunkers. It was evident that the U.S. commander in Afghanistan, Gen. Tommy Franks, had decided to use special forces rather than conventional troops to assault the cave complex. The operation was a limited success, as it is thought that a large number of the enemy escaped by way of a track to the south that had not been sealed off by U.S. and Afghan forces. Particularly frustrating was the fact that intelligence reports placed Osama bin Laden somewhere in the cave complex, but he apparently was able to make his way, with close associates and family, into the frontier district of Pakistan.

Such hunt-and-destroy actions have continued in the mountain regions of southeastern Afghanistan, and scores of al-Qaeda and Taliban fighters have been killed by SAS troops. Since the Tora Bora campaign in December 2001, SAS squadrons have been operating in the mountains on their own and have been involved in a number of clashes with al-Qaeda fighters. In some cases, there have been reports of engagements with well-armed groups of fighters clearly under the influence of drugs, waving their arms and shouting slogans before taking cover from volleys of fire from the SAS.

In April 2002, further operations of special forces from the United Kingdom, the United States, and Australia were mounted under the code name Operation Mountain Lion. This action took place in the mountainous region of Paktia Province and consisted of intelligence gathering to inform Coalition planning for future operations. However, only small, isolated groups of al-Qaeda and Taliban fighters were encountered, and despite fierce fighting, casualties were light on both sides due to the nature of the terrain and the enemy tactic of withdrawing across the border into Pakistan to avoid air strikes or large followups by conventional forces. Patrols were also successful in recovering large caches of arms and munitions.

It is impossible to obtain official confirmation of the accounts of any of the SAS and SBS operations because it is the policy of the Ministry of Defense to never discuss the activities of the special forces. However, it is clear that they were effective in operations against the Taliban and al-Qaeda in Afghanistan before the arrival of conventional ground forces, in operations in cooperation with the opposition to the Taliban, in support of conventional Coalition forces, and especially in independent, ongoing, but undeclared operations.

See also Australian Special Forces; Coalition Land Campaign against the Taliban; U.S. Special Forces

References

Borza, Julien, and Richard Norton-Taylor. 2001. "Special Forces in Afghanistan." *Guardian* (London), 24 September.

Evans, Michael. 2001. "SAS Already Gathering Intelligence in Afghanistan." *Times* (London), 21 September.

Norton-Taylor, Richard. 2002. "Scores Killed by SAS in Afghanistan." *Guardian* (London), 5 July.

UN SANCTIONS

The United Nations had passed a number of resolutions on the situation in Afghanistan in 1988, none of which had an impact on the activities of the Taliban regime that had taken control of the country. On 15 October 1989, the UN Security Council finally adopted a resolution that would impose limited sanctions against the Taliban government unless Osama bin Laden was handed over to a country where he had been indicted for crimes or to a country that would see that he was brought to justice. Earlier resolutions relating to violations of international humanitarian law, human rights, discrimination against women, drug trafficking, and the murder of diplomats were also reaffirmed.

These sanctions were extremely limited: flights owned, leased, or operated by the Taliban were banned from taking off or landing internationally, and the funds and other financial assets of the regime were frozen. Only humanitarian flights and those connected with the hajj were exempted. The Security Council also determined that the Taliban regime should cease to give sanctuary and provide training facilities for terrorists or allow their territory to be used for the planning of terrorist actions.

Sanctions were reinforced on 19 December 2000 by Security Council Resolution 1333, which called again for an end to the practice of providing sanctuary and training for international terrorists, for indicted terrorists to be brought to justice, and for Osama bin Laden to be surrendered. The resolution also required that all states should cease to allow the supply of any military equipment or ammunition to areas controlled by the Taliban or to provide technical assistance or training to armed personnel operating under Taliban control. Member states were also required to withdraw all personnel operating as advisers or under contract to the Taliban working in military or security areas.

On the diplomatic front, member states were instructed to significantly reduce staffing levels at missions and posts and to restrict the movement of all remaining staff. All Taliban offices in member states were to be closed, as would the offices of Ariana Airlines. In addition, all funds of Osama bin Laden, the al-Qaeda organization, and any individuals associated with either were to be frozen. Previous sanctions regarding flying facilities were also reaffirmed, and the Taliban and others engaged in illegal drug activities were required to work to eliminate the illegal traffic.

As with all other sanctions, humanitarian operations were exempt, provided that they were conducted through organizations approved by the United Nations. The Taliban were required to ensure the safe and unhindered access of relief personnel and to guarantee the safety, security, and freedom of movement of all UN personnel.

Sanctions were to remain in force for twelve months but could be reviewed in the light of the actions of the Taliban regime. The Security Council also indicated that further sanctions would be imposed against the Taliban if necessary. The sanction against the international flights of the Ariana airline was lifted as from 16 January 2002 as a gesture of support for the new government

References

UN Security Council. 1999. *Resolution 1560.* New York: United Nations.

———. 2000. *Resolution 1333.* New York: United Nations.

UN SECURITY COUNCIL RESOLUTIONS

The UN Security Council passed a number of resolutions relating to Afghanistan under the Taliban regime from August 1998 forward, with Resolutions 1189 of 13 August, 1193 of 28 August, and 1214 of 8 December all concerned with violations of human rights, opium production, the murder of Iranian diplomats in Mazar-i Sharif, and the continuing refusal to hand over Osama bin Laden and close al-Qaeda terrorists camps.

UN Security Council Resolution 1267
(15 October 1999)

This resolution imposed limited sanctions against the Taliban regime because of its failure to comply with any of the previous sanctions. It reaffirmed all the previous resolutions, reiterated the Security

Council's determination to ensure respect for its resolutions, and laid down the following demands:

1. That the Taliban comply with all previous resolutions, cease providing sanctuary and training for international terrorists and their organizations, and take measures to ensure that Afghan territory was not used for terrorist activities against other states.
2. That Osama bin Laden be turned over without delay to an appropriate country, where he would be arrested and effectively brought to justice.
3. That on 14 November 1999, sanctions would be imposed unless the Security Council had decided, on the basis of a report from the secretary-general, that the Taliban had fully complied with its obligations.
4. That in order to reinforce paragraph 2 of the resolution, all states should:
- Deny permission for any aircraft to take off from or land in their territory if it is owned, leased, or operated by or on behalf of the Taliban, unless the particular flight has been approved, in advance, on the grounds of humanitarian need, including religious obligations such as performance of the hajj.
- Freeze funds and other financial resources controlled directly or indirectly by the Taliban or any undertaking owned or controlled by the Taliban. No funds or financial resources were to be made available to the Taliban or any undertaking controlled directly or indirectly by the Taliban, unless authorized on a case-by-case basis on humanitarian grounds.

All states were called on to act in accordance with the provisions of the resolution and to bring proceedings against powers or entities that violated the measures and impose appropriate penalties.

UN Security Council Resolution 1333
(19 December 2000)

This Security Council resolution called for the closure of terrorist training camps in Afghanistan and the expulsion of Osama bin Laden. In this resolution, the Security Council:

1. Reaffirmed its previous resolutions on Afghanistan and, in particular, Resolution 1267 of 15 October 1999.
2. Reaffirmed its strong commitment to the sovereignty, independence, territorial integrity, and national unity of Afghanistan, together with respect for its cultural and historical heritage.
3. Recognized the critical humanitarian needs of the Afghan people and supported the efforts of the UN special representative to Afghanistan in trying to establish a peace process through the various Afghan parties. The objective was the establishment of a broad-based, multiethnic, and fully representative government. All warring factions were called on to cooperate fully in the process.
4. Strongly condemned the continuing use of areas of Afghanistan for the sheltering and training of terrorists and the planning of terrorist acts. The Security Council reaffirmed its conviction that the suppression of international terrorism was essential for the maintenance of international peace and security.
5. Noted that the Taliban had benefited directly from opium by taxing its production and was able to use these resources to strengthen its capacity to harbor terrorists.
6. Reiterated its deep concerns over the continued violations of international humanitarian laws and human rights, particularly the discrimination against women and girls and the murder of Iranian diplomats and journalists at Mazar-i Sharif.
7. Deplored the continuing safe haven being granted to Osama bin Laden and the continued operation of terrorist training camps as bases for the sponsoring of international terrorist organizations.

The Security Council issued the following demands as part of the resolution:

1. That the Taliban comply with Resolution 1267 and, in particular, cease providing

sanctuary and training for international terrorists and their organizations. The Taliban was also required to ensure that territory under its control was not used for the preparation of terrorist attacks against other states, and it was directed to cooperate with international efforts to bring indicted terrorists to justice.

2. That the Taliban meet the demands of Resolution 1267 to turn over Osama bin Laden to appropriate authorities in a country where he had been indicted or to a country that would see he was effectively brought to justice.

3. That the Taliban close all camps where terrorists were trained in the territory under its control, with the closures to be confirmed by the United Nations.

4. That all states remember that they had an obligation to implement the sanctions imposed under Resolution 1267.

In addition, the Security Council resolved to impose further sanctions on the Taliban regime as follows:

1. States should prevent the direct or indirect supply, sale, and transfer to territory under Taliban control of arms and related material of all types, including weapons and ammunition, military vehicles and equipment, paramilitary equipment, and associated spare parts.

2. No state was to provide technical advice, assistance, or training related to military personnel under control of the Taliban, and all states were to withdraw from Afghanistan any nationals involved in these services.

3. The preceding measures were not intended to apply to supplies of nonlethal equipment or protective clothing required by UN personnel, representatives of the media, and humanitarian workers for their own personal use.

4. All states having diplomatic links with the Taliban were urged to reduce the number and level of the staff at Taliban missions and restrict or control the movement within their territory of Taliban staffers

who remained, including those attached to international organizations.

5. It was also determined that states should take further measures to:
- Close immediately all Taliban offices in their territory
- Close immediately all offices of Ariana Afghan Airlines in their territories
- Freeze without delay all funds and other assets of Osama bin Laden and individuals associated with him, including members of the al-Qaeda organization

6. The Taliban were ordered to halt illegal drug activities and to work to eliminate the illicit cultivation of the opium poppy. All states were to prevent the sale, supply, or transfer of the chemical acetic anhydride to areas under Taliban control.

The resolution concluded by reinforcing the sanctions already imposed under Resolution 1267 and setting up the mechanism to monitor the sanctions and to rule on exceptions on a case-by-case basis. The Taliban regime did not fulfill any of the conditions of these resolutions except for the ban on poppy cultivation, which did not stop the trade because it continued in areas outside of Taliban control and because a great deal of raw opium had been stockpiled.

UN Security Council Resolution 1386 (20 December 2001)

This resolution gave approval for the formation and deployment of the International Security Assistance Force (ISAF) in Afghanistan with an initial mandate for six months, renewable by the Security Council if deemed necessary. The initial force was to be made up of contributions of various sizes and specializations from eighteen countries, later joined by Czechoslovakia with the provision of a military field hospital.

The tasks detailed for the ISAF were as follows:

1. Aid the interim government in the development of national security structures
2. Assist Afghanistan's reconstruction
3. Assist in developing and training future Afghan security forces

The rules of engagement for the force were to be settled by a military-technical agreement between the ISAF and the Afghan Interim Government. The force was initially to be headed by the United Kingdom. The mandate of the ISAF was restricted to Kabul and its immediate environs.

UN Security Council Resolution 1413 (23 May 2002)
This resolution extended the mandate of the International Security Assistance Force for a further six months. Specifically, the resolution:

1. Extended the mandate for a period of six months from 20 June 2002
2. Authorized the member states in the ISAF to take all necessary measures to fulfill the mandate of the force
3. Called on member states to contribute personnel, equipment, and other resources to the ISAF and to the trust fund established to assist elsewhere in Afghanistan
4. Called up the head of the ISAF to provide monthly reports on progress to the UN secretary-general

At the same time, the Security Council recorded its thanks to the United Kingdom for having led the ISAF and welcomed Turkey's agreement to assume leadership over the ensuing six months.

UN Security Council Resolution 1444
(27 November 2002)
This resolution arose from a determination that the security situation in Afghanistan still represented a threat to international peace, and it extended the mandate of the International Security Assistance Force for a further twelve months.
The resolution:

1. Extended the authorization of the ISAF for one year from 20 December 2002
2. Authorized all member states of the force to take all necessary measures to fulfill the mandate of the ISAF
3. Directed all member states to contribute personnel, equipment, and other resources to the ISAF
4. Required the provision of quarterly reports from the ISAF to the UN secretary-general

The resolution also thanked Turkey for taking over leadership of the force from the United King-

dom and acknowledged the willingness of Germany and the Netherlands to assume the leadership function in turn. It was also asserted that the Security Council remained committed to international efforts to root out terrorism and was strongly committed, as well, to the sovereignty, territorial integrity, independence, and national unity of Afghanistan.

References
UN Security Council. 1999. *Resolution 1267 of 15 October*. New York: United Nations.
———. 2000. *Resolution 1333 of 19 December*. New York: United Nations.
———. 2001. *Resolution 1386*. New York: United Nations.
———. 2002. *Resolution 1444*. New York: United Nations.

U.S.-AFGHANISTAN RELATIONS

Relations between the United States and Afghanistan have become particularly close since the U.S. intervention in 2001 and have built upon the results of the Soviet military intervention in Afghanistan in 1979, which led to U.S. backing for the opposition mujahideen forces. However, relations were bad during the Taliban regime from 1996 and became even worse with the appearance in Afghanistan of the wanted terrorist Osama bin Laden and the 11 September 2001 attacks on New York and Washington, resulting in U.S. intervention in Afghanistan and support for the Northern Alliance and other opposition groups in an attempt to rid the country of the Taliban regime and Al-Qaeda fighters.

The United States had been slow to establish diplomatic relations with Afghanistan following its independence, secured by the Third Anglo-Afghan War of 1919, the Mussoorie Conference of 1920, and the 1921 Anglo-Afghan Treaty. A variety of factors contributed to this reluctance, the foremost being the view that Afghanistan was still within the British sphere of influence. In addition, Afghanistan was not seen as a market for U.S. exports or as a source of strategic raw materials. It is also true that most Americans had little or no knowledge of the country, and there was no public interest in the region. Washington therefore relied on Britain to furnish information about the area, and the British government had no desire to encourage U.S. competition in Afghanistan.

In July 1921, a delegation from Afghanistan, led by Wali Muhammad, arrived in Washington after making a tour of European capitals, with the objective of establishing diplomatic relations with the United States. However, the delegation's reception was not auspicious, as the U.S. government merely expressed regret at the death of Amir Habibullah and congratulated King Amanullah on his accession. The delegates left Washington extremely disappointed, for Amanullah had hope to avoid his country's dependency on Britain or the Soviet Union by introducing the United States as a balancing third power and as a provider of Western know-how to further his policy of modernization.

Afghanistan made further overtures to the United States and tried to use commerce to forge closer links by offering attractive incentives to U.S. companies. However, Britain negated some of the attractiveness of these commercial agreements by creating problems in terms of access from Indian ports, insisting that all goods had to be transported by Indian railways—even vehicles capable of proceeding under their own power. The U.S. consul at Karachi was approached about establishing diplomatic relations during a visit to Kabul in 1931, but he could give no reason to the Afghan government for the unwillingness of the United States to open an embassy in Kabul. In 1935, it appeared that some progress was being made: the Afghan foreign minister discussed with a U.S. State Department official the offer of an oil concession to the United States in return for a permanent U.S. legation in Kabul; with such an arrangement, the Afghan government would not have to consider Britain or the Soviet Union as alternative partners. A concession was signed and ratified with the Inland Oil Exploration Company in April 1937, but the company withdrew from the concession in 1938 because of the international situation in Europe.

World War II provided the motivation for the establishment of diplomatic relations between the United States and Afghanistan when, in 1942, the German advance on Stalingrad led to fears that the logistic link through western Iran would be denied to the Allies. Eastern Iran or western Afghanistan were considered as ideal locales for an alternate route, and a U.S. presence in Kabul was seen as an essential prerequisite for securing this route. On 6 June 1942, Cornelius Van Engert became the U.S. first resident ambassador in Afghanistan, even though the German defeat at Stalingrad meant that Afghanistan was not needed as a supply route for the Allies. Following the end of World War II, Afghanistan received economic aid from the United States: loans were made in 1950 and 1954 for the Helmand Valley irrigation and electrification projects, which were led by the Morrison Knudsen Construction Company, a U.S. firm. However, the ambitious project did not achieve the desired results and was a significant drain on Afghanistan's foreign currency reserves.

The Cold War complicated U.S. relations with Afghanistan because, in its quest for allies to contain the Soviet Union, the United States would not guarantee to protect Afghanistan against Soviet aggression, preferring to deal with Pakistan for the defense of the Indian subcontinent. As a consequence, Pakistan became a member of the Baghdad Pact, and Afghanistan was forced to adopt a policy of positive neutrality, which gradually led to a growing dependence on the Soviet Union. The United States continued to provide assistance to Afghanistan via loans and grants of $286 million between 1950 and 1971, with an emphasis on aid for communications infrastructure, education, and agriculture. But it did not provide military support to guarantee Afghanistan's independence. During the same period, aid from the Soviet Union totaled some $672 million and was spread across a range of activities and materials, including some military equipment.

In the latter part of the 1970s, Afghanistan was tacitly left in the Soviet sphere of influence, and the U.S. Department of State downgraded the status of the embassy in Kabul to the category of a mission to a country of least importance to the United States. After the Saur Revolt of April 1978, which brought the Communists to power, Washington recognized the new Marxist government, but relations between the two countries began to deteriorate. They were extremely strained when, in February 1979, the U.S. ambassador, Adolf Dubs, was assassinated by kidnappers during an inept rescue attempt mounted by the Kabul police.

In December 1979, the Soviet Union launched a military intervention in Afghanistan. This intervention almost amounted to an occupation of the country and led the United States to transfer its support to the mujahideen, who were opposing the Soviet presence and the Marxist government in Kabul. Much of the U.S. assistance was provided covertly through the Central Intelligence Agency and channeled through the Inter-Services Intelligence Service of Pakistan. By the beginning of 1989, it was clear that the Soviet presence in Afghanistan was coming to an end due to pressure from the mujahideen forces operating from within Afghanistan and from bases in Pakistan. The U.S. Department of State, fearing a quick collapse of the Marxist government and a possible massacre in Kabul, closed the U.S. embassy for security reasons. Following the civil war and the capture of Kabul in September 1996, Washington reconsidered its decision but opted not to establish diplomatic relations with the new government because of the harshness of the regime and its continuing violations of human rights.

Relations with Afghanistan continued to deteriorate and reached a new low when the Taliban regime gave refuge to Osama bin Laden, who was wanted by the U.S. government for a number of terrorist attacks against U.S. interests and personnel, and allowed him to set up camps in Afghanistan to train al-Qaeda terrorists. This led to U.S. Cruise missile attacks on the al-Qaeda camps in August 1998 and exacerbated tensions between Washington and Kabul. Ultimately, the attacks on 11 September 2001 in New York and Washington by al-Qaeda terrorists brought a complete break in relations due to the failure of the Taliban regime to obey UN resolutions demanding the extradition of Osama bin Laden to face international justice. As a consequence, the United States, with British support, attacked Afghanistan with Cruise missiles and bombing raids on al-Qaeda and Taliban strongholds; it also started to give overt aid to the Northern Alliance and other anti-Taliban forces in Afghanistan.

U.S. involvement in the overthrow of the Taliban and support for the Afghan interim government led by President Hamid Karzai has led to a strengthening of ties between Washington and Kabul. As part of its War on Terror, the United States is now heavily committed militarily, diplomatically, and economically to the future of Afghanistan, though, at the time of writing, it is unclear how that future will develop due to continuing unrest and instability in the country; this is especially true because it is clear that al-Qaeda, although severely weakened, has not been destroyed. Also, the mandate of the new government does not extend much beyond Kabul, and warlords still control the various provinces. Assassination attempts have been made on the president and members of the government, and there is a singular lack of real progress on a program of reconstruction. Washington's use of local warlords and their private armies in the war against al-Qaeda and the Taliban is also causing some resentment within Afghanistan, as it is seen as contributing to instability rather than strengthening the hand of the Kabul government.

See also Anglo-Afghan Treaty of 1921; Central Intelligence Agency and Its Support for the Mujahideen; Coalition Air Campaign against the Taliban; Coalition Land Campaign against the Taliban; Helmand Province; Inter-Services Intelligence Service; Laden, Osama bin; Mujahideen; Mussoorie Conference; al-Qaeda; Taliban; Third Anglo-Afghan War

References
Chase, Robert, et al. 1999. *The Pivotal States. A new Framework for US Policy in the Developing World.* New York: W. W. Norton.
Colley, John K. 2000. *Unholy Wars: Afghanistan, America and International Terrorism.* 2nd ed. Sterling, VA: Pluto Press.
Mackenzie, Richard. 1999. *The United States and the Taliban.* In *Fundamentalism Reborn? Afghanistan and the Taliban,* edited by William Maley. 90–103. London: Hurst.
Margolis, Eric S. 2000. *War at the Top of the World: The Struggle for Afghanistan, Kashmir, and Tibet.* London: Routledge.

U.S. SPECIAL FORCES

U.S. Special Forces fighting in Afghanistan have provided the bulk of the manpower in this area of operations since actions began in 2001. These troops comprise the Green Berets, Rangers, Delta Forces, Seals, and the U.S. Air Force 160th Special Operations Aviation Regiment, together with their Night Stalker helicopters. In company with their UK colleagues the Special Air Service (SAS) and the Special Boat Service (SBS), these forces have been operating in Afghanistan since September 2001, being joined later by detachments from other Coalition partners, such as Australia and New Zealand. The special forces initially linked up with the Afghan fighters opposed to the Taliban to provide advice and intelligence and to help direct B-52 bombing attacks on the Taliban's infrastructure and positions. They were aided by intelligence provided by reconnaissance data from unmanned Predator aircraft, which, unlike in previous operations, were armed with Hellfire antitank missiles, enabling the ground operators to strike at identified potential targets. The U.S. Special Forces also maintained a rescue force based in Afghanistan to intervene in an emergency, using a helicopter-borne rescue unit.

Unconfirmed sources in Washington reported that U.S. forces had entered Afghanistan on 13 September 2001, two days after the terrorist attacks on the World Trade Center and the Pentagon, with orders to capture or kill Osama bin Laden or pin him down until the United States could launch air strikes. The troops had initially landed in Peshawar and Quetta, Pakistan, and were infiltrated into Afghanistan using Black Hawk helicopters. The official confirmation was not released until 29 September, and the activity was described as a routine deployment ahead of a major operation.

An engagement between U.S. Special Forces and the Taliban on 20 October resulted in the loss of two men, and this was followed two days later by the downing of another helicopter, with the loss of between twenty and twenty-five troops. The Taliban claimed that the helicopter had entered Afghanistan from Pakistan and was shot down after the Taliban had moved mobile antiaircraft equipment and rocket-propelled grenades into the mountainous region of Paktia Province. Taliban sources claimed that they were utilizing the same military strategy that was employed against the Soviets and that the United States would pay a high price for any further incursions into Afghanistan.

At the beginning of November 2001, it was announced that the number of U.S. Special Forces had been significantly increased, with the objectives of working with Afghan opposition troops and bolstering U.S. air strikes against the Taliban front lines. Also as part of the campaign against the Taliban and al-Qaeda, U.S. Special Forces worked with their UK counterparts to force back the Taliban toward their Kandahar stronghold, stopping travelers on the road to build up an intelligence picture of Taliban and al-Qaeda locations. Once the data had been analyzed, special forces cut off the occupied area, severed supply lines, and then called in U.S. air strikes to destroy the enemy positions. Local Pashtun tribal leaders opposed to the Taliban were then appointed to control the relieved areas. One example was the capture of Takhteh Pol, 25 miles from Kandahar, which was sealed off by Delta Forces who then called in air strikes; survivors were forced to retreat

toward Kandahar, to be replaced by troops under a local tribal leader, Gul Agha Shirzai, who was opposed to the Taliban but lacked the capacity to take them on militarily.

Evidence also exists that U.S. Special Forces played a role in operations with Northern Alliance troops around Mazar-i Sharif, particularly during the riot by armed Taliban and al-Qaeda prisoners being held in the fort there after the fall of the city. A film shot by an Afghan cameraman showed U.S. and UK Special Forces were involved in the action, which claimed the lives of hundreds of Taliban and al-Qaeda prisoners. During the riot, an operative of the Central Intelligence Agency (CIA) was also killed while interrogating one of the captives. The death toll numbered some 800, with the bulk of the dead being prisoners, as well as some Northern Alliance troops. Both the United States and the United Kingdom rejected calls by Amnesty International that an inquiry into the riot be held.

In December 2001, U.S. Special Forces formed the bulk of the Coalition troops sent to the Tora Bora region on a search-and-destroy mission against Taliban and al-Qaeda fighters believed to be hiding in a complex of caves and bunkers. It was evident that the U.S. commander for Afghanistan, Gen. Tommy Franks, had determined that the Coalition troops would consist of special forces, backed by Afghan forces, and that conventional forces would not be deployed. This operation also signaled the start of a more aggressive ground campaign by the Coalition, with UK and Australian Special Forces also being part of the attacking unit. The terrain in the Tora Bora mountain region is harsh, and because of the altitude, the air is thin; consequently, the operation was slow, as any advance had to be made with care and each cave complex had to be checked for booby traps.

Although the campaign was a success in that a number of the enemy were killed or captured, it was not totally effective due to a tactical error in respect to sealing off the area. Routes to the north of the region had been closed down, but the U.S. and Afghan troops had failed to seal off a snow-covered track to the south, and it is believed that at least 4,000 Taliban and al-Qaeda fighters managed to escape into Pakistan, with a few going to Iran. A particular frustration was the fact that intelligence reports had placed Osama bin Laden in the region, but it is known that he escaped with twenty-six followers and family members into the North-West Frontier Province of Pakistan, having been escorted to safety by frontier tribesmen in return for a large payment.

In April 2002, further operations of special forces from the United States, the United Kingdom, and Australia were carried out under the code name Mountain Lion. This operation took place in the mountainous region of Paktia Province and consisted of intelligence gathering to inform future Coalition planning. However, only small groups of al-Qaeda and Taliban fighters were encountered, and despite fierce fighting, casualties were light on both sides due to the nature of the terrain and the fact that the enemy was quick to withdraw across the border. This was demonstrated by the fact that followups of engagements or sightings using conventional troops failed to locate any enemy presence. There were, however, discoveries of numerous caches of arms and ammunition, indicating that the enemy were active in the area.

The major operations were not the end of such activities, as smaller-scale efforts were launched in the mountains of Paktia Province, near Kandahar and bordering Pakistan. However, no senior members of al-Qaeda were captured, and it was clear that they had gone to ground in the frontier areas of Pakistan, in the cities of Peshawar and Karachi, and in Iran. In July 2002, the U.S. defense secretary, Donald Rumsfeld, was reported to have ordered the head of U.S. Special Forces, Gen. Charles Holland, to assume total control in the hunt for al-Qaeda fighters, in an effort to counter the feeling in the Bush administration that the War on Terror was running out of steam. The classified order included instructions to capture or kill the leading figures in al-Qaeda and to organize the campaign against the terrorist organization.

General Holland made a case for U.S. Special Forces, including Delta Forces, to fight alongside the troops of countries in which al-Qaeda fighters had taken refuge. The action was directed against Osama bin Laden and a number of key al-Qaeda figures who had been identified as posing the greatest threat in the coordination and ordering of new terrorist attacks against the United States and its interests abroad. The classified order allowed special forces to take advantage of the law that permitted them to engage in counterterrorism, or "direct-action," missions to kill enemy forces. Such missions were to be aggressive, unilateral, and secretive and possibly included assassination strikes. Since this change of tactic was introduced, it is apparent that U.S. Special Forces are now operating within Pakistan, working together with the Pakistan army, in actions against al-Qaeda fighters who had sought refuge in the lawless frontier areas bordering Afghanistan. It is not possible to determine whether UK Special Forces are also involved in these operations.

See also Australian Special Forces; al-Qaeda; UK Special Forces

References

Beaumont, Peter. 2002. "Special Forces Take Over Hunt for al-Qaeda." *Observer* (London), 4 August.

Berger, Julian, and Richard Norton-Taylor. 2001. "Special Forces in Afghanistan." *Guardian* (London), 29 September.

Evans, Michael. 2001. "SAS Already Gathering Intelligence in Afghanistan." *Times* (London), 21 September.

UZBEKISTAN

Role in Operation Enduring Freedom

Uzbekistan's policy toward the current situation in Afghanistan has been primarily driven by a desire to guarantee all international frontiers in the region in order to prevent the destabilization of Central Asia. Although there are Afghan refugees in Uzbekistan, they are strictly controlled and only number a few thousand. The border with Afghanistan is seen as important to preventing the secular regime from being opposed by Islamist forces emanating from Afghanistan or, indirectly, Tajikistan, where an Islamic insurgency exists. The Islamic Front of Abdul Rashid Dostum has been backed by Uzbekistan, which sees it as an ally to guard the country's southern border with Afghanistan, not primarily because of ethnic solidarity.

The Uzbek nationalism of the movement is not seen as being in Uzbekistan's interest, for the Tashkent government seeks to preserve the border but feels an alliance is necessary to counter backing for an insurgency similar to that of Tajikstan. Although Uzbekistan's support is limited, it has allowed its base at Termez to be used for landings by Dostum and Coalition forces. However, Uzbekistan's policy will be determined by the future of the Islamic Front, which, if confined to a small part of Afghanistan, would prevent Uzbekistan from having any influence in future political developments in Kabul.

Uzbekistan also allowed the United States to use a former Soviet air base near Tashkent for C-130 cargo planes and AC-130 gunships employed in operations in Afghanistan during the air campaign against the Taliban in October 2001. Bases in Uzbekistan were also used by the Tenth Mountain Division to launch land operations in Afghanistan against Taliban and al-Qaeda forces.

References

Gregory, Feifer. 2002. "Uzbekistan's External Realities." *World Policy Journal* 19, no. 1: 81–89.

Zardykhan, Zharmukhamad. 2002. "Kazakhstan and Central Asia: Regional Perspectives." *Central Asian Survey* 21, no. 2: 167–183.

UZBEKS

The Uzbeks are members of the largest Turki language group in Afghanistan and number about 1.3 million, inhabiting northern Afghanistan from Fariab Province in the west to Badakhshan Province. They mingle with the Turki population, and many of the villages in this area are mixed communities, though the Uzbeks live in separate residential areas. The Uzbeks are Sunni Muslims and speak a central Turki dialect called Uzbeki, which was made a national language by the Marxist government in order to win their support; additionally, the Uzbeks were allowed to use their language in education, the press, and broadcasting. Uzbek society is strictly patriarchal, and the leaders of the tribes, or *khans,* have considerable authoritarian power. Most marriages involve people of the same ethnic groups; although some Uzbeks do marry Turkomans and Tajiks, there is widespread antipathy to marriages with Pashtuns.

The Uzbeks originated in Central Asia, and they became a dominant political force in north Afghanistan in the sixteenth century, following the 1506 demise of the Timurid regime centered on Herat.

They established strong principalities, which sometimes acknowledged the authority of Kabul. But the leaders were constantly vying for power among themselves, though it was not until the reign of Amir Abdur Rahman that they were consolidated into the Afghan state. Fresh immigrations of Uzbeks took place in the 1920s and 1930s due to further unrest in the Soviet Union, but at that same time, Pashtuns also migrated into Uzbek territory, so that the Uzbeks became a minority in the areas they had once dominated. The Uzbeks are mainly sedentary agriculturalists, but the urban dwellers have become astute businesspeople or skilled artisans working in silver, gold, or leather. They are also distinguished by their dress, which consists of a kaftan, a small turban, and soft leather boots that fit over wool stockings and reach to the knees.

During the period of Communist rule (1979 to 1992), some Uzbeks served the government in militia forces in areas largely dominated by the Pashtuns. However, Uzbeks also became part of the mujahideen fighting against the Kabul-based government, and following the rise of the Taliban Uzbek forces, led by Gen. Abdul Rashid Dostum, they joined with the Northern Alliance in the struggle against the Pashtun-dominated Taliban regime.

See also Dostum, Gen. Abdul Rashid

References

Bellew. H. W. 1880. *The Races of Afghanistan: Being a Brief Account of the Principal Nations Inhabiting That Country.* London: Thaker.

Clifford, Mary Louise.1973. *The Land and People of Afghanistan.* Philadelphia:: Lippincott.

Shalinsky, Audrey C. 1994. *Long Years of Exile: Asian Refugees in Afghanistan and Pakistan.* Lanham, MD: University Press of America.

"Uzbeks and Turkoman of Afghanistan." 2002. http://www.afghan-network.net/Ethic-Groups/uzbeks-turkmen.html (cited 7 February 2002).

VICTORY ORGANIZATION (SAZMAN-I NASR)

Victory Organization is a mujahideen group whose membership is drawn solely from the Hazara population. It was formed by Sheikh Mir Husain Sadeqi and three other *ulama* (Islamic scholars) as an outcome of the Saur Revolt of April 1978, which brought the Communists to power. The group was officially announced in 1980 and was originally composed of Hazaras living in Iran, receiving some initial support from the Iranian government but seemingly free from political control. The group became a major force in the Hazarajat region, and it allied with the Guardians of the Islamic Revolution (Pasdaran), to overthrow the traditional Shura (Council). The Shura was headed by Sayyid Ali Beheshti, who supported the unity of the Afghan state, whereas Sadeqi was an advocate of armed action against the Pashtuns as well as the Soviets. Sadeqi had long questioned why the Hazaras were forced to be ruled by non-Hazara appointees from Kabul and had fled to Iran in 1974 because of his political views, becoming involved in the Islamist movement. The group he founded was a radical Islamist organization and ruled through ideological committees; it is now part of the Islamic Unity Party (Hizb-i Wahdat).

See also Beheshti, Sayyid Ali; Guardians of the Islamic Revolution

References

Fuller, Graham E. 1991. *Islamic Fundamentalism in Afghanistan: Its Character and Prospects.* Santa Monica, CA: Rand Corporation.

Roy, Olivier. 1986. *Islam and Resistance in Afghanistan.* London and New York: Cambridge University Press.

VITKEVICH, CAPT. IVAN (?–1838)

In December 1837, the Russian soldier Ivan Vitkevich arrived in Kabul to establish commercial relations with Afghanistan, backed by credentials from the Russian ambassador to Tehran and an unsigned letter that was supposedly from the czar. At the same time, Alexander Burnes was in Kabul as a representative of the British East India Company, and he persuaded Afghanistan's amir, Dost Muhammad, to receive Vitkevich in order to discover his objectives. Meanwhile, the amir was anxious to take the city of Peshawar back from the Sikhs, but Burnes advised that he should forget his claim and make peace with the Sikh ruler. Concerned about lack of support from Britain in the matter of Peshawar, Dost Muhammad negotiated with Vitkevich in hopes of securing Russian assistance for Afghanistan. But the Russian government repudiated these moves, and the captain was recalled to St. Petersburg, where he committed suicide. Given Vitkevich's mission, Britain grew fearful that the amir was going to forge an alliance with Russia, and the leaders in London determined that their nation's interests would be best served by his removal from the throne. This situation led to the Simla Manifesto and the First Anglo-Afghan War (1839–1842).

See also Burnes, Alexander; First Anglo-Afghan War; Simla Manifesto

References

Norris, James A. 1967. *The First Afghan War, 1838–42.* Cambridge: Cambridge University Press.

WAHDAT

Wahdat was a weekly newspaper published in both the Dari and Pashtun languages and was the official publication of the National Unity Party (Wahdat-i-Milli). The party was headed by the poet Khalilullah Khalili, who also edited the newspaper. Due to financial problems, the publication lasted only six months, but in an issue dated 31 January 1966, the manifesto of the party was set out. Specifically, the party was committed to:

- The rule of law
- Constitutionalism
- Nonalignment in foreign relations
- The struggle for human rights
- Peaceful coexistence with Afghanistan's neighbors
- Policies to further agricultural development and an Afghan cultural revival
- Expansion of medical and educational facilities
- Equal rights for women

References
Newell, Richard S. 1972. *The Politics of Afghanistan.* Ithaca, NY: Cornell University Press.

WAKHAN DISTRICT

The district of Wakhan lies in the northeastern part of Badakhshan Province and extends from Ishkashim in the west to the borders of China in the east, separating Tajikistan from the Indo-Pakistan subcontinent. The district had been awarded to Afghanistan by the Anglo-Russian Boundary Commission (1895–1896) in order to create a buffer between the two empires. At first, Amir Abdur Rahman was reluctant to accept this award of territory because of its strategic location, but he eventually agreed when the proposal was sweetened by an annual British subsidy of 50,000 rupees. Until 1882, the area was ruled by an independent amir; there-

W

after, it then came under the administrative control of the governor of Badakhshan. The area is inhabited by some 6,000 Isma'ilis and a small number of Sunni Qirghiz, many of the latter having migrated to Turkey following the Soviet invasion of Afghanistan in 1979. The high valleys of the Wakhan corridor are inhabited by Uzbeks and Wakhis (Isma'ilis), and the Bactrian camel and the yak are the main beasts of burden. The Qirghiz herders live together with the agricultural Wakhis in a mutually dependent way of life.

References
Adamec, Ludwig W. 1972–1985. *Historical and Political Gazetteer of Afghanistan.* 6 vols. Graz, Austria: Akademische Druck-u Verlagsansalt.

WALI, ABDUL (1924–)

Abdul Wali was commander-in-chief of the Central Forces of Afghanistan until 1973 but was imprisoned following the coup led by his cousin Muhammad Daud. He is married to the daughter of the deposed king, Mohammed Zahir, and has been in exile in Rome since 1976. He has been acting as a spokesman for the former king, and in 1995, he went to Pakistan and addressed crowds of Afghan refugees on the monarch's behalf. Wali has also been involved in the king's negotiations with Afghan leaders and the Afghan diaspora following the downfall of the Taliban, as well as the formation of an interim government in December 2001.

Wali was born in 1924, the son of Shah Wali (a cousin of King Zahir), and was educated in France and England. He received a military education in England, attending both Sandhurst and the Command and General Staff College at Camberley.

References

Kakar, Hasan. 1978. "The Fall of the Afghan Monarch in 1973." *International Journal of Middle Eastern Studies* 9, no. 2: 195–224.

WALI, MUHAMMAD (?–1933)

Muhammad Wali was Afghan foreign minister from 1922 to 1924, minister of war from 1924 to 1925, and regent during King Amanullah's journey abroad from 1927 to 1928. He was a descendant of the royal family of the previously independent province of Darwaz and had been appointed to the position of Amir Habibullah's correspondence. In 1922, he headed a mission to Moscow and other European capitals to establish diplomatic relations, but a visit to Washington in July 1922 proved unsuccessful, for the mission failed to convince President Warren Harding to establish relations with Afghanistan. After King Amanullah was deposed and Nadir Shah ascended to the throne in Afghanistan in 1929, Wali was imprisoned and subsequently received a sentence of eight years. In September 1933, he was executed with a number of other supporters of King Amanullah.

References

Khan, Sultan Muhammad. 1980. *The Life of Abdur Rahman, Amir of Afghanistan.* Karachi, Pakistan: Oxford University Press.

WARDAK, ABDUL AHAD (C. 1880–1949)

Abdul Ahad Wardak was an Isma'il Khel Ghilzai who was born around 1880 and served as chief usher to Amir Habibullah from 1909 to 1916. Three years later, he was arrested for complicity in the assassination of the amir and banished but was later acquitted. In 1922, he was restored to favor and became aide-de-camp to King Amanullah, and between 1924 and 1925, he was entrusted with the task of going to Wardak Valley to ensure the loyalty of the Wardakis during the Mangal Rebellion.

In 1927, he became minister of the interior and was a loyal supporter of the deposed Amanullah in his attempts to regain the throne in 1929, fleeing with him into India in May when the attempts failed and then to exile in Iran. However, he returned to Afghanistan in December 1929 and became president of the National Council (Rais-i-Shura-i-milli) in 1930, and in November 1931, he became supreme military and civil administrator of Farah Province. He returned to Kabul in 1932 and was reelected to the National Council that year and again in 1933. Wardak also served on the commission that negotiated with Iran in June 1933 over the Helmand water dispute, which was brought to a satisfactory conclusion, though changes in the water course in later years caused the dispute to flare up again, with final resolution not achieved until 1973. His involvement with the National Council continued, for he was reelected in 1934, from 1937 to 1940, and in 1943. He died in 1949.

See also: Helmand Province

References

Khan, Sultan Muhammad. 1980. *The Life of Abdur Rahman, Amir of Afghanistan.* Karachi, Pakistan: Oxford University Press.

WARDAK PROVINCE

Wardak Province in east-central Afghanistan occupies an area of 3,745 square miles. It has a population of some 310,000, though several thousand have become refugees in Pakistan. The administrative center of the province is the recently constructed town of Maidanshahr, built in the 1970s and located just to the west of the Kabul-to-Kandahar highway. The province is extremely mountainous and is traversed by that road and by the highway west into the Hazarajat region and northwest to Bamian Province. The inhabitants of the province are Ghilzais and Durrani Pashtuns in the south and Hazaras in the north and west. About 89 percent of the province is pastureland, but the farms are extremely small; the majority of the holdings are about half an acre in size. The whole province suffered considerably during the civil war from 1989 to 2001, and the infrastructure that was built up in the 1970s has been largely destroyed.

References

Adamec, Ludwig W. 1972–1985. *Historical and Political Gazetteer of Afghanistan.* 6 vols. Graz, Austria: Akademische Druck-u Verlagsansalt.

WARLORDS

The history of Afghanistan is marked by the lack of a strong central government, with the result that power and authority have been widely dispersed and tribes and factions have long had de facto control of the country outside of Kabul. Local strongmen have dominated since the creation of the modern Afghan state in 1747 and have drawn their power from ethnically homogeneous constituencies, for the country has always been divided primarily along ethnic lines. In essence, the warlords have become regional power brokers, and most often, they are tribal chiefs or militia commanders asserting control over territories of varying sizes and importance.

Regional warlords thrive during periods of war, violence, and political instability—conditions that are necessary for the consolidation of power and the raising of revenues. As a result, they often try to provoke unrest and instability in the interest of self-preservation. Resources are generated not only by taxes imposed on the areas they control but also through duties on trade and, in many cases, criminal activities, including the drug trade. In return, the warlords provided their populations with protection, security, and sometimes a minimal level of public services. Prime examples of regional warlords on the contemporary scene are Abdul Rashid Dostum, with his base at Mazar-i Sharif, and Isma'il Khan, based at Herat, both of whom maintain well-armed militias to enforce their rule.

The tradition of the warlord is well established in Afghanistan, and throughout the country's history, only the threat of foreign invasion has been able to unite the tribes and ethnic groups. In times when no external threats have been present, Afghans have usually withdrawn into their ethnic communities and fought with their rivals over resources or territory. Warlords are very much a feature of contemporary Afghanistan, with many of them having grown in strength since the Soviet withdrawal in 1989 and the civil war between the various mujahideen groups and factions from 1989 to 2001. The most influential factor in generating conflict between rival warlords is the personal ambitions of the warlords themselves. The continued existence of warlords is a violation of the Bonn Agreement of December 2001:— the agreement, which was endorsed by Dostum and Isma'il Khan, stated that all the mujahideen forces and armed groups in the country should come under the control of the Afghan Interim Government.

It is clear that stability in Afghanistan is challenged by the power of the warlords, and their existence poses problems for the regime of President Hamid Karzai. However, attempts by the Kabul government to sideline them or confront their power head on would cause a violent reaction that the central government, with only an embryonic national army, could not handle without assistance from coalition forces. The warlords have filled the security vacuum in the provinces that was created in the wake of the Taliban regime's demise, and in their own areas, they are seen as having the only forces capable of providing security for the populace. Because of this, the Kabul government will probably, in the short term, have to consider allowing them some measure of regional autonomy in order to gain their acquiescence in recognizing the central authority of the government in Kabul.

The work of the Loya Jirga (Great Council) of June 2002, which approved President Karzai's transitional government, was a major achievement after twenty-three years of war, but the process was marred by intimidation, bribery, violence, and the continual harassment of delegates by local warlords pursuing their own agendas. The chair of the Loya Jirga Commission had accorded delegate status to the governors of all thirty-three provinces and a number of major and minor warlords, all of whom should have been excluded under the provisions of the Bonn Agreement because of their past records of violence. Many of the delegates and the Afghan people had hoped that delegates to the Loya Jirga would take the opportunity to distance the government from the warlord culture, but instead, several of the warlords were awarded cabinet posts. Karzai advised delegates that his choices had been dictated by a need to strike an ethnic balance. But Afghans who sought reform felt that the cabinet composition had undermined efforts to distance the government from the warlords; it also did little to reduce the influence of the Panjshiri Tajiks, for members of this ethnic group were given one of the vice-president posts and two of the three most powerful ministries. The Pashtun, Hazara, and Uzbek communities did not welcome the cabinet appointments, and Karzai was charged with failing to use his popularity to usurp the power of the warlords and assert the Kabul administration's control of the country.

Clearly, Karzai had no alternative but to incorporate the warlords and the Panjshiri Tajiks into his administration, as the latter possessed the most powerful military force in the country: to have excluded them would have been a major risk in terms of military instability. The move was also made in the belief that bringing the warlords into the administration would encourage them to see the ballot box as an alternative to civil war. However, the two critical figures, Abdul Rashid Dostum and Isma'il Khan, have resisted efforts to accept the control of the Karzai government and have turned down appointments that would have required them to take up a presence in Kabul. Indeed, both of these regional warlords have flouted the authority of the Kabul government, and it is critical to future stability that they recognize and cooperate with the Transitional Government.

Afghanistan since the fall of the Taliban has been subjected to continuing factional violence, demonstrating the fragility of President Karzai's government. The Karzai administration has a limited mandate that does not extend beyond Kabul, where it is protected by the International Security Assistance Force (ISAF). And despite the presence of the ISAF, Kabul is still insecure. This was made clear by the assassination of Vice-President Abdul Qadir, a Pashtun warlord from the Northern Alliance, on 6 July 2002; this was a serious setback for the administration, as Qadir was considered one of the few people in the government who could have bridged the gap between the Pashtuns and the other ethnic communities. A detailed investigation, aided by the ISAF, has been conducted on this killing, but no real progress has been made on the case, apart from the arrest of several of Qadir's bodyguards for complicity.

After the assassination, President Karzai replaced his Afghan bodyguards with U.S. Special Forces, who were, in turn, replaced by U.S. State Department diplomatic security personnel in September 2002. The Pashtun community has also protested against the killing, holding a big rally on 26 July 2002 in Jalalabad and again on 2 August in Khost, demanding the arrest of the killers in order to avoid unrest among the Pashtuns themselves. Signs of the insecurity of the Kabul government were further demonstrated by an al-Qaeda and Taliban attack on an Afghan army outpost on the edge of Kabul on 7 August 2002 and by an attempt to assassinate President Karzai on 5 September as his motorcade was passing through Kandahar. These attacks have been laid at the door of the Taliban and al-Qaeda but may actually have been joint ventures with the forces of Gulbuddin Hekmatyar's Islamic Party. In 2002, the number of attacks increased throughout Afghanistan, indicating that the Taliban and al-Qaeda are far from beaten.

The situation outside Kabul is even worse. Violence and ethnic tensions, together with economic stagnation, have affected several of the provinces and spawned serious violations of human rights, with women suffering badly in some areas. Indeed, the situation in places such as Paktia Province is so bad that some Afghans look back on the years of the repressive regime of the Taliban as a period of security and law and order.

Northern Afghanistan

The northeast part of Afghanistan is controlled by the Tajik-dominated Islamist Movement, with the rest of the northern provinces being dominated by the Uzbek militia of General Dostum and the Hazara militia of the Islamic Unity Party. Major conflicts have taken place between Dostum, who is the deputy defense minister and the Transitional Government's representative in the north, and Muhammad Ustad Atta of the Islamist Movement, who is corps commander for four northern provinces. In January 2002, dozens were killed in a large battle between the forces of the two factions around Mazar-i Sharif, and further clashes were recorded in May 2002, with fighting at Sar-i-Pul and Sholgara resulting in thirty deaths. A truce brokered by the United Nations was supposed to result in Mazar-i Sharif being policed by a force drawn from all the factions, with everyone else in the city prohibited from carrying arms. However, the truce was short-lived, and since then, there have been numerous clashes in the area. The 2 million people in the region have suffered greatly from this instability, which has damaged the social and economic fabric of the region.

Instability in the region has resulted in a general lawlessness, which has also hampered the work of the humanitarian aid agencies of the United Nations and nongovernmental organizations (NGOs). Assaults have also been made on aid workers; for example, a U.S. aid convoy was attacked, two Afghan members of the Swedish Committee were shot and wounded by militiamen, and a French aid worker was gang-raped near Mazar-i Sharif. The situation became so serious that the United Nations withdrew all female aid workers from the north in May 2002 and issued a warning to President Karzai about the future of humanitarian efforts in the region. The repatriation of refugees to the north has also added to the instability, and there have been several instances of abuses against the minority Pashtun community.

The problem in the north is made worse by the fact that both sides possess heavy weaponry, including tanks and artillery. The situation deteriorated again in April 2003 with further outbreaks of factional fighting in Maimana, resulting in at least seventeen deaths and a number of wounded; some of the casualties were children. The fighting was so severe that the United Nations withdrew all of its aid workers from the area until it was able to organize a cease-fire after a break in the fighting. By 17 April, rival militia had withdrawn from the city, and a neutral police force had been established to ensure security. Another complicating factor is that Dostum receives support from Uzbekistan and Atta is supported by the Afghan Defense Ministry, headed by Gen. Mohammad Fahim, the military leader of the Northern Alliance. Mazar-i Sharif is so significant that the long-term stability of the Kabul government rests, to an extent, on this situation being resolved. But as of March 2003, there were no signs that the hostilities would cease, and efforts to relocate Dostum to Kabul as security adviser to the president also seem to have failed.

In March 2003, at least sixty-four Afghans were killed in factional fighting in Badghis Province; thirty-eight civilians, including women and children, were among those killed. The United Nations also discovered the bodies of twenty-six fighters of a local commander—Juma Khan, from the minority Pashtun ethnic group—executed, with their hands tied behind their backs. Most of the Pashtuns in the province are nomadic herders, and because of the Taliban regime, they have been subjected to human rights abuses from other factions in the area. The bulk of the fighting was in the village of Akazi and the surrounding area, and the Afghan Human Rights Commission also found evidence that women had been raped by factional fighters.

Western Afghanistan

The dominant power in western Afghanistan is Isma'il Khan, the governor of Herat Province, who is being supported by Iran and is an extremely powerful leader: in fact, it would be impossible for the Karzai government to extend its authority over western Afghanistan without his support. Although nominally a member of the Islamist Movement, he is fiercely independent, and his influence also extends into neighboring provinces. However, despite his dominance, the region has not been immune from conflict, for clashes erupted between Isma'il Khan's forces and those of his Pashtun rivals Aman-

ullah Khan and Kareem Khan in July and August 2002.

The first outbreak took place in July 2002 at a former military base some 80 miles west of the city of Herat, an area heavily fought over since the Soviet withdrawal in 1989. The base is located where the Tajik north meets the Pashtun south. The Kabul government mediated in the dispute and arranged a truce, which was brokered by a vice-president and three cabinet ministers. Although Isma'il Khan affirms support for the central government, he has failed to cooperate over the formation of the new Afghan National Army and only remits to Kabul an extremely small percentage of his significant tax revenues, which largely come from cross-border trade with Iran.

In August 2002, there were further clashes between Isma'ili's militia and the Pashtun militia under Mohammed Kareem Khan, with a battle at Ghurian, west of the city of Herat, on 1 August resulting in at least fifty deaths. The administration in Herat stressed that the governor was trying to curb Pashtun involvement in smuggling and looting, but the Pashtuns claimed that they were trying to protect their villages from raids and looting by Tajik forces. Sporadic outbreaks are still occurring, and Isma'il Khan is still operating independently of the Kabul government, which, to date, does not have the capability to impose its control over western Afghanistan.

Eastern Afghanistan

Eastern Afghanistan is predominantly Pashtun but is controlled by a variety of Pashtun commanders. The most prominent is Badsha Khan (also known as Pacha Khan Zadran), who has been a major thorn in the side of the central government. He was initially named governor of Paktia Province, but this appointment was withdrawn and was also rejected by the council of Gardez, the provincial capital. As a result, a new appointment came from Kabul. Throughout 2002, there were continual outbreaks of fighting between the forces of Badsha Khan and those loyal to the Gardez authorities and the new governor. A similar situation existed in Khost Province, where Badsha Khan's brother had also been ousted from the post of governor; President Karzai threatened to send in troops but later withdrew the threat, which again damaged the credibility of the central government.

Badsha Khan's opposition to Karzai was made apparent at the June 2002 Loya Jirga when, as a supporter of the Zahir Shah, he walked out in protest at the former king's withdrawal from the presidential election, warning that bloodshed would follow. Initially, Badsha Khan had exercised control over Paktia, Logar, Paktika, and Khost Provinces and had dreams of creating a greater Paktia. However, these provinces were in a state of anarchy and lawlessness and had little in the way of security. Widespread violence continued throughout 2002, with hundreds of deaths and injuries. The situation was further complicated by Badsha Khan's active support for the U.S. forces in their campaign against the remnants of the Taliban and al-Qaeda in the region.

However, in September 2002, Badsha Khan's forces fell out with the U.S. Special Forces, and Afghan government troops immediately moved in, pushing Badsha Khan's fighters out of Gardez and Khost. These forces are now reduced to manning illegal roadblocks on the road between Gardez and Khost, and they are proving to be an irritant to soldiers and government officials trying to use the road. This area is particularly crucial to the central government due to its proximity to Pakistan and the continuous outbreaks of fighting with remnants of the Taliban and al-Qaeda.

Southern Afghanistan

The southern part of Afghanistan is a Pashtun area controlled by a number of Pashtun warlords, and there was evidence in late 2002 and early 2003 of a resurgence of Taliban and al-Qaeda activity there, in cooperation with fighters from Gulbuddin Hekmatyar's Islamic Party, who have issued a fatwa against U.S. forces and their Afghan allies. An examination of the area shows that the former Taliban administration is largely intact, with Shari'a law being strictly enforced. The city of Kandahar is also being subjected to rampant violence and criminal activity, and there is a general absence of law and order throughout the region. Again, the situation is complicated by the support of the warlords for U.S. military activity; this situation needs to be addressed, as the warlords believe that such cooperation entitles them to behave with impunity.

Instability has increased in the region with the repatriation of Afghan refugees from Pakistan and the problems related to assimilation, humanitarian aid, and ethnic tensions. However, eruptions of violence within the region have resulted in an extremely volatile situation that the Karzai government does not have the capacity to resolve.

Summary

It is clear that the security situation is extremely unstable throughout Afghanistan, with that in the northern area probably presenting the greatest internal threat. Instability in the east and south has led to greater activity on the part of remnants of the Taliban and al-Qaeda; it has also compelled the United States to continue to rely on support from the local warlords, which further complicates the situation. Among the challenges facing the Kabul government is the need to speed up reconstruction aid and use it effectively so that the population can begin to see benefits accruing from Operation Enduring Freedom. The disbursement of aid by the Karzai administration would enhance its prestige and bring warlords under some control in the expectation of receiving funds.

It is also crucial that the United States reconsider its strategy in dealing with local warlords in the ongoing military campaign and convince them that they have not been accorded immunity because of their cooperation. The United States must also avoid civilian casualties in the campaign if it is to win the hearts and minds of the population and not discredit its reputation and that of the Karzai administration. Further, it must make clear its continuing support for President Karzai and underscore its commitment to remain engaged until security and stability have been secured. The training of the new National Afghan Army must also be advanced and expanded to ensure that the Kabul government has the means to impose its authority in the provinces, and a national police force must be created to provide law and order throughout Afghanistan.

It is also essential that the disarmament process be implemented and the militias either recruited into the National Army or reintegrated into society and the civilian economy. A concerted effort must also be made to halt human rights abuses, and the central government must ensure that the Afghan Human Rights Commission, established by the Bonn Agreement, has the power and authority to deal with those guilty of violations. At the same time, efforts to integrate the regional warlords into the central government's decisionmaking process must continue, so that their status is not threatened, though their power is reduced. If problems related to the regional warlords and the general level of insecurity are not resolved, Afghanistan will again descend into total anarchy as soon as the Coalition forces have been withdrawn.

See also: Afghan Army; Dostum, Gen. Abdul Rashid; Isma'il Khan; Paktia Province

References

Baldauf, Scott. 2003. "Once Powerful Warlord Is Shunted Aside." http://www.afgha.com/?af=article&sid=29422 (cited 22 January 2003).

Davis, Anthony. 2002. "Karzai Struggles to Consolidate Afghanistan's Fragile Peace." *Jane's Intelligence Review* (August): 20–23.

Human Rights Watch. 2002. *Return of the Warlords.* New York: Human Rights Watch.

Rashid, Ahmed. 2001. *Taliban: The Story of the Afghan Warlords.* London: Pan.

WATANJAR, MUHAMMAD ASLAM (1946–)

Muhammad Aslam Watanjar held positions as minister of communications, interior, and defense in the Khaliqyar government that assumed power in Afghanistan in May 1990. He was a member of the Khalq faction of the People's Democratic Party of Afghanistan (PDPA) and a leading figure in the 1973 coup by Muhammad Daud, leading the assault on the Royal Palace with armored vehicles. He was also involved in the Saur Revolt of April 1978, again leading the attack on the palace. And he was subsequently joined by Gen. Abdul Qadir in heading the Revolutionary Council, which formed the government until Nur Muhammad Taraki became president. In September 1979, Watanjar was implicated in a plot to remove Hafizullah Amin from power, and he was forced to take refuge in the Soviet embassy in Kabul until the Parcham takeover. Following the revolt of Shanawaz Tanai in March 1990, Watanjar was appointed minister of defense by Dr. Muhammad Najibullah. He fled Afghanistan after the collapse of the Marxist regime in April 1992. Watanjar was born in 1946 in Paktia Province of a Ghilzai family and had been educated at military schools in Kabul and in the Soviet Union.

References

Arnold, Anthony. 1983. *Afghanistan's Two-Party Communism: Parcham and Khalq.* Stanford, CA: Hoover Institution Press.

WAZIRI TRIBE

The Waziris are Ghurghusht Pashtuns whose original home was in Paktika Province, but in the fourteenth century, they migrated eastward to settle in present-day Waziristan, now part of Pakistan, and in the adjacent portions of Afghanistan. The Waziris number about 250,000, most of whom inhabit the Pakistan side of the border, and they are divided into two main branches, the Ahmadzais and the Utmanzais. The tribe had supported Nadir Khan in his war against Habibullah Kalakani in 1929, and their forces had been responsible for the capture of Kabul and the royal palace in October 1929.

References

Hammerton, J. A. 1984. *Tribes, Races and Cultures of India and Neighbouring Countries: Afghanistan, Bhutan, Burma, Ceylon, Nepal, and Tibet.* Delhi, India: Mittal.

WOLUSMAL, MUHAMMAD HASAN (1940–)

Muhammad Hasan Wolusmal had a checkered career as a government official and a journalist, spending several terms in prison because of his journalistic activities. He was born in Gahik in 1940 and at first seemed destined for a career in agriculture, attending an agricultural high school in 1950. However, by 1959, he had changed the course of his career by obtaining a B.A. in journalism from Kabul University, becoming editor of the Pashtu programs for Radio Afghanistan in 1962.

He moved into government service in 1964 as director-general of the Smuggling Prevention Department and later assuming the district governorship in various provinces, including Baghlan, Jozjan, and Herat. He resigned from government service in 1968. He then returned to journalism and owned and edited a publication called *Afghan Weekly,* which was published from 1969 to 1972, when it was banned by the Ministry of Information and Culture. Despite the problem he had with the authorities in regard to the periodical, he returned to government service, becoming district governor of Balkh in 1972 and Kahdaman in 1973.

Wolusmal was unemployed between 1973 and 1976, before returning to government service in 1976 as director of inspection in the Land Development Agency and director-general for coordination in 1977. However, he was then arrested and was a political prisoner from 1978 to 1979 in the Deh, Mazany, and Pul-i Charkhi prisons. One year later, he fled to Pakistan. In Peshawar, he founded another publication, *Afghan Mujahid,* which began publication in 1981 and ceased in 1984 when it was banned by the authorities in Pakistan. In 1985, he became owner and editor of *Afghan Wolus,* but he again ran afoul of the authorities; the publication was banned, and he was sentenced to three months of imprisonment. His brother and brother-in-law were both assassinated in Peshawar in 1983.

References

Guistozzi, Antonio. 2000. *War, Politics, and Society in Afghanistan, 1978–1992.* Washington, DC: Georgetown University Press.

WOMEN IN AFGHANISTAN

Women had long played significant roles in Afghanistan's education, health, and civil service sectors, but they began to figure on the political scene with the arrival of the Marxist regime in Kabul in 1978 and the subsequent Soviet intervention. In 1977, the Revolutionary Association of Women of Afghanistan (RAWA) was founded, with the objective of fighting for human rights and social justice for women in the country. RAWA wanted to involve more women in social and political activities, to acquire human rights for women, and to aid the struggle to establish a government based on democratic and secular values.

However, after the Saur Revolt of April 1978, which brought the Communists to power, and the Soviet intervention in the next year, members of RAWA and other women in Afghanistan became embroiled in the resistance movement, suffered severe deprivation, and were often the victims of acts of violence from forces on both sides of the fight. The ten years of conflict against the Soviets and the Kabul government and the four years of civil war left many women widowed and with dependent families, and they tended to form the bulk of the refugee and internally displaced persons population.

The fall of the mujahideen government in September 1996 brought with it the rise of the fundamentalist Taliban government—a regime based on a strict interpretation of the Koran and the application of Shari'a law. It was the type of regime that women in organizations such as RAWA opposed, just as they had consistently opposed the fundamentalist mujahideen groups from 1979 onward. However, the excesses of the Taliban regime brought the issue of women's rights in Afghanistan to the fore on the international scene; in fact, they were cited as one of the reasons for Coalition involvement in Afghanistan in October 2001, though it had taken the terrorist attacks in the United States to generate real action in this area.

After the fall of Kabul in September 1996, the Taliban set up the Ministry for the Promotion of Virtue and the Prevention of Vice, which placed harsh, systematic restrictions on women's rights. Immediately thereafter, girls over the age of eight were prohibited from attending school, the Women's University of Kabul was closed, and females were forced to leave their employment. Further, all women had to stay at home, out of sight of male passersby, and they were only allowed in public places if they were clad from head to foot in *chadaris* (long garments that covered the entire person) and accompanied by a close male relative. The *burqa* (veil) had been introduced from the Arab world during the Soviet invasion, but the Taliban did not consider use of the burqa alone as sufficient.

A large percentage of women under the Taliban—probably as high as 64 percent—had no access to health facilities because of the problems of finding a female doctor or the high cost of the chadaris they were required to wear in public. Because the chadari is an expensive garment, women in poor villages sometimes shared one such garment and had to take turns to visit the local market, other public places, or their doctors. If no female doctor was available and women had to visit a male doctor, they had to remain fully dressed during the visit, making diagnosis difficult.

This situation represented a radical change in the fortunes of women in Afghanistan: prior to the civil war and the advent of the Taliban, they had been both educated and employed. Indeed, in the early 1990s, women accounted for 50 percent of all students, 70 percent of all teachers, 50 percent of all university lecturers, and 50 percent of all civilian government workers. In Kabul itself, 40 percent of all doctors were female. These figures illustrate the impact the Taliban directives had on the society and economy of Afghanistan. It was also thought that, before the Taliban, some 90 percent of the population believed women had the right to equal access to education, the right to work opportunities, freedom of expression, protection under the law, and opportunities to participate in government. The Taliban maintained that their policy with regard to women

Afghan women wait for food in a refugee camp, at Jallozai, Pakistan, 112 kilometers (70 miles) west of the capital Islamabad, 10 January 2001. The UN says renewed fighting in September displaced more than 70,000 civilians from the northeast Afghan province of Takhar, driving thousands into Pakistan. (Reuters NewMedia Inc./Corbis)

emanated from their religion and culture, but the Afghan belief system demonstrated that the Taliban had no right to claim that their human rights violations of women were culturally validated.

The Taliban government had also blatantly violated all agreements on women's rights, including the International Covenant of Economic, Social, and Cultural Rights (ICESCR), which had been signed by Afghanistan on 24 January 1983. The covenant is supposed to protect women from gender-based violence and guarantee them specific rights: the right to life; the right not to be subjected to torture or cruel, inhuman, or degrading treatment or punishment; the right to liberty and security; and the right to equality before the law, with definitive protection against gender-based discrimination. The treatment of women by the Taliban was in contravention of every agreement that had been entered into by former Afghan governments.

The ban on the employment of females was especially significant because, as a result of the wars, so many women were widows with dependant families who relied on their income for sustenance. It therefore became critical for the UN agencies and NGOs to try to direct aid to women and children, but even this was made more difficult by the edict issued by the Taliban forbidding women to work for NGOs. In addition, male aid workers were not allowed to make contact with women, and as a result, agencies were forced either to withdraw from Afghanistan or to curtail their activities. Throughout this period, areas not under Taliban control did not follow these edicts, and in the Panjshir Valley, Herat, and Mazar-i Sharif, women still continued to fully participate in Afghan life. But once areas came under Taliban control, the situation changed. However, the area controlled by the Northern Alliance in the Panjshir Valley was never under Taliban control, and at the Bonn Conference held in December 2001, one of the representatives of the Northern Alliance was Amena Afzali, a woman.

The fall of the Taliban and the formation of the Interim Government in December 2001 brought new hope for women in Afghanistan. The first evidence of a resurgence of pre-Taliban conditions was the return to education of some 3 million children, 30 percent of them girls, in 2002. In addition, a special scheme was launched in Kabul by the UN Children's Fund (UNICEF) to help females catch up on the lost years of education, with a three-month program during the schools' winter break in 2001and 2002 that attracted some 15,000 girls. The figure far exceeded expectations, and the program was extended to girls whose schooling had also suffered when they were exiled from Afghanistan's long-running conflicts.

The United Nations also launched a campaign, beginning on 26 January 2003, to immunize Afghan women against tetanus, with the goal of having all women of childbearing age immunized by 2005; currently, on a countrywide basis, only 13 percent of women have been inoculated. In February 2003, UNICEF, in cooperation with the Afghan government, launched a teacher-training program aimed at reaching 70,000 educators, with an emphasis on retraining women to enable them to take up their educational professions again. The courses focus on Afghan traditional literature and folklore, new styles of teaching, Afghan languages, child development, and land-mine awareness training. The latter is seen as a important element in education, for land mines and unexploded ordnance cause about 300 deaths or injuries a month in Afghanistan, with the majority of the victims being children.

However, concerns are currently being expressed by human rights and women's groups in regard to the treatment of women in the western province of Herat, under the governor Isma'il Khan. Clearly, women and girls are being forced to live under the very restrictions that were imposed by the Taliban. Human Rights Watch found that women's rights and jobs had improved slightly since the fall of the Taliban but that the improvement had been tempered by growing government repression of social and political life, with women's groups being censored and female leaders being intimidated and also sidelined from the administration in Herat.

Human Rights Watch has also reported that outside of Kabul, government troops and officials are regularly targeting women and girls for abuse and, in some areas, even reimposing Taliban restrictions, including the wearing of the chadari and the banning of music. The group has asked the government in Kabul to prohibit harassment and abuse of women and to appoint new governors in provinces where abuses are taking place. It has also urged international donors to support the work of Afghan women and women's groups throughout Afghanistan. The UN Assistance Mission in Afghanistan has been asked to expand monitoring activities and to make efforts to strengthen the Afghan Human Rights Commission. Human Rights Watch has criticized the Coalition forces, as well, charging that their support of repressive warlords is damaging women's right in Afghanistan and betraying the promises made regarding the liberation of Afghan women.

On 27 January 2003, the Afghan minister of women's affairs, Habiba Suraby, expressed concern about the situation in Herat and announced plans to visit the region. The United Nations also announced plans to send a human rights team into the region to discuss the restrictions on women's education imposed by the provincial authorities. According to these restrictions, for example, men were not able to teach women and girls, mixed-sex classes were no longer allowed, and boys and girls were not permitted to be in school at the same time. Furthermore, because female teachers were in short supply, opportunities for education became severely limited for females. In some areas, schools have been burned or shelled, and pamphlets warn families not to send their daughters to school. The situation had been complicated by the fact that Isma'il Khan's ruling had been upheld by the Afghan chief justice, Maulavi Fazel Hadi Shinwari, who refused to allow mixed-sex education, though it was unclear whether this ruling would be enforced by the Kabul government.

On another front, support for women is being provided by organizations such as the Foundation for International Community Assistance (FINCA), which, on 12 November 2002, announced the establishment of a microcredit program to provide small amounts of capital, ranging from $50 to $300, to begin or expand businesses. In Afghanistan, FINCA aims to provide credit and other financial services for returning female refugees and other women, many of whom are widows with dependent families, and orphans. Although it is recognized that small loans will not make an impact on the country's economy, it is felt that they will have a major effect on individual women. FINCA also intends to introduce village banking to provide seed capital and to ensure that women dependent on their own activities can obtain more reliable sources of income. This operation is similar to that conducted by RAWA, though on a much larger scale and with international backing.

It is evident that women are still suffering at the hands of conservative Islamic judges, who often take a skeptical view of victimized women. A reporter visiting Kabul's women's prison in February 2003 came across several examples of injustice toward women and disproportionate sentences for women as compared to those meted out to men found guilty of the same offense. Women with little status or no education have almost no recourse against actions brought by husbands or in-laws. In the rural areas, some of the restrictions imposed by the Taliban have been lifted, but the fundamental primacy of Islamic and tribal law still prevails. Conditions in the women's prison are harsh, conditions are filthy, food is poor unless supplemented from outside, and women and their children live in a state of hopelessness. Much remains to be done in this area if the basic human rights for women are to be realized.

See also: Humanitarian Relief; Reconstruction Program; Refugee Problem; Revolutionary Association of Women of Afghanistan

References

Coursen-Neff, Zama, and John Sifton. 2003. " Afghan Regression." http://www.postconflict.unep.ch/high1.htm (cited 21 January 2003).

Dupree, Nancy Hatch. 1998. *Afghan Women under the Taliban.* In *Fundamentalism Reborn? Afghanistan and the Taliban,* edited by William Maley, 145–166. London: Hurst.

Lindgreen, Rose V. "Women under the Taliban." *Humanist* 62, no. 4: 21–25.

Marsden, Peter. 1998. *The Taliban: War, Religion and the New Order in Afghanistan.* London and New York: Zed Books.

"'We Want to Live as Humans': Repression of Women and Girls in Western Afghanistan." 2002. http://www.hrw.org/reports/2002/afghanwmn1202/ (cited 2 December 2002).

Y

YALANTUSH KHAN (?–1886)

Until 1837, Yalantush Khan was chief of the Jamshidis of Herat and was then sent by the amir, together with 1,000 families, to colonize Bala Murghab. In March 1884, he was appointed governor of Panjdeh and took part in military actions against the Russians on 30 March 1885 but was then placed under surveillance by the authorities. At the time, the Afghan Boundary Commission was operating in northern Afghanistan trying to resolve boundary issues, and Yalantush was banned from having contact with the team. He was removed as chief of the Jamshidis and replaced by a weak leader, Hadir Kuli Khan, but he still retained the respect of the British officers in the commission. In June 1886, he was taken, with his family, to Kabul, suspected of having been in contact with the Russian authorities. However, it is thought that this charge was fabricated by the governor of Herat to gain control of the Jamshidi and Firozkoti tribes. Nevertheless, Yalantush was believed to have been executed in December 1886.

References
Tate, George Passman. 1975. *The Kingdom of Afghanistan: A Historical Sketch.* New York: AMS Press.

YAQUB KHAN, AMIR MUHAMMAD (C. 1849–1923)

Yaqub Khan was the son of Amir Shir Ali and governor of Herat but had designs on Kandahar and was angered when the amir gave the governorship to another son, Abdullah Jan. In 1871, Yaqub Khan rebelled and marched on Kabul, but he was defeated and forced to return to Herat; he was pardoned by the amir and reappointed as governor. On promise of safe conduct, he went to Kabul, but the amir did not hold to the safe conduct promise, and Yaqub Khan was kept in confinement until December 1978 when the British invaded Afghanistan. Following the British invasion, Amir Shir Ali left for northern Afghanistan to seek Russian support, having appointed Yaqub as his regent. When Shir Ali died on 21 February 1879, Yaqub proclaimed himself amir.

In an attempt to preserve his throne, Yaqub sought to make peace with Britain and signed the Treaty of Gandomak, which forced him to accept a British mission to Kabul under Sir Pierre Louis Cavagnari, who arrived in July 1879. However, on 3 September, rebellious soldiers and Kabul citizens attacked the British mission and killed Cavagnari and his staff. As a result, Yaqub was forced to abdicate in October 1879, to be replaced as ruler by Abdur Rahman Khan. He then left for India, where he died in exile in 1923. Britain, meanwhile, had extricated its troops from Afghanistan for fear of another disastrous involvement similar to the First Anglo-Afghan War.

References
Gregorian, Vartan. 1969. *The Emergence of Modern Afghanistan: Politics of Reform and Modernization, 1880–1946.* Stanford, CA: Stanford University Press.

YAQUBI, GEN. GHULAM FARUQ (1938–1992)

Gen. Ghulam Faruq Yaqubi was a significant figure in the Afghan Security Service, KHAD, from 1980 to 1985, becoming president of the organization in 1985 after Dr. Muhammad Najibullah. He was then upgraded to minister of state security, and he held this position in 1988 and 1990 as an important ally of Najibullah. In 1986, he had also become a member of the Politburo of the People's Democratic Party of Afghanistan (PDPA), probably as a result of his alliance with Najibullah. His formal education had taken place within the Afghan police force, for he had studied at the Kabul police academy, and then in West Germany before becoming a lecturer at the Kabul academy in 1961. He then became director of operations and general director of the criminal department of the Ministry of Interior before moving into state security. Yaqubi is said to have committed suicide on 16 April 1992, but other reports contend that he was assassinated by a Parchami rival.

References

Grover, Verinder. 2000. *Afghanistan: Government and Politics.* New Delhi: Deep and Deep Publications.

YAR MUHAMMAD, WAZIR (?–1851)

Wazir Yar Muhammad was the prime minister under Prince Kamran, who ruled Herat from 1830 to 1842, and in this position, he held the real power. Reputed to be a capable administrator but with a cruel nature, he is best remembered for his defense of Herat against Persian incursions in 1833 and from 1837 to 1838. In the latter siege, the Persians were supported by the Russian General Borovski, whereas the British officer, Maj. Eldred Pottinger, supported Prince Kamran; as a reward, the major was appointed political officer to the ruler. In 1842, the *wazir* (chief adviser to the ruler) had the prince assassinated and embarked on a conquest of the western region of Afghan Turkestan, having allied himself through marriage with Akbar Khan, the son of Amir Dost Muhammad.

References

Pottinger, George. 1983. *The Afghan Connection: The Extraordinary Adventures of Major Eldred Pottinger.* Edinburgh: Scottish Academic Press.

YUSSUF KHAN, MUHAMMAD (1855–?)

Muhammad Yussuf Khan was the son of Amir Dost Muhammad and was with his father at Herat when the elder man died in 1863. In May 1886, after Amir Shir Ali was defeated by Afzal Khan at the Battle of Saidabad, he deserted Shir Ali to join the victor, but when Shir Ali regained power, he switched sides again. In 1877, Yussuf became governor of Girishk, but when Shir Ali fled from Kabul in 1878, he also fled to Herat. However, he was ordered to return to Kabul by Amir Yaqub Khan and dispatched again to Girishk as governor, a post he held until the outbreak of war on 3 September 1879.

Yussuf was a member of a mission sent to meet Abdur Rahman and he remained in Kabul for the proclamation of Abdur Rahman as amir on 22 July 1880. Yussuf was then made governor of Kabul, a post he held until 1881, when he was supposed to take up a post as governor of Kandahar. This move was opposed by factions within the province, and he accompanied the amir in charge of forces to defeat the opposition led by Sardar Ayub. However, rather than moving into the governor's position, he was instead sent by the amir to Herat with a small force of cavalry and infantry to retake the province from the forces of Ayub Khan. He returned from Farah in 1883 when Herat was captured by Quddus Khan and was sent to depose Ibrahim Khan of Chamnkarsur, which he achieved with only a regiment of troops. In April 1884, he was appointed as governor of Farah, a post he held until 1888.

See also: Herat Province

References

Dupree, Louise. 1980. *Afghanistan.* Princeton, NJ: Princeton University Press.

Z

ZABIBULLAH, ABDUL QADIR (1951–1984)

A member of the Organization of Muslim Youth, which became part of the Islamist Movement, Abdul Qadir Zabibullah became a successful mujahideen commander operating with Ahmad Shah Masood, military commander of the Northern Alliance. He was born in Mazar-i Sharif in 1951 and was educated at elementary and secondary school in the town before taking a job as a teacher at Bakhtar High School. He became a supporter of the Jawanan-i-Muslimin (an Islamic movement and forerunner of the Islamic Society of Afghanistan) but left for Pakistan following the Saur Revolt of April 1978, which brought the Communists to power. He returned to Pakistan in 1979 and joined the mujahideen movement, becoming active in the resistance in Baghlan Province and in Mazar-i Sharif, where he linked up with Masood, adopting the nom de guerre Zabibullah. His activities were initially in the Panjshir Valley; he became an extremely capable coordinator of guerrilla activities in the area and an able administrator of the territory controlled by the mujahideen. On 11 November 1984, he was killed when his vehicle struck a land mine. His death led to the collapse of organized resistance in the Mazar-i Sharif area. He was a member of the Islamic Society of Afghanistan.

References
Karp, Craig. 1984. *Afghan Resistance and Soviet Occupation: A Five-Year Summary.* Washington, DC: U.S. Department of State, Bureau of Public Affairs.

ZABUL PROVINCE

Zabul is a province in south-central Afghanistan, occupying an area of 6,590 square miles and having a population of some 181,000. The administrative center is Qalat, which is located 87 miles northeast of Kandahar; the British occupied its fort during the Second Anglo-Afghan War (1878 to 1879). The population of the province is largely Pashtun in the north and Hazara in the south, and the capital has a population of about 40,000, mainly from the Ghilzai tribe. The area is constantly swept by winds and is extremely arid, with the only productive land being in the valleys of the Tarnak and Arghastan Rivers, together with a few areas irrigated by the traditional *qanat* or *kariz* systems. The province is, however, noted for its almond trees: almonds are a major export and important to the economy of the area. The Zabulis are also renowned for their prowess at the traditional game of tent pegging (*maiza bazi*), which requires great skill in spearing pegs that have been fixed in the ground.

References
Adamec, Ludwig W. 1972–1985. *Historical and Political Gazetteer of Afghanistan.* 6 vols. Graz, Austria: Akademische Druck-u Verlagsansalt.

ZAHIR SHAH, MOHAMMED (1914–)

Mohammed Zahir Shah was the only surviving son of Nadir Shah and reigned as king of Afghanistan from 1933 to 1973 before being forced to abdicate. He was educated in Kabul and France, becoming king on 8 November 1933 following the assassination of his father. During the early part of his reign until 1946, real power rested with his uncles Muhammad Hashim and Shah Mahmud Ghazi, with the former holding the position of minister of war and commander-in-chief and the latter prime minister. The king's cousin Muhammad Daud succeeded Ghazi as prime minister in 1953, a position he held until 1963 when the king forced his resignation.

During the early period of Zahir's rule, a proliferation of newspapers and journals instigated a debate among intellectuals on the problems of modernization, the relationship of Islam to society and the individual, and the relationship between modernization and Islam. Archaeological explorations were also taking place in Afghanistan during this period and revealing evidence of the country's past glories, leading modernizers to see the exploration of the past as a means of restoring Afghan glory and diminishing the role of religion. It must be noted, however, that these discussions were restricted to the elite and did not percolate down to the largely conservative general populace.

The economy of Afghanistan also developed during this period, with the introduction of banking institutions, the development of trade in exports of agricultural products, and an increase in the transit trade with Central Asia following improved relations with the Soviet Union. The country had also benefited from remaining neutral during World War II, and it became a haven for refugees from Central Asia, many of whom provided cheap technical expertise for the development program. On the political scene, there was a relaxation of control and an increase in international ties, especially with the United States. Further political reforms were instituted in 1949, resulting in the reformists securing a third of the seats in the new assembly. In addition, laws were passed to establish a free press, and thereafter, new newspapers and journals sprang up overnight, most of them pursuing a reformist agenda while still pledging loyalty to the monarch. A student union was also established at Kabul University, with many of its leading participants having been members of Awakened Youth, an organization founded in 1947. The student union began to pursue an agenda directed against the abuses of the royal family and the misuse of Islam to sustain injustice. However, the government closed the student union in 1951, which was followed by press closures in 1952.

One year later, Muhammad Daud, cousin and brother-in-law of the king, became prime minister, and his policies were very much of a reformist nature: he regarded the government as too conservative, the religious bodies as too reactionary, and the newly emerging capitalists as too powerful. It was Daud's intention to pursue reformist policies by bringing the intellectuals into government and by increasing the strength of the military to ensure stable government. At the same time, he sought to court public support for military expenditures by highlighting the question of Pashtunistan—which the Pashtuns pursued with the objective of either bringing the Pashtun tribes in Pakistan back under

Afghan control or securing independence or autonomy for the region—thus guaranteeing support from the powerful Pashtun tribes.

Daud's policies required outside assistance, but due to the prevailing Cold War politics, the United States was not prepared to meet Daud's needs, especially in the military sector, and he was forced to turn to the Soviet Union for assistance and technical expertise. As a consequence, Afghanistan became ignored by the West and was increasingly drawn into the orbit of the Soviet Union, even as its relations with neighbor Pakistan continued to deteriorate. On the social front, Daud pursued reforms in women's issues and education, though the effects on the female population were mainly restricted to women living in Kabul. A road system connecting all the major cities and providing links with Pakistan was also constructed, with assistance from the United States. Ultimately, however, because of the continued clashes with Pakistan over the Pashtunistan issue and his own autocratic methods, Daud became a liability to the government, and the king forced his resignation in 1963.

In 1964, Zahir Shah promulgated a new constitution, one objective of which was to exclude certain members of the royal family from holding government positions, particularly those of prime minister, Supreme Court judge, or member of parliament. The measure was largely directed against Muhammad Daud, whose foreign policy had been extremely unsuccessful, based as it was on Pashtun nationalism. The constitution had several liberal elements: it provided for a bicameral parliament, free elections, a free press, and the formation of political parties. This period of political tolerance was largely unsuccessful because members of parliament could not establish working coalitions to bring about a stable government. Measures regarding the establishment of political parties were never ratified by the king, and so parties were not legally permitted. They were, however, tolerated, and political manifestos appeared in periodicals and privately printed newspapers. As a result, all members of parliament were independent, and political infighting ensued. It was evident that Zahir Shah had not seized the opportunity of constitutional reform to take a firm grasp on the reins of government, and his rule during this period was characterized by indecision and procrastination.

However, Afghanistan received considerable amounts of foreign aid from both the West and the Soviet Union, and the capital area experienced substantial economic growth. But the economic boom was not experienced throughout Afghanistan or across all strata of society. In July 1973, while the king was abroad, Muhammad Daud staged a successful coup, resulting in the abdication of Zahir Shah and his exile in Rome. At the fall of the Taliban in 2001, there were calls for the king to return from exile to lead the Interim Government, but he indicated an unwillingness to take on this role. However, members of his entourage were involved in the December 2001 Bonn negotiations to establish an interim government, and the Rome group of exiles were represented in the new body. It was also agreed that Zahir Shah would chair the first meeting of the Loya Jirga (Great Council), which was charged with setting up a representative government at the expiration of the Interim Government's mandate. The former king still retains a large measure of political support among some of the Pashtun tribes and elsewhere has been accepted as a leading member of Afghan society, though he still maintains that he has no interest in a position of power within the post-Taliban government.

References
Dixit, J. 2000. *An Afghan Diary: Zahir Shah to Taliban.* New Delhi: Konark Publishers.
Magnus, Ralph, and Eden Naby. 2000. *Afghanistan: Mullah, Marx and Mujahid.* Boulder, CO: Westview Press.

ZALMAI KHAN (?–1960)

Zalmai Khan was one of the leaders of the Khost Rebellion in 1925, which was led by the Mangal tribe and was a protest against the reform program of King Amanullah. After the defeat of the rebel forces, Zalmai took refuge in Kurram, but he was arrested and deported to Abbottabad in 1925. A year later, he was taken back to Kabul as a guest of the king and pardoned, enabling him to return to Khost later that year. He was active in politics again in 1929, aiding Nadir Shah in his successful campaign against Habibullah Kalakani, thus securing the Afghan throne for Nadir Shah. In 1930, he was appointed Naib Sular, and on 30 May, he was responsible for negotiating a successful customs duties agreement with the Ghilzais in Ghazni. In November 1932, he accompanied Shah Mahmud to Gardez in Paktia

Province in a successful quelling of the Dare Khal Revolt. Although he lived most of his life in Kabul, he was nonetheless an important and influential figure in the area occupied by the Mangal tribe.

See also Khost Rebellion
References
Poullada, Leon B. *Reform and Rebellion in Afghanistan, 1919–1929.* Ithaca, NY: Cornell University Press.

ZAMAN, SHAH (1772–1844)

Shah Zaman was one of the twenty-three sons of Timur Shah, and at the time of his father's death in 1793, he was governor of Kabul. He succeeded to the throne. Although he ruled for ten years, most of the period was spent in civil war struggles with his brothers Mahmud and Humayun. He also planned to invade India to defeat the Maratha Confederation (an alliance of Indian rulers opposed to British conquest of India), but the British concluded a treaty with Persia in order to keep the Afghans out of India.

In 1798, the Sikhs revolted in Lahore and massacred the Afghan garrison there, but Shah Zaman restored order and appointed Ranjit Singh governor of Lahore. He also abolished the hereditary posts established by Ahmad Shah Durrani and operated a repressive regime that carried out numerous executions, thus antagonizing much of the population. While he was on a visit to the Punjab, there was a revolt in Kandahar, which brought his brother Mahmud to power, and Shah Zaman was forced to flee to Peshawar. Subsequently, he was captured and taken back to Kabul, where he was blinded and imprisoned. However, he escaped and fled to India, where he lived in exile until his death in 1844.

References
Malleson, George B. *History of Afghanistan from the Earliest Period to the Outbreak of the War of 1878.* London: W. H. Allen.
Schofield, Victoria. 1984. *North West Frontier and Afghanistan.* New Delhi: D. K. Agencies.

ZHAWAR, BATTLE OF (1986)

Zhawar is a village located south of Parachinar in Khost Province, some 6 miles from the Pakistan border. It was the location of a major base along the supply route used by the mujahideen for attacks on the government garrison at Khost; indeed, its significance is illustrated by the fact that 60 percent of mujahideen supplies moved along that route. The base had been built by a Pakistani construction company and featured large, underground facilities with tunnels containing living quarters, medical facilities, and storage for weapons and ammunition. The facility had electricity provided by its own generators, which also permitted radio communications. The base was defended by commanders of the forces of Sayyed Ahmad Gailani, Gulbuddin Hekmatyar, and Muhammad Nabi, with one of the noted commanders being Jalaluddin Hagani.

The base was administered and protected by some 400 mujahideen, and there were some 10,000 mujahideen forces patrolling between Zhawar and Ali Khel, with reinforcements readily available from across the Pakistan border. The base was well defended, as the mujahideen had antiaircraft protection, blowpipe missiles, shoulder-fired SA-7s, heavy artillery, mortars, and an antitank minefield. The base was a thorn in the side of the Kabul government, which sought to destroy the facility and to close off the supply lines of the mujahideen forces.

In April 1986, the government in Kabul, with Soviet assistance, began a campaign against Zhawar, with Gen. Shanawaz Tanai in overall control and the Soviet-Afghan contingent being led by Brig. Abdul Ghafur. The combined forces numbered some 12,000 men, with the Soviets providing one air assault regiment and the Afghans deploying units from the Seventh and Eighth Divisions from Kabul, the Twelfth Division from Gardez, and the Fourteenth Division from Ghazni and Khost. Progress toward Zhawar was slow because resistance was heavy, but the base was reached on 11 April 1986. The Kabul government forces isolated the base and destroyed the underground facilities with laser-guided bombs. Although the base was captured, the government forces withdrew shortly after, and the mujahideen reoccupied the area some forty-eight

hours later. Claims and counterclaims were made with regard to the casualties inflicted, with Kabul saying government forces killed 2,000 mujahideen and wounded 4,000, whereas the mujahideen put their losses at 300 and claimed to have killed or wounded 1,500 of the government forces and taken 100 prisoners. Regardless of these conflicting claims, it is clear that the government campaign was unsuccessful, as the mujahideen were not displaced from the area.

See also Soviet War in Afghanistan

References

Galeotti, Mark. 1995. *Afghanistan, the Soviet Union's Last War.* Portland, OR: Frank Cass.

ZIRAI, SALEH MUHAMMAD (1936–)

Saleh Muhammad Zirai was a founding member of the Khalq faction of the People's Democratic Party of Afghanistan (PDPA) and was a member of PDPA's Central Committee in 1988. In July 1979, he had been appointed minister of health, and in the following May, Babrak Karmal appointed him to the PDPA Politburo and made him secretary of the Central Committee. His success continued under Muhammad Najibullah, who appointed him in 1986 to the Council of Ministers and, in 1988, made him a chair of the House of Representatives. However, he was implicated in the attempted coup staged by Shanawaz Tanai and was expelled from the PDPA on 8 March 1990 and imprisoned.

He was born in Kandahar and educated in the Faculty of Medicine at Kabul University. In 1969, he stood for parliament but was arrested and imprisoned for six years for opposing the government.

References

Brigot, Andre, and Olivier Roy. 1988. *The War in Afghanistan: An Account and Analysis of the Country, Its People, Soviet Intervention, and the Resistance.* New York: Harvester-Wheatsheaf.

Chronology

2000–1000 B.C.	Arians move from northern Afghanistan to northern India
522–486	Afghan region comes under Achaemenid Empire of Darius I
330–327	Alexander the Great arrives and rules Bactria; Balkh becomes province of Greek Empire
50 A.D.–250	Afghanistan region is part of Kushanid Empire
225–600s	Sassanids establish control over region
652–664	First conquests made by Arab Muslims
Eighth–Tenth Centuries	Hindushahis rule Kabul and eastern Afghanistan
997–1150	Ghaznavids rule Afghanistan
1186	Ghorids succeed Ghaznavids
1227–1350	Kurt dynasty rules in Balkh, Ghazni, and Sarakhs
1370	Timur-i-Lang crowned in Balkh
1405–1506	Timurid rule in Balkh and Herat
1504–1525	Region invaded by Babur; Kabul established as capital
1600	British East India Company established
1648	Kandahar captured by Persians
1709–1738	Ghilzais dynasty established; also rules Iran
1713	Mir Wais revolt erupts in Kandahar
1716	Abdali revolt occurs in Herat
1747	Ahmad Shah Durrani crowned, beginning twenty-six-year reign; he will unite Afghan tribes and establish Sadozai dynasty
1748	Durrani attacks Lahore, and India is invaded for third time; Ahmad Shah becomes suzerain ruler of India; coins struck in his name
1761	Afghans defeat Maratha Confederation; Ahmad Shah's empire incorporates Kashmir, the Punjab, and part of Baluchistan
1769–1770	Ahmad Shah advances into Khorasan
1772	Ahmad Shah dies on 16 October
1773	Timur Shah crowned, beginning twenty-year reign; he will move capital from Kandahar to Kabul and wage campaigns in Sind and Bukhara
1793	Zaman Shah comes to power, beginning six-year reign
1798	British policy of containing Afghanistan is established in effort to prevent further invasions of India; Persia seen as partner in this policy; Sikh revolt occurs in Lahore, and Afghan garrison is massacred

1800	Mahmud Shah deposes Shah Shuja, beginning three-year rule		Shah Shuja to restore latter to Afghan throne
		9 September	Siege of Herat lifted
1803	Shah Shuja regains throne from Mahmud Shah	1 October	Britain breaks diplomatic relations with Dost Muhammad and declares war
1805	Persia launches unsuccessful attack on Herat	1839	First Anglo-Afghan War is waged, beginning on 14 April
1809	British envoy Mountstuart Elphinstone and Shah Shuja sign defensive alliance, first official contact between Afghanistan and European power; Shah Mahmud defeats Shah Shuja at Gandomak and will rule until Barakzai revolt in 1817	25 April	British forces under Sir John Keane arrive at Kandahar
		23 July	British forces capture Ghazni
		2 August	Amir Dost Muhammad flees from Kabul
		7 August	Kabul occupied by British Army of the Indus
		15 October	Bengal regiments begin return march to India
1816	Another Persian attack on Herat is unsuccessful	18 October	Bombay regiments begin to move back to India
1818	Civil war erupts in Afghanistan; kingdom becomes a series of virtually independent states; Ranjit Singh seizes Peshawar and conquers Kashmir	1840	
		August	Amir Dost Muhammad leaves Bukhara
		2 November	Dost Muhammad surrenders to British army
		12 November	Dost Muhammad leaves for exile in India
1826	Dost Muhammad, ruler of Ghazni, captures Kabul		
1833	Persians lay siege to Herat	1841	
		2 November	Sir Alexander Burnes and staff of British mission killed in Kabul
1834	Dost Muhammad defeats Shah Shuja and occupies Kandahar; Afghanistan loses Peshawar to Sikhs	7 November	Sardar Muhammad Akbar returns to Bamian
		18 November	Sir William Macnaghten recommends continued defense of Kabul
1835	Dost Muhammad's first period of rule begins	13 December	British forces evacuate Bala Hisar
		22 December	British troops ordered to evacuate Ghazni, Kandahar, and Jalalabad
1837	Lord Auckland appointed governor-general of India; Akbar Khan, son of Dost Muhammad, defeats Sikhs at Jamrud	23 December	Macnaghten assassinated by Sardar Muhammad Akbar; mutiny occurs at Kandahar
August	Eldred Pottinger arrives at Herat	1842	
20 September	Alexander Burnes arrives in Kabul as British emissary	January	Treaty of Capitulation ratified
23 November	Herat besieged again by Persians	6 January	British forces begin retreat from Kabul
19 December	Capt. Ivan Vitkevich arrives in Kabul as an emissary from Russia	13 January	British army makes last stand at Jagdalak; sole survivor, surgeon Brydon, arrives at Jalalabad
1838		5 April	General Pollock's forces cross the Khyber Pass
26 April	Alexander Burnes leaves Kabul		
26 June	Treaty signed between Ranjit Singh, British East India Company, and	7 April	Afghans defeated in Battle of Jalalabad

25 April	Shah Shuja assassinated by Shiya-ud-Daula at Kabul
May	General Pollock arrives at Jalalabad; Kalat-i-Ghilzai relieved; Sardar Akhbar captures Bala Hasir
June	Fateh Khan becomes amir until September
7 August	Kandahar evacuated
20 August	General Pollock moves from Jalalabad, skirmishes with Afghan forces near Gandomak
5 September	British forces reenter Ghazni
15 September	General Pollock arrives at Kabul; bazaar set on fire, city plundered, and much destroyed
19 September	General Nott arrives in Kabul
12 October	British forces leave Kabul
December	Dost Muhammad returns to Kabul, is recognized as amir by Britain, and begins rule of twenty-one years
1845	Akbar Khan dies
1855	Treaty of Peshawar reestablishes diplomatic links between Britain and Afghanistan; Dost Muhammad retakes Kandahar
1856 October	Persian forces capture Herat and occupy city for some months
1857 January	Anglo-Afghan Treaty signed in Peshawar, which guarantees Afghanistan's territorial integrity and provides subsidy for Dost Muhammad
1859	Britain captures Baluchistan, and Afghanistan becomes landlocked
1863	Dost Muhammad retakes Herat but dies shortly afterward; Shir Ali ascends Afghan throne and will spend two years putting down revolts by his half brothers Azam and Afzal and his brother Muhammad Amin; Abdur Rahman and Azam attack Kabul and free Abdur Rahman's father
1865	Russia takes Bukhara, Tashkent, and Samarkand

1866	Afzal becomes amir; Shir Ali flees to Kandahar
1867	Amir Afzal dies
1868	Azam becomes amir
1869	Shir Ali defeats Azam; Abdur Rahman goes into exile in Samarkand; Britain recognizes Shir Ali as amir but refuses to recognize his son, Abdullah Jan, as successor
March	Ambala Conference held between Amir Shir Ali and the viceroy of India, Lord Mayo
1872	Granville-Gorchakoff Agreement between Britain and Russia guarantees Afghanistan is outside of Russia's sphere of influence; Sistan boundary marked by British commission; Abdullah Jan named as heir to throne; Yaqub Khan, eldest son of Shir Ali, revolts and flees to Herat; Russians take Khiva
1872	Ayub Khan imprisoned in Kabul by Shir Ali; Russia establishes boundary between Afghanistan and its new territories and promises to respect Afghan territorial integrity
1876	Quetta occupied by the British
1878 22 July	Russian mission led by General Stolietoff arrives in Kabul for talks with Shir Ali
21 September	British envoy Gen. Sir Neville Chamberlain denied passage to Kabul by Gen. Faiz Muhammad, commander of Ali Masjid; Britain gives Shir Ali an ultimatum, demanding his apology to Chamberlain
November	General Grodekoff arrives in Herat from Samarkand
21 November	Second Anglo-Afghan War begins; Sir Samuel Brown attacks Fort Ali Masjid; General Roberts crosses Afghan border at Thal; Gen. Donald Steward sets out from Quetta for Kandahar

22 November	Fort Ali Masjid captured by British forces
20 December	Jalalabad occupied by General Brown
23 December	Shir Ali leaves Kabul for the north and appoints Yaqub Khan governor of Kabul

1879

12 January	Kandahar captured by General Stewart; Qalat-i-Ghilzai captured thereafter
21 February	Amir Shir Ali dies at Mazar-i Sharif; Yaqub Khan proclaimed as amir
26 May	Treaty of Gandomak signed by Amir Yaqub Khan and British representative, Sir Louis Cavagnari
24 July	Cavagnari takes up post as British envoy to Kabul
3 September	Cavagnari and staff killed by rebellious Afghan soldiers and civilian protestors
6 October	General Roberts's army wins Battle of Charasia
12 October	Roberts occupies Kabul
28 October	Amir Yaqub Khan forced to abdicate
14 December	General Baker driven from Asmai hills with large losses; Roberts abandons positions at Bala Hisar and Kabul and redeploys to Sharpur
15–22 December	Communication lines of British army cut by Muhammad Jan, who lays siege to Sharpur
23 December	Muhammad Jan defeated, and British move back to Bala Hisar

1880

Mid-June	Sardar Ayub Khan moves from Herat to attack Kandahar
10 July	General Burrows and brigade of troops move against Ayub Khan
22 July	Abdur Rahman recognized by Britain as amir of Afghanistan
27 July	Battle of Maiwand occurs; General Burrows is routed, and survivors seek security in Kandahar
6 August	Ayub Khan moves into Kandahar
8 August	British under General Roberts move from Kabul to Kandahar
11 August	General Stewart withdraws from Kabul, and Amir Abdur Rahman moves into city
16 August	Sortie launched on Kandahar by British garrison repulsed, with heavy losses

31 August	General Roberts arrives at Kandahar
1 September	Ayub Khan defeated at Baba Wali by General Roberts
9 September	British troops withdraw from Paiwar Kotal and the Kurram Valley and return to India; withdrawal from Jalalabad begins

1881

21 April	British complete withdrawal from Kandahar, marking end of Second Anglo-Afghan War

1883	Britain annexes Quetta district; Amir Abdur Rahman occupies Shignan and Roshan and is granted a subsidy of 1.2 million rupees by Britain
1884	Britain and Russia begin negotiations on northern boundary of Afghanistan; British mission sent to Herat, and Quetta railway started; Pul-i-Khatun occupied by Russia
1885	Russia takes Zulfikar, Akrobat, and the Panjdeh
1886	Bolan railway to Quetta constructed by Britain; British boundary commission returns to India after visiting Kabul
1887	Russia occupies Karki; final settlement reached between Britain and Russia on demarcation of Afghan-Russian frontier; Ayub Khan escapes from Persia and begins rebellion in Afghanistan, which fails; he surrenders at Mashhad and is exiled to India

1888

January	Quetta railway extended by Britain to Kila Abdullah
July	Ishaq Khan revolts in Turkestan but is forced to retreat to Samarkand

1891	Amir Abdur Rahman introduces oath of allegiance on Koran for his counselors
1892	Hazara uprising suppressed

1893
12 November — Durand Agreement signed between Britain and Afghanistan, demarcating eastern and southern borders of Afghanistan; subsidy to Amir Abdur Rahman is increased, and Britain allows Afghanistan to import military equipment

1896 — Amir Abdur Rahman brings Kafiristan into the Afghan state and renames area as the Province of Nuristan

1900 — Russia presses Britain for right to negotiate directly with Afghanistan over northern borders

1901
1 October — Amir Abdur Rahman dies
3 October — Habibullah proclaimed as amir and begins eighteen-year reign

1902 — Sir Henry Dobbs begins reerection of border pillars on Afghan-Russian border, with work completed in 1903

1903 — Boundary with Sistan demarcated by British mission led by A. H. McMahon; Habibia Secondary School opened in Kabul; Quetta-to-Nushki railroad construction begun by Britain

1905 — Signing of Anglo-Afghan Treaty, under which Amir Habibullah confirms agreements reached between Britain and Amir Abdur Rahman in 1880 and 1893

1905 — McMahon arbitration award over Sistan rejected by Iran

1905
January — Amir Habibullah visits India
31 August — Anglo-Russian Convention signed to agree on spheres of influence in Afghanistan, Iran, and Tibet

1909 — Attempt to assassinate Amir Habibullah fails

1910 — Telephone is introduced in Afghanistan with opening of line between Kabul and Jalalabad

1911 — Afghan Young Movement (Wish Zalmyan) founded by Mahmoud Tarzi, with anti-British and pro-Turkish sentiments

1914 — Afghanistan declares neutrality during World War I; Gen. Muhammad Nadir Khan becomes commander-in-chief of Afghan army

1915
September — German Hentig-Niedermayer Expedition arrives in Afghanistan and remains for nine months; members meet Amir Habibullah in Kabul

1918 — Kabul Museum opens

1919
20 February — Amir Habibullah assassinated in Laghman Province; Nasrullah Khan named amir in Jalalabad
25 February — Amanullah proclaimed amir in Kabul
28 February — Nasrullah arrested by Amanullah
3 March — Amanullah requests treaty negotiations with Britain
13 April — Afghanistan's independence proclaimed by Amanullah.
1 May — Afghan troops under Saleh Muhammad Khan move to Indian border, ostensibly on inspection tour
3 May — British mission to Afghanistan stopped by Afghan troops in disputed border region between Landi Khana and Torkham; Britain responds by issuing ultimatum, and Third Anglo-Afghan War begins
4 May — Afghan troops occupy Bagh and cut water supply to Landi Kotal; jihad is proclaimed
7 May — Afghan positions at Bagh reinforced; Nadir Khan moves with troops to Khost
8 May — Uprising in Peshawar suppressed by Britain
9 May — British advance on Bagh held off by Afghan forces
11 May — Second Battle of Bagh takes place
13 May — British forces occupy Dakka
21 May — Gen. Nadir Khan crosses Indian frontier and advances on Thal
24 May — British Royal Air Force bombs Kabul

27 May	Battle of Spin Boldak occurs
28 May	Wali Muhammad Khan sent to Tashkent, Moscow, and European capitals as envoy of King Amanullah
2 June	Armistice agreed to by Britain and Afghanistan
8 August	Preliminary Anglo-Afghan Treaty signed at Rawalpindi peace conference; Third Anglo-Afghan War ends
September	Soviet envoy arrives in Kabul
10 October	Wali Muhammad Khan arrives in Moscow

1920

17 April	Mussoorie Conference opens with Mahmud Tarzi representing Afghanistan and Sir Henry Dobbs representing Britain
18 July	Mussoorie Conference concludes

1921

	Amir of Bukhara seeks asylum in Afghanistan
20 January	Kabul conference between Afghanistan and Britain opens
28 February	Afghanistan signs Treaty of Friendship with Soviet Union
1 March	Treaty of Friendship signed with Turkey
30 May	Fundamental law of government of Afghanistan comes into force
3 June	Treaty of Friendship signed with Italy
22 June	Treaty of Friendship signed with Iran
2 December	Afghan-Anglo Treaty signed; Britain recognizes Afghanistan as independent state in terms of internal and external relations; diplomatic ties established

1922

28 April	Diplomatic and commercial relations agreed to between Afghanistan and France
9 September	Afghanistan reaches agreement with France on conducting archaeological excavations in Afghanistan

1923

January	Istiqal High School founded
10 April	First Afghan constitution adopted
5 June	British-Afghan trade convention signed
September	French legation opened in Kabul

October	Criminal code adopted by government
November	Statute on marriage issued
December	German legation opened in Kabul

1924

January	Amani High School founded; first hospital for women and children established in Kabul
March	Tribes in Khost Province rise in protest against reforms of Amir Amanullah

1925

January	Khost rebellion put down

1926

	Afghan introduces the Afghani as new monetary unit
3 March	Treaty of Friendship signed with Germany
7 June	Amir Amanullah adopts title of king
15 August	Soviet Union agrees to cede Urta Tagai Islands in the Amu Daria River to Afghanistan
31 August	Treaty of neutrality and nonaggression signed between Afghanistan and Soviet Union

1927

	Anis founded as biweekly newspaper; later becomes main national daily
27 November	Treaty of neutrality and nonaggression signed between Afghanistan and Persia
December	King Amanullah goes on tour of India, Egypt, and Europe

1928

25 May	Treaty of Friendship and Collaboration signed with Turkey
July	King Amanullah returns to Afghanistan and begins to introduce further reforms, particularly regarding dress codes and purdah
November	Uprising of Shinwari tribesmen in Jalalabad area takes place
December	Uprising occurs in Kohistan, led by Habibullah Kalakani

1929

14 January	King Amanullah renounces throne and abdicates; he is replaced by his brother Enayatullah, who abdicates after three days

18 January	Habibullah Kalakani proclaimed amir
14 October	Nadir Khan's forces seize Kabul
3 November	Habibullah Kalakani caught and executed

1930

May	Nadir Shah confirms validity of 1921 and 1923 Anglo-Afghan agreements and all other international treaties
20 September	Nadir Shah agrees to statute governing elections of members to National Assembly

1931

24 June	New treaty of neutrality and mutual nonaggression signed by Afghanistan and Soviet Union
July	National Assembly opened by Nadir Shah
31 October	Nadir Shah confirms adoption of new constitution

1932

	Medical school is opened in Kabul; schools closed under Habibullah Kalakani are reopened
5 May	Treaty of Friendship signed with Saudi Arabia
24 August	Statute sets up new administrative divisions, with five major and four minor provinces formed
October	Further unrest occurs in Khost Province
8 November	Ghulam Nabi executed for complicity in Dar Khel Ghilzai revolt

1933

	Road over Shibar Pass into north of country opened
6 June	Muhammad Aziz, Afghan ambassador to Germany, assassinated
8 November	Nadir Shah assassinated; his son Muhammad Zahir becomes king

1934

16 February	Zahir Shah orders elections for General Assembly
March	Bank-i-Milli established; state takes over control of purchase and export of Karakul skins
21 August	Afghanistan formally recognized by United States
25 September	Afghanistan joins League of Nations

1935

April	W. H. Hornibrook becomes nonresident U.S. ambassador to Afghanistan
May	Turkey begins arbitration over Afghanistan's boundary dispute with Persia
8 June	Zahir Shah opens National Assembly

1936

	Pashtu becomes official language of Afghanistan
March	Treaty of noninterference and commerce signed with Soviet Union
26 March	Treaty of Friendship signed with United States

1937

	Weekly air service between Berlin and Kabul started by Lufthansa; Turkish military mission arrives in Kabul
7 July	Treaty of Saadabad signed by Afghanistan, Iran, Iraq, and Turkey

1938

May	Afghan air force expanded with planes purchased from Britain and Italy; arms purchased from Britain and Czechoslovakia; officers sent to Britain, Soviet Union, and Italy for training

1939

3 September	World War II breaks out; Afghanistan mobilizes as precautionary measure

1940

12 January	National service introduced for all men over seventeen; special taxes imposed to pay for military equipment and radio station in Kabul
May	Joint stock company established to handle all aspects of cotton industry; beet production encouraged by government
29 July	Trade agreement signed with Soviet Union
17 August	National Assembly advised by Zahir Shah that Afghanistan will maintain neutrality in World War II

1941

28 July	Afghanistan restates its neutrality in World War II

19 October	Afghanistan agrees to demands from Britain and Soviet Union to expel German and Italian residents

1942

27 April	Cornelius Van Engert named U.S. ambassador to Afghanistan
5 November	Afghanistan reaffirms World War II neutrality

1943

16 May	Afghanistan consulate opened in New York
5 June	Abdul Husain Aziz presents credentials as ambassador to United States
28 December	Treaty of Saadabad Pact automatically renewed

1944

5 March	Treaty of Friendship signed with China

1946

	Kabul University formed through amalgamation of existing higher education faculties
22 January	Election to National Assembly announced by King Zahir
13 June	Boundary treaty signed with Soviet Union, giving Soviets water rights to Kushka River
9 November	Afghanistan admitted to United Nations
19 November	Abdul Husain Aziz becomes Afghanistan's first UN representative

1947

24 April	Afghan delegation goes to Tashkent to discuss demarcation of Afghan-Soviet border
13 June	Afghanistan writes to Britain and India, stating inhabitants of region between Afghan-Indian border and Indus River are Afghans and must be allowed to decide whether region will be part of Afghanistan, Pakistan, or India or become independent state
3 July	Britain responds to note from Afghanistan, reaffirming Durand Line and asking Afghanistan to refrain from intervention
10 July	Afghanistan reiterates its position on border regions

26 July	Afghan prime minister visits London
3 August	Afghan prime minister visits New York
18 September	Iran claims that Afghan diversion of Helmand River causes crop failures in Sistan
30 September	Afghanistan lodges only vote against Pakistan joining United Nation because of concerns about future of Pashtuns in border regions

1948

1 April	Muhammad Naim named Afghan ambassador to United States
23 April	Sir Giles Squire named British ambassador to Kabul
6 May	Faiz Muhammad named Afghan ambassador to Britain
5 June	United States elevates Kabul legation to embassy status; Ely E. Palmer presents himself as first U.S. ambassador
16 June	Pakistan arrests Abdul Ghaffar Khan and other Pashtun dissidents; Afghanistan begins media campaign for an independent Pashtunistan
29 September	Afghan-Soviet border mission completes demarcation mission, and agreement is signed to fix boundary

1949

24 March	Afghanistan argues against Pakistani claim that tribal territory is integral part of Pakistan
2 April	Afghanistan withdraws diplomats from Karachi after Pakistani bombing in Waziristan
20 April	Louis G. Dryfus named U.S. ambassador to Afghanistan
4 June	Afghanistan institutes border restrictions with Pakistan
12 June	Pakistani plane bombs Moghalgai inside Afghanistan
30 June	Afghanistan National Assembly opens
11 July	Pakistan rejects Afghanistan claim to tribal territory but offers talks on economic issues
26 July	Afghan National Assembly repudiates treaties with Britain, which relate to tribal territory

1950

4 January — Treaty of Friendship signed with India

13 January — People's Republic of China recognized by Afghanistan

8 March — King Zahir visits Europe

26 May — Pakistan asked to recall embassy staff member for breaking Afghan laws

18 July — Afghanistan signs four-year trade agreement with Soviet Union

October — Government authorizes emigration of Afghan Jews to Israel

1951

9 February — Afghanistan signs technical assistance agreement with United States

19 March — George R. Merrell appointed as U.S. ambassador to Afghanistan

25 April — Prime Minister Shah Mahmud visits United States

28 May — United Nations provides assistance to enable drilling of exploratory oil wells in northern Afghanistan

1952

15 January — United States suspends technical assistance agreement, pending signing of Mutual Security Act bilateral agreement

23 September — Soviet Union's objection to oil well exploration in areas near border is rejected by Afghanistan

1953

8 January — United States provides $1.5 million loan to enable Afghanistan to buy U.S. wheat and flour

6 September — Shah Mahmud resigns as prime minister due to illness; he is replaced by Muhammad Daud

November — U.S. Export-Import Bank makes £18.5 million loan to finance development of Helmand Valley

30 December — Offer of U.S. military aid regarded as a grave danger to peace and security by Prime Minister Daud

1954

27 January — Soviet Union grants $3.5 million loan for construction of grain mills and silos and for technical assistance.

8 February — Muhammad Atiq Rafiq named ambassador to Pakistan, and Abdul Husain Aziz made ambassador to India

20 April — Afghanistan joins UN Economic Commission for Asia and the Far East

17 September — Talks held with Pakistan to improve relations between the two countries

7 November — Afghanistan's foreign minister, Muhammad Naim, says issue of Pashtunistan is not one of territory but of allowing Pashtuns to express their wishes

1955

19 January — Relations with People's Republic of China upgraded to embassy status

25 January — National Assembly passes legislation to strengthen armed forces

2 March — Fine Arts College opened in Kabul

29 March — Prime Minster Daud warns Pakistan not to include Pashtun areas of North-West Frontier Province in West Pakistan

30 March — Demonstrations held outside Pakistani embassy in Kabul and the Pakistan ambassador's residence in Kandahar

1 April — Demonstrations staged against Pakistani consulate at Jalalabad; Afghan consulate in Peshawar attacked

12 April — Pakistan rejects Afghan replies to its protests and evacuates families of diplomats and other nationals; consulate at Jalalabad closed

29 April — Afghanistan expresses willingness to apologize and pay compensation for damages, provided similar amends are made by Pakistan

1 May — Pakistan demands closure of all Afghan diplomatic facilities in Pakistan and says it will close all its consulates in Afghanistan

4 May — Afghan forces mobilize

13 May — Afghanistan and Pakistan agree to Saudi-chaired arbitration

21 June — Trade agreement signed with Soviet Union, allowing goods of each nation free transit across each other's territory

28 June — Saudi Arabian arbitration award rejected by Afghanistan and Pakistan

14 July — Afghanistan tells Pakistan it will be held liable for loss or damage to

goods in transit to Kabul or Quetta; Afghanistan becomes member of International Monetary Fund and International Bank

28 July	Afghan army stands down, and state of emergency is ended
14 August	Postal agreement signed with Soviet Union
17 August	India agrees to export four Dakota aircraft for internal use by Afghanistan
9 September	Afghanistan and Pakistan agree to stop hostile propaganda
13 September	Diplomatic facilities reopened in Afghanistan and Pakistan
11 October	Afghanistan requests meeting with Pakistan to postpone incorporation of Pashtun land into Pakistan; Pakistan refuses, and ambassadors are recalled one week later
8 November	Pakistan imposes further restrictions on transit of goods to Afghanistan
20 November	Five-day Loya Jirga approves resolutions calling for plebiscite to determine future of Pashtun area, recommends government find ways to reestablish balance of power following receipt of arms by Pakistan from United States, and refuses to recognize Pashtunistan as part of Pakistan
6 December	Defense Minister Muhammad Arif resigns
15–18 December	Official visit to Afghanistan made by Soviet prime minister Bulganin and Communist Party secretary Khrushchev
16 December	Soviet Union supports Afghan position on Pashtunistan
18 December	Agreements signed with Soviet Union to obtain $100 million loan, extension of 1931 treaty of neutrality and nonaggression, and joint statement on foreign policy

1956

8 January	Pakistan requests recall of Afghan consul from Quetta; Pakistani military attaché asked to leave Afghanistan
24 January	Soviet Union delegation arrives to discuss use of $100 million loan
30 January	Illyushin 14 presented to Zahir Shah by Soviet Union
18 February	Technical cooperation agreement signed with United States
1 March	Technical assistance agreement signed with Soviet Union to cover building of hydroelectric plants, reservoirs, airfields, highway through Hindu Kush, and motor repair facility
6 March	Southeast Asia Treaty Organization (SEATO) declares region up to Durand Line is Pakistani territory and within treaty area
21 March	Afghanistan protests SEATO decision to uphold Durand Line
26 March	U.S. International Cooperation Administration announces $997,000 grant to Teachers College of Columbia University to set up English language program for Afghan secondary schools and to train Afghan teachers of English
31 March	Soviet Union donates 15 buses and equipment for 100-bed hospital in Kabul
4–18 April	Afghanistan sends military mission to Czechoslovakia
7 May	Air agreement with Pakistan opens up regular air service to Europe via Karachi
27 June	Agreement signed with United States, providing $14 million to develop civil aviation in Afghanistan
26 July	Nangarhar irrigation project to be carried out by Soviet Union
7–11 August	Pakistan president, Iskander Mirza, visits Kabul
25 August	Prime Minister Daud announces arms agreements with Czechoslovakia and Soviet Union
12 September	Pan American Airlines begins training flight and ground crews for Ariana Airlines; Kandahar airport to be developed as part of U.S. aid announced 27 June
24 September	Air service to Iran launched
27 September	Military arms and equipment begin to arrive from Czechoslovakia and Soviet Union
17–30 October	Prime Minister Daud visits Soviet Union
28 October	Soviet Union supplies eleven jet planes to Afghan air force
10 November	Gen. Muhammad Oman appointed Afghan ambassador to India

16 November	Afghanistan offers troops for UN peacekeeping force in Suez
24 November	Pashtunistan question discussed in Karachi by Prime Minister Daud

1957

8 January	Trade pact signed with Soviet Union
19–23 January	Chinese prime minister, Chou En-Lai, visits Afghanistan
27 January	M. C. Gillett appointed British ambassador to Afghanistan
10 February	Pashtu language program launched by Radio Moscow
14 April–19 May	Prime Minister Muhammad Daud visits European capitals
27 April	Czechoslovakia agrees to increased aid for Pakistan
8–11 June	Pakistan and Afghanistan agree to restore diplomatic relations
30 June	United States agrees to $5,750,000 loan for Helmand River Authority and $2,860,000 for road building and training program
17 July	Series of communications are issued by Soviet Union concerning aid for Afghanistan in oil exploration, creation of commission to settle boundary issues, and agreement on use of waterways crossing the two countries
28 July	Trade agreement signed with People's Republic of China
31 August	Foreign Minister Naim announces $25 million in military assistance from the Soviet Union under 1956 agreement
22 October	Prime Minister Daud visits China
21 December	Afghan mission sent to Moscow to negotiate new frontier agreement

1958

8 January	Soviet Union agrees to oil deposit survey in Afghanistan
18 January	Treaty signed with Soviet Union regulating Afghan-Soviet frontier
1–6 February	Zahir Shah visits Pakistan
11–27 February	Zahir Shah visits India
26 June	Cultural agreement signed with United States; protocol for utilization of Amu Daria River signed with Soviet Union
30 June	Prime Minister Daud visits United States; agreement announced on aid to improve highway from Spin

	Boldak to Kabul; Pakistan granted $7,708,000 to improve transport links with Afghanistan
17 July	Agreement on transport of goods by road signed with Pakistan
11 September	Contract for Kandahar telephone exchange awarded to Czechoslovakia
18 November	Foreign Investment Law promulgated

1959

1–6 January	Foreign Minister Naim visits Soviet Union
12 January	United States agrees to ship 50,000 tons of wheat to Afghanistan
20 January	Henry A. Byroade named U.S. ambassador to Afghanistan
9 March	Prime Minister Daud calls Baghdad Pact an aggravation of international tension
23 April	Protocol signed with Soviet Union on exchange of goods
18–22 May	Prime Minister Daud visits Soviet Union
28 May	Agreement signed with Soviet Union on Kandahar-Herat-Kushka highway
15 July	Afghan military mission visits Turkey and United Arab Republic
23 August	Soviet Union agrees to provide further aid for Nangarhar irrigation project
31 August	Afghan women appear in public for Jashen celebration without veils
14 September	India prime minister Nehru visits Afghanistan, and women appear without veils at welcoming dinner; thereafter, veil no longer considered obligatory
28 October	Afghan-Soviet Friendship Society founded
1 December	Survey of Amu Daria River is begun with Soviet Union for construction of dam to provide electricity and water for irrigation
21 December	Riots in Kandahar suppressed by police and army; Radio Kabul claims rioters were trying to evade payment of taxes, but other reports state riots were religiously motivated because of unveiling of women and acceptance of Soviet assistance

1960

19 January	Agreement signed with Soviet Union on construction of

irrigation and power project on Kabul River

2–5 March   Soviet prime minister Khrushchev visits Afghanistan to inspect Soviet aid projects, sign a cultural cooperation agreement, and assure Afghanistan of Soviet support over Pashtun question

6 March   Pakistan rejects Soviet stance on Pashtun question

7 March   Prime Minister Daud accuses Pakistan of issuing propaganda against reforms in Afghanistan, especially regarding emancipation of women; announces amir has given Afghans freedom to choose form of government and to organize political parties

3 April   Work begins on Kandahar-Herat-Kushka highway

26 April   Former king Amanullah dies in Switzerland

18 May   Afghanistan protests to Pakistan and United States over violation of airspace by U.S. U-2 plane

15 July   Soviet Union announces petroleum and natural gas finds in northern Afghanistan

4 August   Czechoslovakia announces $200,000 technical assistance grant to Afghanistan

10 August   Two-year barter agreement signed with Soviet Union

13 August   Two Pakistan planes violate Afghan airspace and land at Kandahar; Pakistan apologizes for error, and pilots and planes are returned on 17 September

18 August   Darunta Canal, built with Soviet assistance, opens

21–26 August   Chinese foreign minister, Chen Yi, visits Afghanistan; treaty of friendship and nonaggression signed, and commercial agreements are renewed

3 December   Agreements on trade and transit signed with Iran

1961

5 April   Soviet Union reaffirms support for Afghanistan over Pashtun question

18 April   Cultural agreement signed with Federal Republic of Germany

19 May   Afghanistan denies Pakistan claim that troops are taking part in border unrest

6 June   Afghanistan denies invoking Pashtun revolt and accuses Pakistan of bombarding Afghan populations with arms supplied by United States; 1,200 Pashtun leaders arrested in Peshawar by Pakistan

8 June   National Assembly opens; King Zahir stresses Afghan support for self-determination of Pashtunistan and welcomes economic development

15 June   Pakistan accuses Afghanistan of acts of aggression in border regions

22 June   Pakistan announces ban on entry of nomads unless they possess valid passports, visas, and health certificates

28 June   During visit to London, Foreign Minister Naim states question of Pashtun is only problem in Afghan-Pakistani relations

23 July   Afghan ambassador to United States, Muhammad Hashem Maiwandal, expresses concerns over Pakistan's use of U.S.-supplied arms against Pashtuns

23 August   Pakistan announces closure of Afghan consulates and trade offices and considers banning transit goods

30 August   Afghanistan protests closure of consular facilities and threatens to break diplomatic relations; Prime Minister Daud leaves for Conference of Non-aligned Nations at Belgrade

3 September   Afghanistan seals border with Pakistan; transfer of goods between these countries is suspended.

6 September   Diplomatic relations with Pakistan are severed

12 September   Islamic Congress of Jerusalem appeals for resolution of differences between Afghanistan and Pakistan

18 September   Iran offers to mediate in dispute with Pakistan

19 September   Saudi Arabia agrees to look after Pakistani interests in Afghanistan

21 September   United Arab Republic agrees to look after Afghan interests in Pakistan

27 September   Afghanistan refuses to allow its transit trade to pass through Pakistan unless consular and trade offices are reopened

29 September   President Ayub Khan of Pakistan rejects reopening of consulates and

	trade offices, maintaining they were used for subversive activities
4 October	United States offers to assist in making proposals to improve Afghan-Pakistani relations
11 October	Soviet Union military delegation arrives in Kabul for eleven-day visit
16 October	Afghan-Soviet technical and economic cooperation agreement signed
19 November	Agreement signed with Soviet Union on expansion of facilities for Afghan foreign trade

1962

23 January	Agreement signed with Soviet Union to develop meteorological services
24 January	John M. Steeves named U.S. ambassador to Afghanistan
29 January	Border with Pakistan opened for eight weeks to allow entry of aid goods from United States
14 April	Second Five-Year Plan announced by Prime Minister Daud, with projected expenditure of Afghani 31.3 billion for economic development
20 April	Five-year transit agreement signed with Iran
6 May	Pul-i-Khumri power station, built with Soviet assistance, is commissioned
1 July	Pakistan accepts Iranian arbitration over dispute with Afghanistan
27–31 July	Separate talks held between Iran and Afghanistan and Pakistan
6 August	Pakistan president Ayub Khan proposes confederation of Afghanistan, Iran, and Pakistan
6–15 August	Zahir Shah visits Soviet Union
24 October	Afghanistan and Federal Government of Germany sign agreement for DM 200 million loan to finance various projects, including new power station, sewage network, improved drinking water system, and industrial development

1963

5 February	Government approves establishment of Nangarhar University, to begin with medical school in Jalalabad
12 February	United States decides to ship aid to Afghanistan through Iran because of Afghan-Pakistan dispute

25 February	New trade and assistance agreement signed with Soviet Union
10 March	Prime Minister Daud announces resignation
14 March	Muhammad Yusuf asked to form new government by Zahir Shah
28 March	Constitutional Review Committee established under new minister of justice, Shamsuddin Majruh
18 April	Prime Minister Yusuf states introduction of democracy and improvements to economy are main objectives of government
26 April	United States grants $2,635,00 loan for purchase of aircraft by Ariana Afghan Airways
29 April	Cultural cooperation agreement signed with Soviet Union
25 May	Afghan and Pakistani representatives meet in Tehran to resolve Pashtunistan dispute
28 May	Iran announces agreement between Afghanistan and Pakistan on reestablishing diplomatic and commercial relations
29 May	Afghanistan and Pakistan confirm reestablishment of relations
18 July	On visit to United States, president of National Assembly, Abdul Zahir, announces plans for new form of government, with separation of legislative, executive, and judicial powers
20 July	Afghan consulates reopen in Peshawar and Quetta
25 July	First trucks cross Afghan-Pakistan border, and Ariana Airlines resumes flights
12 August	Afghanistan and Pakistan exchange ambassadors
6 September	Agreement signed with Soviet Union for construction of atomic reactor in Afghanistan and training of specialists in peaceful use of nuclear energy; United States provides $125,000 for surveys of assorted industrial politics
12–17 October	Soviet president Leonid Brezhnev visits Afghanistan and lays foundation stone for new Kabul Polytechnic
16 October	Agreement signed with Soviet Union for technical assistance in extraction and exploitation of

	natural gas in northern Afghanistan
2 December	Border agreement signed with People's Republic of China

1964

29 February	Consultative Constitutional Commission begins hearings
31 May	Aliabad campus of Kabul University, built with U.S. assistance, opens
13 July	Soviet Union grants $25.2 million loan for construction of highway connecting Pul-i-Khumri, Mazar-i Sharif, and Sheberghan
21 July	Zahir Shah announces session of Loya Jirga for 9 September
26 July	Prime Minister Yusuf warns students not to engage in political activity
27 July	Cabinet approves new constitution
4 August	New constitution is released to press; it allows for freedom of speech and formation of political parties, calls for two-house parliament and independent judiciary, and bars members of royal family from key government posts; king is to appoint prime minister and command armed forces
3 September	Zahir Shah and Soviet deputy prime minister, Kosygin, open Kabul-to-Doshi highway, built with Soviet assistance
6 September	Demarcation of border with China completed
9–19 September	Loya Jirga meets and approves constitution
21 September	Federal Republic of Germany loans DM 400, 000 for dental and maternity clinics in Afghanistan
22 September	Afghan-Chinese Friendship Society established
1 October	Zahir Shah endorses new constitution and dissolves National Assembly; transitional government to serve for twelve months
27 October	Soviet Union agrees to provide $6.2 million loan to build Polytechnic Institute in Kabul
19 November	Discovery announced of first Greek city in Afghanistan, at confluence of Kokcha and Amu Daria Rivers; site, abandoned in 130 B.C. now called Ai Khanum

1965

1 January	People's Democratic Party of Afghanistan (PDPA) is founded
12 January	United States agrees to provide $7.7 million loan for construction of Herat-to-Islam Kala highway
18 January	Soviet Union loans Afghanistan $11.1 million to import consumer goods
20 January	UN Special Fund makes grant of $7,178,200 for soil and water surveys, Hazarajat highway survey, telecommunication projects, and teacher-training schools
22 January	Water distribution network for 110,000 Kabul residents is completed, with assistance from Japan
24 February	U.S. ambassador-at-large, Averill Harriman, meets Zahir Shah and Prime Minister Yusuf in Kabul
2 March	New five-year trade transit agreement signed with Pakistan
11 March	Nangarhar irrigation and power project, built with Soviet assistance, is opened
22–25 March	Chinese deputy prime minister, Chen Yi, and foreign minister visit Afghanistan and sign boundary protocol, cultural agreement, and technical cooperation agreement
5 April	All high schools start entrance exams to maintain standards and avoid overcrowding
18 April	World Bank agrees to finance foreign exchange costs to survey Kunduz and Khanabad basins for possible irrigation and agricultural projects
20 April	Cultural agreement signed with Great Britain
28 April	Kunduz airport completed, built with U.S. assistance
11 May	New law implemented providing for universal direct vote by secret ballot for all Afghan men and women over twenty
23 May	Ariana Airlines begins flights to Tashkent
5 June	Mazar-i Sharif airport opens, built with U.S. assistance
6 June	First of three regional appellate courts opened in Kabul; others are planned for Kandahar and Mazar-i Sharif

22 June	Jangalat smelts first iron ore from Afghan mines	
1 July	Land survey and statistics law comes into effect	
7 July	Zahir Shah announces plan to rebuild old Kabul	
15 July	United States agrees to help increase wheat production and provide up to 150,000 tons of wheat; other credits and loans are made available for machinery purchases, construction of Kajakai power plant, importation of diesel generators, and further project planning in Helmand Valley; also provided is a $5 million long-term loan for construction unit of Helmand River Authority	
20 July	Direct telephone link between Kabul, Rawalpindi, and Lahore is inaugurated	
24 July	Soviet Union agrees to build 97-kilometer pipeline from Sheberghan gas fields to Soviet border and 88-kilometer pipeline from fields to fertilizer and power plants in Balkh Province	
28 July	Soviet loans to Afghanistan extended by thirty years and Soviet Union agrees to provide teachers for Kabul Polytechnic	
3–14 August	Zahir Shah visits Soviet Union; treaty on neutrality and nonaggression extended by ten years	
8 August	First census of Kabul reveals population of 435,203	
26 August	Elections held to fill 216 seats in Wolesi Jirga and 28 elective seats in Meshrano Jirga	
9 September	New press law grants freedom of expression but with safeguards for fundamental values of Islam and the constitution	
12 October	Abdul Zahir elected president of Wolesi Jirga; Abdul Hadi Dawai appointed president of Meshrano Jirga by King Zahir; Dawai appoints members on following day	
13 October	Prime Minister Yusuf presents report of Interim Government to king and tenders his resignation; King Zahir asks him to form new government	
14 October	Parliament opened by king	
19 October	Wolesi Jirga decides proposed members of cabinet must declare	

	details of property held before vote of confidence taken
24 October	Presentation of members of cabinet to Wolesi Jirga halted when demonstrators occupy seats of deputies and refuse to leave
25 October	Wolesi Jirga decides to hold vote of confidence for cabinet in closed session; students demonstrate against decision and are dispersed by police and army, with three deaths; all schools are closed and public meetings banned; cabinet approved by Wolesi Jirga
29 October	Prime Minister Yusuf resigns after demonstration, citing poor health; Muhammad Hashem Maiwandal asked to form cabinet
2 November	New cabinet approved by Wolesi Jirga; to ensure transparency, proceedings are broadcast by Radio Afghanistan
4 November	Prime Minister Maiwandal attends condolence ceremony at Kabul University for those killed in 25 October demonstrations; conveys message of sympathy from king and promises to heed student demands; Toryalai Etemadi elected president of Kabul University
7 November	Property holdings of cabinet members debated and accepted by Wolesi Jirga
27 November	Kabul University senate rejects student demands for lower passing grade and postponement of exams
13 December	Kabul University's Science Faculty closed because of disturbances
14 December	Ministry of Interior bans public gatherings after demonstrations

1966

31 January	*Wahdat,* first privately owned newspaper for fourteen years, is published in Kabul in both Dari and Pashtu languages
10 February	Ghulam Muhammad Sulaiman appointed ambassador to Afghanistan
11 February	*Payam-i Imruz,* twice-weekly newspaper published by Ghulam Nabi Kater, is first issued
15 February	Muhammad Asif Sohail named Afghan ambassador to People's Republic of China

23 February	Nasir Zia appointed Afghan ambassador to India
2 March	Cabinet approves new constitution for Kabul University
15 March	Khalilullah Khalili appointed ambassador to Saudi Arabia
5 April	*Afghan Millat*, a Pashtu newspaper, is published by Ghulam Muhammad Farhad
11 April	*Khalq*, owned by Nur Muhammad Taraki, is published in Pashtu and Dari
13 April	Wolesi Jirga begins discussion of political parties draft law
4 May	Meshrano Jirga debates publication of *Khalq* and determines any publication against values of Islam should be stopped
22 May	Wolesi Jirga asks government to take action against *Khalq*
23 May	*Khalq* distribution banned by government under Article 48 of Press Law
25 May	*Payam-i Imruz* ceases publication on instructions of Ministry of Information and Culture; lack of editor constituted breach of press law
20 June	Foreign Minister Etemadi and Interior Minister Shalizi named first and second deputy ministers
19 July	Wolesi Jirga approves political parties draft law
20 August	Supreme Judiciary Committee set up as foundation for future Supreme Court
28 August	Former prime minister Yusuf named ambassador to Federal Republic of Germany
20 September	Abdul Rahman Pazhwak, Afghan representative to United Nations, elected president of UN General Assembly

1967

25 March–9 April	Prime Minister Maiwandal visits United States
10 May	Deal reached with Soviet Union on export of natural gas; anticipated to earn £320 million over following eighteen years, with production target of 3 billion cubic meter by 1971
30 May–2 June	Nikolai Podgorny, chair of Presidium of Supreme Soviet of the Soviet Union, visits Afghanistan

20 August	Direct telephone line between Kabul and Herat completed
11 October	Prime Minister Maiwandal resigns due to ill health; Abdullah Yaflati appointed acting prime minister
15 October	Supreme Court inaugurated
1 November	King Zahir asks Nur Ahmed Etemadi to form government
13 November	New cabinet submitted to Wolesi Jirga; will be approved on 15 November, after three-day debate

1968

25 January	Commission established to determine national education policy for Afghanistan
4 February	Chakhansur Province renamed Nimruz, after name given in Pahlavi literature
22 April	Sheberghan gas pipelines officially opened by Second Deputy Prime Minister Yaftali and president of Soviet Union's Council of External Affairs

1969

25 May	U.S. Secretary of State Rogers visits Kabul for talks with government
22 June	All primary and secondary schools in Kabul closed after student unrest and student boycott of Kabul University
17 July	Soviet military delegation begins visit to Afghanistan
25 December	Soviet military delegation, led by Defense Minister Grechko, arrives for official visit

1970

21 January	Soviet Union signs protocol for export of 2.5 billion cubic meters of natural gas in 1970
26 January	Defense Minister Khan Mohammed visits United States

1971

17 May	Government of Prime Minister Nur Ahmed Etemadi resigns but remains in power pending formation of new government
8 June	Abdul Zahir, former ambassador to Italy, asked to form a new government
26 July	National Assembly gives Abdul Zahir vote of confidence after seventeen-day debate

August	Afghanistan is in middle of worst recorded drought in its history

1972

3 January	Soviet Union signs agreement to expand natural gas operations in northern Afghanistan
16 May	Kabul Radio broadcasts demand for creation of independent Pashtunistan
21 July	U.S. special envoy John Connolly tells Afghan government no further aid commitments will be forthcoming
25 August	Major natural gas discovery made at Jarquduq
5 December	Muhammad Zahir resigns as prime minister and is replaced by Musa Shafiq

1973

17 January	Diplomatic relations established with East Germany
13 March	Agreement signed with Iran to settle dispute over Helmand River
8 July	King Zahir leaves for vacation in Italy
17 July	King Zahir deposed by cousin Muhammad Daud; Afghanistan proclaimed as a republic
18 July	Daud proclaimed president and minister of defense
19 July	New government accorded diplomatic recognition by Soviet Union and India
27 July	Parliament dissolved and constitution abrogated
2 August	New cabinet announced, with Daud holding portfolios of prime minister, defense minister, and foreign affairs minister
24 August	King Zahir announces abdication
23 September	Number of senior army officers arrested because of plot to overthrow government; Pakistan accused of complicity in plan

1974

5 April	New trade and payments agreement reached with Soviet Union
19 July	Soviet Union agrees to assist with development of Jarquduq gas field and further oil exploration
24 July	Agreement reached with Iran over joint development of Helmand River region

1975

26 February	Government protests U.S. decision to lift arms embargo on Pakistan
1 May	All banks and associated financial services nationalized by government
28 July	Terrorist group captured in Panjshir; Pakistan accused of providing arms to group
2 December	Afghanistan denies mobilizing troops on border with Pakistan

1976

23 April	About 100,000 Afghanis left homeless by earthquakes, torrential rain, and floods
7 June	President Bhutto of Pakistan meets with President Daud
4 July	Indian premier Indira Ghandi arrives in Kabul for three-day visit
9 December	At least fifty people arrested by Afghan security service, accused of plotting to overthrow government

1977

30 January	Loya Jirga convened by President Daud to approve draft of new constitution
14 February	New constitution approved
15 February	Daud sworn in as president, and Loya Jirga is dissolved
24 February	Constitution promulgated
29 March	Agreement reached to restore air links between Afghanistan and Pakistan
16 November	Minister of Planning Ali Ahmad Khurram assassinated in Kabul

1978

24 February	Trial of twenty-five people accused of plotting to assassinate President Daud begins
17 April	Mir Akbar Khaibar, a founder of PDPA, assassinated in Kabul
20 April	Funeral of Khaibar turns into demonstration against government
26 April	PDPA leaders arrested on orders of president
27 April	Pro-Communists stage coup in Kabul, known as the Saur Revolt, with support from military; Nur Mohammad Taraki becomes prime minister; President Daud is overthrown and killed by PDPA supporters

29 April	Kabul Radio reports a number of ministers in former government also killed in coup	28 March	Revolts break out across Afghanistan, and army collapses
30 April	Revolutionary Council is established, and Nur Muhammad Taraki is installed as president	2 April	Soviet Union accuses United States of arming mujahideen; Washington denies involvement
May	First mujahideen camp established in Pakistan	30 April	President Taraki accuses Pakistan of involvement in unrest in eastern provinces
6 May	Afghanistan declared to be nonaligned and independent	23 June	Kabul Radio announces that antigovernment protests by Hazaras in Kabul were put down, with a number killed
17 August	Taraki assumes minister of defense portfolio		
18 August	Government announces plot to overthrow government is foiled; Defense Minister Abdul Qadir arrested for his role in conspiracy	5 August	Heavy fighting occurs between government troops and rebellious units at Bala Hissar Fort in Kabul; authorities impose curfew
23 August	PDPA Politburo orders arrest of Planning Minister Sultan Ali Keshtmand and Public Works Minister Muhammad Rafi'i for their roles in conspiracy	19 August	Presence of 1,600 Soviet advisers in Afghanistan is confirmed
		14 September	Taraki removed from power by Hafizullah Amin
17 September	Diplomatic relations with South Korea broken	15 September	Interior and frontier affairs ministers removed from their posts;. explosions and gunfire in Kabul follow announcement
22 September	Taraki dismisses six ambassadors who were members of Parcham faction of PDPA	16 September	Hafizullah Amin becomes president after reports of Taraki being ill
19 October	Red flag adopted as new national emblem	8 October	Death sentences passed on former defense minister Abdul Qadir and former planning minister Sultan Ali Keshtmand are commuted to fifteen years of imprisonment; rebellious tribes claim to have cut road between Kabul and Gardez after fighting with government troops
5 December	Twenty-year Treaty of Friendship and Cooperation signed with Soviet Union		
1979			
28 January	Guerrilla action begins against government in eastern provinces	9 October	Taraki assassinated by supporters of Amin; President Amin publishes a list of 12,000 killed by the Taraki regime
2 February	Reports say mujahideen are beginning to train at Pakistani military establishment near Peshawar	14 October	Fighting breaks out at Rishkhur barracks near Kabul, but mutiny crushed by government troops two days later; Soviet forces move in to Shindand air base
14 February	U.S. ambassador Adolph Dubs killed in rescue attempt after being taken hostage by terrorists in Kabul; United States protests Afghanistan's use of force to free hostages		
		9 November	Two hundred government troops and mujahideen killed in ambushes near Kabul
19 February	Foreign Minister Hafizullah Amin rejects protest from United States	7 December	Soviet special forces occupy Bagram air force base
22 February	President Carter announces cut in aid to Afghanistan	21 December	Soviet Union moves forces to border with Afghanistan, and 1,500 troops are sent to Bagram air base
16 March	Revolt erupts in Herat, with support of military garrison; it is put down by government troops, but thousands are believed killed	24 December	Soviet invasion of Afghanistan begins
27 March	Hafizullah Amin becomes prime minister	26 December	Large-scale Soviet airlift into Kabul is reported

27 December	Further fighting breaks out in Kabul; President Amin is overthrown and assassinated, reputedly by Soviet special forces
28 December	Babrak Karmal becomes president and announces offer of political, moral, economic, and military aid by Soviet Union

1980

January	Administration of President Carter requests $30 million to provide covert aid to mujahideen groups; Soviet-made weapons are secretly channeled to mujahideen in Pakistan by CIA
1 January	President Karmal announces Soviet forces have been invited into Afghanistan because of aggressive stance of enemies of the state
2 January	Karmal calls on people to support the revolution
5 January	United Nations opens debate on situation in Afghanistan
7 January	UN resolution calling for withdrawal of all foreign forces in Afghanistan is vetoed by Soviet Union
14 January	UN General Assembly votes for total withdrawal of foreign troops from Afghanistan
23 January	United States announces sanctions against Soviet Union, including significant wheat embargo
29 January	Conference of Islamic Foreign Ministers condemns Soviet military intervention in Afghanistan
13 February	Egypt announces it will provide some training to mujahideen
14 February	UN Human Rights Commission condemns Soviet aggression in Afghanistan
15 February	U.S. press reports indicate United States has begun to supply mujahideen with light weapons
19 February	European Community proposes Afghanistan be declared a neutral country, guaranteed by international community, if Soviet forces are withdrawn
22 February	Soviet Union agrees to withdraw forces if all forms of outside interference are terminated; demonstrations and rioting against government erupt in Kabul

25 February	All commercial premises in Kabul are closed, and civil servants strike
26 February	Mass arrests of demonstrators in Kabul
28 February	Shops reopen, and civil servants return to work
3 March	Gulbuddin Hekmatyar announces his group will withdraw from negotiations to form alliance of six mujahideen groups
7 March	Soviet forces appear on streets of Kabul
10 March	Government announces arrest of forty-two associates of former president Hafizullah Amin
22 May	Conference of Islamic Foreign Ministers in Islamabad calls for immediate withdrawal of Soviet forces from Afghanistan
24 May	Further demonstrations against Soviet presence held in Kabul
8 June	Kabul Radio announces execution of ten supporters and aides of former president Amin
14 June	News reports mention execution of three ministers in former president Amin's government
2 July	Soviet Union argues that peace settlement in Afghanistan will only be achieved if incursions from adjoining states ceased
14 September	Foreign Affairs Minister Faiz Muhammad killed while trying to obtain tribal support for government
October	Masood supplied with SAM-7 missiles by CIA
13 November	President Karmal threatens expulsion from PDPA for anyone not working for good of the party, regardless of their past records
20 November	UN General Assembly calls for unconditional withdrawal of all foreign troops from Afghanistan
21 November	Afghanistan rejects UN resolution as interference in Afghanistan's internal affairs
25 December	President Anwar Sadat of Egypt confirms he is supplying weapons to the mujahideen

1981

January	Pakistan government announces it will recognize only six mujahideen groups

9 March	U.S. president Ronald Reagan says mujahideen requests for weapons will be considered seriously
7 April	Saudi Arabia announces severing of diplomatic links with Afghanistan
9 May	At least 2 million Afghan refugees are in Pakistan
11 May	Sultan Ali Keshtmand becomes prime minister
12 July	Gen. Fateh Muhammad, member of the national committee of the National Fatherland, is killed by rebels
22 July	Heavy fighting reported between mujahideen and Soviet forces at Paghman, 16 miles from Kabul
12 August	Government lifts acreage restrictions on land held by religious and tribal leaders
22 August	President Sadat announces United States had been buying old Soviet weapons from Egypt to supply mujahideen forces in Afghanistan
18 November	UN General Assembly votes, for third time, that Soviet Union must withdraw forces from Afghanistan

1982

6 January	Soviet troops in Afghanistan are estimated to be between 110,000 and 120,000
20 February	Archer K. Blood rejected as U.S. chargé d'affaires to Kabul; U.S. State Department imposes travel restrictions on Afghan diplomats in Washington
1 April	WFP announces additional $18.5 million in aid for Afghan refugees in Pakistan
16 May	PDPA conference in Kabul endorses purging of dissidents and a continuing program of land reform
8 June	Soviet and government forces succeed in driving mujahideen out of Panjshir Valley
16–25 June	UN-sponsored direct talks between Afghanistan and Pakistan held in Geneva
2 August	Afghan government extends length of service for conscripted troops
30 October	More than 1,000 people, including 700 Soviet troops, killed by explosion in Salang Tunnel

December	CIA increases volume and range of weapons sent to mujahideen

1983

19 January	UN deputy secretary-general begins peace mission to Geneva, Tehran, Islamabad, and Kabul to try to resolve Afghan crisis
21 March	Bomb explodes in Kabul mosque, with four dead and seven injured
14 May	Afghanistan announces boycott of 1984 Summer Olympics in Los Angeles
17 May	U.S. vice-president George Bush visits Khyber Pass and voices support for Afghan resistance movement
26 July	Intelligence sources announce U.S. House of Representatives approved $50 million in covert aid for mujahideen
27 August	Afghanistan and Pakistan foreign ministers meet UN intermediary in separate talks in Geneva
31 August	Bomb explodes at Kabul airport
4 November	Nine people executed after being convicted of Kabul airport explosion

1985

18 January	United States announces it will increase aid to mujahideen to $280 million; aid also said to be coming from China, Israel, and Saudi Arabia
26 January	Mujahideen leader Khan Gul sentenced to death in Paktia Province
29 January	A leader of Islamist Movement, Zabiullah, killed when his jeep strikes land mine
3 March	Iran announces merger of four Shi'a mujahideen groups: Nasr, Pasdaran, Guardians of the Islamic Revolution, and United Front of the Islamic Revolution
23 April	Loya Jirga convened by Babrak Karmal to win support for war against mujahideen
10 May	Mujahideen leaders in Peshawar reject attempt by Abdul Rasul Sayyaf to appoint himself leader of Alliance of Afghan Mujahideen
20 June	UN-sponsored proximity talks held in Geneva between Afghan and Pakistani governments; they will conclude on 25 June and be described as intense and fruitful

30 August	United Nations announces progress of plan for peace in Afghanistan but stresses stumbling point on withdrawal of Soviet troops
23 October	All Afghan males up to forty years of age ordered to enlist for three years of military service; Afghani foreign minister stresses withdrawal of Soviet troops can only be discussed in direct negotiations with Pakistan
13 November	UN General Assembly again votes for withdrawal of Soviet troops from Afghanistan
22 November	Abdul Qadir, Ghulam Dastagir Panjshiri, and Ismail Danesh removed from PDPA Politburo
6 December	Ghulam Faruq Yaqubi named as director of KHAD (Afghan secret police)
13 December	United States agrees to act as guarantor of peace in Afghanistan, based on Soviet troop withdrawal and termination of U.S. aid to mujahideen
31 December	UN-sponsored talks at Geneva lead to Afghan government drawing up informal table for withdrawal of Soviet troops as part of an overall accord

1986

11 January	President Karmal rejects U.S. offer to act as guarantor for a peace settlement
4 February	Kandahar-based mujahideen group led by Asmatullah Achakzai Muslim changes allegiance and backs government
20 February	Revolutionary Council sets up commission to draft new constitution
17 March	Foreign Ministry rejects UN report on human rights violations as groundless
20 March	Pakistan denounces Afghan attack on border post and refugee camp at Khurram, which resulted in six deaths
2 April	United States reported to be supplying hundreds of Stinger missiles to mujahideen
6 April	Car bomb in Kabul reported to have wounded twenty-two civilians

11 April	Joint Afghan-Soviet operation launched against Zhawar
4 May	Babrak Karmal resigns as secretary-general of PDPA on grounds of ill health and is replaced by Najibullah, former head of KHAD
5 May	Further round of UN-sponsored peace talks between Afghanistan and Pakistan open in Geneva
15 May	Collective leadership in Afghanistan announced by Najibullah, with himself as party leader, Babrak Karmal as head of Revolutionary Council Presidium, and Sultan Ali Keshtmand as prime minister
19 May	Seventh round of UN-sponsored indirect talks between Afghanistan and Pakistan resume in Geneva
28 May	Najibullah announces that bicameral parliament will be established, based on free and democratic elections
16 June	President Reagan meets mujahideen leaders in Washington and reaffirms commitment to their cause
17 June	Gulbuddin Hekmatyar and Abdul Rasul Sayyaf criticize mujahideen meeting in Washington

1987

26 February	Further round of peace negotiations between Afghanistan and Pakistan opened in Geneva by United Nations
4 March	Soviet territory attacked by mujahideen rockets from Imam Sahib in Kunduz Province
20 July	President Najibullah meets with Soviet leader Gorbachev and raises prospect of Soviet withdrawal
11 August	UN special human rights investigator allowed to visit Afghan political prisoners in three prisons
10 October	Najibullah announces government will pay mujahideen fighters who surrender their weapons
18 October	Maulawi Yunis Khales elected spokesman of the seven-party mujahideen alliance
24 October	New alliance of Shi'a mujahideen groups based in Iran is announced
10 November	Revolutionary Council Presidium announces endorsement of decree providing for formation and registration of political parties

24 November	Lt. Gen. Muhammad Nabi Azimi commits suicide after failure of an offensive against mujahideen
29 November	Loya Jirga called to approve new constitution
30 November	Najibullah confirmed as president by Loya Jirga under new Islamic constitution
6 December	Mujahideen alliance refuses to accept any Communist participation in Afghan government
10 December	UN envoy Cordovez opens talks between exiled King Zahir and mujahideen leaders on formation of transitional coalition government

1988

6 January	Soviet foreign minister, on visit to Kabul, states he hopes Soviet forces will leave Afghanistan by end of year, provided United States ceases to aid mujahideen
12 January	Pakistan states members of pro-Moscow Afghan government must be able to participate in any future government as a condition of the withdrawal of Soviet forces
17 January	Mujahideen leader Yunis Khales refuses to accept Pakistani insistence on a role for Communists in Afghan government
20 January	President Najibullah pledges continuance of nonalignment policy following a withdrawal of Soviet forces
22 January	Bombs explode at funeral of Khan Abdul Ghaffar Khan in Jalalabad, killing at least seventeen
8 February	Soviet leader Gorbachev promises a pullout on 15 May if settlement is reached in Afghanistan by March
10 February	President Reagan says United States will cease support for mujahideen sixty days after peace settlement and concurrent with Soviet withdrawal
11 February	Head of Afghan Information Office in Peshawar, Sayyid Baha'uddin Majruh, assassinated
23 February	Mujahideen alliance in Peshawar announces formation of Interim Government
4 March	U.S. administration states aid to mujahideen will stop only when

	Soviet Union ceases arms supplies to Kabul government
14 March	Gulbuddin Hekmatyar appointed spokesman of mujahideen alliance
24 March	Reports state Pakistan has withdrawn demand that interim government be formed to oversee a Soviet withdrawal
26 March	Reports from United States say supplying of Stinger missiles has ceased in anticipation of peace settlement at Geneva
29 March	President Najibullah promises opposition leaders will get seats in new parliament if they participate in forthcoming elections
30 March	President Najibullah's offer of a coalition government rejected by mujahideen
3 April	Sari-Pul Province is created by Kabul government as part of the Hazarajat; Gharib Husain appointed as governor
9 April	Mujahideen refuse to be bound by any agreement reached at Geneva
14 April	Geneva Accords signed by Afghanistan, Pakistan, Soviet Union, and United States; under the agreement, Soviet Union will withdraw troops within nine months, and United States will be guarantor of the agreement; military aid to both sides will be halted, and provision will be made for return of Afghan refugees
25 April	UN group arrives in Islamabad to assist in overseeing implementation of Geneva Accords
28 April	President Najibullah announces Soviet military advisers will remain in Afghanistan following Soviet troop withdrawal
11 May	UN appoints Sadruddin Aga Khan to coordinate relief and resettlement in Afghanistan
15 May	Soviet troops begin to withdraw from Afghanistan
19 May	Afghan army's Maj. Gen. Fazil Ahmad Samadi defects to mujahideen
25 May	Soviet Union announces losses of 13,310 killed, 35,478 wounded, and 311 missing in action in Afghanistan

31 May	United States announces continued aid for mujahideen because of Soviet plans to leave $1 billion of equipment for Kabul government
7 June	In address to United Nations, President Najibullah accuses Pakistan of violating Geneva Accords
9 June	President Najibullah announces 243,900 soldiers and civilians had died in war in Afghanistan
15 June	Pir Sayyid Ahmad Gailani, head of National Islamic Front, becomes spokesman for mujahideen alliance
16 June	President Najibullah announces formation of new government
18 July	UN envoy Cordovez proposes peace plan based on formation of a neutral government; proposal is endorsed by Sabghatullah Mujaddidi, leader of National Front for the Liberation of Afghanistan, and Sayyid Ahmad Gailani, leader of National Islamic Front of Afghanistan
21 July	Creation of Nuristan Province approved by President Najibullah
23 July	Formation of new political party, the Self-Sacrificing Afghan People's Solidarity Movement, approved by President Najibullah
27 July	Government announces approval for formation of a new party, the Union of God's Helpers
8 August	Soviet troops begin to withdraw from Kabul
17 August	Lt. Gen. Shanawaz Tanai appointed defense minister
25 September	U.S. administration appoints Edmund McWilliams special envoy to mujahideen
5 October	Hekmatyar's forces in Nejrab kill Maulawi Zahir, a commander in forces of Burhanuddin Rabbani
17 October	Rabbani becomes spokesman for mujahideen alliance
21 October	UN special representative for Afghanistan calls on former king Zahir to assist in establishing a government of national reconciliation
26 October	Governor of Herat Province, Khaliqyar, also appointed governor of Badhis and Ghor Provinces
17 November	Reports indicate Deputy Foreign Minister Abdul Ghafur Lakanwal and Deputy Director in the Foreign Ministry Sayyid Kamaluddin have defected to mujahideen
19 November	Soviet commander in Afghanistan warns mujahideen that escalation in conflict could halt Soviet withdrawal
28 November	Muhammad Gul, brigadier general in KHAD and cousin of President Najibullah, reportedly defects

1989

2 January	Sabghatullah Mujaddidi succeeds Rabbani as spokesman for mujahideen alliance
18 January	Mujaddidi visits Tehran but fails to gain Shi'a mujahideen participation in an interim government
21 January	West Germany withdraws diplomatic staff from Kabul
25 January	United States announces intention to close embassy in Kabul
26 January	Mujahideen delegation, led by Gulbuddin Hekmatyar, visits Tehran to meet with Iranian foreign minister
27 January	Britain, France, Japan, and Italy announce they will withdraw diplomats from Kabul
28 January	Meeting between Soviet defense minister and President Najibullah reiterates continued Soviet support for regime
30 January	U.S. embassy in Kabul is closed
2 February	Closure of Western embassies denounced by President Najibullah; large demonstration occurs in Peshawar, staged by Afghan refugees calling for return of King Zahir
13 February	President Bush pledges continued support for mujahideen
14 February	Soviet troop withdrawal completed; seven-party alliance of mujahideen in Peshawar announces formation of Afghan Interim Government, with Sabghatullah Mujaddidi as president
15 February	United States rejects Soviet demands to end arms shipments to mujahideen
18 February	State of emergency declared by Kabul government; Muhammad Muhammadi becomes spokesman for mujahideen alliance
20 February	Prime Minister Sharq resigns
21 February	Sultan Ali Keshtmand appointed chair of Council of Ministers' executive committee

23 February	Interim Government is set up by mujahideen commanders in Peshawar, with Abdul Rasul Sayyaf as acting prime minister, Sabghatullah Mujaddidi as acting president and remainder of portfolios spread around other groups; legitimacy of government challenged by Pir Sayyid Gailani
5 March	Major offensive launched by mujahideen against Jalalabad
20 March	Mujahideen attack on Jalalabad repulsed
24 March	Government convoy breaks through mujahideen positions and reaches Jalalabad
27 March	Mujahideen commanders offered autonomy if they end armed resistance; offer rejected by council of thirty-five commanders
12 April	Cabinet of Interim Government holds meeting on Afghan territory
23 April	Report in *New York Times* states that the 5 March attack on Jalalabad was made by Pakistan government against advice of the Inter-Services Intelligence Service of Pakistan
24 April	Afghan protests against Pakistani aggression
9 May	Sayyid Ahmad Gailani challenges legitimacy of Interim Government
16 May	Reports indicate head of KHAD, Abdul Rahman, defected to mujahideen group led by Yunis Khales
17 May	Kabul-Jalalabad road reopened by government forces
21 May	President Najibullah invites mujahideen leaders to participate in a loya jirga
24 May	Government again offers regional autonomy to mujahideen
5 July	Tor Kham recaptured by government forces
19 July	Fighting occurs between groups led by Burhanuddin Rabbani and Muhammad Nabi Muhammadi over territory in Helmand Province
24 July	Defense Minister Shanawaz Tanai placed under house arrest
1 August	Tanai implicated in attempted coup
7 August	Haji Abdul Latif, a commander with National Islamic Front, poisoned by

	two bodyguards, who are arrested and executed
11 August	Prime minister of Interim Government, Abdul Rasul Sayyaf, rejects suggestion by Hekmatyar that mujahideen seize power through backing an army coup
14 August	Government announces 183 civilians killed in Kabul by rocket attacks in one week
20 August	Maj. Gen. Muhammad Faruq Zarif defects to opposition
25 August	Ahmad Shah Masood accuses Islamic Unity Party of colluding with government
29 August	Groups headed by Sayyaf and Muhammadi battle for control of bridge in Helmand Province to secure tax and toll revenues
30 August	Gulbuddin Hekmatyar withdraws his group from mujahideen alliance
11 October	Muhammad Asghar becomes president of National Salvation Society, which seeks peaceful end to the war
7 November	Fighting breaks out at Kandahar, and Lt. Gen. Ali Akbar is killed
14 November	Three-pronged assault launched by mujahideen on Jalalabad; attack is repulsed
21 November	Government extends state of emergency for six months
30 November	Rabbani and Hekmatyar agree on a cease-fire and exchanging prisoners and territory
2 December	127 people arrested in Kabul, accused of plotting coup; Brig. Gen. Ghulam Haidar killed in renewed fighting at Jalalabad
21 December	Islamist Movement executes four members of Islamic Party, including Sayyid Jamal, for ambush on Islamic Movement commanders
31 December	President Najibullah calls for change of name for PDPA

1990

24 January	President Najibullah promises to stand down if defeated in UN-supervised elections
2 February	Demonstration of some 10,000 Afghan refugees takes place in Quetta, Pakistan, in favor of return of King Zahir

12 February	Farid Ahmad Mazdak becomes acting chair of National Front's Central Council
5 March	Trial begins of Afghans arrested in December, accused of plotting coup
6 March	Defense Minister Tanai launches coup against President Najibullah
7 March	Hekmatyar announces support for Tanai coup
9 March	Government forces recapture Bagram air base; other mujahideen refuse to back Tanai coup
18 March	Twenty-four members of PDPA expelled for treachery against party and country
6 April	Supposed mujahideen surrender talks result in death of two generals and eleven others when mujahideen troops open fire on government troops; governor of Herat, Fazl Haq Khaliqyar, wounded in exchange of fire
14 April	United Nations accused by government of failing to police Geneva Accords
21 May	New government formed by Prime Minister Khaliqyar
28 May	Government convenes a loya jirga to consider proposals to amend constitution
29 May	Najibullah announces formation of multiparty system
16 June	Nine Shi'a mujahideen groups unite to form Islamic Unity Party
30 June	Meeting held between former prominent government officials, President Mujaddidi of Interim Government, and representatives of Islamic Unity Party
18 July	Italy reopens embassy in Kabul
25 July	United Nations begins repatriation of Afghan refugees from Pakistan
29 July–25 August	President Najibullah visits Moscow, and Abdur Rahim Hatef becomes acting president
4 September	Forces of Islamist Movement and Islamic Party clash near Kabul, and sixteen deaths are recorded
5 September	Government forces expel militias from Kabul
11 September	Legalization of political parties announced by President Najibullah
5 October	Administrative capital of Oruzgan Province, Tirin Kot, captured by mujahideen
15 October	Masood visits Pakistan for meeting with Pakiststani president and Gulbuddin Hekmatyar
25 October	U.S. Congress scales down assistance to mujahideen
19 November	President Najibullah visits Switzerland for discussions with exiled Afghan personalities to try to form coalition government in Afghanistan

1991

9 January	General Hashim is captured and executed by mujahideen forces
22 January	Head of progovernment militia, Esmat Muslim, dies
23 January	Embassy of the resistance opened by Rabbani in Khartoum
5 February	Severe problems recorded in southwestern Afghanistan due to floods
8 February	Afghan resistance sends 300 fighters to Saudi Arabia to participate in war with Iraq; decision opposed by Sayyaf and Hekmatyar
31 March	Khost captured by mujahideen, with 2,200 prisoners taken, including seven government generals
2 April	Government declares day of mourning
6 April	Muhammad Nurzad elected mayor of Kabul following defection of Abdul Karim Misaq, who fled to Germany
10 April	Vice-President Sultan Ali Keshtmand dismissed
16 April	President Najibullah offers amnesty to all Afghan exiles who agree to return home
20 April	Explosion occurs at headquarters of Wahhabi movement in Kunar Province, with some 500 dead and 700 wounded, including Arabs and Pakistanis; reports suggest explosion was a car bomb, but Wahhabis claim it was Scud missile attack
26 April	Geneva meeting held between representatives of Pakistan's intelligence services and Kabul government
21 May	UN secretary-general issues five-point proposal for political settlement in Afghanistan; AIG rejects any compromise with Najibullah government

27–28 May	Soviet-Pakistan talks about Afghanistan held in Moscow
31 May	Ammunition depot explodes in Nowshera, Pakistan
22 July	Masood captures Jahkashem, followed by Wakhan Corridor
30 August	Jamilur Rahman, chief of self-proclaimed Wahhabi republic in Kunar Province, assassinated in Pakistan
13 September	United States and Soviet Union agree to end all arms supplies to Afghanistan on 1 January 1992
14 October	Supreme justice in Kabul declares all legal decisions must conform to Islamic law
4 November	Former king Zahir slightly wounded in assassination attempt
5 December	United Nations agrees on solution for transfer of government in Afghanistan
15 December	Soviet Union stops arms shipments to Afghanistan

1992

14 January	President Najibullah annuls decree that confiscated property of royal family
6 February	Generals Dostum, Naderi, and Momen rebel against government
15 March	Samangan Province captured by mujahideen
18 March	President Najibullah agrees to step down as soon as Interim Government is installed
29 March	National Unity Party captures Sar-i-Pul
8 April	General Dostum takes control of Mazar-i Sharif
12 April	Masood takes over Salang Tunnel
15 April	Kabul airport captured by militia of General Dostum
16 April	President Najibullah takes refuge in UN compound in Kabul; Gardez and Ghazni captured by mujahideen, military junta takes control of Kabul, and mujahideen seize Herat
18 April	Kunduz and Jalalabad fall to mujahideen; Rahim Hatef nominated as interim president
21 April	Pul-i-Alam in Logar Province taken by Islamic Party

24 April	Mujahideen leaders set up interim Islamic Council, headed by Mujaddidi, with fifty-one members
25 April	President Najibullah resigns in order for UN-brokered, broad-based government to be formed; mujahideen forces enter Kabul; fighting breaks out between Islamic Party of Hekmatyar and forces of Masood
26 April	Masood's forces take control of presidential palace and oust Hekmatyar's forces from military barracks;. Shi'a forces take missile base at Darulaman
28 April	Mujaddidi arrives in Kabul and proclaims an Islamic state of Afghanistan, together with general amnesty
29 April	Islamic Party fighters expelled from Ministry of the Interior; Masood arrives in Kabul
May	Ahmad Shah Masood named Afghan defense minister
3 May	Egypt formally recognizes Islamic state of Afghanistan; Hekmatyar's forces threaten to attack Kabul unless General Dostum leaves capital
6 May	First meeting of Islamic Council held under Rabbani
10 May	Sayyid Ahmad Gailani arrives in Kabul
21 May	Yunis Khales arrives in Kabul; Masood and Hekmatyar agree to a cease-fire
30 May	Fighting occurs between Dostum and Hekmatyar for control of district of Karte Nau
19 June	Clashes reported between forces of Dostum and Masood
28 June	Mujaddidi surrenders presidency to Rabbani
4 July	Artillery battle erupts between forces of Dostum and Hekmatyar
2 August	Yunis Khales resigns from Islamic Council
15 August	United Nations withdraws a number of staff from Kabul
27 August	Rabbani concludes cease-fire with Hekmatyar
5 September	Uzbek militia of General Dostum leaves Kabul
17 September	Rabbani and Hekmatyar reach agreement at Paghman over

December | Rabbani elected president under multiparty agreement
designation of assembly to select Rabbani's successor

1993

19 January | Rabbani's forces launch attack on Gulbuddin Hekmatyar, who responds with rocket attack on Kabul

3 February | United Nations suspends aid shipments through southern and eastern Afghanistan for security reasons

5 February | India withdraws diplomats from Kabul

6 February | General Dostum nominated deputy defense minister

7 February | Fighting breaks out in Soviet embassy compound between rival groups

8 February | Turkish embassy in Kabul is closed

11 February | Imam of Kabul University issues plea for mujahideen to cease fighting among themselves

16 February | Kabul has first peaceful day since entry of mujahideen in January

7 March | Islamabad Accord reached between Afghan parties, except Dostum and Khales; Rabbani nominated as president for eighteen months; Hekmatyar nominated as prime minister; OIC, Pakistan, and Afghan parties are to supervise cease-fire

8 March | Islamic Unity and Islamic Party of Khales subject Kabul to missile attack

11 March | Afghan leaders meet in Mecca to agree on details of Islamabad Accord and power of Uzbek militia; King Fahd of Saudi Arabia endorses accord

19–20 March | Meeting of Afghan parties at Jalalabad fails to resolve differences

22 March | Fighting between Islamic Union for the Liberation of Afghanistan and Islamic Party continues in Kabul

28 March | Spokesperson for General Dostum declares peace is impossible without Uzbek representation in Kabul government

1 April | Islamic Unity Party and Islamist Movement form committee to resolve differences, and one day later,

they agree to exchange prisoners and maintain a cease-fire

7 April | Claim made by Kabul government that Islamic Unity Party and Islamic Party of Hekmatyar had been supplying arms to insurgents in Tajikistan

9 April | Cease-fire between Islamic Unity Party and Islamist Movement breaks down

15 April | Agreement reached between governors of Herat in Afghanistan and Khorasan in Iran on cooperation to halt drug traffic

25 April | Hekmatyar's mujahideen fighters blockade Kabul

3 May | Some fifty fighters from Shi'a Islamic Unity Party killed in fighting in Tajikistan

9–10 May | Major clashes in Kabul between forces of Rabbani and Hekmatyar

11 May | Kabul Museum set on fire during intergroup fighting

12 May | Hekmatyar's forces continue rocket attacks on Kabul

13 May | General Dostum agrees to assist Masood in struggle against Hekmatyar

19 May | Hekmatyar and Rabbani agree to cease-fire

20 May | Masood resigns as defense minister

6 June | Hekmatyar presides over first meeting of his government at Charasyab

17 June | Government meets in Paghman; Hekmatyar formally sworn in as prime minister

21 June | Meeting of Council of Ministers in Darulaman

23–28 June | Heavy fighting between Islamists and forces of Masood

3 July | Meeting held between President Rabbani and General Dostum

12 July | Dostum and Hekmatyar agree to cease-fire

15 July | Further fighting between Hekmatyar's and Masood's forces around airport

26 July | Masood's forces capture Bagram air base from Hekmatyar

31 August | Cease-fire agreed to between Rabbani's group and Islamic Unity Party

14 September	Islamic Party again bombards Kabul
2 October	Islamic fighters active again in Tajikistan; force reportedly composed of about 300 fighters
19 October	Kabul-Jalalabad highway reopened
24 October	Agreement signed with Tajikistan for export of natural gas
9 November	U.S. undersecretary of state for South Asia visits Kabul to discuss humanitarian and economic aid; meetings held with Rabbani, Hekmatyar, Dostum, and Masood
23 December	Sher Khan Bandar retaken by General Dostum

1994

1 January	Dostum and Hekmatyar ally to attack Rabbani's forces in Kabul
5 January	Rabbani's forces capture Kabul airport
6 January	Fighting breaks out in Bala Hisar and Microrayon areas, with forces of Mujaddidi joining Dostum-Hekmatyar alliance
10 January	Mosque at Pul-Khishti destroyed during fighting
2 April	UN emissary, Mestiri, arrives in Kabul for discussions with Rabbani, Masood, and Hekmatyar
4 April	Masood launches attack on Pul-i-Khumri, which has been held by forces of Dostum and Hekmatyar
6 April	UN emissary leaves Afghanistan without agreeing to cease-fire
19 April	President Rabbani announces intention to extend his mandate until December 1994 due to refusal of opposing groups to respect agreements reached at Jalalabad in March
27 April	International Committee of the Red Cross estimates civil war in Kabul has killed 2,500, left 17,000 injured, and made 632,000 refugees since January 1994; at least 20,000 houses had been destroyed
1 May	Hekmatyar's offensive against Kabul is stopped
9 May	Kabul government air force bombs Mazar-i Sharif and Pul-i-Khumri
13–14 May	Dostum's forces bombard government troops at Qargha, near Kabul

18 May	Forces of Abdul Rasul Sayyaf oust Hekmatyar's troops from Maidan Shahr
21 May	General Dostum claims to have downed two aircraft of Rabbani's forces, using Stinger missiles
22 May	General Jali, head of Dostum's air force, claims to have 32 operational planes, 100 pilots, and large supply of bombs
28 May	Internecine conflict erupts within Islamic Unity Party, involving groups loyal to Akbari and Mazari
3 June	Clashes occur between forces of Dostum and Isma'il Khan at Shindand; Herat bombed by Dostum
8 June	Rabbani proposes his successor should be selected by a loya jirga
10 June	Renewed fighting erupts in Kabul
15 June	Rabbani arbitrarily extends his mandate by six months
19 June	Assassination attempt on Isma'il Khan fails
25 June	Islamic Revolutionary Movement recaptures Darulaman palace from Islamic Party
26 June	Dostum's forces expelled from Bala Hisar and Maranjan hill by Rabbani's forces
17 June	Yunis Khales declares himself interim president
8 July	Commission formed between Dostum, Gailani, Hekmatyar, Mazari, Muhammadi, and Muhseni, to negotiate with Rabbani and Sayyaf
20 July	Herat Assembly opens with 700 participants
24 July	Rabbani visits Herat but does not address assembly
29 July	BBC reporter, Mir Wais Jalil, killed in area controlled by forces of Hekmatyar
7 August	Meeting held in Kabul between Rabbani, Gailani, Muhammadi, and Muhseni
16 August	Ariana Airlines banned from flying over Pakistan because of breach of international regulations
8 September	Islamic Party takes control of Khenjan, north of strategic Salang Pass
12 September	Fighting occurs at Darulaman between Islamic Unity Party and Islamic Revolutionary Party; Akbari

reported to have defected from Islamic Unity Party

25 September — Iran brokers a cease-fire between various Shi'a mujahideen groups

October — Kandahar falls to militia composed of religious students led by Mullah Omar

2 October — Pakistan holds transit goods for Afghanistan due to security concerns

11 October — Red Cross announces 1,100 people were killed and 23,000 wounded in Kabul during September

2 November — Pakistani convoy destined for Turkmenistan stopped by troops between Spin Boldak and Kandahar; clash occurs between mujahideen and Taliban forces over convoy

5 November — Kandahar captured by Taliban, and leader of defenders is executed

7 November — Uzbekistan accused of interference in Afghanistan's internal affairs due to supplying thirty tanks to General Dostum

11 November — United Nations appeals for $106.4 million to meet humanitarian needs of Afghanistan for twelve months

13 November — Taliban repel counterattack on Kandahar

5 December — First delivery of aid to Kabul for six months arrives by convoy of sixty-four trucks; aid equally split between Rabbani and his opponents

12 December — Rabbani leaves for OIC meeting in Morocco

13 December — First UN aid convoy for two years arrives in Kunduz

19 December — India prepares to reopen embassy in Kabul

20 December — Dostum goes to Islamabad for discussions

28 December — UN envoy Mestiri arrives in Islamabad to reopen peace efforts

30 December — Sudanese delegation arrives in Afghanistan for talks with Hekmatyar

1995

1 January — Rabbani refuses to step down as president at end of term; UN peace envoy endeavors to find a solution; Maulawi Yunis Khales returns to Jalalabad after a nineteen-year exile

4 January — UN envoy Mestiri opens new UN office in Jalalabad and begins talks with Hekmatyar; Rabbani meets with U.S. ambassador to Pakistan

10 January — Rabbani offers to hand over presidency to UN-brokered interim administration if Hekmatyar forces stop shelling Kabul

12 January — Cease-fire announced, on condition that Rabbani relinquishes power

17 January — UN aid convoy plundered by Hekmatyar's forces in Sarobi

19 January — Hekmatyar's forces bomb Kabul, resulting in twenty-two deaths and many injuries

22 January — Access to Kabul again closed by forces of Hekmatyar

24 January — Ghazni captured by Taliban

26 January — Heavy fighting occurs in Kunduz Province between government forces and Ahmad Rashid Dostum; at least 100 troops die, and 120 are injured

28 January — United Nations announces plans are being finalized to transfer power from Rabbani to interim council of all opposing factions

27–31 January — Hekmatyar forces pushed out of Ghazni Province by alliance between Rabbani and Taliban forces;. Hekmatyar suffers large loss of men and armor

5 February — Uzbek forces of Dostum take Kunduz town; widespread looting of city occurs

10 February — Hekmatyar's stronghold of Maydan Shar in Wardak Province falls to Taliban

11 February — Taliban claim to have captured Pul-i-Alam and to control Logar Province

13 February — Kunduz recaptured by forces of Rabbani; capital of Loghar Province, Pul-i-Alam, captured from Hekmatyar forces by Taliban

14 February — Hekmatyar's forces defeated by Taliban at Charasyab headquarters in Logar Province;. Hekmatyar's troops cease to be major factor in civil war

15 February — Taliban occupy Pul-i-Charkhi and Khost

16 February — Kunduz recaptured by forces of Rabbani

17 February — Kabul airport reopens after year's closure

19 February — Taliban take Sharan in Paktika Province and Gardez in Paktia Province

22 February	Rabbani refuses to step down until 21 March unless Taliban included in interim administration; talks unsuccessful due to Taliban demands for participation
25–27 February	Forces of Rabbani and Hizb-i Wahdat fight for control of southwestern areas of Karte Seh, Kote Sangi, and Karte Chahar
6–10 March	Action against Hizb-i Wahdat continues, and on 8 March, Wahdat leader strikes deal with Taliban who were blocking his escape routes; Taliban move into Darulaman and occupy Wahdat front lines, disarm forces of Abdul Ali Mazari, and attack Rabbani forces; casualties are heavy, with at least 100 to 1,500 killed and 1,000 wounded, the majority being civilians
9 March	After discussions with Taliban, Harakat leader Muhammad Nabi withdraws support from Rabbani, and members resign from government
12 March	Rabbani launches attack on Taliban and drives them out of Karte Seh and back to Charasyab; Taliban shell Kabul during their retreat;. reports indicate Rabbani forces wreak vengeance on Hazara population of Karte Seh, with looting, beating, rape, and murder of civilians
	Iran announces plans to repatriate 500,000 Afghan refugees over ensuing year, withdraws temporary living permits, refuses to renew work permits, and withdraws welfare facilities
13 March	Ali Mazari, Wahdat leader, dies under unclear circumstances while a captive of Taliban; Karim Khalili named provisional leader, but split develops in party
14 March	Taliban claim to have complete control of Ghor and Nimruz Provinces
16 March	Rabbani delays resignation, and transfer of power scheduled for 21 March is delayed for fifteen days
19 March	Government forces expel Taliban from Charasyab headquarters into hinterland of Logar Province
20 March	Taliban expelled from Kabul by government forces following killing of Abdul-Ali Mazari, Shi'a mujahideen leader
26 March	Ali Mazri buried in Mazar-i Sharif
30 March	Mass grave discovered at Charasyab, with twenty-two male corpses all shot in head, most of whom were Shi'a Hazaras; since town changed hands between Hizb-i-Islami, Taliban, and Rabbani, it is not possible to ascribe guilt for killings
1 April	Hekmatyar removed as head of anti-Rabbani alliance and replaced by Mujaddidi, head of Jabha-yi-Najat-yi Milli-yi Afghanistan
4 April	About 800 Rabbani soldiers killed and 300 captured by Taliban forces in Farah Province; Shindand air base and Herat also attacked by Taliban
7 April	Iran bans commercial transit to Afghanistan
19 April	Taliban impose fuel blockade on Kabul
27 April	Taliban free 300 prisoners of Dostum's forces
May	Rabbani forces continue actions against Taliban around Maydan Shahr, where they regrouped following retreat from Kabul
3–4 May	India and Pakistan agree to reopen diplomatic missions in Kabul
5 May	Kabul offices of independent weekly *Subh Omid* raided by militants; in October, Rabbani will replace entire editorial staff and control its content
11 May	Forces of Rabbani and Jamiat governor Isma'il Khan complete recapture of Farah Province from Taliban
15 May	Taliban lose Helmand Province to Rabbani and Isma'il Khan forces; Nimruz Province falls on 16 May
24 May	Negotiations between representatives of Dostum and Rabbani continue, covering opening of Salang highway and lifting of fatwa proclaiming holy war against Dostum
5 June	General Dostum attacks Rabbani forces in Samangan Province, and fighting continues in Baghlan Province
9 June	Government and Taliban agree to ten-day truce to allow for exchange

	of prisoners, free movement of civilian traffic, and extension of peace talks	September	Northwestern province of Badghis lost by government to forces of Dostum
15 June	Dostum carries out bombing raids over Kabul and Kunduz City	2 September	Taliban capture province of Farah and city of Shindand, site of largest air force base
20 June	Rabbani forces and pro-Rabbani faction of the Wahdat, Akbari, capture town of Bamian from Khalili Wahdat faction	3 September	Supreme Coordination Council of opposition warns that its airspace is closed and nonapproved flights will be forced down or shot down
22 June	Iran begins repatriation of 400,000 Afghan refugees through Herat	5 September	Herat falls to Taliban; Governor Isma'il Khan flees to Iran; city had
29 June	Fighting resumes in Maydan Shahr between Taliban and forces of Rabbani; envoy of former king Zahir holds talks in Islamabad with Afghan tribal leaders and Pakistani officials, and indicates former king's willingness to participate in peace process		been bombed by Dostum, and observers felt alliance between Taliban, Dostum, and Hekmatyar was responsible for fall of city; regime now controls thirteen of thirty provinces, SCC holds eight, and Rabbani has Kabul and five other provinces
23 July	Forces of Dostum and Khalili Wahdat faction recapture Bamian Province	6 September	Iran closes border with Afghanistan after fall of Herat; repatriation of refugees halted; Afghanistan complains about Pakistani
30 July	Rabbani proposes to United Nations setting up commission of intellectuals to form grand assembly for a year, elect leader, draft new constitution, and form parliament from among commission members		interference in Afghan affairs; 5,000 attack Pakistan embassy in Kabul, and one member of staff is killed and twenty-six injured, including ambassador; embassy closed by Pakistan, though diplomatic ties not severed
3 August	Taliban hijack Russian cargo plane in Kandahar loaded with arms for Rabbani, and crew taken prisoner; they demand release of all Afghan prisoners in Russia in return for release of Russian crew; Russians will be held for a year	7 September	Taliban take Ghor Province
		15 September	Anti-Taliban explosions occur in Herat
		16 September	BBC correspondent Kasra Naji expelled from Herat by Taliban, accused of biased reporting
17 August	Further repatriation of Afghan refugees from Iran's Sistan Province takes place	21 September	Taliban force down Ariana airliner in Kandahar carrying military spare parts; Pakistan expels thirteen Afghan diplomats without explanation
21 August	Kabul cinemas closed for month to halt spread of immoral films, all centers of cultural corruption are closed, foreign videos are destroyed, and female singers are banned from media	24 September	More explosions and acts of sabotage by enemies of Taliban occur in Herat
28 August	Government forces capture Girishk and Helmand Province from Taliban, but Girishk will be retaken on 30 August	9 October	Ambassador to Pakistan Masud Halili expelled, and six more Afghan diplomats will be expelled on 18 October in retaliation for 6 September attack on Pakistan embassy in Kabul
31 August	Female delegation banned from leaving Afghanistan to attend World Conference on Women in Beijing due to un-Islamic nature of the agenda—for example, family planning, abortion, premarital sex	11 October	Taliban capture Charasyab and attack Kabul; large numbers of civilians killed and injured by heavy shelling; National Reconciliation Commission

	presents peace proposals to Rabbani and plans to show them to officials in other provinces
15 October	Rabbani's forces lose Bamian to Taliban but capture Sanglakh Valley, close to Taliban-held Maydan Shahr
6 November	President Rabbani advises United Nations he is prepared to resign in exchange for immediate cease-fire by Taliban and end to foreign intervention; fighting breaks out in Kabul before offer can be considered, and talks are suspended
10 November	UNICEF suspends education and training programs in Taliban-held territory in protest against closure of girl's schools in Herat and Jalalabad
11 November	Taliban attack Kabul with rockets and shells, cause widespread damage, and kill at least thirty-five civilians; Rabbani's forces retake Balashiar, Abdolabad, Zerka, Madrasa, and Labani regions of Balkh Province from forces of Dostum
13 November	Taliban again shell Kabul, and at least another twenty-one civilians killed
26 November	Taliban launch air strikes on Kabul; at least 40 civilians are killed and 140 wounded; Rabbani's forces push Taliban back
27 November	Jabha leadership withdraws from SCC, and Mujaddidi resigns as SCC president
30 November	Taliban again shell Kabul, resulting in seventeen deaths and at least twenty-six wounded, all civilians
1 December	Government forces bomb Taliban positions outside Kabul; Taliban return fire and hit residential areas and airport
5 December	Demonstrations take place in Kabul against civil war and bombing of residential areas; submit resolution to United Nations seeking action to prevent attacks on civilians
9 December	Government forces bomb Taliban positions at Charasyab; residential areas and civilians hit, and thirty-seven Taliban fighters are killed
12 December	Taliban shell Kabul again, with much destruction of property and heavy civilian casualties; another attack will be launched on 19 December

25 December	Further rocket attacks hit Kabul, repeated on 27 and 30 December
30 December	Delegation from Rabbani meets with Dostum in Mazar-i Sharif to try to reach negotiated settlement

1996

2–3 January	Taliban rocket attacks hit residential areas of Kabul, with twenty-four dead and fifty injured; government claims attack was aimed at undermining peace proposals
10 January	Government makes peace offer to Taliban and opposition; it calls for cease-fire, exchange of prisoners, and peace talks; Rabbani makes no move to resign
10–12 January	Residential areas of Kabul again shelled by Taliban
14 January	All routes from Kabul blocked by opposition forces; Rabbani government and Shi'a party of Hizb-i Wahdat, Khalili faction sign peace agreement that includes cease-fire, exchange of prisoners, and reopening of Kabul-Bamian road; Kabul suffers from lack of food and fuel
20 January	Bitter fighting reported between Taliban factions in Kandahar and the provinces of Ghazni, Wardak, and Logar; rift caused by Mullah Omar's faction wishing to hold peace talks with Rabbani, the Mullah Borjan faction wishing to continue the struggle, and the faction of Mullah Rabbani remaining neutral
29 January	Demonstrations by Kabul civilians against Rabbani take place, demanding he hand over presidency to interim government; Taliban again launch rocket attacks on Kabul
1 February	Taliban bomb residential area near Kabul's grand mosque; ten civilians killed and many injured
3 February	Red Cross emergency food supplies reach Kabul to supply 100,000 citizens, via planes from Peshawar
6 February	400 trucks arrive in Kabul with basic food supplies and fuel; militias demand bounty on all trucks traveling highways from Pakistan, through Jalalabad to Kabul
11 February	Taliban and government forces engage in area of southern Kabul

13 February	Mujaddidi rejoins SCC
14 February	At initiative of Pakistan and United Nations, peace talks held in Islamabad between Hekmatyar, Dostum, Taliban, Shi'as, and Isma'ilis but end without agreement
22 February	Rabbani attempts new set of talks with Hekmatyar in Kabul and Sarobi
26 February	Fighting breaks out in Baghlan Province between various opposition faction, with hundreds of deaths, injuries, and refugees
27 February	UNHCR report 391,000 Afghan refugees were repatriated in 1995 but 400,000 internal refugees are still living in camps near Jalalabad
March	Opposition forces report that in Taliban-controlled areas, one member of each household is forced into hard labor, a tax of 10 percent is levied on all earnings, and vehicles are commandeered
4 March	Save the Children, UK suspends all operations in Taliban- controlled areas because of restrictions
7 March	Rabbani government and Hekmatyar sign agreement to take joint action against Taliban; agreement also signed to restore electricity to Kabul
12–13 March	Government forces bomb Taliban positions in towns of Charasyab and Muhammad Agha
13 March	Iran announces further repatriation of 250,000 Afghan refugees to northern Afghanistan via Turkmenistan; Taliban shell Kabul, and government bombs Taliban positions
30 March	Taliban call a meeting of 1,000 ulama in Kandahar to determine future policy; Mullah Omar elected leader on 3 April, but SCC rejects this
3 April	Mullah Omar elected by 1,000 clergy as "commander of the faithful"
11 April	Government forces capture Taliban-controlled district of Saghar in Ghor Province, but Taliban retaliate by capturing Sharak district, with heavy government losses
18 April	Civil servants in Herat forced to wear turbans and grow beards or lose jobs
4 May	Iranian embassy in Kabul shelled by Taliban; two embassy staffers are wounded
12 May	Forces of Hekmatyar arrive in Kabul to assist Rabbani in defending city against Taliban
20 May	Iran reports Taliban have executed their commander in Wardak Province, Mullah Abdur Rahman, for establishing contact with opposition forces
24 May	Rabbani and Hekmatyar sign peace agreement and agree to organize elections and form "real Islamic government"; Taliban call a counter meeting of Yunis Khales, Muhammad Nabi, Ahmad Gailani, and representatives of General Dostum
30 May	Afghans demonstrate at UN offices in Kabul, requesting UN and international aid in mine-clearing operations
1 June	Taliban take Chaghcharan, capital of Ghor Province
7 June	SCC suspends Hekmatyar's membership because of alliance with Rabbani
11 June	General Dostum creates Balkh airline to transport passengers and freight between Mazar-i Sharif and Pakistan, Iran, and Central Asia; Pakistan grants landing rights at Peshawar
18 June	Taliban take government positions at Nimruz
19 June	Hekmatyar and Rabbani sign peace accord; Hekmatyar becomes prime minister in Kabul
24 June	Rasool Pahalwan, an influential northern warlord, killed in ambush near his base in the Shor desert, Mazar-i Sharif
26 June	Hekmatyar becomes prime minister in Rabbani's government; Taliban respond by bombing Kabul, killing about 60 people and wounding about 150
3 July	Rabbani names broadly based, ten-member cabinet but leaves twelve places for other Afghan factions not present in Kabul
22 July	Prime Minister Hekmatyar closes cinemas in Kabul and bans music and television broadcasts as un-Islamic; women are ordered to dress modestly, but restrictions on work

and education imposed by Taliban are not emulated

18 July Islamic National Front for Peace in Afghanistan formed by parties headed by Gailani, Dostum, Mujaddidi, Khalili, and Saiq Moddabir, to work for broad-based government

5 August Fierce fighting reported in provinces of Paktia, Paktika, Nimruz, and Ghor; opposition forces accuse Taliban of forcible recruitment of young people and levying heavy taxes to support war

8 August Opposition captures Chaghcharan, capital of Ghor Province, but it is immediately retaken by Taliban; Taliban arrest people who cooperated with opposition forces and fire on women protesting arrests, with five women shot dead

13 August Hekmatyar's government and General Dostum agree to formal cease-fire agreement allowing for reopening of Salang highway from Kabul to the north

14 August Pakistan reopens embassy in Kabul

16 August Russian crew of plane hijacked in Kandahar by Taliban in 1995 escape and return to Russia via United Arab Emirates

28 August Eastern provinces of Laghman, Nangahar, and Nuristan declare neutrality in war between forces of Taliban and Rabbani

29 August Salang highway linking Kabul to north of Afghanistan reopens

4 September About 200 women participate in march in Kabul, protesting Taliban restrictions on females; march is supported by Afghan Women's Islamic Movement (AWIM) and Afghan Women's Islamic Renaissance (AWIR); letter submitted to UN secretary-general, Boutros Boutros-Ghali

5 September Taliban launch attack in eastern Afghanistan

11 September Jalalabad, capital of Nangahar Province, falls to Taliban; route from Kabul to Peshawar is cut, and majority of population flees to Pakistan; all UN offices temporarily shut to protect staff

12 September Government forces bomb Jalalabad; Taliban advance on Sarobi, which controls access to Bagram airport, the only airport open to government; government reinforces Sarobi in anticipation of assault; Taliban capture Mehtarlam, capital of Laghman Province

15 September Iran announces intention to repatriate 250,000 Afghan refugees to northern Afghanistan via Turkmenistan with cooperation of United Nations and UNHCR

16 September Rabbani sends emissaries to Tashkent Uzbekistan to try to secure support from General Dostum

22 September Taliban take province of Kunar

25 September Taliban capture Sarobi and large quantities of arms from fleeing government troops

26 September Kabul attacked by Taliban from southeast and southwest; hundreds of citizens flee to Mazar-i Sharif in the north; Rabbani, Hekmatyar, and Masood withdraw forces from capital and are declared national criminals by Taliban; Masood and Rabbani regroup forces at Masood's base at Jalal Saraj

27 September Kabul falls to Taliban, and Taliban declare Shari' a law throughout Afghanistan; thousands of civilians flee city; Mullah Muhammad Rabbani appointed to head six-man ruling council; amnesty offered to all former government soldiers in Kabul and Kandahar; former president Najibullah and brother Shahpur Ahmadzai forcibly removed from UN compound and executed, with their bodies hung on public display from lampposts

28 September Taliban issue decree compelling women to wear *burqas* when outside the home; women are also prohibited from working, and girls are banned from attending school; films, music, television, cassette recorders, and videorecorders are also banned; Mujaddidi announces his support for Taliban

29 September Taliban take Jabal-us-Siraj; civil servants and military personnel given six weeks to grow beards of

	acceptable length or face dismissal and punishment
30 September	Taliban announce continued salary payments for women no longer allowed to work, but no detail given as to time limit; Kapsia Province captured by Taliban, followed by towns of Charikar and Jabal Saraj; Masood retreats to Panjshir Valley, but Taliban advance is halted by forces of General Dostum
3 October	Schools and colleges in Kabul remain closed because of ban on female teachers and insufficient number of male teachers; hospitals also suffer—although women are allowed to work in female-only hospitals, many stay away from work for fear of harassment
7 October	UNHCR ceases operations in Afghanistan because of staff shortages caused by women not being allowed to work; Save the Children suspends its land-mine awareness program: Taliban introduce a 9:00 P.M. TO 4:00 A.M curfew on Kabul; Rabbani, Dostum, and Khalili form anti-Taliban alliance, the Council for the Defense of Afghanistan
12–19 October	Masood's forces retake strategic towns of Jabul Siraj and Chaikar, north of Kabul, from Taliban
14 October	Taliban accused of conscripting young men to fight at front from mosques and bazaars and "press-ganging" young men arrested for being sympathizers of former government
15 October	Pakistan offers to broker peace talks and sends minister of the interior, Naseerullah, to meet with Taliban leaders in Kabul and General Dostum; market town of Qara Bagh retaken by Taliban, without resistance, but seized again on 19 October by forces of Dostum and Masood; Rabbani's forces lose Bamian to Taliban but recapture Sanglakh Valley
18 October	Bagram air base retaken by forces of Dostum and Masood
20 October	Masood's forces take Hussein Kot, 12 miles from Kabul, and mount rocket attacks on Kabul airport; Dostum also advances on Kabul from northeast
21 October	Dostum proposes cease-fire to Taliban, using Pakistan interior minister as intermediary; Masood also accepts proposal, subject to Kabul being demilitarized, but Taliban insist on exchange of prisoners and commission to monitor cease-fire; talks collapse without any agreement
22–30 October	Anti-Taliban forces stall in their advance on Kabul
22 October	Village of Sar Cheshma, 5 miles north of Kabul, destroyed by Taliban as collective punishment due to shelling from village by Masood's forces, who then withdraw
23 October	Women in Mazar-i Sharif demonstrate against Taliban and wear Western-style dress
25 October	Taliban claims to have captured Badghis Province rejected by Dostum
27–28 October	Anti-Taliban alliance again attacks Kabul but is repulsed
29 October	Regional conference held in Tehran to try to bring about peace in Afghanistan, but talks fail; Pakistan, Saudi Arabia, and Uzbekistan refuse to attend
30 October	Anti-Taliban forces take Dar-ye Nur, administrative capital of Nangarhar Province, but Taliban forces soon retake it
30 October–3 November	Heavy fighting occurs in Badghis Province with both sides claiming victory, but independent reports claim a stalemate; anti-Taliban forces are led by Dostum and former governor of Herat Isma'il Khan, who had troops flown in from Iran to take part in offensive
1 November	Taliban announce girls can return to school in Kabul, as fighting has ceased around city; indication given that women might be allowed to return to work
4 November	Dostum calls for peace talks, but call is rejected by Taliban unless cease-fire and exchange of prisoners takes place first; anti-Taliban alliance air force bombs Herat airport and takes control of Mangoi district in Konar

	Province, but it is soon retaken by the Taliban
5 November	General Taina, former defense minister in Najibullah government, comes out in support of Taliban
9 November	Dostum's air force bombs Taliban positions at Kabul airport
10 November	Several hundred refugees flee north because of heavy fighting around Kabul, but there is little movement in the frontline positions
11–16 November	Further heavy fighting in Badghis Province, resulting in some 50,000 refugees moving on Herat and Qale-e-Naw; as nearly all refugees are Pashtuns, UNHCR and other aid agencies maintain their move is outcome of ethnic cleansing
17 November	Taliban regime calls on United Nations to recognize it as legitimate government in Afghanistan and to allocate UN seat to a Taliban representative
18 November	UN-sponsored one-day conference on Afghanistan held in New York, with delegates from nineteen countries and groups, including Security Council, but no representatives of warring factions; conference calls for an immediate cease-fire and demilitarization of Kabul
20 November	UNHCR suspends operations in Kabul due to arrest of four staffers but resumes activities after they are released on 11 December
23–24 November	Taliban claim to have captured Mir Bachakot and Guldra, north of Kabul, representing first movement of front line since October
26 November	Sixty people arrested in Jalalabad by Taliban for failure to attend prayers regularly
27 November	Dostum's forces capture Bala Morghab region in Badghis Province, and 10,000 Pashtun refugees flee to Turkmenistan; Taliban capture villages of Kalakan and Istalif, moving front line north by some 10 miles, but heavy fighting continues in area
29 November	Taliban push back former government troops
4 December	Taliban decree that the *chadari* does not conform to requirements of

	Islam and that women must wear the full burqa
7 December	Taliban forbid women to work for relief agencies
9 December	Reports from Kabul seem to indicate ethnic minorities are being targeted by Taliban, with increased harassment of non-Pashtun inhabitants; Norbert Holl, UN envoy, holds separate meetings with Dostum, Masood, and Taliban to try to secure cease-fire; claims are made of success and agreement to establish a commission to begin direct talks between factions, but some Taliban officials deny this
18 December	Public executions held by Taliban in Herat and Kabul
21–22 December	Anti-Taliban demonstrations held in Herat by women demanding aid from international organizations; demonstrators are dispersed by Taliban militia; this leads to violent clashes, arrest of twenty women, imposition of curfew, and streets patroled by tanks and personnel carriers
24 December	Clashes between different factions of Islamic Unity Party break out in Wardak Province, resulting in seventeen deaths
27–28 December	Taliban launch major offensive against Bagram air base and by 28 December control all access to base; they also take Qarabagh, Kalakan, and Istalif; opposition retaliates by launching air strikes on Kabul and the airport

1997

2 January	Taliban warn that failure to pray five times a day will result in punishment
5 January	Dostum's air force strikes against Wazir Akbar suburb of Kabul, with four deaths and ten people wounded; Taliban threaten to hang anti-Taliban alliance prisoners if attacks continue
9 January	Taliban decree that nonobservance of Ramadan will result in sixty days of imprisonment; two men are subsequently charged for not meeting their obligations

9–14 January	Fierce fighting continues between Dostum's forces and Taliban in Badghis Province
13–15 January	UN-brokered talks take place on possible peace negotiations with Taliban and anti-Taliban delegates; Taliban indicate a willingness to negotiate but refuse to accept demilitarization of Kabul, a key alliance demand
16 January	Bagram air base recaptured by Taliban, as is Charikar, capital of Parwan Province; people in town and surrounding villages are ordered to evacuate to eliminate any uprising from pro-Masood Tajik population
17–18 January	Taliban forces continue to advance northward and take several towns and villages in Kapsia Province
21 January	Thousands of refugees head south to Kabul due to heavy fighting near Charikar
21–22 January	UN-sponsored forum on aid held in Ashgabat, capital of Turkmenistan, and donor countries and agencies agree to continue aid
22 January	United States refuses to recognize Taliban government in Kabul
23 January	Taliban capture Jebul Siraj and Gulbahar, which had been strongholds of Masood; first town is close to strategic Salang Pass and was a gateway to Dostum's power base in northern Afghanistan; Gulbahar lies at mouth of Panjshir Valley, Masood's traditional power base; alliance forces blast hillsides near Salang Pass to slow Taliban advance; UNHCR reports arrival of about another 30,000 refugees in Kabul from frontline towns and villages
25–26 January	Peace talks held in Tehran but without Taliban representation; Rabbani, Hekmatyar, and representative of General Dostum call for cease-fire, exchange of prisoner, and safe, secure environment in Kabul; without Taliban presence, no real progress is made
26 January	Taliban are accused of ethnic cleansing of Tajiks in Gulbahar to prevent uprising; Taliban claim to have captured Shinwari and Siagird

	in Ghorband Valley from Islamic Unity Party of Khalili
27 January	Alliance forces blow up part of Salang highway to slow Taliban advance; Taliban propose cease-fire and prisoner exchange; refugees are arriving in Kabul in such large numbers that aid agencies cannot cope; some refugees also head for Jalalabad and Peshawar
28 January	Alliance jets bomb the Taliban-held town of Jebel Siraq, with at least three civilians killed; UNHCR reports refugees in Badghis are dying from hunger and cold, and continued heavy fighting is causing number of refugees to swell
29 January	Taliban troops continue evacuation of frontline villages as they advance along Salang highway; as most inhabitants are Tajiks, ethnic cleansing is suspected; refugees are totally reliant on outside agencies, as Taliban show no real interest in problem
30–31 January	Taliban continue to advance north in Ghorband Valley and capture Chardehi and Bakhan, some 80 miles north of Kabul
2 February	Taliban radio announces Shi'a residents of Tagab and Behsoud districts in Wardak Province have rebelled against Islamic Unity Party forces led by Karim Khalili; Taliban forces take Hazara districts of Shekali and Sorkhi Parsa in Parwan Province from forces of Khalili; Khalili gathers fresh troops in Bamian Province in preparation for Taliban assault
19 March	Major explosion at ammunition depot in Jalalabad kills fifty, injures hundreds, and destroys many houses; explosion is thought to have been an accident
13 May	Opposition, under Rabbani, forms new government in Mazar-i Sharif
19 May	Gen. Abdul Malik, governor of Fariab Province, mutinies and allies with Taliban; Dostum flees to Turkey
24 May	Taliban forces enter Mazar-i Sharif; Dostum moves to Uzbekistan
25 May	Pakistan, Saudi Arabia, and United Arab Emirates recognize Taliban government

28 May	General Malik turns on Taliban and drives them from Mazar-i Sharif; hundreds are killed, and 2,000 Taliban troops are captured
30 May	Islamic Unity Party troops capture Ghorband Valley; forces of Masood take Jabul Siraq
June	Mazar-i Sharif falls to Taliban, and General Dostum flees to Turkey; city is retaken shortly after by forces of General Malik
20 July	Masood leads anti-Taliban forces to retake areas north of Kabul
24 July	Masood-led forces advance to within 12 miles of Kabul
29 July	Opposition advance held back by Taliban north of Kabul
21 August	Taliban lose ground north of Kabul; fighting erupts in Mazar-i Sharif between forces loyal to Dostum and Malik
August	Taliban begin blockade of Hazarajat
8 September	Mazar-i Sharif besieged by Taliban
12 September	Dostum returns from Kabul to northern base; order restored in Mazar-i Sharif
4 October	Taliban forces expelled from air base at Mazar-i Sharif; massacre of Taliban militia takes place in city; grave of 2,000 Taliban militia will be discovered
November	General Malik and family flee into exile
18 November	Taliban treatment of women condemned by United States

1998

4 February	Earthquake hits Takhar in northern Afghanistan, leaving at least 5,000 dead and more than 1,500 homes destroyed
23 February	Osama bin Laden calls on Muslims to kill Americans and their allies
25 March	United Nations withdraws staff from Kandahar
17 April	U.S. ambassador to the United Nations holds peace talks with Taliban
26 April	Talks begin between Afghan factions in Pakistan
3 May	U.S.-Taliban peace talks collapse; Taliban launch offensive against Northern Alliance

13 July	Two UN staff members murdered in Jalalabad
21 July	Foreign nongovernmental organizations leave Kabul
7 August	U.S. embassies in Kenya and Tanzania attacked; 224 people are killed and 5,000 wounded
18 August	Mazar-i Sharif falls to Taliban; between 4,000 and 5,000 people killed, including 9 Iranian diplomats
20 August	United States launches Cruise missile attack against bin Laden's training camps in Afghanistan, near Khost, following attacks on U.S. embassies in Kenya and Tanzania
21 August	UN observer murdered in Kabul; UN and International Committee of the Red Cross withdraw all foreign staff
27 August	UN representatives attacked at Jalalabad in protest against U.S. missile attacks
30 August	Taliban recapture Mazar-i Sharif
September	Saudi Arabia withdraws diplomats; Taliban capture Bamian
13 September	Taliban take control of the Hazarajat region from Islamic Unity Party, giving them 80 percent of country; only Pakistan, Saudi Arabia, and United Arab Emirates recognize Taliban regime as legitimate government
21 October	United Nations defers decision on recognition of Taliban regime
8 November	United States posts $5 million reward for capture of Osama bin Laden; Taliban offer to try him in Afghanistan, and they find him innocent of all charges by end of month

1999

12 February	United Nations returns to Kabul; Taliban announce disappearance of Osama bin Laden
14 March	Taliban and opposition meet in Turkmenistan and agree to create shared government, exchange prisoners, and open negotiations
21 April	Taliban recapture Bamian
4 July	bin Laden found at Jalalabad
6 July	United States imposes trade sanctions on Taliban regime
28 July	Taliban launch three-pronged assault on forces of Masood; Bagram air base captured

4 August	Ethnic cleansing across Shomali Plain conducted by Taliban; Masood launches successful counterattack
24 August	Attempted assassination attack made on Mullah Omar at Kandahar
7 October	Pakistan Inter-Services Intelligence unit denounces presence of terrorist training camps on Afghan soil
13 October	Gen. Pervez Musharraf becomes president of Pakistan after military intervention
14 November	UN sanctions against Taliban come into effect, including air embargo

2000

1 February	Taliban maintain they do not support terrorism but reject demands for expulsion of Osama bin Laden; opposition accuses Taliban of atrocities again Hazara, Tajik, and Uzbek minorities in Gosfandi and claim eighty are dead; CIA warns bin Laden is acquiring biological, chemical, and nuclear weapons and accuses him of involvement in hijacking of Indian airliner by Kashmiri separatists in December 1999
3 February	New UN representative to Afghanistan, Fransec Vendrell, arrives in Pakistan for tour of region
6 February	Ariana airliner hijacked on route to Mazar-i Sharif by Afghans and flies to London via Uzbekistan, Kazakhstan, and Moscow; some hostages freed at various stops, but 165 passengers on board when plane arrives in London on 7 February; hijackers demand release of opposition leader Isma'il Khan from Taliban imprisonment; incident ends on 10 February
7 February	Taliban delegation received in France; French government takes firm line on international terrorism, opium production, human rights, and position of women
9 February	Bomb explodes outside Ministry of Interior in Kabul; opposition rejects Taliban claims of responsibility; Taliban arrest number of airport workers, including women, allegedly complicit in 6 February Ariana hijacking; UN Sanctions

	Committee approves Ariana flights for the hajj
10 February	Mullah Omar demands hijackers in Britain face British or international law for action
11 February	UN World Food Program warns of food crisis in Afghanistan, with a million-ton shortfall of wheat in relation to demand
12 February	Taliban guarantee safe passage for all Ariana hijacking hostages who wish to return to Afghanistan
14 February	Seventy hijacked hostages fly back from London to Afghanistan; Taliban air force bombs Panjshir Valley, and at least eight civilians are killed
17 February	United Nations condemns death of civilians in Panjshir Valley, bombed by Taliban air force on 14 February
23 February	Pakistan seeks world assistance to curb opium production in Afghanistan, which has reached 4,600 tons (75 percent of world supply)
25 February	President Nazarbayev of Kazakhstan complains about drug trafficking and acts of terrorism emanating from Afghan and Pakistani refugee camps; UN report on human rights accuses Taliban regime of serious human rights violations.; UNHCR announces repatriation of 200,000 refugees from Iran and Pakistan after agreement with Taliban; logistical support to be provided by United Nations
28 February	NGOs in Afghanistan express concern about effects of UN sanctions on civilian population
29 February	Bomb explodes outside Ministry of Information and Culture; opposition forces deny responsibility; killings and looting of Kabul money market also reported
1 March	Forces of Taliban and Masood clash north of Kabul in first serious action for some months; Taliban claim to have seized river port of Sher Kan Bandar on border with Tajikistan
2 March	Further fighting between Taliban and forces of Masood, with exchanges of artillery in Shomali Plains near Kabul and on Tajikstan border; Iran's police force demands better border security from all Afghan neighbors to combat drug trafficking

3 March	Taliban consolidate position in Sher Khan Bandar and Imam Sahib; Russia assists Tajikstan with troops to guard border as a result of fighting in Afghanistan; UN Security Council demands end to Taliban military action and threatens further, unspecified sanctions
7 March	Peace talks sponsored by Organization of the Islamic Conference attended by warring parties
8 March	UN representative to Afghanistan sees some softening of Taliban policy toward women, particularly on access to health facilities and education
26 March	Isma'il Khan, the "Lion of Herat," escapes Taliban custody after three years of imprisonment in Kandahar, together with Abul Zaher, another opposition leader
27 March	Afghan drug traffickers shot dead by Iranian police in eastern Iran; UNHCR begins repatriation program from Pakistan, with each family receiving $100, food, and plastic sheets for shelter
28 March	Bomb blast in Torkam on border with the Khyber Pass kills four people, and a number are injured
29 March	UN operations halted in southern Afghanistan following Taliban raid on UN offices in search for Isma'il Khan; Iran announces Khan is in Iran
31 March	Afghan opposition forces of Dostum, Malik, and Masood combine to oppose Taliban; pro-Western government in Afghanistan is favored, and new grouping is backed by Iran and Russia
4 April	Taliban governor of Kunduz Province, Mohammad Arif Khan, killed in Peshawar, Pakistan
5 April	Taliban governor of Nangarhar Province begins implementation of decree by Mullah Omar to reduce poppy cultivation by one-third, with poppy fields along Jalalabad-Pakistan border road plowed up
7 April	Reports from Afghanistan indicate military buildup on both sides in preparation for spring offensive;

further clashes reported from Nejran district, north of Kabul

8 April	Taliban warned of further UN sanctions unless fighting and human rights abuses of minorities cease and bin Laden is extradited; Taliban capture Darra-i-Kalan Valley in Nejrab district, but fierce counterattacks launched by opposition forces
12 April	Taliban warn Russia not to become involved in Afghanistan's internal affairs
13 April	Opposition forces claim to have captured Sagha and Sharak districts of Ghor Province; intense fighting reported around Albak, capital of Samangan Province; UN team returns to Kandahar following guarantees of security from Taliban regime
18 April	U.S. secretary of state Madeline Albright and President Karimov of Uzbekistan agree Taliban regime is threat to regional stability
19 April	Food prices in Afghanistan rise 25 percent due to taxes imposed by Taliban regime, collapse of Afghan currency, drought-affected poppy crop, threat of further UN sanctions, and printing of currency by opposition forces; UN representative meets Masood in Tajikistan, who agrees to negotiate with Taliban, but no formal proposals follow
21 April	All warring factions agree to three-day truce to enable UNICEF polio vaccination program to take place
24 April	Maulavi Mohammed Siddiquillah assassinated by unknown gunmen in Peshawar; Siddiquillah was a mujahideen commander in alliance with Hekmatyar
25 April	European Union provides $26 million to aid displaced Afghan refugees
May	Taliban torture and kill civilians in Robatak Pass area on border between Baghlan and Samangan Provinces
8 May	Indirect peace talks sponsored by OIC at Jeddah, Saudi Arabia, begin between Taliban and opposition
9 May	At OIC peace talks, Taliban and opposition agree to exchange

prisoners; United States provides $4 million for UNHCR Afghan operations

18 May United States supports plan by former king Zahir to hold Loya Jirga to bring peace to Afghanistan; proposal rejected by Taliban

19 May President Putin of Russia and President Karimov of Uzbekistan pledge to fight terrorism and regional effects of Taliban regime; Pakistan and Taliban agree to fully recognize Durand Line and streamline refugee repatriation, and Pakistan agrees to close mujahideen training camps; United States donates $500,000 for emergency drought relief in southern Afghanistan

20 May Taliban bomb opposition-held town of Taloqan in Takhar Province; UN aid worker and six children killed

22 May Russia accuses Taliban of supporting and training Chechen guerrillas; preventive strikes against Afghanistan not ruled out if there is perceived threat to Russia's security

23 May Taliban claim to have captured area around strategic Salang Tunnel from Masood after two days of intensive fighting

26 May Major explosion occurs at Taliban ammunition store in Kabul; opposition denies responsibility; United States and Russia agree Security Council must take further action against Taliban regime if it continues to ignore world opinion

27 May U.S. undersecretary of state, Thomas Pickering, meets Taliban deputy foreign minister, Abdul Jallil, to press for handover of Osama bin Laden

28 May Mullah Omar denies presence of terrorist training camps in Afghanistan; Pakistani and Western intelligence agencies identify Rishkor base and camps in Laghman and Khost Provinces as training camps

2 June Repatriation of Afghan refugees to southern Afghanistan suspended because of drought

4 June Taliban accuse opposition of breaking cease-fire in Parwan and Gorband Provinces during UNICEF vaccination program

7 June Pressure mounts in United Nations for tougher sanctions because of Taliban refusal to extradite bin Laden

10 June Taliban mass troops in north of Afghanistan, ready for attack on Northern Alliance territory; Uzbekistan reinforces border

14 June UN Security Council considers use of "intelligent" sanctions against Taliban leaders to protect general population, but doubts expressed about Pakistan's commitment; opposition sources claim Northern Alliance has taken Chaghcharan, capital of Ghor Province; Central Asian Economic Association leaders contend international community not doing enough to end conflict in Afghanistan

23 June UNHCR warns drought could cause massive population displacement to Pakistan and Iran unless aid is forthcoming. U.S. agrees to donate further $6 million to drought program in Afghanistan and parts of India and Pakistan

26 June Opposition forces claim Taliban is preparing for summer offensive and say attack has started on Dara-i-Suf in Samangan Province; Taliban agree to stop poppy production, provided international aid is received to repair damaged infrastructure

30 June OIC emphasizes impossibility of solving Afghan conflict by military means, calling for end to hostilities and for all states to cease supplying arms

1 July Fighting flares up near Bagram, north of Kabul, which spoils plans for exchange of some 4,000 prisoners and delays opening of OIC-sponsored peace talks

4 July U.S. consul-general in Karachi states sanctions will remain in force until bin Laden is handed over by Afghanistan

6 July Turkmenistan signs contract with Taliban to supply electricity to city of Herat

9 July Opposition admits losing ground to Taliban in fighting north of Kabul

10 July Anti-Taliban forces blamed for bomb attack on Pakistani embassy in

Kabul; Taliban issues ban on NGOs using female workers, but it is unclear as whether ban applies only to Afghan employees

12 July Iran seals border with Afghanistan to stop flow of drugs; U.S. aid worker Mary MacMakin expelled from Afghanistan after being accused of spying for United States; United Nations begins negotiations with Taliban in attempt to lift ban on female relief workers

15 July Mullah Omar refuses to hand over Osama bin Laden to United States

17 July Opposition blamed for bomb attack on house of Pakistani diplomat in Kabul

18 July Pakistan footballers playing in Kandahar arrested by religious police for wearing shorts, and their heads are shaved as punishment; Taliban apologize after protests from Islamabad; UN World Food Program announces major relief operation to aid 1.6 million Afghanis threatened by famine because of drought

20 July United Nations admits no progress on talks to reinstate female NGO workers

21–22 July Bomb explosions in Kabul blamed by government on opposition forces

25 July Pakistan requests extradition of Pakistanis suspected of involvement in terrorist activities and sectarian violence; Taliban agree, if evidence is produced; Taliban arrest commander in northern Baghlan Province on suspicion of collusion with opposition; opposition claim arrest was due to refusal by Bashir Baghlani to supply recruits to Taliban forces

28 July Intense fighting breaks out in eastern Baghlan Province; ban on cultivation of opium poppy announced by Mullah Omar

29 July Taliban forces cut communications between Masood's stronghold in Panjshir Valley and Takhar Province on Tajikistan border

30 July Strategic district of Burqa seized by Taliban

31 July Some 65,000 illegal Afghan refugees expelled by Iran under plan aided by United Nations

3 August Taliban capture strategic town of Ishkamish in Takhar Province, regarded as great setback for Masood; United Nations again pressures Taliban to ease ban on female NGO workers

5 August Opposition forces claim to recapture of territory along Salang highway, exposing Khinjan to artillery; seven workers of Organization for Mine Clearance and Afghan Rehabilitation killed in Herat Province; Taliban blame opposition for attack

6 August Taliban take town of Banji in Takhar Province from opposition

7 August Taliban forces advance on opposition stronghold of Taloqan, with heavy casualties on both sides

8 August United Nations calls for arrest and punishment of those responsible for OMAR murders

9 August Fighting near Taloqan escalates; opium prices in Afghanistan rise steeply because of drought and Taliban ban on opium production

10 August Fighting near Taloqan abates, and opposition declares willingness to accept UN mediation

11 August Russia claims most fighters in Chechnya Province are Afghan mercenaries; Russian border troops aiding Tajikistan repel attempt by Afghan fighters to cross border

13 August Taliban intensify assault on Taloqan and make further ground

16 August Taliban authorities close WFP bakeries for women in Kabul due to ban on female NGO workers; decision is reversed on 17 August after UN protests

19 August Opposition forces announce capture of Daray-i-Noor district in Jalalabad and parts of Khiva district; Taliban authorities reaffirm decision not to extradite Osama bin Laden

21 August WFP delivers emergency supplies to besieged, opposition-held Dara-i-Suf in Samangan Province

22 August UN Security Council receives report stating Afghan people would not be able to sustain further sanctions, except for arms embargo

25 August Forces allied to Masood make gains in fighting northeast of Kabul

26 August	Taliban appeal for lifting of sanctions because of suffering to Afghan people
30 August	Taliban indicate willingness to begin peace talks and release some political prisoners; peace proposals initiated by Turkmenistan
31 August	Afghan opposition claims capture of strategic territory in Baghlan Province; Turkmenistan peace proposals are backed by Pakistan
1 September	Pakistan embassy in Jalalabad hit by bomb attack; UN land-mine clearance program threatened by lack of funds
2 September	Masood meets Turkmenistan officials to discuss ending of civil war
4 September	Taliban launch all-out assault on Taloqan, which falls on 6 September to a combined Taliban-Pakistani-Arab force; thousands of refugees flee to Tajikistan and Pakistan borders
9 September	Taliban forces attempt to clear opposition forces from outskirts of Taloqan
10 September	Fighting erupts again around Bagram air base, north of Kabul
13 September	Rocket attack hits Kabul airport, suspected to have come from nearby villages due to nature of weapons
14 September	Iranian police kill eleven Afghan bandits near town of Tobat-e-Heydarieh; opium production declines 28 percent, but Afghan remains world's largest supplier
15 September	UNHCR high commissioner, Sadako Ogata, raises issue of Taliban regime's treatment of women
17 September	Opposition forces claim to have seized hilltops around Taloqan; Taliban offer to hold peace talks with Masood
18 September	At meeting with UNHCR high commissioner, Taliban press for lifting of economic sanctions and for international recognition
19 September	WFP launches operation to supply food to civilians displaced by fighting around Taloqan; Taliban capture Imam Sahib district in Kunduz Province, further cutting off supply route to Masood's territory; ground retaken by opposition on following day
21 September	Hazarbagh, north of Taloqan, and Khawajaghar airport captured by Taliban
22 September	Taliban appeal for international aid as compensation for losses due to cuts in opium production and protest UN decision to cease supply of substitute crops to farmers; Tajikistan complains its stability is threatened by Islamic extremists trained by Taliban militia; Taliban make significant gains by capturing Shir Khan border port on the Oxus River, the Imam Sahib and Dashte Archi districts in Kunduz Province, and the Ai Khanoum border area of Takhar Province; President Rabbani appeals for aid to rid Afghanistan of Taliban, arguing neighboring states will pay high price if Afghanistan becomes extreme Islamic state
23 September	Two men publicly executed by Taliban, accused of working for opposition and carrying out bomb attacks in Kabul
28 September	Italy proposes setting up humanitarian corridor in Afghanistan to allow aid to all areas controlled by warring factions
29 September	Bomb attack launched on offices of Al-Rasheed Trust aid agency and a weekly religious newspaper that backs Taliban movement; 8,000 Afghan refugees flee into Pakistan to escape fighting
30 September	Taliban captures Karkhar gorge east of Taloqan after fierce fighting; gorge links Taloqan with Badakhshan Province, heartland of Northern Alliance
1 October	Uzbekistan opens dialogue with Taliban to bolster security in Central Asia
2 October	Taliban publicly hang two men in Kandahar for murder and robbery
5 October	UN special envoy Vendrell arrives in Kabul for talks with Taliban and finds regime willing to hold peace talks with opponents to secure political settlement
6 October	Opposition commanders meet in Iran and form the United Front to combat Taliban regime

8 October	Masood urges international community to pressure Pakistan to end Afghan civil war
9 October	Crossfire on border of Tajikistan kills one Russian border guard and wounds five Tajik soldiers
12 October	United States warns Taliban government Afghanistan will be attacked if Osama bin Laden found responsible for strike on the USS *Cole* in Yemen
15 October	Bomb explodes outside Ministry of Communications in Kabul; opposition forces make gains in Khoja Ghar district in Takhar Province and Imam Sahib and Dashti Archi districts in Kunduz Province
16 October	Taliban deny al-Qaeda was involved in Yemen attack on U.S. warship that killed seventeen sailors
19 October	UNHCR criticizes effects of religious extremism in Afghanistan
20 October	United Nations estimates drought and antidrug measures on Afghans borders have reduced opium poppy revenue from £230 million to $90 million
23 October	Former president Rabbani urges Pakistan to stop arming Taliban regime and predicts opposition will mount offensive before winter; however, Rabbani feels a revolt in Taliban areas will be necessary, in addition to international pressure, for negotiations to take place; opposition takes river crossing near Taloqan, cutting off Taliban-held city of Kunduz
24 October	United Nations reports renewed fighting has resulted in another 60,000 displaced persons
26 October	Russian defense minister, Sergeyev, meets with Masood; Taliban warns Russia against supporting Northern Alliance; Masood's forces begin shelling Taloqan, but Taliban deny loss of territory
27 October	WFP warns that hundreds of thousands of Afghans will not survive winter unless more funding is forthcoming to support emergency food supply program
29 October	Taliban issues edict banning poppy planting in following season

2 November	U.S. and Taliban ambassadors meet in Islamabad to discuss drug trade and try to resolve impasse over Osama bin Laden
3 November	Taliban and opposition agree to peace talks backed by United Nations
6 November	Edict issued by Mullah Omar banning men without beards from employment or any other services; Kazakhstan advises it is ready to talk to Taliban, despite its opposition to regime, for purely pragmatic reasons
7 November	United Nations votes against recognition of Taliban, and Afghan UN seat remains with opposition; Iranian police kill thirteen Afghans in drug battle in border region
9 November	Russia refuses to negotiate with Taliban and urges sanctions be intensified; North-West Frontier Province of Pakistan bans entry of more Afghan refugees on economic and security grounds; move welcomed by Taliban but opposed by opposition
10 November	British and Taliban ambassadors meet in Islamabad for wide-ranging discussions; mortar bombs from Afghanistan land in Tajikistan, provoking threat of retaliatory action from Russia
12 November	Taliban threaten Russia and its Central Asian allies if support for Masood is not withdrawn; Taliban request Pakistan to withdraw ban on refugees
13 November	Opposition commander in Samangan Province, Paydel Pahlwan, joins Taliban with 150 soldiers due to Russian support for Northern Alliance
14 November	Former king Zahir and opposition leaders meet in Rome to prepare peace proposals, including holding of a loya jirga to determine future of Afghanistan; overtures rejected by Taliban
17 November	United Nations asks Pakistan and Tajikistan to reopen borders to refugees
19 November	Pakistan agrees to allow entry of Afghan refugees with relevant documentation
20 November	Taliban reject peace proposals put forward by former king Zahir from

	exile in Rome; heavy fighting occurs around Taloqan, with rival claims on gains and losses
21 November	India and Russia press for intensified sanctions if Taliban do not stop violence
22 November	Ministry of Information in Kabul rocked by explosion
23 November	UN special envoy and Taliban foreign minister meet in Kandahar to discuss agenda for peace talks
24 November	Taliban accuses Russia of providing Northern Alliance with ammunition to sustain attack of Taloqan
26 November	Taliban detain foreign aid workers in Kabul because of perceived irregularities in papers
27 November	Russia reports Afghan refugees have been fired on at border with Tajikistan
28 November	United Nations says $229 million in emergency relief is needed for Afghanistan; Pakistan claims part of funding is required for dealing with 2.6 million refugees
30 November	Taliban condemn further sanctions on Afghanistan, claiming ordinary people will suffer; they again refuse to extradite bin Laden, arguing that ban on his activities in Afghanistan is sufficient
30 November	Iran says drug traffickers from Afghanistan will be shot on sight in attempt to halt drug trade across border, with its accompanying violence
10–19 December	UN and NGO foreign staff withdraw from Afghanistan for fear of reprisals
20 December	UN sanctions renewed by Security Council and tightened, with arms embargo imposed, Taliban offices abroad closed, and Taliban officials forbidden to leave Afghanistan; Taliban leave peace talks and threaten to shut UN offices in retaliation
28 December	Heavy fighting resumes in Bamian Province around Imam Sahib, Taloqan, and Panjshir Valley, with claims of territorial gains by opposition forces

2001

7 January	Taliban retake Yakaolang in Bamian Province, and accusations of war crimes against Hazaras follow
9 January	Yemeni authorities suspect al-Qaeda link in attack on U.S. warship in 2000
10 January	Religious groups in Pakistan back Taliban because of UN sanctions
31 January	United Nations reports 110 people have died in Herat from cold and hunger
9 February	Pakistan refuses entry to new refugees; United States closes Taliban office in New York despite protests from United Nations
10 February	Anti-Taliban Alliance offers to hold peace talks with Taliban
14 February	Taliban regime closes UN offices in Kabul in retaliation for closure of its New York office; opposition captures Bamian town, but it is retaken by Taliban three days later
19 February	Human Rights Watch issues report on Taliban atrocities in May 2000 and January 2001
20 February	United Nations warns of starvation conditions in Afghanistan
26 February	Mullah Omar orders destruction of all statues in Afghanistan and arouses condemnation from international community
1 March	Despite world pressure, Taliban begin destruction of giant statues of Buddha at Bamian
2 March	UNESCO asks Taliban authorities to halt destruction of pre-Islamic heritage and begins series of international visits, which are ignored by Taliban
13 March	Destruction of statues at Bamian confirmed by Afghani freelance photographer
5 April	Abdul Shah Masood goes on European tour to elicit support for Northern Alliance
22 May	Taliban issue edict requiring non-Muslims to wear identifying badges on clothing
July	Taliban arrest eight international aid workers on charges of Christian propaganda activities
7 August	Taliban refuse outside access to aid workers arrested for preaching Christianity
27 August	Delegation of diplomats and relatives visit detained foreign aid workers

5 September	Trial begins for eight foreign aid workers arrested by Taliban and charged with preaching Christianity	
9 September	Suicide bombers, posing as Arab journalists, assassinate Masood with bomb concealed in videocamera; attack now thought to have been an al-Qaeda operation on behalf of Taliban	
11 September	About 4,000 people killed as hijacked planes are flown into World Trade Center in New York and Pentagon in Washington	
14 September	U.S. and British governments name Osama bin Laden and Al-Qaeda as prime suspects in U.S. terror attacks	
15 September	Death of Masood announced by Northern Alliance; all foreigners ordered to leave Afghanistan by Taliban	
20 September	President Bush calls on Afghanistan to hand over Osama bin Laden; mullahs call on Taliban to ask bin Laden to leave Afghanistan voluntarily to avoid U.S. action; Taliban agree to act on ruling but plead for time	
24 September	Taliban admit loss of Zaare, near Mazar-i Sharif	
25 September	Saudi Arabia cuts ties with Kabul	
26 September	Pakistan abandons official support for Taliban and agrees to cooperate in War on Terror	
1 October	Opposition decides to form Interim Government after talks with former king Mohammed Zahir in Rome	
2 October	Taliban regime again rejects demands to expel bin Laden; Rome Accord agreed to by opposition	
4 October	British government releases dossier of evidence linking bin Laden to attacks of 11 September; President Bush pledges another $320 in humanitarian aid for food, medicine, blankets, and shelter before winter	
5 October	U.S. Army sends 1,000 troops of Tenth Mountain Division to Uzbekistan	
6 October	Taliban offer release of eight imprisoned foreign aid workers if United States will ensure Afghanistan will not be attacked and provided propaganda war against regime ceases; offer is rejected by	

Washington; 1,000 U.S. Special Forces arrive in Uzbekistan

7 October	Operation Enduring Freedom begins; first U.S.-led air and missile strikes hit Afghanistan; videotape released by bin Laden, praising 11 September terrorist attacks on United States
8 October	United States begins humanitarian aid drops in Afghanistan, using C-17 cargo planes; Kabul and Kandahar attacked by U.S. Air Force
9 October	U.S. bombing of Afghanistan continues, including first daylight raids
11 October	United States mounts daylight raid on Kabul and on suspected al-Qaeda compound at Kandahar
13 October	Taliban reject further U.S. demands to expel bin Laden; Kabul airport subjected to U.S. airstrikes; four civilians killed in adjoining neighborhood
15 October	Further daylights raids occur near Kabul and on suspected training camps near Jalalabad
16 October	U.S. air strikes hit Red Cross warehouses outside Kabul; Taliban positions at Jalalabad attacked by U.S. gunships; UN World Food Program announces plans to restore supply route to Northern Afghanistan, and first Russian aid shipment arrives in region
18 October	Further air strikes on Kabul made by United States, and opposition forces announce intention to advance on Kabul
19 October	U.S. Special Forces arrive in Afghanistan
21 October	Taliban positions north of Kabul bombed by United States to aid advancing northern forces
22 October	U.S. air strikes hit Taliban front lines at Mazar-i Sharif and north of Kabul to aid opposition advance
24 October	U.S. forces continue to bomb Taliban forces north of Kabul; fierce fighting takes place between Taliban forces and opposition south of Mazar-i Sharif
25 October	Heavy U.S. airstrikes hit Taliban forces north of Kabul and the capital itself

26 October	Abdul Haq executed by Taliban following mission to persuade Pashtuns to rise against regime; United States again bombs Red Cross warehouses outside Kabul
27 October	U.S. Air Force mounts daylong strike on Taliban positions in northern Afghanistan; armed militants move from Pakistan into Afghanistan to join Taliban forces
28 October	United States bombs Taliban positions near border with Tajikistan, near Kakala River
30 October	Opposition forces deployed near Taliban lines north of Kabul
31 October	Taliban front line in northern Afghanistan pounded by U.S. heavy bombers
5 November	Heavy U.S. air assaults occur in Samangan and Balkh Provinces and on Taliban positions near Taloqan
6 November	Further heavy bombing occurs at Mazar-i Sharif; town of Ogopruk seized by Northern Alliance
8 November	Eighty-five Pakistani militants killed in U.S. air strike near Mazar-i Sharif; Northern Alliance forces move in from south of city
9 November	Mazar-i Sharif captured by Northern Alliance, and gains made elsewhere in northern Afghanistan, including city of Herat
12 November	Anti-Taliban forces capture city of Herat; UK ground forces operate alongside Northern Alliance
13 November	Kabul entered by Northern Alliance forces after overnight withdrawal by Taliban
14 November	Opposition forces capture Jalalabad; al-Qaeda military chief Mohammed Atef killed in air strike
15 November	Eight foreign aid workers held by Taliban freed by anti-Taliban forces at Kunduz, which has been besieged by Northern Alliance forces aided by U.S. air strikes
17 November	Former president Rabbani returns to Kabul, promising to form broad-based government
19 November	Northern Alliance attacks Chagatai Ridge to open up assault on Taloqan; United States continues bombing of Kunduz, last northern Taliban stronghold

23 November	Taliban still resist in Kunduz, and heavy bombing by United States continues; 15,000-pound "Daisy Cutter" bombs dropped around Kandahar
26 November	After two-week siege of Kunduz, last remaining Taliban stronghold falls to Northern Alliance; 500 U.S. Marines arrive in Afghanistan and seize air base near Kandahar
30 November	Uprising by Taliban prisoners at Mazar-i Sharif ends; hundreds killed, including CIA operative; anti-Taliban forces, with U.S. air support, move on Taliban stronghold at Kandahar
December	World Food Program moves 90,000 tons of wheat into Afghanistan to avert famine
3 December	Caves of Tora Bora and surrounding area bombed by U.S. forces in support of anti-Taliban troops' attack on airport near Kandahar
4 December	U.S. Marines occupy air base southwest of Taliban stronghold of Kandahar; United Nations pulls international staff out of Mazar-i Sharif due to factional fighting
5 December	Four rival Afghan groups sign Bonn Agreement to form Interim Government under UN auspices; royalist, Pashtun leader Hamid Karzai appointed head of interim administration; Coalition position near Kandahar bombed in error, with three U.S. Special Forces killed and Karzai injured
6 December	Taliban surrender their last stronghold of Kandahar on guarantee of general amnesty by Karzai
7 December	U.S. troops and U.S. air strikes hit al-Qaeda and Taliban positions in Tora Bora caves in eastern Afghanistan
10 December	U.S. Marines reoccupy U.S. embassy in Kabul; Dostum voices opposition to Bonn Agreement
16 December	After two weeks of fighting by U.S. troops and Afghan militia, together with U.S. bombing raids, al-Qaeda fighters are cleared from Tora Bora caves
19 December	Agreement reached on international peacekeeping force for Kabul, to be

known as International Security Assistance Force and headed by Britain

20 December British Royal Marines arrive to spearhead ISAF; al-Qaeda fighters leave Tora Bora area

21 December Opposition captures Pul-i-Khumri, north of Kabul, and Qala-i-Nau in Badghis Province

22 December Karzai sworn in as head of interim administration, together with thirty other members

29 December Six-hour bombing raid kills 110 Paktia villagers, probably the result of bad intelligence from local warlord Pacha Khan Zadran

2002

1 January U.S. forces airlifted from Kandahar air base to Helmand Province in search for Mullah Omar

4 January Agreement signed between Afghan interior minister, Younus Qanooni, and British general John McColl on deployment of international security force

7 January U.S. bombing occurs near Khost in hunt for Taliban leader, Jalaluddin Haqqani, who is high on U.S. most-wanted list

9 January Karzai calls for creation of national army to unite country

11 January Governor of Kandahar announces surrender of three Taliban leaders: Mullah Obaidullah, former minister of defense, Mullah Nooruddin Rurabi, former minister of justice, and Mullah Saadudin, former minister of mines and industry; Mullah Haqani, former ambassador to Pakistan, also surrendered

21 January Tokyo Conference pledges $2.6 billion in aid for reconstruction of Afghanistan.

24 January U.S. ground action in Oruzgan Province results in sixteen deaths and the capture of twenty-seven, but none turn out to be Taliban or al-Qaeda fighters

31 January Forces of governor of Paktia Province, Padsha Khan, defeated by rival warlord Saif Ullah, Pashtun tribal leader who had taken control after withdrawal of Taliban

5 February U.S. air strikes hit Mafazatoo area of Gorboz district, 12 miles south of Khost, in hunt for remnants of Taliban and al-Qaeda

14 February Afghan aviation minister, Abdul Rahman, killed by angry Muslim pilgrims at Kabul airport; crowd angered by delays in flights to hajj

21 February Thousands of Pashtuns reported to be fleeing northern Pakistan in face of ethnic cleansing by anti-Taliban forces

1 March Operation Anaconda launched with 1,000 U.S. troops, Coalition special forces, and Afghan militias at Shah-i-Kot to oust Taliban and al-Qaeda fighters

3 March Chinook helicopter destroyed in heavy fighting with Taliban and al-Qaeda forces, with deaths of seven U.S. troops

6 March U.S. troops airlifted to Tora Bora cave complex to flush out Taliban and al-Qaeda forces

10 March U.S. troops involved in fierce battle with Taliban and al-Qaeda in the Shah-i-Kot Valley, near Gardez, as part of Operation Anaconda

20 March Al-Qaeda attack hits U.S. and other Coalition forces at Khost

Mid-April Operation Snipe launched by UK commandos and Afghan forces in southeast Afghanistan

11 April Al-Qaeda attack on mosque in Tunisia results in nineteen dead, most of them German tourists

15 April Operation Mountain Lion launched in eastern Pakistan by Coalition special forces

16 April Operation Ptarmigan launched by UK troops in conjunction with Operation Mountain Lion

17 April Four Canadian soldiers killed by U.S. aircraft while engaged in live-fire exercise, having been mistaken for Taliban forces

18 April Former king Mohammed Zahir Shah returns to Afghanistan

29 April Turkey announces it will head up Kabul International Security Assistance Force, taking over from Great Britain

2 May Loya Jirga Independent Commission announced by Interim Government and United Nations in Kabul; British marines begin Operation Snipe in southeast Afghanistan

15 May   UN high commissioner for refugees highlights plight of 500,000 refugees who have returned to Afghanistan

23 May   512 Taliban prisoners freed from Sheberghan prison in northern Afghanistan in liaison with International Committee of the Red Cross

24 May   Bomb attack in Kandahar targets music shop

25 May   Five hundred Taliban prisoners freed from Sheberghan prison under the supervision of International Committee of the Red Cross

26 May   U.S. forces raid compound near Gardez and hold two suspected Taliban members

29 May   Operation Buzzard launched by UK and Afghan forces in Khost region of southeast Afghanistan

19 June   President Karzai inaugurated by Loya Jirga as head of transitional government

28 June   Major explosion in ammunition store near Spin Boldak, near Pakistan border, kills at least ten, injures thirty-five, and damages property

1 July   United States bombs villagers celebrating a wedding in central Afghanistan after reports indicate military unit came under fire; at least forty villagers are killed, but United States maintains antiaircraft gun had been firing from nearby compound

3 July   Four al Qaeda militants and three Pakistani police killed in gunfight at checkpoint at Kohat in North-West Frontier Province

6 July   Afghan vice-president Abdul Qadir, veteran Pashtun leader, assassinated by gunmen

12 July   Six Afghan governors demand United States obtain permission to mount military operations in their provinces

13 July   U.S. convoy attacked on road linking Bagram air base with Kabul

29 July   Fighting occurs between U.S. forces and al-Qaeda at village of Ab Khail, 10 miles east of Khost

8 August   Thirteen escaped al-Qaeda killed in gun battle with Afghan security forces in Kabul; group consists of twelve Pakistanis and one Kyrgyz

9 August   Explosion, thought to be a car bomb, hits Jalalabad construction firm's building; ten are killed and twenty-five injured

14 November   Kabul University students are threatened and beaten by police;. many injured are in hospital

2 December   Kabul government brokers truce between ethnic Pashtun commander Amanullah Khan and Isma'il Khan, Tajik governor of Herat Province, after fighting at Zer-e-Koh near Shindand air base, leaving sixty dead (mostly civilians); conference on Afghanistan held in Bonn, Germany, to discuss security and reconstruction issues

11 December   Factional fighting breaks out between rival warlords for control of Gardez in Paktia Province

2003

13 January   Joint regional teams established by United States to operate in key cities to improve security and begin reconstruction programs

21 January   World Bank announces grant aid of $100 million for projects in Afghanistan

26 January   Police vehicle escorting UNHCR convoy attacked some 25 miles west of Jalalabad; two police and four attackers dead; UN staff returns safely to Jalalabad

27–28 January   Taliban and al-Qaeda force of eighty fighters attacked by U.S. and Afghan forces in the mountains near Spin Boldak; eighteen rebels killed in air and ground assault on cave complexes

28 January   Government announces political parties will not be allowed in new legislature designed to serve until 2004; conference of Afghan elders in Peshawar criticizes performance of Karzai government

29 January   Interior Minister Wardag replaced by Ali Ahmad Jalali due to Wardag's handling of student unrest in November 2002

31 January	Eighteen civilians killed in bus blown up by bomb on Rambasi Bridge, near Kandahar; incident thought to have been aimed at Afghan troops and mounted by Taliban and al-Qaeda
13 February	U.S. operation launched in Helmand Province, with seven suspected fighters arrested, but troops are accused of killing civilians; Afghan government opens investigation
14 February	Audiotape purported to be by Osama bin Laden broadcast by al-Jazeera television; in it, he announces support for people of Iraq and urges attacks on United States and Israel
16 February	Pakistan's army provides submachine guns, mortar rockets, and ammunition to new Afghan army
19 February	Gulbuddin Hekmatyar designated by United States as global terrorist
20 February	Fifteen Tajik generals reassigned in Defense Ministry and replaced by Hazara, Pashtun, and Uzbek generals; Gen. Gul Zarak Zadran, a Pashtun, appointed as fourth deputy defense minister; major demobilization conference held in Tokyo
22 February	Conference held in Tokyo to discuss demobilization and disarmament of Afghan militias; fighting occurs in Fariab Province between forces of Rashid Dostum and Ustad Atta Mohammed, leaving six dead
24 February	Five suspected terrorists arrested by Afghan police at Spin Boldak; clashes take place between U.S. forces and unidentified attackers at Tarin Kot in Oruzgan Province and near Wazir in Nangarhar Province; road between Gardez and Khost blocked by forces of Bacha Zadran in retaliation for government seizure of vehicles being used for illegal checkpoints
25 February	Taliban fighter killed in Ata Ghar region of Zabal Province in clash with Afghan security force; Afghan minister for mines and industry, Juma Mohammed Mohammedi, killed when plane crashes in Arabian Sea on flight to southwestern Pakistan; bomb attack hits home of education minister, Dawood Barak, in Kandahar but with no casualties

26 February	Afghan government forces find huge cache of weapons at Bander in Nangarhar Province, including missiles, antitank mines, mortars, guns, and ammunition
27 February	Afghan police make seven arrests in Kandahar and recover stock of explosives and land mines
28 February	Two rockets explode in Kandahar, but no casualties are reported; regional leaders in northern Afghanistan, Gen. Abdul Rashid Dostum, Gen. Ustad Atta Mohammed, and Saradar Saeedi, agree to end ethnic conflict at meeting convened by United Nations in Mazar-i Sharif
1 March	Khalid Sheikh Mohammad, thought to be al-Qaeda's planner of 11 September atrocities, among other actions, arrested by Pakistani security with CIA cooperation in Rawalpindi, Pakistan
3 March	United States announces new anti-Taliban push in a second valley in Helmand Province; Taliban claim responsibility for recent attacks in Afghanistan
4 March	Group from University of Colorado announces it will rebuild Farza village, north of Kabul
10 April	Afghanistan applies to join World Trade Organization
11 April	Afghan national army troops engage Taliban fighter in battle 108 miles south of Kabul; former Taliban minister Amanullah killed; further outbreak of fighting between forces of Dostum and Atta Mohammed in Maimana, Fariab Province; four of Atta's soldiers killed and at least four wounded, United Nations and other aid agencies evacuate personnel; eleven Afghan civilians killed in U.S. bombing raid at Shkin near the Pakistan border; bombing was in response to attack on Afghan military checkpoint in Paktia Province; U.S. forces mount raids in southern Helmand Province in area where two U.S. Special Forces ambushed and killed on 29 March 2003; arrests made, and cache of weapons and explosives seized;

Afghan authorities announce launch of National Solidarity Program designed to deliver $95 million in grants to 4,000 villages with the objective of reaching every village in three to four years

12 April Two Afghan soldiers shot near Khost when hand grenades thrown at an Italian patrol; one Taliban suspect arrested; car loaded with explosives blows up near Khost, killing occupants, two Pakistanis, a Yemeni, and a former intelligence officer of the Taliban suspected of planning a terrorist attack on an unidentified target; U.S. commander in Afghanistan calls for joint U.S.-Afghan forces and Pakistani border patrols to halt infiltration of Taliban

13 April Relatives of governor of Kandahar, Gul Agha Sherzai, killed by Taliban militants in Pakistani border town of Chaman; complaints made to Pakistan about continued support for Taliban; Pakistan authorities seize ton of drugs being brought through the Murda Karez Mountains near border town of Chaman, and 1,100 pounds of morphine seized in former Afghan refugee camp at Chaghi district, 130 miles west of Quetta

15 April Commander Shahi and two bodyguards from militia of General Dostum ambushed and killed on the way to Mazar-i Sharif, but assailants not identified; some 500 Afghan refugees leave Pakistan under repatriation program sponsored by United Nations; pamphlets released in Afghan refugee camps in Pakistan's North-West Frontier Province urge Afghans to revolt against Karzai government and U.S. allies; leaflets unsigned but thought to be work of Taliban; UNICEF begins three-day immunization program against polio, aimed at reaching 6 million Afghan children; FAO announces outbreaks of animal diseases are major threat to food security in Afghanistan

16 April NATO announces takeover of command of UN peacekeeping

mission in Kabul as of late summer 2003; three caches of heavy ammunition, including antitank rockets, antiaircraft rounds, and rocket-propelled grenades discovered by Coalition forces at Khar Bolah in Ghazni Province; Romanian troop find cache of weapons near Qalat in Zabul Province

17 April Afghan-Pakistani security forces exchange fire across border at Ghulam Khan; no casualties reported, and accounts of size of Pakistani incursion confused; bomb explodes in Kabul while bomb-disposal team defusing second bomb; grenade attack hits UNICEF offices in Jalalabad; Afghan forces announce arrest of Maulawi Qalamuddin, fomer deputy head of Taliban religious police, in area south of Kabul, but no details released; United Nations brokers agreement to secure withdrawal of rival militia from Maimana, and UN offices reopened

19 April U.S. special representative to Afghanistan warns Pakistan that border clash that threatens the stability of Afghanistan is also a challenge to U.S. interests; border dispute resolved in meeting between Afghan and Pakistani officials

20 April Five reported dead in floods in Baghran district of Helmand Province; Afghan military leaders agree on need for national army at meeting in Kabul

21 April Cable television in Kabul resumes broadcast of programs banned by Supreme Court in January 2003; Afghan authorities announce arrest of five former Taliban supporters for killing four foreign journalists at Tangi Abishu, 55 miles east of Kabul, in November 2001

22 April President Karzai, on visit to Pakistan, stresses more must be done to seal porous border and prevent Taliban incursions; U.S. forces kill one Taliban fighter and arrest seven others in raid in southern Afghanistan; UN Development Fund for Women launches research program to determine how disadvantaged women are in Afghanistan; U.S. forces believed to have killed Taliban fighter responsible for death of International Red Cross worker in March 2003 in Shah Wali Kot district of Kandahar

23 April   NATO announces takeover of command of the ISAF in summer 2003 under UN mandate; two Afghan soldiers and three Taliban killed in ambush in the Gizab district of Oruzgan Province, 50 miles north of Tarin Kot; Pakistan announces agreement to train Afghan security personnel and offers to establish free industrial zone near Torkim and Chaman on Pakistan border to aid economic development in Afghanistan

24 April   National Emergency Employment Program started under UN auspices to secure employment for Afghans, particularly in rural areas, on labor-intensive works programs

25 April   Public consultations begin on new draft constitution designed to pave way for democratic elections in 2004; Hindu businessman becomes first non-Muslim appointed to commission to examine draft constitution

27 April   UN and Afghan Human Rights Group discover twenty-six prisoners executed with hands tied behind backs after fighting in Badghis Province

28 April   Two U.S. soldiers killed after gun battle with twenty rebels at Shkin in eastern Afghanistan; Pakistani authorities seize huge cache of weapons in North-West Frontier Province, including mortar shells, remote-controlled fuses, missiles, and guns, and promise to act against Taliban leaders operating out of Pakistan while denying presence of Mullah Omar in Pakistan

29 April   Preliminary survey by UN and Afghan antinarcotics division shows rise in poppy production, making Afghanistan world's largest producer again

30 April   Six al-Qaeda suspects arrested in Karachi, thought to be planning terrorist attack in Pakistan; explosives, detonators, and weapons seized in the raid and Yemeni suspected of complicity in attack on USS *Cole* among those detained; Human Rights Department formed to train police in observance of human rights

2 May   Sixty Taliban rebels arrested in Helmand Province after unsuccessful attack on Kajakai Dam in north of province

5 May   Eight fighters from Hekmatyar's Islamic Party arrested in Wardak Province following attack on Afghan Development Agency group engaged in mine clearing

6 May   Small protest in Kabul complaining that United States has not done enough to rebuild country or provide jobs and security

8 May   Further violence reported in Gardez, and United Nations complains about increasing attacks on aid workers and Afghan civilians

9 May   Two Afghans, including former Taliban official, arrested by Pakistani police in Karachi, and weapons and satellite telephone seized; U.S. troops call up air support in Helmand Province to calm clash between two rival Afghan forces

10 May   Muslim cleric Mullah Habibullah, close to President Karzai, killed outside of mosque 90 miles north of Kandahar; two Afghan soldiers wounded when bomb explodes outside governor's residence in Helmand Province

11 May   Customs raid in village of Zard, 300 miles west of Quetta, seizes 200 pounds of heroin smuggled across border from Afghanistan; demonstration staged in Kabul against Karzai's decision to offer amnesty to former members of Taliban who are "not stained with Afghan's blood"; one Afghan soldier killed and U.S. soldier injured in firefight near Khost, two rebel fighters killed in action, and remainder killed in subsequent air strike

12 May   British army announces establishment of provincial

reconstruction team to be based in Mazar-i Sharif to work on rebuilding and security in area

22 May U.S. troops kill five of an attacking force near Gardez

1 June Some 2,000 Afghan refugees return home from Chitral Valley in Pakistan as part of voluntary program; refugees are returning to Jalalabad, Nangarhar, and Kunar

2 June Governor of Kunar Province asserts poor people are being paid about $10 dollars by guerrillas to launch rockets on U.S. and government bases

3 June Fighting near Spin Boldak between rival Afghan factions results in four deaths; Isma'il Khan agrees to hand over $2 million in customs revenues from Herat to central government, enabling defense force salaries to be paid; home of Ahmad Wali Karzai bombed in Kandahar, but no casualties reported; four fuel trucks on way to U.S. forces at Urgan base in Paktia Province attacked, but no reported casualties

4 June Forty-seven Taliban killed in battle with troops loyal to governor of Kandahar at Populzai, near Spin Boldak

5 June Homemade bomb explodes near U.S. Special Forces convoy on Gardez highway but with no casualties

6 June World Bank announces grant of $59.6 million to provide health care for women and children

7 June Four German peacekeepers from ISAF killed and thirty-one injured in suicide car bomb attack on bus in Kabul; troops were heading to Kabul airport at end of tour of duty

9 June Karzai blames foreign elements for car bomb attack on ISAF troops and vows to step up activity against terrorist elements; leaflets distributed in Zabul Province urging police and military to join Taliban in antigovernment and anti-U.S. campaign

10 June National debate launched on proposed new constitution to determine form of government, which interpretation of Islam to adopt, and power of central government

16 June Taliban circulate leaflets in Spin Boldak promising suicide attacks on Coalition forces and members of Afghan government

17 June al-Qaeda suspect arrested by Pakistan authorities in Peshawar; suspect is Arab national thought to be top facilitator in terrorist network; Afghanistan to begin disarmament program of Afghan fighters in July 2003, and Karzai promises reform of Defense Ministry

18 June Report by Council on Foreign Relations states United States could lose the peace in Afghanistan due to lack of control over warlords and slow process of reconstruction

19 June Pakistan president calls for increase in size of international force in Afghanistan to fill growing vacuum outside of Kabul

21 June Air assault launched in eastern Afghanistan to clear area for troop deployment to seal border with Afghanistan in attempt to prevent Taliban and al-Qaeda incursions; Afghan court to try two journalists for blasphemy; weekly newspaper *Aftaab* closed down

22 June Bomb attack on U.S. military base in city of Kunduz but with no casualties

24 June Taliban announce formation of ten-man leadership council to organize resistance against Coalition and Afghan forces; council consists primarily of former Taliban military commanders from southwest Afghanistan

25 June Journalists charged with blasphemy released on bail on instructions of Karzai; two Afghan soldiers killed in ambush by Taliban 3 miles from U.S. base at Spin Boldak; Afghan soldier wounded in attack on home of militia commander in Maruf district, 110 miles northeast of Kandahar; U.S. Special Operations soldier killed and two wounded on patrol near Gardez in Paktia Province

26 June Karzai states on visit to Poland that bin Laden probably alive and living as fugitive in Afghan-Pakistan borderlands; at forum in Switzerland, Karzai delivers upbeat speech on Afghanistan's reconstruction, saying country starting to rise from ashes as result of national and international cooperation

27 June   U.S. military begins Operation United Resolve in border areas of eastern Afghanistan, primarily in Nangarhar Province, to prevent Taliban insurgents from crossing into Afghanistan to launch attacks; military objectives combined with program to assess humanitarian needs in area; Pakistan troops begin coordinated series of patrols in Mohmand tribal region of North-West Frontier Province, much to anger of Islamist parties in Pakistan; Mullah Malang charged by Taliban with organizing mobile training camps for new generation of fighters

28 June   Fresh outbreak of violence between Tajik and Uzbek forces in three villages in Samangan Province but no reports of casualties

30 June   Several rockets fired into city of Jalalabad, hitting a house and military compound and near UNICEF office; bomb blast at Kandahar mosque injures nine worshipers at evening prayer, thought to be because preacher, Malawi Abdullah Fayaz, refuses to sanction Taliban call for jihad against government; follows battle by Afghan forces against Taliban fighters north of Kandahar

4 July   U.S. forces launch Operation Haven Denial against Taliban fighters in Paktia and Khost Provinces

5 July   Explosion in Kabul kills three Dutch members of International Security Assistance Force

6 July   Fighting erupts again between forces of Gen. Abdul Rashid Dostum and Ustad Atta Mohammad in the Dara-i-Suf district of Samangan Province; forces of Dostum and Atta Mohammad agree to a cease-fire in the Shalgara district of Balkh Province after intervention by UN officials

7 July   Cross-border fire between Afghan and Pakistani forces confirmed in Nangarhar Province

8 July   Afghans hold demonstrations in Kabul to protest Pakistan's alleged "invasion" of Afghanistan; Pakistan embassy is attacked, computers and phones are smashed, and embassy is closed by Pakistan in protest against the outrage; attack is condemned by President Karzai

10 July   Senior ousted Taliban official seized in Kandahar city, and detonators and light and heavy machine guns are also found; official is not identified but is thought to be brother of former Taliban defense minister, Mullah Obaidullah

11 July   Governor of Ghazni Province, Hajj Asadullah, warns of coordinated Taliban strikes in Ghazni, Khost, Paktia, Paktika, and Wardak Provinces; governor claims this was outcome of planning meeting in Pakistan held between Taliban commanders and Gulbuddin Hekmatyar

12 July   UN refugee transit center in Jalalabad attacked by explosive device, but no injuries reported; Bagram air base attacked by rocket, but no damage or casualties reported

13 July   Afghan forces seize 300 rocket-propelled grenades, antitank rifles, AK-47 rifles, ammunition, and explosives in raid on Taliban training camp 6 miles from Spin Boldak

14 July   5 Afghan policemen killed in attack by Taliban on police station in Ghorak district of Kandahar Province; among those killed was the chief of police, Sahak Mama; car carrying Coalition personnel is bombed in Kabul, but no casualties reported

15 July   Census teams are being deployed across Afghanistan to count civilians in preparation for 2004 elections; after meeting with the U.S. secretary of state, Colin Powell, Foreign Minister Abdullah Abdullah expresses belief in U.S. commitment to Afghanistan reconstruction and the road to democracy; representatives of Afghanistan, Pakistan, and United States meet in Kabul to discuss border clashes between Afghanistan and Pakistan

16 July   Afghan soldiers and police launch house-to-house searches in Ghorak district of Kandahar Province for gunmen who killed five policemen on 14 July

17 July   Afghan Ministry of the Interior announces that four Afghans were arrested for planning 8 July attack on Pakistan embassy in Kabul

18 July   Three Coalition soldiers hurt when improvised bomb explodes in middle of their convoy near Bagram; remote-controlled mine in Khost Province kills eight Afghan soldiers; rockets also fired at border checkpoint, but no casualties reported

19 July   U.S. forces launch air strike on Taliban position close to Pakistan border, near Spin Boldak; about 200 guerrillas, thought to be led by former Taliban minister Mullah Abdul Razaq, attack government checkpoint

21 July   NGOs stress urgent need for medical treatment for at least half of Afghanistan's population; women and children, especially those who have lost husbands and fathers, are considered extremely vulnerable

22 July   UNHCR uses iris validation tests to weed out refugees who try to effect multiple repatriations in order to receive multiple aid packages

23 July   B-52 bomber raid is made on suspected rebel position near Asadabad, Kunar Province; new Afghan army launches sweep in Sumad district, Paktia Province, code-named Warrior Sweep; Pakistan and Afghanistan representatives, meeting in Islamabad, vow to enhance cooperation in fight against terrorism; Iran announces it is holding a large number of al-Qaeda members but refuses to release identities; John Abizaid, U.S. general, meets President Musharraf of Pakistan and praises him for cooperation in War on Terror

24 July   Pilot project to launch public Internet service announced by Afghanistan Ministry of Communications, backed by finance from France and UN Development Program

25 July   Telecom Development Company of Afghanistan announces launch of new mobile phone service called Roshan (meaning "light"); Coalition sweep in Zormat region of Paktia Province locates no guerrillas but uncovers hundreds of rockets and other weapons; Afghan aid groups plead for international security forces to operate throughout country, as poor security is slowing reconstruction efforts

26 July   U.S. military spokesman, Col. Rodney Davis, warns of Taliban and al-Qaeda terror attacks in Afghanistan

27 July   Six Afghan policemen killed by Taliban and al-Qaeda guerrillas in ambush in Girishk district of Helmand Province; Afghans in Zabul Province plead for major Coalition operation to rid area of at least 500 Taliban fighters operating freely in Deh Chopan district; Taliban spokesman admits one of group's leading commanders, Mullah Abdur Rahim, was severely wounded in clash with Afghan forces three months earlier, near Spin Boldak

28 July   Human Rights Watch warns that Afghan warlords are creating climate of fear that could threaten drafting of new constitution and elections in 2004; United States announces $1 billion aid package to speed reconstruction in Afghanistan, with emphasis on schools and roads; Taliban issue posters and pamphlets naming twenty-eight collaborators who will be killed unless they stop supporting government; most of those listed live in Spin Boldak and are members of Nurzai tribe

29 July   Progovernment Mullah Jenab killed by Taliban gunmen outside mosque in Kandahar; three Afghan troops killed in Taliban ambush at Naish, 40 miles north of Kandahar

30 July   UN Food and Agriculture Organization announces bumper harvest for Afghanistan but warns of

	problems caused by continued drought in southern part of country
31 July	U.S. Special Forces base near Spin Boldak attacked, with attackers withdrawing across border into Pakistan; U.S. troops in Kabul fire on taxi and wound three Afghan soldiers; three guerrillas killed by U.S. troops near their base in Asadabad, capital of Kunar Province; Afghanistan interior minister promises intensified training of police and border guards to create disciplined, nationwide, nonpartisan force; Russian border guards seize 1.5 tons of Afghan heroin on border with Tajikistan; President Karzai announces urgent reforms in Defense Ministry that will pave way for implementation of demobilization program; China trade company opens office in Kabul to market imported Chinese goods
1 August	U.S. gunships kill four guerrillas north of Kandahar city, but others in group cross back into Pakistan; UN secretary-general, Kofi Annan, says Afghanistan will need international security presence for some years; severe flooding causes twenty deaths in Panjshir Valley of Parwan Province
2 August	Operation mounted by Afghan troops backed by U.S. forces and helicopters kills four Taliban fighters, with twelve others arrested, in Tora Ghar Mountains, 6 miles north of Kandahar; three Taliban mullahs among those arrested; Afghan women's group Negar presents document to commission drafting new constitution, calling for equal rights for women under that constitution
3 August	United Nations and NGOs warn of deteriorating security situation in Afghanistan, though President Karzai does not think violence is of serious concern; reports indicate increasing levels of political violence, especially in Kandahar Province, and marked rise in Taliban activity; UNICEF announces that campaign to vaccinate millions of Afghan children cut measles deaths from 400 a month to 50 a month over 18-month period
4 August	Explosion among weapons handed in as part of voluntary disarmament process kills thirteen and injures twenty-one at Mazar-i Sharif but is thought to be an accident; Farouq Khan, of Northern Alliance in Jozjan Province, refuses to participate in disarmament process, which was instigated by General Dostum in advance of national program
5 August	Fresh outbreak of fighting occurs between militias of General Dostum and Ustad Atta Mohammad in Fariab Province
7 August	Government offices in Deshu district of Helmand Province attacked, with six Afghan soldiers and an Afghan driver for U.S. aid group killed; thirty women graduate from business training course in Kabul and hope to start their own small businesses
8 August	Afghan troops mount operation in Helmand Province to hunt Taliban fighters responsible for attack on government offices in Deshu district.
9 August	Six rockets fired on U.S. base at Shkin, Paktia Province, near Pakistan border; no casualties reported, and U.S. forces return fire with unknown results; ex-king, Zahir Shah, returns to Kabul from France, where he had been recovering from a broken leg, thus dispelling rumors of his death
10 August	Mohammad Amin, Taliban spokesman, announces in Peshawar that Taliban intends to extend guerrilla attacks to northern Afghanistan, under command of Mullah Mohammad Asim Muttaqi, who has already moved into Fariab Province; United Nations announces suspension of missions in southern Afghanistan due to rise in attacks on aid workers and general deterioration in security
11 August	NATO formally takes over command of ISAF in Kabul but with no expansion of mandate; Pakistan announces arrest of Hajji Jamil, former mujahideen commander from Khost and close ally of Gulbuddin Hekmatyar

Abbreviations and Acronyms

AGSA	Afghan Security Department
AIG	Afghan Interim Government
APA	Afghanistan Peace Organization
ASDP	Afghan Social Democratic Party
AWIM	Afghan Women's Islamic Movement
AWIR	Afghan Women's Islamic Renaissance
CAEA	Central Asian Economic Association
CIA	Central Intelligence Agency
FINCA	Foundation for International Community Assistance
GRU	Chief Intelligence Directorate (Soviet Union)
ICESCR	International Covenant of Economic, Social, and Cultural Rights
ICRC	International Committee of the Red Cross
INFPA	Islamic Front for National Peace in Afghanistan
ISAF	International Security Assistance Force
ISI	Inter-Services Intelligence Service (Pakistan)
JRT	Joint regional teams
JSTARS	Joint Surveillance Target Attack Radar System
KAM	Workers' Security Institution
KGB	Soviet State Security Committee
KHAD	State Information Service
LCSFA	Limited Contingent of Soviet Forces in Afghanistan
NIFA	National Islamic Front of Afghanistan
NNF	National Fatherland Front
NRP	National Revolutionary Party
NWFP	North-West Frontier Province (Pakistan)
OIC	Organization of the Islamic Conference
OMAR	Organization for Mine Clearance and Afghan Rehabilitation
PDM	Progressive Democratic Movement
PDP	Progressive Democratic Party
PDPA	People's Democratic Party of Afghanistan
PKK	Kurdistan Workers Party
RAWA	Revolutionary Association of Women of Afghanistan
SAMA	Organization for the Liberation of the Afghan People
SAS	Special Air Service—UK Special Forces
SBS	Special Boat Service—UK Special Forces
SAZA	Organization of Revolutionary Toilers of Afghanistan
SCC	Supreme Coordination Council
SCN	Supervisory Council of the North
SEALS	Sea Air Land—U.S. Navy Special Forces
SEATO	Southeast Asia Treaty Organization
UNHCR	UN High Commissioner for Refugees
UNICEF	UN Children's Fund
WAD	Ministry of State Security
WATAN	Homeland Party (formerly the PDPA)
WFP	World Food Program of the United Nations

Glossary

Amir   Commander, nobleman, prince, ruler, or chief. Used by the mujahideen for a commander with civil and military powers.

Burqa   Woman's garment that covers the face. Wearing the burqa was considered insufficient by the Taliban regime, which required women to be covered from head to foot.

Buzgars   Farm managers employed by wealthy landowners, usually of the Durrani tribe.

Chadari   Woman's garment that completely covers the wearer from head to foot. The requirement that women wear this garment was strictly enforced by the Taliban.

Eid al-Azha   Feast held to celebrate the end of Ramadan.

Fatwa   A legal ruling based on the Koran and the Sunnah and issued by an Islamic scholar in response to a specific question.

Ghazis   Holy warriors.

Hajj   Pilgrimage to Mecca

Hizbullah   A small Shi'a mujahideen group led by Sheikh Ali Wusuki, with a presence in Herat and other scattered areas in the province. Also known as the Party of Allah, it has close ties to the Guardians of the Revolution (Pasdran) in Iran.

Jihad   Holy war.

Laskhars   Afghan tribal armies.

Madrasa   Religious school.

Maulwai   A graduate from a college of Islamic studies, or, *madrasa*.

Meshrano Jirga   House of Elders in Afghan Parliament.

Mir   A chief of the Hazaras in the Hazarajat.

Muhammadzai tribe   A branch of the Barakzai of the Durrani tribe, who ruled Afghanistan from 1826 until the Marxist coup of April 1978.

Pamirs   A mountain range running north to south and dividing the River Oxus from the plains of Kashgar, China.

Qarliq   A small ethnic community of Sunni Turks in Badakhshan, Kunduz, and Takhar Provinces.

Qazi   A judge with jurisdiction in cases of civil and criminal law.

Qirghiz   A Turki Sunni community from the Qirghiz Soviet Republic; some members of this community lived in eastern Badakhshan. After the Soviet invasion in 1979, most fled to Pakistan and thence to Turkey.

Rais-i-Shura-i-milli   National Council.

Safi   A tribe located in northeast Jalalabad of Nuristani origin and one of the last tribes to convert to Islam. From 1947 to 1949, the Safis rebelled against the government and were forcefully resettled in northern Afghanistan.

Shura   Shi'a elected ruling council in the Hazarajat.

Spetsnaz   Russian Special Forces.

Sunnah   A collection of sayings and actions of the prophet Muhammad, designed to explain the meaning of the Koran.

Ulama   Muslim clergy.

Wolesi Jirga   House of the People in Afghan Parliament.

Bibliography

Bibliographies

Black, Joseph Laurence. 1984. *The Soviet Union and Afghanistan: A Select List of Titles Published Before 30 December 1983, With Subject Index.* Ottawa: Institute of Soviet and East European Studies, Carleton University.

Hall, Lesley A. 1981. *A Brief Guide to Sources for the Study of Afghanistan in the India Office Records.* London: British Library, Oriental and India Office Collection.

Hanifi, Mohammed Jamil, and Donald Newton Wilber. 1982. *Annotated Bibliography of Afghanistan.* 4th ed. New Haven, CT: HRAF Press.

Jones, Schuyler. 1966, 1969. *An Annotated Bibliography of Nuristan (Kafiristan) and the Kalash Kaifirs of Chitral: Selected Documents From the Secret and Political Records, 1885–1900.* Parts 1 and 2. Copenhagen: Royal Danish Academy of Sciences and Letters.

———. 1992. *Afghanistan.* Oxford and Santa Barbara, CA: ABC-CLIO Press, World Bibliographical Series.

McLachlan, Keith Stanley, and William Whittaker. 1983. *A Bibliography of Afghanistan: A Working Bibliography of Materials on Afghanistan With Special Reference to Economic and Social Change in the Twentieth Century.* Cambridge: Middle East and North African Studies Press.

Miller, Eugene Willard, and Ruby M. Miller. 1989. *The Third World: Afghanistan and Pakistan: A Bibliography.* Monticello, IL: Vance Bibliographies.

Ovesen, J. 1979. "An Annotated Bibliography of Sources Relating to the Pashai People of Afghanistan." *Afghanistan* 32, no. 1:. 87–98.

Rahimi, Wali M. 1991. *Status of Women: Afghanistan.* Bangkok: UNESCO Principal Regional Office for Asia and the Pacific.

Wahab, Shaista. 1995. *Arthur Paul Afghanistan Collection Bibliography.* Vol. 1, *Pashto and Dari Titles.* Lincoln, NE: Dageforde Publishing.

———. 1995. *Arthur Paul Afghanistan Collection Bibliography.* Vol. 2, *English and European Languages.* Lincoln, NE: Dageforde Publishing.

White, Anthony G. 1986. *A Military Look at the Afghanistan Invasion: A Selected Bibliography.* Monticello, IL: Vance Bibliographies.

Wilber, Donald N. 1968. *Annotated Bibliography of Afghanistan.* New Haven, CT: Human Relations Area Files.

Witherell, Julian W. 1986. *Afghanistan: An American Perspective—A Guide to U.S. Official Documents and Government-Sponsored Publications.* Washington, DC: Library of Congress.

Biographies

Adamec, Ludwig W. 1987. *A Biographical Dictionary of Contemporary Afghanistan.* Graz, Austria: Akademische Druck-u Verlagsansalt.

———. 1975. *Historical and Political Who's Who of Afghanistan.* Graz, Austria: Akademische Druck-u Verlagsansalt.

Habib, Mohammad. 1951. *Sultan Mahmud of Ghaznin.* Delhi, India: G. S. Sharma.

Habibullah, Amir. 1990. *My Life: From Brigand to King—Autobiography of Amir Habibullah.* London: Octagon Press.

Khan, Sultan Muhammad. 1980. *The Life of Abdur Rahman, Amir of Afghanistan.* Karachi, Pakistan: Oxford University Press.

Lockhart, L. 1988. *Nadir Shah: A Critical Study Based Mainly on Contemporary Sources.* London: Luzac.

Nazim, M. 1931. *The Life and Times of Sultan Mahmud of Ghazne.* Cambridge: Cambridge University Press.

People's Democratic Party of Afghanistan. 1978. *A Short Biography of Noor Mohammad Taraki: Secretary General of the Central Committee of the People's Democratic Party of Afghanistan, President of the Revolutionary Council and Prime Minister of the Democratic Republic of Afghanistan.* Kabul: Political Department of the People's Democratic Republic of Afghanistan.

Singh, G. 1959. *Ahmad Shah Durrani, Father of Modern Afghanistan.* Bombay, India: Asian Publishing House.

Wild, Roland. 1933. *Amanullah: Ex-King of Afghanistan.* London: Hurst and Blackett.

Agriculture

Allen, R. H. 1965. *Agricultural Development in Afghanistan.* Kabul: Nathan Associates.

Amin, H. 1974. *Agricultural Geography of Afghanistan.* Kabul: Kabul University Press.

Arez, G. J. n.d. *The Pattern of Agriculture in Afghanistan.* Kabul: Kabul University.

Assifi, A. Tawab.1970. *Helmand Valley Shamalan Land Development Project Plans.* Kabul: Communications Media, USAID.

Baron, Lloyd, and David Levintow. 1973. *Sector Analysis-Helman-Argandah Valley Region: An Analysis.* Kabul: USAID.

Coleman, J. C. 1967. *Afghanistan: Helmand-Argandab Valley Project Executive Management.* Kabul: USAID.

Dawlaty, Khairullah, Zarghuna Saleh, and Gerald P. Owens. 1970. *Wheat Farming in Afghanistan: Cost of Production and Returns.* Kabul: University of Kabul, Faculty of Agriculture.

Democratic Republic of Afghanistan. n.d. *The Democratic Land Reforms in Afghanistan: Full Action to Uproot Feudalism.* Kabul:. Government Press.

Field, Neil C. 1954. "The Amu Daria: A Study in Resource Geography." *Geographical Review* 44, no. 2: 528–542.

Food and Agriculture Organization of the United Nations. 1971. *Kunduz-Khan Abad Irrigation Feasibility Study, Afghanistan, Final report.* New York: Development and Resources Corporation.

———. 1972. *Report to the Government of Afghanistan on the Improvement and Development of Marketing of Table Grapes and Raisins in Afghanistan.* Rome: Food and Agriculture Organization of the United Nations.

Gul, Azam. 1994. *The Agricultural Survey of Afghanistan: Eighteenth Report, Reference Manual, Agricultural Surveys.* Peshawar, Pakistan: Swedish Committee for Afghanistan.

Ministry of Agriculture and Irrigation. 1957. *First Five Year Plan of the Ministry of Agriculture.* Kabul: Government Printer.

Pastidis, Stelios L. 1964. *Report to the Government of Afghanistan on Agricultural Marketing.* Rome: Food and Agriculture Organization.

Pillsbury, Harold W., and Noorgul Hamzakheyl. 1970. *An Afghan Farmer's Guide to How Plants Grow.* Kabul: Faculty of Agriculture, University of Kabul.

———. 1974. *An Afghan Farmer's Guide to How Vegetables Grow.* Kabul: Faculty of Agriculture, University of Kabul.

Senzai, M. O., and R. K. Harlan. 1965. *Agri-Facts: Report on Economic Survey of Agriculture in Nangarhar Province.* Kabul: Kabul University.

Stevens, I. M., and K. Tarzi. 1965. *Economics of Agricultural Production in the Helmand Valley, Afghanistan.* Denver, CO: U.S. Department of the Interior, Bureau of Reclamation.

Swedish Committee for Afghanistan. 1993. *Agricultural Survey of Afghanistan: Repatriation and Rehabilitation of Afghan Refugees.* Peshawar, Pakistan: Swedish Committee for Afghanistan.

Tkachev, N. D. 1965. *Survey of Land and Water Resources: Afghanistan, General Report.* Rome: UN Food and Agriculture Organization.

United States Mission to Afghanistan. 1972. *Agricultural Research in Afghanistan: Report of Survey and Recommendations.* Kabul: USAID.

Whiting, Gordon C., Rufus B. Hughes, and Robert Nathan Associates. *The Afghan Farmer: Report of a Survey.* Washington, DC: Robert Nathan Associates.

Architecture

Bechhoefer, William B., and Tami Beth Katz. 1975. *Serai Lahori: Traditional Housing in the Old City of Kabul.* College Park: University of Maryland School of Architecture.

Edelberg, Lenart. 1984. *Nuristani Buildings.* Jutland, Denmark: Archaeological Society Publications.

Etemadi, Goya. 1953. "The General Mosque of Herat." *Afghanistan* 8, no. 2: 40–50.

Frye, R. N. 1946. "Notes on the History of Architecture in Afghanistan." *Ars Islamica* 11, no. 12: 200–202.

Hallet, Stanley Ira, and Rafi Samizay. 1980. *Traditional Architecture of Afghanistan.* New York: Garland Publishing.

Najimi, Abdul Wasay. 1988. *Herat: The Islamic City: A Study in Urban Conservation.* Copenhagen: Scandinavian Institute of Asian Studies.

Scherr-Thoss, Sonia P., and Hans Christoph Scherr-Thoss. 1968. *Design and Colour in Islamic Architecture: Afghanistan, Iran, Turkey.* Washington, DC: Smithsonian Institution Press.

Sofi, Lutfullah. 1982. "Historical Development of Cities in Afghanistan." *Afghanistan* 34, no. 1: 54–69.

Szabo, Albert, and Brenda Dyer Szabo. 1991. *Afghanistan: An Atlas of Indigenous Architecture.* Austin: University of Texas Press.

Culture, Arts, Folklore, and Music

Ali, Mohammed. 1964. *A Cultural History of Afghanistan.* Lahore, Pakistan: Punjab Educational Press.

———. 1958. *Manners and Customs of Afghans.* Lahore, Pakistan: Punjab Education Press.

Allchin, F. R., and N. Hammond. 1978. *The Archaeology of Afghanistan from the Earliest Times to the Timurid Period.* New York: Academic Press.

Anderson, Ewan W., and Nancy Hatch Dupree. 1990. *The Cultural Basis of Afghan Nationalism.* London and New York: Pinter.

Auboyer, Jeannine, and Dominique Darbois. 1968. *The Art of Afghanistan.* Translated from the French by Peter Kneebone. London: Hamlyn.

Baily, John. 1988. *Music of Afghanistan: Professional Musicians in the City of Herat.* Cambridge and New York: Cambridge University Press.

Ball, Warwick. 1982. *Archaeological Gazetteer of Afghanistan.* 2 vols. Paris: Editions Recherches sur les Civilisations.

Barfield, Thomas Jefferson. 1981. *The Central Asian Arabs of Afghanistan: Pastoral Nomadism in Transition.* Austin: University of Texas Press.

Bellew, H. W. 1880. *The Races of Afghanistan: Being a Brief Account of the Principal Nations Inhabiting That Country.* London: Thaker.

Bray, Denys. 1913. *The Life and History of a Brahui.* London: Royal Asiatic Society.

Bruce, C. E. 1929. *The Tribes of Waziristan.* London: India Office.

Centlivres-Demont, Micheline. 1976. *Popular Art in Afghanistan: Paintings on Trucks, Mosques, and Tea-Houses.* Graz, Austria: Akademische Druck-u Verlagsansalt.

Clifford, Mary Louise. 1973. *The Land and People of Afghanistan.* Philadelphia: Lippincott.

General Staff, India. 1910. *A Dictionary of the Pathan Tribes on the North-West Frontier of India.* Calcutta: Government of India.

Hammerton, J. A. 1984. *Tribes, Races and Cultures of India and Neighbouring Countries: Afghanistan, Bhutan, Burma, Ceylon, Nepal and Tibet.* Delhi, India: Mittal.

Harvey, Janet. 1996. *Traditional Textiles of Central Asia.* London and New York: Thames and Hudson.

Institute for Afghan Studies. "How the Precious Statues of Afghanistan Got Destroyed." http://www.institute-for-afghan-studies.org (cited 26 April 2001).

Jarring, Gunnar. 1939. *On the Distribution of Turki Tribes in Afghanistan: An Attempt at a Preliminary Classification.* Lund, Sweden: Gleerup.

Jettmar, Karl. 1974. *Cultures of the Hindukush.* Wiesbaden, Germany: Franz Steiner.

Komnieczny, M. G. 1979. *Textiles in Baluchistan.* London: British Museum.

Mark, William Rudolph Henry. 1984. *The Mohmands.* Lahore, Pakistan: Vanguard Books.

Marsden, Peter. 2001. *Afghanistan—Minorities: Conflict and the Search for Peace.* London: Minority Right Group International.

Mills, Margaret Ann. 1978. *Cupid and Psyche in Afghanistan: An International Tale in Cultural Context.* New York: Afghanistan Council of the Asia Society.

———. 1990. *Oral Narrative in Afghanistan: The Individual in Tradition.* New York: Garland Publishing.

———. 1991. *Rhetorics and Politics in Afghan Traditional Storytelling.* Philadelphia: University of Pennsylvania Press.

Olesen, Asta. 1994. *Afghan Craftsmen: The Culture of Three Itinerant Communities.* London: Thames and Hudson.

Oudenhoven, N. J. A van. 1979. *Common Afghan Street Games.* Lisse, the Netherlands: Swets and Zeitlinger.

Rapin, Claude. 1996. *Indian Art from Afghanistan: The Legend of Sakuntala and the Indian Treasure of Eucratides at Ai-Khanum.* New Delhi: Manohar.

Raverty, Henry G. 1976. *Notes on Afghanistan and Part of Baluchistan, Reprint from 1888 Edition.* Quetta, Pakistan: Gosha-ye Adab.

Rice, Frances Mortimer, and Benjamin Rowland. 1971. *Art in Afghanistan: Objects from the Kabul Museum.* London: Allen Lane, the Penguin Press.

Robertson, George Scott. 1974. *The Kafirs of the Hindu-Kush.* Karachi and New York: Oxford University Press.

Robinson, J. A. 1978. *Notes on Nomad Tribes of Eastern Afghanistan.* Quetta, Pakistan: Nisa Traders. (Reprint of 1934 edition)

Sakata, Hiromi Lorraine. 1983. *Music in the Mind: The Concepts of Music and Musician in Afghanistan.* Kent, Ohio: Kent State University Press.

Schurmann, H. F. 1962. *The Mongols of Afghanistan.* Gravenhage, the Netherlands: Mouton.

Shahrani, M. Nazif Mohin. 1979. *The Kirghiz and Wakhi of Afghanistan: Adaptation to Closed Frontiers.* Seattle: University of Washington Press.

Slobin, Mark. 1976. *Music in the Culture of Northern Afghanistan.* Tucson: University of Arizona Press.

Storr, Lillian A. 1920. *Frontier Folk of the Afghan Border–and Beyond.* London: Church Missionary Society.

Economy

"Afghanistan Starts Arduous Task of Rebuilding Kabul." 2002. http://www.afgha.com/article.php?sid=17391 (cited 3 November 2002).

Ahmed, Akbar S. 1980. *Pukhtum Economy and Society: Traditional Structure and Economic Development in a Tribal Society.* London and Boston: Routledge and Kegan Paul.

———. 1977. *Social and Economic Change in Tribal Areas, 1972–1976.* Karachi, Pakistan: Oxford University Press.

Barry, Michael. 1972. *Personal Account of Famine Conditions in North-Western Afghanistan.* Kabul: USAID.

Christensen, Hanne. 1995. *Aiding Afghanistan: The Background and Prospects for Reconstruction in a Fragmented Society.* Copenhagen: NIAS Books.

———. 1990. *Afghan Refugees in Pakistan: From Emergency towards Self-Reliance: A Report on the Food Relief Situation and Related Socio-Economic Aspects.* Geneva, Switzerland: UN Research Institute for Social Development.

Conolly, Violet. 1933. *Soviet Economic Policy in the East: Turkey, Persia, Afghanistan, Mongolia and Tana Tuva, Sin Kiang.* London: Oxford University Press.

Ekker, M. H. 1952. *Economic Aspects of Development in Afghanistan.* New York: United Nations.

Fry, Maxwell J. 1974. *The Afghan Economy: Money, Finance, and the Critical Constraints to Economic Development.* Leiden, the Netherlands: Brill.

———. 1973. *The Financial Institutions of Afghanistan: Description and Analysis.* Kabul: USAID.

———. 1973. *Kabul and Kandahar Money Bazaars: Their Role in Afghanistan Foreign Trade.* Kabul: USAID.

Glassner, Martin Ira. 1983. *Transit Problems of Three Asian Land-Locked Countries: Afghanistan, Nepal, and Laos.* Baltimore: School of Law, University of Maryland.

Gopal, Darvesh, and M. A. Qureshi. 1987. *Science, Technology and Development in Afghanistan.* New Delhi: Navrang.

Helmand River Delta Commission. 1951. *Report of the Helmand River Delta Commission: Afghanistan and Iran.* Washington, DC: Helmand River Delta Commission.

Hinrichs, Harley H. 1967. *The Role of Public Finance in Economic Development in Afghanistan.* Washington, DC: Robert R. Nathan Associates.

Hobbs, Frank B. 1988. *Afghanistan, a Demographic Profile.* Washington, DC: Center for International Research, Bureau of the Census, U.S. Department of Commerce.

Kamrany, Nake M. 1969. *Peaceful Competition in Afghanistan: American and Soviet Models for Economic Aid.* Washington, DC: Communication Service.

Lake, Anthony, and Selig. S. Harrison. 1990. *After the Wars: Reconstruction in Afghanistan, Indochina, Central America, Southern Africa, and the Horn of Africa.* New Brunswick, NJ: Transaction Publishers.

Lalvani, G. H., and Amiruddin Shahed. 1972. *The Fact Book on Manpower in Afghanistan.* Kabul: UNESCO Educational Planning Team and Afghanistan Ministry of Education.

Lieberman, Samuel S. 1980. *Afghanistan: Population and Development in the Land of Insolence.* New York: Population Council.

McChesney, R. D. 1968. "The Economic Reforms of Amir Abdur Rahman Khan." *Afghanistan* 21, no. 3: 11–34.

Maierhofer, Charles R. 1961. *Drainage and Related Problems of the Helmand Valley Development Project Afghanistan.* Denver, CO: U.S. Department of the Interior, Bureau of Reclamation.

Manly, Robert. 1961. *Investment Opportunity List: Basic Data on Projects Which May Be Feasible for Afghanistan.* Kabul: Ministry of Commerce.

Michel, Aloys Arthur. 1959. *The Kabul, Kunduz, and Helmand Valleys and the National Economy of Afghanistan: A Study of Regional Resources and the Comparative Advantages of Development.* Washington, DC: National Academy of Sciences.

Najafi, Abdul Wasay. 1988. *Herat, the Islamic City: A Study in Urban Conservation.* London: Curzon.

Newberg, Paula R. 1999. "Politics at the Heart: The Architecture of Humanitarian Assistance to Afghanistan." http://www.ceip.org/files/Publications/wp2.asp?from=pubauthor (cited 3 January 2000).

Noorzoy, M. Siddieq. 1976. *Planning and Growth in Afghanistan.* London. Pergamon Press.

Norvell, Douglas G. 1973. *Markets and Men in Afghanistan.* Kabul: U.S. Agency for International Aid.

Opic, James. 1992. *Tribal Rugs: Nomadic and Village Weaving from the Near East and Central Asia.* Portland, OR: Tolstoy Press.

People's Democratic Party of Afghanistan. 1979. *Kabul: The Cradle of Revolution, the Capital of Afghanistan towards Development under Twenty-Five Years Master Plan.* Kabul: Government Publishing House.

Poulin, Roger. 1990. *Private Sector Agribusiness Support.* Peshawar, Pakistan: Development Alternatives.

Salim, Malik Arshad. 1986. *The Socio-Economic Impact of Afghan Refugees on the Rural and Urban Population of Peshawar District.* Peshawar, Pakistan: Institute of Development Studies, North-West Frontier Province Agricultural University.

Strauss, A. A. 1965. *Industrial Development in Afghanistan: A Forward Look.* Washington, DC: Robert R. Nathan Associates.

Tabibi, Abdul Hakim. 1970. *The Right of Transit of Land-Locked Countries: A Study of Legal and International Development of the Right of Free Access to the Sea.* Kabul: Afghan Book Publishing House.

Thompson, Jon. 1988. *Oriental Carpets: From the Tents, Cottages and Workshops of Asia.* New York: Dutton.

Geography

Abdullah, Shareq. 1977. *Mineral Resources of Afghanistan.* Kabul: Ministry of Mines and Industries.

Ali, Muhammad. 1953. "Afghanistan's Mountains." *Afghanistan* 8, no. 1: 47–52.

Amin, Hamidullah, and Gordon B. Schiltz. 1976. *A Geography of Afghanistan.* Omaha: University of Nebraska, Center for Afghan Studies.

Arez, G. J. 1970. "Geography of Afghanistan." *Kabul Times Annual,* pp. 19–28.

Bowersox, Gary W., Richard T. Liddicoat, Bonita E. Chamberlain, and Peter C. Keller. 1995. *Gemstones of Afghanistan.* Tucson, AZ: Geoscience Press.

Desio, Ardito. 1975. *Geology of Badakhshan (North-East Afghanistan) and Surrounding Countries.* Leiden, the Netherlands: E. J. Brill.

Dupree, Nancy Hatch. 1967. *The Road to Balkh.* Kabul: Afghan Tourist Organization.

Field, Neil C. 1954. "The Amu Daria: A Study in Resource Geography." *Geographical Review* 44, no. 2: 528–542.

Formoli, Tareq A., M. Afzal Rashid, and James P. Du Bruille. 1994. *An Overview and Assessment of Afghanistan's Environment.* Sacramento, CA: Afghanistan Horizon.

Gopalakrishnan, Ramamoorthy. 1980. *The Geography and Politics of Afghanistan.* New Delhi: Concept.

Hahn, Helmut. 1962. "Geography in the Frame of the Social Sciences. *Geographical Review of Afghanistan* 1, no. 2: 38–40.

Latkovich, Vito J. 1968. *Activities of the Senior Field Engineer, Surface-Water Research Project, Afghanistan, 1964–68.* Washington, DC: U.S. Geological Survey.

McClymonds, N. E. 1972. *Shallow Ground Water in the Zamin Dawar Area, Helmand Province, Afghanistan.* Reston, VA: U.S. Geological Survey.

Maraini, Fosco, and Peter Green. 1964. *Where Four Worlds Meet: Hindu Kush, 1959.* London: Hamish Hamilton.

Matthai, James. 1966. *A Geographical Introduction to Herat Province.* Kabul: Faculty of Education, Kabul University.

Michaud, R., and S. Michaud. 1972. "Winter Caravans to the Roof of the World." *National Geographic Magazine* (April): 435–465.

Reshtya, Sayed Qasim. 1947. "The Rivers of Afghanistan." *Afghanistan* 2, no. 2: 8–14.

Robert Nathan Associates and Louis Berger International, Inc. 1992. *Final Report: Mineral Resources in Afghanistan.* Arlington, VA: Robert Nathan Associates and Louis Berger International.

UN Environment Program. 2003. *Afghanistan: Post-Conflict Environmental Assessment.* Geneva, Switzerland: UNEP.

U.S. Central Intelligence Agency. 1985. *Afghanistan: Major Insurgency Groups.* Washington, DC: Central Intelligence Agency.

U.S. Office of Geography, Geographic Names Division. 1971. *Afghanistan: Official Standard Names.* Washington, DC: U.S. Board on Geographic Names.

Volin, M. E. 1950. *Chromite Deposits in Logar Valley, Kabul Province, Afghanistan.* Washington, DC: U.S. Department of the Interior, Bureau of Mines.

Weippert, Dietrich, Hanspeter Wittekindt, and Reinhard Wolfart. 1970. *On the Geological Development of Central and South Afghanistan.* Kabul: Afghan Geological and Mineral Survey.

Westfall, Arthur O. 1969. *Surface Water Investigation in Afghanistan: A Summary of Activities from 1952 to 1969.* Washington, DC: U.S. Geological Survey.

Zanettin, Bruno. 1964. *Geology and Petrology of Haramosh–Mango Gusor Area.* Leiden, the Netherlands: E. J. Brill.

History and Politics

Abdul, Ghani. 1989. *A Brief Political History of Afghanistan.* Edited by Abdul Jaleel Nafji. Lahore, Pakistan: Najaf Publishers.

Abu Khalil, A. 2002. *Bin Laden, Islam and America's New "War on Terrorism."* Washington, DC: Seven Stories Press.

Adamec, Ludwig W. 1967. *Afghanistan, 1900–1923: A Diplomatic History.* Berkeley: University of California Press.

———. 1974. *Afghanistan's Foreign Affairs to the Mid-Twentieth Century: Relations with the USSR, Germany and Britain.* Tucson: University of Arizona Press.

———. 1996. *Dictionary of Afghan Wars, Revolutions and Insurgencies.* Lanham, MD: Scarecrow Press.

———. 1972–1985. *Historical and Political Gazetteer of Afghanistan.* 6 vols. Graz, Austria: Akademische Druck-u Verlagsansalt.

———. 1991. *Historical Dictionary of Afghanistan.* Metuchen, NJ: Scarecrow Press.

———. 1985. *Kabul and Southeastern Afghanistan.* Graz, Austria: Akademische Druck-u Verlagsansalt.

"Afghan Interim Government." 2001. http://www.afghanland.com/history/interim.html (cited 5 January 2002).

Afghan National Liberation Front. 1978. *The Declaration of the Afghan National Liberation Front.* Peshawar, Pakistan: Afghan National Liberation Front.

———. 1981. *The Objectives of the Afghan National Liberation Front.* Peshawar, Pakistan: Afghan National Liberation Front.

"Afghan Peace Accord or the Islamabad Accord of March 1993." 1993. http://www.forisb.org. afghan_docs/15islbad.htm (cited 11 April 2003).

"Afghan President Says He May Not Be a Candidate in Elections." 2003. http://www.afgha.com/?af=article&side=29914 (cited 15 May 2003).

"Afghan Transitional Government." 2002. http://www.afghanland.com/history/transitional.html (cited 6 January 2003).

Ahmad, N. D. 1990. *The Survival of Afghanistan, 1747–1979: A Diplomatic History with an Analytic and Reflective Approach.* Lahore, Pakistan: Institute of Islamic Culture.

Ahmad, Syed Iqbal. 1992. *Balochistan: Its Strategic Importance.* Karachi, Pakistan: Royal Book.

Aitchison, C. U. 1933. *A Collection of Treaties, Engagements and Sanads Relating to India and Neighbouring Countries.* Vol. 13, *Persia and Afghanistan.* Calcutta, India: Superintendent of Government Printing.

Alder, G. J. 1963. *British India's Northern Frontier, 1896–95: A Study in Imperial Policy.* London: Longman.

Alexiev, Alexander. 1988. *Inside the Soviet Army in Afghanistan.* Santa Monica, CA: Rand Corporation.

———. 1988. *The United States and the War in Afghanistan.* Santa Monica, CA: Rand Corporation.

———. 1984. *The War in Afghanistan: Soviet Strategy and the State of Resistance.* Santa Monica, CA: Rand Corporation.

Ali, Mohammed. 1959. *Afghanistan (the Mohammadzai Period): A Political History of the Country since the Beginning of the Nineteenth Century with Emphasis on Its Foreign Relations.* Lahore: Pakistan. Punjab Educational Press.

———.. 1958. *Afghanistan: The National Awakening.* Lahore, Pakistan: Punjab Educational Press.

———. 1955. "The Battle of Maiwand." *Afghanistan* 10, no. 2: 26–38.

Ali, Sharifah Enayat. 1996. *Afghanistan.* New York: Marshall Cavendish.

Amnesty International. 1995. *Afghanistan: International Responsibility for Human Rights Disaster.* New York: Amnesty International.

———. 1986. *Torture of Political Prisoners.* New York: Amnesty International.

———. 1988. *Afghanistan: Unlawful Killings and Torture.* New York: Amnesty International.

———. 1983. *Democratic Republic of Afghanistan: Background Briefing on Amnesty International's Concerns.* New York: Amnesty International.

Amstutz, J. Bruce. 1986. *Afghanistan: The First Five Years of Soviet Occupation.* Washington, DC: National Defense University Press.

Anderson, Ewan W., and Nancy Hatch Dupree. 1990. *The Cultural Basis of Afghan Nationalism.* London and New York: Pinter.

Anderson, J. H. 1991. *The Afghan War, 1878–1880.* London: R. H. Keach.

Ansary, Mir Tamin. 1991. *Afghanistan: Fighting for Freedom.* New York: Dillon Press.

Anwar Khan, M. 1963. *England, Russia and Central Asia: A Study in Diplomacy, 1857–1878.* Peshawar, Pakistan: Institute of Central Asian Studies, University of Peshawar.

Anwar, Raja. 1989. *The Tragedy of Afghanistan: A First-Hand Account.* London and New York: Verso.

Arghandawi, Abdul Ali. 1989. *British Imperialism and Afghanistan's Struggle for Independence, 1914–21.* New Delhi: Munshiram Manoharlal Publishers.

Arney, George. 1990. *Afghanistan.* London: Mandarin.

Arnold, Anthony. 1985. *Afghanistan: The Soviet Invasion in Perspective.* Stanford, CA: Hoover Institution Press.

———. 1983. *Afghanistan's Two-Party Communism: Parcham and Khalq.* Stanford, CA: Hoover Institution Press.

———. 1993. *The Fateful Pebble: Afghanistan's Role in the Fall of the Soviet Empire.* Novato, CA: Presidio Press.

Ashitov, Vladimir, Karen Gevorkian, and Vladimir Svetozarov. 1986. *The Truth about Afghanistan.* Moscow: Novosti Press Agency Publishing House.

Asia Watch Committee. 1991. *Afghanistan: The Forgotten War—Human Rights Abuses and Violations of the Laws of War since the Soviet Withdrawal.* New York: Asia Watch.

Astute, J. Brice. 1986. *Afghanistan: The First Five Years of Soviet Occupation.* Washington, DC: National Defense University.

Baker, Anne, and Ronald Ivelaw-Chapman. 1975. *Wings over Kabul: The First Airlift.* London: Kimber.

Baldauf, Scott. 2003. "Once Powerful Warlord Is Shunted Aside." *http://www.afgha.com/?af=article&sid=29422* (cited 22 January 2003).

Banuazizi, Ali, and Myron Weiner. 1986. *The State, Religion and Ethnic Politics: Afghanistan, Iran, and Pakistan.* Syracuse, NY: Syracuse University Press.

Baryalay, Mahmood, Abdullo Spantgar, and V. F. Grib. 1984. *Afghanistan: The Revolution Continues.* Moscow: Planeta Publishers.

Beaumont, Peter. 2002. "Special Forces Take Over Hunt for al-Qaeda." *The Observer* (London), 4 August.

Bellew, Henry W. 1979. *Afghanistan and the Afghans.* London: Sampson Low.

Bennigsen, Alexandre. 1981. *The Soviet Union and Muslim Guerrilla Wars, 1920–1981: Lessons for Afghanistan.* Santa Monica, CA: Rand Corporation.

Bergen, Peter L., and Rachel Klayman, eds. 2001. *Holy War Inc.: Inside the Secret World of Osama bin Laden.* New York: Free Press.

Berger, Julien, and Richard Norton-Taylor. 2001. "Special Forces in Afghanistan." *Guardian* (London), 29 September.

Bilgrami, Asghar H. 1972. *Afghanistan and British India, 1793–1907: A Study in Foreign Relations.* New Delhi: Sterling Publishers.

"Blowback." 2001. *Jane's Intelligence Review* (August): 42–49.

Bocharov, G. 1990. *Russian Roulette: Afghanistan through Russian Eyes.* New York: Hamish Hamilton.

Bodansky, Yossef, and Helen Deliel Bentley. 1999. *Bin Laden: The Man Who Declared War on America.* Rocklin, CA: Forum.

Bokari, Farhan. 2003. "Poverty Fuels Afghanistan's Drug Trade." http://www.japantimes.co.ip/cgi-bin/getedp/5?eo2002024b.htm (cited 24 February 2003).

Bonosky, Phillip. 1985. *Washington's Secret War against Afghanistan.* New York: International Publishing.

Borovik, Artem. 1990. *The Hidden War: A Russian Journalist's Account of the Soviet War in Afghanistan.* New York: Atlantic Monthly Press.

Borza, Julien, and Richard Norton-Taylor. 2001. "Special Forces in Afghanistan." *Guardian* (London), 24 September.

Bosworth, Clifford E. 1963. *The Ghaznavids: Their Empire in Afghanistan and Eastern Iran, 944–1040.* Edinburgh: Edinburgh University Press.

Bradsher, Henry St. Amant. 1999. *Afghan Communism and Soviet Intervention.* London and New York: Oxford University Press.

Brentjes, Burchard. 2000. *Taliban: A Shadow over Afghanistan.* Varanasi, India: Rishi Publications.

Brigot, Andre, and Olivier Roy. 1988. *The War in Afghanistan: An Account and Analysis of the Country, Its People, Soviet Intervention and the Resistance.* New York: Harvester-Wheatsheaf.

Bruce, George Ludgate. 1969. *Retreat from Kabul.* London: Howard Baker Publishers.

Burrell, Robert Michael, and Alvin J. Cottrell. 1974. *Iran, Afghanistan, Pakistan: Tensions and Dilemmas.* Beverley Hills, CA: Sage.

Canfield, Robert Leroy. 1977. *Hazara Integration into the Afghan Nation: Some Changing Relations between Hazaras and Afghan Officials.* New York: Afghan Council of the Asia Society.

Cardew, F. G. 1908. *The Second Afghan War, 1878–80.* London: J. Murray.

Carew, Tom. 2000. *Jihad: The Secret War in Afghanistan.* Edinburgh: Mainstream.

Caroe, Olaf. 1958. *The Pathans, 550 B.C.–A.D. 1957.* London: Macmillan.

Chase, Robert, Emily B. Hill, and Paul Kennedy, eds. 1999. *The Pivotal States: A New Framework for US Policy in the Developing World.* New York: W. W. Norton.

Chopra, V. D. 1988. *Afghanistan, Geneva Accord and After.* New Delhi: Patriot Publishers, on behalf of Indian Centre for Regional Affairs.

Coalition Information Center. 2001. "Fact Sheet: Al-Qaeda and Taliban Atrocities." http://www.usinfo.state.gov/regional/nea/sasia/afghan/fact/1123tlbn (cited 15 January 2002).

Cogan, Charles. 1993. *Holy Blood: An Inside View of the Afghan War.* Westport, CT: Praeger.

Collins, Joseph J. 1985. *The Soviet Invasion of Afghanistan: A Study of the Use of Force in Soviet Foreign Policy.* Lexington, MA: Lexington Books.

Cooley, John K. 1999. *Unholy Wars: Afghanistan, America and International Terrorism.* New York: Free Press.

Cordovez, Diego, and Selig S. Harrison. 1995. *Out of Afghanistan: The Inside Story of the Soviet Withdrawal.* New York: Oxford University Press.

Cranfield, Robert L. 1977. *Hazara Integration into the Afghan Nation: Some Changing Relations between Hazaras and Afghan Officials.* New York: Afghan Council of the Asia Society.

Curzon, G. N. 1967. *Russia in Central Asia in 1889 and the Anglo-Russian Question.* New York: Barnes and Noble.

Czacka, Tony. 2002. "Afghanistan Conference Sets Track for Army, Election, a Year after Taliban Ousted." http://www.story.nes.yahoo.com/news?tmpl=story2%cid:524=u=/ap/200221202/ap (cited 2 December 2002).

Daraglai, Borzov. 2002. "Afghan Governor Spurns Instability Fears." http://www.washingtontimes.com (cited 2 December 2002).

Data Collection for Afghan Repatriation Project. 1989. *Laghman Province.* Islamabad: UN High Commissioner for Refugees.

———. 1989. *Logar Province.* Islamabad: UN High Commissioner for Refugees.

———. 1989. *Nangahar Province.* Islamabad: UN High Commissioner for Refugees.

Davis, Anthony. 2002. "Karzai Struggles to Consolidate Afghanistan's Fragile Peace." *Jane's Intelligence Review* (August) 20–23.

———. 2002. "Makeover for a Warlord." *Time Atlantic* 159, no. 22: 60–63.

De Gaury, Gerald, and Harry Victor Frederick Winstone. 1981. *The Road to Kabul: An Anthology.* London: Quartet Books.

Democratic Republic of Afghanistan. 1980. *Babrak Karmal's Speeches.* Kabul: Government Press.

———. 1982. *Documents and Records of the National Conference of the People's Democratic Party of Afghanistan.* Kabul: Government Press.

Dey, Kelly Prosono. 1881. *The Life and Career of Major Sir Louis Cavagnari, C.S.I., K.C.B., British Envoy at Cabul, with a Brief Outline of the Second Anglo-Afghan War.* Calcutta, India: J. N. Ghose.

Diver, Maud. 1924. *The Hero of Herat.* London: John Murray.

Dixit, J. 2000. *An Afghan Diary: Zahir Shah to Taliban.* New Delhi: Konark Publishers.

Dorn, Allen E. 1989. *Countering the Revolution: The Mujahideen Counterrevolution.* New York: Afghanistan Forum.

Duffield, Mark, and Patricia Grossman. 2001. *Review of the Strategic Framework for Afghanistan (Final Draft): Report Commissioned by the Strategic Monitoring Unit Afghanistan.* Islamabad: UNOCHA.

Dundas, A. D. F. 1938. *Precis on Afghan Affairs, 1927–1936.* New Delhi: Government of India.

Dupree, Louise. 1980. *Afghanistan.* Princeton, NJ: Princeton University Press.

Dupree, Louise, and Linette Albert, eds. 1974. *Afghanistan in the 1970s.* New York: Praeger.

Dupree, Nancy Hatch. 1977. *An Historical Guide to Kabul.* Kabul: Afghan Tourist Organization.

Durand, Algernon George Arnold. 1974. *The Making of a Frontier.* Graz, Austria: Akademische Druck-u Verlagsansalt. (Reprint of 1899 edition. London: John Murray)

Edwardes, Michael. 1975. *Playing the Great Game: A Victorian Cold War.* London: Hamish Hamilton.

Edwards, David B. 1993. "Summoning Muslims: Print, Politics and Religious Ideology in Afghanistan." *Journal of Asian Studies* 52, no. 3: 609–628.

Effendi, M. A. 1948. *Royals and Royals Mendicant: A Tragedy of Afghan History, 1791–1947.* Lahore, Pakistan: Lion Press.

Eliot, Theodore L. 1988. *Gorbachev's Afghan Gambit.* Cambridge, MA: Institute for Foreign Policy Analysis.

Elliot, H. M., and J. Dowson. 1953. *History of Ghazni.* Calcutta, India: Sasil Gupta.

Elliott, Michael, Mike Billips, Tim McGirk, Michael Ware, Sean Scully, and Mark Thompson. 2002. "The Battle over Peacekeeping." *Time Atlantic* 158, no. 9: 33–34.

Elphinstone, Mountstuart. 1815. *An Account of the Kingdom of Caubul, and Its Dependencies in Persia, Tartary and India.* London: Longman.

Emadi, Hafizullah. 1998. "New World Order or Disorder: Armed Struggle in Afghanistan and United States' Foreign Policy Objectives." *Central Asian Survey* 18, no. 1: 49–64.

———. 1990. *State, Revolution and Superpowers in Afghanistan.* New York: Praeger.

Entekhabi, Camelia. 2002. "Iranian Leader Plans Visit to Afghanistan." http://www.eurasianet.org/ departments/insight/articles/eav052402.shtml (cited 24 May 2002).

Evans, Michael. 2001. "SAS Already Gathering Intelligence in Afghanistan." *Times* (London), 21 September.

"Examination of Human Rights Violations." 2000. http://www.ishr.ch/About%20UN/Reports%20 Analysis/Sub%2053%20.%20examination.htm (cited 2 August 2001).

Eyre, Vincent. 1879. *The Kabul Insurrection of 1841–42.* London: W. H. Allen.

Farr, Grant M., and John G. Merriam, eds. 1987. *Afghan Resistance: The Politics of Survival.* Boulder, CO: Westview Press.

Fazelly, Mohammad K. 1990. *La Loya Djirqa.* Paris: Centres de Recherches et d'Etudes Documentaire sur l'Afghanistan.

Fletcher, Arnold. C. 1965. *Afghanistan: Highway of Conquest.* Ithaca, NY: Cornell University Press.

Forbes, A. 1982. *The Afghan Wars, 1839–42 and 1878–80.* London: Seeley.

Fraser-Tytler, W. Kerr. 1953. *Afghanistan: A Study of Political Developments in Central and Southern Asia.* London: Oxford University Press.

Fuller, Graham E. 1991. *Islamic Fundamentalism in Afghanistan: Its Character and Prospects.* Santa Monica, CA: Rand Corporation.

Fullerton, John. 1984. *The Soviet Occupation of Afghanistan.* Hong Kong: Far Eastern Economic Review.

Galeotti, Mark. 1995. *Afghanistan, the Soviet Union's Last War.* Portland, OR: Frank Cass.

———. 2001. "Business as Usual for Afghan Drugs." http://www.theworldtoday.com (cited 10 January 2002).

Galiullin, Rustem. 1988. *The CIA in Asia: Covert Actions against India and Afghanistan.* Moscow: Progress Publishers.

Gall, Carlotta. 2003. "Holdout Afghan Warlord May Join Karzai Camp." http://www.iht.com/articles/83722. html (cited 18 January 2003).

Gall, Sandy. 1988. *Afghanistan, Agony of a Nation.* London: Bodley Head.

———. 1984. *Behind Russian Lines: An Afghan Journal.* New York: St. Martin's Press.

Galster, Steven R. 1990. *Afghanistan: The Making of U.S. Policy, 1973–1990: Guide and Index.* Alexandria, VA: Chadwyck-Healey; Washington, DC: National Security Archive. (Accompanies set of 424 microfiches with the same title.)

Ganjoo, Satish. 1990. *Soviet Afghan Relations*. Delhi, India: Akashdeep Publishing House.

Garrity, Patrick J. 1982. *The Soviet Penetration of Afghanistan, 1950–1979*. Claremont, CA: Claremont Institute.

"Geneva Accords of 1998 (Afghanistan)." 1988. http://www.institute-for-afghan-studies.org/Accords%20Treaties/geneva_accords_1988_pakistan_afghanistan.htm (cited 2 August 2001).

"Genocide in Afghanistan." 1991. http://www.members.tripod.com/MillateHazara/ (cited 12 February 2002).

Ghani, Abdul. 1989. *A Brief Political History of Afghanistan*. Edited by Abdul Jaleel Nafji. Lahore, Pakistan: Najaf Publishers.

Ghaus, Abdul Samad. 1988. *The Fall of Afghanistan: An Insider's Account*. Washington, DC.: Pergamon-Brassey.

Ghobar, G. 1968. *Afghanistan dar masir-i-tarikh* (Afghanistan in the path of history). Kabul: Government Press.

Gibbs, David. 1987. "Does the USSR Have a Grand Strategy? Reinterpreting the Invasion of Afghanistan." *Journal of Peace Research*, 21, no. 4.

———. 1986. "The Peasant as Counter-Revolutionary: The Rural Origins of the Afghan Insurgency." *Studies in Comparative International Development* 21, no. 1: 36–59.

Giradet, Edward. 1985. *Afghanistan: The Soviet War*. New York: St. Martin's Press; London: Croom Helm.

Giustozzi, Antonio. 2000. *War, Politics and Society in Afghanistan, 1978–1992*. Washington, DC: Georgetown University Press.

Gohari, M. J. 2000. *The Taliban: Ascent to Power*. Karachi, Pakistan: Oxford University Press.

Goodhand, Jonathan. 2000. "From Holy War to Opium War? A Case Study of the Opium Economy in North Eastern Afghanistan." *Central Asian Survey* 19, no. 2: 265–280.

Goodson, Larry P. 2001. *Afghanistan's Endless War: State Failure, Regional Politics, and the Rise of the Taliban*. Seattle: University of Washington Press.

Goodwin, Jim. 1987. *Caught in the Crossfire*. New York: Dutton.

Graham, Stephen. 2003. "Afghan Leader Appeals for More Security." http://www.afghan.com (cited 20 May 2003).

Grasselli, Gabriella. 1966. *British and American Responses to the Soviet Invasion of Afghanistan*. Aldershot, VT: Dartmouth Publishing.

Grassmuck, George, and Ludwig W. Adamec. 1969. *Afghanistan: Some New Approaches*. Ann Arbor: University of Michigan, Center for Near Eastern and North African Studies.

Gregorian, Vartan. 1969. *The Emergence of Modern Afghanistan: Politics of Reform and Modernization, 1880–1946*. Stanford, CA: Stanford University Press.

Gregory, Feifer. 2002. "Uzbekistan's External Realities." *World Policy Journal* 19, no. 1: 81–89.

Griffin, Michael. 2001. *Reaping the Whirlwind: The Taliban Movement in Afghanistan*. London and Sterling, VA: Pluto Press.

Griffiths, John C. 1967. *Afghanistan*. London: Pall Mall Press.

Grover, Verinder. 2000. *Afghanistan: Government and Politics*. New Delhi: Deep and Deep Publications.

Gulzad, Zalmay. 1994. *External Influences and the Development of the Afghan State in the Nineteenth Century*. New York: P. Lang.

Gunaratna, Rohan. 2001. *Inside al-Qaida: Global Network of Terror*. New Delhi: Roli Press.

Gupta, Bhabani Sen. 1986. *Afghanistan*. London: Francis Pinter.

Habberton, William. 1937. *Anglo-Russian Relations Concerning Afghanistan, 1837–1907*. Urbana: University of Illinois Press.

Halliday, Fred. 1989. *From Kabul to Managua: Soviet-American Relations in the 1980s*. New York: Pantheon Books.

Hamilton, Angus. 1906. *Afghanistan*. London: Heinemann.

Hammond, Thomas Taylor. 1984. *Red Flag over Afghanistan: The Communist Coup, the Soviet Invasion, and the Consequences*. Boulder, CO: Westview Press.

Hanna, Henry B. 1910. *The Second Afghan War, 1878–1880: Its Causes, Its Conduct, and Its Consequences*. 3 vols. London: Constable.

Harpviken, Kristian Berg. 1995. *Political Mobilization among the Hazara of Afghanistan*. Oslo: University of Oslo, Department of Sociology.

———. 1999. "The Taliban Threat." *Third World Quarterly* 20, no. 4: 861–870.

Harrison, Selig S. 1981. *In Afghanistan's Shadow: Baluch Nationalism and Soviet Temptations*. New York: Carnegie Endowment for International Peace.

Hauner, Milan, and Robert Leroy Canfield, eds. 1989. *Afghanistan and the Soviet Union: Collision and Transformation*. Boulder, CO: Westview Press.

Heathcote, T. A. 1980. *The Afghan Wars, 1839–1919*. London: Osprey.

Hekmatyar, Gulbuddin. 1998. *Clues to the Solution of the Afghan Crisis*. Peshawar, Pakistan: Directorate of International Affairs.

Herda, D. J. 1990. *The Afghan Rebels: The War in Afghanistan*. New York: Franklin Watts.

Hiro, Dilip. 2002. *War without End: The Rise of Islamist Terrorism and the Global Response*. London and New York: Routledge.

"Hizb-i Wahdat (The Unity Party)." 2000. http://www.fas.org/irp/world/para/hizbi_wahdat.htm (cited 10 December 2001).

Hopkirk, Peter. 1990. *The Great Game.* London: John Murray.

Huldt, Bo, and Erland Jannson, eds.1988. *The Tragedy of Afghanistan: The Social, Cultural, and Political Impact of the Soviet Invasion.* London and New York: Croom Helm.

Human Rights Watch. 1991. *Afghanistan, the Forgotten War: Human Rights Abuses and Violations of the Laws of War since the Soviet Withdrawal.* New York: Human Rights Watch.

———. 2002. *Return of the Warlords.* New York: Human Rights Watch.

Hussain, Syed Shabbir. 1982. *Afghan Refugees in Pakistan: The Long Wait.* Islamabad: Kamran Publishing House.

Hussein, Waseem. 1999. *Afghan-Pakistani Relations: The Afghan Perspective.* Bern: Swiss Peace Foundation for Conflict Resolution.

Hyman, Anthony. 1984. *Afghan Resistance: Danger from Disunity.* London: Institute for the Study of Conflict.

———. 1984. *Afghanistan under Soviet Domination, 1964–83.* New York: St. Martin's Press.

Ikbal, Ali Shah. 1939. *Modern Afghanistan.* London: S. Low, Marstons.

Ilinskii, Mikhail Mikhailovich. 1982. *Afghanistan, Onward March of the Revolution.* New Delhi: Sterling Publishers.

ILO, Office of the United Nations High Commissioner for Refugees. 1982. *Tradition and Dynamism among Afghan Refugees: Report of an ILO Mission to Pakistan, November 1982, on Income-Generating Activities for Afghan Refugees.* Geneva, Switzerland: International Labor Office, UN High Commissioner for Refugees.

"Insecure and Suddenly Even the Capital Is Dangerous." 2002. *Economist* (London) 364, no. 8289: 42–43.

Institute for Afghan Studies. 2001. "Masoud's Role as a Political Leader Questioned." http://www.institute-for-afghan-studies.org (cited 28 November 2001).

"Internal Displacement in Afghanistan: New Challenges." 2001. http://www.hspl.harvard.edu/hpct (cited 28 March 2002).

International Crisis Group. 2001. *Afghanistan and Central Asia: Priorities for Reconstruction and Development.* Asia Report no. 26. Brussels: ICG.

Isby, David C. 1986. *Russia's War in Afghanistan.* London: Osprey.

"Islamabad Accord." 1993. http://www.ariaye.com/islamabad.html (cited 11 February 2003).

Jalali, Ali A., and Lester W. Grau. 2001. "Expeditionary Forces: Superior Technology Defeated—The Battle of Maiwand." *Military Review* 81, no. 3: 71–82.

———. 1999. *The Other Side of the Mountain: Mujahideen Tactics in the Soviet-Afghan War.* Quantico, VA: U.S. Marine Corps, Studies and Analysis Division.

Jamiat-i-Islami. 1961. *Aims and Goals of Jamiat-i-Islami Afghanistan.* Peshawar, Pakistan: Jamiat-i-Islami Afghanistan.

Jannson, Eland. 1981. *India, Pakistan or Pakhunistan?* Uppsala, Sweden: Almquist.

Jasjet Singh. 1990. *Superpower Detente and Future of Afghanistan.* New Delhi: Patriot Publishers.

Jawad, Nassim. 1992. *Afghanistan: A Nation of Minorities.* London: Minority Rights Group.

Joffe, Lawrence. 2001. "Abdul Haq: Veteran Afghan Leader Seeking Post-Taliban Consensus Rule." http://www.guardian.co.uk (cited 26 October 2001).

Jones, A. 1967. *The First Afghan War, 1838–42.* London: Cambridge University Press.

Kakar, M. Hasan. 1971. *Afghanistan, a Study in International Political Developments, 1880–1886.* Lahore, Pakistan: Punjab Educational Press.

———. 1995. *Afghanistan: The Soviet Invasion and the Afghan Response, 1979–1982.* Berkeley: University of California Press.

———. 1978. "The Fall of the Afghan Monarch in 1973." *International Journal of Middle Eastern Studies* 9, no. 2: 195–224.

———. 1979. *Government and Society in Afghanistan: The Reign of Amir Abd al-Rahman Khan.* Austin: University of Texas Press.

Kamrany, Nake M. 1983. *The Six Stages of the Sovietization of Afghanistan.* Boulder, CO: Economic Institute for Research and Education.

Kaplan, Robert D. 1990. *Soldiers of God: With the Mujahideen in Afghanistan.* Boston: Houghton Mifflin.

Karp, Craig. 1984. *Afghan Resistance and Soviet Occupation: A Five-Year Summary.* Washington, DC: U.S. Department of State, Bureau of Public Affairs.

Kartha, Tara. 2000. "Pakistan and the Taliban: Flux in an Old Relationship." http://www.institute-for-afghan-studies.org . . ./2001_kartha_idsa_pakistan_and_the_taliban.ht (cited 12 December 2001).

Keddie, N. R., ed. 1993. *An Islamic Response to Imperialism: Political and Religious Writings of Sayyid Jamal al-Din 'al-Afghani.* Berkeley: University of California Press.

Khaflin, N. A. 1958. "The Rising of Ishaq Shah in Southern Turkestan (1888)." *Central Asian Review* 6, no 2: 253–263.

Khalilzad, Zalmay. 1980. "Soviet-Occupied Afghanistan." *Problems of Communism* 29, no. 6: 23–40.

———. 1991. *Prospects for the Afghan Interim Government.* Santa Monica, CA: Rand Corporation.

Khan, Riaz Mohammad. 1991. *Untying the Afghan Knot: Negotiating the Soviet Withdrawal.* Durham, NC: Duke University Press.

Khurassani, Hamid. 1986. *Facts and Fiction: Human Rights in the Democratic Republic of Afghanistan.* Kabul: Kabul Peace Publishing House.

Klass, Rosanne. 1990. *Afghanistan, the Great Game Revisited.* Lanham, MD: Freedom House.

Klass, Rosanne, and Theodore L. Elits. 1989. "The Geneva Accords, Excerpts and Short Commentaries." *Defence Journal* 15, no. 1-2: 49–57.

Kleiner, Jurgen. 2000. "The Taliban and Islam." *Diplomacy and Statecraft* 11, no. 1: 19–32.

Krushelnycsky, Askold. 2002. "Afghanistan: Human Rights Abuses Threaten Peace Process." http://www.rferl.org/nca/features/2002/04/11042002 083542.asp (cited 11 April 2002).

———. 2002. "Afghanistan: Musharraf and Karzai Exchange Warm Words and Pledge Cooperation." http://www.rferl.org/nca/features/2002/04/02042094 053.asp (cited 2 April 2002).

Laber, Jeri, and R. Rubin Barnett. *A Nation Is Dying: Afghanistan under the Soviets, 1979–87.* Evanston, IL: Northwestern University Press.

Labeviere, Richard. 2000. *Dollars for Terror: The United States and Islam.* New York: Algora Publishing.

Lal, M. M. 1978. *Life of Amir Dost Mohammad Khan of Kabul.* 2 vols. Karachi, Pakistan: Oxford University Press.

Lansdell, Henry. 1887. *Through Central Asia; with a Map and Appendix on the Diplomacy and Delimitation of the Russo-Afghan Frontier.* London: S. Low, Marston, Searle and Rivington.

Lessing, Doris May. 1987. *The Wind Blows Away Our Words, and Other Documents Relating to the Afghan Resistance.* New York: Vintage Books.

———. 1984. *Jihad: Holy War.* Washington, DC: Regnery Gateway.

Lockhart, Laurence. 1958. *The Fall of the Safavi Dynasty and the Afghan Occupation of Persia.* Cambridge: Cambridge University Press.

Lohbeck, Kurt. 1993. *Holy War, Unholy Victory: Eyewitness to the CIA's Secret War in Afghanistan.* Washington, DC: Regnery Gateway.

Ma'aroof, Mohammad Khalid. 1990. *United Nations and Afghanistan Crisis.* New Delhi: Commonwealth Publishers.

McGirk, Tim. 2002. "Lonely at the Top." *Time Atlantic* 159, no. 9: 36–38.

———. 2002. "Murder in the Airport." *Time Atlantic* 159, no.8: 25.

McGirk, Tim, Hannah Bloch, and Massina Calabresi. 2002. "Has Pakistan Tamed Its Spies." *Time Atlantic* 159, no. 18: 54–57.

McGirk, Tim, Massimo Calabresi, Mark Thompson, Ron Stodgill II, and Charles P. Wallace. 2001. "The Great New Afghan Hope." *Time Atlantic* 158, no. 25: 41–42.

McMichael, Scott. 1991. *The Stumbling Bear: Soviet Military Performance.* London: Brassey's.

MacMunn, George Fletcher. 1929. *Afghanistan, from Darius to Amanullah.* London: Bell and Sons.

Maconachie, R. R. 1928. *Precis on Afghan Affairs, 1919–1927.* Simla: Government of India.

Macrory, Patrick Arthur. 1986. *Kabul Catastrophe: The Story of the Disastrous Retreat from Kabul, 1842.* Oxford and New York: Oxford University Press.

Magnus, Ralph H. 1997. "Afghanistan in 1996: Year of the Taliban." *Asian Survey* 37, no. 2: 111–117.

Magnus, Ralph H., ed. 1985. *Afghan Alternatives: Issues, Options and Policies.* New Brunswick, NJ.: Transaction Books.

Magnus, Ralph H., and Eden Naby. 2002. *Afghanistan: Mullah, Marx and Mujahid.* Rev. ed. Boulder, CO: Westview Press.

Male, Beverley. 1982. *Revolutionary Afghanistan: A Reappraisal.* New York: St. Martin's Press.

Maley, William. 1999. *Fundamentalism Reborn? Afghanistan and the Taliban.* London: Hurst.

———. 1996. "Taliban Triumphant." *World Today* 52, no. 11: 275–276.

Maley, William, and F. S. Saikal. 1992. *Political Order in Post-Communist Afghanistan.* Boulder, CO: Lynne Rienner.

Malleson, George B. 1879. *History of Afghanistan from the Earliest Period to the Outbreak of the War of 1878.* London: W. H. Allen.

Manuel, Anja, and P. W. Singer. 2002. "A New Model Afghan Army." *Foreign Affairs* 81, no. 4: 44–89.

Manz, Beatrice F. 1988. *Central Asia in Historical Perspective.* Boulder, CO: Westview Press.

Manzar, A. M. 1980. *Red Clouds over Afghanistan.* Islamabad: Institute of Policy Studies.

Maprayil, Cyriac. 1983. *Britain and Afghanistan: In Historical Perspective.* London: Cosmic Press.

———. 1982. *The Soviets and Afghanistan.* London: Cosmic Press.

Margolis, Eric S. 2000. *War at the Top of the World: The Struggle for Afghanistan, Kashmir and Tibet.* London and New York: Routledge.

Marsden, Peter. 1998. *The Taliban: War, Religion and the New Order in Afghanistan.* London and New York: Zed Books.

Martin, Frank A. 2000. *Under the Absolute Amir of Afghanistan.* New Delhi: Bhavana Books and Prints.

Matinnusin, Karmal. 1999. *The Taliban Phenomenon: Afghanistan, 1994–1997.* Karachi, Pakistan: Oxford University Press.

Maxwell, Leigh. 1979. *My God—Maiwand! Operations of the South Afghanistan Field Force, 1878–80*. London: Leo Cooper.

Mehreban, Abdullah. 1982. "National Jirgas (Assemblies) and Their Role in the Socio-Political Life of the People of Afghanistan." *Afghanistan Quarterly* 35, no. 2: 50–58.

Mendelson, Sara Elizabeth. 1998. *Changing Course: Ideas, Politics, and the Soviet Withdrawal from Afghanistan*. Princeton, NJ: Princeton University Press.

Migration and Refugee Services. 1984. *Refugees from Afghanistan: A Look at History, Culture, and the Refugee Crisis*. Washington, DC: U.S. Catholic Conference, Migration and Refugee Services.

Miller, Charles. 1977. *Khyber: British India's North West Frontier*. London: Macdonald and James.

Miller, George Boris. 1985. *Refugees from Afghanistan*. London: Cleveland Press.

Ministry of Foreign Affairs (Afghanistan). 1984. *Achievements of the April Revolution in Afghanistan*. Kabul: Democratic Republic of Afghanistan, Ministry of Foreign Affairs.

———. 1984. *Undeclared War: Armed Intervention and Other Forms of Interference in the Internal Affairs of the Democratic Republic of Afghanistan*. Kabul: Information and Publications Department, Ministry of Foreign Affairs.

Ministry of Foreign Affairs, Information and Press Department (Afghanistan). 1985. *White Book: China's Interference in the Internal Affairs of the Democratic Republic of Afghanistan*. Kabul: Information and Press Department, Ministry of Foreign Affairs.

Misra, Kashi Prasad. 1981. *Afghanistan in Crisis*. New York: Advent Books.

Mitchell, Richard P. 1969. *The Society of Muslim Brothers*. London: Oxford University Press.

Moaveri, Azadeh. 2002. "In Bush's Shadow." http://www.ahran.org/2002/600/re4.htm (cited 10 December 2002).

Mohana, Munshi Lala. 1846. *Life of the Amir Dost Muhammad Khan of Kabul: With his Political Proceedings towards the English, Russian, and Persian Governments, Including the Victory and Disasters of the British Army in Afghanistan*. London: Longman.

Molesworth, George Noble. 1962. *Afghanistan, 1919: An Account of Operations in the Third Afghan War*. London and New York: Asia Publishing House.

Monks, Alfred L. 1981. *The Soviet Intervention in Afghanistan*. Washington, DC: American Enterprise Institute for Public Policy Research.

Morgan, Gerald, and Geoffrey Wheeler. 1981. *Anglo-Russian Rivalry in Central Asia, 1810–1895*. London and Totowa, NJ: Frank Cass.

Muhammad Daud, Sardar. 1973. *The Republic of Afghanistan: Statements, Messages, and Press Interviews of the National Leader and the Founder of the Republic*. Kabul: Government Press.

Muhammad, Fayz. 1999. *Kabul under Siege: Fayz Muhammad's Account of the 1929 Uprising, Translated, Abridged, Re-worked, and Annotated by R. D. McChesney*. Princeton, NJ: Markus Wiener Publishers.

Mukherjee, Sadhan. 1984. *Afghanistan from Tragedy to Triumph*. New Delhi: Sterling.

"National Islamic Movement of Afghanistan and Its Indispensable Duties at Present." 2001. http://www.angelfire.com/ny/Chapandaz/index.html (cited 12 December 2001).

Newell, Nancy Peabody, and Richard S. Newell. 1981. *The Struggle for Afghanistan*. Ithaca, NY: Cornell University Press.

Newell, Richard S. 1972. *The Politics of Afghanistan*. Ithaca, NY: Cornell University Press.

Nikolayev, Lev. 1986. *Afghanistan: Between the Past and the Future*. Moscow: Progress Publishers.

Noelle, Christin. 1997. *State and Tribe in Nineteenth-Century Afghanistan: The Reign of Amir Dost Muhammad Khan*. London: Curzon Press.

Nojumi, Neamatallah. 2002. *The Rise of the Taliban in Afghanistan: Mass Mobilization, Civil War and the Future of the Region*. New York: Palgrave.

Norris, James A. 1967. *The First Afghan War, 1838–42*. London: Cambridge University Press.

Norton-Taylor, Richard. 2002. "Scores Killed by SAS in Afghanistan." *Guardian* (London), 5 July.

O'Ballance, Edgar. 2002. *Afghan Wars: Battles in a Hostile Land*. New York: Brassey's.

———. 1993. *Afghan's Wars, 1839–1992: What Britain Gave Up and the Soviet Union Lost*. London and New York: Brassey's.

Objectives of the Afghan National Liberation Front. n.d. Peshawar, Pakistan: National Liberation Front.

Oleson, A. 1995. *Islam and Politics in Afghanistan*. London: Curzon Press.

"Once Powerful Warlord Is Shunted Aside." 2003. http://www.afgha.com/?af=article&side=25422 (cited 25 April 2003).

Ottaway, Marion, and Anatol Leven. 2002. "Rebuilding Afghanistan: Fantasy versus Reality." http://www.ceip.org/pubs (cited 16 January 2002).

Overby, Paul. 1993. *Holy Blood: An Inside View of the Afghan War*. Westport, CT: Praeger.

Oxfam. 2000. "Crisis in Afghanistan: Humanitarian Situation." http://www.oxfam.org.uk/atwork/emerg/afghanprogramme.htm.

Pazhwak, Abdur Rahman. 1955. *Pakhtunistan*. Hove, England: Key Press.

People's Democratic Party of Afghanistan. 1980. *Fundamental Principles, Democratic Republic of Afghanistan.* Kabul: Ministry of Information and Culture.

Perry, Alex, and Johnny Michael Spann. 2001. "Inside the Battle at Qala-i-Jangi." *Time Atlantic* 158, no. 24: 28–35.

"The Peshawar Accord (March 1993)." 1993. http://www.institute-for-afghan-studies.org/Accords%20Treaties/peshawar_accord_1993.htm. (cited 15 April 2003).

Poladi, Hassan. 1989. *The Hazaras.* Stockton, CA: Mughal Publishing.

Porter, Charlene. 2003. "Afghanistan Improves Performance in International Anti-drug Cooperation." http://www.washingtonpost.com (cited 25 April 2003).

Pottinger, George. 1983. *The Afghan Connection: The Extraordinary Adventures of Major Eldred Pottinger.* Edinburgh: Scottish Academic Press.

Poullada, Leon B. 1995. *The Kingdom of Afghanistan and the United States: 1828–1973.* Lincoln: University of Nebraska, Omaha.

———. 1970. *The Pushtun Role in the Afghan Political System.* New York: Afghanistan Council of the Asia Society.

———. 1973. *Reform and Rebellion in Afghanistan, 1919–1929.* Ithaca, NY: Cornell University Press.

———. 1969. "Some International Legal Aspects of Pashtunistan Dispute." *Afghanistan* 21, no. 4: 10–36.

Quinn-Judge, Paul. 2001. "So Many Warlords, So Little Time." *Time Atlantic* 159, no. 4: 23.

Rais, Rasul Bux. 1994. *War without Winners: Afghanistan's Uncertain Transition after the Cold War.* New York: Oxford University Press.

Rasham, G. Rauf. 2001. "Loya Jirga: One of the Last Political Tools for Bringing Peace to Afghanistan." http://www.institute-for-afghan-studies.org (cited 8 June 2002).

Rashid, Ahmed. 2000. *Taliban: Islam, Oil and the New Great Game in Central Asia.* London: I. B. Tauris.

———. 2001. *Taliban: The Story of the Afghan Warlords.* London: Pan.

———. 1999. "The Taliban: Exporting Extremism." *Foreign Affairs* 78, no. 6: 22–35.

Ratnesar, Romesh, Hannah Beech, Anthony Davis, Michael Fathers, Terry McCarthy, Alex Perry, Johanna McGeary, and Rahimullah Yusufzai. 2001. "The Afghan Way of War." *Time Atlantic* 158, no. 21: 28–37.

Ratnesar, Romesh, Massimo Calabresi, James Carney, Mark Thompson, Karen Tumulty, J. F. O. McAllister, Hannah Beech, Anthony Davis, Alex Perry, Johanna McGeary, and Rahimullah Yusufzai.

2001. "Bombs Away." *Time Atlantic* 158, no. 20: 22–28.

Raverty, H. G. 1976. *Notes on Afghanistan and Baluchistan.* Quetta. Pakistan: Gasha-a-Adeb.

Reeve, Simon. 1999. *The New Jackals: Ramzi Yousef, Osama bin Laden, and the Future of Terrorism.* Boston: Northeastern University Press.

Reid, Robert H. 2003. "Man Thought to Be Osama bin Laden Urges Followers to Back Saddam; US Says It Shows Iraqi Ties to al Qaeda." http://story.nes.yahoo.com/news (cited 15 April 2003).

"Repeated Massacres of Hazaras." 2002. http://www.members.tripod.com/MillateHazara (cited 30 June 2002).

Reshtia, Sayed Qassem. 1990. *Between Two Giants: Political History of Afghanistan in the Nineteenth Century.* Peshawar, Pakistan: Afghan Jehad Works Translation Centre.

———. 1984. *The Price of Liberty: The Tragedy of Afghanistan.* Rome: Bard Editore.

Richards, Donald Sydney. 1990. *The Savage Frontier: A History of the Anglo-Afghan Wars.* London: Macmillan.

Richardson, Bruce G. 1996. *Afghanistan: Ending the Reign of Soviet Terror.* Bend, OR: Maverick Publications.

Rittenberg, Stephen Alan. 1988. *Ethnicity, Nationalism and the Pakhtuns: The Independence Movement in India's North-West Frontier Province.* Durham, NC: Carolina Academic Press.

Roashan, G. Rauf. 2002. "Is the Afghan Government Meeting the Challenge." http://www.institute-for-afghan-studies.org/Contribution/Commentaries/DRRoshan/7-12-01 (cited 7 December 2002).

Robson, Brian. 1986. *The Road to Kabul: The Second Afghan War, 1878–1881.* New York: Arms and Armour Press.

Rogers, Tom. 1992. *The Soviet Withdrawal from Afghanistan: Analysis and Chronology.* Westport, CT: Greenwood Press.

Rostar, Mohammed Osman. 1991. *The Pul-i-Charkhi Prison: A Communist Inferno in Afghanistan, Translated and Edited by Ehsomullah Azari.* Peshawar, Pakistan: Writers' Union of Free Afghanistan.

Roy, Olivier. 1994. *From Holy War to Civil War.* Princeton, NJ: Princeton University Press.

———. 1998. *Has Islamism a Future in Afghanistan?* In *Fundamentalism Reborn? Afghanistan and the Taliban,* edited by William Maley, 199–211. London: Hurst..

———. 1986. *Islam and Resistance in Afghanistan.* London and New York: Cambridge University Press.

———. 1991. *The Lessons of the Soviet/Afghan War*. London: Brassey's for the International Institute for Strategic Studies.

———. 1988. "The Origin of the Afghan Communist Party." *Central Asian Review* 7, nos.2–3: 77–99.

———. 1984. "The Origins of the Islamist Movement in Afghanistan." *Central Asian Survey* 3, no. 2: 117–127.

Rubin, Barnett R. 1999. "Afghanistan under the Taliban." *Current History* 98, no. 625: 79–91.

———. 2002. *The Fragmentation of Afghanistan: State Formation and Collapse in the International System*. 2nd ed. New Haven, CT: Yale University Press.

———. 1992. "Political Elites in Afghanistan: Rentier State Building, Rentier State Wrecking." *International Journal of Middle East Studies* 24, no. 1: 77–99.

———. 1995. *The Search for Peace in Afghanistan: From Buffer State to Failed State*. New Haven, CT: Yale University Press.

———. 1988. "Soviet Militarism, Islamic Resistance, and Peace in Afghanistan." Typescript. Afghan Research Center, University of Nebraska, Omaha.

Rubinstein, Alvin Z. 1982. *Soviet Policy toward Turkey, Iran, and Afghanistan*. New York: Praeger.

Ryan, Nigel. 1983. *A Hitch or Two in Afghanistan: A Journey behind Russian Lines*. London: Weidenfeld and Nicolson.

Saikal, Amin. 1999. "The Rabbani Government, 1992–1996." In *Fundamentalism Reborn? Afghanistan and the Taliban*, edited by William Maley, 29–42. London: Hurst.

Saikal, Amin, and William Maley. 1991. *Regime Change in Afghanistan: Foreign Intervention and the Politics of Legitimacy*. Boulder, CO: Westview Press.

———. 1989. *The Soviet Withdrawal from Afghanistan*. Cambridge and New York: Cambridge University Press.

Salahuddin, Sayed. 2002. "Karzai Arrives at Loya Jirga for Inauguration." http://www.afgha.com/asp/yest.html (cited 19 June 2002).

Sale, F. 1843. *A Journal of the Disasters in Afghanistan, 1841–1842*. London: John Murray.

Samad, Omar. 2001. "Ismail Khan Opens Up New Front." http://www/afghan-info.com (cited 12 February 2003).

———. 1999. "UN Rapporteur Tells of 'Evidence of Widespread Human Rights Violations' by Taliban; Accuses 'External Forces' of Interference and Calls for Total Comprehensive Solution." http://www.afghanvoice.org/ARTICLES/SAMAD.shtml (cited 12 February 2003).

Samdani, Zafar. 1980. *Afghan Refugees: The Long Wait*. Islamabad: Pakistan Publications.

Sarin, Oleg Leonidovich, and Lev Semenovich Dvoretskii. 1993. *The Afghan Syndrome: The Soviet Union's Vietnam*. Novato, CA: Presidio Press.

Schofield, Victoria. 1984. *North West Frontier and Afghanistan*. New Delhi: D.K. Agencies.

Sen Gupta, Bhabani. 1986. *Afghanistan: Politics, Economics, and Society*. Boulder, CO: Lynne Rienner Publishers.

Shah, Ikbal Ali. 1982. *Afghanistan of the Afghans*. Quetta, Pakistan: Nisa Traders.

———. 1933. *The Tragedy of Amanullah*. London: Alexander-Ouseley.

Shah Wali, Sardar. 1970. *My Memoirs*. Kabul: Education Press.

Shahrani, M. Nazif, and Robert L. Caufield, eds. 1984. *Revolutions and Rebellions in Afghanistan*. Berkeley: Institute of International Relations, University of California.

Shalinsky, Audrey. 1979. *Central Asian Emigrés in Afghanistan: Problems of Religious and Ethnic Identity*. New York: Afghan Council of the Asia Society.

———. 1994. *Long Years in Exile: Central Asian Refugees in Afghanistan and Pakistan*. Lanham, MD: University Press of America.

Shams, Abdul Halim. 1987. *In Cold Blood: The Communist Conquest of Afghanistan*. Boston, MA: Western Islands.

Sikorski, Radek. 1989. *Dust of the Saints: A Journey to Herat in Times of War*. London: Chatto and Windus.

———. 1987. *Moscow's Afghan War: Soviet Motives and Western Interests*. London: Alliance Publishers for the Institute for European Defence and Strategic Studies.

Singhal, D. P. 1963. *India and Afghanistan, 1876–1907: A Study in Diplomatic Relations*. Melbourne, Australia: University of Queensland Press.

Smucker, Philip. 2002. "New Afghan Leader Faces a Rouges Gallery." http://www.csmonitor.com/2002/p07s02-wsosc.htm (cited 21 June 2002).

Spain, J. W. 1962. *The Way of the Pathans*. London: Hale.

Srivastava, Mahavir Prasad. 1980. *Soviet Intervention in Afghanistan*. New Delhi: Ess Publications.

Stewart, Rhea Talley. 1973. *Fire in Afghanistan, 1914–1928: Faith, Hope and the British Empire*. New York: Doubleday.

Stone, Andrea. 2002. "Afghan Governor De Facto Ruler in West." http://story.news.yahoo.com/news?templ:story2&sid=675&u=ustoday/20021219/ts (cited 19 December 2002).

"Summit to Tackle Afghan Woes." 2002. http://www.afgha.com (cited 19 December 2002).

Supreme Council of the Afghan Social Democratic Party. 1988. *Aims and Objectives of the Afghan Social Democratic Party.* Peshawar, Pakistan: Afghan Social Democratic Party.

Swing, John Temple. 1990. *Afghanistan after the Accords: What Happens Now?* New York: Council on Foreign Relations.

Sykes, Sir Percy. 1940. *History of Afghanistan.* London: Macmillan.

Tabibi, Abdul Hakim. 1985. *Afghanistan: A Nation in Love with Freedom.* Cedar Rapids, IA: Igram Press.

———. 1986. *The Legal Status of the Afghan Resistance Movement.* Cedar Rapids, IA: Igram Press.

"Tashkent Declaration on Fundamental Principles for a Peaceful Settlement of the Conflict in Afghanistan." 1999. http://www.institute-for-afghan-studies.org/Accords%20Treaties/tashkent_declaration_1999.htm (cited 28 June 2002).

Tate, George Passman. 1975. *The Kingdom of Afghanistan: A Historical Sketch.* New York: AMS Press.

Trousdale, William. 1985. *War in Afghanistan, 1879–80.* Detroit, MI: Wayne State University Press.

United Nations. 1988. *Geneva Accords.* New York: United Nations.

———. 2002. "Immediate and Transitional Assistance for the Afghan People, 2002: Updated Financial Requirements." http://www.reliefweb.int (cited 12 March 2002).

———.. 2000. *Security Council Resolution 1383.* New York: United Nations.

———. 2001. *Security Council Resolution 1386.* New York: United Nations.

———. 2002. *Security Council Resolution 1413.* New York: United Nations.

———. 2002. *Security Council Resolution 1444.* New York: United Nations.

———. 1999. *Security Council Resolution 1560.* New York. United Nations.

Urban, Mark. 1988. *War in Afghanistan.* London. Macmillan; New York: St. Martin's Press.

U.S. Congress, House Committee on International Relations. 2001. *The Future of Afghanistan: Hearing before the Committee on International Relations, House of Representatives, One Hundred Seventh Congress, First Session, 7 November 2001.* Washington, DC: U.S. Government Printing Office.

U.S. Congress, House Committee on International Relations, Subcommittee of Asia and the Pacific. 1996. *Afghanistan: Civil War or Uncivil Peace? Hearing before the Subcommittee on Asia and the Pacific of the Committee on International Relations, House of Representatives, One Hundred Fourth Congress, Second Session, 9 May 1996.* Washington, DC: U.S. Government Printing Office.

U.S. Department of the Army. 1980. *Afghanistan: A Country Study.* Area Handbook Series. Washington, DC: U.S. Government Printing Office.

Ved, Sreedhar Mehedra. 1998. *Afghan Turmoil: Changing Equations.* New Delhi: Himalayan Books.

Vogel, Renate. 1976. *Die Persien und Afghanistan expedition: Oskar Ritter Von Niedermayer, 1915–16* (The Persian and Afghanistan expedition: Oskar Ritter Von Niedermayer, 1915–16). Osnabruck, Germany: Biblio-Verlag.

Volodarski, Mikhail I. 1994. *The Soviet Union and Its Southern Neighbours: Iran and Afghanistan, 1917–1933.* Portland, OR: Frank Cass.

Wakman, Mohammad Amin. 1985. *Afghanistan, Non-alignment and the Super Powers.* New Delhi:. Radiant Publishers; London: Sangam Books.

Waller, John H. 1990. *Beyond the Khyber Pass: The Road to British Disaster in the First Afghan War.* New York: Random House.

Warman, Mark. 1982. "Kabul's Urban Guerrillas: Killing Russians House-to-House." *Soldier of Fortune* (November): 28–33.

Watkins, Mary Bradley. 1963. *Afghanistan: Land in Transition.* Princeton, NJ: Van Nostrand.

Weinbaum, Marvin G. 1994. *Pakistan and Afghanistan: Resistance and Reconstruction.* Boulder, CO: Westview Press.

Wilber, Donald Newton. 1962. *Afghanistan: Its People, Its Society, Its Culture.* New Haven, CT: HRAF Press.

Yapp, Malcolm E. 1964. "The Revolutions of 1841–1842 in Afghanistan." *Bulletin of the School of Oriental and African Studies* 26, no. 2: 338–345.

———. 1980. *Strategies of British India: Britain, Iran and Afghanistan, 1838–42.* New York: Clarendon Press.

Yate, Charles Edward. 1888. *Northern Afghanistan; or, Letters from the Afghan Boundary Commission.* London: Blackwood and Sons.

Yonak, Alexander, and Michael S. Swetnan. 2001. *Usama bin Laden's al-Qaida: Profile of a Terrorist Network.* New York: Transnational Publishers.

Yousaf, Mohammad, and Mark Adkin. 1992. *The Bear Trap: Afghanistan's Untold Story.* Lahore, Pakistan: Jang Publishers.

Yunas, S. Frida. 1977. *History of People's Democratic Party of Afghanistan (PDPA) Watan Party of Afghanistan.* Peshawar, Pakistan: University of Peshawar.

Zardykhan, Zharmukhamad. 2002. "Kazakhstan and Central Asia: Regional Perspectives." *Central Asian Survey* 21, no. 2: 167–183.

Language and Literature

Badakhshi, Shah Abdullah. 1960. *A Dictionary of Some Languages and Dialects of Afghanistan*. Kabul: Government Press.

Bellew, Henry Walter. 1986. *Pusht Instructor: A Grammar of the Pukkhto or Pukshto Language, on a New and Improved System*. Peshawar, Pakistan: Sacred Book Bank and Subscription Agency.

Bray, Denys. 1986. *The Brahui Language: An Old Dravidian Language Spoken in Parts of Baluchistan and Sind*. Delhi, India: Gian Publishing House.

Chaveria-Aquiler, Oscar Luis. 1962. *A Short Introduction to the Writing System of Pashto*. Ann Arbor: University of Michigan Press.

Dames, Mansel Longworth, and Jamiat Rai. 1911. *Text Book, Part I and II of the Baluchi Language*. Lahore, Pakistan: Punjab Government Press.

Dorn, Boris Andreevich. 1982. *A Chrestomathy of the Pushto or Afghan Language: To Which Is Subjoined a Glossary of Afghan and English*. Osnabruck, Germany: Biblio Verlag.

Dulling, G. K. 1973. *The Hazaragi Dialect of Afghan Persia*. London: Central Asian Research Centre.

Dvorjankov, N. A. 1966. "The Development of Pushtu as the National and Literary Language of Afghanistan." *Central Asian Review* 14, no. 3: 210–220.

Edelman, D. I. 1983. *The Dardic and Nuristani Languages*. Moscow: Nauka.

Elfenbein, J. H. 1966. *The Baluchi Language: A Dialectology with Texts*. London: Royal Asiatic Society of Great Britain and Ireland.

Foreign Service Institute. 1957. *Spoken Afghan Persian*. Kabul: U.S. Embassy.

Gilbertson, George W. 1923. *The Baluchi Language: A Grammar and Manual*. Hartford, CT: Gilbertson.

Habibi, A. H. 1967. "Pashto Literature at a Glance." *Afghanistan* 20, no. 4: 51–64, and 21, no. 1: 53–57.

Jarring, Gunar. 1938. *Uzbek Texts from Afghan Turkestan, with Glossary*. Lund, Sweden: W. K. Gleerup.

Lorimer, D. L. R. 1915. *Pashtu, Syntax of Colloquial Pashtu, with Chapters on the Persian and Indian Elements in the Modern Language*. Oxford: Clarendon Press.

Miran, M. Alan. 1977. *The Functions of National Language in Afghanistan*. New York: Afghanistan Council of the Asia Society.

———. 1974. *Some Linguistic Difficulties Facing Dari Speakers Learning Pashto*. New York: Afghanistan Council of the Asia Society.

Morgenstienne, G. 1967. "The Language of Afghanistan." *Afghanistan* 20, no. 3: 81–90.

Penzl, Herbert. 1965. *A Reader of Pashto*. Ann Arbor: University of Michigan Press.

Raverty, Henry George. 1980. *Dictionary of the Pukhto, Pushto, Language of the Afghans*. Karachi, Pakistan: Indus Publications.

———. 1986. *The Pushto Manual: The Language of the Afghans*. New Delhi: Cosmo.

Trummp, Ernest. 1969. *Grammar of the Pashto or Language of the Afghans, Compared with Iranian and North-Indian Idioms*. Osnabruck, Germany: Biblio Verlag.

Law

Amin, Sayed Hassan. 1991. *Law, Reform and Revolution in Afghanistan: Implications for Central Asia and the Islamic World*. 3rd ed. Glasgow, Scotland: Royston Publishers.

Anwar Khan, Mohammed. 1977. *The New Constitution of Afghanistan*. Peshawar, Pakistan: Institute of Central Asian Studies, University of Peshawar.

Cerkel, David, and Ralph LeRoy Miller. 1958. *Petroleum Law for Afghanistan*. Kabul: Ministry of Mines and Industries.

Chishti, Nighat Mehroze. 1998. *Constitutional Development in Afghanistan*. Karachi, Pakistan: Royal Book.

Committee on Constitution Secretariat. 1964. *Draft of the New Constitution of Afghanistan*. Kabul: Franklin Book Programs.

Constitution of Afghanistan. 1964. Kabul: Franklin Book Programs.

English Translation of Some of the New Laws Promulgated by the Republic of Afghanistan. 1975. New York: Afghanistan Council of the Asia Society.

Huqugi, Walid A. 1971. *Judicial Organization in Afghanistan*. Kabul: Government Press.

Kamali, Mohammad Hashim. 1985. *Law in Afghanistan: A Study of the Constitutions, Matrimonial Law and the Judiciary*. Leiden, the Netherlands: E. J. Brill.

Khan, Sultan Muhammad. 1900. *The Constitution and Laws of Afghanistan*. London: J. Murray.

Vafai, Gholam H. 1988. *Afghanistan: A Country Law Study*. Washington, DC: Law Library, Library of Congress.

Religion

Canfield, Robert Leroy. 1973. *Faction and Conversion in a Plural Society: Religious Alignments in the Hindu Kush*. Ann Arbor: Museum of Anthropology, University of Michigan.

Dupree, Louise. 1966. "Afghanistan, Islam in Politics: A Symposium." *Moslem World* 46, no. 2: 269–276.

Gaulier, Simone, Robert Jera-Bezard, and Monique Maillard. 1976. *Buddhism in Afghanistan and Central Asia*. Leiden, the Netherlands: E. J. Brill.

Ghani, Ashraf. 1978. "Islam and State Building in a Tribal Society." *Modern Asian Studies* 12, no. 2: 269–284.

Jettmar, Karl, Adam Nayyar, Schuyler Jones, and Max Kliburg. 1986. *The Religions of the Hindukush*. Warminster, England: Aris and Phillips.

Keddie, N. R., ed. 1983. *An Islamic Response to Imperialism: Political and Religious Writings of Sayyid Jamal ad-Din al-Afghani*. Berkeley: University of California Press.

Nawid, Senzil K. 1999. *Religious Response to Social Change in Afghanistan, 1919–29: King Amanullah and the Afghan Ulama*. Costa Mesa, CA: Mazda Publishers.

Roy, Olivier. 1994. *The Failure of Political Islam*. Cambridge, MA: Harvard University Press.

———. 1998. *Has Islamism a Future in Afghanistan?* In *Fundamentalism Reborn? Afghanistan and the Taliban*, edited by William Maley, 199–211. London: Hurst.

Tabibi, A. H. 1977. "The Great Mystics of Afghanistan." *Afghanistan* 30, no. 2: 25–39.

Wilber, D. N. 1952. "The Structure and Position of Islam in Afghanistan." *Middle East Journal* 6, no. 1: 41–48.

Mousavi, Sayed Asker. 1998. *The Hazaras of Afghanistan: An Historical, Cultural, Economic, and Political Study*. London: Curzon Press.

Pedersen, G. 1994. *Afghan Nomads in Transition*. London: Thames and Hudson.

———. 1981. "Socio-Economic Change among a Group of East Afghan Nomads." *Afghanistan Journal* 8, no. 4: 115–122.

Poladi, Hassan. 1989. *The Hazaras*. Stockton, CA: Mughal Publishing.

Robinson, J. A. 1978. *Notes on Nomad Tribes of Eastern Afghanistan*. Quetta, Pakistan: Nisa Traders.

Shalinsky, A. 1979. *Central Asian Emigrés in Afghanistan: Problems of Religious and Ethnic Identity*. New York: Afghanistan Council of the Asia Society.

———. 1994. *Long Years of Exile: Asian Refugees in Afghanistan and Pakistan*. Lanham, MD: University Press of America.

Strand, R. F. 1975. "The Changing Herding Economy of the Kom Nuristani." *Afghanistan Journal* 2, no. 4: 123–134.

Swinson, A. 1979. *North-West Frontier: People and Events, 1839–1947*. London: Hutchinson.

Tapper, Nancy. 1991. *Bartered Brides, Politics, Gender, and Marriage in an Afghan Tribal Society*. Cambridge and New York: Cambridge University Press.

Tapper, R., ed. 1983. *The Conflict of Tribe and State in Iran and Afghanistan*. London: Croom Helm.

Society

Afghan Network. 2001. "Pashtuns." http://afghan-network.net/ethnic-groups (cited 28 November 2001).

Ahmed, A. S. 1977. *Social and Economic Change in Tribal Areas*. Karachi, Pakistan: Oxford University Press.

Anderson, J. 1978. "There Are No Khans Anymore: Economic Development and Social Change in Tribal Afghanistan." *Middle East Journal* 32, no. 2: 167–183.

Bacon, E. E. 1951. "An Enquiry into the History of the Hazara Mongols of Afghanistan." *Southwestern Journal of Anthropology* 7, no. 2: 230–247.

Broguetti, Michele. 1982. *The Current Situation in the Hazarajat*. Oxford: Oxford University Press.

Ferdinand, K. 1962. " Nomad Expansion in Central Afghanistan: A Sketch of Some Modern Trends." *Folk* 4: 123–159.

Harpviken, Kristian Berg. 1995. *Political Mobilization among the Hazara of Afghanistan, 1078–1992*. Oslo: Oslo University, Department of Sociology.

Hart, David M. 1985. *Guardians of the Khaibar Pass: The Social Organization and History of the Afridis of Pakistan*. Lahore, Pakistan: Vanguard Books.

Women

Amnesty International. 1995. *Women in Afghanistan: A Human Rights Catastrophe*. London and New York: Amnesty International.

Boesen, I. W. 1980. "Women, Honour and Love: Some Aspects of the Pashtun Woman's Life in Eastern Afghanistan." *Afghanistan Journal* 7, no. 2: 50–59.

Christensen, Hanne. 1990. *The Reconstruction of Afghanistan: A Chance for Rural Women*. Geneva, Switzerland: UN Research Institute for Social Development.

Ellis, Deborah. 2000. *Women of the Afghan War*. Westport, CT: Praeger.

Schultz, J. J, and L. Schultz. 1999. "The Darkest of Ages: Afghan Women under the Taliban." *Peace and Conflict* 5, no.3: 237–254.

Tapper, Nancy. 1991. *Bartered Brides: Politics, Gender and Marriage in an Afghan Tribal Society*. Cambridge and New York: Cambridge University Press.

———. 1977. "Pashtun Nomad Women in Afghanistan." *Asian Affairs* 64, no. 2:, 163–170.

"'We Want to Live as Humans': Repression of Women and Girls in Western Afghanistan." 2002.

http://www.hrw.org/reports/2002/afghanwmn 1202/ (cited 2 December 2002).

Woodsmall, Ruth Frances. 1960. *Women and the New East.* Washington, DC: Middle East Institute.

Web Sites

http://www.afgha.comhttp://www.afghan-network.net

http://www.AfghanistanPeace.com

http://www.afghanland.com

http://www.ahran.org

http://www.bbc.co.uk/news

http://www.bbc.co.uk/news/southasia

http://www.ceip.org/files/Publications

http://www.cnn.worldnews.com

http://www.csmonitor.com

http://www.defenselink.mil

http://www.eurasianet.org

http://www.globalspecops.com/oefportal.html

http://www.guardian.co.uk

http://www.gulf-news.com

http://www.hrw.org/reports

http://www.institute-for-afghan-studies.org

http://www.nytimes.com

http://www.operations.mod.uk/veritas

http://www.pm.gov.uk/news-asp?Newsld=2601

http://www.rawa.org

http://www.rferl.org

http://www.time.com

http://www.unhcrich

http://www.un.org.pk/unhcr

http://www.washingtonpost.com

http://www.whitehouse.gov/news/releases

http://www.whitehouse.gov/response/military.response.html

Index

About the Authors

Professor Ludwig W. Adamec of the University of Arizona is the author of a number of books on Afghanistan, Iran, and Islam.

Frank A. Clements is director of information services at the College of St. Mark and St. John in Plymouth, England.